Middle Kingdom and Empire
of the Rising Sun

Middle Kingdom and Empire of the Rising Sun

Sino-Japanese Relations, Past and Present

JUNE TEUFEL DREYER

UNIVERSITY PRESS

Oxford University Press is a department of the University of Oxford. It furthers the University's objective of excellence in research, scholarship, and education by publishing worldwide. Oxford is a registered trade mark of Oxford University Press in the UK and certain other countries.

Published in the United States of America by Oxford University Press
198 Madison Avenue, New York, NY 10016, United States of America.

© Oxford University Press 2016

First issued as an Oxford University Press paperback, 2018

All rights reserved. No part of this publication may be reproduced, stored in a retrieval system, or transmitted, in any form or by any means, without the prior permission in writing of Oxford University Press, or as expressly permitted by law, by license, or under terms agreed with the appropriate reproduction rights organization. Inquiries concerning reproduction outside the scope of the above should be sent to the Rights Department, Oxford University Press, at the address above.

You must not circulate this work in any other form
and you must impose this same condition on any acquirer.

Library of Congress Cataloging-in-Publication Data
Names: Dreyer, June Teufel, 1939– author.
Title: Middle kingdom and empire of the rising sun : Sino-Japanese relations, past and present / June Teufel Dreyer.
Description: New York, NY: Oxford University Press, 2016.
Identifiers: LCCN 2015043811 (print) | LCCN 2016006841 (ebook) |
ISBN 978-0-19-537566-4 (hardcover : alk. paper) |
ISBN 978-0-19-069220-9 (paperback : alk. paper) |
ISBN 978-0-19-970490-3 (E-book) |
ISBN 978-0-19-060359-5 (E-book)
Subjects: LCSH: China—Foreign relations—Japan. |
Japan—Foreign relations—China.
Classification: LCC DS740.5.J3 D74 2016 (print) | LCC DS740.5.J3 (ebook) |
DDC 327.51052—dc23
LC record available at http://lccn.loc.gov/2015043811

For Edward, Always

Contents

Part One

1. **Getting to the Present** — 3
   - Introduction — 3
   - The Establishment of the Chinese World Order — 4
   - The Establishment of the Japanese State — 6
   - Early Sino-Japanese Contacts — 7
   - China Gains Influence over Japan — 8
   - The Taika Reforms — 9
   - Eighth-Century Reforms — 11
   - Nativist Elements Return — 12
   - Not Quite Separate, Whether or Not Equal — 14
   - The Ming, the Fall of the Ashikaga, and the Reunification of Japan — 19
   - Sino-Japanese Relations in the Early Tokugawa Era — 21
   - The Sakoku Period — 24
   - Arai Hakuseki's Proposed Reforms — 25
   - Fall of the Ming Dynasty — 28
   - Kokugaku — 29
   - Conclusions — 32

2. **China, Japan, and the Coming of the West, 1835–1945** — 33
   - The West Intrudes — 33
   - The Macartney Mission — 34

The Opium War and the Unequal Treaties ... 35
  The Tongzhi Restoration, 1862–1874 ... 36
  Matthew Perry Arrives in Japan ... 38
  The Meiji Restoration, 1868–1912 ... 40
  Sino-Japanese Relations During the Restorations ... 41
  Sino-Japanese Tensions Build ... 43
  Japan Ponders Its Relationship with China and Korea ... 44
  The Sino-Japanese War, 1894–1895 ... 45
  The Effect of Defeat on China ... 50
  Sino-Japanese Relations after the 1895 War ... 52
  Sino-Japanese Diplomacy, 1898–1911 ... 55
  The Russo-Japanese War ... 57
  A New Balance of Power ... 59
  The Siberian Intervention ... 64
  Shidehara Diplomacy ... 65
  Sino-Japanese Relations in the Post-Sun Yat-sen Era ... 66
  The Mukden Incident ... 68
  Expansion in North China ... 70
  A Chinese Communist-KMT Alliance against Japan ... 71
  The Marco Polo Bridge Incident, 1937 ... 72
  Wang Jingwei ... 75
  The Second Sino-Japanese War ... 77
  The Chinese Civil War ... 79
  Conclusions ... 80

3. **Wary Engagement, 1945–1969** ... 82
   Finding a Place in the Post-War Balance of Power ... 82
   The New Japanese Government Regards China ... 82
   The New Chinese Government Regards Japan ... 86
   Negotiations for a Post-World War II Settlement ... 87
   Sino-Japanese Relations during the Korean War ... 88
   The Bandung Era ... 95
   The Nuclear Issue ... 98
   Resurgence on the Left ... 99
   Irritants Continue ... 100
   The Communist Monolith Splinters ... 106
   The French Connection ... 111
   Intra-Left Disputes ... 112

China Becomes a Nuclear Power	114
Satō Takes the Helm	115
Chinese Foreign Relations during the Cultural Revolution	119
The LDP Reassesses Its China Policy	121
U.S. Concerns	124

4. The Tortuous Path to Normalization, 1969–1972 — 127
- Satō Tries to Engage China — 127
- The Soviet Connection — 130
- Chinese Reaction — 131
- The Okinawa Reversion Agreement — 132
- Business as Usual — 132
- Denouement of the Normalization Issue — 148

5. The Golden Age of Sino-Japanese Relations, 1972–1989 — 156
- Negotiating the Details — 156
- The Peace and Friendship Treaty — 159
- Friendship and Friction — 166
- The Euphoria Ends — 166
- The Diaoyu/Senkaku Issue and the Yasukuni Shrine — 167
- Great Power Politics — 169
- The Textbook Issue — 171
- Strains Accumulate — 172
- Hu Yaobang Reestablishes Amicable Relations — 173
- The Kokaryo/Guanghua Dormitory Case — 176
- The Demise of Hu Yaobang — 177
- Insensitive Remarks by Japanese Officials — 179
- The Tiananmen Demonstrations and Sino-Japanese Relations — 182
- Aftermath of the Tiananmen Demonstrations — 184

6. Tarnished Gold, 1990–2006 — 188
- Returning to the Status Quo Ante — 188
- Familiar Tensions Return — 191
- Maritime Issues — 193
- The Asian Currency Crisis — 195
- Jiang Zemin Visits Japan — 196
- Trade Difficulties — 200
- The Koizumi Era — 201
- Mutual Distrust Grows — 203

    Voices of Moderation in China   205
    New Frictions Are Added to Old Irritants   207
    The Japanese View   209
    Anti-Japanese Riots in China   211
    Rivalry for Energy Resources   213

7. Contradictions Deepen, 2006–2015   215
    Efforts to Mend Bilateral Relations   215
    Fukuda Takes the Helm   223
    Asō as Prime Minister   226
    Hatoyama   231
    The Diaoyu/Senkaku Issue Redux   233
    Japan's Triple Disaster and New Pressures from China   235
    The Islands Controversy Intensifies   236
    Chinese Domestic Factors   239
    Abe Returns to the Prime Ministership   240
    Efforts to Manage Tensions   244

Part Two

8. Economic Rivalry   249
    Economic Relations before Normalization   249
    Economic Consequences of Normalization   255
    Japanese Concerns Grow: Rivalry Rekindled   261
    Trade Imbalances   262
    Japan as Number One   263
    Effect of the Tiananmen Incident   267
    The Chinese Economy Recovers   268
    And the Japanese Economy Falters   268
    The Search for an Explanation   271
    Official Development Assistance to China Is Terminated   272
    Koizumi's Attempts at Restructuring Fall Short   273
    Current Economic Relations   274

9. Mutual Military Apprehensions   281
    The Demilitarization of Japan   281
    The Korean War   283
    China Rearms . . . and Regresses   285
    Cautious Security Steps in Japan   287

	The Sword Reemerges in Japan	288
	China Complains	292
	Tiananmen Square Incident and Its Aftermath	294
	Effect of the Gulf War	295
	North Korean Missile Tests	296
	Crisis in the Taiwan Strait	297
	New Japanese Defense Legislation	300
	The North Korean Military Issue Resurfaces	302
	Dueling Defense White Papers	304
	New Powers for the SDF	305
	Effect of the War Against Terrorism	305
	The Third National Defense Program Outline	308
	Beijing Responds	312
	Abe's Defense Program	313
	The Debate on Amending the Constitution	315
	The Nuclear Debate Rekindled	316
	Conclusions	318
10.	**Taiwan between Two Powers**	320
	Multicultural Influences and the Qing/Manchu Annexation	320
	Taiwan under Japanese Rule	324
	The Kuomintang Assumes Control	329
	The De-Recognition of the ROC and Sino-Japanese Relations	335
	Restoration of Japanese Influence in Taiwan	337
	Taiwan Politics Poised between China and Japan	339
	Conclusions	352

Part Three

11.	**Conclusions**	357
12.	**Epilogue**	381
	Acknowledgments	391
	Notes	393
	Bibliography	441
	Index	455

Part One

1

Getting to the Present

INTRODUCTION

Sino-Japanese tensions have gone through several turbulent periods since the end of World War II. The Beijing government has attributed the problems to the Tokyo government's insufficient expressions of remorse over Japan's responsibility for the war and to politicians' persistent refusal to foreswear visits to the Yasukuni Jinja, Japan's shrine to its war dead. Relations will not improve, they warn, unless China receives adequate apologies and visits to the shrine cease.

The central theme of this book is that these issues are merely symptoms of an underlying problem that stretches back to the beginning of relations between the two states: the unwillingness of either China or Japan to accept the other as an equal, and the refusal of either to accept a position of inferiority to the other. The roots of this tension can be found as early as the seventh century, in some of the earliest contacts between the two cultures. China treated Japan, as it did all of its neighbors, as a cultural and political inferior. Although Japan had indeed borrowed its written language, its institutional structure, and parts of its philosophical tenets from China, this assertion of superiority engendered anger and resentment in Japan. However, in the premodern era, the ocean that separated the two, the relatively minor interest of each in trade and commerce, and the fact that when one of the two was strong the other was generally not, served to mitigate these tensions.

By the mid-nineteenth century, the shrinking distances afforded by advances in technology and the intrusion of Western powers brought the two into closer proximity in ways that alternately united and divided them, with adversarial relationships frequently outweighing ties of amity. The current Chinese government regards the period from the late nineteenth to the mid- twentieth century, when Japan was clearly stronger, as part of its "century of humiliation." In the immediate aftermath of World War II, both sides were weak. Japan quickly developed into an economic power, but rejected concomitant military capabilities, preferring to rely on security commitments from the United States. China, after emerging from the shadow of Stalin's Soviet Union, began a tortuous journey toward modernization hindered by ideological and leadership struggles that lasted until the death of revolutionary leader Mao Zedong in 1976.

When the Japanese economic bubble deflated at the same time as the People's Republic of China (PRC) experienced a period of strong economic and military growth, the Beijing government again began to treat Japan in an apparently condescending manner, to the intense annoyance of influential members of the Tokyo establishment. A very different situation has taken shape. In the PRC, as communist ideology declined, Chinese nationalism became more important. At the same time, latent nationalism was rekindled in Japan. Both China and Japan are now interested in commerce. With the two currently the world's second and third largest economic powers and possessing potent military forces, rivalries have intensified. They compete for energy sources, raw materials, markets for their goods, and both regional and international stature. Each is an important international actor. Unless China and Japan can learn to co-exist, either as co-equals or with one accepting the primacy of the other, the stability of both regional and global systems will be jeopardized.

THE ESTABLISHMENT OF THE CHINESE WORLD ORDER

The entity currently known as China, and hereafter referred to by that name, had a concept of state (*guo*) from the beginning of the Zhou dynasty, which is traditionally dated from 1122–256 B.C. but actually commenced around 1000 B.C. As defined by Confucius's disciple Mencius, the three treasures of a state ruler were land, people, and government. It was the duty of the king (*wang*) to align the three levels of heaven, earth, and man through his righteous example, as can be seen in the ideograph for king of a vertical line connecting three horizontal lines. According to this tradition, a dynasty was founded by a righteous man designated by Heaven. Should his successors prove unworthy, the Mandate of Heaven would be removed and pass to another dynastic founder designated by Heaven.

A distinction was made between inner and outer realms: China was the central state, *Zhongguo*, with others regarded as populated by uncivilized barbarians. Properly speaking, Confucian society did not conceive of a China, or of a Chinese civilization: there was only civilization and barbarism, with one defining another. What was not civilized was barbaric. The emperor, *huangdi* as he was called after the founding of the Qin dynasty (221 B.C.E.), was not simply the ruler of one state among many, but the mediator between heaven and earth, the apex of civilization, and a being who was unique in the universe. As the son of heaven, the rituals he performed were not particularistic but universal. As the embodiment of virtue, the emperor carried out the rites (*li*) that were necessary for the continuing harmony of the universe. In this capacity, he ruled All under Heaven (*tianxia*). Should the rituals not be properly performed, this was an indication that the emperor had betrayed his role as the son of heaven; the result would be disharmony in the universe.[1]

Although Confucianism was elaborately hierarchical, it contained elements of egalitarianism as well. In theory, the Mandate of Heaven could fall on any male, depending in part on his ethical standards. Indeed, mythical sage rulers of antiquity such as Yao and Shun did not choose to pass the mandate to their own sons. And uncivilized barbarians could become civilized barbarians, with proper observance of the rites. Presentation of tribute to the emperor was the ritual appropriate to acknowledging the universality of the Sinitic world order and one's place in it. Entry into the emperor's presence required proper obeisance, as exemplified by the performance of the kowtow (*ketou*)—the three kneelings and the nine prostrations. Since this entailed not only bowing but hitting one's head repeatedly on the floor, it can be presumed to induce the feelings of humility that were considered appropriate to the situation. Refusal to carry out this act would not have been regarded as mere *lesemajesté*, or an insult to the emperor's person, as Western tradition would see it, but as an affront to the preordained order of the universe.

The proper rituals having been performed, envoys from these less civilized states presented tribute in the form of local products, and received gifts from the emperor in return. Typically, the gifts exchanged were of the finest workmanship and often quite rare in the society of the recipient. Some scholars have speculated that the exchange constituted trade in disguise, since Confucius had great contempt for commerce, and also since it was difficult for an entity that considered itself the apex of civilization to regard the products of barbarian lands as having intrinsic value. They had interest as curiosities, but little more. It is probably more accurate to say that the tribute–gift exchange was neither purely ceremonial nor purely commercial. One analyst opines that, by the time of the Qing dynasty (1644–1911), the two had become so intertwined as to be separable only analytically.[2]

The barbarian ruler might also receive a patent of office, *biao*, from the emperor, thus confirming the legitimacy of his administration, and would receive a title that was deemed consonant with his status. The more important of these rulers received the title of king, *wang*. The enfieffment process involved acceptance of the Chinese dynasty's calendar to date letters and official documents; this indicated that the ruler had accepted vassal status as well. During the Qing, the vassal state was required to send embassies to Beijing at regular intervals to "receive the calendar" (*fengshuo*), a term that can also be translated "receiving the commands of the Son of Heaven."[3]

It should not be assumed that all who participated in the tribute system did so from the same motives. The various Korean kingdoms seem to have been the most sincere in their acceptance of a position of inferiority in the Sinitic hierarchy, with Vietnam much less so. Thailand's motivation might best be described as pragmatic. That country's longstanding foreign policy was to accommodate to the dominant outside power in the region that, until the arrival of the West in the mid-nineteenth century, was generally China. With its civilization deriving from Indic rather than Sinitic roots, Thailand could accommodate Confucian concepts without accepting them.[4] While other states may have accepted the system either sincerely or cynically, Japan, as will be seen, participated episodically, but was never entirely comfortable with, and sometimes openly defiant of, it.

THE ESTABLISHMENT OF THE JAPANESE STATE

In contrast to the Chinese polity, with its early development of a written language, we know very little about early Japan, and much of that is contained in records compiled later using the Chinese language. These are assumed to have been influenced by Chinese categories of thought and philosophical concepts, rather than accurate accounts of the events and conditions of the times they describe. Additionally, the narratives differ somewhat in their account of events. Even taking these factors into account, the picture that emerges is of a polity very different from China.

In contrast to the down-to-earth descriptions of early Chinese records, supernatural and cosmological features play an important part in Japanese narratives, as does the aristocratic theme.[5] The Japanese islands are said to have been created through the union of the god Izanagi and the goddess Izanami, who stand on a floating bridge of heaven. They produced the sun goddess Amaterasu, who invested Ninigi, the immediate ancestor of the imperial line, with the sacred regalia: the three treasures of the mirror, the jewel, and the sword. Amaterasu also endowed Ninigi with the explicit charge, according to some accounts, that his dynasty should endure forever.[6] Ninigi, in turn, endowed his own progeny, the first human emperor, Jinmu Tennō, with the regalia and the responsibilities of office.

In this narrative, the human emperor is a direct descendant of the gods rather than, as in China, the holder of a mandate from heaven that is contingent on proper performance of his duties. While there seem to have been not one but three different Japanese dynasties, early compilers of the legends wove together the rulers thereof into one single lineage extending back from those ruling at the time they wrote to the age of the gods.[7]

EARLY SINO-JAPANESE CONTACTS

Archaeological evidence indicates similarities between stone tools that may have made their way from China to Japan 20,000 years ago.[8] Chinese bronze culture reached Japan by about 200 B.C., modifying the existing Neolithic civilization. Bronze culture itself was soon supplanted by the Iron Age. The presumptive channel to Japan was not direct, but through Paekche, one of the three Korean kingdoms of the time. The earliest Japanese mission mentioned in Chinese records came to China in 57 A.D. According to the records of the Later Han, the Guangwu emperor presented a seal with a decorative ribbon to the envoys of a king of Wa as a token of investiture. In 1784 a peasant redigging an irrigation ditch in Shinkanoshima Island on the northwest coast of Kyushu accidentally unearthed such a golden seal inscribed to a "[Vassal of] Han," which has been accepted as the object referred to in the Chinese record.[9]

Because of its proximity of access to the Korean peninsula, the northwest coast of Kyushu was a traditional contact point in that era. Some immigrants from what are now China and Korea arrived as well. Collectively known as the Toraijin, they brought cultural influence and serve as a partial refutation to later nationalist claims of Japanese racial homogeneity. What we now know as Japan was not at that time unified, but rather divided up into a number of small tribal units, each under the rule of a hereditary high priest or priestess. While it is reasonable to assume that the king of Nu was one of these, there is no way of knowing whether he was an ancestor or relative of the hereditary line of chieftains that by the fifth or sixth century had evolved into the Japanese imperial family.[10]

Again according to Chinese records, the next Japanese embassy arrived in 107 A.D. It is said to have presented 160 slaves. The Later Han fell in 220, after a period of disruption, and the next embassies are recorded in the first half of the third century, visiting the court of the Wei dynasty that ruled in the north of a divided entity. A mirror found in Luoyang, capital of the Wei, in 2009 confirms written records of contact between emissaries of the Wa queen Himiko and the court.[11] Missions also appeared in Nanjing in the fifth century, at the court of the Liu-Song (429–479), southern dynasties that were based there. The records do not reveal which of these embassies actually represented the group that was in the process of establishing itself as the central government of Japan. Nor is it certain which, if any, were official missions at all: it was not unknown for groups of private businesspeople to represent themselves as emissaries from a foreign ruler in order to obtain the imperial recognition that would afford them better trading opportunities.

Chinese travelers also on occasion visited Kyushu, though one expert opines that it is likely that they did not see very much, and perhaps did not understand all that they saw and heard.[12] Still, accounts of the strict discipline of the people, the signs of respect paid by inferiors to superiors, their impressive martial spirit, and the emphasis on cleanliness and ritual purification are all consonant with Japanese culture as it existed in later centuries.

CHINA GAINS INFLUENCE OVER JAPAN

By the time China had been reunited under the Sui dynasty in 589, missions were being recorded in Japan's own records as well as those of China. The Japanese seem never to have been comfortable in their relations with China, resenting the subservient attitude expected of them and regarding themselves as the center of their own diplomatic order.[13] In behavior considered beyond shocking at the time, Prince Shōtoku, as regent for Empress Suiko (554–628; r. 593–628), wrote to the Sui emperor in 607 on her behalf, saying, "The emperor of the land where the sun rises sends a letter to the emperor of the land where the sun sets."

This tacit assumption of equality between the barbarian empress and the son of heaven greatly upset the Sui emperor and his court. According to the understated language of the Sui dynastic history, "When the emperor read this he was not pleased, and he said to the President of the Court of Diplomatic Reception, 'This letter from the barbarians contains improprieties. Do not call it to my attention again.'"[14]

Note, however, that Shōtoku is using a name for his country that could only have been bestowed by the Chinese or by orienting Japan with reference to China, given the position of the sun. *Nihon* (*Riben* in Chinese), whose ideographs signify "origin of the sun," is still the name both countries use to designate Japan today. The Sui, however, typically referred to Japan as *woguo*, or "country of the dwarves," rather than the state of Yamato, Great Peace, as the Japanese would have described themselves at the time. Despite this awkwardness, Japanese missions to China continued because they brought back material goods and, more importantly, useful information about Chinese culture.

It is interesting to speculate on what Prince Shōtoku might have done had an early death not cut short his career. Not a nativist by any means, he had supported the introduction of Buddhism from Korea against the opposition of clans who did not approve of foreign ideas and wanted to adhere to indigenous Shintō practices—as well as because they wanted to preserve a certain degree of autonomy from the imperial court. Power and religion were, as is often the case in other cultures, intertwined. Additionally, while Prince Shōtoku refused to acknowledge that Japan was subservient to China, he clearly believed that his country should learn from it. There was a strongly pragmatic element to his desire to do so. The major challenge confronting Shōtoku was the establishment of the central power of the imperial court, and the teachings of Confucianism were very helpful in that regard.[15]

THE TAIKA REFORMS

In 645 a coup overthrew the dominant Soga clan. The coup's leaders, a future emperor assisted by the founder of the powerful Fujiwara lineage of future imperial consorts and regents, proclaimed direct imperial rule. 645 was designated the first year of Taika, meaning Great Transformation. Significantly, this represented the first use in Japan of the Chinese-style dating system.

The new rulers proceeded to transform Japanese institutions along the model of China's Tang dynasty (618–907), then at the peak of its power. While useful in consolidating the rule of the new Japanese leaders, the Taika reforms were also a response to a perceived danger from abroad. In the nineteenth century, the Meiji reforms would be impelled by a similar perception of external threat.

In this case, the threat was from the Korean peninsula, where the three kingdoms of Silla, Koguryŏ, and Paekche contended. One of these, Silla, was backed by the powerful Tang dynasty. Another, Paekche, had close ties to Japan. After a combined Silla–Tang force conquered the Paekche capital, the Japanese responded by dispatching a force whose mission was to restore the Paekche kingdom. It was decisively defeated in 663. Silla went on to conquer Koguryŏ,[16] thus creating the first unified Korean kingdom. A twentieth-century analyst deemed the sense of crisis in Japan occasioned by its defeat in the wars of Korean unification to be comparable in magnitude only to the Mongol invasions of the thirteenth century and the arrival of Commodore Matthew Perry's black ships in the nineteenth.[17] Heightening the sense of danger, the Tang sent five separate embassies to Japan in less than a decade, the last of which included over 2,000 men. It is conceivable that the missions were intended to placate Japan and perhaps gain its acquiescence to China's control of the Korean peninsula. But it is clear from both Japanese sources and the feverish defensive preparations taken during this period that the Japanese considered their purpose to be hostile.[18]

Silla and its successors, the Wang dynasty Koryŏ (935–1392) and Yi dynasty Chŏson (1392–1916), adopted a deferential posture toward China that, as will be seen, enabled Korean states to call on China for assistance against Japan in the 1590s and again in the decade before 1894. Korea, in addition to its role in transmitting Chinese culture to Japan, was to continue to be the object of competition between the two for power and influence, as well as an active participant in the rivalries between them. Japan viewed a Korea unified under Silla and backed by Tang dynasty military might as threatening its own security. This was a major factor in the Japanese desire to emulate the institutions that produced Tang power.[19]

EIGHTH-CENTURY REFORMS

The early eighth century saw three important developments in this borrowing from China. In the first of these, in 701, the country's first comprehensive criminal and administrative codes were promulgated. Called the Taihō *ritsuryō*, they were based on Chinese theories and, with minor revisions, remained the basis for civil administration for centuries to come. A seventeen-point document conceived by Prince Shōtoku was promulgated. Although generally referred to as a constitution, it would not be recognizable as such by today's standards. Second, in 710, a new capital was built at Nara. It was laid out in accordance with the Chinese ideal of symmetrical architecture for administrative centers. A successor capital established at Heian, later known as Kyōto, in 794 also used this plan.

The third project was the compilation of Japan's first national history, the *Nihon Shoki* (Chronicles of Japan), according to Chinese historiographical models. Completed in 720, the *Nihon Shoki* was written in stylistically proper Chinese. It attempted to establish the legitimacy of the imperial family and the recently Sinified court government. By contrast, the earlier *Kojiki* (Records of Ancient Matters), completed in 712, focused more on ancient legends and was written in a hybrid language that interspersed Chinese with Japanese elements. About this time also, the Japanese began to refer to their country as *Nihon*, the land of the rising sun, as Prince Shōtoku had done in his sixth-century letter.

While the new administrative system was in most respects a copy of that of the Tang dynasty model, there were small but important differences. The Department of Worship, for example, outranked the Council of State, such that precedence was given to the priestly functions of the sovereign over secular administrative matters. In essence, this indicated the unwillingness of the reformers to abandon their national tradition that the claim to the throne is established solely on the basis of descent, in favor of the Chinese notion that the mandate of heaven is given on the basis of moral worthiness. The hierarchy of offices also depended far more on birth than, as Chinese theory had it, talent. An edict of 682 said bluntly that, when selecting men for office, the consideration must be birth first, then character, and, lastly, capacity.[20]

In the educational area, the influence of Korea in the transmission of Chinese ideas was also important. Many of the professors at the Confucian academy were émigrés from the destroyed Paekche kingdom or their descendants. So as well were many of those who sat for the civil service examinations. Japan's first university admitted students from higher and lower ranks of noble families as well as commoners. In this sense, it was actually more egalitarian than its Chinese counterparts in the same era, since the Tang system was highly aristocratic and hereditary. However, this changed over time. As Japanese court offices became increasingly hereditary, the examination system, which had never functioned on more than a limited scale, atrophied into insignificance. Meanwhile, the Chinese examination system was evolving into the normal path for selection to high office.[21]

NATIVIST ELEMENTS RETURN

In the eighth and ninth centuries, the Japanese court attempted to preserve its Sinified appearance, though in practice, as seen above, elements of Chinese and native culture co-existed. In poetry, which has enjoyed an honored place in Japanese culture, the *Kaifusō* (Fond Recollections of Poetry) was published in Chinese in 751, and the *Man'yōshū* (Collection for Ten Thousand Generations), containing what many Japanese consider the most pristinely pure of their native poetry, in 759. In general, for a period of two centuries, the court attempted to govern according to Chinese principles, somewhat modified by nativist ideas. Court culture was Sinified.

Beginning in the mid-ninth century, the court gradually abandoned this commitment to functioning in the Chinese manner. Politically, a single lineage from the northern house of the Fujiwara family came to dominate high court offices. Lesser posts became hereditary preserves as well, in contrast to the Confucian ideal of a bureaucratically organized meritocracy. Economically, land that was supposed to be controlled by the government and distributed to peasants increasingly accumulated into large, privately managed estates known as *shōen*. The revenue from these shōen went to powerful court families rather than into the government treasury, thus decreasing the dependence of these families on the central government. Although the ritsuryō codes were not revoked and interest in Chinese culture remained, they gradually lost their positions of preeminence.[22]

Despite the slow diffusion of power away from the court, the imperial capital at Kyōto remained the unrivaled center of culture. Interest in Chinese forms declined. Japanese literature, which had almost disappeared after the publication of the *Man'yōshu*, began to flourish again. When the imperially sponsored *Kokinshū* (Collection of Ancient and Modern Times) was compiled in 905, the native poetic tradition was given the official recognition that had previously been given to Chinese literature alone. As a general statement, during the middle and late Heian periods, from about 900 to 1185 A.D., a more noticeably Japanese culture arose. A native script that was better suited to writing the Japanese language was developed. Novels such as the still popular classic *Tale of Genji* employed this script, as well as exemplifying traits that later developed into a distinctively Japanese aesthetic tradition.

The divide between China and Japan should not be overstated. Certain accommodations were made by each to the other. For example, the Japanese, regarding the requirement to bring tribute and make obsequious oaths of fealty to be offensive, had taken to dispatching their embassies with gifts but not documents. This was apparently accepted at certain ports of entry where Chinese officials were familiar with Japanese customs, although not at others. The records of a court scholar named Kiyokimi state that, when he arrived at the inland Tang capital of Chang'an in 804, he found that his compatriots who had traveled on another ship were absent. His inquiries revealed that they had been detained because their ship had been blown off course and landed at a port where Japanese customs were not understood.[23] And, complaints about the distasteful nature of Chinese attitudes aside, when a scholar/poet named Ono no Takamura wrote a tract attacking the whole purpose of embassies to China, he was deemed to have insulted the memories of the emperors who had dispatched them, and banished forthwith.[24]

However, the dispatch of embassies began to decline. The last, in 838, on which Ono no Takamura had served as second in command, is the best known, since Ennin, a Buddhist monk who participated in it and traveled widely in China over a period of nine years, kept a meticulous diary of his observations. Part of the reason for the lesser number of missions was that the Tang dynasty itself was in decline. Members of Kiyokimi's embassy had reported unstable conditions at the turn of the ninth century; these can also be inferred from Ennin's diary, though what is more remarkable are his descriptions of the impressive attention to organization and the observance of ritual even in a period of dynastic deterioration.[25] Other reasons for the decline in embassies were their expense and the dangers inherent in the treacherous journey across the sea. But most important may have been the conviction that the purposes of the embassies could better be achieved by other means.

Here again, the role of Korea is important. In the view of the Japanese court, the primary reasons for sending missions to China were political and cultural. They were intended to demonstrate that the country was a civilized member of the East Asian community of nations, and to bring back additional learning from China. At least in theory, the exchange of goods was a secondary concern. If, therefore, the economic functions of the missions were taken over by private traders, then the more important political and cultural functions could be fulfilled by relations with Parhae, a newly arisen kingdom that included ethnic Korean and Manchurian, non-Han Chinese, peoples. Japan could add substance to its claim of equality with, or even superiority to, China, using Parhae as a surrogate.

Since Parhae was willing to place itself in a nominally inferior position to Japan, the Kyōto court's ties with it were more gratifying than with China, where Japanese envoys had several times run into problems for their refusal to take a properly subservient posture. Since Parhae also continued to have regular contacts with China, its missions were a way, although possibly not the best one, to follow developments in China. Moreover, the Parhae government was willing to send embassies to Japan even when these were not reciprocated, thus reducing the danger and the expense involved in mounting missions to that kingdom.[26] Between 794 and 929, Parhae sent twenty of its thirty-three missions to Japan, whereas Japan sent only two embassies to China. By 894 no official missions had been sent to China for more than half a century,[27] although some merchants and members of the Buddhist clergy continued contacts. The cessation of the missions is considered a major turning point in early Japanese history.

NOT QUITE SEPARATE, WHETHER OR NOT EQUAL

In Japan, the gradual devolution of power away from the imperial court led to a struggle among the major clans for actual power, as opposed to the titular power of the emperor. A bloody contest for military ascendancy between the Taira and Minamoto lineages ended in 1192 with the establishment of a military government in Kamakura that effectively terminated rule by the court at Kyōto. Minamoto Yoritomo wielded power with the title of *shōgun* (meaning "general"). Yoritomo's headquarters, the *bakufu*, literally translated as (military) tent government, is also referred to by later English-language scholars as the shōgunate. As commander-in-chief of the entire warrior class, the shōgun ordered that all disputes from members of this class be submitted to him, rather than to the imperial court. Clearly, this endowed the shōgun with immense power that went far beyond the literal translation of his title. The separation of rule between bakufu and court was geographic as well: the largely powerless court remained in Kyōto, with the bakufu in Kamakura and, later, Edo. At that time, the warrior class would even be prohibited from entering the imperial capital. This development was to have profound significance not only for the future of Japan, but also for Japan's relations with China.

In China, a period of internal division and invasions by less civilized neighbors culminated in conquest by one of the least civilized, the Mongols, in the thirteenth century. Ruling as the Yuan dynasty, the Mongols conquered all of China, as well as a number of contiguous territories. Although consciously resisting pressures toward adopting Han Chinese practices, even changing the location of the capital city and repairing to a more northern location in the summer months in the fashion of their nomadic forebears, the Mongols/Yuan were interested in receiving both tribute and the submission of their neighbors. Unlike the Han Chinese dynasties, they actively sought out both. A Mongol envoy appeared in Japan in 1268 to demand tribute, but was rebuffed. The Mongols retaliated by mounting an invasion in 1274, which the Japanese fought off. A second, and stronger, force was sent in 1281, but was destroyed just off the coast by a typhoon. Collectively, the invasions reinforced national consciousness in Japan. Shintō clerics fostered the belief that the winds were divinely sent (*kamikaze*), interpreting them as evidence of the protection that the indigenous deities, principally the sun goddess Amaterasu, and Hachiman, the god of war, afforded to Japan.

Less than a half century later, a political leader and scholar named Kitabatake Chikafusa wrote the *Records of the Legitimate Succession of Divine Sovereignty*, in which he proclaimed the superiority of Japan over China, as well as India, because of Japan's single line of emperors descended from the gods. At approximately the same time or even a bit earlier, there appeared the *Five Classics of Shintō*, forgeries that were supposedly set in remote antiquity that attempted to provide a Shintō philosophy and ethics. Since Shintō, which has been compared to nature worship, had not actually possessed these attributes, Kitabatake's argument borrowed extensively from Buddhism. Advocates of what came to be called primal Shintō would later contend, based on these classics, that the Japanese gods were the original substance and Buddha and the boddhisattvas merely the manifested traces.[28]

Although the Mongol invasions had a positive effect on Japanese consciousness of national solidarity, this did not accrue to the benefit of the Kamakura bakufu. Repelling the intruders had been extremely expensive and, in contrast to previous struggles, which had been among and between factions within Japan, there were no lands to distribute to the victors in return for their services. The Kamakura bakufu was badly weakened. Meanwhile, in Kyōto, Go-Daigo became the first adult male to become emperor in over a hundred years. Eager to reclaim the glory of his ancestors, Go-Daigo proclaimed the restoration of direct imperial rule. Some warriors joined him, and in 1333, the Kamakura bakufu was overthrown.

Ashikaga Takauji was the most prominent of the warriors who supported Go-Daigo, doing so with the expectation that he would be named shōgun. When Go-Daigo did not award him the office, Takauji seized Kyōto and installed a puppet emperor on the throne who granted him the coveted title. Go-Daigo, however, took the imperial regalia and fled to Yoshino, in the southern part of the country. From then until 1391, there were two rival emperors. In 1392 an agreement was reached under which the southern emperors were declared to have been legitimate, but yielded the regalia and the throne to the northern claimants.

The Yuan dynasty fell in 1368, and was replaced by an indigenous Han Chinese dynasty, the Ming. There were pressures to resume relations with China. Even unofficial trips had been difficult under Mongol rule, and merchants and Buddhist leaders on both sides were in favor of resuming contact. Coming to agreement on the circumstances under which this could be effected was another matter. Ming envoys who arrived prior to 1392 took note of unsettled conditions, prompting a letter from the founder of the dynasty, the Hongwu emperor that intended to convey support for the legitimate ruler and condemn the rebels. Hongwu appeared, however, to be unsure which was which.

The Japanese officials who read the letter were offended by phrases such as "it is the common rule of propriety that barbarians should respect the Middle Kingdom." Hongwu, in turn, was offended by their response, which was not phrased in a sufficiently deferential manner, and was moreover dated according to Japanese chronology, rather than employing a calendar based on the founding of the Great Ming. Successive correspondence became more overtly rude. A letter from the Ming emperor, dated 1376, contained an explicit threat if compliance were not forthcoming:

> [Y]ou ... make it clear that you do not obey the order of Heaven ... The distance which separates us from Japan is nothing but the high seas. It takes only five days and nights to sail with favorable winds. It would be a great advantage for you to respect Heaven's will by practicing a benevolent rule in order that you may escape the disaster of an invasion by China.[29]

Another letter, written by the Hongwu emperor himself, reads in part:

> You stupid eastern barbarians! Your king and courtiers are not acting correctly; you have disturbed neighboring countries in all directions. In former years, you created dissensions with ungrounded statements. ... [T]his year your people come ... and want to determine which of us is the stronger. Oh! living so far across the sea, you are unmindful of the wonderful land that Heaven has given you; you are haughty and disloyal. ... [W]ill this not inevitably bring disaster upon you?[30]

A Japanese reply of 1382 was defiant and provocative, openly denying the primacy of the Chinese emperor, with such statements as

> [H]ow should only the Middle Kingdom have its master while the barbarians do not have their rulers? Heaven and earth are vast; they are not monopolized by one ruler. The universe is great and wide, and various countries are created each to have a share in its rule. ... [T]he world does not belong to a single person.

Its author, Prince Kanenaga, says that he has heard that the emperor is planning to invade "my territory" and warns that China might receive an unpleasant surprise if such action were taken.[31] In this vein, Kanenaga notes that "this small country" possesses the literary works of Confucius and Mencius as well as the military works of Sun Zi and Wu Qi. How would the Japanese kneel to pay respect to China's best generals?[32] The implication is that, although the Japanese had enormous respect for the sages named, this did not translate into feelings of subservience to the state that had produced them.

The Chinese emperor, perhaps mindful of the fate of Mongol attempts to invade Japan, apparently decided against invasion, but he remained angry. In 1386 Hongwu refused to receive a Japanese envoy, and a break in relations occurred between the two countries. There was an additional irritant to the Ming court's pique over Japanese arrogance in claiming a position of equality: the more concrete issue of raids on the Chinese coast by Japanese pirates. Since the common, and disparaging, name for Japan was land of the dwarves, the sea raiders were known as dwarf pirates, *wokou*.

In 1398 the Jianwen emperor succeeded to the throne after his grandfather, Ming Hongwu's, death. The new ruler apparently looked favorably on a memorial to him from Ashikaga Yoshimitsu in 1401. Couched in submissive language, it resulted in Jianwen's ordering that Chinese Buddhist monks accompany the embassy on its return voyage to Japan. Jianwen's favorable attitude toward Japan may have been influenced by the civil war he found himself embroiled in and ultimately lost. He was killed by his uncle, who became the third Ming emperor, Yongle. In 1405 Yongle accepted Yoshimitsu as a vassal of Great Ming.

Although this act of submission would later cause Yoshimitsu to be heavily criticized, there were tangible immediate benefits. The Ashikaga bakufu received a monopoly on legal trade with China, as regulated by tallies issued by the Chinese authorities. These consisted of slips of paper numbered to whatever level had been decided upon—typically one hundred—with the first half of the Chinese name for Japan written at the top and the other at the bottom. The papers were then torn and placed in stub books, one for each side. If they fit, the ship's cargo was deemed legitimate. Persons without valid tallies were regarded as unauthorized and subject to arrest.[33] Although the agreement provided for only one tribute-bearing voyage per decade and put limits on the number of ships, their crews, and their passages, all these restrictions eventually came to be disregarded.

In return for this recognition of his legitimacy, at least from the Chinese, and trade arrangements that would enrich his treasury, Yoshimitsu agreed to suppress piracy. This was a more nuanced issue than surface appearances might indicate. Particularly after the Ming sea voyages ceased in 1433,[34] the dynasty's attentions were internally focused and official external contacts were carefully regulated. Ming Hongwu had gone so far as to decree that no Chinese should be permitted to go overseas, and that those who sailed abroad on ships of more than two masts—presumably meaning that fishing boats would be allowed to practice their trade—would be executed.[35] However, local interests in coastal areas were frequently eager to trade. These included not only merchants and their wealthy customers, but also officials, quite a few of whom were willing to support the wokou activities in return for a share of the profits. Ming sources indicate that Chinese craftsmen, with their superior maritime engineering skills, helped Japanese seamen to improve the quality of their ships. They also reveal that some Chinese joined the wokou, as did a few Portuguese. In time, Chinese pirates would become more numerous than Japanese. Some merchants and wealthy families became heavily indebted to the pirates, whose raids might therefore have the aim of retribution for defaulted debts.[36] The collusion between vested interests on China's coast and the pirates complicated the difficulties of apprehending and suppressing them. Nonetheless, Yoshimitsu appeared to undertake the task with some relish. He presented a group of captives to the Ming emperor, who politely returned them to Yoshimitsu. Yoshimitsu then boiled them alive. According to a Chinese document of 1402, the copper cauldron used therein was preserved in situ.[37]

As restrictions on trade eased, piracy declined. In the words of one Ming official,

> The pirates and the traders were the same people. When trade flourished, the pirates became traders; when trade was banned, the traders became pirates. At first it was trade that was banned, later it was piracy that was suppressed. The more strictly enforced was the ban [on trade], the fiercer piracy became.[38]

In the fifteenth century, as would occur again 500 years later, when there were profits to be made, merchants would find ways to forge ties despite the obstacles imposed by their respective governments.

Frictions between the highest levels of government continued, as did at least some level of pirate activity. In a 1418 imperial rescript, the Yongle emperor complained that since pirates continued to invade, "we do not know whether your conduct is virtuous or not." He carefully distinguished the Ming military from the Mongols, "who were strong in riding and shooting but weak in seamanship," averring that the Ming forces were skilled in both.[39] Several decades later, the Japanese government would discover that this was not an idle boast.

THE MING, THE FALL OF THE ASHIKAGA, AND THE REUNIFICATION OF JAPAN

Gaining Ming recognition of its legitimacy and consequent control of trade revenue did not sustain Ashikaga rule for very long. As members of the Ashikaga family and their generals engaged in intrigues in the capital, power drifted away from the central government. In the provinces, warlords of the great families, *daimyō*, were becoming increasingly autonomous. Such control as the Ashikaga possessed, which was never as much as it desired, disappeared after the Ōnin War of 1467–1477. A period of disunity extended from the mid-fifteenth to the early seventeenth century. It is known as the Sengoku, or Warring States, era, in conscious imitation of the 200-year period before China was unified by Qin Shi Huangdi in 221 B.C.E. An important difference with China, however, is that in Japan conflict was not among states or even provinces, but among the daimyō warlords. The Ashikaga shōguns became puppets of the most powerful of these families, even as previous shōguns had made puppets of emperors.

As might be expected, little that could be called Japanese foreign relations occurred in this time frame. In 1547 licensed trade lapsed. Japanese were excluded from China, and Chinese were forbidden by Chinese law from going to Japan.[40] But the daimyō of the western regions were able to conduct foreign relations of their own with neighboring states, including China. The same areas were also visited by Christian missionaries from the Western Hemisphere. Of the so-called three unifiers of the period, Oda Nobunaga, the first, was able to seize Kyōto and, a few years later, in 1573, abolished the shōgunate. He was assassinated by one of his own generals in 1582.

Nobunaga was succeeded by the second unifier, and arguably the outstanding figure of this period, Toyotomi Hideyoshi. Hideyoshi was able to establish control over all of Japan, although he never assumed the title of shōgun. In 1592 he invaded Korea. Fleeing Seoul in the face of advancing Japanese troops, the Korean king appealed to the Ming emperor for help. A Chinese force, fielding heavier cannon than the Japanese possessed, defeated the invaders at Pyŏngyang, though it did not pursue the retreating Japanese. A truce was arranged, with Hideyoshi demanding an imperial daughter as consort; resumption of licensed trade between China and Japan; Korean princes to be sent to Japan as hostages; and sworn promises from high Korean officeholders that they would never attack Japan. In return, Japan would promise to return the four northern provinces and the capital of Korea to the king. Implicitly, therefore, the southern provinces would belong to Japan.

These were amazing terms from a defeated leader, and the Ming court either was unaware of the conditions or decided to ignore them. In the closing days of 1596, a Chinese ambassador reached Kyōto for the investiture ceremony of Hideyoshi as king of Japan and vassal of the emperor. When the envoys read a patronizing letter from the court rather than the submissive document Hideyoshi expected, he became abusive and, a few hours later, announced his intention to declare war on China. Again, the fighting took place in Korea, with the outnumbered Japanese, mostly from the western domain of Satsuma, inflicting enormous destruction.[41] Japanese naval forces did not fare nearly as well. The Koreans had developed "turtle boats," so named because their sides were covered with iron plates and spikes. These thwarted Japanese skills at grappling and boarding. Korean ships were also equipped with cannon on all sides, whereas the Japanese ships had very few. Although the Koreans did not have many turtle boats, other Chinese and Korean ships proved more maneuverable than their Japanese counterparts, which were essentially merchant vessels that had been pressed into wartime service. And the square sails used by the Japanese were less effective than Chinese and Korean designs with fore and aft sails.[42]

Despite the bravery with which its military fought, the Japanese position on land may not have been sustainable. Hideyoshi, whose health was failing, appears to have been considering a withdrawal. When he died, in 1598, a peace agreement was quickly concluded. Rivalry for preeminence on the Korean peninsula had again brought China and Japan into conflict.

SINO-JAPANESE RELATIONS IN THE EARLY TOKUGAWA ERA

The third unifier, Tokugawa Ieyasu, defeated his adversaries in the epic battle of Sekigahara in 1600 and set about establishing control over all of Japan. Even after his success at Sekigahara, Ieyasu's legitimacy was in doubt due to the existence of Hideyoshi's son and designated heir. On his deathbed, Hideyoshi had had his generals swear allegiance to the boy. Ieyasu maneuvered carefully. He rewarded the daimyō, mostly from eastern Japan, who had fought on his side; took the title of shōgun; and established his headquarters at Edo. Ieyasu also cultivated good relations with the imperial court. He installed a deputy in Kyōto to serve as a channel of communication between the court and the shōgun, also charging the official with keeping a close eye on the daimyō of western Japan, in which area Kyōto is located.

The ability to control foreign relations was a major building block in establishing the legitimacy of the new shōgun's government. Reestablishing control was not as simple as it might sound. The revival of relations with China was fraught with familiar difficulties. Ieyasu could have petitioned the Chinese emperor for vassal status, thereby opening the way for trade that could be used to reward the loyalty of his retainers. But doing so would have made Ieyasu vulnerable to the same kind of criticism that Ashikaga Yoshimitsu had been subjected to. In any case, the Ming court, with memories of Hideyoshi's invasion fresh in mind, was understandably wary of Japan. Piracy problems, though not exclusively attributable to Japanese, much less to the Japanese government, continued to be an irritant.

There were internal pressures to resume trade. The lord of Tsushima, a poor island whose prosperity depended heavily on trade with Korea, needed an agreement between Ieyasu and the Korean king to conduct the trade. Knowing that Korea, as a vassal state of China, would insist that the letter be phrased in ways that Ieyasu would not accept, the lord in 1606 took the unusual step of forging one. Since the missive was dated according to the Ming calendar and referred to Ieyasu as king, a title he had rejected, the Korean king saw through the ruse immediately. In due course, word of Tsushima's ruse reached Ieyasu.

Appropriate punishments were meted out, with all the daimyō present in Edo ordered to attend the sentencing so that neither they nor their descendants would be tempted to engage in similar conduct.[43] Ieyasu had learned a lesson as well. He responded by establishing the *sankin kōtai*, or alternate residence system, which required daimyō to spend part of the year at the shōgun's castle in Edo and leave their families in the area when they returned to their domains. This formed an important part of the Tokugawa system of control.

A series of exchanges between China and Japan covering the years 1611 and 1625 might best be characterized as shadow-boxing. The first letter, written by an adviser rather than Ieyasu himself, was dated according to the Japanese calendar, not signed by the shōgun, and did not take the form of a petition. Its statement that the Ryūkyūan kingdom calls itself Japan's vassal, whereas the Chinese consider Ryūkyū its vassal state, implies that Japan has taken China's place in the celestial order. A reply of sorts, not from the Ming court but from the military governor of Zhejiang province, offered direct trade in return for the suppression of piracy. But it was discovered that this letter to the shōgun was worded identically to a letter to his deputy at the trading port of Nagasaki, thus violating the distinction between superior and inferior. Further, it addressed the shōgun in a manner deemed disrespectful to his status. The effort to reestablish relations failed.

The Tokugawa, in essence, sought to establish a separate world order centered around itself rather than China. Relations with the Korean and Ryūkyūan kingdoms thus took on special significance. Early shōguns took care to entertain their foreign embassies lavishly on Japanese soil, to establish not only their international but also domestic legitimacy. They attempted to lure Korea out of the Chinese ambit and subordinate itself to Japan. The Koreans were resistant, as evidenced by their insistence on using the Ming calendar. However, as the Manchu presence on their borders increased and the decline of the Ming dynasty left their protector state less able to defend them, Korean leaders were understandably reluctant to antagonize Japan. When the Manchus displaced the Ming in 1644, so did Korea's use of the Chinese dating system. It was never resumed.

In general, missions from Korea were treated as peers of the bakufu, whereas those from Ryūkyū were addressed as vassals, received less elegant lodgings than the Koreans, and, unlike the Koreans, did not receive lavish ceremonial banquets. The Dutch were received at Edo in a still simpler fashion, since they were not regarded as representing a king or country. Having rejected official government-to-government relations with China in 1621, the bakufu relegated the Chinese to the lowest level of its foreign relations. The Chinese were not allowed to visit Edo at all: matters concerning them were handled by the Nagasaki magistrate's office in Kyūshū. As explained by a shōgunal adviser,

> Dealing with barbarians is like dealing with slaves, which is the reason why these matters [of correspondence with China] were handled by low-ranking vassals like [Hasegawa] Fujihiro and [Gotō] Mitsutsugu.[44]

Chinese merchants calling at Nagasaki were required to present a kind of passport issued by the Nagasaki Office of the Chinese Interpreters that used language demeaning to the Chinese, was dated according to the Japanese calendar, and bore what was called a split seal that was reminiscent of the trading tallies that the Ming dynasty had required of Japanese vessels wishing to trade on the China coast. A seal was stamped such that it overlapped the passport and the Office of the Interpreters' registry, enabling the edges to be compared for authenticity. Documents referred to

China as "Tang," which had vulgar connotations, rather than Great Ming or, later, Great Qing, as the Chinese would have referred to their country.[45] The obvious intent was to force the appearance of subordination—for example, if the "Tang" merchants accepted the use of the Japanese calendar, they were implicitly accepting Japan's central role in the world.

It is clear that the merchants did not lightly accept this interpretation. When, in order to reduce the number of Chinese ships calling at Nagasaki, some were sent home empty, the merchants complained to their Japanese handlers not that they were being excluded from the trade, but that if they accepted the calendar of the foreign barbarians, meaning Japan, this was tantamount to subordinating themselves to Japan. Since that was precisely the intent of the regulations, the merchants' protests received little sympathy from the Nagasaki authorities.[46]

THE SAKOKU PERIOD

In a conscious attempt to achieve separation, the shōgun issued three sets of orders, in 1633, 1635, and 1639, respectively, that closed Japan to most foreign interaction. No vessel without a valid license could leave Japan for a foreign country, no Japanese could leave for a foreign country unless he or she had received approval, and Japanese who resided abroad were to be executed if they tried to return. An exception would be made if the returnee had been held abroad against his or her will, had lived in a foreign country for less than five years, and would agree to never attempt to leave Japan again.

A few Dutch, whose shipbuilding skills the Tokugawa recognized their need for in view of the problems the Japanese naval forces had encountered in their invasion of Korea, were allowed to stay, but they were confined to tightly controlled areas that included the artificial island of Deshima. Likewise, the shōgun granted some privileges to the Portuguese, whose arms and ships were also of interest. He had noted the rivalry between the two European groups, and was able to play one off against the other, the better to receive foreign goods and knowledge.[47] In consequence of the three decrees, Japan became known as a "closed country" *sakoku*. Although it has been convincingly argued that this term arose later and implies far more closure than actually existed, given trade through Nagasaki and contacts with the Dutch and Portuguese,[48] the exclusions did provide space for the Japanese government to refine its worldview.

A number of protocol problems arose in the course of constructing this Japan-centric world order. One of the more intractable was what the Tokugawa ruler should be called in terms of external relations. Clearly, "king" was unacceptable, since it not only implied subordination to the Chinese emperor, but would also put the shōgun on the level of the ruler of Korea, whom it was trying to induce to accept vassal status. *Shōgun*, since it meant only "general," was a title even less prestigious in the Chinese world order. Obviously, the shōgun could not use the title "emperor," since there was already an individual with that title installed in Kyōto, and one who moreover was believed to be the direct descendant of the gods. The solution finally arrived at, in the 1630s, was Great Prince of Japan, Nihon-koku Taikun, which became the standard diplomatic title for the shōgun in foreign relations. Parenthetically, it is also the origin of the English-language word "tycoon." Japanese scholars have argued that the establishment of Great Prince diplomacy represented a declaration of independence from the Sinocentric world order that had dominated East Asia, and that it was a major factor in Japan's ability, alone among the nations of East Asia, to escape colonization or being parceled out among the European powers in the nineteenth century.[49]

A Western scholar goes further, believing that the choice of Great Prince of Japan was more than a declaration of independence from the Sinocentric world order: it represented the articulation of a Japan-centric world order. This new, self-sufficient domestic legitimacy structure was henceforth willing to meet with others autonomously in the diplomatic arena. There were problems in explicating this structure, not least among which was that it relied on Chinese norms and terms. There was also the difficulty of rationalizing the Confucian notion of one ruler under heaven with the Japanese reality of a ruler that was bifurcated between emperor and shōgun. While the imperial house was endowed with the symbolism of national authority, it was almost devoid of power. The opposite was true of the institution of shōgun.

ARAI HAKUSEKI'S PROPOSED REFORMS

A Confucian scholar of the era, Arai Hakuseki, attempted an ambitious synthesis of the imperial and military institutions, in order to prove that the authentic ruler should exercise comprehensive authority and that, in the situation of the time, the shōgun was the authentic person. One of the first problems he encountered was dealing with the cosmological origins of the imperial house as described in accounts of the *Kamiyo*, or Age of the Gods. Hakuseki tried to establish that this age actually existed historically, in the manner of the beginnings of Chinese rulership found in the revered classic Book of History (*Shu Jing*).

He did this by arguing that the meaning of words does not remain constant, but rather evolves continuously. Hence, given the fact that Japan did not at first have its own written language but employed the Chinese system instead, the original meaning of Japanese words had become overlaid with Chinese connotations that distorted the written accounts. Also, Hakuseki pointed out, early compilers were not consistent. Sometimes they chose characters for their phonetic value, and sometimes for their meaning. Later commentators built on these errors, providing fanciful interpretations of the kamiyo accounts solely on the meaning of the characters and ignoring the original Japanese terms that these characters had been intended to transcribe. Since there are multiple accounts of particular incidents in the *Kojiki, Nihon Shoki*, and other accounts, Hakuseki believed that none should be regarded as definitive.

While this is a plausible argument, Hakuseki chose only those interpretations that fit the conclusions he wanted to reach. The view of the kami as deities is mistaken, he says: they were actually quite human. Due to a misconstruction of the sound of a word used in the early compilations, the floating bridge of heaven that Izanagi and Isanami stood on was not actually a bridge but a line of warships on the sea. Similarly, the establishment of a pillar on the island of Onogorojima represented the posting of a symbol of sovereignty. And the intercourse that Izanagi and Isanami are said to have engaged in was in reality a pledge to join their armies in battle. According to this reasoning, the two were human beings who extended civilized rule over the realm in much the same way as Yao, Shun, and Yü had, according to the Book of History, brought the regions of China under their rule.

Hakuseki also downplayed the significance of the regalia in order to weaken those elements of the Ninigi myth that bolstered the idea that sovereignty was legitimately exercisable only in the imperial line. Hence, he extrapolated, the emperors were neither endowed with an eternal mandate to rule Japan nor exempt from accountability to heaven. Hakuseki believed that the imperial line had lost heaven's trust because the emperors had proved themselves unworthy. From the mid-fourteenth century on, he pointed out, the court existed only as a façade. The mandate had passed to the shōgun. Having established the shōgun as the appropriate holder of the mandate, however, created another conceptual problem: successive shōguns had accepted the legitimacy of bifurcated sovereignty.

Hakuseki attempted to solve this problem by referring to the pre-Tokugawa shōguns as *ha*, or hegemons, rather than shōgun. Here, he borrows from Chinese history again: in the Spring and Autumn period of the middle Zhou dynasty, the hegemons showed the legitimate rulers the respect that subjects owe to their sovereign, but, in fact, they transformed kingly authority into a hollow shell, thus contributing to further decline of kingly government and opening themselves to charges of usurpation. Clearly, Hakuseki's intent was to establish the philosophical basis for the legitimacy of the Tokugawa as possessors of the Mandate of Heaven. It is somewhat ironic that Chinese history is used as the model for a Japanese world order that its proponents felt to be far superior to the original. The Chinese court, inwardly oriented and confident in its own superiority, took no notice.

That Hakuseki believed Japan to be at least the equal of China is beyond doubt. He avoided referring to the country as Chūgoku, with its literal meaning of Central Kingdom and associated overtones of superiority. Hakuseki employed a variety of other designators, including a dynasty name, as in "Great Ming"; "the foreign court"; "the other country"; or—in the first usage of what was regarded as a derogatory term—Shina.

There were, he believed, great sages in Japan, too. Therefore, it was absurd that China should be referred to as the Central Kingdom or the Central "Flowery" (meaning civilized) Kingdom, as if Japanese civilization were somehow less civilized. He asserted that China and Japan were equal in their sovereign status, and that the shōgun was equal in status to the Chinese emperor. And that, despite China's claim to exemplify civilization, many of the authentic rites of antiquity were better preserved in Japan than in China.

Even in antiquity, Hakuseki continued, people in China had noticed that Japan had maintained rites that had been lost in the decadent days of the later Zhou dynasty. Moreover, authentic forms of weapons and armor that were lost after the Qin conquered the Zhou had survived in Japan, as had items of clothing. In China, said Hakuseki, clothing had changed to reflect barbarian influence. Although the word "barbarian" was also frequently used to refer to Chinese, Hakuseki obviously had in mind groups like the Tangut and Jurchen, who conquered parts of China in past history as the Xixia and Jin dynasties, respectively.

Hakuseki also initiated construction projects whose aim was to make the shōgunal premises in Edo the equivalent of the imperial court in Kyōto. At the same time, he attempted to fuse the lines of authority. Drawing on the model of the Chinese sage Yao voluntarily choosing Shun rather than his own son to succeed him, and Shun, in turn, choosing Yü, Hakuseki arranged for the retired emperor Reigen to present Ietsugu, the son and heir of the recently deceased shōgun Ienobu, with his cap of adulthood. The intent was to establish a symbolic father–son relationship that implied Ietsugu might act as the emperor's heir in other ways as well.

Hakuseki also arranged the marriage of an imperial daughter to a military leader. This was unprecedented. Although the daughters of military leaders had previously married emperors, and the children of such unions had succeeded to the throne, never before had the daughter of an emperor married down into a military household.[50]

The court was in other ways loath to cooperate with Hakuseki's efforts, however. The emperor most assuredly did not volunteer to transfer power to the shōgun in the manner attributed to Yao and Shun, and could not have been happy with Hakuseki's analysis that imperial decadence had caused his lineage to forfeit the Mandate of Heaven. In the end, Hakuseki's reforms were almost completely overturned when a new shōgun, Yoshimune, restored traditional norms. The bifurcation of sovereignty remained, with the shōgun, at least in theory, exercising power by a grant from the emperor. At a later date, the bifurcation of sovereignty would be challenged again, in the direction of restoring power to the emperor.[51]

FALL OF THE MING DYNASTY

As these events were taking place in Japan, in China, the Ming had from the early seventeenth century on been exhibiting the classic signs of dynastic decline. The costs of defending Korea from Japan had sapped the imperial treasury, and Chinese scholars of the time described the Wanli emperor as selfish and inattentive to affairs of state. Barbarian enemies, in this case, the Manchus, were attacking. All of these were considered indications that the Mandate of Heaven was being lost. Japanese officials were aware of this, and watched developments in China with growing apprehension. Though referring to the Chinese as "barbarians," they were obviously aware of distinctions among barbarians, and ranked the Manchus significantly below the Chinese. There were also vivid memories of the attempted Mongol invasions. Although their failure was interpreted as a manifestation of the commitment of Japanese gods to protect the territory of the sun goddess, no one appeared anxious to test the willingness of the gods to protect the country from a Manchu repeat of the Mongol actions.

In the forty-year period following the fall of the Ming in 1644, the bakufu received a series of letters from Ming loyalists requesting help. At least one argued that the "Tatars" had been enemies of Japan from ancient times, and pointed out that it was the Ming who had defeated the Mongols/Tatars. The author thereby implied that there was a debt to be paid and reasoned that, in light of "historic friendship" an alleged between Japan and the Ming, it was only proper for troops to be dispatched to help restore the dynasty. These requests were rejected on various grounds, including the facts that no formal relations had existed between the countries for a hundred years, and that Japan had formally adopted a policy of exclusion.

An equally important reason may have been that the numerous letters came from different individuals, each claiming to represent the true Ming claimant to the throne. Although there was considerable support for sending troops, the shōgun and his advisers could not be sure to whom they should be sent. Moreover, the various claimants appeared to be as eager to fight each other as the Manchus.[52] There seemed little serious hope that a restoration was feasible; one of the last of the pretenders, seemingly oblivious to the erosion of his position, was described as "madly singing in a leaky boat."[53] In hindsight, the decision not to send troops was a wise one: the Manchus, ruling as the Qing dynasty, did not attack or even harass Japan.

KOKUGAKU

Under the Tokugawa, Japan experienced an unusually long respite from war, either internal or external. A kind of proto-industrialization evolved. The transportation infrastructure that had been improved to meet the needs of the *sankin kōtai* system was used by many others besides lords and their retinues. It facilitated the circulation of merchants and their wares, books, theatrical performances, and works of art among the different areas of the country. With relatively high literacy rates, rising prosperity, and a highly urbanized population—Edo, at over a million people, has been described as the largest city in the world at the start of the eighteenth century, with Kyōto and Ōsaka comparable in size to London and Paris—a vibrant popular culture developed. Since Japan was relatively isolated from the outside world, this culture developed with very little external influence.

One of the manifestations of this synergy of literacy, urbanity, prosperity, infrastructure, and isolation was the development of a keen interest in the past. This included a rethinking of the relationship between nativism and Confucianism, which had co-existed reasonably comfortably throughout the seventeenth century. Japanese scholars of Confucius found verification for the sage's premises in Japanese history, tried to harmonize Confucian truths with the native truths of Shintō, and attempted to apply Confucian political principles to their government's structure. They might even, as Arai Hakuseki had done, argue that Japanese history had respected such Confucian virtues as loyalty and obedience in a way that was superior to China.

Nativists and Confucianists shared a number of basic tenets: that there was a Way; that conformity to it yielded blessings to both individuals and their communities; and that life in the past was preferable to life in the present. Therefore, one should seek to resurrect the elements of this ancient perspective within the present. However, with the development of *kokugaku*, or national studies, in the mid- and late eighteenth centuries, scholars tended to hold the introduction of foreign doctrines such as Confucianism and Buddhism responsible for the disruption of this ancient perfection. They argued that these alien doctrines had disturbed the spiritual harmony that existed in the distant past and continued to do so. Different schools of analysis, and differences of opinion within each school, compound the difficulties of summarizing kokugaku. For example, some kokugaku scholars believed that it was acceptable to study Confucianism, but only after one had properly purified one's mind of the unconscious accretions of its categories of thought. Others felt that Confucianism should be ignored as dangerous and misleading. Some argued that an indigenous written language had existed prior to the introduction of Chinese characters, others that the ancient Japanese had no need for a writing system, relying instead on their powers of memorization, while developing superior intellects in the process.[54]

Nonetheless, one common theme was the desire of kokugaku scholars to ascertain the character of the society before the intrusion of foreign doctrines, to probe what was purely Japanese. The ambiguities inherent in doing so have been discussed above, and kokugaku scholars had the same tendency as Arai Hakuseki to find justification for what they wanted to through selective interpretation of the available texts. As the movement progressed, there was a tendency to cast foreign doctrines in more of an antagonistic relationship to what was typically portrayed as a naive, unlettered, and purer past. This had been guided by Shintō, the Way of the Gods, that was sufficient for all their needs, from ordering both daily lives and the governance of the realm.

As a case in point, writing in the late seventeenth century, Tokugawa Mitsukuni (1628–1701), daimyō of Mito and patron of kokugaku, could say merely that, although it was natural for the people of China to call their country "central flower [civilization]," Japanese should speak of their own land as the central flower,[55] positing an equality between the two countries. Later scholars, however, would assert that Japanese civilization was not only equal but also superior to Chinese civilization. Shintō revival was a common feature of kokugaku scholarship as the eighteenth century progressed. One of its advocates argued that Shintō should not be known by that name, a Chinese-derived pronunciation of the characters that caused confusion with the Way of the Chinese sages, but as "kami no michi," the Way of the [Japanese] Gods. This was not so much an attempt at Shintō revival as Shintō restoration, since its central concern was to return the doctrine to its original form—unaffected by interaction with foreign thought systems.[56]

One of the most renowned of the kokugaku scholars, Kamo no Mabuchi, writing in the mid-eighteenth century, posited the existence of a "true heart," *magokoro*, or ancient Japanese heart, *yamatogokoro*, juxtaposing it with the Chinese heart, *karagakoro*, that had corrupted it. Reminding later scholars of French postmodernist thinker Michel Foucault, Mabuchi and others felt that, through careful analysis of ancient texts, the true Way could be intuited.[57] However, they would have differed sharply with Foucault in his rejection of the notion that norms and standards existed, and that there was a preordained order to the right governance of human beings.

Mabuchi's true Way of Heaven and Earth believed Buddhism to be evil, since it "made men stupid," but felt Confucianism to be far worse. It was a human invention that reduced the spirit of heaven and earth to something exceedingly trivial. Another prominent scholar, Sadao Miyahiro, believed that many of the ills that had befallen Japan were due to the wrath of the kami in protest against the malevolent influence of Buddhism. Among its bad effects was the stagnation of population growth, since so many people had entered monasteries or nunneries.[58]

As kokugaku developed, there was a tendency to look down upon and reject Chinese civilization as a whole. China had had a succession of dynasties; Japan—putatively, at least—only one. Moreover, whereas Japan had always been ruled by Japanese, China had many times been conquered and administered, in whole or in part, by barbarians. A cultural chauvinism developed that would exacerbate Chinese–Japanese relations. Kokugaku would also lead to calls to restore the emperor. In an era when the quality of the reigning shōgun tended to decline, scholarship that supported a return to the original, pre-Chinese influenced Way could and was used to return to a putatively superior time when the emperor ruled supreme. Since one of the evidences that Japan was superior to China was the assertion that Japan had had only one line of emperors, descending directly from the sun goddess, a return to first principles demanded a return to imperial rule.

A Japanese scholar has described kokugaku as Japan compensating for feelings of inferiority by defining itself through its relationship with the "unforgettable other" of China in order to achieve parity.[59] A Western scholar of Japan characterizes the background against which this intellectual discourse took place as the working out of oedipal feelings about Chinese civilization.[60]

CONCLUSIONS

China and Japan had constructed essentially similar worldviews, save that each was at the center of its own world order, regarding the other as inferior. Since Qing China and Tokugawa Japan essentially ignored each other, and since certain countries such as Korea and Ryūkyū were willing to maintain relations with each, separately, this caused little conflict. This smug self-satisfaction and splendid isolation were about to be challenged by a different set of newcomers with a very different concept of world order, the Westphalian notion of numerous sovereign states interacting on the basis of equality. Initially regarded by the Chinese as barbarians who came by sea, the newcomers would neither allow themselves to be ignored nor acknowledge a position of inferiority to China or Japan. The two countries reacted very differently to their presence, with consequences of immense magnitude to the Asian balance of power in the nineteenth and twentieth centuries.

2

China, Japan, and the Coming of the West, 1835–1945

THE WEST INTRUDES

There had been contacts between East and West for centuries, although they were sporadic and typically involved individuals or small groups. When Marco Polo, perhaps the most famous of the Western visitors, arrived at the court of the Great Khan of the Mongol (Yuan) dynasty in the thirteenth century, he found European artisans already employed there. In the sixteenth and seventeenth centuries, priests such as Matteo Ricci, Johann Schall, and Ferdinand Verbiest brought their mathematical and medicinal skills to the court while they were seeking converts to their faith. Saint Francis Xavier, among others, was active in Japan.

Maritime trade between China and European states began during the sixteenth century, and with it requests from Western states whose commercial sectors were rapidly expanding. Though Chinese officialdom rejected the idea that the Celestial Empire had any need for barbarian products, the empire's entrepreneurs and their customers were often happy to engage in such transactions.

At first, the scale was small and could be accommodated within traditional structures. The great sailing empires of the day, the Spanish and the Portuguese, exchanged silver from their colonies in the Americas for Chinese silks. As their power declined, that of the Dutch and British grew. Initially, trade took place at several ports, but in 1757 the Qing government confined it to Guangzhou (Canton). An officially authorized group of merchants, the *cohong*, paid for the privilege of trading with the foreigners, under the watchful eye of a superintendant of maritime customs for Guangdong, better known in the West as the *hoppo*. The hoppo was then responsible for levying and collecting duties on this trade and forwarding them to the Board of Revenue in Beijing. As the demand for Chinese goods grew, Western traders increasingly chafed under restrictions that included, but were not limited to, having to deal through the cohong rather than communicating directly with Chinese officials; prohibitions against stationing an envoy in the capital, learning the Chinese language, or hiring Chinese servants; and strictures that precluded payment in any other currency except silver.

THE MACARTNEY MISSION

Hence, in 1792, the British dispatched a mission headed by Lord George Macartney to the court of the Qing emperor to try to mitigate these conditions. His audience with the Qianlong emperor in the following year was less than satisfactory to both sides. Each saw the mission in terms of its own worldview. To the Chinese, Macartney's delegation was a tribute mission, and the costly gifts Macartney presented were the standard curios of such missions: interesting, but nothing to be particularly impressed with. Macartney was expected to perform the *ketou*. Conversely, members of Macartney's delegation considered themselves representatives of a co-equal monarch, and therefore entitled to the considerations due to such a group. Ritual prostrations were not part of the protocol. According to Chinese sources, Macartney did perform the ketou; his lordship reported that he had gone down on one knee only.

The letter Macartney carried back from the Qianlong emperor to the British monarch, though polite by Chinese standards, was by Western standards humiliating in the extreme. The emperor felt he had already been most gracious; British desires to trade at more ports and to station an envoy in Beijing ran counter to established procedures and were completely unnecessary. The "strange and costly objects" presented by Macartney, said the emperor, did not interest him. The Celestial Empire possessed all things in prolific abundance and had no need to import the manufactures of outside barbarians. His majesty could not overlook the inexcusable ignorance of "your island," and had instructed his ministers to enlighten the British envoy on proper demeanor. Should the island's vessels touch shore in contravention of established procedures, the barbarian merchants would be immediately expelled. Qianlong admonished the British monarch to "tremblingly obey and show no negligence."[1]

THE OPIUM WAR AND THE UNEQUAL TREATIES

Despite the Qianlong emperor's statement that all things were produced in abundance by China, British companies soon discovered consumers eager for one in particular of their manufactures: opium. Already produced within China, albeit in smaller quantities, the drug could be less expensively fabricated in British India. When, in 1833, the British government cancelled its East India Company's trade monopoly, cheap opium flooded the market. American companies became active in the opium trade as well. The number of addicts soared into the millions.

The opium influx also reversed the balance of trade to China's detriment. By 1837 the drug constituted 37 percent of Chinese imports; for fiscal year 1835–1836, there was an outflow of 4.5 million silver dollars. With silver scarce, its price rose relative to the copper that peasants used for everyday transactions. Due to a requirement that they pay their taxes in silver, taxes became increasingly burdensome. Concerned that this would lead to mass rebellions, the imperial government pleaded with the Western powers, who countered by pointing out that China produced opium itself: were they to cease exporting opium, the demand would simply be met through domestic sources.

In 1839 an imperial commissioner acting on behalf of the Daoguang emperor seized nearly 3 million pounds of British raw opium and flushed it out to sea. Outraged business interests prevailed over more moderate voices in parliament who believed the Chinese had acted properly. A fleet was dispatched. Its modern steam-powered vessels and long-range guns quickly demolished the Chinese defenses. The Opium War was the most serious defeat the dynasty had ever suffered, though other and worse defeats were to follow. A series of settlements gave foreigners substantial concessions in trade, tariffs, rights of residence, extraterritoriality,[2] most favored nation status,[3] and redress for damages. Hong Kong island was also ceded to Britain in perpetuity. These settlements were the first of the unequal treaties that were to become a sore point with latter-day Chinese patriots.

The Chinese court spent the next decade trying to avoid compliance with the treaties it had signed. Several reasons were involved. One was ignorance of the true strength of the barbarians. The unwillingness of those at the top of the hierarchy to communicate directly with inferiors, the penchant of officials to avoid transmitting bad news lest it harm their careers, and an imperial system that had made the monarchs all but prisoners in their own palaces, all contributed to this lack of knowledge. When Cixi, known to history as the empress dowager, became the de facto ruler of China, she was further constrained by rules that forbade women to leave the imperial enclave. A second factor was psychological: most officials simply refused to believe that anything the barbarians possessed was worth having. A third was preoccupation with serious domestic problems that included three large, separate rebellions with the potential to topple the dynasty.[4]

Wearying of Chinese evasive strategies, the British and French seized on a fairly minor incident in 1856 to recommence hostilities. Another rout of Chinese forces ensued; a joint Anglo-French force then fought its way into the imperial capital that had heretofore been closed to them. The Qing emperor fled the city. The ensuing 1860 Treaty of Beijing—actually a series of treaties since, through the most favored nation clause, the privileges won by the victors extended to other countries as well—constitutes the second set of unequal treaties. Having wasted more than two decades ignoring the barbarian threat, Chinese officialdom at last realized that something would have to be done.

THE TONGZHI RESTORATION, 1862–1874

Not surprisingly, this learned group devised a response that derived from their education and knowledge of history. The cause of the empire's decay and weakness lay in the deterioration of its adherence to Confucian tradition. Restoration of traditional principles would halt this decay, strengthen the empire, and save the dynasty. The ensuing self-strengthening movement, which began in 1862, was known as the Tongzhi (unified government) Restoration, after the then-emperor's reign title. The restoration was conceived as a self-strengthening movement conducted within the parameters of Confucian tradition. Within this broad rubric, there were differences of opinion among officials on details, and some of the tactics suggested were plainly naive—for example, sending swimmers with torches to burn foreign boats at their waterlines would not have been effective. Most agreed, however, that it was acceptable to borrow Western military techniques. This was sanctioned by the aphorism of ancient China's preeminent military sage, Sun Zi, to "know yourself, know your enemy; win ten thousand battles." One would study the barbarians the better to outmaneuver the barbarians.

The slogan of the self-strengthening movement was "Chinese essence (*ti*) for the foundation; Western learning (*yong*) for practical use." At least one conservative, a Manchu expert on the ancient classics, saw the flaw in this argument immediately, arguing that Western learning possesses its own essence, which would eventually overwhelm the Confucian. But his view was not widely shared.[5]

The Tongzhi Restoration had a number of positive accomplishments. The Grand Canal, as well as some lesser waterways that had been allowed to silt up, were dredged and reopened to transportation. A new transit tax, called *likin* (*lijin* in pinyin transliteration) by westerners, was instituted. Based on one-thousandth of value, likin was too small to make avoidance worthwhile. Though much resented and misused, it nonetheless provided the government with an additional source of revenue. Regionally based armies and navies were founded, funded by both likin and customs revenues. The latter were collected by a Western consortium on behalf of the Beijing government to prevent the revenues from being siphoned off by avaricious officials.

In an effort to reverse the traditional Chinese saying "As one does not use good iron to make nails, one does not use good men as soldiers," literate members of the gentry class were sought as officers and strong peasants as soldiers. Army officers were sent to Germany to study military science, and a group of young men was dispatched to the United States to study at Yale University. A coal mine, a steamship company, and some arsenals and shipyards were established; so as well was a school for the study of foreign languages. A proto-foreign office was set up: none had existed before, since other countries were considered too inferior to warrant it.

However, rationalizing reforms in terms of tradition had limitations that interfered with the self-strengthening movement. When Westerners suggested building railroads and telegraph networks to speed communications, officials replied that the existing system of courier service was sufficient; the only reason for faster communication was to facilitate commercial transactions, and since Confucianism held commercialism in low regard, they were unnecessary. A foreign consul whose requests to build a telegraph system were repeatedly rebuffed finally received permission to build one that connected only treaty ports, provided that all the lines were immersed in water and all the terminals housed on ships.[6] This reduced much of the system's value to China. After repeated delays, a railway was finally built in 1876, with a length of only 10 miles. However, the government destroyed it after peasants complained that the *fengshui*, the spirits of the wind and water, had been violated: the livestock were terrified, and hens refused to lay eggs.[7]

The steamship company failed when its initial profits, instead of being reinvested, were used to buy land and other unproductive goods,[8] a practice that was more consonant with Confucianism than Adam Smith's philosophy. The education mission was recalled from Yale after its students failed to ketou when visited by a supervisor. And the regionally based armies proved disastrous to central power. With several internal rebellions as well as foreign pressure to be concerned with, the Qing government reluctantly appointed regional army commanders as governors of the provinces their armies defended. The governors then began to appoint their own subordinates, deriving support as well from the local gentry and creating power bases that became to varying degrees autonomous from central control. Since Beijing formally appointed both leaders and staffs to office, the regional entities remained part of the official bureaucracy even as they were dissolving central authority. After the internal rebellions had been defeated, Beijing attempted to break or at least reduce the autonomy of the new leaders. But, once established, regional powers were generally able to sustain themselves.[9]

While the accomplishments of the Tongzhi Restoration are undeniable, the infrastructure to meld them together and even the decision-makers' mindset to do so were lacking. Individuals who realized what needed to be done definitely existed. For example, Li Hongzhang, generally regarded as the greatest statesman of the late Qing, had a markedly practical mindset. His biographers judge that Li actually paid little more than lip service to the idea of Chinese learning as the essence, Western learning for practical use. In a riff on the traditional formula, he joked about using barbarian ways to change China.[10] But Li's efforts to implement reforms were stymied by the resistance of vested interests.

MATTHEW PERRY ARRIVES IN JAPAN

As an emerging commercial power that had been engaged in trade with China from its earliest days, the United States viewed British expansion in

Asia as a potential hindrance to its own ability to expand. Matthew Perry, a naval officer and the brother of Oliver Perry who became a national hero after he defeated the British at the battle of Lake Erie in 1812, advised President Millard Fillmore that the United States should take active measures to secure ports of refuge in Japan. Fillmore agreed, empowering Matthew Perry to negotiate with the Japanese and awarding him the rank of commodore to facilitate the negotiations.

Perry prepared carefully in order to make the maximum impression on the exclusionist government of the shōgun. In July 1853 four of the U.S. Navy's most modern steamships, bearing guns notable for both their size and number, unexpectedly appeared in Edo Bay, just off the epicenter of Tokugawa power. The black ships, belching steam, stunned Japanese officials who had never seen ships not powered by sail, or guns so large. Quickly calculating that its own defenses would be useless against those of the intruders, the government did not attempt to engage the foreigners in battle. Perry's preparations, his adamant refusal to meet with anyone of lower rank, and the meticulously staged panache with which he carried off the delivery of Fillmore's message, had the desired effect.

The Japanese government temporized in order to take stock of its own defenses. When Perry returned seven months later, this time with eight black ships, he got the concessions he wanted. The shōgunate agreed to open two ports for trade, to the purchase of such supplies as the ships needed, and to provide for the care of shipwrecked crews. It also acceded to the American request for a most favored nation clause. Russia and Britain soon concluded similar treaties.[11]

While the arrival of the West was in general unwelcome, it also introduced Japan to a different and more appealing concept of world order. Whereas previous efforts had aimed at challenging the Chinese conception of world order, Japan now had the option of joining the Westphalian system: a community of at least theoretical equals that operated without a morally and ethically dominant center or Middle Kingdom. For example, the ideas of eminent Dutch international legal theorist Hugo Grotius, known to Japanese as Hyūgo of Holland, were attractive to intellectuals because they applied to all nations alike, rather than dividing the world into two categories: Middle Kingdom and barbarians.[12] The conceptual leap from a unipolar to a multipolar worldview was much easier for the Japanese: for Chinese intellectuals, there could be no other centers, since the sinic view of truth and morality was valid for all under heaven. To deal with other states on a basis of equality would necessitate the unthinkable: imputing value to their radically different institutions and standards.[13]

The shōgunal government, unlike the Chinese court, was fully aware of the dangers as well as the opportunities presented by the West and took immediate steps to enhance the country's defenses. People were sent abroad to study Western experiences, and plans made for building railroads. When a tsunami destroyed Russian ships, the government helped the stranded Russians to build a new vessel, hoping thereby to learn their techniques.

However, restive daimyō, principally from Satsuma and Chōshū, sought to capitalize on the humiliation that foreigners had visited Japan for their own purposes. Although the shōgun had no choice but to acquiesce to the demands of the Western powers, they argued that he was failing to protect the emperor. Under the slogan *sonnō jōi* ("Revere the emperor; expel the barbarians"), a coalition of fiefs forced the shōgun from power and "restored" the emperor. The imperial seat was moved from Kyōto to Edo, which was renamed Tokyo (eastern capital), although actual power was exercised not by the emperor but by a small group that would later be referred to as the *genrō*, or elder statesmen. Composed of nobles and former samurai, nearly all from Satsuma and Chōshū, the genrō immediately set about the task of strengthening Japan.

THE MEIJI RESTORATION, 1868-1912

Surprisingly, the antiforeignism inherent in the sonnō jōi slogan did not result in the expulsion of foreigners. The new leaders assured envoys that their government would honor the previous government's treaty obligations. Nor did their vows to return to more ancient and legitimate traditions like imperial rule portend antimodernization. In 1868 the young emperor, given the reign title of Meiji ("enlightened government"), proclaimed the Charter Oath, pledging that all governmental matters would be determined by public discussion; that deliberative assemblies would be established at all levels; that evil past customs were to be discarded; and that knowledge would be sought throughout the world to promote the welfare of the empire.

Another surprise, considering that the revolt against the Tokugawa had been led by powerful fiefs, was the rapid abolition of feudalism. As power in China became more regionalized, that in Japan became more centralized. Only a year after the restoration began, the daimyō returned their land registers to the throne, later being rewarded with pensions and ranks in a newly established nobility. The *sankin kōtai* routes (see Chapter 1) became the national road system, and commoners received family names. Samurai special privileges of rank, hairstyle, clothing, and, eventually, even sword-wearing were abolished. Such diminutions of status engendered resistance: that of disgruntled samurai erupted into the Satsuma rebellion of 1877 in which an army that included conscripts defeated the samurai.

While visits to the West, at first clandestine and later open, had taken place even under the late Tokugawa, the process of seeking knowledge abroad now became better focused and occurred on a larger scale. Less than two years after the Meiji Restoration, the new government dispatched a group led by the vice-president of the country's Council of State, Iwakura Tomomi. The Iwakura mission spent eighteen months abroad and included several of the country's most important leaders, such as Itō Hirobumi. The mission failed in its goal of renegotiating the unequal treaties, but succeeded in learning a great deal about other countries, choosing which institutions and practices they believed were best suited to the Japanese context. Western legal systems and commercial treaties were studied and codified. The educational system was modeled on that of France, with German influences added as well. Universal education was instituted. The British parliamentary system, with its House of Commons and House of Lords, became the inspiration for the bicameral Japanese Diet. Prussia's military and its conscript system were also admired and modified to suit the Japanese context.

Useful insights were reported back to Tokyo, which acted on a number of them. For example, a later group, on noticing that the citizens of Paris tried to defend their city in the Franco-Prussian War of 1870, advised that patriotism should be promoted in Japan so that commoners would feel as ready to fight for their country as samurai had. A plan of action was formulated and implemented. The Shintō religion was chosen as a vehicle in the endeavor. It had the advantage of being native to Japan, whereas both Buddhism and Christianity had been imported from abroad. Shintō was adapted to bolster the status of the emperor as a symbol of Japan and focus of loyalty.

SINO-JAPANESE RELATIONS DURING THE RESTORATIONS

Despite tensions between China and Japan, there was a significant degree of awareness that they were geographically neighbors who faced a common danger and might profitably combine to resist it. When, for example, the expanding Russian Empire announced in 1891 that it planned to construct a trans-Siberian railway, both China and Japan could see an incipient threat to their security. Nonetheless, each country appears to have felt that it would assume the lead and the other would follow. Li Hongzhang opined that "if we have some weapons with which to stand on our own feet, [the Japanese] will attach themselves to us and watch the shortcomings or strength of the westerners."[14] Li could also be condescending, as in his statement that

> the Japanese today are the dwarf pirates of the Ming period. They are far away from the Western countries and are close to us. If we can stand our ground, they will be subordinate to us and we can watch for opportunities to compete with the westerners. If we have no wherewithal to strengthen ourselves, then Japan will follow the westerners and share their sources of profit [at our expense].[15]

Note the sense of competition that underlies the discussion of the usefulness of cooperation. As the Japanese reforms began to achieve visible progress while China's foundered, the contempt that Chinese officials felt for their eastern neighbor became tinged with a degree of envy. Japanese could also be condescending. As seen in Chapter 1, already by the late Tokugawa, nativist thinkers had become convinced that China had long ago relinquished its right to be known as the Middle Kingdom: unlike Japan, it did not have an unbroken line of imperial succession.[16] In their view, Japan had always exhibited greater military valor than China; unlike China, it had never been conquered from abroad. And, according to nativists, Japan had better retained and nurtured ancient virtues.

Moreover, the Chinese distinction between themselves as civilized and all others as barbarians was, they argued, absurd, given the reality that barbarians had several times conquered China and the barbarian leader was then anointed as the son of heaven. Who, then, should be considered barbarian?[17] To nativists, the logical conclusion was that Japan had become the true Middle Kingdom. While one might revere China's past accomplishments, China had declined into an entity that was no longer worthy of emulation. The term *Shina*, later to be interpreted in a highly pejorative sense by Chinese patriots, began to be used to signify that China was no longer the Middle Kingdom, *Zhongguo* or *Chūgoku*. The country's difficulties in modernizing did not so much lead nativist thinkers to a new attitude toward China as validate what they had already concluded.

As China continued to weaken while Japan strengthened, the feeling that their country had surpassed it spread beyond nativist thinkers. A Japanese visitor to Shanghai in 1862, for example, confided to his diary that talented Chinese who should have held positions of authority were working in the most menial jobs. Although the city was technically part of China, in reality, it should be said to belong to the English and the French. Owing to "obstinateness and idleness," the Chinese still lacked any understanding of Western ways and therefore could offer no effective resistance.[18]

China and Japan had already clashed over control of Okinawa and Taiwan (see Chapter 8), alerting Li Hongzhang to Japan's expansionist tendencies. Still, the matter was soothed after an agreement brokered by the British minister to Beijing, under which Japan received an indemnity for Okinawan seamen killed by Taiwanese natives. Japanese special envoy Ōkubo Toshimichi proposed that a portion of the indemnity be returned to China to pay for the administration of areas of Taiwan occupied by aborigines, and for measures to protect other countries' seamen in the future. Presumably, he did so in order to allay Chinese suspicions as well as to show Japan's goodwill. Both in this and other instances, Ōkubo expressed his desire to reach a rapprochement with China in the belief that good relations could better ensure Japan's prosperity.[19] Commonalities of culture and race (*tongwen, tongzhong* in Chinese; *dōbun, dōshu* in Japanese) would be a commonly heard slogan, albeit falling short of an accurate description of reality.

Li Hongzhang was initially receptive, not because he failed to recognize the danger posed by Japan but because he believed the Western powers to be a greater threat. After Japan's annexation of the Ryukyus in 1879, however, the opposite began to seem a real possibility.

SINO-JAPANESE TENSIONS BUILD

As China and Japan attempted to modernize in order to protect themselves from the West, their rivalry with each other came to focus on an age-old issue: the control of Korea. By the late nineteenth century, Korea's Yi dynasty was faction-ridden and corrupt. A succession of underaged monarchs was dominated by in-laws and queens; the tax burden on the peasantry conduced toward rebellions. Such weaknessese as well as its strategic location made Korea tempting prey in this age of imperialism. Consonant with the strategy of using barbarians against barbarians, Qing officials had advised their vassal state to sign treaties with the Western powers in order to counterbalance Japan. There was little support for this in Korea, whose leaders tended to prefer maintaining its status as the Hermit Kingdom.

While seeking to rid itself of unequal treaties with the West, Japan presented Korea with commercial demands that imposed more stringent conditions than the West had imposed on Japan: for example, it did not even offer to pay tariffs. The Korean government signed the treaty, which also proclaimed Korea to be a sovereign state—that is, no longer a vassal state of China—though the Yi continued to consider the kingdom a Chinese tributary. In what is perhaps an oversimplification of highly convoluted political and personal relationships, a pro-China group, Korean conservatives, tried to maintain traditional tributary relationships, while a pro-Japan group wanted to end the traditional system and institute reforms along the lines that the Meiji government had begun.

Friction between members of these factions threatened to escalate into a major conflagration that officials of both China and Japan wanted to avoid at this time. An agreement negotiated between Li Hongzhang and Minister Plenipotentiary Itō Hirobumi in 1885 tried to preclude this eventuality. According to the Li-Itō Convention, also known as the Treaty of Tianjin, China and Japan would withdraw their troops from Korea within four months, though either could send in troops should there be future uprisings or other serious disturbances, contingent on prior notification of Korea and each other, and with the further stipulation that the troops would be withdrawn completely once the problem had been settled.

JAPAN PONDERS ITS RELATIONSHIP WITH CHINA AND KOREA

In March 1885 an unsigned editorial appeared in a Japanese newspaper that was to have a profound influence on Japan's international relations. Assumed to have been written by author and educator Fukuzawa Yukichi, since it is included among his collected works, the title *datsu-a ron* has been variously translated as a call to "leave Asia," for "de-Asianization," and as "good-bye Asia." Fukuzawa's argument was that Western civilization was an unstoppable wind, which the Chinese and the Koreans were attempting in vain to resist. Rather than stay with "bad Asian friends" or wait for them to develop enlightenment so that the group could develop jointly, it was preferable for Japan to leave the ranks of Asian nations and cast its lot with the civilized nations of the West.

In various forms, the debate about Japan's place in Asia forms a leitmotif in the country's politics that continues into the present. Having successfully modernized itself, what obligation did Japan bear for the rest of Asia, and particularly for China and Korea as other Confucian-based societies? If those states continued to resist reform, should Japan employ patient tutelage or was it acceptable, as Fukuzawa himself would later argue, to force reform through military means. And what were the consequences of each for Japan's security? Finally, would the Western states accept Japan as an equal and, if not, what should the Japanese reaction be? How much Japan should be part of Asia and how much a part of the West continue to be debated today.

THE SINO-JAPANESE WAR, 1894-1895

Several highly significant events occurred in 1894. Foreign Minister Mutsu Munemitsu's negotiations with Britain to revise the unequal treaties began to make progress, finally reaching success with the signing of a more equitable commercial agreement that summer. This treaty became the basis for revision of the remaining unequal treaties Japan had had to agree to with other powers, hence excising a humiliation to the national honor.[20]

Meanwhile, a more explosive sequence of events began when the pro-Japanese Kim Ok-kyun was assassinated in Shanghai in April. The Chinese government declined to release the body to Kim's Japanese friends, instead returning it to Korea, certainly in full knowledge of what was likely to happen and how the Japanese government would react. The corpse was draped in a shroud inscribed "arch rebel and heretic." On the same ship was the assassin, who received a hero's welcome when the ship docked. The Korean king then mutilated Kim's body in a particularly grisly manner, and punished his family members as well. While this treatment was considered appropriate for traitors, which from China's and Korea's point of view, Kim certainly was,[21] the Japanese government perceived the manner in which it was carried out to have been designed to humiliate their country.

Japanese public opinion, fanned by angry articles in the nation's newspapers, was infuriated. The Japanese military, already resentful over the more conciliatory policies of the country's statesmen, determined that it was necessary to intervene. Defeating Li Hongzhang's well-regarded Beiyang army would free Korea definitively from the Chinese sphere of influence as well as silence domestic critics who criticized their government's unwillingness to take action. It might also serve to dissuade the Russian government from trying to establish a sphere of influence on the Korean peninsula, which Japan regarded as vital to its own security. Since the trans-Siberian railway would give Russia a direct conduit to the Pacific Ocean, Japanese statesmen were concerned that its completion would be tantamount to a Russian version of America's Monroe Doctrine.

When the Tonghak (Eastern Learning) Rebellion broke out in Korea in 1894, the tinderbox of tensions was ignited. The Korean king, on the advice of Li Hongzhang's representative in Korea, Yuan Shikai, requested that China send troops to help suppress it. In accordance with the Li-Itō Convention, China notified Japan that it was doing so. Ignoring the Korean king's request that Japan not send troops, Japan immediately dispatched them nonetheless. Although the official explanation was that soldiers were needed to protect Japanese nationals and property, the large number of troops that were sent and their instantaneous dispatch indicated prior preparations. Japanese troops moved into Seoul and captured the king.

Tokyo announced that it would not withdraw the troops until the Korean government had implemented a program of thorough reform. Li Hongzhang, realizing that his troops would be unable to stand up to those of Japan, tried unsuccessfully to persuade foreign powers to mediate. There was considerable feeling among Western powers that the weak, corrupt Korean government was badly in need of reform; perhaps Japanese pressure was what was needed. At the end of July, the ship *Kowshing*, carrying more than a thousand Chinese troops, was intercepted by Japanese naval vessels and refused the commander's orders to follow its ships to port. After several hours of negotiations, the commander, Tōgō Heihachirō, later to become the hero of the Russo-Japanese War, ordered the *Kowshing* sunk.[22]

On August 1, 1894, each country declared war on the other. Japan's declaration accused China of interfering in Korea's domestic affairs, of refusing Japan's offer to jointly sponsor reforms, and of opening fire on Japanese ships. China's declaration repeatedly referred to the Japanese as dwarfs, *woren*, or dwarf pirates, *wokou*. Adding insult to insult in this face-conscious culture, the Chinese side had the declaration translated into English, accompanied by a note explaining that the word was used in an "opprobrious sense."[23] In her definitive study of the Sino-Japanese War, S. C. M. Paine characterizes such language as equivalent to repeatedly spitting in the emperor's face.[24] At first, foreign observers assumed that Chinese forces would win. This was quickly proved wrong, as Japanese forces achieved victory after victory in what could only be considered a humiliating defeat of their larger neighbor. China's regionally based armies had a tendency to avoid battle, feeling that they did not have a stake in the outcome. Battleships, including some modern vessels whose capabilities exceeded those of the Japanese, were hoarded rather than used. Corruption siphoned money meant for military modernization into luxury items for dishonest officials. A subordinate of China's most outstanding admiral, Ding Ruchang, disobeyed Ding's order to put the flagship in a position to fire on the Japanese fleet and instead fired the main guns at the bridge on which Ding was standing. The admiral escaped death, but his leg was crushed, seriously affecting his ability to direct the battle. [25]

Incredibly, the Chinese managed to sustain the attitude of superiority even in the face of defeat. For example, in November 1894, an eminent scholar-official wrote:

> The island barbarian Japanese have inscrutable temperaments and petty dispositions. Their hearts are like those of jackals and wolves, and they possess poison like the bees and the scorpions.... They dare to title their emperor as the son of heaven in the land of the rising sun. It took them 48,000 years before they made contact with China, while in 3,600 years they still have not accepted our celestial calendar.... [I]llegitimately assuming the reign title of Meiji [i.e., Enlightened Rule], they in reality abandon themselves all the more to debauchery and indolence. Falsely calling their new administration a reformation, they only defile themselves so much the more.... As for Korea, all the world knows it is a vassal of China. And yet Japan took military action there without reason. Is this not deliberately provocative?... How can we tolerate this willingness to act like the dog of the ancient tyrant Chieh barking at the sage-king Yao? Both the immortals and human kind are angry, the entire world takes offense.[26]

This stoked the anger of Japanese, who were already passionate to become treated as equals if not superiors. The image of China among ordinary Japanese citizens also suffered. When soldiers whose educations had taught them that China was the land of the sages encountered the poverty and illiteracy of the Chinese countryside, and shared these observations through letters and conversations with relatives and acquaintances at home, the once revered land came to be regarded as far inferior to their own.[27]

While some responded with their own disparaging characterizations of the Chinese, generally based on nativist views, others tended to be compassionate once victory had been secured. A case in point is the dialogue between Admiral Itō Yūkū and his opposite number Admiral Ding Ruchang after the latter's defeat at Weihaiwei. Though fate had made them adversaries, the two had previously had cordial relations. Itō pointed out that the defeat had not been Ding's fault, but that of a government which preferred to choose its officials on the basis of their literary accomplishments rather than their military expertise. He then invited Ding to come to Japan rather than return to Beijing to accept responsibility for the defeat.[28] Ding responded by committing suicide, thereby earning the highest respect of the Japanese. As commented by a newspaper columnist of the time, enmity is temporary, respect endures forever. Admiral Itō ordered Ding's body returned to China, with flags flying at half-mast and ships firing a salute as the vessel bearing his body left port. Knowing that the war was essentially over at this point, Itō also returned Ding's surviving officers. Ding's own government did not react as well: his corpse was denied proper burial until 1912, and the emperor ordered his surviving officers beheaded.[29]

A similar exchange of views occurred when Li Hongzhang again met Itō Hirobumi, this time to negotiate the terms of the peace treaty at Shimonoseki. Itō reminded Li that, at Tianjin a decade before, he had spoken with Li about reform, regretted that nothing had actually been reformed, and asked why. Li replied that "affairs in my country have been so confined by tradition that I could not accomplish what I desired."[30]

In a third example, also from the Shimonoseki negotiations, Premier Itō inquired of one of the Chinese translators, the brilliant Luo Fenglu, why China had not learned more from the West. Luo replied, "You see, in our younger days we knew each other as fellow students, and now you are prime minister in your country and I am an interpreter in mine."[31] As summarized by an astute observer, for years Japanese diplomats had offered the same advice to Chinese diplomats, only to see it ignored. From the Chinese point of view, "They would be damned before they would take advice from 'dwarfs.' And damned they were."[32]

Even in defeat, the Chinese government refused to treat the victors as equals. The negotiations were stalled when the Japanese, confronted with a delegation of relatively low-ranking individuals who had arrived without power to make decisions, refused to deal with them. Meanwhile, a group of officials in China who clearly did not comprehend the difficult position that the devastation of their armies and ships had put them in, urged fighting on. A few days after the envoys' ship set sail, *The Peking Gazette*, the official organ of the Chinese government for the publication of memorials and edicts, referred to the Japanese by an even more demeaning term than dwarfs: "dwarf pirates"[33] (see Chapter 1). After a member of the delegation asked the highly inappropriate question of when he could expect an audience with the emperor, the Japanese sent the delegation back.

Eventually, with the Japanese threatening to advance into Beijing—an action that was easily within their military's capacity but that civilian statesmen preferred to avoid, fearing Western powers' reaction—the Chinese dispatched an acceptable delegation.[34] In the resultant Treaty of Shimonoseki, signed in 1895, China recognized the full and complete independence and autonomy of Korea, which was henceforth to refrain from paying tribute and performing ceremonies to China that were incompatible with this independence and autonomy. Taiwan, the Pescadores, and the Liaodong peninsula were ceded to Japan. China was to pay an indemnity of 200 million Kuping taels [35] (about 7.5 million kilograms of silver). Four new cities, Shashi, Chongqing, Hangzhou, and Suzhou, were to be opened to Japanese trade, and China granted most favored nation status to Japan.

The mood in Japan was ecstatic; the military had not only assuaged past slights but also brought much honor to the country. However, almost immediately a consortium of three European states—France, Germany, and Russia—intervened. Apprehensive for their own interests in the wake of the Japanese victory, the parties to the Triple Intervention advised Japan to retrocede the Liaodong peninsula. Aware that their military could not withstand the combined forces of the three, Japanese diplomats agreed. A concession that China would have to pay an additional 30 million Kuping, or 1.12 million kilograms, of silver for the retrocession of Liaodong, for a total indemnity of over 9 million kilograms of silver, was scant consolation. An imperial rescript urged the people to "bear the unbearable" and to refrain from rash acts of revenge. Although a number of ritual suicides were reported, citizens in general obeyed the emperor's command. However, the intervention had other, very serious consequences.

Public opinion was outraged, charging that diplomats had surrendered a valuable prize that had been won through the sacrifices of thousands of valiant young men. The prestige of civilian government fell; that of the military rose. As did support for larger military budgets, so that Japan could never again be humiliated in this fashion, and the desire for revenge. Additionally, the Triple Intervention was interpreted as meaning that the Western powers had not yet accepted Japan as their equal, its impressive reforms notwithstanding. In the Japanese view, this attitude extended beyond the three intervening powers: Tokyo had approached other Western powers for help against the consortium, but had been rebuffed. The conclusion was that Western powers understood only military force, and that Japan had best ready itself for such a confrontation. Japanese decision-makers were aware of the so-called Willy-Nicky letters, in which the German kaiser and his cousin, the Russian czar, discussed the dangers of the "yellow peril."[36]

THE EFFECT OF DEFEAT ON CHINA

China, too, had been humiliated. To a significant extent, its problems were of its own making. Not only had the Middle Kingdom been defeated by the contemptible dwarfs, but its image among the Western powers had suffered as well. In these countries, the defeat brought about a keener awareness of China's deficiencies and the opportunities it presented them with. In what was termed a scramble of concessions, Western powers sought, and were generally granted, grants of territory and improved opportunities for trade.

France received non-alienation agreements for Hainan Island, Guangdong, Guangxi, and Yunnan provinces, border adjustments with regard to its foothold in northern Vietnam, and railway concessions. Germany acquired a ninety-nine-year lease in Qingdao as well as railway and mining concessions in Shandong; Russia got railway concessions in Manchuria that were far beyond those granted to any other power. It also received a twenty-five-year lease on the Liaodong peninsula, which along with France and Germany, it had only three years before forced Japan to return to China. Japan was awarded a non-alienation agreement for Fujian province, directly opposite its newly acquired colony of Taiwan, and a concession in Shashi, on the Yangtze River. Observers commented that China was being carved up like a melon.

Britain, which had traditionally favored China, now moved closer to Japan, even incorporating the latter into its balancing strategy against the rising power of a recently united Germany. The Qing dynasty had been weakened not only militarily but also psychologically, since military defeats were considered to be a sign that the dynasty was losing the Mandate of Heaven. Some Chinese began to blame the Manchus, as foreigners, for these defeats.

The Tongzhi Restoration was recognized as a failure, and the need to deal not only with Western powers but Japan as well was now deemed imperative. A variety of different opinions emerged on how best to do so. These views may be briefly summarized as reformist, reactionary, and revolutionary.

The first group to take action was the reformers. Kang Youwei[37] and Liang Qichao,[38] outstanding scholars who had passed the examination system at young ages but who had also studied Western ways, gained access to the Guangxu emperor and convinced him of the need for thorough reforms along the lines that had so enhanced Meiji Japan. Salient items in their reinterpretation of Confucianism were the creation of a constitutional monarchy and the reorganization of the examination system into an assessment of substantive knowledge rather than literary skills.

Flattered because attention was usually centered on the power behind the throne, the empress dowager Cixi, the Guangxu emperor enacted their program in 1898. Known as the Hundred Days' Reforms, since that is the short duration they were in effect, the program aroused the immediate enmity of the literati officials, whose power and prestige the reforms would have undermined. They appealed to the empress dowager who, with the help of the aforementioned Yuan Shikai, carried out a military coup and rescinded the reforms. The Guangxu emperor was placed under house arrest, where he remained until his death ten years later. Kang and Liang fled to Japan to escape the death of a thousand cuts. Receiving refuge there, they continued to agitate for constitutional monarchy.

Next to act were the reactionaries, in the form of the Boxer Rebellion of 1900. This xenophobic movement attempted to expel all foreigners, including the Japanese, from China. A particular source of their venom was Christianity; Chinese converts to the religion as well as foreigners were subjected to grotesque mutilation. After the Boxers besieged the legation quarter in Beijing, where foreigners were required to live, the Western powers and Japan sent in a joint military force to protect their nationals. As it neared Beijing, the empress dowager, dressed as a peasant, fled the city hiding in a wooden cart. Through no fault of her own, she had been confined to the palace for decades, and had little comprehension of conditions in the land she ruled.

When Cixi returned, she was converted to reform, enacting in 1902 most of the reforms that were contained in the 1898 program. The consensus, however, is that these reforms were too few and came too late. The program was underfunded; the government had a huge foreign debt, was having difficulty collecting taxes, and had to contend with powerful regional forces who had their own armies and their own priorities.

Meanwhile, revolutionaries, who aimed to overthrow the dynasty and replace it with a democratic republic, were also becoming active. The most famous of these, Sun Yat-sen, had been educated at the prestigious Iolani School in Honolulu before taking his medical degree in Hong Kong. A Christian, he received strong support from Chinese living overseas and frequently traveled abroad on fundraising tours. After an unsuccessful coup attempt in 1895, Sun fled to London, where he was captured the following year by Qing authorities. About to be deported and executed, he escaped only through the efforts of his former medical school professor, who had returned to the United Kingdom. Arriving in Japan in 1897, Sun assumed a Japanese name to avoid detection and continued his activities.

SINO-JAPANESE RELATIONS AFTER THE 1895 WAR

The Hundred Days' Reforms had attracted favorable attention in Japan, which had become alarmed by the Western powers' expansion in China after the 1895 war and wanted, for the sake of its own security, to help strengthen the dynasty. For interlocking reasons of self-interest and altruism, the preservation of China became a cause. Under the Ōkuma Doctrine, formulated by former prime minister and foreign minister Ōkuma Shigenobu, Japan would repay its debt to China for borrowing its culture by helping to stave off Western depredations until China had had time to strengthen its own institutions and defenses. Itō Hirobumi had visited Beijing during the Hundred Days period and been received by the Guangxu emperor, who inquired about the Meiji reforms. After the empress dowager's coup, Itō instructed Japanese representatives to help the fugitive reformers.

The two decades after the Sino-Japanese War were characterized by Chinese-Japanese cooperation. A contrarian view of the period argues that the surface harmony was not all that it seemed. For one thing, despite talk of dōbun, dōshu, Japanese politicians spoke out against a formal relationship with China. And talk of a Japanese Monroe Doctrine could be seen as no different from Western-style power politics masquerading as benign protection of a fellow Asian state. Dōbun, dōshu notwithstanding, sympathy for China existed only when no other power was watching.[39]

In any case, the first Chinese students, a group of thirteen, arrived in Japan in 1896, just a year after the peace treaty had been signed. Japan was attractive for several reasons: transportation was faster and cheaper than to Western countries, and although the two languages are not as alike as most nonspeakers suppose, they at least have a number of characters in common. It was easier for a Chinese to learn Japanese than English, French, or German. Tuition fees were also lower in Japan than in Western countries.

Chinese central and provincial governments also sought Japanese expertise on topics relating to modernization, hiring hundreds of Japanese to advise them. A wide variety of fields was represented, including law, finance, military, science, education, and engineering. Most advisers lived and worked in China for several years. Japanese terms for modern concepts entered the Chinese language though, confusingly, they sometimes shifted meanings in the process.[40] For most Chinese, Japanese imperialism was not yet seen as a problem.

Any explanation of why this era of relative comity did not blossom into a long-term relationship runs the risk of imposing a post hoc, ergo propter hoc solution on a complex topic. Scholars who have examined the diaries and conversations of the participants in this cooperative enterprise point to the frustration of Japanese who were well disposed to both the Chinese and their reforms. As might be expected, different individuals interpreted events through the prism of their own personalities as well as with reference to the particular circumstances in which they found themselves.

As a case in point, Hattori Unokichi arrived in Beijing in 1899, eager to study Chinese culture firsthand.[41] However, he found himself snubbed by an antiforeign elite and, when the Boxer Rebellion broke out, lived in fear that he would be one of its victims. He was surprised to find that China had no special category of Asian friends and that he was considered as much a foreigner as the Christian Westerners. At first, Hattori found it ironic that, as a non-Christian nation, Japan should have to help defend against the siege of the legation quarter. By the end of the ordeal, however, he came to feel a sense of unity with the other foreigners and against those who would destroy them.

Sounding much like the mutually patronizing members of the preceding Itō Hirobumi-Li Hongzhang generation, Hattori wrote that Japan must guide the Chinese so that they abandoned their antiforeign sentiment, since it could only be dangerous for themselves and Asia as a whole. After a time, his sense of frustration began to show: the Chinese were "inherently racist, treating all outsiders as culturally inferior, taking this attitude toward the Europeans with their indisputably superior technology is a losing proposition."[42] Hattori returned to Japan ambivalent about China's long-term development prospects.

He recognized that some of China's top leaders were genuinely committed to reform, but felt that the government was not using its newly trained people properly, and that the pace of change was too slow. Hattori identified the reasons as a fundamental close-mindedness to outside ideas, and a smug certainty that anything worthy in human culture had a made-in-China label on it.[43] Beyond the mindset problem, he continued, even those Chinese who sincerely supported reform faced enormous communications problems. For example, enforcing the criminal code, which had been drafted with Japanese help and distributed in 1906, was difficult because officials were confused by Japanese versions of Western legal terms: common characters did not necessarily mean the same thing in Chinese and Japanese. Distrust abounded: when the Japanese government decided in 1923 to apply the unpaid portion of the Boxer indemnity to Sino-Japanese cultural projects, many Chinese saw cultural imperialism in disguise rather than an effort at cooperation, and opposed the move.

These suspicions were not without basis. As has been seen with the nativists, it was possible to combine both profound admiration for Chinese culture and civilization with utter contempt for contemporary China. Thus, Naitō Konan, a renowned expert on traditional Chinese painting who identified with the Confucian literati, believed that the China of his day could not advance on its own and should relinquish its sovereignty to Japan. In his view, Chinese resistance to this was short-sighted. When Chinese students protested against Japanese imperialism in 1919, an angry Naitō remarked that "we no longer need to ask when China will collapse. It is already dead, only its corpse is wiggling."[44] In essence, Japan was now denying to China the equality that Japan had for so many centuries sought from China.

Chinese students in Japan also felt the sting of Japanese contempt from their Japanese peers. Teased because of their different clothing and hairstyles—even after the fall of the Qing, when queues had been abandoned, they were taunted as "pig tails"—the students told of being hooted at by groups of small children. For some, education in Japan made them into nationalists rather than encouraging Sino-Japanese cooperation. Their writings exude what one analyst characterized as an "anything you can do, I can do better" quality: if Japan, poorly endowed with natural resources and weak, could so quickly become strong and prosperous, China, with its greater resources and superior culture, could achieve more in less time.[45]

SINO-JAPANESE DIPLOMACY, 1898–1911

In the period after the failure of the Hundred Days' Reforms, the Japanese government tried to carefully calibrate its dealings with both the Qing dynasty and its opponents. This was quite difficult, due to a mixture of motives. At the highest levels of Japanese decision-making, there was a consensus between liberals, who wanted to help China for essentially idealistic motives, and expansionists, who wanted allies to further their great power and anti-Western motives. This alliance would prove temporary, however. Meanwhile, questions arose about whom Japan should support: the dynasty, for which even Chinese conservatives now accepted the need for some change; the constitutional monarchists, who wanted faster and more thoroughgoing change; or the revolutionaries. It would be best to bet on a winner, but no one could be sure which group would emerge triumphant. The resultant policies tended to reflect shifting opinions of the fortunes of each group as well as a desire not to become too firmly tied to any of them.

Although certain sympathetic Japanese responded favorably to requests for arms from various Chinese groups, the Tokyo government was chary of such aid: it wanted a friendly China, but definitely not a militarily powerful China. Should China disintegrate, Japan wanted its share of the spoils; should it survive, under whatever government, that government should have a close relationship with, and preferably be a client state of, Japan in order to create a bulwark against further Western depredations.[46]

After Kang Youwei and Liang Qichao were given refuge in Japan, they used it as a base to pursue their activities, hoping to get Japanese support for the Guangxu emperor's reforms that had been suppressed by domestic conservatives. The Japanese leadership, sensing that the conservative viceroys were what was holding the Qing dynasty together and not wishing to be seen by either them or by the Western powers as seeking to destabilize the dynasty, sought to assure the Chinese power holders that they were doing no more than international law required in giving shelter to political refugees. They warned Kang and Liang against assuming too high a profile, with only Liang appearing to respond positively. Eventually, Kang was asked to leave, and provided with funds to defray the cost of his voyage to Canada.[47]

The Japanese were similarly wary of Sun Yat-sen, the revolutionary, though he appears to have had an easier time working in Japan than Kang, the reformer. Sun was originally approached by two men, Miyazaki Tōten and Hiranuma Shū, who had been hired by an associate of Prime Minister Ōkuma to keep track of the revolutionary movement in China. The men developed a genuine friendship that endured for many years after the fall of the Ōkuma cabinet ended their financial stake in a relationship with Sun. Miyazaki and Hiranuma introduced Sun to influential Japanese, publicized his cause, and helped him to raise money.

The Japanese also facilitated meetings for Sun with Kang and Liang, hoping to get them to join forces. The effort failed for several reasons. The two groups had different ideologies, since the latter two favored a constitutional monarchy, while Sun and his followers wanted to overthrow the dynasty and replace it with a democratic republic. They were also in competition for funding. Finally, and perhaps most importantly, the tensions were a matter of style: Kang and Liang, both accomplished Confucian scholars in addition to their knowledge of the West, regarded the Western-educated Sun as ignorant and uncultured.

Uncultured or not, Sun proved more successful in organizing Chinese students in Japan on behalf of his cause. After he founded his Tongmenghui, variously translated as Alliance Society or United Allegiance League, in Tokyo in 1905, students formed up to 90 percent of its membership.[48] Openly dedicated to the overthrow of the Manchu dynasty and the establishment of a republic, both the organization specifically and Sun's activities in general were closely watched by the Qing authorities. They were given an opportunity for a formal protest by a particularly fiery speech in January 1907 in which Sun reportedly intimated that, since the revolution aimed at the Manchus and the revival of China, he would not object if Japan claimed the territory north of Changchun—that is, in Manchuria, the homeland of the Manchus—in return for its help. The Beijing government then demanded that Tokyo expel Sun.[49] Sun was duly invited to leave, doubtless with no favorable feelings toward those who had asked him to do so.

Despite causing problems for the Japanese government at the time, memories of both reformers and revolutionaries, and even their progeny would be useful to Sino-Japanese relations in later years. The construction of monuments to them, and the defacement thereof, provide a rough index of the state of bilateral relations at the time the incidents occur. For example, in mid-2010—just months before intense enmity in China because of an unforeseen incident (see Chapter 7)—the city of Nara dedicated a statue to the son of Liang Qichao, described as "believed" to have interceded with the U.S. military to protect Nara and Kyōto from the air raids that destroyed so many of Japan's other urban centers.[50]

By this time, Japan had developed a vested interest in the status quo in China, and the aging Meiji leaders had come to feel more comfortable dealing with their elite peers in Beijing. Japanese advisors were sent to help the Qing reform into a constitutional monarchy along Meiji lines, the better to prevent the sort of revolution Sun and his followers aimed at. By the time that revolution broke out in 1911, most observers expected Japan to intervene on the side of the Qing.[51] Although some Japanese conservatives favored this course of action, Tokyo did not intervene. The nationalists succeeded in overthrowing the Qing, and showed that Japanese oligarchs had bet on the wrong party.

Hence, a period that might have been extended into long-term Sino-Japanese cooperation for mutual benefit ended instead in anger and mutual hostility. After friendships between Chinese nationalists and Japanese nationalists ended in enmity, both came to regret their former intimacy. On the Chinese side, there was a tendency to read back into events a consistent Japanese plan for future aggression: they had not been helped, but used. Conversely, the Japanese tended to conclude that the Chinese had proved themselves inept and ungrateful.[52]

THE RUSSO-JAPANESE WAR

Within Japan, as liberal forces lost ground, forces for expansionism gained. A major concern was the expansion of Russian power in Korea and Manchuria in proportion to the decline of Chinese power in both. In Korea, certain politicians began courting the Russians as a counterweight to Japanese influence, though aggressive Russian demands for commercial concessions and a naval base backfired. Koreans also learned that the Russians and Japanese were holding secret negotiations to delineate their respective spheres of influence on the peninsula. With each side wary of the other, however, negotiators were unable to reach agreement.

When the Boxer Rebellion broke out in 1900, the Russian government, like many others, sent troops to protect its nationals and property. Unlike the other governments, however, Russia did not withdraw its forces after the rebellion had been defeated. Moscow asked for an agreement that would enhance the privileged position it already enjoyed in Manchuria through the aforementioned railway concessions it had obtained after the 1895 Sino-Japanese War. Positing a connection between the enhanced Manchurian railway concessions and the completion of the trans-Siberian railway, Japanese leaders concluded that Russia wanted to expand into Manchuria, and also Korea, while minimizing Japanese influence in both. Those Japanese who favored expansionism argued that the alternative was exclusion.

In 1902 Japan concluded an alliance with Great Britain. From London's point of view, Japan would serve as a counterweight to rising German power, and would also reduce the need for British naval protection of its possessions in Asia. The advantage for Tokyo was the reassurance that Britain would not side with Russia in a Russo-Japanese confrontation. In the same year, Russia agreed to a three-stage evacuation of its troops from Manchuria. It abided by the first stage, but not the second, and also presented the Chinese government with several additional demands.

Japanese expansionists, who had for many years been critical of their government for what they considered spineless policies, urged action. Manchuria and Korea were considered to be connected, and no trade-off between the two seemed likely to ensure Japanese security: Russia would regard Japan's dominance in Korea as a threat to its position in Manchuria, just as Japan regarded Russian dominance in Manchuria as a threat to its position in Korea. Moreover, they added, Korea was "a dagger pointed straight at the heart of Japan." In any case, Russia did not seem inclined to agree to such a trade-off. The time for war seemed at hand. The Tokyo government had devoted a large part of the indemnities it received from China to enhancing its military forces, but czarist Russia was expanding its military presence in Manchuria.[53] If the moment were not seized, expansionists believed, the balance of power might tip in Russia's favor.[54]

Ultra-nationalist organizations proliferated in Japan after the turn of the century. The most famous of these was the Kokuryūkai, or Black Dragon (Amur River) Society. Founded in 1901, it advocated greater emphasis on Eastern values; the country as a nation in arms; and the rise of the "Yamato race." Kokuryūkai members advocated a permanent Japanese presence in Korea, and some of them were actively involved in political activities there.

The genrō and large business interests continued to hope that a negotiated settlement could be reached, but when Russia both failed to meet the third deadline for withdrawal of its troops and set unacceptable conditions, including the establishment of a neutral zone in Korea north of the thirty-ninth parallel and complete control of trade and resources in southern Manchuria, the position of the genrō became untenable. In February 1904 the war began with a Japanese surprise attack on the Russian fleet at Port Arthur, in southern Manchuria. The Japanese won several victories while taking heavy losses, with the siege of Port Arthur being particularly difficult. In May 1905 Russia's Baltic fleet, which had sailed 18,000 miles to relieve Port Arthur, was annihilated by Admiral Tōgō's forces in the battle of Tsushima. With Russia bereft of victories though unwilling to admit defeat[55] and Japan economically exhausted, the two sides agreed to accept the services of American President Theodore Roosevelt to mediate a peace settlement.

Under the Treaty of Portsmouth, concluded in September 1905, Russia agreed to terminate its twenty-five-year lease on Port Arthur, including its naval base and the surrounding Liaodong peninsula. Japan's forced retrocession of a decade before had been avenged. In addition, Russia ceded the southern half of Sakhalin to Japan. Due to wartime censorship, the Japanese public was unaware of the real costs of the war to their country, and had anticipated a much more advantageous settlement that included the payment of a large indemnity and the cession of all of Sakhalin. Encouraged by a patriotic press and nationalist expansionist elements, they expressed their disappointment at a protest meeting in Hibiya Park in Tokyo that turned violent and was repeated in cities in many other parts of Japan.

The disturbances were quelled by the near-simultaneous issuance of an imperial rescript accepting the settlement and the arrival of heavy rain.[56] But, as with the Triple Intervention of a decade before, there were serious consequences. Once again, expansionists argued, the heroic sacrifices of the military had been undercut by the timidity of the nation's political leaders, as well as by America in the person of mediator Roosevelt. Force, they concluded, was the only way for Japan to attain its rightful role as leader of Asia, guardian of Eastern values, and a major player in the international community of states.

A NEW BALANCE OF POWER

For a time, stability seemed to have returned to the East Asian area, and specifically to Sino-Japanese relations. The imperialist powers seemed reasonably satisfied with their territorial gains, focusing on participation in a consortium of loans to the Qing for their mutual gain and, presumably, the development of China, rather than further partitions of it. The empress dowager had committed the dynasty to reforms and instituted a number of measures that confirmed the seriousness of her intent. In 1907 Japan and Russia reached an agreement under which southern Manchuria and Inner Mongolia were recognized as the former's sphere of influence and northern Manchuria and Outer Mongolia as the latter's. Japan's annexation of Korea in 1910 caused little foreign concern, and even some sentiment that proven Japanese skills at organization and modernization might prove beneficial to Korea.

Very soon, however, a concatenation of unrelated events was to end this period of stability and facilitate the ability of the Japanese nationalist expansionist elements to further their agenda. Within the space of a few years, the Qing dynasty fell, the Meiji emperor died, World I began, and a revolution replaced Russia's Romanov dynasty with a larger, and communist, Soviet Union. With the old order definitively gone, already extant questions about what a new one should look like, and what Japan and China's respective places in it and with each other should be, were revived.

The outbreak of the 1911 revolution took the Japanese government by surprise. Also taken by surprise was Sun Yat-sen, who was in the United States fundraising when a bomb accidentally detonated in Hankou, setting off a chain of events catastrophic to the Qing dynasty. By the time Sun arrived back in China, Yuan Shikai, the military leader who had been instrumental in quelling the Boxer Rebellion, had seized power. This put Sun in the position of having to try to wrest power from Yuan. Yuan, aware of Sun's past residence in Japan, his many friends there, and the fact that Chinese students in Japan strongly supported Sun, understandably distrusted the Japanese government.

At the same time, age was depleting both the ranks of the genrō and their ability to control policy. Less cautious forces were gaining strength. The death of the Meiji emperor in 1912 was followed by the enthronement of his only surviving son. The Taishō emperor, in poor physical health and afflicted with mental illness as well, could not match his father's prestige and was not able to keep the new forces in check. In addition to nationalist expansionists, political parties and public opinion also became more assertive. How to react to the new power structure in China posed a major dilemma.

Given Yuan Shikai's hostility, Sun Yat-sen was a logical choice. A professed pan-Asianist—with the salient exception of the Manchus, whom he blamed for most of China's ills—Sun had special appeal to those Japanese who shared his pan-Asian views. But decisions on how much aid to give him, and what form it should take, were not as clear-cut. Nor was it clear that Sun could succeed.

Sun also gained supporters who were less idealistic than those who had previously befriended him. As a case in point, when Sun was engaged in trying to overthrow Yuan in 1913, a leading Japanese industrialist offered Sun 20 million yen in return for ceding Manchuria to Japan. He readily agreed.[57] Yuan was able to use Sun's aid from Japan against Sun, pleading for patriotic national unity to defend the new republic and arguing that Tokyo's support had ulterior motives. This succeeded in increasing anti-Japanese feelings in China. Yuan then offered an amnesty to revolutionaries who would return from Japan and help resist Japanese aggression. A number of Sun's followers, hard-pressed for funds, took advantage of Yuan's offer. Apparently, a number of them also received cash rewards for doing so. Solvent patriotism was clearly a more attractive option than pecunious pan-Asianism: Sun's followers all but disappeared.[58]

Yuan's troops had little difficulty in suppressing Sun's effort at revolt. In the process, they committed atrocities against Japanese, both military and civilian, which Japanese nationalist expansionists seized on as justification for more aggressive actions against China. As it had in 1905 after the peace settlement with Russia proved less than anticipated, a large crowd gathered in Hibiya Park, its anger growing as its numbers increased. A foreign ministry bureaucrat was assassinated by a young man who then seated himself on a map of China and committed *seppuku* (hara-kiri) in such a manner that his blood poured onto Manchuria and Mongolia. His sacrifice was applauded by public opinion, forcing the foreign minister to demand an apology and financial compensation from Yuan's government. It got them, though Tokyo's dissatisfaction with Yuan's leadership did not abate.

Nor did either the government or public opinion feel any sense of solidarity with the Western powers, due to repeated slights and ethnic slurs. Also in 1913, as public anger against Yuan was mounting, the U.S. state of California enacted discriminatory legislation against Japanese immigrants acquiring land there, further inflaming nationalists who accused their own government of weakness in the face of yet another humiliation.[59]

The outbreak of World War I in 1914 gave Japanese expansionists other opportunities to implement their agenda. Keenly sensitive to the probable reaction of Western powers to Japanese expansion in China since the Triple Intervention, Tokyo now perceived those states as not only distracted by war in Europe, but also at odds with each other. It joined the war on the Allied side, seizing German possessions in Shandong and in the South Pacific, thereby also gaining revenge for Germany's role in the Triple Intervention.

During the following year, Tokyo secretly presented Yuan Shikai's government with a list of desiderata known as the Twenty-One Demands. Loosely based on a memorandum on how to solve "the China problem" that nationalist expansionist Uchida Ryōhei had prepared for Prime Minister Ōkuma a few months before, the demands comprised five parts that, if accepted, would have transformed China into a de facto protectorate of Japan. Included were concessions on railway and mining operations in Manchuria, Shandong, and Fujian. China was to agree not to lease or cede any part of its territory to any other power. Particularly controversial and presented as "desires" rather than demands was the fifth group, under which the Chinese central government agreed to engage influential Japanese as political, financial, and military advisers. Local police forces would operate under joint Japanese-Chinese administration.

Yuan proved a wily negotiator through such tactics as temporizing and leaking the demands to foreign powers, who were not so preoccupied with the war in Europe that they were loath to protest. Japan was once again forced to back away from the more secure position in China that it desired.

While these negotiations were taking place, Sun Yat-sen, who was even more eager to displace Yuan than the Tokyo government, offered the Japanese better terms than those they had asked Yuan for. These included a Sino-Japanese alliance that granted far-reaching commercial concessions: Japanese would receive the right of unrestricted residency in China, and there would be a customs union. Rather than view this as evidence that Sun was a collaborator, it should be seen as indicative of his desperation.

According to a leading analyst of the period, Sun's willingness to concede China's sovereignty to Japan is likely to have been a temporary stratagem on his part. His Japanese supporters such as the aforementioned Uchida Ryōhei could not know that Sun envisioned Japanese guidance as a transitional stage of tutelage toward a truly independent Chinese republic. Conversely, Sun could not know that Uchida's support for the revolution was a prelude to the establishment of a constitutional monarchy.[60]

To be sure, Japan did not favor any truly independent government, even a constitutional monarchy, or it might have tried harder to make common cause with Yuan Shikai. A number of Japanese nationalists began to speak of the restoration of the Manchus, possibly with a government headed by Sun in the south and a revived Manchu dynasty in the north. Both were expected to be under Japanese tutelage. Hence, although Sun and many Japanese sincerely believed in pan-Asianism, it meant different things to each side. In the words of an ancient Chinese proverb, "Same bed, different dreams." In essence, Japan was now denying the equality of treatment to China that the Chinese empire had denied to Japan.

As it turned out, Yuan was soon overthrown in a revolt that owed nothing to either Sun or the Japanese. After Yuan proclaimed himself emperor later in 1915, there arose such resistance that he was forced to resign. Broken in spirit, Yuan died in mid-1916. With him died any realistic possibility of the revival of a monarchy in China, constitutional or otherwise. China entered a period of regionally based warlordism. Control of Beijing was considered the prize among contending warlords. In addition to its symbolism as the capital city, the foreign powers had determined that the incumbent government of Beijing would receive the customs revenue they collected on behalf of China. Warlords accepted loans and advice from foreign powers. Since some foreign powers, unsure whom to back, aided more than one warlord, they perhaps inadvertently aided the warlords to better fight one another. Sun Yat-sen and his Kuomintang (KMT), ensconced in southern China, appeared little different from the other contenders for power, except that Sun at this time had no army.

As the war proceeded, Japan continued its efforts to obtain other powers' acquiescence to its special position in China. Only the United States evinced resistance. Prime Minister Terauchi dispatched Viscount Ishii Kikujirō to Washington, DC with a proposal: if the United States agreed not to challenge Japan's primacy in Manchuria, Japan would allow U.S. investment there. President Woodrow Wilson rejected this, with the two sides eventually agreeing to a somewhat ambiguous joint statement signed by Ishii and Under-secretary of State Robert Lansing in November 1917. According to the Lansing-Ishii agreement, the United States and Japan affirmed the "open door" principle and respect for Chinese integrity, while affirming Japan's special interests in China "particularly in the part to which her possessions are contiguous."[61]

While Terauchi felt he had solidified Japan's position in the post–World War I era, a new and powerful player was about to enter the Asian power equation, in the form of the Soviet Union. The victory of the Bolshevik revolution in Russia in 1917 brought a communist party to power, and with it new risks for Japan. Sun continued to express warm feelings for the Japanese people. But he had no reason to feel the same way about the Japanese government, its numerous pronouncements about the need for China and Japan to live together notwithstanding.

The Chinese nationalistic sentiment that had been encouraged by Yuan Shikai received added stimulus after Yuan's death when, in 1919, the Versailles Conference awarded German possessions in China to Japan. Although the peace settlement was arrived at by all parties to World War I and accepted by the Chinese delegate—who, of course, had no real choice—a groundswell of anger arose that had Japan as its focus. It coalesced into the May Fourth Movement, whose anniversary is still celebrated each year in Beijing. A multifaceted protest, the May Fourth marchers opposed Confucianism and their own government as well as Japanese imperialism. A successful boycott of Japanese goods was organized. Some Chinese patriots saw in the Versailles settlement confirmation of Karl Marx's theories on the exploitation of states by imperialist powers. Two years later, the Chinese Communist Party was founded in Shanghai, determined to implement Marx's theories and rid China of imperialist domination.

Sun turned for help to the Soviet Union. The USSR's Communist International (Comintern) had been established precisely in order to fan the spark of revolution that Lenin hoped would start a prairie fire of worldwide proletarian seizures of power. The Comintern arranged an alliance between Sun's KMT and the newly founded Chinese Communist Party (CCP), formalized with the signing of the Sun-Joffe Manifesto of 1923. As a consequence, the Comintern supplied funds and advisers to the KMT as well as the CCP. Among other activities, they packaged Sun's ideology, the "Three Principles of the People," into book form, and backed the establishment of a military academy, Whampoa, to train and indoctrinate loyal officers.

THE SIBERIAN INTERVENTION

The Japanese government, by contrast, viewed international communism as an imminent threat. It joined with several Western powers, including the United States, in the Siberian intervention of 1918–1922 on behalf of the White opposition to the Bolsheviks. In addition to intense ideological hostility to communism, Tokyo was motivated by a desire to avenge previous losses to Russia and the opportunity to secure additional territory either through creation of a buffer state or outright annexation. The Bolsheviks' eventual victory not only thwarted these aims but also rendered Japan ill positioned to deal with the now more securely established government of the Soviet Union. In that Tokyo's aims in Siberia were not precisely the same as Washington's, there was friction between them as well. Moreover, the intervention took the lives of 5,000 Japanese soldiers and had cost nearly 100 million yen.[62]

SHIDEHARA DIPLOMACY

While Japan had prospered during World War I as its factories turned out products needed by the combatants, the inevitable postwar economic slowdown and the costs of the Siberian intervention dictated a policy of fiscal and diplomatic prudence that was bitterly resented by the armed forces, and particularly by the army. During the 1920s, under a series of prime ministers, Foreign Minister Shidehara Kijūrō attempted to pursue a conciliatory policy toward Washington. A fluent English speaker and open admirer of the United States, he advocated non-intervention in China despite the wishes of the military. Shidehara backed the reinstatement of China's tariff autonomy, originally announced in 1925 and ultimately effected five years later.[63] The term "Shidehara diplomacy" became synonymous with Japan's liberal foreign policy of the 1920s.

Western powers, and particularly the United States, did not make Shidehara's task easy. In 1919 the Versailles conference had rejected an eminently reasonable Japanese request to have a racial equality clause inserted in the League of Nations Covenant. Then the Washington naval treaties of 1921–1922 had forced Japan to accept an unfavorable battleship ratio of 5:5:3 for the United States, Great Britain, and Japan. And in 1924 the U.S. Congress passed the Japanese Exclusion Act to stem Japanese immigration to the United States. Nor were the Western powers willing to accept the premise that Japan had special interests, and therefore special rights, in Asia. Surely most galling was when the United States, the originator of the Monroe Doctrine, flatly rejected Japanese claims for an Asian Monroe Doctrine in which Tokyo would lead the nations of the East forward toward modernization and economic development.[64]

Such slights gave credence to the arguments of ultranationalists and militarists. Having established Japan's clear primacy over China, Japan had also become a first-rate country (*ittō koku*) in every way save acceptance of that fact by the Western powers; it was now necessary to establish that fact by force if need be. They found the arguments of the *kokugaku* scholars useful in this endeavor. For example, the term *hakkō ichiu*, literally meaning "eight cords, one dwelling," was understood as a synonym for "all the world under one roof." It was pieced together by early-twentieth-century ultranationalist Tanaka Chigaku from parts of a statement that the *Nihon Shoki* had attributed to the legendary First Emperor Jimmu at the time of his ascension. Tanaka interpreted the phrase to mean that the rule of the Japanese emperor was divinely ordained to expand until it united the entire world. While Tanaka saw this in the same relatively benign light as China's *tianxia*, according to which the emperor ruled all under heaven through his moral suasion, more militant types extended Tanaka's interpretation to mean that the Japanese were a divine race destined to rule, by force if need be.

SINO-JAPANESE RELATIONS IN THE POST–SUN YAT-SEN ERA

Sun died in 1925, just two years after the signing of the manifesto, mourned by his Japanese friends despite the Soviet connection. At his bedside was his trusted lieutenant Wang Jingwei. Wang had first visited Japan in 1903 as one of the students sent by the Qing dynasty. Two years later, he joined Sun's Tongmenghui. Arrested for plotting the assassination of the Qing regent, Prince Chun, he was saved from execution only by Japanese intervention. Wang, like Sun, held Japan in high regard. Regarded as Sun's heir apparent, he presided over his mentor's will. However, Wang had no army and was soon eclipsed for leadership by Chiang Kai-shek, who had a power base in the Whampoa Military Academy and had married the younger sister of Sun's wife.

Chiang had ties with several major countries in the China power equation. He had attended a military academy in Japan; his wife, for whose sake he had converted to Christianity, was American-educated; and his elder son studied and worked in the Soviet Union, where he married a Russian woman. Chiang appeared to distrust all these countries, but willing to cooperate with any as the circumstances seemed to warrant.

Despite a tendency to read later Chinese-Japanese hostility back into history, and the existence of very real tensions between Chiang and the Japanese, actual relationships during this period were far more fluid. In the fall of 1927, Chiang visited Tokyo to talk with Prime Minister Tanaka Giichi. Tanaka held forth the promise of Japanese help if China could block the spread of communism, which he believed required Chiang to focus on southern China. For Chiang to have focused on the south, however, would have meant abandoning his major immediate goal: the Northern Expedition to unify China under his and KMT control. Though declaring himself open to cooperation as long as the Japanese ceased to favor the Manchurian warlord Zhang Zuolin, Chiang told Tanaka that failure to move north would further radicalize patriotic elements. The negotiations were amicable, but solved nothing.

Like Japan, other foreign powers were less than enthusiastic about Chiang's unification of China, for different reasons. At that time, Chiang appeared to the United States as more leftist than Washington was comfortable with. As for the Soviet Union, its policies were enmeshed in the power struggle between Stalin and Trotsky. The USSR was supporting the warlord Feng Yuxiang, also known as the "Christian general," in addition to the aid it was providing to the KMT. Some Soviet advisers wanted to delay Chiang's Northern Expedition to unify the country so that Feng's, and presumably the USSR's, power could be enhanced. Some wanted the communists to try for control of the north before Chiang Kai-shek's forces arrived there; others felt Soviet efforts should focus on territory already held by left-wing elements in Wuhan. The Japanese, consonant with their perception of the importance of Manchuria, had heretofore concentrated on forging ties with Zhang Zuolin.

As it turned out, all parties' expectations were proved wrong. Chiang Kai-shek became markedly more conservative in the process of becoming more powerful and Feng Yuxiang would later forge an alliance with Chiang. When Feng was still receiving Soviet aid, Japanese forces denied him access to the South Manchurian Railway area, thus enabling Zhang Zuolin to move into Beijing. Zhang understandably anticipated that the Japanese would also aid him against Chiang Kai-shek's army as it approached Beijing, but this help did not materialize. The Kwantung army wanted to separate Manchuria from northern China, and decided that Zhang was expendable. In June 1928, acting without authorization from the Tokyo government, nationalist expansionist elements of the army blew up the train on which Zhang was withdrawing from Beijing en route to Mukden/Shenyang, killing him. The goal was to provoke disorder so that they could claim the need for Japanese intervention in Manchuria.

The anticipated disorder did not materialize. Moreover, Zhang's death removed the major impediment between Chiang Kai-shek and the conquest of Beijing, which then passed into KMT hands. Zhang was succeeded by his son Zhang Xueliang who, though in no position to challenge Japan directly and immediately, was determined to avenge his father's murder, even at the cost of making common cause with Chiang Kai-shek. Japanese aggression proved a useful bonding element for the otherwise divided elements of Chinese society. To paraphrase an ancient Chinese proverb, the Japanese expansionists had picked up a rock, only to drop it on their own foot.

It should not be imagined that divisions within the ranks of the Chinese disappeared. First, rather than conquer many of the warlords he encountered on the Northern Expedition, Chiang had simply absorbed them into his government scheme. Several were designated governors of the provinces they had previously controlled as warlords. For another, there were sharp divisions within the KMT. Wang Jingwei, Sun's erstwhile heir apparent, had cast his lot with the left wing of the party, his favorable disposition toward Japan notwithstanding. Differences of opinion and goals on all sides provided fertile ground for semi-official and unofficial negotiations with each other and with foreign powers, as well as for other actions that had serious consequences.

In Japan, the world depression that began with the crash of the U.S. stock market in late 1929 had a devastating effect, deepening distrust of the West and encouraging extremist elements in the army. Statesmen who preferred to reach an accommodation with China and the West placed themselves and their families in a difficult position. A number of them were, in fact, murdered, prompting one analyst of the era to title his study of Japanese politics *Government by Assassination*.[65]

THE MUKDEN INCIDENT

One of the most serious of the clashes between ultranationalists in the Japanese army and Chinese forces, known as the Mukden, or Manchurian, incident, occurred on September 18, 1931. Ishiwara Kanji, the guiding force behind the incident, was a follower of Tanaka Chigaku, and espoused a military interpretation of Tanaka's hakkō ichiu. Extremist elements in the Kwantung army were concerned that Chiang Kai-shek's Northern

Expedition would jeopardize Japan's privileged position in Manchuria, particularly in light of Zhang Xueliang's move toward the KMT.

The unsolved murder of Japanese Army Captain Nakamura by Zhang Xueliang's troops a few months earlier gave ultranationalists fresh ammunition to use against Shidehara's accommodative diplomacy. Learning that a military envoy was being sent from Tokyo to soothe the tense situation, they arranged for him to be entertained at a geisha house the evening before negotiations were to begin. As the party proceeded, a bomb explosion occurred outside Mukden, on the main line of the South Manchurian Railway and not far from a company of Zhang Xueliang's troops. Japanese forces provoked a confrontation with these troops, following it with a full-scale attack that took Mukden with the loss of only two Japanese lives.

Japanese public opinion was strongly on the side of the seizure: a few months later, the cabinet that had tried to forestall the incident fell. Extremists thus brought an end to Shidehara's accommodative stance. In early 1932 the last Qing emperor was enthroned as titular head of a Manchu state, Manchukuo, surrounded by Japanese advisers.

Although U.S. Secretary of State Stimson wanted to mount a united opposition effort to the invasion of Manchuria, he found Western powers disinclined to intervene. *The Times* of London, for example, opined that Chinese sovereignty over Manchuria was a "legal phantom" that had not existed in 1922 and did not exist today [1933].[66] Stimson, feeling compelled to act unilaterally, let it be known that the United States no longer felt obliged by earlier promises that it would not further fortify Guam and the Philippines. He also dispatched U.S. ships to Shanghai. The Japanese interpreted these responses as indicating that American and Japanese aims were irreconcilable.

Chiang Kai-shek, knowing that his troops were no match for the imperial Japanese army, avoided confrontation, at first preferring to concentrate his military attentions on fighting the Chinese communists. When assailed by patriots for this, Chiang famously described the Japanese as but a disease of the skin, whereas the communists were attacking the internal organs of the body politic. While Chiang was undoubtedly correct in his assessment of the futility of attacking the Japanese, it enabled the CCP to seize the patriotic high ground of protector of China from foreign invasion.

Indiscriminate dislike of all foreigners in China was quickly becoming focused on the Japanese, and reached a high pitch after the Mukden incident. Boycotts of Japanese goods began in the treaty ports, with the most effective occurring in Shanghai. This prompted the commander of Japanese forces in the area, General Shiozawa, to notify the mayor of Shanghai that all boycott activities must cease by the end of the month. The mayor agreed, but before the boycott could be implemented, Shiozawa, without Tokyo's prior knowledge or permission, provoked a skirmish by sending Japanese marines into a Chinese district. Although there were no serious injuries, Shiozawa claimed the incident was an insult to the Japanese empire and ordered an aerial bombardment of the area.

Stimson feared that the Japanese would use the Shanghai incident as an excuse to declare war on China, but again found little support among other Western powers, or even from his own president, Herbert Hoover, for a strong stand. Despite their distaste for what Shiozawa had done, the Western powers were loath to take action. In effect, however, the Shanghai incident ended more moderate Japanese politicians' hope of settling the Manchurian issue.[67]

Linking the Shanghai incident to Japan's actions in Manchuria, Stimson, in a public letter to the ranking member of the Foreign Relations Committee, Senator William Borah, implied that the United States should no longer feel bound by previous treaty commitments on battleship construction and fortifications in Guam and the Philippines. The Tokyo government, in turn, interpreted this as further evidence of the irreconcilability of U.S. and Japanese policies. In February 1933 a League of Nations commission presented a report critical of Japan's actions in Manchuria. Tokyo's representative Matsuoka Yōsuke countered that, since China was a bandit-ridden hopelessly disorganized country, the Chinese central government was a legal fiction. Chinese violations of international treaties were frequent, whereas Tokyo had always upheld the principles of international law. Moreover, communism was a looming menace to East Asia: the possibility of a USSR allied with a communist China could not be ignored. His country had special rights and interests, and responsibilities in the area, one of which was to help China. Therefore, the League should recognize the status of Manchukuo. When the delegates denied Matsuoka's appeal, Japan left the League of Nations.

EXPANSION IN NORTH CHINA

At the same time, the Kwantung army advanced south of the Great Wall and forced the Tanggu[68] Truce, under which all Chinese troops were to leave the

Tianjin area. In 1935 two additional accords, the Ho-Umezu and Jin-Doihara agreements, resulted in the withdrawal of Chinese troops from Hebei and Chahar. Also in that year, the KMT government agreed to Japanese demands to establish a Hebei-Chahar Political Council, with General Song Zheyuan, who was regarded as pro-Japanese, as head. Contrary to Japanese hopes, however, the council remained loyal to Chiang's government in Nanjing.

The army's goal was to protect Manchukuo from both communist activities instigated from Moscow and from those emanating from anti-Japanese patriotic elements in China. In this, it had succeeded: Japan now controlled north China up to the outskirts of Beijing, then known as Beiping (Northern Peace), since Chiang Kai-shek had established his capital (*jing*) at Nanjing (Southern Peace). But it had deepened the isolation between Japan and the Western powers. On the expiry of the London and Washington naval treaties in 1936, Tokyo withdrew the country from both. In the same year, it signed an anti-Comintern pact with Hitler's Germany.

A CHINESE COMMUNIST–KMT ALLIANCE AGAINST JAPAN

Chiang Kai-shek meanwhile continued his efforts against the communists. He succeeded to the extent of forcing the group from its base in Jiangxi in 1934 and onto a convoluted year-long epic trek northward known to history as the Long March. It ended in Yan'an in Shaanxi. Determined to exterminate the CCP, Chiang flew to Shaanxi to confer with the powerful warlord there. However, Zhang Xueliang's priority was to recoup his base in Manchuria and avenge his father's murder: he made common cause with the CCP and arranged to kidnap Chiang. After tense negotiations, agreement was reached on a CCP–KMT united front against Japanese aggression. While Zhang was undoubtedly motivated by a desire to regain his satrapy in Manchuria, Chiang placed him under house arrest, where he remained until 1990. The CCP got the better end of the bargain: Chiang pledged to end his attempt to destroy it and granted the party territory in which to govern. Neither side observed the terms of this truce completely: Chiang still nourished hopes of destroying the CCP, and the CCP was able to expand well beyond the bases of operation it was formally granted.

Recent research based on Chiang Kai-shek's diary and presidential papers indicates that Chiang decided on war not because he reached an agreement with the CCP to resist, but because while at Xi'an he had received a signal from Josef Stalin that the Soviet Union would support him in a war with Japan.[69] In any case, the CCP–KMT alliance, precarious though it was, allowed Japanese extremists to argue that, in fighting for control of China, they were opposing the spread of communism as well. Even had the Xi'an incident never happened, extremist elements in Japan had redefined policy toward China in ways that infinitely complicated any amicable accommodation with Chiang's KMT government.

Domestically, assassinations continued. In August 1935 a lieutenant colonel entered the office of the chief of the army's Bureau of Military Affairs, General Nagata Tetsuzan, drew his sword, and hacked the general to death. The colonel's ire was provoked because the Ministry of War had acceded to a China policy that sought a modus vivendi based on the status quo in Manchuria, and because General Nagata had acted quickly to deal with a plot by several extremist officers to subvert the policy. The trial of the assassin provoked a major army rebellion that included more assassinations. The General Staff, backed by the emperor in whose interests the insurrectionists claimed to act, suppressed the rebellion and dealt swiftly with the perpetrators. This placed the General Staff in a more powerful position in the Japanese government and, perversely, resulted in an increasing conviction that Tokyo needed to take a more assertive position in China.[70]

THE MARCO POLO BRIDGE INCIDENT, 1937

With nationalist emotions running high in both China and Japan, incidents were to be expected. On July 7, 1937, the Japanese army stationed near Marco Polo Bridge, south of Beijing, was holding unscheduled maneuvers, shooting blanks. Shots were heard from the other side, and a soldier was discovered missing. The Japanese telegraphed nearby KMT forces, asking for permission to search for him. Since the bridge ran by the Pinghan (Wanping-Wuhan) railway, as well as being the only passage from Beijing to KMT-controlled areas from the south, its location was strategically important. The Chinese side was reluctant to agree, and although the missing soldier reappeared unharmed, a skirmish ensued.

Elements on both sides appeared to favor settlement, with even some army leaders contending that the real danger to Japan came from the Soviet

Union, and that therefore a confrontation with China would be counterproductive. Just as an agreement seemed possible, on July 17th, Chiang Kai-shek, presumably acting on the above-mentioned promise of help from the Soviet Union, declared a policy of no retreat. If Beijing fell, which seemed likely, then Nanjing would be next. Chiang ordered his troops into the area prohibited under the terms of the Tanggu Truce.

Tokyo responded by demanding an apology for these illegal actions and guarantees that they would not recur. Both sides moved in troops. When the Japanese ordered General Song Zheyuan, hitherto regarded as friendly to them, to evacuate south of Beijing, he refused. Serious fighting began on the 27th, with the Chinese taking heavy casualties. On the following day, the Chinese Peace Preservation Corps, a group sponsored by a Japanese-affiliated East Hebei government, murdered their Japanese officers as well as at least 230 Japanese civilians. This silenced army leaders who wanted a settlement. Beijing and Tianjin fell on July 29th.

At this point, the emperor himself stepped in, ordering the prime minister to begin negotiations with Chiang's government. However, a further complication was added when, on August 9th, a Japanese marine corps officer and his driver were killed by sentries of the local Peace Preservation Corps as they tried to enter the Shanghai airport. The mayor of Shanghai, arguing that the Japanese had brought the incident on themselves by reinforcing the marine contingent and moving warships to the area, rejected demands that the Peace Preservation Corps be moved to the outskirts of the city.

In the end, the Japanese consul-general did apologize for the marine's actions and the commanding admiral ordered an end to night patrols. Just as settlement again seemed possible, the mayor announced he could no longer speak for the Chinese government, because authority now rested with the KMT military.[71] On August 14th, Chiang's air force bombarded Japanese naval installations at Shanghai.

There followed several months of negotiations. Although the League of Nations would do no more than appoint a committee to investigate, several foreign powers offered their good offices. The two sides agreed to accept German mediation. In November Ambassador Herbert von Dirksen presented Chiang with terms that included:

- an autonomous government in Inner Mongolia
- a new demilitarized zone in North China running from the border of Manchukuo to south of the line between Beiping/Beijing and Tianjin

- a larger demilitarized zone in the Shanghai area
- the cessation of anti-Japanese activities in China
- a common fight against Bolshevism
- a reduction in customs duties on Japanese goods
- a guarantee of political and economic rights for Japanese nationals in China

These demands were presented as non-negotiable. Chiang was warned that failure to accept them meant Japan would prosecute the war until China was totally defeated, at which point it would exact far more sweeping demands. Chiang refused, demanding that Tokyo restore the status quo ante of July 7th. This confirmed the view of Japanese leaders who felt he needed further punishment. As the respective sides conferred, regional Japanese armies in China acted without Tokyo's permission to set up client regimes headed by men who took orders from them rather than Tokyo. A month later, with Japanese troops advancing on his capital of Nanjing, Chiang agreed to accept the November terms.

Within Japanese ruling circles, there was consensus that Nanjing could easily be taken, but markedly different opinions on the consequences. Some thought that defeat would cause the collapse of Chiang's government, at which point it could be replaced with a regime more amenable to Japanese direction. Admiral Suetsugu opined that in this way the Chinese could be made allies against the real enemy, the white race, and Foreign Minister Hirota noted that the regional armies would now expect to exact more stringent conditions from Chiang.

Others thought that the defeated government would not collapse, forcing Japan to extend the war into south China. The real enemy, the Soviet Union, would take advantage of this diversion of Japanese energies to encroach on north China. In the end, Chiang was asked to accept still more stringent terms: to extend de facto recognition to Manchukuo; agree to the establishment of special administrative areas in north and in central China; and pay reparations.

On December 13, 1937, Nanjing fell as predicted, amid horrifying carnage carried out by Japanese troops. Foreigners were unharmed, with some managing to photograph and film the unfolding human tragedy. Estimates of casualties range from a low of 13,000 to a high of 300,000. If, as reported, one motive behind the atrocities was to break the will of the Chinese population to continue to fight, it backfired badly. The event remains to this day both highly controversial and a massive impediment to efforts at Sino-Japanese reconciliation.[72]

Japanese leaders who doubted that the fall of Nanjing would bring the collapse of Chiang Kai-shek's regime were correct. After protracted discussion among decision-makers in Tokyo, those favoring continued efforts to reach a settlement with Chiang were outmaneuvered by those favoring the annihilation of his government. The Germans were told that their efforts at mediation were no longer required, with Ambassador von Dirksen predicting presciently that Tokyo's policy would lead to the Bolshevization of China.[73] After Chiang turned down Japan's conditions for peace, the Japanese government announced it would no longer deal with him. Astonishingly, even while each side was publicly committed to destroying the other and Tokyo had refused to speak with Chiang, the channel for negotiations remained open.

WANG JINGWEI

Deprived of its capital, Chiang's government left Nanjing for Chongqing, in southwest China where the KMT held out despite regular bombardments by Japanese planes. Chinese victories were few and far between. Often these were due to the arrogant overconfidence of the Japanese military as much as by the skills of the Chinese forces, who were typically poorly organized and equipped with inferior arms. For example, at Taierzhuang, in eastern China, overconfidence led the Japanese to overlook the presence of infiltrating "farmers" who cut their communications lines. This meant resupply had to be carried out by air, and therefore in much smaller amounts than needed. Apparently still convinced of his force's superiority, the Japanese commander then attacked far larger numbers of KMT troops frontally, resulting in an embarrassing defeat.

The same contempt allowed the Chinese Communist forces to prevail at Pingxingguan in the northern province of Shanxi. The Japanese commander marched his troops through a narrow pass between mountains without having checked the security of the heights on either side. Communist forces attacked from front, center, and rear, throwing hand grenades into the mass of soldiers trapped inside. These two battles were, however, the exception rather than the rule, and had little strategic value.[74] By mid-1939 Japanese forces had taken the densely populated, urban, and more foreign-trade-oriented parts of China that had formed the mainstay of the KMT's support. Japan also controlled most of the rail lines. Nonetheless, since Japan was only a fraction of the size of China in terms of land area and population, there were limits on how closely it could control such a large territory.

With open dialogue precluded and the prospect of an endless struggle looming, private channels were sought. Wang Jingwei, as someone who had ties to both the KMT and the Japanese, was approached as an intermediary. Pessimistic about China's chances to win a war against Japan, Wang favored negotiation as a means for China's survival. Though Wang was castigated as a traitor, subsequent research indicates that the truth is far more complicated. In order to further a peace scheme originated not by himself but by Chiang Kai-shek, Wang left Chongqing for Japanese-occupied Shanghai in 1938. If a settlement could be effected, Chiang would not have to take responsibility for concessions to Japan, which the communists and various Chinese patriotic groups who wanted to fight to the bitter end would have opposed.

An exhaustive study of the negotiations concludes that each side was trying to dupe the other. Chiang was trying to maneuver a Japanese commitment to withdraw troops from China. He was able to play on the Japanese penchant for believing they "understood" China and Chinese politics. Chiang not only allowed the Japanese to think that Wang would organize an anti-Chiang military uprising, but actually told the Japanese so.[75]

Convoluted negotiations ensued with Wang, for example, insisting that Japanese troops be stationed only in Inner Mongolia, which would be designated a special anti-Comintern area for joint defense against Bolshevism, and the Japanese refusing. While Tokyo proved unwilling to agree to Wang's conditions, the Chongqing government worried that he had gone too far. On January 1, 1939, Wang was expelled from the KMT and soon thereafter denounced as a traitor.

Repudiated by one side, Wang lost his leverage with the other. Eventually, he capitulated to Japanese demands, agreeing to the severance of Manchuria/Manchukuo from China; the indefinite stationing of Japanese troops in north China, Amoy, and Hainan; the cessation of anti-Japanese activities; and economic concessions in the lower Yangtze Valley. Japanese troops would be withdrawn from central and southern China once peace had been established, but only after a two-year delay.[76]

In March 1940 Wang became head of a Japanese-sponsored government based in Nanjing. He accepted the need for China to follow the Japanese in a common effort to preserve an alleged Asian culture from the depredations of European colonialism, justifying his stance on the basis of Sun Yat-sen's pan-Asianism.[77] This sentiment was not mere rhetoric. One of Wang's aides, about to be executed for treason by Chiang's side, stated forcefully that history would prove him right to have worked with the Japanese against the white race. He believed that he had been sentenced to death in order to placate the whites.[78]

Although Wang had little ability to bargain with the Japanese, the resultant regime was not a purely Japanese creation. A scholar of the period characterizes it as the product of "a political process of negotiation, misrepresentation, and subterfuge in which Chinese were involved as more than passive puppets of their Japanese masters."[79] Even so, Wang's government was never able to eclipse Chiang's: Tokyo's effort to replace Chiang's regime with a more compliant one had failed. Chiang, infuriated that the Wang regime had been established, became even more difficult to deal with.

In 1940 also, Prime Minister Konoe Fumimaro's administration issued a White Paper entitled "Fundamental National Policy," which opened with the words hakkō ichiu and in which Konoe declared that the first step in Japan's goal to secure world peace was the establishment of a new order in East Asia. This was the genesis of the "Greater East Asia Co-Prosperity Sphere," under which Japan would lead the hemisphere forward for the good of all. Fortuitously, the 2600th anniversary of Emperor Jimmu's ascension to the throne happened to occur in 1940 as well. Preparations for a grand celebration included frequent mentions of Japan's divine mission and the new East Asian order.

THE SECOND SINO-JAPANESE WAR

From 1939 through late 1941, the battle lines in China did not change greatly. Retrospective myth-making by both KMT and CCP governments notwithstanding, the idea of a single China at war with Japan is not consonant with historical reality. Closer scrutiny reveals a highly fragmented mosaic of competing regimes whose populations struggled to survive by whatever means possible. Both Japanese and local peoples adapted to changing circumstances that were not within their power to control, with as many compromises as confrontations in existence. Cynical bargains were made with local elites, and conflicting loyalties were common. Resistance was not the polar opposite of collaboration.

For example, the fall of Wuhan contrasted sharply with the horrendous carnage at Nanjing. Returned students from Japan ran a relatively orderly administration. Even in communist-controlled areas, there was trade with the enemy.[80] Simultaneously, however, the Japanese were carrying out grisly medical research on a scale that rivaled and, were comparisons of such bestialities even possible, possibly even exceeded that of Nazi Germany. Nationals of half a dozen countries were subjects of the research, with Chinese constituting the overwhelming majority of victims. Though rumored, the experiments were not widely known until a Japanese researcher working in an American archive found and exposed them in 1980. At the postwar Tokyo War Crimes Trials, prosecutors from the countries involved were aware of the issue, but chose to remain silent because the data would be valuable and could not be independently collected due to "scruples attached to human experimentation."[81]

The Chinese communists used the relative lull in fighting to expand. By 1940 their increase in strength was such that they launched a coordinated attack known as the Hundred Regiments offensive. It failed badly, with the party's troops taking casualties estimated at 22,000, compared to only 3,000–4,000 for the Japanese. Tokyo's answer to the CCP's notion of military-civilian cooperation, "The people are the fish and the army is the water, the water must always support the fish," was "drain the pond." The "three alls"—kill all, burn all, destroy all—did not distinguish between fish/soldiers and civilians/water.

Though Japanese forces were successful in quashing resistance, as they did in the Hundred Regiments campaign, neither the CCP nor Chiang's KMT government (as opposed to Wang Jingwei's KMT government) would accept defeat. Nor did either do much fighting, though the KMT forces did considerably more than the CCP's. Where Japanese troops behaved with great cruelty, resistance was stimulated. Japanese control has been compared to a net: they controlled the nodes, but not the spaces within.

CCP expansion was also noticed by Chiang Kai-shek whose forces began blockading the major communist base area in 1939. In January 1941 KMT units attacked the communist New Fourth Army, ending the united front against the Japanese that had been agreed upon after the Xi'an incident. The civil war, which had never really ceased, intensified. After Pearl

Harbor and the U.S. declaration of war against Japan, both Chiang Kai-shek and Mao Zedong anticipated that America would conquer Japan, thereby facilitating their ability to fight each other.

Washington, wanting Chinese to engage Japanese troops regardless of their political affiliation, pledged help. U.S. aid was dispersed to Chiang Kai-shek, as head of the officially recognized government of China. However, Chiang was angry and disappointed when the United States changed its strategy from a campaign against Japanese troops in China to an island-hopping one: capturing selected Japanese-held Pacific islands en route to an invasion of the Japanese home islands. American diplomats stationed in Chongqing reported persistent rumors that Chiang was threatening to make a separate peace with Tokyo.[82] While this is likely to have been a negotiating ploy by Chiang, the U.S. side could never be totally sure.

Chiang also endeavored to block the delivery of American supplies to the Communist base areas. At one point, President Roosevelt had to tell Chiang that unless hostilities between the CCP and KMT ceased, American aid would end. This appears to have been a bluff: foreign eyewitnesses confirm that neither the fighting nor the aid actually did cease.[83]

American observers sent to the communist base areas were impressed with the relative lack of corruption and dedication to fighting the Japanese, as compared to those of Chiang Kai-shek's government. Subsequent research has revealed that appearance was not necessarily reality; one scholar describes the "brilliant" Potemkin village that the CCP constructed for the visiting Dixie Mission, dispatched in 1944 to try to get the KMT and CCP to stop fighting and coordinate their efforts.[84] The head of the mission himself later admitted that he had been deceived about the nature of the government and its intentions.[85] Cynicism about the motives of its leadership aside, however, the CCP was able to create and mobilize substantial numbers of dedicated anti-Japanese patriots to fight for it.

THE CHINESE CIVIL WAR

America's island-hopping strategy achieved a string of hard-fought successes in the Pacific, and advanced upward through Okinawa. The coup de grace to a rapidly failing Japanese defense came with America's dropping hitherto secret nuclear weapons on Hiroshima and Nagasaki in August 1945. Emperor Hirohito, using the same language his grandfather had in announcing the retrocession of the Liaodong peninsula fifty years earlier, asked his subjects to bear the unbearable and surrender. An orderly evacuation of most of the Japanese troops in China took place, and fighting between KMT and CCP forces proceeded uninhibited in spite of American efforts to mediate.

Inflation is a common postwar phenomenon, as people, with the large amounts of money earned during the typically high-employment conditions of wartime, seek to purchase the too few goods that are available. Urban areas suffer more than rural ones, because the latter produce food that can be bartered without recourse to currency. Since the KMT's bases of support were in cities, the ensuing inflation affected it more than it did the CCP, which was ensconced in the countryside. Speculators, who included leading members of the KMT and persons directly or indirectly connected to the Chiang family, made enormous profits while less well-positioned citizens suffered—and held the Kuomintang government responsible.

By contrast, morale in the Communist-held areas was high and corruption low. Dispirited KMT forces surrendered so much of their U.S.-supplied equipment to CCP forces that Red Army commanders joked about their logistics command being located in Washington. On October 1, 1949, Mao Zedong entered Beijing in a captured American jeep and proclaimed the founding of the People's Republic of China. Ambassador von Dirksen's prediction had come true: Japan's refusal to compromise with Chiang had led to the Bolshevization of China.

CONCLUSIONS

Even when Japan's military victory became increasingly unlikely, Tokyo was never prepared to offer Chiang's government peace terms consistent with Chinese nationalism.[86] A study of the responsibility for the war undertaken by a major Japanese newspaper sixty years after its end concluded that, because Japanese leaders were obsessed with traditional ways of Chinese thinking, they had failed to understand Chinese nationalism.[87] For its part, China had badly failed to understand and respect Japan, treating it as an inferior until the first Sino-Japanese war began to illustrate beyond argument how erroneous that view was. Conversely, the contempt that Japan had shown for China since the first Sino-Japanese war had caused it to underestimate the staying power of the Middle Kingdom. China did not defeat Japan in World War II: the Western powers, and particularly the United States, were responsible. But it was Japan's refusal to stop expanding within China that ultimately brought it into conflict with the Western powers.

The initial steps toward war can be traced to the Japanese leadership demanding recognition of a client state it set up in Manchuria, ostensibly to ensure the security of the empire, and both Chinese and Western refusal to accept either that client state or Japan's special place in Asia. By increments, the mindset of superiority that had been developed to overcome feelings of inferiority led to conflict with not only China but the Western powers as well. Halting the step-by-step expansion that progressively widened the confrontation would mean accepting the status of less than first-class power, and was therefore unthinkable in terms of the mindset they had created. The result was the destruction of the Empire of the Rising Sun on a scale hitherto unimaginable. Large swaths of the Middle Kingdom lay in ruins as well.

3

Wary Engagement, 1945–1969

FINDING A PLACE IN THE POST-WAR BALANCE OF POWER

In the years following World War II, Japan and China became part of the bipolar configuration of power on opposite sides. Neither was entirely comfortable with this position and each, though constrained by its immediate postwar weaknesses, cautiously attempted to stake out a position independent of its stronger partner. In the case of Japan, where the United States occupation government encouraged free speech, this was more obvious than in China, where Stalin's government and Mao Zedong suppressed the expression of views that deviated from the party line set down by the leader. Chinese media made frequent mention of Japanese cruelties during World War II and the valiant struggle that the Chinese people had waged to defeat them. The CCP took full credit for leading the masses, as it then referred to the Chinese people, to victory.

THE NEW JAPANESE GOVERNMENT REGARDS CHINA

Mutual antagonisms notwithstanding, Prime Minister Yoshida Shigeru felt strongly that the CCP leadership was Chinese first and communist second. He believed that in time the CCP government would become as nationalistic as its predecessors and that, rather than contributing to the USSR's power in Asia, it would diminish Soviet power. Some American officials expressed private concerns about this possibility, reasoning that a Sino-Soviet rift could result in the formation of a Sino-Japanese force that was inimical to U.S. interests. At one point, the then-adviser to the Secretary of State John Foster Dulles felt it necessary to fly to Tokyo to obtain pledges of Japanese loyalty to Chiang Kai-shek's Republic of China (ROC) on Taiwan.[1]

Yoshida argued that Japan could play an important part in loosening the ties between Moscow and Beijing; as a nation with longstanding ties to China, Japan could guide Washington out of the situation on China that it had boxed itself into. Dulles countered that this was pure fantasy: China was the major threat to Japanese security, and its isolation was the best way to deal with the threat. In the end, an agreement was reached that Japan would recognize the ROC as *a* government of China rather than *the* government of China, and that any treaty would be restricted to the area under actual ROC jurisdiction. Yoshida, unconvinced but in no position to argue, tried to negotiate good relations with both Chinas. Since each claimant to the title of China reacted negatively to acknowledgment of the other's right to exist, this was no easy task.

As Japanese policy hoped to wean mainland China away from the Soviet Union, Chinese policy aimed at undermining Japan's alliance with the United States. Mao hoped to draw Japan, with its strategic location, skilled population, and advanced industrial base, into the communist camp. While railing against the Japanese government and its capitalists and militarists, the Chinese media expressed sympathy for the country's masses, whom they portrayed as being oppressed by these exploitative forces. To reach them, Beijing attempted to work through leftist organizations in Japan, whose revival had been permitted by the U.S. occupation in order to further its goal of democratizing the country.

In this endeavor, the CCP was able to call upon the services of both Chinese who had been educated in Japan during the prewar period and Japanese with experience in China. The best-known member of the latter group was Nosaka Sanzō, head of the Japanese Communist Party (JCP), who had spent the war years in exile with Mao in Yan'an: he returned to a victory celebration in Tokyo in December 1945. Perhaps to assuage concerns, Nosaka declared that there could be peaceful roads to communism: violent revolution was not the only path.

Supplementing the ties that Japanese communists and socialists had forged with CCP members during the war were the Japanese contacts made by Sun Yat-sen. Both proved useful in building bridges between China and Japan. Miyazaki Tōten's son Miyazaki Seimin played a prominent role in establishing friendly ties in the absence of formal diplomatic relations. Most prominent was Liao Chengzhi, the son of Sun Yat-sen's close friend Liao Zhongkai, and his mother He Xiangning. The Liao family's social cachet was enhanced through Madame He's close friendship with Sun's wife Soong Qingling. Liao, born in Tokyo, spoke the Edo dialect better than many Japanese from outside the area. Though often forced to defend himself against discrimination—his memoirs describe a teacher who referred to him as "a little Chinese pig who didn't know anything," Liao apparently survived the experience with no ill will. He also recalled that a Japanese classmate had defended him against the taunts of others.[2]

The Liao family returned to China for a time in the 1920s, during which the elder Liao was assassinated, presumably by a right-wing KMT member.[3] This qualified his survivors for the status of revolutionary martyr family, which was to serve them well during Mao's several post-1949 purges. Returning to Japan after the assassination, Liao Chengzhi became active in communist political activities and demonstrations against Japan's increasing involvement in China, which resulted in his expulsion from the country in 1928.

In addition to sanctioning the legitimacy of the communist party, the occupation authorities also encouraged socialists to regroup and labor unions to re-form. The Japan Socialist Party (JSP) became the standard-bearer of the socialist cause; the General Council of Trade Unions of Japan, typically referred to by its abbreviated name Sōhyō, was formed in 1950. Labor laws were formulated to protect workers' interests and permit collective bargaining. Many of the Americans involved in these activities were alumni of President Franklin Roosevelt's New Deal legislation, leading more conservative Japanese to conclude ruefully that their country was being used as a social laboratory to implement reforms that the New Dealers had been unable to enact in the United States.[4] Yoshida was immensely relieved when occupation head General Douglas MacArthur countermanded their activities, praising the general's power and good sense.[5]

Meanwhile, Japan's postwar leaders, mainly conservatives who would by 1955 come together to form the dominant Liberal Democratic Party (LDP), worried about a communist revolution that would be abetted by the newly enfranchised leftists. Yoshida's memoirs describe the Americans as "an unsuspicious race"—perhaps a carefully chosen euphemism for hopelessly naive—who initially seemed to think that the Japanese communists were their friends but soon became aware of the price to be paid for that friendship.

Relations between Japanese leftists and China were carried out through a variety of unofficial organizations such as Sino-Japanese friendship groups, trade union organizations, youth leagues, and professional groups. These were coordinated from the Chinese side by the CCP's United Front Work Department (UFWD) and its Overseas Chinese Affairs Commission (OCAC). Liao Chengzhi's mother Madame He was appointed head of the OCAC; Liao himself soon became vice-chair and was thus technically, though not actually, subordinate to his mother.

Beginning from 1953, Radio Beijing broadcast to Japan for ten and a half hours a week, though an American scholar resident in Japan at the time termed its messages ineffectual.[6] Press releases from Xinhua, the PRC's official news agency, were distributed by another communist outlet, the Asia News Service, but the Japanese press typically relied more on its own wire services as well as those of the United States and Great Britain.

Beijing's Foreign Languages Press produced several magazines, pamphlets, and books in Japanese, shipping them in via Hong Kong in the absence of formal diplomatic recognition. These were available in many bookstores, with their rather crude messages appealing more to left-wing readers than to the uncommitted, much less to conservatives. Bookstalls in major Japanese cities carried such literature as the selected works of Mao Zedong, speeches by other high-ranking CCP leaders, and books by well-known Chinese authors like Guo Moruo and Lu Xun. A few Chinese films were smuggled into Japan, but their blatantly propagandistic messages did not attract wide audiences.[7]

Propaganda conducted through the medium of traditional Chinese culture had far better results. When the influential center-left newspaper *Asahi* sponsored the performance of a theatrical troupe headed by acclaimed Chinese opera star Mei Lanfang, it was an enormous popular success. Troupe members cultivated contacts with Japanese stage and screen actors and other cultural leaders, many of whom were sympathetic to left-wing causes. And several of the books published by the Chūgoku Kenkyūjō (China Research Institute) became basic sources of information on China, serving as standard reference works in libraries, newspaper offices, and universities.[8]

THE NEW CHINESE GOVERNMENT REGARDS JAPAN

After defeating Chiang Kai-shek's KMT (Nationalist Party) forces, Mao Zedong proclaimed the founding of the People's Republic of China (PRC) on October 1, 1949. In a ringing victory speech, Mao is commonly quoted as having said, "China has stood up."[9] At the time, this was more hortatory than a description of reality: the newly founded PRC had been economically devastated by decades of civil war and felt menaced by foreign enemies as well. The Soviet Union was its sole meaningful source of external sustenance, leading Mao to journey to Moscow to seek help. There, he was treated coolly by Soviet leader Josef Stalin, who reportedly did not even contact Mao for the first few days of the chairman's residence at the state guesthouse.

Many weeks went by, indicating that difficult negotiations were taking place. Anti-communists' hopes that this indicated the existence of a Tito-like split between the leaderships of the PRC and the Soviet Union proved overly optimistic. The agreement that was announced on Valentine's Day 1950 showed that, beneath a thin veneer of intimate socialist friendship, Stalin had driven a hard bargain. According to the terms of the Sino-Soviet Treaty of Friendship, Alliance, and Mutual Assistance, China would receive $300,000,000 in credits for weapons, and economic and technological assistance that included advisers and machinery. Stalin also agreed to return property the USSR had seized from Japanese owners in Manchuria. In return, the PRC gave the Soviet Union continued use of a naval base at Lüda (Port Arthur/Dalian or, when under Japanese control, Dairen) in Liaoning province, as well as concessions on the Chinese Eastern Railway and in Xinjiang, in northwest China. The economic agreement had a five-year duration, with the loan to be repaid at 1 percent interest and tied to the purchase of Soviet rail and mining equipment. Mao, who had made resistance to unequal treaties a rallying cry of his revolution, had to settle for exactly that with the USSR. Although apparently assenting voluntarily to Stalin's "lean to one side," that is, the side of the Soviet Union, policy, Mao would have had no other choice.

With regard to Japan, the newly pledged alliance partners stated their objective of "frustrate[ing] jointly any revival of Japanese militarism and repetition of aggression by Japan, pledging mutual aid in the event of aggression by Japan" or "any other state directly or indirectly associated" with Japan. They declared their intention to conclude a peace treaty with Tokyo "in the shortest possible time."[10] It was widely believed that the real terms of the alliance were contained in secret protocols. In Japan, there were rumors that these included a provision for the invasion of Japan by a "Japanese Liberation Army" of former Japanese soldiers armed by the Soviets and trained by the Chinese.[11] Most commentators believed that the treaty dealt a virtual death blow to the already dim chances of Chinese and Soviet participation in the Japanese peace conference.

NEGOTIATIONS FOR A POST–WORLD WAR II SETTLEMENT

While no invasion by a Japanese Liberation Army materialized, the prediction that the communist states would not take part in the peace conference proved accurate. Japanese officials reacted to the Sino-Soviet agreement with a mixture of anger and anxiety, fearing that Tokyo had been warned against cooperating with Western states in any way lest the country be branded an aggressor. Japanese officials disclaimed any intentions to become an aggressor, and cited General MacArthur's statement that it would take the country at least a generation to menace its neighbors even were it to harbor any plans to do so. They believed that the principal object of the treaty was to aid the cause of communism by reviving hatred of Japan among Asian peoples who had suffered in the war.

Meanwhile, Japanese leftists united to oppose a peace treaty that excluded the USSR and the PRC, while less radical elements favored the separate treaty as the best way to end the occupation of the country at the earliest possible date.[12] To foreign criticism that he had "leaned to one side," Mao replied that indeed he had: there was a clear choice to be made between following the path of communism and the path of imperialism, and the People's Republic would steadfastly adhere to the former.

In its efforts to cultivate good relations with the PRC while guarding against leftist-inspired subversion from within, the Japanese government (GOJ) was helped by a change in the American attitude toward leftist forces. This began when left-wing organizations threatened a general strike in 1947, causing U.S. officials to take seriously the possibility that a mobilized militant worker movement could help deliver the country into the hands of communist expansionism. Moreover, since these activities would cripple Japanese economic recovery, the United States would have to prolong aid to its former enemy, thus reducing its own prosperity by whatever amounts it was required to expend in Japan. The strike was banned by MacArthur's headquarters.[13]

Two years later, with leftists still instigating labor unrest and encouraging anti-American sentiment, MacArthur's Fourth of July message raised the issue of whether communists should be able to use the democratic freedoms they had been granted in order to destroy those freedoms. If, as seems likely, this was intended as a warning to left-wing activists, it was not heeded. A series of events including the murder of the head of Japan's national railways and the derailment of two trains, causing several deaths, implicated radical unionists.[14] Communist activities became still more radical after early 1950, when the Comintern criticized Nosaka for daring to suggest that the socialist revolution could be carried out by other than violent means.

A further escalation of violence that followed the outbreak of the Korean War in June 1950 convinced Japanese leaders that some action would have to be taken. One of the communists' motives appeared to be to tie down as many American troops as possible in Japan so that they could not fight the North Korean military and, later, Chinese forces as well. This ran directly counter to the Japanese government's desire to reduce the number of American troops and end the occupation as soon as possible. Discussion of whether to declare the communist party illegal fell athwart the constitution's provisions on fundamental freedoms. The government decided against banning the party outright, opting instead to terminate communists and their sympathizers from government positions, the press, and industries in order to prevent them from engaging in destructive activities within the organizations that employed them.

This was no easy matter: mere membership in a union sympathetic to communism did not automatically mean that the member was a Communist. Conversely, committed communists often concealed their views. Chinese and Soviet media denounced the "Red Purge." As the vetting proceeded, Nosaka Sanzō and several other high-profile leftist leaders disappeared, and were presumed to have returned to exile in China.

SINO-JAPANESE RELATIONS DURING THE KOREAN WAR

The outbreak of the Korean War in June 1950 and subsequent entrance of China, backed by the Soviet Union, into the conflict led to United States/United Nations/South Korean forces facing off against Chinese and North

Korean troops. Japanese bases were crucial to the Western effort, and even the most optimistic proponent of a comprehensive peace treaty could no longer consider it realistic that such a settlement could be concluded. Chinese media continued to rail against any treaty that excluded the socialist powers. An open letter published in Shanghai's *Dagong Bao* in August 1951 warned Japan that a separate peace was tantamount to a declaration of war against the PRC and the Soviet Union, and urged the Japanese people "to rise up and take the fate of your country into your own hands, not letting a small number of people sell out your nation ... [and] not letting imperialists cause mutual slaughter among the Asian peoples."[15]

In September, after eleven months of negotiations, the San Francisco Peace Conference convened, culminating with Japan signing a peace treaty with most of its remaining adversaries of World War II. A separate bilateral mutual security concluded on the same day officially ended the American occupation, to take effect in the following year. It also declared that the United States was, in the interest of peace and security, willing to maintain certain of its armed forces in and around Japan, albeit in the expectation that Japan would increasingly assume responsibility for its own defense against direct and indirect aggression. An additional clause pledged American military intervention in the event of Japanese domestic instability instigated by an outside power.

Although this intervention could occur only by request of the Japanese government, which was indeed worried at this time by such a possibility,[16] these provisions represented a diminution of full sovereign rights of nations and reminded many Japanese uncomfortably of the unequal treaties of the nineteenth century that they had painstakingly managed to erase before World War II. Nonetheless, there was comfort in knowing that America would protect Japan against communist invasion and subversion.

Predictably, the treaty was denounced by Beijing, though with a vehemence that surprised foreign observers, even temporarily eclipsing Chinese reporting on the Korean War. Radio Beijing and *Renmin Ribao* (People's Daily) portrayed the agreement as an alliance between Japanese and American reactionaries for the purpose of waging war against China and the rest of Asia. In essence, they declared, the treaty had solidified an alliance between Japanese and American reactionary capitalism.[17]

Chinese Premier Zhou Enlai excoriated the agreement as an open insult and an act of hostility toward the Chinese people. It had revived Japanese militarism, extended aggression to elsewhere in Asia, prepared for war, sold out Japanese sovereignty, and brought all Japan to an "unprecedented state of crisis." Zhou extended his sympathy to the patriotic people of Japan in their struggle against the traitorous San Francisco Treaty, their efforts to bring an early end to the state of war between China and Japan, and to ensure peaceful co-existence between the two countries. Japan's reactionary rulers, he averred, had not the least intention to atone for their crimes during World War II, but were determined to invade China again, revive their imperialist rule, and extend beyond China throughout all of Asia. Zhou also demanded that all occupation troops be withdrawn from Japan.[18]

Notwithstanding these decidedly unflattering comments about his administration, Yoshida, on returning from San Francisco, expressed interest in opening an official overseas office in Shanghai similar to the one that was to open in Taipei; he invited the Chinese to establish a similar office in Tokyo, provided only that it must avoid propaganda and conflict-related activities. Apart from arousing the ire of Chiang Kai-shek's government in Taipei and concerns in Washington, this offer had no substantive results. It indicated, however, that Yoshida had, in effect, postponed rather than abandoned his efforts to reestablish ties with Beijing. After the U.S. Senate ratified the peace treaty, Nishimura Kumao, a close adviser to Yoshida, suggested that Japan, as an old nation familiar with the Far East, could guide America, inexperienced in foreign policy, to extricate itself from the difficult position it had put itself in with regard to China. Reportedly, he felt that, apart from the Japanese, only the British understood China well.[19]

During the Korean War, there was no official engagement between Beijing and Tokyo, though American troops equipped with provisions sourced from Japan fought Chinese military units, and the Japanese coast guard performed minesweeping activities along the Korean coast. U.S. procurement needs were a significant stimulus to Japan's postwar economic recovery. Some discourse between Beijing and Tokyo did take place on a quasi non-official basis on issues that concerned the two, which may be briefly summarized as trade, reparations, and fisheries.

Trade

Beijing's militant rhetoric on the need to expand the communist cause notwithstanding, it also made known China's interest in commerce. Cognizant that the key to prosperity was revived trade, but constrained by U.S. pressure from political recognition of the PRC, Tokyo adopted a policy of separating politics and economics (*seikei bunri*). This was vigorously opposed by Beijing, which was as eager to have the CCP recognized as the legitimate government of China as Tokyo was to expand its trade. Each side played on the desires of the other to achieve maximum advantage for its aims.

Toward the end of the occupation, Japan's Ministry of International Trade and Industry (MITI) brought up the matter of negotiating with Washington to loosen export restrictions on trade with China. Other GOJ officials, however, argued that China's actions were political rather than economic. Businesses and financial institutions were also reluctant to become involved because it might complicate their dealings with American firms. Given their geographical proximity and, at this stage, economic complementarity, each was a logical market for the other, political differences notwithstanding. This will be dealt with in greater detail in Chapter 7.

Repatriation

In contrast to the limited opening of trade that occurred in the spring of 1952, the issue of repatriation achieved significant results. At the time of surrender, over a million and a half Japanese lived in China. These included soldiers, administrators, and colonists, the latter mainly settled in Manchukuo. Though nearly all in this category had been impoverished farmers in their native land, they appeared to take their superiority over the natives for granted. Hence, both their presence and their attitudes were much resented. Sometimes prosecuted by Manchukuo authorities for various infractions of law, the colonists tended to receive light sentences. In one of the most serious cases, the Manchukuo authorities declined to continue the prosecution of a Japanese who admitted killing a Chinese man, citing the interests of ethnic harmony. Apparently unrepentant, the self-confessed perpetrator explained that his sense of his racial superiority (*nihonjin no yūetsukan*) became inflamed after the man declined to accept a job he had offered.[20]

Those who felt mistreated by their self-styled overlords were surely not pleased by Chiang Kai-shek's post-surrender plea to treat Japanese residents with kindness:

> . . . we must not . . . impose insults on the innocent civilians . . . if we . . . repay with insults their mistaken superiority complex . . . then the spirit of revenge shall be interminably perpetuated.[21]

and many of the colonists were in fact not well treated by those whom they had looked down upon. The worst-treated, however, appear to have been those who were taken prisoner by Soviet troops. The USSR sent able-bodied male colonists to forced labor camps in Siberia, where many of them died as a result of the harsh conditions there. Those captured by the Chinese fared somewhat better, though only by comparison. Prisoners with skills needed by the CCP such as engineering and medicine were absorbed into Chinese institutions regardless of their wishes.

Most colonists were, however, simply stranded, as the communist forces advanced. Aware of the dangers inherent in this and knowing that the GOJ was in no position to respond, Washington arranged for repatriation through Huludao, the only seaport in northeast China still under KMT control. From May 1946 until August 1948, when the advancing communist military ended the effort, an estimated 1.05 million Japanese were repatriated. Those who died on arrival at Huludao were buried with their graves facing east, toward their homeland.

In mid-2006, a low point in Sino-Japanese relations, an elaborate ceremony at Huludao commemorated the repatriation of the 1.05 million. In an interesting twist of historical reality, none of the assembled dignitaries on either side, who included a Chinese state councillor and a former Japanese prime minister, mentioned that the effort had been undertaken by the United States and the KMT government of China. Nor did they say that the reason the repatriation fell short of completion was because of the imminent arrival of communist troops.[22] Participants signed their names to a peace declaration at the site of a proposed park dedicated to the repatriation effort and posed for pictures in front of a commemorative monument. A Japanese newspaper speculated that Beijing wanted to underscore the humanitarianism of the Chinese people and show its commitment to friendly ties.[23] Ironically, because the park and monument are located in a restricted area of the Huludao submarine base, they cannot easily be visited.

Perhaps it is just as well that the site is not easily accessible. In 2011 a memorial to the settlers that had been erected by the local government of a Heilongjiang county in order to attract Japanese investment was defaced by angry nationalists amid widespread protests that the inhabitants had plundered Chinese land and discriminated against other races. The monument was later removed.[24]

The plight of those Japanese who remained in China weighed heavily on their family members as well as the government. Hence, when in

December 1952, *Xinhua* reported that the Chinese Red Cross Society had asked three Japanese organizations—the Japanese Red Cross Society, the Liaison Committee of the Japanese Peace Committee, and the Japan-China Friendship Association—to form a delegation to discuss the issue, the response was immediately favorable.

According to Beijing, there were about 30,000 Japanese residents in China, not counting those who had been deemed war criminals. The statement went on to say that repatriation had been delayed because of lack of shipping. This was not true: two British passenger ships made regular trips between Tianjin and Hong Kong, from which there were connections to several Japanese ports, and the Japanese government had had vessels available for years for direct trips. Hence, there were suspicions that Beijing was using an issue that would be popular in Japan as a wedge to reopen negotiations on closer ties.[25] The negotiations hit several snags, with one side refusing to accept one or another of the proposed delegation members. For example, Tokyo accepted the Beijing government's rebuff of a delegation member it had proposed because he was likely to check the influence of the leftist friendship association and liaison committees, but then declined to issue a passport to another member of the delegation since she had traveled to the USSR and the PRC in early 1952 without carrying an official passport.[26]

The talks were completed in March 1953, with the first contingent of 4,000 repatriates arriving back in the west coast port of Maizuru at the end of the month. They encountered a wary reception in their homeland that included both a sanitation quarantine and investigations into their backgrounds: the government was concerned that the returnees might undertake subversive activities on behalf of ccommunist causes. The Japanese Communist Party was forbidden to stage a welcoming ceremony.[27] The JCP and affiliated pro-communist groups responded by arranging to greet the returnees at the train stations that brought them to their respective hometowns. Waving welcoming banners and bearing leaflets, members attempted to recruit the repatriates into their organizations.[28] This confirmed Japanese government officials' suspicions that the CCP's apparently softer attitude toward repatriation was motivated by a desire to turn the Japanese public into advocates for normalization of relations.

Repatriation continued into 1958, interrupted by periodic disputes between the two countries on matters that were generally unrelated to the returnees themselves. In one instance, a Japanese prime minister's remark about China that Beijing deemed disrespectful was the cause; in another, a dispute over fishing rights.

The issue of those held as war criminals—Japanese soldiers who had been incarcerated after being captured by Chinese communist forces—was handled separately and took much longer. The PRC's treatment of these detainees was reportedly astonishingly lenient. They received three Japanese-style meals a day, whereas their guards got only two meals. When ill, the prisoners were provided with scarce foreign medicines. Their guards were forbidden to use violence against them under any circumstances, and they had no obligation to work. This contrasted sharply with the extremely severe conditions that Japanese incarcerated in Soviet forced labor camps had to endure. [29]

The CCP's aim was to give the soldiers time to reflect on what they had done to Chinese victims, and to inculcate feelings of shame. Socialized since earliest childhood to believe that any deeds done on orders from representatives of the empire and emperor were praiseworthy and even glorious, they were re-educated—critics would call it brainwashed—to recognize that they had, in fact, committed heinous crimes. Some reportedly asked for the death penalty, which the authorities graciously declined to impose.

Those not prosecuted were sent back to Japan in July 1956. Reporters who went to meet the 335 individuals commented that they looked healthy and cheerful, but that they had given stereotyped answers to questions and spoke as if they feared someone were behind their back. Several had contracted tuberculosis. Having been told that Japan had become no more than an American military base and that 12 million of their countrymen were unemployed, the repatriates were surprised to discover that U.S. forces had been drastically reduced and that the country was prosperous.[30] Despite the former detainees' shock at having been deceived, Chinese re-education succeeded to the extent that many of the former detainees joined pacifist organizations as well as supporting diplomatic recognition with the PRC.[31] Not until mid-1964 would all of the forty-five individuals who had been indicted be repatriated.

Fishery Issues

Washington's attempts to convince reluctant Japanese officials, militantly opposed domestic pacifist forces, and foreign victims of Japanese aggression during World War II that rearmament was necessary began to seem more credible when the nation's fishing boats began to be seized by Chinese, Soviet, and Korean forces. South Korea announced that any boats seized would not be returned, but would be sold in Korea to the highest bidder. It was in this context that Tokyo requested that Washington lease to it seventeen warships, including destroyers and submarines. There were hints that an aircraft carrier was also being discussed and that it might be necessary for the new platforms to venture outside territorial waters and skies.[32] In the end, it was decided that the fishing fleet would be protected only within territorial waters and not on the high seas.[33]

The partial relaxation of international tensions that began in the mid-1950s allowed the negotiation of several agreements that reduced the incidence of seized fishing boats, though not without a recurrence of unpleasant incidents. A Chinese suggestion to visiting socialist Diet members that exchanges take place resulted in the formation of a civilian Japan-China Fishery Council to promote the settlement of differences. The Japanese fishing industry indicated that, in addition to dealing with problems arising from seized vessels, it wanted to discuss the establishment of zones where the fishing fleets of both sides could work without harassment and areas that could be jointly exploited.[34]

In the spring of 1955, the two sides reached agreement on a one-year pact. This set up six authorized fishing areas in the Yellow and East China seas and designated a seventh area just north of Taiwan as a military operations zone where the safety of Japanese boats was not guaranteed. Each country would provide three ports of refuge for ships that developed problems. Japan was allocated 188 ships; the PRC, 248.[35]

THE BANDUNG ERA

The year 1953 saw a modification of communist militant rhetoric in general. Many colonies who were about to gain their independence had expressed strong desires to remain aloof from Cold War politics, indicating that the previous communist policy of insisting that countries must "lean to one side"—meaning they must side with communism or they would be considered to have sided with capitalism—might be counterproductive to advancing the revolutionary cause. Additionally, Josef Stalin, the architect of this rigid policy, had passed away in March 1953.

Stalin's death enabled China to divest itself of several manifestations of the subservient position it occupied under him. In 1954 the USSR's new leader, Nikita Khrushchev, agreed to withdraw Soviet troops from Port

Arthur/Dalian in northeast China as well as to dissolve the companies that operated civil air routes and exploited mineral resources in the Xinjiang area in China's far northwest. New railroads would connect Alma Ata[36] in the USSR to Lanzhou in the PRC and Ulan Bator, capital of the Mongolian People's Republic, to Jining, in Shandong, with each country to build its own portion. The communiqué expressed deep sympathy for the people of Japan, caught in a semi-colonial dependency on the United States and expressing the wish that they would be able to liberate themselves.[37]

Skeptical Japanese sources saw a demonstration effect meant for them: acting Prime Minister Ogata Taketora opined that Moscow had made symbolically important concessions to show Japan that good neighbor Russia had retreated from infringing on Chinese sovereignty. Beijing could now assure the world, and Japan, that it was an independent actor rather than a satellite of Moscow, whereas, by implication, Tokyo remained in thrall to Washington.[38] Moreover, the new era of good feeling did not prevent the Soviet Union from continuing to veto Japan's application for membership in the United Nations.

In addition to abandoning previous insistence that countries lean to the communist side, Chinese and Soviet media toned down their strident calls on the need to promote revolution in non-communist countries. The new emphasis was on creating a united front of third world countries to oppose imperialism, a message that would have far more appeal to former colonies. Revolutionary rhetoric abated. At a summit of Afro-Asian nations held at Bandung, Indonesia, in 1955, Premier Zhou Enlai, responding to the concerns of Laotian and Cambodian delegates about Chinese interference in their affairs, articulated what was to become a touchstone of the PRC's foreign policy: the Pancha Shila, or Five Principles, that included peaceful co-existence and non-interference in the domestic affairs of other countries.[39] Beijing maintained that it would stand side by side with Asian states to oppose Washington's plot to establish an "aggressive block" that included Japan, the Philippines, South Korea, and Taiwan.[40]

The softer rhetoric emanating from Bandung somewhat mitigated, but did not completely erase, the concerns of Japanese officials about native left-wing forces abetting a revolution instigated by international communism. Their scenarios included an attempted invasion of Japan by Soviet and/or Chinese forces; a grave internal economic crisis that would enhance the appeal of a revolution; or an American effort to use Japan as a base of operations against China or the USSR.

Should any of these scenarios occur, the director of the security division of the national police speculated that leftists would stage a general strike on a scale never before seen. Communications and transportation would be suspended and important power stations sabotaged. Next, leftists would take over newspapers, urge farmers to refuse to deliver their rice quotas to the state, and attempt to win over the police to their cause. Authorities claimed to have seized documents indicating that the JCP had a military structure that paralleled its political institutions. Divided into nine regional commands and in control of self-defense forces and guerrilla units, it was conducting extensive training in mountain hideouts using weapons stolen from police units and U.S. military bases as well as smuggled in from China.[41]

Leftist behavior did little to dispel these dire predictions. Strikes intensified in the spring of 1954, with the explicit aim of overthrowing the Yoshida government and ending its pro-American policies. After a cease-fire was announced in the Korean conflict, military procurement orders abated, contributing to unemployment and reinforcing labor union militance. On the other side of the political spectrum, ultra-nationalist right-wing groups re-emerged. While fiercely opposed to all communism, whether Chinese or Soviet, they were equally opposed to a close relationship with the United States.

Yoshida was replaced in late 1954 by a caretaker government headed by fellow conservative Hatoyama Ichirō. Hatoyama announced his willingness to establish friendly relations with China, arguing that isolation from one's neighbors was neither normal nor natural. Trade was the best way to avoid World War III. Hatoyama envisioned a three-stage process, beginning with loosening restrictions on travel, followed by removing the ban on selling certain strategic goods to communist countries, and finally the formation of trade groups to promote the exchange of products.[42]

Shortly after announcing this plan, Hatoyama added that any normalization of relations would depend on acceptance of what amounted to a two-China policy—that is, Tokyo's recognition of both the PRC government in Beijing and the ROC government in Taipei.[43] Neither government was receptive. When Zhou Enlai suggested that Japan would be welcome to join, albeit informally, a friendship pact that India, Burma, and China had concluded the year before, Foreign Minister Shigemitsu Mamoru replied that Beijing would first have to prove by its actions that it intended to pursue its avowed policy of peaceful co-existence.[44] Zhou did actually go some way to meet these concerns at Bandung, stating that China respected the way of life as well as the political and economic systems chosen by other people. Zhou added that he had told the Japanese delegation that China recognized the Yoshida government as legitimate representatives of the Japanese people, and the current Hatoyama government as well.[45]

Japan was not able to function as a bridge between East and West at Bandung, where Zhou and Indian Premier Jawaharlal Nehru emerged as leading figures and peacemakers. Nor did Hatoyama's plans to institute policies that amounted to having good relations with both Chinas prove possible to implement. A Chinese delegation invited to Japan under Hatoyama government's plan to loosen travel regulations was delayed when the invitees reached Hong Kong and discovered to their dismay that their visas read "China" rather than "the People's Republic of China."[46] Trade talks bogged down in a dispute over the participation of government banks, which was not feasible in the absence of official diplomatic relations.[47]

THE NUCLEAR ISSUE

In March 1954 an incident occurred that greatly benefited the alliance between the Japanese left and the Chinese government. An American nuclear test at Bikini Atoll proved twice as powerful as predicted, with changes in weather patterns dispersing radioactivity beyond the danger zone that had been declared beforehand. An estimated 100 fishing vessels received varying degrees of contamination. The *Fukuryū Maru* (Lucky Dragon) *Number 5*'s crew was the worst affected. Though realizing what had happened, its crew chose to retrieve the boat's fishing gear before fleeing and hence were exposed to radiation for several hours. They returned to Japan suffering from burns, bleeding from the gums, eye pain, and other symptoms of radiation poisoning. The ship's chief radio operator died six months later.

That Washington quickly agreed to compensation did little to mitigate the emotional outrage over the incident, which took on the proportions of a satanic epic after the release of the first of the Godzilla films.[48] It also provided a convenient rallying point for China, at that time a non-nuclear power, and the Japanese left, whose stridently antinuclear stance resonated well with domestic public opinion. Since the United States was the only country ever to have used nuclear weapons against another state, this issue was perfectly suited to the anti-American agenda of both sides. A large antinuclear group, Gensuikyō, the commonly used abbreviated name for the Japan

Council Against Atomic and Hydrogen Bombs, was founded. After holding its first congress in September 1955, Gensuikyō proceeded to produce antinuclear informational materials and sponsored peace marches and a major rally each year on the anniversary of the attack on Hiroshima. While most attendees were present to honor the dead and express their hope that nuclear weapons would never again be used, rather than because they were socialists or communists, Gensuikyō was from the beginning manipulated by a coalition of the JSP, JCP, and Sohyō with the enthusiastic support of China. The commemorations were convenient venues at which to remind the participants who had employed these weapons, and to denounce the Japanese government's spineless sycophancy to the Americans.[49]

RESURGENCE ON THE LEFT

Japanese communists remained few in numbers and votes, but were able to exercise influence far in excess of their membership. In the mid- to late 1950s, Japanese internal security sources estimated avowed communists at a modest 100,000 out of a total population of almost 90 million. Only about 60,000 were believed to be registered party members, of whom 25,000 were engaged in JCP activities. Donors to the party were estimated at 120,000. Still, candidates who ran on the communist ticket received 1.7 million votes, at least some of which had been cast due to the candidates' personal popularity rather than their political beliefs or those of their constituents. Although only two communists served in each house of the Diet, many socialists had been elected with the support of the JCP.[50]

The party's finances were opaque and hence of great interest to Japanese authorities. Although in theory every member was supposed to contribute 1 percent of her or his income to the party, only about 15 percent did so regularly and another 30 percent occasionally. The JCP's official newspaper *Akahata* (Red Flag) was clearly being run at a loss, with declining circulation. Contributions from the USSR and China were assumed to make up the difference, as well as to subsidize the JCP's other activities.

The Tokyo government was less concerned with the leftists' numbers than with their ability to influence public opinion on issues like nuclear energy, the security treaty with the United States, the return of Okinawa, and labor legislation. Since strikes for higher wages and expanded workers' rights had the potential to cripple the economy, these would play directly into Moscow's and Beijing's plans.[51]

IRRITANTS CONTINUE

A series of contentious issues arose that caused tensions between Chinese and Japanese governments despite the softer foreign policy line enunciated by Beijing. A Japanese foreign ministry inquiry asking for the return of 7,000 of the country's citizens still in China, as well as information related to an additional 40,000 Japanese known to have been there at the end of the war, languished for a month before receiving a denial that they existed.[52] The PRC replied that only about 7,000 Japanese remained in China, including 6,000 who had expressed their desire to stay there and 1,069 war criminals. *Xinhua* accused Hatoyama's government of having raised the issue to divert attention from domestic pressure to normalize relations with China and brought up the issue of tens of thousands of Chinese civilians living in Japan whose legitimate rights and interests had not been properly cared for. Moreover, said *Xinhua*, their contacts with their homeland and families had been obstructed.[53] Discussions with the United States on relaxing items on the list of commodities banned from sale to the PRC also proved difficult.

By the summer of 1955, the right and left wings of Japan's socialists had united for the purpose of overthrowing the Hatoyama administration, explicitly charging that it had failed to live up to its preelection promise to normalize relations with the PRC and USSR, as well as that it was too subservient to Washington.[54] At the same time, Zhou Enlai told visiting correspondents that Beijing wanted to normalize relations with Tokyo and had taken a series of steps toward this end, which the premier did not elaborate on. It was regrettable, Zhou continued, that the Japanese government had not made corresponding efforts and stated that if the Japanese side showed sincerity comparable to China's, it would be possible to find the road that could lead to normalization of the two countries' relations.[55]

Tokyo officials responded in kind: in a statement to the Japanese press foreign minister, Shigemitsu replied that the only question Japan cared to consider with the PRC was that of repatriation of captives. And the director of the Japanese Defense Board, Sunada Shigemasa, suggested that Japan undertake research toward the manufacture of hydrogen and cobalt bombs. A few days before, Sunada had proposed that the country's military affairs be placed under a full-fledged ministry of defense.[56] Chinese media interpreted these statements as indicative of a return to the militarism that had characterized the governments of the pre–World War II period.

Withal, trade between the two countries continued to rise and delegations, albeit theoretically unofficial, continued to be exchanged.[57] Despite the anti-communist focus of rhetoric from Washington, diplomatic records indicate that American interest in Sino-Japanese relations was grounded in geopolitical considerations. Memoranda of conversations described the United States as a country with permanent interests in the Western Pacific rather than an Asian power, whereas Japan, as a clearly Asian power and a major one, should exercise a greater influence there. In this case, confident of Tokyo's ability to serve as a stabilizing force in Asia, Washington would be happy to exert less influence.[58]

However, Secretary of State Dulles expressed disappointment to British Foreign Secretary Harold Macmillan that the Japanese had not "pulled themselves together" for a role of greatness as the Germans were doing under Chancellor Konrad Adenauer.[59] On the other hand, U.S. diplomats voiced ambivalent feelings on what they saw as an increasing Japanese desire for more freedom of international action. They believed that this nationalist trend, "rooted in racial pride, a longing for national prestige and a desire for greater maneuverability in the event of conflict between Communist China or the USSR and the United States," was important to Japan's recovery as a major power. However, they also regarded the issue of how to accommodate nationalism within the context of the U.S.-Japanese alignment as a basic problem for U.S. policy. In the short term, they felt that Tokyo considered its alignment with America and cooperation with other democratic nations to be in Japan's national interest: it was the best way to regain a position of international importance and economic strength, as well as to ensure American protection to defend their country against external attack.[60]

U.S. officials saw China as using Japan's desire for trade for primarily political purposes: to lure Tokyo away from alignment with Washington. They tended to dismiss the notion that the two were natural market partners, pointing out that in the past, most of Japan's trade with China had been with Manchuria and other areas it brought under its control during the war. Moreover, Beijing did not wish to buy Japanese consumer goods, but rather materials that contributed to the development of heavy industry and war potential.[61] Worries that the sale of Japanese consumer goods to China would generate good will toward Japan were discounted. The items such as rubber shoes and straw hats that were likely to be sold would not reach Chinese consumers directly, but rather be sold to a government monopoly, which would then resell them to the population. Hence, there was very little likelihood that such trade would contribute to advancing understanding between peoples.[62] Further, U.S. officials opined, since Tokyo's recognition of Beijing would have a demonstration effect for the rest of Asia and would reduce those countries' will to resist communist expansionism, it should be guarded against.[63]

The next several years were characterized by a series of Chinese diplomatic demarches in which the Japanese leadership, consonant with Washington's view, attempted to keep separate outstanding issues such as trade, repatriation, and fisheries from political recognition of Beijing, while the Chinese leadership attempted to use them to obtain recognition. In a typical scenario, Mao Zedong or Zhou Enlai would grant an interview to a visiting Japanese delegation, generally but not always composed of leftists, suggesting something that appeared to represent a more conciliatory posture on some issue that had divided the two governments. The Japanese government would react positively, perhaps making a concession of its own, only to find that its demarche had been rejected. Left-wing Japanese groups would then join the PRC media in denouncing the Tokyo leadership, and Beijing would announce punitive measures.

As a case in point, socialist leader Asanuma Inejirō reported that during a lengthy meeting with Mao Zedong in April 1957, Mao held out the prospect of much improved relations that included joint arrangements for meteorological, postal, and fishing operations; a more permanent trade agreement to replace the temporary unofficial arrangements; an offer to purchase fishing vessels from Japanese shipyards; imports of Japanese fishing nets and the establishment of a factory in China to manufacture the fibers used in the nets; an agreement on cooperation to develop iron ore on Hainan Island with Japanese technical assistance. The Chinese government had also expressed a desire for an increase in the number of cultural delegations exchanged, and for relaxed restrictions on passport restrictions on Japanese visiting the PRC.[64] All of these were attractive to most Japanese; in fact, Tokyo was already pressing Washington for a lifting of the prohibitions against selling many items to China.

However, in late July, as negotiations were taking place, Zhou Enlai surprised the GOJ by telling a visiting labor union delegation that Premier Kishi Nobusuke was a lackey of the United States, hostile to China and an impediment to the development of friendly relations between the two countries.⁶⁵ This was somewhat surprising, since Kishi's longstanding support of Chiang Kai-shek government was well known. Echoing Zhou, Lei Renmin, a vice-minister of foreign trade, immediately issued a similar barrage of criticism in an interview with the Japanese press agency Kyodo.⁶⁶ Japanese Foreign Minister Fujiyama Aiichirō told parliamentary committees before which he appeared that it would be "the height of folly" to take the denunciations at face value. An underlying motive, opined Fujiyama, was to hinder any advance of Japanese influence into South and Southeast Asia, though the connection between the denunciation of Kishi and hindering a Japanese advance into other areas of Asia seemed obscure to outside observers.⁶⁷

Other areas of friction also inhibited the establishment of more cordial relations. In August, the fingerprinting issue was raised. Although at that time fingerprinting was a standard practice applied to all foreign visitors who intended to stay in Japan for more than a brief visit, the Beijing government protested strongly. It warned that Tokyo's insistence on fingerprinting members of a Chinese trade delegation who went to Japan to arrange for a trade fair in the fall was an insult that must never be repeated.⁶⁸ Tokyo offered a compromise whereby five officials and their families would be exempt from the fingerprinting requirement, which was refused. A week later, Beijing announced that it had closed the Bohai Bay, Yellow Sea, and East China Sea to Japanese ships.⁶⁹ In December, Japanese police moved against a spy ring that, working through North Korea, had smuggled JCP members out of China back into Japan.⁷⁰

These obstacles notwithstanding, a non-official private trade agreement with a one-year duration was signed in early March 1958.⁷¹ Any feelings of relief were short-lived. The Taipei government immediately suspended its trade discussions with Tokyo, threatening to sever ties completely if the Chinese trade group were given diplomatic privileges such as an exemption from fingerprinting rules and the right to fly the PRC flag, arguing that these would be tantamount to diplomatic recognition of the PRC.⁷² In the United States, the influential pro-Chiang Kai-shek regime Committee of One Million Against the Admission of Communist China to the United Nations, which included twenty-two senators and eighty-eight members of the House of Representatives, urged Tokyo to reconsider the pact.⁷³

China, for its part, expressed anger over the visit of a Japanese newspaper delegation to Taipei and threatened to retaliate against Japanese reporters in the PRC.⁷⁴ In the midst of this, the Japanese police seized a fishing vessel they believed to be the flagship of a communist fleet engaged in clandestine operations between China and Japan. Ten crew members were arrested and what was described as large numbers of communist documents were found aboard. The operation, known as the peace fleet, had been transporting important Japanese communists to and from China for the past six years. Nosaka Sanzō and others, seeking to circumvent charges that they had violated immigration laws, denied that they had ever left Japan.[75]

Two weeks later, in April, Beijing announced it had suspended the visit of trade representatives to Japan under the agreement made the previous month, since its mission had not been guaranteed the right to fly the PRC's flag.[76] Kishi attempted a compromise, stating that the flying of the flag would not be recognized as a right, but would be protected under the domestic laws of Japan, a less than forthright way of saying that the flag could be flown. He then assured the Taipei government that this did not mean de facto recognition of the Beijing government. Taipei did not press the matter further. Presumably, it did not want to embarrass Kishi and his party in the forthcoming elections, thereby creating votes for the socialists, who wanted to recognize Beijing as not only the de facto but also de jure government of China.

Beijing, however, reacted sharply, accusing Kishi's "two-faced" government of deliberate efforts to sabotage the agreement and stating that its attempt to equate the PRC's national flag with ordinary property was a gross insult and a deliberate invitation to damage it.[77] Chief Cabinet Secretary Aichi Kiichi responded that Japan had made all the concessions it could, and would take a wait-and-see attitude.[78]

For a time, quiet seemed to prevail. Scarcely a week later, the liner *Hakusan Maru* sailed from Tianjin with 420 Japanese to be repatriated. However, on May 2nd, a member of a Japanese right-wing organization pulled down a Chinese flag that was flying over a philatelic exhibition sponsored by the China-Japan Friendship Organization at a Nagasaki department store. The Chinese government was infuriated. On May 7th, the Chinese navy seized 14 Japanese fishing boats and 170 sailors in the East China Sea. Several of the vessels were fired on before being boarded. Beijing charged that the Japanese trawlers had repeatedly encroached on Chinese waters, damaged its fishermen's nets, and rammed their boats, causing one death.[79] This was the first such seizure since July 1954, and had seemingly been prompted by strained relations over other issues. A few days later, Beijing announced it was suspending all business with Japan due to Kishi's hostile attitude toward China.[80]

Icy relations prevailed for the next several months: in June, Beijing, citing Japan's "blatant policy of extreme unfriendliness and hostility," announced its decision not to extend the fishery agreement that had been signed in 1955 and renewed twice thereafter. It also stated its intention to modernize the country's fishing fleet so that it would outstrip that of Japan[81]—a clear challenge that raised hackles in Japan—and suspended the repatriation program.[82] The arrival of the *Hakusan Maru* was delayed as well. Since the ship had already sailed, Japanese Red Cross officials on board were reduced to tossing notes to reporters who had come out in launches. They reported that they had been subjected to an hour-long diatribe against the Kishi government.[83]

Japanese authorities then learned that the ship's passengers included sixty-six JCP members as well as others who were union leaders. Since these individuals had presumably departed surreptitiously from Japan earlier, GOJ officials pondered whether they should charge the arrivals with violation of the country's immigration laws.[84] Osaka merchants began to worry that Chinese cotton producers, whose prices were 10 to 20 percent lower, would push them out of established markets.[85] They renewed pressure on Tokyo for better Sino-Japanese relations.

At the end of July, socialist leader Sata Tadataka, with the blessing of the Japanese Foreign Ministry, met with Zhou Enlai to try to break the deadlock in relations. His visit, however, occurred at an inopportune time. On August 1st, the anniversary of the founding of the Red Army, later renamed the People's Liberation Army, Marshal Zhu De delivered a vituperative address calling for a stronger defense that would wipe out the imperialist system forever.[86] While one would not expect to hear conciliatory words at Army Day addresses, Zhu's speech struck observers as unusually strident and did, in fact, signal a harder line. Three weeks later, China began bombarding the offshore islands held by Taiwan. Tokyo officials publicly downplayed the significance of this as a local issue, although there were private concerns that, because of the security treaty and the presence of U.S. military bases in Japan, American support of the ROC government would involve the country in a war with China.

When Sata reported back to the foreign ministry at the end of August, he conveyed three non-negotiable Chinese conditions: the Kishi government must issue a formal apology for the Nagasaki flag incident, make amends, and officially work to restore normal Sino-Japanese relations. Not until all of these were fulfilled would Beijing entertain the possibility of an official delegation to China to discuss what it referred to as future problems. The Japanese foreign ministry regarded these as unacceptably humiliating, and there were wry jokes that the conditions represented China's Twenty-One Demands, in reference to the humiliating terms Japan had sought to exact from China in 1915.[87]

THE COMMUNIST MONOLITH SPLINTERS

Mao Zedong's decision to take a harder line internationally was prompted by a number of factors, of which one major aim was believed to be the derailment of Khrushchev's policy of peaceful co-existence with the capitalist powers. If this were the case, it failed. Khrushchev, like the Japanese leadership, feared being drawn into war by his country's alliance partner. He infuriated Mao by references to trading space for time, as the newly founded Soviet Union had done in the Treaty of Brest-Litovsk in 1918. Only when he was sure that the Chinese did not intend to take the islands, which Eisenhower had pledged the United States to defend, did Khrushchev publicly back Mao.[88] Latent Sino-Soviet tensions began to become more publicly visible, with some observers perceiving the depth and significance of the rift sooner than others.

At the same time, Mao embarked on an ambitious domestic policy to institute communism in the PRC. The population, intimidated by an anti-rightist purge carried out in 1957, meekly acceded to policies that many sensed would be disastrous. Communes were founded on the basis of Marx's "to each according to his ability, to each according to his need," thus destroying incentives to work hard. Communes vied with each other to announce higher and higher crop yields, with the government then collecting as taxes the alleged bounty of bogus bumper harvests. Millions starved, and production levels dropped precipitously. Because the statistics had been falsified, often at more than one level, not even the government could say with any certainty what they were. The government simply stopped reporting production levels for several years afterward.

For Sino-Japanese relations, the events of 1958 had two important consequences. First, Chinese domestic difficulties made the country seem far less menacing. Second, the Sino-Soviet split reverberated throughout the Japanese left wing, leading to open rifts within its always fractious membership. The latter confirmed Yoshida's earlier observation that, soon after becoming prime minister, he came to realize that the left did not operate on a simple pattern. Socialists and communists had as much animosity for each other as for conservatives.[89] As quickly became obvious, strong differences of opinion within the left on relations with China caused serious cleavages that would blunt its appeal to Japanese voters and help the LDP.

An initial tendency in both China and abroad to accept at face value the CCP's claims of unprecedented gains in production soon gave way to skepticism. Domestically, the PRC's citizens soon began to experience shortages of food and fuel, followed by widespread starvation. Attempts to suppress the news were only partially successful; those who managed to cross the border from China into Hong Kong brought frightening tales of disease, desperation, and even cannibalism.[90] The reason for a sharp decrease in the PRC's exports that first puzzled outsiders now became obvious: there was nothing to send abroad. The PRC defaulted on contracts, thus dampening, at least temporarily, Japanese attraction to the lure of the Chinese market.

While the failure of the Great Leap Forward cost the PRC dearly both economically and in terms of international prestige, Japan forged forward on both indices. It had regained its prewar place as the world's leading fishery nation as early as 1948; in 1956 it became the world's largest shipbuilding nation,[91] maintaining this position even as other countries experienced declines. In 1959 another milestone was achieved when the International Olympic Committee (IOC) awarded the 1964 summer games to Tokyo. There was special symbolism in the IOC's choice: Tokyo had originally been chosen as the site of the 1940 event, but the decision was rescinded and the games awarded to Helsinki in retaliation for Japanese aggression against China. Subsequently, the event was cancelled altogether because of the outbreak of World War II. Hence, recovering the honor of hosting the games seemed emblematic of Japan's reacceptance into the community of nations.

With these accomplishments came renewed self-confidence and, for a number of Japanese, a sense of their superiority. A tomb to the unknown soldier was dedicated, with both the imperial couple and Prime Minister Kishi in attendance.[92] At the same time, many began to question what Japan's new international role might be. While a general consensus existed that the country should assume a more prominent posture, there was also hesitation about what form this might take and some misgivings about the greater responsibilities this might entail. A foreign observer compared this to a child offering food to a strange animal at the zoo: afraid of getting bitten and yet fearful that the food might be refused.

In 1959 also, JSP leader Asanuma Inejirō journeyed to Beijing, reporting Zhou Enlai's three preconditions for normalization of relations and resumption of trade in commodities that were not at that time available:

- the GOJ must repudiate its hostile attitude toward China.
- it must not divide China into communist and nationalist Chinas.
- it should not stand in the way of normalization between the Chinese and Japanese peoples.

On the same trip, Asanuma was moved to make a statement, in deference to Zhou's wishes, that would haunt his party for years to come: that the United States was the common enemy of Japan and China. This shocked the right wing of the JSP as much as it did the conservatives in the LDP. Anger over what right-wing socialist leader Nishio Suehiro referred to as humiliating capitulationism to the Chinese was a major factor in the secession of many of its members and the formation of the Democratic Socialist Party (DSP).[93]

Major Japanese newspapers referred to the trip as a failure.[94] Mainstream media and, apparently, public opinion interpreted what came to be known as the Asanuma statement as China's attempt to sweep Japan into the communist net. The elation socialists and communists and their Chinese supporters felt over a Tokyo district court ruling finding that the Self-Defense Forces were unconstitutional also proved transient, since the country's supreme court reversed the decision on appeal.[95]

Another wave of anti-China feeling was generated by the PRC's suppression of the revolt in Tibet in March 1959. The PRC's decision in the following month to return fifty-one Japanese fishermen who had been seized that year did not succeed in ameliorating these sentiments: the sailors returned in Japanese boats that had been painted with pro-communist slogans. Reporters described the men with adjectives such as "brainwashed," "tight-lipped," and "glum."[96]

While the public reaction to events in China may have been adverse, policymakers tended to be more concerned with the international balance of power and to continue to seek a formula for better relations with China that would not unduly upset the United States. They were, however, concerned about the choices voters made at the polls. These were expressed in elections held in April for the lower house of the Diet and in June for the upper house, resulting in impressive victories for the LDP, with the

Asanuma statement and the suppression of the revolt in Tibet both considered important factors. Still, the JSP managed to hold on to one more seat in the lower house than the one-third it needed to retain the ability to block changes in the constitution.

While united in their desire to oppose amendments to the constitution, since it was feared that they would ease the way to a more conventional military role for Japan, there were major differences within the left on most other matters. One of the more explosive, both literally and figuratively, involved nuclear weapons. Fault lines within the left became fissures when in late 1963 Washington, London, and Moscow agreed to a partial nuclear test-ban treaty, leading some observers to comment that the Sino-Soviet dispute was being fought on Japanese soil. Indeed, Mao Zedong, eager to enlist Japan on the side of China, went so far as to declare that the Kuril Islands, which had come under Soviet control after World War II and referred to as the Northern Territories in Japan, belonged to Japan and should be returned to it. As will be seen, this support would change in tandem with Beijing's relations with Moscow.

The JCP, after some debate, backed Beijing's position that the pact was part of an Anglo-Russian plot against China in order to create a condominium to divide the world between them. To oppose all nuclear tests was tantamount to forgiving imperialism and therefore weakening the democratic forces of the world. The socialists engaged in a much more fractious debate, with a majority deciding to back the Soviet position. Most JSP members favored Khrushchev's view that co-existence between the United States and the USSR was possible, as opposed to Beijing's position that it was unthinkable. They were also aware that Moscow had made good on Beijing's losses for terminating trade with Japan.[97]

The need to renew the security treaty with the United States provided a convenient issue for the left to come together—briefly, as it turned out—in opposition. China made known its strong opposition, with analysts observing that, whereas the original treaty could have been portrayed as forced on Japan by the occupation, ratification of the new one would be harder to explain to either China or the Soviet Union.

In December 1959 leftist groups stormed the Diet in one of the most serious demonstrations since the end of World War II. Protests continued as the treaty made its way past various milestones in the legislative process. In July 1960 a student at Tokyo University was killed in the melee, leading to recriminations that set one faction of leftists against another. When the left-wing student activist organization Zengakuren charged that the police were responsible for the young woman's death, the JCP newspaper *Akahata* responded that the death had been due to the organization's own extreme tactics. Zengakuren members then staged a raid on the headquarters of the JCP, demanding that *Akahata* retract its statement. The newspaper's editors refused, engendering a controversy that led to a three-way split in Zengakuren. Some students argued that the police were responsible and others that the organization itself was at fault; a third, smaller group appeared to prefer to skirt the issue by advocating that Zengakuren adopt methods that were more appealing to the general public.[98]

The government claimed that the violence, which also permeated the annual commemoration ceremony at Hiroshima, was perpetrated by communist extremists incited from abroad who had infiltrated the educational system and the labor unions; Chinese Foreign Minister Chen Yi subsequently denied this and other similar accusations as "shameless fabrications."[99]

The treaty passed, though the level of unrest succeeded in thwarting U.S. President Dwight Eisenhower's plans to visit Japan for the signing. As well, Prime Minister Kishi resigned to take responsibility for the violence. Ikeda Hayato succeeded him, becoming Japan's ninth postwar prime minister. Ikeda adopted a low-profile posture that was understandable under the circumstances. While making clear that he rejected neutrality and intended that Japan continue its partnership with the West, Ikeda also indicated the importance of cultural and economic ties with China, though adding that this could be done only if Japan were respected. It would not be fooled into dealing with communist countries.[100] Zhou Enlai did not appear eager to reciprocate, stating that trade could be gradually resumed but that agreements could be signed only when "normal" relations had been established.[101]

Indicative of the importance Ikeda attached to reestablishing trade relations, Takasaki Tatsunosuke, who had been head of MITI in the Kishi cabinet, was dispatched to Beijing to discuss the issue. While he was there, JSP leader Asanuma was assassinated in Japan by a teen-aged right-wing fanatic wielding a samurai sword. Sympathy for the slain leader combined with concern about an economic downturn as the United States decided to reduce its aid purchases in response to a dollar outflow, thus enhancing the lure of better ties with China. In a tentative first step, it was announced that athletic exchanges between the two countries, suspended since 1958, would be resumed in 1961.[102]

While there was a great deal of talk, relatively little changed over the next two years: China was experiencing a painful recovery from the disastrous Great Leap Forward and had few exportable items. In Japan, there was increasing criticism of Ikeda's low posture, with the famously outspoken former Prime Minister Yoshida comparing Japan to a frog in a well who knows nothing of the great ocean. Some opinion leaders argued that, for the sake of duty and gain, Japan should take a more active international role, suggesting plans to offer economic and technical assistance to the newly independent nations of Africa and Asia. Others were more hesitant, fearing that a higher international posture might revive memories of Japan's wartime aggression, and also that economic and technical investment in these countries might result in setbacks for Japan's own economy. In any case, anxiety about the status of relations with China and the Soviet Union seemed to have abated.

THE FRENCH CONNECTION

French President Charles de Gaulle's announcement in January 1964 that he intended to establish formal diplomatic relations with Beijing provided another issue on which the Japanese left could agree: Japan should do so as well. De Gaulle's decision raised anxieties in Washington, as policymakers wondered that, should Tokyo follow France, it would create a domino effect in other Asian states. Since de Gaulle chose to reveal the news to the American ambassador on the anniversary of the day he had vetoed Britain's application to enter the European Common Market, his demarche to Beijing was interpreted as a carefully calculated insult by Le Grand Charles, well known for his animosity toward "les Anglo-Saxons," whether British or American.

Signs that Beijing wanted better relations than it had had with the Kishi administration were not lacking. *The Japan Times*, whose articles were believed to reflect the views of the country's foreign ministry,[103] noted that the Chinese media had ceased to attack seikei bunri, the separation of politics from economics, and that the last three Japanese war criminals it had held had been returned.[104] The Ikeda administration took a detached position, with the prime minister announcing that recognition would come when Beijing showed itself to be a peace-loving nation that would adhere to international agreements.[105] The latter statement was a veiled reference to China's abrupt cancellation of trade relations in 1958. Withal, progress was made in Sino-Japanese relations: in June, the first PRC ship to visit Japan arrived,[106] and in September, an agreement was reached to exchange news correspondents, albeit as a result of "private" negotiations. In a significant concession, the GOJ agreed to exempt Chinese journalists from the fingerprinting requirement it imposed on other foreign visitors.[107]

There was considerable doubt in Tokyo that France could expect much gain from recognition: since the PRC was recovering from the reverses of the Great Leap Forward, it was considered still convalescent and therefore unable to buy much from France. Although the PRC did not issue official statistics in their period, Japanese analysts estimated the 1963 grain harvest as about the same as that in 1957, though observing that, due to population growth, China had many more people to feed in 1963 than in 1957. Cotton and steel production were believed to be 45 and 33.33 percent, respectively, below previous peak years.[108] Conservatives went further, with one commentator opining that, although France's motive appeared to be to build a bridge between the free world and China, it was apt to find that the bridge was a drawbridge controlled from one end: Beijing's.[109] By September, it was reported that French diplomats were disappointed at the results of the decision to normalize relations.[110]

INTRA-LEFT DISPUTES

Though concurring on the desirability of recognition of China, the left agreed on very little else. At the end of February, at a Japan-China Diet Members Association welcoming party for Chinese trade negotiator Zhao Anbo, DSP official Nagasue Eiichi's speech alluded to his party's stand for one China, one Taiwan. An infuriated Zhao responded that this constituted interference in the internal affairs of his country, and that a small party had no right to say such things. Apparently equally incensed, Nagasue responded that Zhao's words were out of line: the size of his party was irrelevant, since it still represented the will of the Japanese people.

Zhao also clashed with members of Komeitai, when one of its Diet members indicated that the religious group Komeitai represented, Sōka Gakkai, would like to expand its missionary work in the PRC. Zhao denied that the group had any members in China and added that, if they were present, they would be suppressed as representing an illegal religious organization. Japanese newspapers, whether liberal or conservative, were highly critical of these comments, pointing out that it was against the principles of democratic government in Japan or anywhere else to belittle voices because they were small, and inexcusable to suppress any form of religion. Zhao, they commented, had undercut support for recognition of Beijing, the very cause he had come to Japan to promote.[111]

The JCP did not participate in Gensuikyō's commemoration of the anniversary of the *Fukuryū Maru* incident.[112] A few days later, the JSP postponed a mission to China, accusing Beijing of interfering in its internal affairs. The proximate cause was a *Xinhua* criticism of the JSP for having abandoned the party's policy of anti-Americanism and favoring the creation of two Chinas.[113] Since Beijing was known to be pressing the JSP, now dominated by a more moderate group, to reaffirm the Asanuma statement, it is likely that *Xinhua*'s blast was aimed at strengthening the more pro-Beijing wing of the JSP. Just as Zhao's remarks had, *Xinhua*'s attack aroused adverse reaction, with critics commenting on the discrepancy between these incidents and the PRC's vaunted devotion to the Pancha Shila, with its principles of respect for sovereignty and noninterference in the internal affairs of other states. The center-left *Tokyo Shimbun* editorialized that

> there is an air of arrogance in the attitude of forcing one's own stand upon others. In presupposing diplomatic normalization between a Free World member and a communist nation, the question of respecting mutual positions assumes the greatest importance. . . . [Such actions] make one uneasy on this score.[114]

The 1964 commemoration ceremony at Hiroshima was marred by disputes among the different factions. In the end, one ceremony was held by the pro-China group, with three other groups belonging, respectively, to the JSP group favoring the anti-proliferation treaty, the DSP, and Gensuikyō, each scheduled to hold separate rallies the following week.

For its part, the GOJ, having received an unofficial invitation from the Indonesian government to attend a planning meeting to commemorate the 10th anniversary of the Bandung conference, declined to attend. Although no official reason was given, Tokyo bureaucrats privately stated that such conferences had fallen under "monolithic Red Chinese influence."[115] The GOJ also refused entry to a *Xinhua* correspondent Wu Xuewen, whom the Chinese side had included in a trade delegation, pointing out that Wu had previously made frequent remarks on Japanese government policy and U.S. imperialism that clearly constituted engaging in undesirable political activities.[116] The PRC responded angrily, and became angrier still when a right-wing youth hurled an ink-filled egg at a picture of Japan-China Friendship Association head Liao Chengzhi.[117]

CHINA BECOMES A NUCLEAR POWER

Pressures for recognition received another sharp setback in mid-October, when China detonated its first nuclear weapon. More was at issue than Japan's understandable nuclear allergy and the fact that it could expect radioactive fallout to drift over its territory. At the end of April, Japan proudly became the 21st member of the Organization for Economic Co-operation and Development (OECD) as well as, if one discounts geographically bifurcated Turkey, the OECD's only non-Western member. At the time of the nuclear detonation, Japan was also basking in the prestige of having been the first non-Western state to have hosted the Olympic games. The atomic blast deflated newly revived feelings of superiority over China as well as raising anxieties about how this would affect Japan's security. With its self-image jolted and, due to Article 9 of the constitution as well as strong pacifist sentiment in certain segments of the population, politically unable to develop its own nuclear weapons, the government contemplated its position. Both the decision to go ahead with construction of a nuclear-powered ship, the *Mutsu*, and place a satellite in orbit by 1968 or 1969 were believed to be responses to the Chinese challenge.[118]

A JSP delegation visiting Beijing at the time was taken unawares. After what must have been contentious internal debate, members agreed to affirm the Asanuma statement, which Beijing had attached great importance to doing, but refused to endorse the nuclear explosion. Only the JCP did so, on grounds that the PRC had acted out of purely defensive motives. The Ikeda administration, as well as all political parties but the JCP, issued protests. At this crucial juncture, Prime Minister Ikeda resigned: he had been diagnosed with a precancerous throat tumor that demanded immediate attention. Satō Eisaku, a protégé of Yoshida Shigeru, was named his successor.

SATŌ TAKES THE HELM

Satō proved at least as distasteful to Beijing as Kishi, who was in fact his elder brother.[119] Announcing immediately that he thought Japan's voice in international affairs had been too small, Satō described his country as one of the three pillars of the world, along with the Western countries and the USSR and other communist states.[120] In what must have been galling for Beijing, Satō implicitly claimed parity for Japan with the West and the USSR, but did not accord the same status to China. Not wanting to appear to sanction the nuclear tests, the Satō government then further angered Beijing by barring a high-level Chinese delegation from attending a JCP party conference in Tokyo.

Beijing retaliated, charging that Satō was more reactionary than his predecessors. It withdrew its invitation for an LDP Diet member delegation to visit Beijing, and cancelled a trip by Kuno Chūji, a Satō confidant who was deputy chair of the LDP's parliamentary policy committee. An unusually vituperative series of attacks in *Renmin Ribao* ensued. Among other ripostes, the articles dismissed official criticism of the PRC's tests as "ravings," saying that they were nobody's business but China's own. The PRC had been forced to develop nuclear weapons because of U.S. and Soviet imperialism. Moreover, *Renmin Ribao* warned, if war should break out, Japan, as an American base, would "inevitably bear the brunt of a nuclear holocaust."[121]

Possibly because of the still-hidden power struggle that was taking place at the highest levels of the CCP leadership, Beijing chose to ignore the real efforts Satō was taking to improve relations. En route to a meeting with U.S. President Lyndon Johnson, Satō had explicitly stated that he thought American policy toward China was too rigid, and that he hoped Johnson would understand Japan's desire for better relations with Beijing. China's admission to the United Nations could not be put off indefinitely, though Satō believed that the chances were slim at the moment.[122] Japanese newspapers voiced their approval, with the center-left *Asahi* commenting that Satō's statements should bring new light to the Diet debate on the China issue and the center-right *Yomiuri* opining that, since U.S.-Chinese antagonism was a primary source of tension in Asia, Satō should more aggressively promote peaceful co-existence between Beijing and Washington.[123]

Satō also told a parliamentary committee that he would like to hold talks with Chinese leaders themselves should the occasion arise. Despite the ambiguity of the last four words, this was quite a concession in light of the efforts that Japan had made to ensure that contacts be unofficial.[124]

While there was no noticeable abatement in the Chinese media's attacks on Satō, it is true that certain of his actions must have made Beijing leaders question the sincerity of his professed desire for better Sino-Japanese relations. As a case in point, a delegation led by Satō's elder brother Kishi visited Taipei for a meeting of the Committee for the Promotion of China (meaning, of course, the Republic of China on Taiwan)-Japan Cooperation. Former Prime Minister Kishi not only criticized the Chinese nuclear test but also pointed out that Japan was fully capable of making its own nuclear weapons.[125] Amazingly, in the midst of these mutually insulting exchanges, Beijing backed down on its demands for more concessions on trade. An agreement to purchase Japanese steel was signed on the same day Kishi made his speech.[126]

In addition to apparently sanctioning his brother's visit to Taipei, Satō, although approving the sale of the Nichibō vinylon textile plant to China, did not grant Japanese banks permission to make loans that would assist the sale; Nichibō was instructed to obtain private financing.[127] Beijing angrily cancelled the agreement, as it had previously warned it would do.[128] Chagrined Osaka merchants asked why their government had refused the same terms to Nichibō that it had accorded to a previous sale of a similar plant.[129] Japanese analysts believed Satō's seemingly inconsistent decision had been prompted by a desire to soothe relations with the anti-communist right wing of the LDP as well as to avoid renewed frictions with the Taipei government.

And, although it may not have been known to the Chinese at the time, on the same visit to Washington where Satō appealed for U.S. understanding of better Sino-Japanese relations, he also asked that the United States be ready to launch an immediate nuclear attack on the PRC if war broke out between them. This request became public only in December 2008, when the relevant documents were declassified by the Japanese Foreign Ministry. The revelation was quite shocking, since Satō had won the 1974 Nobel Peace Prize for his rejection of nuclear arms.[130] While trying to appease several different constituencies with conflicting agendas, Satō's actions risked offending those whose interests were adversely affected while laying himself open to charges of inconsistency as well.

In any case, Beijing's attacks on the Satō administration continued unabated. Acerbic exchanges notwithstanding, each side continued to feel the other out, the better to effect closer relations on its own terms. Despite its obviously economically inferior status at the time, China was in a far better position. Japanese frequently expressed views about their country's need to trade in order to survive, and on the necessity of dealing with China because of its size and geographical proximity. No similar sentiments emanated from the PRC. Partly this was because the CCP tightly controlled expressions of public opinion. As well, Chinese officials took a position that was, mutatis mutandis, not dissimilar to the reply that the Middle Kingdom had given to Western powers: that the People's Republic produced all that was needed within its borders—however dissonant this may have been with reality. Its modern iteration implied that China could afford to wait until the Japanese approached Beijing on Beijing's terms.

Japanese expressed multifaceted emotional reactions to China, in contrast to the publicly monolithic view of Japan emanating from Beijing, where the official media frequently reminded citizens of Japan's wartime cruelties toward Chinese and portrayed its current status as subservient to American imperialism. A number of Japanese felt strongly that their country owed a debt of gratitude to China for its culture, and should accord its modern-day incarnation a degree of respect on that basis. Many expressed feelings of profound guilt over Japanese wartime behavior, with one going so far as to say that he thought Japanese had committed patricide. Others expressed a less extreme version of this, insisting that a Japan cut off from relations with China was like an orphan.

Yet another scoffed at this, commenting that the orphans did not appear to miss the parent very much, and that the average Japanese today knew more about American and other Western cultures than he or she did about China. Moreover, current-day communist China's culture, with its crude propaganda and simplistic art and literature, could hardly be considered the inheritor of the sophisticated civilization many Japanese professed to admire. U.S. Ambassador Edwin Reischauer, a leading authority on Japan, described the average Japanese as viewing China like a gawky adolescent who would some day come to his senses and agree to normal trade and other relations with his country.

At the other end of the spectrum were those who felt that Japan had long ago surpassed China in all areas from cultural to economic, and viewed it as unworthy of sustained attention: Japan should concentrate on strengthening its ties with the advanced democratic nations of the West. Here, one finds echoes of the *datsu-a* of nineteenth-century intellectual Fukuzawa Yukichi (see Chapter 2). A more militant group worried about the threat posed by China, pointing to its actions in Tibet in 1959, toward India in 1962, and most recently its acquisition of nuclear capabilities in 1964. They urged a higher military profile. In this view, Japan's inability, despite its stunning economic achievements, to command the international respect it once had indicated that only the acquisition of a military force would enable the country to recoup the country's lost prestige.[131] For a minority, this included the development of indigenous nuclear capabilities.

Meanwhile, China, putatively because its leadership was engaged in an internal power struggle, was also giving off mixed signals. In the midst of the Nichibō controversy, Foreign Minister Chen Yi announced that Beijing had repeatedly urged Moscow to return the Kuril Islands to Japan,[132] and Zhou Anbo, in his capacity as secretary-general of the Japan-China Friendship Association, hinted that China would not seek reparations as a condition of establishing normal diplomatic negotiations.[133]

On the other hand, Liao Chengzhi, as chair of the Afro-Asian Solidarity Conference, discounted the possibility that important contacts between Chinese and Japanese officials could take place at the conference's Algiers meeting because of the Satō government's hostile attitude toward China. He compared trade relations between the two to an automobile with a flat tire, with Tokyo responsible for repairing the puncture.[134] Paradoxically, at exactly the same time, a Japanese delegation in Beijing to arrange a trade fair reported that officials had been remarkably cooperative: Their drafts of a basic policy and plans for the commodities to be sold were accepted without revision, and the Chinese had even promised special payments to cover the cost of preparing the fair sites at Beijing and Shanghai.[135] The Chinese government also announced its desire to increase tourism, opening more cities to Japanese tour groups and producing new glossy brochures to promote their attractions.[136]

In yet another surprising development, the left wing of the JSP gained strength over more moderate factions, facilitated by the resignation of incumbent head Kawakami Jōtarō due to ill health. The historically pro-China Sasaki Kōzō ran uncontested, immediately declaring that U.S. imperialism was the common enemy of all the people of the world, thereby considerably expanding the scope of the already controversial Asanuma statement. The JSP moved away from its earlier stance of condemning all nuclear testing to adhere to the PRC's position that China had been forced to develop the weapons. The influence of American escalation of the war in Vietnam, plus Washington's invasion of the Dominican Republic, may have enabled the left to gain more traction, but the JSP's defense of China's nuclear arsenal had the opposite effect on the Japanese public at large, with commentators suggesting that what the average voter wanted from the JSP was a constructive policy to counter the LDP.[137]

In China also, radicals were gaining power, with adverse reactions on the PRC's relations with Japan. Though it was never definitively proved, many Japanese believed that Beijing was complicit in an attempted coup in Indonesia in September 1965, leading those who were already suspicious of the PRC to wonder if there were plans to do the same in Japan. In the same month, and in explicit commemorization of the 20th anniversary of Japan's World War II surrender, Chinese Defense Minister Lin Biao issued a well-publicized call for a worldwide people's war to destroy the United States just as China had, according to Lin, defeated Japan in World War II even though it was militarily weaker. In Lin's analysis, the United States had stepped into the role vacated by Japan's defeat. This startled most Japanese, while seemingly confirming right-wing predictions that Beijing had a blueprint for world domination.[138]

CHINESE FOREIGN RELATIONS DURING THE CULTURAL REVOLUTION

As the Chinese power struggle ripened into the Great Proletarian Cultural Revolution, militant rhetoric antagonized many neutral or formerly friendly countries, with a *New York Times* correspondent commenting that "the Chinese communists are quarreling with most of the world."[139] Cuba, Indonesia, Upper Volta (now Burkina Faso), Dahomey, and Kenya all broke relations with the PRC, typically accusing Beijing of meddling in their internal affairs. The president of the Central African Republic ordered the expulsion of all Chinese in the country on grounds that the PRC was building a revolutionary army that was staffed by Chinese and pro-PRC nationals. A cache of arms and documents and a firing range had been discovered near the capital city, Bangui.[140]

Since Japan did not have formal diplomatic relations with the PRC, it was more insulated from such concerns than the countries who did maintain relations. Nevertheless, the threat of China attempting to export its revolution to Japan continued to be a concern. A meeting of the chiefs of the country's public security investigation bureaus was convened in which

Justice Minister Ishii Mitsujirō warned participants of the possibility of operations by international communism. Yoshikawa Mitsutada, head of the National Public Security Investigation Agency, was more explicit, calling for caution in personnel exchanges with China in trade and culture. The PRC, he predicted, would escalate its anti-American and anti-GOJ efforts using the Japanese Communist Party and various left-wing youth organizations as the vanguard of the revolution it hoped to foment.

Due to infiltration by individuals sympathetic to Chinese communism, Yoshikawa opined, discussions on such unobjectionable topics as peace, cultural exchange, and trade were, in fact, designed to create general mistrust of the government among the people, thus alienating them from the leadership. He noted that the JCP had recently claimed to have a membership of over 200,000, and that the circulation of its flagship newspaper *Akahata* exceeded 300,000 copies. The public security director indicated that he was aware of some differences of opinion between the JCP and the CCP—for example, JCP Secretary-General Miyamoto Kenji had failed to form a united front with the CCP to support Vietnamese communists. Still, Yoshikawa did not believe that these would adversely affect their cooperation with regard to Japan.[141]

Left-wing student groups did become far more active, staging frequent demonstrations and closing major campuses while expressing great admiration for Chairman Mao. However, Yoshikawa's dire predictions were not borne out, no doubt to his great relief. The JCP mainstream decisively rejected Beijing's request to prepare for armed struggle. A few months after the meeting of public security investigation agency heads, Japan's police chiefs were apprised that Beijing had lost favor within the JCP, and that its leaders had warned party members that the failure of the attempted coup in Indonesia and subsequent bloody near-eradication of the Indonesian Communist Party should serve as an object lesson for those who might be tempted to heed China's call for armed struggle. *Akahata* ceased to reprint articles from PRC media, ran editorials condemning "dogmatism"—a code word for Chinese tactics—and refused to accept advertisements for Chinese films and publications. Chinese publications disappeared from JCP bookstores, though they were still available at other Japanese stores, and the Party began a purge of members who were considered to be pro-Chinese.[142] The Beijing government responded by adding the JCP to its enemies list, where it joined the previous big three: U.S. imperialism, Soviet revisionism, and Japanese monopoly capitalism.

Not everyone believed that the open hostility between the JCP and the CCP meant the end of their collusion to threaten Japan's security. The lead article in the January 1967 issue of *Keizai Ōrai* (Economic Comings and Goings), entitled "The JCP and Red Chinese Funds," noted that these funds had been very large—400 to 500 million yen over an unspecified time period—and that there was still a cooperative relationship through Japanese companies who expressed pro-PRC sentiments. Its author, Koito Chūgo, strongly hinted that the PRC was buying trade with Japan. He claimed that "friendly firms" who did business with China received a commission in advance based on estimates of annual exports, which was not refunded if the business were not actually transacted. One percent was standard, although in at least one case, a JCP member had received a 20 percent token of gratitude. This, said Koito, was not recorded in the annual assets of the trade association promotion group that he was an officer of. Koito also reported that China gave 2 percent rebates, called "participation expenses," to Japanese businesses who attended the Guangzhou trade fair.[143]

All of China's strained relations in this period paled in import with the Sino-Soviet dispute, which threatened to erupt into war, and perhaps nuclear war. Japan, as a close neighbor to both, feared for its security. At the same time, however, the Sino-Soviet dispute caused both parties to become more eager to court Japan and, since trade between the two dropped drastically, created more interest in Japanese markets. Militant anti-Satō rhetoric notwithstanding, Sino-Japanese trade went up by 50 percent in 1965, though still amounting to only 6.1 percent of Japan's total trade.[144] The USSR was eager to enlist Japanese technical and managerial expertise in developing its Siberian resources but, although Soviet-Japanese trade increased, negotiations were inhibited by the two sides' inability to reach agreement on the disposition of the Kuril Islands.

THE LDP REASSESSES ITS CHINA POLICY

As fissures deepened not only between the USSR and the PRC but among Japanese leftists as well, communism appeared less menacing to the security of Japan, and hence closer ties with the PRC appeared more feasible to certain members of the ruling party. In mid-1966 senior LDP leader Matsumura Kenzō returned from a visit to Beijing denouncing Prime Minister Satō's "negative" attitude toward China to a receptive group of thirty-odd other members. Satō, whose position mandated that he be sensitive to both relations with the United States and the Soviet Union, pointedly did not attend. Professing his amazement "at the phenomenal change in every aspect of Chinese life," Matsumura declared that Japan could ill afford to ignore the PRC.[145]

The JSP, dominated by its pro-Beijing wing, quickly announced its intention to take advantage of this split within the LDP on China policy by initiating a nationwide drive to normalize relations with Beijing. Liaison councils were to be established throughout the country as part of a drive to collect 30 million signatures in favor of recognizing the Beijing government; the JSP claimed to have 2.5 million signatures from an earlier drive. The party also announced its intention to press local governments to adopt resolutions urging recognition. Large-scale teach-ins were to be held under the supervision of leftist organizations of educators and student groups; the JSP would step up its demands on the government to admit PRC delegations on goodwill missions.[146]

The desire for closer relations took place against the backdrop of the ideological extremism and physical violence of the Cultural Revolution. Several Chinese who were regarded as close friends of Japanese leftists were purged, including Guo Moruo and Liao Chengzhi. While reports of the purges and violence were reported by Japanese newspapers, the stories were matter-of-fact and, in general, nonjudgmental. The impression was that journalists and editors regarded what was happening as a passing phase, to be tolerated until the perpetrators came to their senses and business could resume as usual. Although two-way trade declined in the second half of 1966,[147] the outlook for an upturn remained optimistic. It did not happen quickly: in 1968 *Sankei Shimbun* announced that China had drastically reduced exports to Japan. The paper attributed this partly to political reasons and partly to what it delicately referred to as the country's confused transportation situation. Ship departures from major ports had, for example, been delayed for about two weeks.[148]

The reasons for the media's complaisant attitude did not emerge until 1972, when it was revealed that, as a condition of their reporters being able to remain in China, the newspapers had agreed to three conditions: "not to pursue a hostile policy toward China," not to participate in any plot to create "two Chinas," and not to obstruct the restoration of normal Japan-China relations. These conditions were interpreted as a mandate to accentuate positive news and minimize anything unfavorable. Reporters whose articles exceeded Beijing's tolerance level were usually expelled,[149] though at least one of them, *Nihon Keizai Shimbun*'s Samejima Keiji, spent a year and a half in prison on espionage charges.[150]

The expulsions did not further the cause of Sino-Japanese relations, since after returning to Japan, the reporters were able to write still more frankly about what they had seen. Some reported being roughly handled by Red Guards; several Japanese business representatives revealed they had received similar treatment. Others reported that Zhou Enlai had told them that the government was aware that Japanese intelligence activities were being conducted by newsmen and trade representatives, and that it would deal sternly with the perpetrators.[151]

It is ironic that the major exception to this accommodative media attitude toward the Chinese Communist Party should be *Akahata*, the house organ of the Japanese Communist Party. Red Guard publications responded to a negative comment by JCP Chair Miyamoto by calling him an idiot: he and *Akahata* had attacked both the Guards and Chairman Mao. Moreover, *Akahata*'s account of the negotiations between Chinese and Japanese leaders was distorted: what the JCP called its independent stance was a poorly disguised effort to split "real" Marxism-Leninism and tantamount to surrendering to Soviet revisionists, U.S. imperialists, and Japanese reactionaries.[152] *Akahata* responded by calling the Red Guards childish and ignorant in their accusations, which constituted bullying and interference in the affairs of another country.[153] A series of further accusations and counter-accusations in the same vein ensued.

Throughout this period, a steady succession of Japanese left-wing groups appeared in Beijing, and were feted by their host organizations. Typically, Mao Zedong and Zhou Enlai met with them as well. According to Chinese news media, all visitors were impressed with socialist China. Several reportedly described the Japanese masses as becoming angrier with their government daily. Occasionally, the Chinese media could find specific referents for this anger, such as peasants refusing to allow their land to be bought for the construction of new airports[154] or fishermen complaining that their activities were being impeded by naval patrol boats. *Xinhua* described the Japanese masses as "realiz[ing] deeply that Mao Zedong's thought is nourishing them as crops are being nourished by the sun and the rain [and that] it is essential to depend on the invincible thought of Mao Zedong in making revolution."[155]

Particularly well received in China were the performers of the Matsuyama Ballet and the Haguruma theater group. The messages of the former were often political. Included in its repertoire were the Chinese revolutionary opera *White-Haired Girl* and a fictionalized account of an uprising against a ruler in medieval Kyōto. Haguruma, which means "cogwheels" or "gears," took its name from a classic story by Akutagawa Ryunosuke about a brilliant mind watching its own descent into madness. The group performed its signature piece, *Prairie Fire*, to packed audiences in several major cities. Its plot line, about an actual nineteenth-century peasant uprising against an evil capitalist landlord, fit in perfectly with the message of the Cultural Revolution.[156]

After protracted negotiations, the Liao-Takasaki agreement was extended in March 1968, with *Xinhua* reporting that the Japanese side had agreed, in contravention of the GOJ's policy, that politics and economics were inseparable. Although the Chinese had initially insisted that the Satō government be clearly identified in the communiqué as subservient to U.S. imperialism, the final version had the Chinese side pointing out that "all obstacles existing in the China-Japan relations have been brought on by U.S. imperialism and the hostile policy toward China pushed by the Japanese authorities." Satō was not named. The Japanese side showed "deep understanding" of the PRC position and pledged to work harder for the removal of such obstacles and accelerate the normalization of Japan-China relations. Henceforth, the agreement would be known as memorandum trade rather than the L-T agreement.[157] However, a week later, Kyodo reported that Japanese industrial trade fairs that had been scheduled for the fall of 1968 had been postponed until the spring of 1969.[158]

U.S. CONCERNS

Washington watched Sino-Japanese efforts to reach a mutually advantageous modus vivendi with some interest, evincing concern both at a Japan that might loosen its ties with the United States and at an intensifying Sino-Japanese rivalry that could bode ill for international stability. In an addendum to a later declassified National Intelligence Estimate (NIE) that was completed in January 1968, Fred Greene, head of East Asian affairs in the State Department's Bureau of Intelligence and Research (INR), opined that the NIE had not given adequate weight to the emerging regional and global importance of Japan in coming years. Greene believed that Japan's international political position would catch up to the powerful economic rank it already held and that, while it was unlikely to attain parity with the United States and USSR, the country would be at least as important in world affairs as Great Britain, France, and West Germany. Also, that the GOJ would take more and more active steps to contain and compete with communist China; the country would be drawn into the more dynamic role to which its leadership already aspired. Tokyo would likely seek to avoid unnecessary provocation to Beijing while working through mainly economic means to limit its influence.[159]

At the same time, INR Director Thomas Hughes wrote to Secretary of State Dean Rusk describing Japan's overriding concern as its relationship with communist China. While China remained militant and threatening, Japan would rely on the United States; should the PRC take on a less menacing aspect, it would rival Japan for Asian influence and leadership. Given China's efforts to develop a nuclear arsenal, the pressures on Japan to either accommodate or compete were bound to increase; Hughes had no doubt that Tokyo intended to compete. At this stage, at least, the GOJ hoped that U.S. protection would be sufficient to allow it to do so without nuclear weapons.[160]

Japanese faith in Washington received a rude shock only two months later when President Lyndon Johnson announced a unilateral de-escalation of hostilities against North Vietnam and his intention not to seek re-election. According to U.S. Ambassador to Tokyo U. Alexis Johnson, the speech was "widely misinterpreted" as an admission of defeat and a reversal of policy, "pulling the rug out from Satō." The United States was expected to withdraw from Asia and to move toward more cordial relations with the PRC. Johnson added that "many Japanese friends of the U.S." began to advocate that Japan immediately loosen its ties with the United States, including its security relationship, and adopt a more independent foreign policy. Satō came under heavy attack, not only from his political opposition but also from within his own party, for having tied himself too closely to the United States and then being left out on a limb by the reversal of American policy in Vietnam. The ambassador subsequently went to Satō's retreat in Kamakura on a Sunday for a five-hour private meeting to allay the prime minister's concerns that President Johnson's speech signaled a forthcoming change of policy toward China and that the United States would alter its position precipitously and unilaterally.[161]

Although the drama surrounding Johnson's announcement disappeared from mention in the Japanese media, American concerns about future Japanese relations with China did not. A telegram from the U.S. Embassy in Tokyo to the Department of State in June opined that years of peace, economic prosperity, and political stability had resulted in increased self-confidence and restlessness at reliance on others, and particularly on the United States. Though the LDP was still the largest party in the Diet, its share of the vote had been eroding. Within the past year, the opposition parties had tended to find more and more common ground in neutrality, opposition to the security pact, and an opening to China. There were some signs that the conservative leadership would find it increasingly necessary to try to capture this rising nationalist sentiment and pull back at least somewhat from ties with America and toward China.[162] Although the telegram did not say so, there were good reasons for Japan to want to detach somewhat from the United States and edge toward the PRC: Washington, increasingly concerned with the steady rise of the U.S. international balance of payments deficit, of which that with Japan was a major part, was responding to public calls for protectionist measures. Hence, U.S.-Japanese trade talks had been characterized by considerable friction, thus increasing the ever-present lure of the Chinese market.

Due in considerable part to the disruptions of the Cultural Revolution, there were limited opportunities to expand Sino-Japanese trade at that time. The embassy's telegram concluded that, although emotional attitudes toward China might strengthen pressures for more trade, trade with China offered less potential gratification for Japan's nationalistic desire to assert leadership than did economic assistance to Southeast Asian nations. "Chances of communist China's ever acknowledging any degree of Japanese leadership seem nil, and Japan certainly will not play second fiddle to China."[163]

The Chinese media also interpreted Japanese aid as Tokyo's effort to assert leadership, though in a far less flattering light: it was trying to fill the vacuum left by British imperialism's decision to withdraw west of Suez and working with the United States to complete the encirclement of China.[164] Aid to individual countries was termed exploitation and plunder in the name of economic cooperation.[165]

At times, the degree to which certain Japanese would go to trade with China upset the United States. After one such incident in 1957 involving sensitive electronic equipment, a high-level briefing team had been sent to Tokyo to convey U.S. concerns; another was dispatched in November 1967. American diplomats complained about Japan "punching holes in the nuclear umbrella" under which the U.S. sheltered them.[166]

4

The Tortuous Path to Normalization, 1969-1972

SATŌ TRIES TO ENGAGE CHINA

By 1969 the violence of the Cultural Revolution seemed to be abating. Although the power struggle behind it went on, Zhou Enlai continued to present its public face with his customary aplomb, allowing diplomatic negotiations to continue with some semblance of normalcy. In late January, Satō delivered a major foreign policy speech to the Diet. While the major topic of immediate interest to the delegates was the prime minister's announcement of his firm determination to obtain the reversion of Okinawa, Satō also offered a cautious overture to China. Japan would "welcome a situation in which Communist China could be widely received as a member of the international community" as it emerged from the Cultural Revolution, and "would keep various doors for contact open, as heretofore." Analysts observed that Satō had omitted the usual caveat about separating politics from economics.[1]

In addition to the usual reasons for wanting to improve relations with China, one motivating factor behind Sato's words may have been the news that came only a day before that Italy was about to extend diplomatic recognition to Beijing. Japanese officialdom reacted with outward unconcern and private dismay: the Canadian government had already indicated that it intended to enter into serious discussions with the same end, and Tokyo did not want to be the last of the non-communist countries to normalize relations with its near neighbor and putative competitor.[2]

Meanwhile, some Japanese sources were optimistic that the economic stagnation of the Cultural Revolution had ended and there were profits to be made. China had placed sizeable orders for scrap iron with France and Britain, indicating that the PRC's steel output was about to rise, and Japanese companies wanted to be in a position to satisfy it. Other Japanese business interests were more circumspect, noting that China had few products to sell apart from agricultural items such as rice and beef, and that due to the LDP's policy of protecting domestic agricultural products, such sales could not easily be transacted. Moreover, increasing economic relations with the PRC jeopardized existing lucrative trade with the ROC on Taiwan. Italy and Canada, by contrast, had very little trade with Taiwan. At this time, smaller enterprises tended to see greater value in China; big businesses were more likely to attach greater value to Taiwan's economic development prospects as well as to Taipei's greater influence over large segments of the Overseas Chinese entrepreneurs.[3] The Chinese government made no public acknowledgment of Satō's attempt to better relations, continuing to attack both his government and Satō personally. Instead, *Renmin Ribao* devoted a full page to commemorating the fifth anniversary of the publication of Chairman Mao's statement supporting the Japanese people's just patriotic struggle against U.S. imperialism. An article by "commentator," signaling that the author was considered an authoritative source, noted that the revolutionary mass movement had "shaken the islands of Japan like spring thunder."[4] A few weeks later, another *Renmin Ribao* article by "commentator" described Satō as "hostile to the Chinese people and a traitor who was enthusiastic about United States imperialism."[5] *Xinhua* reported Japanese left-wing protests again the government in minute detail.

In April, the latest of the unofficial Sino-Japanese trade agreements was signed, replacing the agreement that had expired in December. Headed by LDP stalwart Furui Yoshimi, described as attending in a private capacity, the delegation, which had been in Beijing since mid-February, found that the Chinese side wanted to resolve political issues before it agreed to discuss the trade-related items the Japanese had come for.[6]

As the talks proceeded, the industrial exhibition that had originally been scheduled for the previous spring opened, staffed by Japanese trade organizations that had been deemed friendly toward China. It had been postponed after the Japanese government refused permission to display nineteen items, including electronic computer components and a measuring device for semiconductors, on the grounds that they were on the COCOM (Coordinating Committee for Export to Communist Countries) embargo list, with *Xinhua* referring to an unspecified "host of obstacles put up by the U.S.-Japanese reactionaries."[7]

Although Japanese sources did not mention it, *Xinhua* described the opening of the exhibit as accompanied by angry shouts against the U.S.-Japanese reactionaries' anti-China activities in collusion with the USSR. The meeting room was flanked by slogans in both Chinese and Japanese reading, "The U.S.-Japanese reactionaries will come to no good end by opposing China in coordination with the Soviet revisionists!" and "Long live the militant friendship between the Chinese and Japanese peoples!" A giant portrait of Chairman Mao hung from the ceiling.[8] The closing ceremony two weeks later was followed by a highly ritualized protest meeting in which representatives of the friendly firms praised the opening of the CCP's Ninth Party Congress and vehemently denounced the Satō administration, U.S. imperialism, Soviet revisionism, and the Japanese Communist Party. *Xinhua* concluded tersely that the end of the protest meeting "was followed by an evening party."[9]

The Furui delegation had hoped to obtain a five-year agreement calling for larger amounts of trade, and to include the inauguration of unscheduled, nongovernmental air links between the two countries.[10] What it got was a one-year agreement for a total of only $70 million, as opposed to the $110 million recorded for 1968.[11] Further, the communiqué stated that the Japanese side had "admitted frankly that all the responsibility for straining Chinese-Japanese relations rested with the Japanese government" and, in contravention of GOJ policy, had agreed to Beijing's one-China policy, that the PRC was the legitimate government of China and that Taiwan was a part of it.[12]

The capitulation of the Furui delegation in order to achieve what was, from the Japanese point of view, a less than optimum agreement, aroused considerable resentment at home, with center-left *Tokyo Shimbun* commenting that the stance taken by the Japanese side in the communiqué reminded one of a master–slave relationship rather than the result of a negotiation between equals.[13] A slightly more charitable view was that acceptance of the humiliating terms represented *fumie* diplomacy, meaning an affirmation of a loyalty the affirmer does not voluntarily accept.[14]

Satō, in response to questions in the Diet, expressed regret over the wording of the communiqué, but added that he thought it was "very fine" that contacts with China had been preserved. This was interpreted as meaning that the prime minister regarded keeping lines of communication, however, slender, open with China weighed more heavily than considerations of national or personal prestige.[15]

THE SOVIET CONNECTION

At the same time Satō was making these largely fruitless efforts to warm relations with China, his administration was doing other things that annoyed Beijing. These included substantial increases in the defense budget, justified because of the need to defend Okinawa once it reverted to Japanese rule, but interpreted by China as a further step toward remilitarization. The prime minister took actions indicating that he favored a two-Chinas policy, such as receiving the ROC ambassador at diplomatic functions. Further, Satō sought better relations with the Soviet Union, now the PRC's arch-enemy. *Xinhua* denounced these as the USSR's "ardently flirting with the Japanese reactionaries out of its anti-China and counterrevolutionary needs." It described a Soviet-Japanese aviation agreement as an example of Moscow's penchant for concluding "one dirty deal after another," which was tantamount to selling out the USSR's state sovereignty and national interests to Japan.[16]

In essence, Japanese foreign policy during this period was attempting to maneuver among the United States, the USSR, and the PRC. As described by an unnamed senior Japanese diplomat, when the Sino-Soviet alliance appeared monolithic, Tokyo had no choice but to align the country tightly with the United States. While the Sino-Soviet split had the potential to undermine Asian stability, it had given Japan more flexibility in the immediate present.[17]

Soviet overtures were enticing: high-ranking conservatives were honored guests of the Kremlin, with hints that the prime minister had an open invitation. Leningrad's renowned Kirov Ballet toured Japan, and the Soviet Union sponsored an oratory contest for Japanese students of Russian. Economic results were, however, decidedly below both sides' expectations. Japanese were dissatisfied with the large imbalance of trade in favor of the Soviet Union: in 1968, for example, the USSR exported $463 million in goods to Japan but imported only $169 million. Soviet negotiators were unable to get Japanese agreement to develop Siberian resources at the price they wanted. The projects being contemplated—a trans-Siberian pipeline built through permafrost, development of natural gas on Sakhalin Island, and construction of a copper mine at Udokan—would be extremely costly. For the Udokan mine alone, the Soviets estimated that an investment of $1.8 billion would be required, requesting that the Japanese side contribute half. The Japanese demurred, replying that only $400 to $500 million would be required, of which they were prepared to advance only a fourth. In the words of one business leader, "Resources that cannot be developed on a paying basis are not resources at all."[18]

There was also no progress on the disposition of the Kuril Islands question. With U.S. agreement on the return of Okinawa to Japanese jurisdiction expected imminently, Japanese public opinion was expected to shift to the disposition of the northern islands as the last unresolved territorial claim. Given the Soviet interest in courting Japan, which could only have increased after Chinese and Soviet troops clashed over an island in the Ussuri River in March 1969, this intransigence on the islands claimed by Japan presumably indicated the importance the Kremlin and, more specifically, the Soviet military leadership, placed on maintaining jurisdiction over them.

CHINESE REACTION

The lack of progress in Soviet–Japanese relations did not lessen Chinese attacks on both. That the Soviets were "selling out" their country's resources to Japanese monopoly capital showed both their true nature as revisionists and the desperate straits that their erroneous policies had reduced them to.[19] *Xinhua* regularly denounced the reactionary policy of the United States, Japan, and the USSR in "a vain attempt to ... rig up an anti-China ring of encirclement." Satō and his ilk would, *Xinhua* predicted, "suffer a more ignominious fate than his [sic] predecessor Tōjō Hideki,"[20] Tōjō having been executed in 1945 for war crimes. A meeting between Satō and West German Chancellor Kurt Kiesinger produced a similarly extreme response. Pointing out that Kiesinger had once belonged to the Nazi Party, *Xinhua* argued that U.S. imperialism was encouraging the revival of the World War II Axis powers. It interpreted the agreement to hold periodic German-Japanese meetings on foreign aid as an alliance to suppress national liberation movements in Asia.[21] Clearly, although the

Chinese government did not want to deal with Satō's government, it had real concerns about Japan drawing closer to any other government.

THE OKINAWA REVERSION AGREEMENT

A November 1969 agreement between U.S. President Richard Nixon and Sato to return Okinawa to Japanese control in 1972 met with similar scorn from Beijing. This was, the Chinese media argued, merely a paper transfer: U.S. bases would remain on the island, and it refused to believe—correctly, as it turned out[22]—that nuclear weapons would be removed after the reversion. Since the reversion agreement refuted the Chinese media's prior contention that Washington would ever agree to the return of Okinawa, some revision of that view was needed. The rationale the media decided on was that Washington's underlying motive was the "Okinawazation" of all of Japan. In *Renmin Ribao*'s somewhat stretched reasoning, if all Washington were doing was turning over to Japan the administrative rights to Okinawa while the United States retained rights over the island's military bases, on which nuclear weapons could be stored even after the island had technically become part of Japan, then nothing could stop the United States from doing the same to the rest of Japan. Hence, the whole country would become "Okinawaized."[23]

Nixon, as part of his new Asia policy, had told Satō that he expected Japan would play a major part in maintaining peace and stability in Asia. This particularly angered Beijing, which it interpreted as Nixon deputizing Tokyo to "rule supreme in the Asian and Pacific region," with Japan serving as the "gendarme" of Asia to the disadvantage of the valiant revolutionary masses of China and other Asian states.[24]

Satō's speech at his triumphant return from the negotiations mentioned that he wanted China to recognize that the United States and Japan were making efforts to reduce tensions in Asia, and urged closer Tokyo–Beijing ties.[25] Although hoping for reciprocal gestures, he received none.

BUSINESS AS USUAL

Meanwhile, Chinese media reported, the valiant revolutionary workers and peasants of Japan were eagerly snapping up copies of Lin Biao's brilliant report to the Ninth Party Congress; bookstores had sold out of copies of the issue of *Beijing Review* that included the important documents of the Congress; and the masses were studying the works of Mao Zedong with renewed enthusiasm.[26]

Underneath the rhetoric, trade continued to take place. The Fishery Association of China sent a cable to its Japanese counterpart severely criticizing the behavior of both the Tokyo government as well as violations of Chinese territorial waters by Japanese fishing boats, but extended the agreement for six months while it waited to see an improvement in the behavior of both.[27] Friendly Japanese companies were active at the mid-April to mid-May Guangzhou Trade Fair. Difficult negotiations took place on the medium of exchange for contracts. These had been conducted using the British pound but, due to the continuing instability of that currency, difficulties had arisen. Although Japanese companies lost a great deal of money after the pound was devalued in 1967, it continued to be used because the two sides could not agree on a yuan–yen exchange rate.[28]

Differences of opinion continued to exist on how much the Chinese market could mean for Japan. In a discussion with two individuals who enjoyed the status of friends of China, Furui Yoshimi and Utsonomiya Tokuma, Zhou Enlai was encouraging, saying that although some people in China did not realize that Chinese machines could make anything beyond imagination by depending on the creativity of Chinese workers, this did not mean that China had no need for imported machines. What one country has may not be in another country's possession. Therefore, the two should trade in order to supplement each other's shortages in raw materials, processed goods, and equipment.[29]

A few weeks later, the Japanese foreign ministry released what was described as an exhaustive survey of the PRC's economy, noting that the losses in economic growth and human education caused by the Cultural Revolution would hobble industrial development in future years. It assessed the PRC's basic problems as, first, low agricultural productivity that limited industrial development and, second, ongoing increases in population that kept the unemployment problem perpetually unsolved. Because of the resultant inability to achieve rapid economic development through capital and technical investment, the Chinese authorities had tried to break through these barriers by effecting a basic reform of human nature in the form of the Cultural Revolution. The effort failed.[30]

This pessimism did not noticeably diminish the Japanese interest in establishing normal diplomatic relations with the PRC. At the first Diet meeting of 1970, JSP Chair Narita Tomomi challenged Satō on whether he really meant to make good on his avowed desire to improve relations with the PRC. In what amounted to an open letter to the LDP, Narita suggested three steps toward achieving the better relations:

- cancellation of the Yoshida letter, in which the former prime minister had pledged that the GOJ would not permit the use of Export-Import Bank loans to finance sales to the PRC.
- discontinuation of Japan's co-sponsoring a motion that deemed the issue of China's representation in the United Nations an important question, meaning that it would require a two-thirds majority for approval.
- refusal of any U.S. request to deploy American troops from Okinawa and Japan to the Taiwan Strait.

Narita also noted that, in order to improve relations with the PRC, the GOJ would have to abide by Beijing's three preconditions: to not be hostile to China, not participate in any plot to create two Chinas, and not obstruct any efforts to improve Chinese-Japanese relations. Satō's refusal to do any of these would indicate that his words about bettering relations were merely propaganda.[31]

Satō, basking in the LDP's biggest electoral win in a decade—the party won 288 seats of a 486 seat total outright, and gained another 12 from party members who had not received official backing—had no need to defer to the JSP requests, particularly since the JSP had lost more than 30 seats. But, in his first news conference following the inauguration of the third Satō cabinet, the prime minister indicated that the improvement of Sino-Japanese relations would be a major task facing the country in the new decade; it was undesirable for the two countries to "glare . . . and turn a cold shoulder to each other."[32] However, he also reiterated that he intended to maintain relations with Chiang Kai-shek's government. Analysts noticed that Satō had referred to the PRC as "the Beijing government" for the first time, and that neither he nor Foreign Minister Aiichi had used the hitherto standard term "communist China" at all.[33]

Within Japan, pressure for normalization was clearly building. With the exception of the far right and the Japanese Communist Party, it spanned the political spectrum. Demands increased when Canada, which had been rumored to be on the verge of establishing full diplomatic relations with the PRC, actually did so in the fall of 1970. The GOJ publicly welcomed the news that the Chinese and American ambassadors had been meeting in Warsaw,[34] the Polish capital having become an informal meeting venue in the absence of official relations between the two countries. But privately, there were concerns about what this meant for Japan. A nervous joke circulated in which Tokyo's ambassador to Washington is awakened one morning by a call from the Department of State announcing that the United States has just recognized the People's Republic of China.

The PRC raised its order for Japanese steel in February without attaching any political conditions, which was highly unusual. Still, this was not believed to be a signal that Beijing's attitude toward the Satō administration was softening, but rather because China urgently needed steel. Supplies of that commodity from Europe were constrained, and Beijing, worried about further confrontation with the Soviet Union, wanted to ensure that it had adequate quantities on hand.[35] The PRC was also an active buyer of other metals on world markets.[36] A memorandum trade agreement for 1970 was signed in April, again negotiated by Furui Yoshimi, and again confirming adherence to China's three principles.[37]

Perhaps to assuage domestic annoyance at the subservient tone of the agreement, the LDP issued a point-by-point refutation of the communiqué expressing "deep regret" over what it termed Beijing's high-handed criticism and attack against the GOJ, characterizing its accusation of resurgent militarism in Japan as an outrageous distortion of facts and malicious slander against the Japanese people, and suggesting that such accusations could arouse suspicions that the PRC was trying to impede friendly relations between Japan and other Asian countries as well as with the United States. It was perfectly reasonable for Japan to hope for peace in the Taiwan Strait, since the area was an important factor affecting Japan's security. Moreover, the prediction of the "Okinawanization" of Japan was absurd and ignored both the natural desire of the Japanese people for the restoration of control over Okinawa and the goodwill that existed between the United States and Japan on the issue.[38]

A few days after the steel agreement was signed, the GOJ proudly announced that Japan had lofted a 50-pound space satellite into orbit, thus becoming the fourth nation to do so, after the USSR, the United States, and France.[39] Beijing immediately accused Tokyo of developing missiles for use in nuclear warheads. Western analysts speculated that the Chinese pique might have been prompted by its own lack of progress in this field, which had been lagging.[40]

The skill level of the Sino-Japanese scientific competition was raised again at the end of April, when China sent a 380-pound satellite into orbit. Foreign sources pointed out that the same capabilities needed to produce the launch rocket for the satellite would enable China to create a missile that could deliver the nuclear weapons that the PRC was already producing.[41]

Politically, the attacks on Satō not only continued but also increased. He was regularly denounced as the "new Tōjō," either because he was, according to accusers, a Tōjō-like militarist or because he cherished the dream of re-creating the Greater East Asian Co-prosperity Sphere that had been a goal of the expansionist Japanese government of the interwar period, or both. In one of the stronger attacks, Xinhua likened Satō to a crazy dog barking at the sun ... [and] embarked on the old path once traversed by the Japanese militarists. In May 1970 Zhou Enlai announced four new conditions for trade: Japanese manufacturers and traders would be excluded from dealings with the PRC if they

- did business with South Korea and Taiwan.
- had "vast" capital investments in South Korea and Taiwan.
- supplied military weapons and explosives to the United States that could be used in Indochina.
- were associated with joint ventures with American companies and the subsidiaries of American business corporations in Japan.

Still, according to the *New York Times*, Japanese business circles remained optimistic about the future of Japan's trade with Beijing. Japanese manufacturers were uniquely positioned to supply products that met the PRC's specific requirements; the continued blockade of the Suez Canal helped make Japanese products more price-competitive than similar goods manufactured in Europe; and the PRC was concerned to increase its stockpiles of many commodities that Japan could supply.[42] Japan had been the PRC's largest trading partner in 1969, accounting for 16 percent of China's total foreign trade; two-way trade had reached a postwar high of $625,343,000, an increase of 13.8 percent over 1968. About 90 percent of this was conducted by firms designated "friendly" by Beijing, with more than half of this negotiated at the twice yearly Guangzhou trade fairs.[43] Clearly, this gave such firms every incentive to comply with Beijing's new conditions. The remaining Sino-Japanese trade was carried out under the memorandum trade agreement, whose Japanese negotiators had already proven themselves compliant.

Satō's reaction to Beijing's attacks on him was to "regret" the harsh criticism and urge patience so that Beijing could get a better understanding of his country's position.[44] Meanwhile, Japan's opposition parties seemed to be vying with each other for visits to Beijing, where they would enthusiastically agree to Beijing's conditions. Sometimes this risked peril to their parties, as JSP Chair Narita Tomomi's did to his group's always fractious membership. A particularly contentious intra-JSP issue was adherence to Beijing's four principal enemies. While it was easy to denounce two, U.S. imperialism and the reactionary Satō government, a declaration that the other two, the Japanese Communist Party and the Soviet Union, were enemies, threatened to split the party and did indeed end a fragile period of cooperation between the JCP and the JSP.[45]

Some members of Sato's LDP also became more vocal on the desirability of establishing relations with Beijing. Former foreign minister and millionaire businessman Fujiyama Aiichiō, who had been trying to visit China for more than a year, finally received Beijing's permission to do so. Journeying there in March 1970 with former minister of education Matsumura Kenzō, Fujiyama said bluntly that Japan needed a new China policy, even at the risk of rupturing relations with the ROC. Export-Import Bank credits should be extended to Chinese businesses even without withdrawing diplomatic relations with Chiang Kai-shek's government. If doing so risked a rupture of relations with the ROC, as Chiang had threatened, then so be it. The break would hurt Taiwan more than it would hurt Japan.

While Fujiyama was not saying anything that had not been said before, his words carried additional weight since, unlike previous LDP advocates of improving relations with the PRC, he could not be dismissed as a "Beijingya," or professional go-between, a term that carried somewhat pejorative overtones, and as Matsumura and Furui definitely had been classified.[46]

In August, Saionji Kinkazu, often referred to as Japan's unofficial ambassador to China, announced his intention to return to Japan after twelve years, explaining that his country now sent so many delegations to the PRC that his presence was no longer necessary. Saionji, a courtly presence—his grandfather was Prince Saionji Kinmochi, one of the *genrō* of the Meiji era—had been a member of the Sorge spy ring; he went to China in 1958 after being expelled from the JCP over ideological differences, and enjoyed good relations with Zhou Enlai.[47]

At the end of October, several non-mainstream LDP members announced that they planned to set up a supra-partisan Diet Members' League for Early Restoration of Japan-Communist China Relations. This action defied an internal party directive barring members from joining an outside organization with views that differed from the LDP's formal position. The leader of the mavericks, Utsonomiya Tokuma, was the son of prominent Sun Yat-sen supporter General Utsonomiya Tarō.[48] LDP Secretary-General Tanaka Kakuei attempted to set up a counter group in which party members could discuss their differences on China policy, but Utsonomiya's group vowed to press ahead nonetheless.[49]

With sinking popularity ratings and deserted by Diet members in his own party, Satō was in a difficult position. While a majority favored recognition of Beijing, there were many differences of opinion on what the specific circumstances of the agreement should be. An influential group within the LDP, many of them strongly pro-ROC, were adamantly opposed to normalization. The reaction of the United States had to be taken into account. And, finally, Beijing had announced that it would not deal with Satō at all. Hence, despite the will to move forward, the result was stasis. Japan again supported the designation of the question on admission of China to the United Nations as an important one requiring a two-thirds vote, though diplomats quietly told reporters that it would be necessary for the GOJ to reevaluate its position the following year.[50]

As the Satō administration worried about Japan's future, foreigners expressed mixed admiration and concern about what the country's apparently inexorable rise meant for them. Herman Kahn's *The Emerging Japanese Superstate: Challenge and Response*, published in 1970, predicted that Japan would surpass the United States in per capita income by 1990, equal its Gross Domestic Product by 2000, and become a major player in international affairs.[51] The book became a best-seller, as Westerners discussed what the resurgence of this former enemy meant for their own security and conception of a comfortable world order. Meanwhile, Japanese officials fretted about what textile negotiations with an increasingly protection-minded Nixon administration would do to their country's economic health. Greeting the new year, Satō appealed to the domestic textile industry to accept temporary losses for the sake of future trade relations with the United States.[52]

Nixon's call in his February 1971 State of the World speech for Japan to play a "unique role in the development of the new Asia" elicited mixed reactions, particularly given the uncertain relationship of both the United States and Japan to China. Did Washington intend to withdraw from Asia, hoping that Japan would continue its anti-communist stance in the region, as the Chinese media indeed did interpret Nixon's message? This could put Japan on a collision course with its larger neighbor, rather than improve ties with it, and could upset other countries as well. In some quarters, they observed, we are already known as "the ugly Japanese." Would this more assertive posture entail a greater military role and therefore exacerbate an already unfavorable image? No less an advocate of rearmament than right-wing author Ishihara Shintarō declared himself ambivalent because he could not be sure where the country would stop if it embarked on such a road.[53]

Worries that Japan was not ready for a more activist role were disputed by more confident personalities who argued that it was high time for their country to step out of its posture of humility and assume the place among the great nations of the world to which its postwar achievements entitled it. A tentative step was announced: the emperor and empress would visit Europe later in the year; the first time that Hirohito had left his country since he had ascended to the throne. It was noticed, but little remarked upon outside official circles, that in the same State of the World speech, Nixon had, in a first for him, referred to China as the People's Republic of China—several times.[54]

At the same time, Satō continued to search for a formula that would allow recognition of the PRC while retaining normal diplomatic relations with the ROC. A new year's address called relations with Beijing the "central core" of Japanese diplomacy. The initial draft of the speech, worked out by the foreign ministry, called for proceeding cautiously in a manner that would protect the national interest while contributing to the easing of tensions in the Far East. Satō himself added the phrase "so as to respect international faith," whose abstract words belie its underlying meaning: "respect for international faith" was a veiled commitment to maintaining the peace treaty that Tokyo had signed with the Taipei government,[55] and whose immediate abrogation the Beijing government had made a precondition for normalization.

U.S. officials judged that Chinese aspirations on the international scene would be constrained, as already vastly superior American and Soviet strength were joined by the increasing economic strength and growing self-confidence of its traditional rival, Japan. They predicted, erroneously as it turned out, that Beijing's "rigid and vituperative propaganda attacks on Japan's leaders, their policies, and their alleged ambitions in Asia ... would do little good for China's cause in Japan itself."[56]

Rivalry there certainly was, but also distinct feelings of inferiority. Okazaki Kaheita, for example, reacted to Satō's call for negotiations with the PRC by saying it was impudent and arrogant for Japan, which had been defeated in World War II, to propose talks as equals.[57] An academic commentator opined that "from ancient times, the Chinese have looked down on us 'eastern barbarians' ... there is a world of difference in their attitude toward the Japanese and toward the Americans, to whom they display grudging respect. Japanese often rail against American imperialism while taking a surprisingly low posture toward the CCP. However, how can such an association with China continue if they start by looking down on us?" The scholar concluded that Beijing was practicing the traditional Chinese policy of friendship with distant countries while attacking those nearby: trying to drive a wedge between Tokyo and Washington and between Washington and Moscow, the better to compete with Japan for the leadership of Asia.[58] And former ambassador Reischauer wrote that

> Chinese have traditionally paid scant and largely contemptuous attention to Japan which, in their eyes is a late and distorted offshoot of China's ancient civilization. There is a general feeling at this time that an important reason China wants better relations with the United States is to keep a resurgent Japan in check.[59]

Assertions of Japanese superiority could be found alongside those of inferiority: a poll of nearly 2,000 university students indicated that they viewed Japanese as considerably superior to Chinese, French, Mexicans, and Indonesians and slightly superior to Americans. The only country they felt inferior to, and that by only a small margin, was Germany.[60]

The fact that the United States and China appeared to be drawing closer also raised the stakes for improving Sino-Japanese relations. The foreign ministry publicly hailed the news that envoys for Washington and Beijing were holding talks in Warsaw, while privately expressing concerns that Tokyo was being abandoned. In April, the Chinese men's ping-pong team, returning from a six-year absence from international competition, bested defending champion Japan on home territory in Nagoya, with the Japanese press taking small solace from the triumph of the country's women's team.[61] When, just after the game, Beijing invited the American team to visit China to play, some Japanese saw symbolism in their being summoned directly from a Japanese city. Two months later, U.S. President Nixon eased the two-decades-old trade embargo to allow American companies to sell a range of products from food to zoo animals and to buy whatever the Chinese had for sale.[62]

Even as Satō appeared to be eager to make concessions—at the end of January, he referred to China as the People's Republic of China for the first time, and a few months later offered to go to Beijing personally to talk[63]—Chinese policy continued to court Satō's opposition while keeping up attacks on the prime minister himself. This could be advantageous: the JSP reversed its electoral decline in the House of Councillors contest of June 1971, with other opposition parties also making gains.[64]

It could also be dangerous. Kōmeitō, at that time the country's second largest opposition party after the JSP, received a long-sought invitation to Beijing only days after party chair Takeiri Yoshikatsu announced that his party advocated recognition of Beijing as the only legitimate government of China and abrogated the country's 1952 peace treaty with the ROC.[65] A few months later, while returning from the party's annual convention, he was seriously wounded in a knife attack by a rightist who told police that he was "displeased" with Kōmeitō's policy toward China.[66] Although Takeiri survived, observers were uncomfortably reminded that JSP leader Asanuma Inejirō had been assassinated in 1960 after he criticized the Japanese government during a visit to China.

Plans were announced to form a supra-partisan group favoring early relations with Beijing, duly constituted in February, and Miki Takeo, who coveted the prime ministerial position, stated flatly that Beijing represented China.[67] In a later campaign speech, he received only polite and perfunctory applause from his mainly LDP listeners until he mentioned better relations with Beijing, at which point the audience became noticeably more energized.[68]

Trade agreements were signed as usual during this period, with the Chinese side extracting the by-now expected humiliating clauses. Compromise was not tolerated. For example, LDP leader Fujiyama Aiichirō, visiting China at the same time the 1971 trade negotiations took place, agreed that the PRC was the sole legitimate government of China but said that he thought that abrogation of the Japan-ROC treaty should be not be considered a precondition for normalization talks. He also voiced his disagreement with some of the more humiliating phrases that appeared in the final communique, such as that the revival of Japanese militarism was already an established fact. Fujiyama's status notwithstanding he was excluded from the signing ceremony for the trade agreement, nor did Zhou not invite him to the reception thereafter. With exquisite understatement, a commentator for the Japan Times wrote "Some people say that Premier C(Z)hou's attitude toward Fujiyama was not necessarily warm."[69]

Particularly after it became obvious that U.S. businesses were courting China, Japanese corporations, even those with large financial interests in Taiwan, began to consider ways to enhance their dealings with the PRC. A record 791 firms applied for permits to attend the spring fair in Guangzhou, and an increasing number voiced willingness to subscribe to Zhou Enlai's four principles if that would serve as their entrée to the Chinese market.[70] The PRC had announced its fourth five-year economic construction plan, which would entail larger foreign purchases, and Japanese businesses were eager to maximize their market share.[71]

Into this charged situation burst the first of the "Nixon shocks." In mid-June, Nixon appeared on U.S. television announcing that his chief foreign policy adviser Henry Kissinger had conducted a series of heretofore secret talks with Chinese leaders, and that Nixon himself would visit Beijing in 1972. The way in which this was announced caused shock waves on both sides of the Pacific: Nixon had disrespected a loyal ally by failing to even inform the Japanese government, much less discuss with it the merits, of a step with the potential to change so drastically its international position. The government's public position was subdued, with acting Foreign Minister Kimura Toshio averring that he had been informed beforehand. Ambassador Ushiba Nobuhiko confirmed that the State Department had tried to contact him three hours beforehand, but had been unable to make contact until an hour before the announcement. *The Japan Times* commented that while it might be technically true that the GOJ was informed, there had certainly been no prior consultation, in contravention of longstanding agreements between the United States and Japan.[72] *Asahi*, a notable exception, argued that the GOJ had had ample evidence over the past six months that China and the United States were approaching each other through various channels and that, if the government had not noticed them, it should be accused of stupidity.[73]

Satō and his party were caught in a difficult position. The LDP suggested sending an official delegation to China; Sato offered to go himself. The Beijing government curtly rebuffed both initiatives, adding yet another affront to Japanese pride. How, Japanese media asked, could Mao Zedong's government agree to accept a visit from the American president without preconditions, while refusing what amounted to entreaties from the Japanese government? Perhaps, the feeling lurked, Kissinger and Zhou Enlai had reached some private understanding that had not been shared with the GOJ. One commentator, noting that Nixon was going to Beijing rather than Mao coming to Washington, concluded that

> the historical past in which China was the central kingdom where the world paid proper homage appears to be in the process of being revised in the Chinese communist mind. [The Nixon trip] would signify recognition [of China] as one of the world's superpowers.[74]

In a placatory gesture, Nixon proposed that he fly to Alaska to meet the emperor and empress on their way to Europe, which the GOJ agreed to. U.S. diplomats also attempted to soothe agitated feelings, assuring their wary Japanese counterparts that Nixon's trip did not imply a change of American policy toward Japan and promising the closest consultation on the details of the trip. Former under-secretary of State George Ball opined that care would have to be taken to ensure that America did not exchange friendship with a superpower for a fragile relationship with a potential superpower.[75]

In an address to a National Press Club gathering in Washington, Ambassador Ushiba stated that U.S. explanations would not easily satisfy the Japanese media and public. He suggested that the two countries try to coordinate their policies on China rather than compete with each other for Beijing's favor. Much would depend on how consultative and cooperative Washington was in the future.[76] However, a few days later, Nixon announced his second shock, scarcely a month after the first: the dollar was to be delinked from gold and a 10 percent surcharge added onto imports that were not subject to quotas. Again, there was no prior notification or consultation. It was clear that the revaluation of the yen was a major goal of the policy. Japanese businesses, heavily dependent on exports, feared devastating losses: the Tokyo stock market immediately fell 20 percent, with cumulative losses of over $11 billion.[77]

Renewed fears at a diminution in trade with the United States whetted the already eager appetite of Japanese businesses toward the PRC. Barely a week after Nixon's announcement that he would visit China, several major Japanese companies including such behemoths as Nippon Steel and

Komatsu, offering varied explanations, canceled their scheduled participation in economic conferences with the ROC/Taiwan and South Korea. The underlying motive was clear: they expected U.S.-Chinese normalization soon, and none wanted to be associated with countries likely to arouse ill feelings in Beijing. Large financial institutions such as Fuji Bank and trading firms like Mitsui and Mitsubishi reacted similarly.[78] Of six major Japanese shipping companies that regularly served Taiwan ports, only one, Kinkai Yusen, a small subsidiary of the giant Nippon Yusen Kaisha, continued to call at the island's ports.[79]

Toyota Motors announced that it would do nothing that contravened Zhou Enlai's four principles on trade, and that it planned to send a vice-presidential-level envoy to discuss doing business in the PRC.[80] Its rival, Honda, which had already exported small power generators to the PRC, revealed that it was hoping to exhibit its cars and motorcycles at the fall Guangzhou trade fair.[81]

Politically, delicate negotiations were being conducted by all parties both domestically and internationally. Satō continued efforts to better relations with Beijing while retaining ties with Taiwan, meeting implacable resistance from Zhou Enlai. Although they were invisible to the outside world and certainly did not appear to affect the continuity of foreign policy, elite politics in China were troubled as well. Lin Biao, Mao Zedong's designated heir-apparent, who had been explicitly named his successor in the constitution ratified at the CCP's Ninth Plenum in 1969, had fallen afoul of his enemies, both those more radical and more conservative, with one possible point of contention being his alleged preference for mending ties with the Soviet Union and opposition to bettering relations with the United States.

Lin was not seen in public after May 1971, and was later described as having been killed in a mysterious plane crash in Mongolia in September. He was accused of plotting to kill Mao and attempting to flee to the USSR after the plan was discovered. Chinese sources released information on Lin's alleged crimes piecemeal and sometimes in ways that appeared to conflict with each other. For example, in speaking with a Japanese delegation in 1972, Liao Chengzhi stated that Lin's aim had been to oust Zhou.[82] Remarkably, Zhou was able to remain the public face of Chinese diplomacy throughout this period of internal disarray within the leadership group.

Satō, deserted by many in his own party who wanted closer relations with China as quickly as possible, also had to contend with a vocal right wing that was strongly opposed to doing so. Groups with names such as the International Federation for Victory over Communism staged rallies that expressed doubt on whether there really was a split between the Soviet Union and China, and predicted that normalization would be followed by renewed attempts to export their revolutions to Japan.[83] An influential anticommunist group in the Diet argued forcefully that breaking relations with Taiwan would damage international faith in Japan's credibility and call into question its adherence to other agreements it had made. The foreign ministry itself was divided on the wisdom of recognition of the PRC.[84]

Meanwhile, Zhou Enlai conducted multifaceted diplomacy designed to reassure other countries that the imminent shifts in the balance of power would be beneficial to international stability. He assured visiting Canadian Trade Minister Jean-Luc Pepin, among others, that China did not seek superpower status and was interested solely in economic development.[85] In a series of interviews with *New York Times* reporter James Reston, Zhou attempted to counter allegations that the PRC was trying to create a wedge between Japan and the United States to destroy the security treaty between the two—a demand that Beijing and Japanese leftist parties had consistently made in the past. To the contrary, Zhou wanted the United States to remain tied to Japan, saying that this would place limits on Japan's militaristic ambitions; the Japanese left was unrealistic. Without its ties to the United States, Japan would, he opined, become a nuclear power and again threaten world peace.

Zhou portrayed Japan under American tutelage as using its economic growth to create military power rather than, as in the interwar period, using military power to enhance its economic growth. In essence, he argued that Washington was to blame and should therefore make amends by restraining Tokyo. The U.S.-Japan security treaty should be retained as the building block for the future Asian security system: American withdrawal from the area, as Nixon had earlier envisioned, would increase rather than alleviate Asian security tensions. As he had with Kissinger earlier in the year, Zhou accused Japan of harboring imperialistic ambitions toward both Korea and Taiwan.[86]

These remarks elicited considerable adverse comment in Japan. *Sankei Shimbun* declared itself surprised at the severity of the remarks, wondered if Zhou really meant what he said or whether he had some other motive, and pointed out that his comments came close to interference in another country's domestic affairs.[87] Ambassador Ushiba, in language unusually blunt for a diplomat, characterized Zhou's words as "the biggest nonsense I have ever heard."[88]

Less than two weeks after this acrimony, there was an unexpected positive signal. After the death of senior LDP statesman and long-time advocate of improved Sino-Japanese relations Matsumura Kenzō, the GOJ informed Beijing that a Chinese representative would be welcome to attend his funeral. The Chinese government not only accepted the invitation but also named Wang Guochuan, who had represented the PRC in the Warsaw ambassadorial-level talks with the United States when he was ambassador to Poland, to attend. The decision to send so highly credentialed an official, plus the announcement that Wang would stay for fifteen days, far exceeding his condolence obligations, seemed to portend a softening in Beijing's attitude.[89] Wang shook hands with Prime Minister Satō at the funeral, raising hopes that this might lead to Chinese agreement to hold talks on better relations.[90]

Apart from the handshake, Wang did not meet with Satō, though he did hold extensive talks with important business interests and influential members of all political parties except the JCP, which remained hostile toward any contacts with the CCP leadership. *Nihon Keizai Shimbun* commented that Wang's visit showed that Beijing was prepared to cooperate with those who were opposed to Satō's China policy, and that if the GOJ really wished to improve ties, it would have to acknowledge Beijing as the only legitimate government of China.[91]

Meanwhile, President Nixon met with the emperor and empress in Alaska in what was deemed a successful, if purely symbolic, visit. The Japanese press commented that the appearance of an aurora, rare at this time of year, just at the time their majesties' flight took off for Denmark, was a good omen.[92] It was also considered important that the meeting had taken place, albeit on U.S. territory, before Nixon visited China.

The White House also made considerable efforts to deny that a Kissinger trip to China that was scheduled for October would have substantive content, reiterating that the purpose of the visit was merely to discuss the administrative details attendant on Nixon's forthcoming trip. *The Japan Times* commented that it would be more useful for Kissinger's dealings with China to "make a more recent and first-hand observation" of Japan, since it was such an important factor in the U.S.-China relationship. Kissinger would find it helpful to call in Tokyo en route to Beijing, which was "even more important at this moment than having President Nixon making a stopover in Tokyo."[93]

Additional anxiety was generated by the announcement that Nixon would go to Moscow. The Japanese press, while applauding his efforts to reduce international tensions and apparent desire for equidistance between Beijing and Moscow, took a tone best summarized as "but what about us?" From the Japanese standpoint, this development underscored yet again "the distance that lies between this nation and the seat of the world power structure. It is not that Japan should aspire to a place among the supernations, but the contrast cannot go without being noticed." What the press did notice was that, in the press conference announcing his trip, Nixon mentioned Japan only once, and then only in the context of the textile agreement that was being negotiated.[94]

Satō, anxious to avoid exacerbating friction with a U.S. administration angry about textiles as well as other trade matters, decided to side with Washington in sponsoring resolutions deeming the issue of China's entry into the United Nations as an important question requiring a two-thirds majority. To the dismay of LDP leaders, for whom being on the losing side of the UN vote appeared to weigh at least as heavily if not more so than the actual issue, the resolutions failed, with the Chinese press crowing that they had "lifted a rock only to drop it on their own feet" and "behaved like ants on a hot pan."[95]

In yet another blow to Japan's long quest for at least equality for China, Tokyo's bid for a permanent seat on the UN's Security Council was also rebuffed; it had argued that Japan, not China, is the major economic and political, though not military, power in Asia.[96] The People's Republic of China, displacing the Republic of China on Taiwan, was now the only non-Western nation among those colloquially known as the perm five. Satō, who bore the burden of responsibility, managed to defeat three separate motions of no confidence, two in the House of Representatives and one in the House of Councillors. Some LDP members, angry at Japan's humiliation in the UN, sided with the opposition.[97]

The cadence of attacks on Satō and Japanese militarism continued, even as China conducted its twelfth nuclear test. With radioactive fallout expected to reach Japan in a few days, Zhou Enlai received several of the country's leading businessmen, telling them that China and Japan could coexist, but warning them that what Zhou called the abnormal expansion of the Japanese economy could lead to militarism whether or not Japan wanted it.[98] *The Japan Times* editorialized on the irony of residents of Okinawa protesting the possibility that U.S. weapons *might* remain in Okinawa after reversion, while no one was demonstrating against the "ashes of death from China" that were actually falling over the main island of Honshu.[99]

DENOUEMENT OF THE NORMALIZATION ISSUE

With the parameters of the debate within Japan fairly clear and the protagonists identified, the ensuing months saw skirmishes and debates as each side tried to maximize its bargaining position. Satō opened the year by reiterating that he wanted better relations with China but did not want to abandon Taiwan. A few days later, he met with Nixon at the latter's home in San Clemente, with one major topic being the positions Nixon intended to take during his trip to Beijing the following month. Of more immediate importance to the Japanese was a firm date for the reversion of Okinawa to Tokyo's control, which the two men agreed would be May 15, 1972.

That the GOJ was not reassured by Nixon's statements that it could expect no surprises for the trip is obvious in that Ambassador Ushiba continued to tour the United States, warning civic groups that Nixon's trip might result in the unraveling of the two countries' mutual security arrangements in the Far East. Satō was reported as visibly irritated while watching televised coverage of Nixon's arrival in Beijing, and an unnamed Japanese foreign ministry official told U.S. Ambassador Armin Meyer that his country felt it had been left behind. Anonymous American officials in Tokyo described GOJ leaders as "holding their breath and praying something dramatic won't happen."[100] Though expressing relief that the communiqué issued as a result of the visit was quite limited, the Japanese press nonetheless accused America of betrayal and Satō of allowing himself to be outstripped by Washington in establishing ties with Beijing. *Asahi* reiterated that the GOJ should think seriously about why Beijing had completely disregarded its attempts to establish government-level contacts with the PRC.[101]

Satō, under intense questioning in a parliamentary interpellation a few days later, made a statement that Taiwan was part of the People's Republic of China, causing a furor that Foreign Minister Fukuda could only partially smooth over (see Chapter 10). Even before Fukuda's attempt at damping down criticism that the prime minister had gone too far, the Chinese delegate to the UN Security Council had denounced Satō for not going far enough.[102]

In a tearful address to the Diet in June, Satō announced that he planned to resign, expressing regret that he had been unable to establish relations with China. At a press conference immediately thereafter, he accused reporters of being biased, refused to answer their questions, and stalked out of the room.[103] Since the revelation of a secret agreement between Japan's major newspapers and the Beijing government had become public only a few weeks before,[104] the prime minister's remarks were not so much unfair as out of character with his normally even-tempered mien.

Although the likely successors to the prime ministership had already declared that establishing relations with the PRC would be a priority, all had avoided the minefield of the conditions under which this would take place. Meanwhile, controversy continued to swirl on how normalization should be effected. At the extreme were groups who would acquiesce to Beijing's conditions before normalization talks began, and groups demanding that Beijing acquiesce to what amounted to a two-Chinas solution. A less conservative group suggested that Tokyo put forth preconditions of its own, with *Sankei Shimbun* advocating that talks must

- be held on an equal footing (which acceptance of Beijing's preconditions would decidedly not be).
- not be held at the expense of relations with a third country.
- accept the principle of economic freedom.
- include mutual pledges on the non-use of force.[105]

The candidate who would have to create a consensus, Tanaka Kakuei, was selected as LDP chair, and hence prime minister, in mid-July. Tanaka, only 54 and a self-made man from a poor family, was considered unusually outspoken—not generally considered a virtue in Japan—and lacked a university education. On all counts, he was an oddity among postwar prime ministers.

Beijing immediately signaled that it was open to talks. On the day that Tanaka was sworn in, *Asahi* reported that Zhou Enlai had communicated to Tanaka through a mutually trusted intermediary that negotiations could be held "if the new government decides to earnestly take up the normalization issue."[106] PRC ambassadors in other capitals had begun to engage their Japanese counterparts in conversation, and in Geneva, the Chinese representative to the UN's Economic and Social Council had for the first time attended a reception hosted by Japanese diplomats.[107]

Except in the sense that it had apparently been unwilling to deal with Satō under any circumstances, this did not actually constitute a softening of Beijing's conditions, since both *Asahi* and later dispatches by other papers indicated that acceptance of the three principles remained a prerequisite for talks. In mid-July, the GOJ for the first time said it would "study concrete measures for the normalization of relations that would be mutually acceptable to the two sides," which was taken as an indication that it was ready to accept Beijing's conditions.[108] Urged by JSP leader Sasaki to accept Zhou Enlai's invitation, Tanaka replied that he would go to Beijing "when the time comes."[109]

Though Tanaka did not say so, he could not go in the absence of a consensus within his fractious party. In one of the more visible manifestations of discontent, Fukuda, leader of a powerful LDP faction and the man whom Satō had clearly preferred to succeed him, had flatly refused Tanaka's offer for members of his group to serve in the cabinet. With Satō's exit from the prime ministership, the hawks went from leadership faction to antileadership faction, but they nonetheless represented 40 percent of LDP Diet members.

While political pundits advised against hasty moves that might disadvantage Japan in talking with China, Zhou Enlai had made it plain that delay would be considered tantamount to endorsement of the previous government's hostile policy. He also specified that Tanaka's visit take place before October 1st, saying that he did not want the occasion to interfere with the celebration of the PRC's national day.[110] In effect, this created a window of opportunity of about six weeks—a formidable challenge even for Tanaka, whose nickname was "the computerized bulldozer."

The antileadership faction managed to change some of the language of the original draft of Japan's conditions for normalization, and a consensus was finally reached on five points:

- Chinese-Japanese relations should be in accord with the UN Charter and the Bandung agreement on peaceful co-existence.
- Japan and China should respect each other's political systems and refrain from interfering in each other's internal affairs.
- the two nations should refrain from the threat or the use of armed force.
- economic and cultural exchanges should be promoted equally and without discrimination.
- Japan and China should cooperate for peace and prosperity in Asia.

With consensus achieved in his own party, Tanaka quickly completed the easier task of soliciting support from opposition parties, since all save the JCP were already in favor of rapid normalization.

In early August, Tanaka said publicly for the first time that it was "inevitable" that Japan would sever relations with the ROC, and sent emissaries to Taipei and Seoul to explain the government's position.[111] The LDP's Council on the Normalization of Japanese-Chinese Relations approved Tanaka's trip to Beijing and hence, tacitly, of his plans for normalization.[112] Two days later, Tanaka accepted Zhou Enlai's invitation.[113]

Japan having conceded on the ROC/Taiwan, the media hoped for some concession from Zhou who, openly at least, did not give any immediately. Meeting with representatives of the Japan-China Cultural Exchange Association, he had harsh words for Japanese extremists of both left and right who opposed ties with the PRC.[114] The JCP, incensed at Zhou's lumping them together with right-wingers, denounced his statement as "an act of unpardonable interference" in Japanese affairs.[115] The JCP remained on the PRC's four great enemies list, along with U.S. imperialism, Soviet revisionism, and the now-dissolved reactionary Satō cabinet. Meeting with representatives of a Kōmeitō group, Zhou did make plain that China did not intend to demand war reparations.[116] This had been hinted at in the past, though with the clear understanding that some kind of acknowledgment of debt was expected. Since Chiang Kai-shek had already foresworn any demands for reparation, it would have been difficult for the PRC to re-open the question.

In early September, Tanaka met with Nixon in Honolulu—quite literally meeting him half way, albeit on U.S. territory. Japanese media carefully noted, however, that the prime minister had ensconced himself and his entourage in a Japanese-owned hotel. In essence, Tanaka received the U.S. seal of approval for normalization, with Nixon reportedly telling the prime minister that it would not hurt American interests in Asia and that he hoped the trip would contribute to relaxing tensions in the region.[117]

A week later, an advance party left Tokyo for Beijing: an odd collection of Diet members, airline executives, technical personnel for the television hookup, a medical team, two chimpanzees. and a brace of black swans.[118] Those not reminded of Noah's ark might have thought of the ancient tribute system that Japanese leaders of past centuries had felt so demeaned by. The Chinese were expected to reciprocate with rare animals of their own, as indeed President Nixon had been presented with pandas on the occasion of his pilgrimage to Beijing.

Tanaka arrived in Beijing on September 25th, amid intense media scrutiny of the most minute details of protocol. It was noted, for example, that the band at the welcoming ceremony at the airport played the Japanese national anthem, whose first line, "May the emperor's reign last until pebbles become rocks and moss grows on them," had often been construed as justifying a return to imperial rule, and that Tanaka, pleading fatigue, had not attended a revolutionary ballet in which Chiang Kai-shek was ridiculed.

At a banquet, the prime minister duly delivered the expected message of apology for Japanese actions in World War II. In what was assumed to be an attempt to mollify Japanese hawks, the language of the apology was carefully calibrated, with Tanaka expressing "profound self-examination" (*fukai hansei no nen* 深い反省の念), which was said to be a traditional form of apology. Although this fell short of the abject expression of regret that the Chinese side would have preferred, *Kyodo* described Premier Zhou as nodding approvingly and applauding. His response to Tanaka's statement that "we should not submerge ourselves in the dark blind alley of the past" was a bit less than enthusiastic agreement: "We must bear in mind the saying that one should not forget bygones, but use them as a warning for the future."[119]

On the morning of Friday September 29, just under Zhou Enlai's deadline, the two sides signed the normalization agreement, formally ending the legal state of war between them. The preamble said that Japan "is keenly aware" of its "responsibility" for causing "enormous damage" to the Chinese people through war and "deeply reproaches itself." Taiwan was disposed of in the body of the document, using language similar to that of the U.S.-Chinese communiqué of seven months before: the GOJ "fully understands and respects" the stand of Beijing that "Taiwan is an inalienable part of the territory" of China. The communiqué also said that China declared its renunciation of its demand for war indemnities from Japan. The two sides agreed to establish "durable relations of peace and friendship . . . on the basis of the so-called five principles of peaceful coexistence," which were listed. The parties averred that normalization was not directed against third countries, so that neither should seek hegemony in the Asia-Pacific region.[120]

The clause on the principles of peaceful co-existence is recognizable as part of the demands of Japanese conservatives, who were resentful of Beijing's regular pronouncements on their country's politics as well as mindful of its efforts to promote revolution there. The clause on hegemony was a Chinese suggestion. The Japanese side may have regarded it as innocuous, or even helpful, since Tokyo was concerned both to erase memories of its hegemonic activities in the interwar period, and to forestall foreign countries' fears that normalization foreshadowed the formation of a Sino-Japanese axis. However, the clause would later cause considerable difficulty when, as pledged in the communiqué, the two sides began to negotiate a treaty of peace and friendship.

This was not noticeable amid the smiles and clinking champagne glasses at the signing ceremony. Zhou Enlai even requested that Tanaka convey his best regards to the emperor, which, in the context of decades of invective against the imperial institution as a focus of militarism, was taken as a positive sign.[121] Media on both sides used phrases like "the dawn of a new era" and "historic rapprochement."

Still, concerns remained. The PRC celebrated its 23rd birthday the day after Tanaka and his party left, but in a subdued manner. Although a bit more festive than in 1971 when Lin Biao's mysterious disappearance caused the cancellation of most observances, the massive parades, impressive fireworks, and floats of past years were replaced with smaller political entertainments in people's parks in major cities.

Tanaka, in a widely watched televised news conference held on his return, chose his words carefully. Zhou had, he said, agreed that every country should carry out its own revolution, conveying the implication that the PRC would not attempt to export its revolution to Japan.[122] Zhou had also waved off questions about the islands contested between Japan and China, suggesting that it was not important the issue be resolved immediately. How normalization would affect Japan's commitment to the Mutual Security Treaty with the United States was also an open question, as was the form of Japanese-Taiwan relations.[123]

Despite a "China fever" among some segments of the population, the Japanese media saw an incipient rivalry issue, with the generally pro-China *Asahi* suggesting that Japanese would be well advised to start thinking about economic competition with the PRC under the new conditions.[124] One of Japan's premier sinologists, Nakajima Mineo, worried about the effect that normalization would have on his country's relationships with other countries. Nakajima predicted that frictions were bound to develop with the United States as Japan moved closer to China, that the Soviet leadership would interpret the antihegemony clause as directed against the USSR, and that Asian neighbors would fear that the coming together of a major political power and a major economic power posed a threat to them. He added that Tokyo should end its overly ambitious economic policy if it wanted its newfound friendship with China to last.¹²⁵

Political commentator Hirasawa Kazushige echoed many of these same sentiments. Noting that the Tanaka cabinet had sent three special envoys to nine Asian countries to soothe concerns over the restoration of Sino-Japanese relations, he expressed doubts that this could be done. Other Asian states' worries included sometimes overlapping and sometimes mutually incompatible fears that Tokyo had embarked on a new policy that gave priority to big nations while ignoring smaller ones; that Japan and China would conspire with each other to dominate Asia; that Japan might come under the influence of China, with the latter becoming regional hegemon; and that, with China presumably no longer critical of Japanese militarism, Japanese would feel freer to dominate Asia economically. Citing the clauses in the normalization agreement that said normalization was not directed against third countries, and that neither Japan nor China should seek hegemony in the Asia-Pacific region would not, Hirasawa predicted, suffice to abate these concerns.¹²⁶

A prominent professor at Keio University, Kamiya Fuji, noted a slight but, he felt, meaningful difference in the wording of the Sino-Japanese communiqué and the communiqué that had been signed between Tanaka and Nixon at Honolulu three weeks before. Whereas the former said that normalization would contribute to the relaxation of tension in Asia and the safeguarding of world peace, the latter merely expressed hope that this would be so. Kamiya also took issue with the widely held assumption that Tokyo, having abandoned Taiwan, was no longer encumbered, whereas Washington continued to have its diplomatic hands tied because it continued to bear the burden thereof. In Kamiya's analysis, the opposite was true: Japan had surrendered a strong bargaining chip with the PRC, while the United States continued to be able to wield it. Moreover, Washington had avoided having its credibility with other Asian nations eroded by having abandoned Taiwan. Hence, Tokyo's diplomatic freedom had not necessarily been advanced by agreeing to normalization. Henry Kissinger, Kamiya concluded, "probably will not be able to refrain from smiling to himself whenever the subject of Asia comes up these days, and for some time to come."¹²⁷

The question of which side profited more from normalization continued to be debated. Some argued that Chinese diplomacy had brilliantly manipulated Japanese "guilt and greed" into an overly hasty decision that made needless concessions.¹²⁸ This is certainly an oversimplification. The desire to expand markets was important, and guilt about Japanese wartime actions did indeed exist, though the major Japanese decision-makers do not appear to have been especially troubled by it. But unquestionably, Chinese good cop–bad cop diplomacy was skillful, holding out the promise of more and better trade conditions after normalization and withholding them as a way of modifying Japanese behavior in other spheres.

Beijing also worked through left-wing groups in Japan, using them to mobilize Japanese public opinion in favor of normalization and other pro-Chinese positions. The apparently endless procession of visits by "Japanese friends," accompanied by banquets and cameo appearances by Mao Zedong and Zhou Enlai, also helped to win favor among the groups and individuals honored with such invitations. Equally skillful was the way in which Beijing played opposition parties against the dominant LDP, as well as nonmainstream LDP politicians against prime ministers. Secret agreements between Japanese media outlets and Beijing ensured that their coverage of events in China was biased in favor of the PRC.[129]

Meanwhile, Japan, as a pluralistic and more open society, could not easily resist such tactics nor practice them itself. Nonetheless, others have argued that its methods were also creative and adaptive. In essence, Tokyo had used good cop–bad cop techniques as well. Pro-Chinese individuals were dispatched to Beijing, where they behaved obsequiously and readily agreed to whatever humiliating conditions Zhou Enlai imposed in order to maintain and expand trade relations. This was reminiscent of certain phases of Japanese behavior in the era of the tribute system. Indeed, Japanese conservatives castigated such behavior as *ketou* (kowtow) foreign policy: 土下座外交 *dogeza gaikō*. Others termed it *fumie* diplomacy. Their argument was that by conceding style, Japan maintained substance.

Whichever view one chooses to hold, beneath the public euphoria, each side began the normalization period with a good deal of wariness about the intentions of the other.

5

The Golden Age of Sino-Japanese Relations, 1972–1989

NEGOTIATING THE DETAILS

The first seventeen years after normalization of have been characterized as the golden age of Sino-Japanese relations.[1] Although the period appears so in light of what superseded it, the relationship seemed far more stressful at the time. A number of difficult issues had been left for future negotiation; neighbors who were apprehensive about how a Sino-Japanese rapprochement might affect them had to be reassured; and the details of a new economic and political partnership painstakingly worked out. Additionally, there were domestic political issues that caused each side to harbor misgivings about the stability of the arrangement it had made.

Tanaka faced strong opposition not only from other parties but also within his own LDP, and soon became embroiled in corruption charges. In China, the aging leaders who had agreed to the conditions of the rapprochement agreement were suffering from serious health problems, raising questions about who would succeed them and what policies they were apt to pursue. A major power struggle between those who would have preferred to mend relations with the Soviet Union and those who felt that the PRC's security would be better served by a close relationship with the United States had already claimed the life of Mao's chosen heir apparent, Lin Biao, though at the time he was known publicly only to have mysteriously disappeared.

Uncertainties, both within each country and toward each other, were barely visible behind an outward appearance of reciprocal good will and mutual admiration. In Japan, this reached a pitch the domestic media referred to as "China fever." Exchange groups proliferated, with each expressing delight at the friendliness of the people, the beautiful scenery, and the unique culture of the other. Museum exhibits, exotic flora and fauna, theatrical performances, and film festivals helped satisfy the curiosity of those who were unable to leave their own countries. Handicrafts from the PRC enjoyed brisk sales at local department stores, and millions of Chinese were eager to buy Japanese electronics.

With an election for the lower house of the Diet scheduled for December 1972, the LDP sought to capitalize on its position as the party that would effect normalization of relations. The panda was used as the party's campaign symbol, and its election headquarters featured a large plush panda bear along with the traditional daruma doll.[2] The tactic did not work, with the party losing more than two dozen seats, hanging onto its majority only with the addition of independently elected candidates who later joined the party. Two LDP members who had spearheaded the call for normalization were actually defeated, though observers tended to attribute this to their neglecting campaign activities because they were preoccupied with lobbying for diplomatic recognition of the PRC.

Officially, the respective central governments set about the housekeeping details of opening embassies in each other's capital, appointing ambassadors, and the like. Speeches at a seemingly endless round of dinners and receptions repeated the mantra that the two countries were separated only by a narrow strip of water, touching lightly if at all on the "problems" of the past. When mentioned, they were treated as unfortunate blips in a long history of amicable relations.

The Japanese government sent delegations to nine countries to calm concerns that rapprochement would mean the emergence of a Sino-Japanese juggernaut that would affect their security, and that Tokyo would continue to help subsidize their economic development. Though received politely, the envoys were aware that the recipient countries' leaders remained apprehensive.

Since Sino-Soviet relations had since 1969 several times erupted into border skirmishes that threatened to escalate, Tokyo was at pains to let the USSR leadership know that its new friendship with China would not come at the expense of ties with Moscow. Apart from security considerations—Soviet planes entered Japanese airspace with enough regularity to be jokingly referred to as "the Tokyo Express," and Soviet ships and submarines sometimes patrolled uncomfortably close to Japanese waters—Tokyo still cherished hope of effecting the return of the Northern Territories, that is, the Kuril Islands.

Japanese businesses were also interested in participating in the USSR's ambitious plans to develop Siberia's oil and natural gas resources. In addition to the profits to be made, the oil and gas that were produced would help to meet energy-deficient Japan's need for fuel. Hence, even before leaving for Beijing to formalize the Sino-Japanese agreement, Prime Minister Tanaka, in his capacity as head of the LDP, wrote a personal letter to Party General Secretary Leonid Brezhnev, marking the first time that a Japanese leader had communicated directly with the head of the Communist Party of the Soviet Union. Brezhnev replied in a cordial tone.[3]

For its part, the Chinese leadership was eager for Japanese technology and managerial expertise, but for reasons of pride and past prickly relations did not want to play the role of younger brother to Japan. PRC officials insisted, and constantly reminded delegations of would-be investors, that any agreement must be made on the principles of equality and mutual benefit. Yet, at the time the rapprochement was taking place, Japanese economic primacy seemed unchallengeable. The structural weaknesses pointed out in Zbigniew Brzezinski's *The Fragile Blossom* (1972) were acknowledged but appeared to be unimportant: the economy continued to grow by double digits. In 1972 Japan was the world's leading shipbuilder for the seventeenth straight year.

The Chinese were aware that the reversion of Okinawa had stimulated Japanese nationalism, and had vivid memories of the dangers that this had posed for Japan in the pre–World War II period. Hence, as a U.S. official confided to the author at the time, behind the bonhomie of the meeting of the two countries' leaders, there was less warmth than cold realism in the renewed dialogue.

Strong differences of opinion emerged in negotiating agreements on reciprocal air routes, fertilizer sales, fisheries, textiles, and numerous other issues. In January 1974 a trade agreement was signed, marking the first of the four that the normalization agreement called for. Of the others, reaching consensus on a civil aviation pact was complicated because of Japanese uncertainty over whether the routes to China would be profitable and Chinese insistence that Japan give up flying its lucrative routes to Taiwan. Negotiations on maritime transport and fisheries proved difficult as well. China was initially reluctant to allow Japanese participation in oil-drilling ventures. The two also found themselves on different sides of negotiations on the United Nations Convention on the Law of the Sea (UNCLOS), with China favoring and Japan opposing placing research and development in the hands of the riparian state.[4] Less than two years after normalization, China fever had subsided into a difficult process of mutual adjustment of expectations.

THE PEACE AND FRIENDSHIP TREATY

Perhaps most troublesome to the relationship were negotiations over a treaty of peace and friendship. At the suggestion of the Chinese side, this had been mentioned in the joint communiqué that established diplomatic relations, and, sounding completely innocuous, was readily agreed to by the Japanese negotiators. In October 1975 Deng Xiaoping told a visiting cultural exchange group that the People's Republic was ready to start talks, seemingly taking Japanese officials by surprise. The conservative *Sankei Shimbun* opined that, although it was not clear why Beijing seemed to want such a treaty so urgently, the three most plausible reasons were, first, that it was apprehensive over Japan's future leadership: Tanaka, the most pro-China prime minister the LDP had ever produced, was likely to be succeeded by someone less sympathetic to the PRC. Second, since Japanese negotiations with the USSR had made little progress due to Soviet refusal to turn over the disputed Kuril Islands/Northern Territories, Beijing hoped to conclude a treaty with Tokyo before the Soviets could do so. And third, China might be hoping to include a statement on Taiwan in the pact.[5]

If the first were Beijing's motive, the Chinese leadership must have been disappointed. Mired in accusations of accepting large bribes from the U.S. aircraft manufacturer Lockheed, Tanaka resigned in November, succeeded by Miki Takeo.[6] To Tokyo's great relief, Beijing announced that it would not discuss Taiwan, the third of *Sankei*'s list of probable factors, at this time. The second issue, the Soviets, turned out to be critical. Early in 1975, to Tokyo's surprise, Beijing invited Hori Shigeru, a prominent supporter of former prime minister Satō's China policy, to visit. Analysts speculated that the Chinese might be seeking a new route to the Japanese government after the collapse of its Tanaka channel, and that it might be trying to win over supporters of the Taipei government. In any case, Hori accepted the invitation, met with Zhou Enlai, and assured him that Japanese fears that Chinese-Japanese normalization would lead to communism in their country were now gone.[7]

Negotiations proved difficult nonetheless. One concern centered on the moribund 1950 Sino-Soviet treaty's hostile language on Japan. A second, and more intractable, issue was the Chinese side's insistence that the treaty contain a clause opposing hegemony. Since the hegemon Beijing had in mind was indisputably the Soviet Union, and since Japan continued to hope for the return of the Northern Territories as well as participate in the USSR's plans to develop Siberia, agreement to the clause would certainly adversely impact both these goals.

The talks were carried out against a backdrop of uncertainty on the leadership in both capitals. In China, a campaign was in full flower to oppose Lin Biao and Confucius, the former deceased since 1971 and the latter since 479 BC. The object of the diatribes against Lin appeared designed to thoroughly discredit not only the man who had been constitutionally designated as Mao's successor but also those who had been associated with Lin. The attack against Confucius was of greater concern to Japanese policymakers, since it was understood to be directed against Zhou Enlai, who had overseen the normalization talks. Although the party congress of 1973 indicated that some stable modus vivendi had been reached among the factions competing for primacy, rumors soon began to circulate that Zhou was suffering from an incurable form of cancer. For whatever reasons, the Chinese position remained intransigent on the hegemony issue.

In Japan, Miki proved a weak and vacillating prime minister. Hawks in his LDP insisted that the word "peace" be removed from the draft, that China delete the anti-Japan clause from the 1950 Sino-Soviet treaty, that Beijing explicitly recognize Japan's sovereignty over the Diaoyu/Senkaku Islands, and that Tokyo reopen the lucrative Taiwan-Japan air route that the PRC insisted be ended. This would effectively have scuttled the treaty, which was undoubtedly precisely what the hawks had in mind. The first condition, removing the word "peace," was a nonstarter and was never seriously considered; the second was resolved by saying that when Deng Xiaoping asserted the issue be put off for another generation, the issue of the disposition of the islands had been settled. This was either a disingenuous ruse designed to assure passage of the treaty or a most unwise leap of faith. Regardless of motive, the decision would cause severe problems in the future.

Trying to address the opposition's third condition, the Japanese foreign ministry suggested asking the government of China to "declare in a certain official manner" that it did not harbor hostility toward Japan, rather than asking it to repudiate the treaty outright.[8] The fourth issue, the air route, was partially solved through artful name changing and giving Taiwan's national carrier landing rights at a different airport than China's (see Chapter 9). More middle-of-the-road sources asked why it was necessary to quickly conclude a treaty because of the blandishments of an eager neighbor,[9] claimed that the treaty was redundant,[10] and warned that it was highly unwise to risk good relations with the Soviet Union by again making explicit what was already apparent in the 1972 joint communiqué.[11]

In addition to broad agreement that there was uncertainty over just what obligations would arise under the anti-hegemony law, the slightly left-of-center *Mainichi* added another concern: the definition of hegemony. Were the term to be construed to include expansion of economic interest in addition to military conquest, Japan might be subject to Beijing's criticism on even such matters as its economic contributions to developing nations.[12]

A series of talks repeatedly faltered. Sometimes this was due to anger, as when Beijing objected to sympathetic obituaries in the Japanese media on Chiang Kai-shek's death, and when high-level mourners attended his funeral. At others, the reason was deadlock due to simple failure to agree on specific points. Beijing reacted by stepping up people-to-people diplomacy, hoping to use the Japanese public to put pressure on an argumentative Diet, but in the process arousing Japanese concern that China was interfering in the country's domestic affairs. The JSP, with its pro-Soviet and pro-Chinese wings in an uneasy coalition, was put in a particularly difficult position by Beijing's tactics.

Summarizing the situation thirty months after normalization, *Sankei Shimbun* opined that Japanese had outgrown their unbridled adoration of things Chinese and formed an unbiased picture of the PRC: a totalitarian state under the control of the communist party. Beijing's open support of Tanaka when the former prime minister was in well-earned disgrace for his involvement in financial scandals had transcended the bounds of propriety. *Sankei* tempered its harsh judgment somewhat by observing that Beijing had completely ceased its constant harangues about the growth of Japanese militarism and now even expressed approval of the security treaty with the United States.[13]

Hesitations about concluding agreements with the Chinese were also reinforced by comments from within the Japanese foreign ministry that they were regularly outmaneuvered by their counterparts. A participant who took part in several negotiations from 1972 through 1975 commented that, although much of the rest of the world appeared to regard the process as one group of inscrutable Orientals jousting with another, "The Chinese are skilful negotiators. They are skilful not only in extracting maximum concessions from foreigners but also in creating the appearance of their own generosity."[14]

The stop-and-start negotiations dragged on against a backdrop of serious concern within Japan of economic contraction. Competition from lower-wage developing economies caused shoemakers in Nara to destroy their machines, and several shipyards declared bankruptcy, as did the country's largest plywood manufacturer. In 1977 the unemployment rate exceeded 1 million for the first time since World War II. At the same time, African countries were asking for more aid, while the United States and Great Britain were declaring that Japan's trade surpluses with them should be cut. Difficult fishing talks were taking place with the Soviet Union, which refused to budge on the Kurils/Northern Territories issue.[15] These were powerful motivators for enlarging Japan's market share in the PRC's development. Fukuda Takeo had succeeded Miki as prime minister, and in China, the uncertainty following the deaths of Mao Zedong and Zhou Enlai seemed to have been cleared with the elevation of Hua Guofeng to leadership of the party and government and the arrests of the ultra-leftist Gang of Four.

Deng Xiaoping was rerehabilitated in mid-1977. The signing of a $20 billion trade accord reflected a new degree of confidence on both sides, with *Xinhua* comparing it to "laying a long, thick pipeline" of friendship between the two and hence smoothing the way for resumption of talks.[16] Favorable economic data were announced: after a sharp drop in 1976, trade rebounded to its second-highest level, with, according to statistics compiled by the government-funded but autonomous Japan External Trade Organization (JETRO), the PRC having a favorable balance of $1.4 billion, following a similar figure of $1.2 billion in 1976.[17]

At this juncture, Moscow offered its own good-neighbor treaty, accompanied by a letter from Party General Secretary Leonid Brezhnev saying that his government wanted an accord because of a "third force that sought to damage Soviet-Japanese relations."[18] To Beijing's great relief,[19] the Japanese government rejected what Chinese media referred to as the so-called treaty, explaining that a treaty could not be concluded until the Northern Territories had been returned to Japan. Interestingly, the demands of LDP conservatives notwithstanding, the Japanese government did not make a similar condition with regard to the Senkaku/Diaoyu Islands.

Deng Xiaoping, evincing impatience, then announced a four-point proposal stating that, first, the Chinese government had not changed the position expressed in the 1972 joint communiqué, and second, that it did not see the treaty as directed against any third country but rather to promote friendly relations between the two signatories. However, if a country were to express its opposition to hegemony but then did not oppose a hegemonic country, its position would be illogical. Third, to take an antihegemonic position did not mean that the two countries should take joint action against hegemony, since each had its own foreign policy and neither would interfere in the internal affairs of the other. Fourth, the Chinese side saw no obstacle to resuming negotiations: Foreign Minister Sunoda would be welcome in the PRC if the prime minister wished to resume negotiations.[20]

Japanese commentators reacted favorably to Deng's statement that hegemonism did not imply joint action, but objected to the idea that it was illogical not to state opposition to a third country's hegemonism. There was ongoing concern about angering the Soviet Union, stoked by periodic statements from Moscow that hinted of dire but unspecified unpleasant consequences should Tokyo succumb to Chinese blandishments and sign a treaty it regarded as hostile to the USSR. Japanese analysts countered that they found Moscow's reaction puzzling: if the USSR did not think of itself as a hegemon, why would it object to the agreement?[21]

Southeast Asian states, particularly Vietnam, viewed renewed steps toward negotiations apprehensively, fearing a possible increase in Chinese influence in the area.[22] China, however, claimed that the Southeast Asian states were concerned with Japan's future moves in the region.[23] Beijing's penchant for delivering messages through visiting groups of Japanese opposition parties or friendly nongovernmental groups continued to irritate Tokyo officials.

In July, the Japanese government tabled its own draft treaty, referring to opposing hegemony throughout the world rather than limiting it to the Asia-Pacific region, just as had the 1972 joint communiqué on normalization. In addition to an article stating that the pact was not directed against any third nation, Tokyo asked Beijing to agree to a postscript declaring that each party could interpret the meaning of hegemonism in terms of its own policy.[24] At this point, the Chinese government, perhaps because it was eager to get an agreement that would encourage Japanese investment, put forth three major initiatives that seemed to indicate willingness to compromise on the treaty language:

- proposing for the first time that Japan participate in developing offshore oil fields in the East China Sea, thereby reversing its previous policy of restricting Japan to technical and financial aid only[25]
- departing from its longstanding policy that the Chinese government would not accept foreign loans by notifying a visiting Japanese mission that the government would allow bank loans to finance industrial development[26]
- inviting representatives of Japanese arms manufacturers to visit Beijing to discuss sales to China, although Tokyo had previously declared a policy that deemed such exports incompatible with its constitution[27]

As an added incentive, Deng expressed his willingness to personally visit Japan for the formal signing of the treaty, thus ending the one-way diplomacy of Japanese leaders visiting China without reciprocation that reminded some Japanese uncomfortably of the imperial tribute system.

At the end of July, treaty talks resumed. The Chinese side flatly refused to agree to the clause that the treaty would not be directed against any specific third country,[28] with the CCP-financed Hong Kong newspaper *Wen Wei Po* emphasizing that the fault lay entirely with Japan and that China would never change its stand. Oddly, and out of character for a PRC-backed paper that typically took a somewhat harder line than the Beijing government, putatively because it was not considered official, *Wen Wei Po* declared that the anti-hegemony clause was only a general statement that was not aimed at any specific country.[29] Also surprising was that, against this backdrop of acrimony, good-will delegations and Buddha images traveled back and forth between the two countries, and major deals were concluded for the massive Baoshan iron and steel complex. Nonetheless, when Foreign Minister Sunoda asked his Chinese counterpart Huang Hua to support his country's application for nonpermanent membership on the United Nations Security Council, Huang replied only that the matter "would be carefully studied."[30]

Just as it appeared that the talks would end deadlocked once more, Beijing offered a compromise: while it would not accept the Japanese draft treaty's inclusion of a third-party clause as part of the article on anti-hegemony, it did consent to the inclusion of a separate article specifying that the treaty would not affect the position of either party in its relations with other countries. The agreement was signed on August 12th,[31] with Chinese media reports emphasizing its anti-hegemony content without mentioning the separate article.[32] The CCP-sponsored Hong Kong daily *Ta Kung Pao* described the treaty as a great defeat for the Soviet Union and creating a precedent for future international treaties.[33] Chinese media made frequent reference to the historic friendship between the two countries and the narrow strip of water separating them.

A commune on the outskirts of Beijing was renamed in honor of Sino-Japanese friendship, with the ceremony attended by dignitaries including Vice-Premier Chen Yonggui, a peasant who had attained his high office after the government lauded his service as leader of the model Dazhai brigade, and perennial icon of Sino-Japanese friendship Liao Chengzhi. To the accompaniment of drums, gongs, and fireworks, twin pine and cypress trees were ceremonially planted in the courtyard of the China-Japan Friendship Commune to symbolize the evergreen relationship between the two.[34]

Deng Xiaoping duly visited Japan for the signing, eliciting mixed feelings in Tokyo. Pleasure at the departure from one-way diplomacy that it symbolized was tempered by concern on other issues. First, there might be a "Deng boom" akin to the China fever that had followed the conclusion of the 1972 normalization agreement, thereby complicating hard bargaining by Japanese officials. Second, Prime Minister Fukuda might use Deng's visit to enhance his personal popularity in order to fend off a challenge from rival LDP faction leader Ohira Masayoshi. Japan's left-wing parties, pacifist to varying degrees, were apprehensive lest Deng voice his support for the country's Self-Defense Forces and the U.S.-Japan mutual security agreement.

As it turned out, Fukuda got only a mild boost in popularity from Deng's visit and was replaced as prime minister by Ohira scarcely a month later. Deng did endorse both the Self Defense Forces (SDF) and U.S.-Japan agreement, to the annoyance of Japan's otherwise pro-China but also pro-pacifist leftist elements. Fears over foreign country reactions proved unfounded. The Soviet Union complained vigorously that Japan had jumped on a tiger's back—that is, once mounted, it would be virtually impossible to get off— but took no hostile actions. Other Asian nations reacted with equanimity.

Optimists even dared to hope that the treaty would usher in a new era of quadrilateral great power relations.

FRIENDSHIP AND FRICTION

A small cloud on the horizon appeared in the form of an unattributed column in the leftist Hong Kong *Hsin Wan Pao* entitled "There Is No Tacit Consent Regarding the Diaoyutai Islands." Taking issue with former prime minister Nakasone's contention that Deng Xiaoping had given his tacit consent to Japanese ownership of the Diaoyu/Senkaku group, the anonymous author conceded that outsiders did not know what Deng had said. However, he was certain that if Deng had given any assurance, it was to be interpreted in light of Section 1, Article 1 of the Peace and Friendship Treaty: "The two signatories affirm that in mutual relations all disputes will be solved by peaceful means that they will not resort to armed force or threat of armed force." That, the writer said, "is all there is to it." Nakasone's words, the author continued, were a distortion based on his own wishful thinking. Seemingly in contradiction to the statement about peaceful resolution, the author concluded that even though the islands were small, "China will fight for every inch."[35]

Although China did not support Japan's bid for one of the UN Security Council's rotating seats, which went to Bangladesh, bilateral relations were otherwise harmonious. Fukuda's visit to the Yasukuni Shrine on the anniversary of the end of the war, the second prime minister, after Miki Takeo in 1975, to do so aroused more adverse comment in Japan than China.[36] Deng Xiaoping continued to favor Japan having its own defense capability, and many Japanese, noting that the 1978 clause on hegemony differed only slightly from the 1972 joint declaration, wondered what the controversy had been about.[37] The pace of business agreements between the two countries accelerated to a degree that worried Japanese financial planners, who preferred a more cautious approach.

THE EUPHORIA ENDS

A series of unpleasant shocks that began in early 1979 jolted relations. The Chinese decision to invade Vietnam in February seemed to many Japanese to undermine the spirit of peace and friendship they hoped was inherent in the treaty that had been signed only a few months before. The Japanese Socialist Party, long a supporter of China, was particularly embarrassed, with its chair, Asukata Ichirō, publicly accusing Beijing of betraying its commitment to the Five Principles of Peaceful Coexistence.[38] The cost of the war, when added to the consequences of the PRC's ambitious industrialization program, forced the Beijing government to order a series of plant cancellations and postponements that adversely affected multimillion dollar contracts already signed with Japanese companies.[39]

In Japan, the decision brought back memories of other business agreements that had been aborted, beginning with the Nagasaki flag incident of 1958. Their misgivings were at least partially alleviated by Chinese leaders' repeated assurances that this was but a temporary delay in the country's ongoing commitment to industrialization. At the end of March, the two sides had agreed to extend their long-term trade agreement to 1990 and to expand the amounts involved threefold.[40]

THE DIAOYU/SENKAKU ISSUE AND THE YASUKUNI SHRINE

Only a few days later, however, new problems arose, with the Diaoyu/Senkaku Islands again the focus. On April 2nd, the Japanese Maritime Safety Agency reported that an estimated fifty Chinese fishing vessels were operating off the main island of Uotsurijima. Perhaps intending to send a signal, Prime Minister Ohira, though a Christian, made a well-publicized visit to the Yasukuni Shrine, with the chief priest remarking afterward that he had spent a longer time there than any of his predecessors.[41] Although every post–World War II prime minister save Ishibashi Tanzan had visited the shrine, Ohira's visit was notable in that it was made shortly after the revelation that fourteen Class-A war criminals had been enshrined there the previous fall.[42] The visit of Ohira's predecessor, Fukuda Takeo, had also caused controversy within Japan because it both occurred on the August 15 anniversary of Japan's surrender and because he had signed his name in the visitors' book at the shrine. While the Beijing media all but neglected this last detail, it would become a major issue in years to come.

The intrusion of the fishing boats also gave impetus to previously mooted Japanese plans to build a heliport on the island to strengthen its claim to sovereignty. The foreign ministry expressed misgivings, saying that there were other ways to strengthen the claim, but failed to specify what those ways might be. Personnel and materials were unloaded on Uotsurijima a few months later, and the office of the prime minister announced the initiation of a formal scientific survey of the area.[43] Beijing protested, saying that these actions violated the 1972 normalization agreement's understanding that the disposition of the islands would be shelved.[44] The study proceeded nonetheless, reporting a few months later that lighthouses and other land facilities could be constructed there, but deemed the islands unsuitable as a port of shelter for ships during storms.[45]

Diplomatic sources noted that Beijing had chosen a verbal representation, the mildest form of diplomatic protest, to express its views, and a few days later Deng Xiaoping told a former Japanese cabinet minister that the issue could remain untouched for some years if it could not be settled at present.[46] Since Deng also mentioned the need for more Japanese government loans as well as commercial credit to finance the PRC's modernization programs, it may be surmised that economic issues provided the emollient to soothe territorial problems, and indeed, agreements, visits by technical personnel, and cultural exchanges continued to be everyday items in the media of both countries.

In August, the two sides were discussing joint development of undersea oil resources in the area, with Beijing quickly rejecting Tokyo's conditions that

1. the islands be recognized as an integral part of Japan.
2. the areas to be developed were outside the 12-mile territorial waters around the islands.
3. the part of the areas designated for development that faced Taiwan would be kept intact "to avoid any unnecessary disputes."[47]

If the GOJ had any doubts about the strength of Beijing's commitment to its claims of sovereignty, they should have been dispelled during Vice-Premier Gu Mu's visit to Tokyo. Although the purpose of Gu's visit was to seek financial assistance, he stated unequivocally that the islands belonged to China. Japanese press agencies pointed out that this was the first time a Chinese leader had laid claim, in public and in Japan, to China's title to the islands, adding that it was unusual for someone seeking a financial favor to accompany the request with so strident a pronouncement.[48] Japanese officials also took note of Beijing's warning to other claimants of the Spratly

Islands in the South China Sea, regarding this as another indication of its resolve on the issue of contested territories.[49]

On the Japanese side, the promise of eventual economic gain evidently outweighed hesitation about loans, despite concerns over the contested islands and whether the obvious, though not publicly acknowledged, tensions within the Chinese leadership would result in a drastic reversal of PRC policies. Though the general direction of Japanese policy was never in doubt, the composition of the personalities at the top continued in flux. Ohira's party obtained only a bare majority in the fall 1979 Diet elections and the JSP also lost ground, while the more moderate Japan Communist Party more than doubled its strength. Chinese media reported on Ohira's programs without editorial commentary, simply citing Japanese newspapers.

Shortly thereafter, Ohira visited China, with *Xinhua* quoting him as saying that he hoped China would make steady progress and become a strong power,[50] and that no third country would be disadvantaged by the growing Sino-Japanese friendship. Behind Ohira's positive message were serious issues. The Japanese Ministry of International Trade and Industry (MITI) and the country's foreign ministry differed on whether aid should be tied or not. MITI argued the former as a way to ensure that the country reaped maximum advantage from its largesse, as well as helping to ensure that the funds were well used. The foreign ministry countered by pointing out that advanced countries, most vocally the United States, opposed tied aid because it would give Japan an unfair advantage in the China market. Association for Southeast Asian Nations (ASEAN) members feared that Japanese aid to the PRC would create economic entities that would adversely affect their traditional markets in Southeast Asia as well as lead to a reduction of Japanese loans to their countries. Soviet specialists argued that creating the impression of a Japan strongly committed to the PRC would irritate the USSR unnecessarily.[51]

GREAT POWER POLITICS

Beijing continued to try to draw Tokyo into a more assertive anti-Soviet stance, arousing resistance and occasionally resentment. In an uncharacteristically blunt statement, the Japanese ministry of foreign affairs termed Deputy Chief of the General Staff Wu Xueqian's statement urging Prime Minister Nakasone to strengthen Japan's defense capabilities "none other than an act of interfering with the domestic affairs of this nation ... the usual ploy of a major power." *The Japan Times* opined that the intent of the statement was to use Japan for China's own purpose in global strategy.[52] The center-left *Tokyo Shimbun*, though stating that Sino-Japanese relations had never been better, added that Wu's demarche constituted "uncalled for meddling in Japan's internal affairs,"[53] and the generally pro-China *Asahi* urged Prime Minister Ohira to "frankly express [to Chinese leader Hua Guofeng, during Hua's impending visit to Tokyo] that Japan cannot agree to China's anti-Soviet stance."[54]

This did not happen quite according to script, since the Ohira cabinet fell, and Ohira himself succumbed to a heart attack, just before Hua's state visit. Hua soothed the issue by saying that he appreciated that Japan had its own interests to protect as well as its own opinions on how to deal with the Soviet Union. He had no intention of meddling in Japanese affairs; the country needed "a certain level of defense," but that was a matter for the Japanese themselves to decide.[55] Hua held forth the promise of limitless possibilities for Sino-Japanese trade, while stressing that the PRC would remain self-reliant.

Both sides expressed satisfaction with the visit, the first ever of the formal Chinese head of state. Among other festivities, the son of celebrated author Lu Xun unveiled a monument to the Japanese professor who had taught his father. The PRC press ran stories of Marshal Nie Rongzhen's ordering in mid-war that two orphaned Japanese girls be properly cared for, and the two sides discussed plans for new student exchanges.

Still, a curious dichotomy existed between government pronouncements that all was well and the obvious frictions that existed. As 1981 drew to a close, Japan's leading business daily, *Nihon Keizai Shimbun*, declared that "relations between Japanese political, economic, and cultural circles and their Chinese counterparts can hardly be cooler than at any time since normalization. ... Sino Japanese relations are at the crossroads."[56] Two weeks later, *Xinhua* quoted with obvious approval the Japanese prime minister's statement that Sino-Japanese relations "have never been as good as they are today," and added that "we must take good care of them."[57]

Domestically, leadership instability continued in both states. Hua, whom a number of other Chinese leaders considered socially awkward and a diplomatic embarrassment,[58] was pushed aside in favor of Deng Xiaoping protégés. In Japan, Ohira's successor Suzuki Zenkō was having a difficult time coordinating the contentious LDP factions. Hua was replaced by Hu Yaobang in 1981; Suzuki by Naksone Yashuhiro the following year.

There were also leadership changes in the Soviet Union, with former KGB head Yuri Andropov succeeding Leonid Brezhnev in 1982. Andropov then passed away only fifteen months later; and his successor Konstantin Chernenko thirteen months after that.

THE TEXTBOOK ISSUE

In 1982 a new and highly contentious issue burst into Sino-Japanese relations, ironically initiated from within the Japanese side. Friction had existed for decades between the left-leaning Japanese teachers' union Nikyōso and the conservative bureaucrats of the country's education ministry, frequently focusing on how Japan's activities in World War II were depicted. As early as 1965, historian Ienaga Saburō had filed suit against the ministry's censorship of texts he had authored, the first of several attempts to end such actions.

Hence, when in late June, several Japanese newspapers reported that high school history textbooks had replaced the word *shinryaku*, meaning "aggression," with *shinshutsu*, "advancement," to describe the Japanese military's actions in China during World War II, their reports were plausible and quickly escalated into an multinational incident that continued even after it turned out that the reports were distorted—no textbooks had been revised that year—and *Sankei Shimbun*, among other media, issued apologies to its readers.

In Japan, some suspected that there had been collusion between Nikyōso and Beijing to contrive the issue.[59] Other Japanese scholars of China opined that the militant Chinese attitude, even after the apology and the Tokyo government's promise to re-revise texts that had never actually been revised, reflected the unsettled leadership conditions within the highest levels of the CCP.

Whatever the reasons, the Beijing biweekly *Hongqi* (Red Flag) linked the alleged textbook revisions with a recently released patriotic Japanese film and excoriated the Tokyo government for glorifying war. *Xinhua* provided additional details and hinted that Prime Minister Suzuki's scheduled state visit to Beijing might not take place. Adding to Chinese outrage were the revelations in a book published by a Japanese author the year before in which he detailed the ghastly wartime biological experiments of Unit 731 of the Imperial Japanese Army.[60]

Suzuki's visit did take place, though the textbook issue and revelation of gruesome medical experiments put him in a poor negotiating position. The Chinese government had obtained two valuable additional levers to use against its Japanese counterpart, and proceeded to wield them skillfully. A museum was founded in Harbin, the epicenter of Unit 731's experiments: it quickly became a standard part of visits by both domestic and foreign tourists as well as a staple of field trips for schoolchildren. Beijing also paid more careful attention to Japan's yearly textbook decisions, commenting in detail about what it found objectionable.

STRAINS ACCUMULATE

Chinese attention also extended to who attended periodic ceremonies at the Yasukuni Shrine, how this compared with the number and rank of officials who had paid their respects in previous years, and whether the individuals attended in a personal or official capacity. Closely watched as well were periodic discussions in Japan about how sacrosanct the self-imposed 1 percent of GNP limit on defense expenditures was. Chinese media invariably interpreted such discussions as indicative of growing remilitarization. This scrutiny, however, came at the cost of arousing a backlash among Japanese who resented being told what to do by foreign sources.

The Japanese government's desire to pursue a foreign policy of equidistance proved difficult to operationalize, with the United States pressing for a stronger Japanese defense commitment and the Soviet Union railing against it. Chinese relations with the Soviet Union began a warming trend in 1981, causing concern in Tokyo. At first denied by Deng Xiaoping and Zhao Ziyang,[61] the signs became increasingly obvious. Moreover, the Chinese leadership began to send mixed signals, sometimes saying that they continued to support the U.S.-Japanese security treaty and at other times that they had never done so: Deng Xiaoping's remarks that the USSR was the major stumbling block to peace in Asia and had massed troops on the PRC's border as well as in Afghanistan and Mongolia were followed by Sun Pinghua, vice-president of the China-Japan Friendship Association, saying in October 1982 that China had never supported the U.S.-Japan security treaty.[62] A month later, the organization's president, Liao Chengzhi, told a former ambassador to Beijing that "China has never opposed or supported the … treaty."[63]

Declarations of support for Japanese ownership of the Kurils/Northern Territories also disappeared.

Japanese unease continued despite repeated assurances from Beijing leaders that closer Sino-Soviet relations would not come at the expense of China's relations with Japan. Tokyo also noted with some apprehension Washington's successive decisions to assist China militarily, wondering if this portended an American trend toward abandoning Japan in favor of a Sino-American alliance to counter the Soviet Union. This concern was lessened by the "Ron-Yasu" friendship that developed between Prime Minister Nakasone Yasuhiro and U.S. President Ronald Reagan.

HU YAOBANG REESTABLISHES AMICABLE RELATIONS

As U.S.-Japanese ties warmed, so also did Sino-Japanese relations. Hu Yaobang had already received high marks for his conciliatory policies toward Tibet when he arrived in Japan for an unusually long official visit that seemed to reflect the new leader's genuine desire to get to know the country better. Hu's disarmingly down-to-earth style was much praised. In one speech, for example, he remarked that Japanese journalists had made two comments about him: first, that he was frank, and second, that he was not familiar with Sino-Japanese relations. [64] He vowed to continue to be frank and to try hard to improve his knowledge. More substantively, Hu publicly supported Japan's right to defend itself. He further suggested that, since youth would be the peacemakers of the future, the youth exchange program should be greatly expanded: he would welcome 10,000 Japanese young people to visit China. Also, the PRC would be willing to accept so-called Silver Volunteers: retired engineers, professors, business managers, and scientists who would stay in China for periods ranging from a few months to a year giving guidance at factories, research institutes, and agricultural development projects.

However, the Chinese media continued a litany of alliterative complaints on trade, technology transfer, textbooks, temples, Taiwan, and war guilt, albeit in a more muted form. Chinese officials also became more willing to acknowledge the problems that the PRC's economic structure posed to potential donors and investors, with economic planning head Song Ping and Finance Minister Wang Bingqian telling delegates to the country's National People's Congress that much of the country's industry was hopelessly inefficient and outdated, turned out shoddy unsalable goods, had expanded heavy industry too quickly relative to light industry, and lacked managerial expertise due to past rigid state control, thus causing poor supervision of staff and finances.[65] Japanese sources, who had complained about these factors for some time, expressed pleasure that they were being acknowledged and hoped they would be remedied.

Diagnosing the problems as emanating from transitioning so huge an economy from one that was centrally planned to one that was market-based was, however, easier than solving the problems. Strong, though publicly muted, differences of opinion emerged within the elite on how to do this, even as the inflation rate soared and popular anger, scarcely heard of in the Mao era, mounted. Acutely sensitive to spiraling inflation, since post–World War II hyperinflation had been a major factor enabling the CCP to seize power from the ruling KMT, the authorities tried various measures to cool the economy. The results were unsatisfactory, with students becoming particularly restive.

In August 1985, after Nakasone became the first post–World War II prime minister to visit the Yasukuni Shrine in his official capacity, the official Chinese response was muted: the deputy director of the party's propaganda bureau stated that the Chinese people felt no hatred toward Japan and noted that the Japanese people had different opinions on this matter (of visiting Yasukuni). The official's comments elicited a strong negative reaction among students, who had perhaps received behind-the-scenes encouragement of hard-liners within the leadership who regarded such views as traitorous.[66] Anti-Japanese protest rallies were held in several large cities with the demonstrators railing, sometimes violently, against revived Japanese militarism and Tokyo's attempt to re-create the Greater East Asia Co-prosperity Sphere of the 1930s, by which they meant placing the Chinese economy in thrall to that of Japan, with the collaboration of complaisant PRC officials.

Protests continued sporadically for the next two months, raising questions of what role the Chinese leadership, or a portion thereof, played in them. The students' mention of officials who collaborated with Japanese militarists and capitalists was eerily reminiscent of charges made during the Cultural Revolution, arousing suspicions that there was a power struggle within the elite. According to a Beijing University wall poster, an official had visited campus the day before, urging the students to be prudent and not damage Sino-Japanese relations. But he did not forbid the students to demonstrate, and clearly knew the demonstrations were going to happen. There was speculation that party and government, or factions therein who considered themselves vulnerable to charges of collaboration, were attempting to deflect public anger away from themselves by scapegoating Japan.

A respected Hong Kong magazine devoted a special edition to protests and their relationship to Japan, making the point that Beijing University students, in the process of forming a core organization to establish ties with students elsewhere in the country, had purposely adopted the slogans of the December 9, 1935, anti-Japan demonstrations it was ostensibly commemorating. The date was chosen for protective cover, since the PRC had officially designated the December 9 uprising to be a patriotic movement. The 1935 protest had been occasioned by the then-KMT government's signing an agreement with Japan to form a client state for the latter in China. The use of the December 9th slogans, which included "Protest against bureaucratism and unhealthy tendencies" and "Oppose those who seek wealth and power by betraying their country," were now, however, implicitly directed against the CCP. Under the umbrella of protests against Japan, other grievances were also noticeable, with rising prices and official corruption most prominent among them.

The mention of student liaison groups establishing ties with like-minded groups elsewhere also added to the leadership's concern. To questions of how to handle inflation was now added the specter of a return to the days of the Cultural Revolution, when rampaging Red Guards roamed the country in search of enemies to destroy.[67] After several days during which protestors in Sichuan province destroyed Japanese cars and Japanese businesses, authorities there moved to disabuse the networking students of any idea that repetition of 1935 slogans conferred immunity in the present day: they ruled that there had been no patriotic students among the rioters. The media declared that those who blindly rejected foreign things without clear understanding of historical conditions and China's trade policy were not patriotic, but narrowly nationalistic. Trade with Japan, they pointed out, had always been premised on the principle of equality and mutual benefit.[68] Readers were presumably expected to understand this as a refutation of charges that party and government were allowing Japan to gain control over China.

Conservative Japanese meanwhile speculated that Beijing had raised the Yasukuni Shrine issue as a bargaining chip ahead of Foreign Minister Abe Shintarō's visit, adding that, coming from a country with a nuclear arsenal, and whose naval commander had recently boasted that his country's submarine fleet now constituted an "underground Great Wall," the charges of Japanese militarism were ludicrous.[69]

Student concerns about a Japanese economic invasion notwithstanding, the PRC leadership continued to value Japanese participation in the economy: Deng Xiaoping observed to a visiting delegation that, if the volume of Sino-Japanese trade were 25 percent of Japan's total foreign trade, as opposed to the 6.2 percent it constituted at the beginning of 1986, this would benefit China while bringing no harm to Japan.[70]

THE KOKARYO/GUANGHUA DORMITORY CASE

The following year, a new issue entered the long list of Sino-Japanese frictions, involving a Kyōto University student dormitory that the government of the Republic of China, that is, Taiwan, had purchased in 1952, at the time Tokyo acknowledged it as the legitimate government of China. When, after normalization, the Beijing government laid claim to the facility, the issue entered the Japanese court system, accompanied by a steady stream of complaints from Beijing that this was an administrative matter, not one for the judicial authorities, and that any allegations to the contrary were part of a plot to create the "two-Chinas" policy that Tokyo had pledged never to support.

A lower court ruled that the dormitory belonged to the PRC, after which Taiwan appealed the case to the Osaka Intermediate Court. The latter ordered the lower court to reconsider its judgment. It did so, angering Beijing by reversing itself and awarding the facility to Taiwan. Nakasone, whose words sometimes indicated that he would have liked to settle the issue administratively, replied that Beijing must respect Japanese law on this matter. The case was appealed to the Japanese Supreme Court, which failed to rule on it for twenty years before finally awarding ownership on the facility to the PRC. In the interim, the dormitory issue became one more irritant in Sino-Japanese relations, to be raised intermittently when Beijing deemed it appropriate. So as well did the issue of "comfort women," a euphemism for women whom the Japanese military supplied to troops for sexual purposes, and whom the GOJ at first attempted to deny, and later, to apologize and compensate the survivors. Certain efforts were subsequently made to address the issue, but complicated by the revelation that at least some of the evidence advanced on behalf of the women had been falsified.[71]

THE DEMISE OF HU YAOBANG

In December 1986 new student demonstrations, not directed against Japan, broke out. Beginning in Hefei, Anhui, they quickly spread to seventeen cities including Beijing and Shanghai. Student grievances focused on a number of factors that included complaints about poor conditions on campus, advocacy of political and economic reforms, and demands for a crackdown against corruption. Hu Yaobang appeared to be sympathetic to the students, and the authorities at first took no actions to quell them. By the time the demonstrations became so large as to attract world attention, conservative leaders accused Hu Yaobang of mismanagement. He resigned in mid-January.[72]

The underlying reasons for removing Hu from office were related to the power struggle within the top leadership:his efforts to rejuvenate the elite, which had been a Deng Xiaoping initiative, put Hu at odds with senior officials in the party, government, and military. The PLA's high command had always been dubious about Hu, since he had had no military experience, and was able to block Deng's efforts to make him chair of the Central Military Commission, an action that separated the position of head of party and state from the commander-in-chief of the PRC's armed forces. Though unmentioned in public discourse, this ran directly counter to Mao Zedong's often cited dictum that the party must always control the gun, the gun must never control the party.

Hu was also blamed for championing the "rash advance" into industrialization that had caused many of the PRC's current problems, "presumptuously" making speeches without the prior approval of the CCP Central Committee, opposing the campaign against spiritual pollution, and a long list of other policies that were now regarded as, at best, misguided.[73]

Japan, though not included in the initial list of accusations against Hu, soon entered the litany of complaints against him. His opponents charged that Hu had "rashly" invited far too many Japanese students than the PRC could afford to host and that his Japan policy had been "arbitary." Japanese sources interpreted this to mean that Hu had not taken a tough enough stance against Tokyo.

In Japan, Nakasone, who had invested much time in Sino-Japanese relations as represented by Hu, was criticized by his opponents for the way in which he did so. Nakajima Mineo, perhaps the country's most prominent China specialist, said he had several times warned the prime minister against such a personal involvement with Hu, but that his administration, in haste to strengthen ties with China, had "not only willfully disregarded warning signs but failed to take prudent precautions in the face of political uncertainty in China."

The student demonstrations, Nakajima continued, had caught Deng Xiaoping and other top CCP leaders off guard; when they moved to suppress the demonstrations, they were simultaneously signaling the end of the assumption that economic reform would soon be followed by political reform. To make matters worse, Nakasone had taken a hastily arranged trip to Beijing to lay the cornerstone at the ceremonial opening of the Sino-Japanese Youth Center and had also apologized for the unfortunate remarks of one of his ministers.

Without thinking through its implications, Nakasone delivered a speech stating that young people are always the motivating force behind human progress, and that it had been the selfless struggle by a large number of Japanese young people that transformed feudal Japan into a fight against conservatives who wanted to block the path of reform. Conservative Chinese leaders saw Nakasone's blatant siding with the reformers as taking Hu's side in a domestic factional dispute and inciting the audience to fight against conservatives who were blocking the path of reform. According to Nakajima, this humiliated Hu, with PRC conservatives comparing him with Wang Jingwei, the KMT leader who attempted to make peace with the Japanese invaders in 1937 and is reviled in China as a traitor for having done so (see Chapter 2).[74]

Chinese sources continued to vigorously deny the existence of any power struggle,[75] and to reassure foreign investors that the open door to foreign investment would remain open. Indeed it did, though with numerous complaints from both sides about the shortcomings of the other, as detailed in Chapter 8. The two sides continued to bicker about visits to the Yasukuni Shrine, the disposition of the Kokaryo/Guanghua dormitory, the (un)fairness of Japanese restrictions on high-tech exports to the PRC as a result of the Toshiba corporation having violated restrictions on the sale of certain items to the Soviet Union, and whether or not Japan was remilitarizing. The Chinese side was able to marshal considerable evidence in favor of the last-named from Japanese sources. Whether Tokyo should participate in America's Strategic Defense Initiative (SDI) was heatedly debated within Japan, with the Chinese media devoting special attention to reporting the protests against it.

When, in 1985, the Ministry of Education instructed all prefectural boards of education to raise the *hinomaru* (rising sun) flag and sing the Kimigayo, which had served as the country's national anthem prior to 1945, there was vocal opposition that, like the textbook revision issue, reflected the ideological divide between education ministry bureaucrats who were predominantly conservative and the left-wing teachers' union. The former argued that these were no more than symbols of pride in one's nation that were common in all nations; the latter that they were symbols of past militarism and incipient ultra-nationalism. In the sense that the Kimigayo "glorifies" the emperor (the words merely wish him long life and praise his rule), the anthem's opponents regard it as unconstitutional, since the constitution clearly states that sovereignty belongs to the people. Hence, by simply quoting Japanese newspaper reports of protests against the flag and anthem, the Chinese media could circumvent charges of interfering in the domestic affairs of another country.

The same restraint was not always noticeable in the case of the Yasukuni Shrine, with Foreign Minister Wu Xueqian, on an official visit to Tokyo while Hu Yaobang was still in power, calling on cabinet ministers to stop visiting the shrine. His counterpart Abe Shintarō defended the visits by citing a prior agreement that neither nation should hurt the feelings of the other. Japanese regret for the war had been written into the 1972 communiqué, and neither the government of Japan nor the country's people were praising the war criminals; they were simply mourning those who had died.[76]

Evidence that might indicate a militarization of China was also present: the PRC was becoming a space power and an arms exporter. The disastrous explosion of America's *Challenger* space shuttle and the failure of a French Ariane launch had created an opening for Chinese satellite launches, which the PRC hastened to take advantage of.

INSENSITIVE REMARKS BY JAPANESE OFFICIALS

As these events were unfolding, a series of unfortunate remarks, some of which appeared to be intentionally provocative, exacerbated existing tensions. In 1986 Minister of Education Fujio Masayuki not only went to the Yasukuni Shrine on the anniversary of the World War II surrender, but also arrived in an official car with a police escort and commented publicly that visits by cabinet ministers ought to be acceptable and furthermore carried out with confidence. On the matter of Japan's invasion of China, Fujio said that the entire history of the world was one of invasion, and that it was time for Japan, which was certainly not the only country in the world to have committed acts of aggression, to shed its timidity. "Those guys (*yatsu*) who complain about [the textbooks] should look back themselves to see if they didn't commit similar acts in world history." He added that the Nanjing Massacre was intended to break down enemy resistance, that war means killing people, and that as far as international law was concerned, this did not constitute slaughtering. For good measure, Fujio added that Korea itself was partially responsible for Japan's 1901 annexation.

Unrepentant, and unwilling to acknowledge that his remarks had been a slip of the tongue (*shitsugen*), the minister refused to resign. Nakasone subsequently dismissed Fujio, stating that it was regrettable that his remarks had caused disorder in the country's foreign policy. *Renmin Ribao* applauded the dismissal, commenting that it was "the inevitable result of Fujio's perverse refusal to face present-day realities."[77]

Less than a year later, a Japanese official, later identified as Vice-Minister of Foreign Affairs Yanagiya Kensuke, was reported as responding to Deng Xiaoping's comments rejecting the right of Japanese courts to rule on the dormitory issue by saying he was "a man above the clouds." This did not seem out of line in Japan, since Deng's remarks were widely regarded as interference in the country's internal affairs, and the still-unnamed official had not spoken in a public context.

The Chinese press, however, reacted sharply, construing the remarks as indicating that the patriarch's age had left him mentally infirm and accused the official of "openly launching a malicious attack" that would adversely impact on bilateral relations.[78] It rejected explanations the reference was a carefully chosen term of respect, *keigo*, intended to convey that Deng had become such an awesome figure that Chinese diplomats may have become too reticent to brief him on the true state of bilateral relations. Even if true, said the Chinese media, it would not explain why, as reported in some sources, the minister had added that "anyone who gets old becomes hard-headed." An entire litany of grievances was attached to the remarks, including, among others, Japanese arrogance, the number of people killed in World War II, and the trade imbalance. Yanagiya announced his decision to take early retirement, with the Ministry of

Foreign Affairs stating unconvincingly that his resignation had nothing to do with the controversy about his remarks.[79]

New insensitive remarks occurred in 1988, with *Xinhua* quoting Watanabe Michio, director of the LDP's powerful Policy Coordination Council stating in an Osaka campaign speech that "lots of people in China's Shanxi[80] province are digging holes and living there. China is a country like that. It is because the politics are not so good."[81] Hong Kong's CCP-funded *Wen Wei Po* railed against this latest "attack." The ridiculous remarks showed Watanabe's ignorance that cave residences—which are quite different from Watanabe's description of digging holes—had won praise from international experts on human dwellings. *Wen Wei Po* added that the director's words "could have a new impact on the already unstable Japanese-Chinese friendship."[82] Watanabe subsequently apologized for his mistake, saying, according to *Xinhua*, that he should have shown more respect for China's historical background, its expansive territory, and the diversity of its people.[83]

However, a scant few weeks later, tempers flared over yet other comments. Referring to Deng Xiaoping's remarks that Chinese regret the existence of a handful of Japanese people who did not wish to see improvements in Sino-Japanese relations, head of the National Land Agency Okuno Seisuke, on an April visit to Yasukuni, opined that the Japanese people had been "twisted around" by such comments. Japan, he continued, fought World War II in order to secure its safety. Asia had been colonized by Caucasians at that time: Japan was no by no means a nation of aggression.[84]

Japanese right-wing groups responded to barrages of criticism in the PRC through protests when visiting dignitaries arrived, and by repeatedly defacing monuments to Sino-Japanese friendship. A hitherto unknown group calling itself Hotaru (firefly) took responsibility for a shooting incident at the Chinese consulate-general in Fukuoka in which no one was hurt.[85] The government, as distinct from some of its ministers, took an apologetic tone.

The same peculiar pattern of statements, that Sino-Japanese relations had never been better,[86] "generally good,"[87] or without "delicate problems,"[88] were interspersed with the heated arguments noted above, and statements that relations were not as good as might be wished. Still, the general attitude appeared to be that problems could be solved.[89]

THE TIANANMEN DEMONSTRATIONS AND SINO-JAPANESE RELATIONS

Official statements on good relations stretched into 1989, even as tensions grew. Chinese complaints about the trade imbalance were mitigated, though they did not disappear, after 1988 statistics revealed that Japan had run a trade deficit with China for the first time in five years. When Emperor Hirohito died in January, Beijing extended its condolences but sent only its foreign minister to the funeral, disappointing Tokyo's hopes for a higher-level personage. Qian Qichen's designation as envoy is likely to have represented a compromise between Japanese hopes and the distaste expressed by nationalistic Chinese that a man they believed responsible for Japan's wartime aggression should be honored in any way. In Fujian, a signature drive that must have received approval from at least some high-ranking officials urged the government to boycott the emperor's funeral completely and demanded that Japan pay compensation for its aggression against China during the war.[90]

Meanwhile, domestic discontent simmered in China. Unruly confrontations between Han Chinese and African students occurred in Beijing and Nanning, with the Africans charging racial discrimination.[91] Tibetans staged pro-independence demonstrations in Lhasa in March. The former confrontation was settled by deporting the students; the latter by the imposition of martial law and harsh punishments.

Resentment stemming from the pressures and imbalances that accompanied rapid economic development was rising among Han Chinese, particularly in urban areas. Inflation continued to increase as citizens scoffed at the government's statistics and expressed anger over corruption. There were also calls for political reform. The leadership debated how to handle these issues, being broadly divided between those who felt that more rigid control was needed and others who felt that the solution was more reform.

The mass demonstrations that began in Beijing and an estimated hundred other cities in April, hardly seemed to deter the Chinese media from their standard list of critical comments on Japan. Indeed, some Japanese believed that the Chinese leadership was using complaints against Japan to deflect its citizens' discontent with their own government.[92] When the Tokyo government suggested a 5.9 percent increase in the 1989 defense budget, the Chinese government, whose increase for defense that year was 12.6 percent,[93] protested vigorously.[94] The head of the CCP's United Front Work Department accused "Japanese groups" (i.e., not the Japanese government) of training and funding Tibetan demonstrators to provoke unrest in Lhasa.[95]

Simultaneous with these harsh criticisms, a mid-April article in *Beijing Review* entitled "Plum and Cherry Blossoms Jointly Blossom" described a warming trend in Sino-Japanese relations that was akin to the actual coming of spring, noting that bilateral relations had in recent years taken a down-to-earth, mature approach. The bases of healthy development had been established; more than a hundred Chinese cities had signed sister-city agreements with Japanese counterparts, and there was a "Japanese-learning craze" that reflected the desire of Chinese citizens to learn more about the country.[96] Premier Li Peng, regarded as a hard-liner, visited Tokyo, promising that his country's investment environment would improve and denying rumors of a power struggle that Party General Secretary Zhao Ziyang was rumored to be losing.[97]

As China's anti-party and government protests escalated in size and spread to more cities, the Japanese government maintained a business as usual attitude, interspersed with occasional expressions of concern for the safety of its nationals and those of its investments in the PRC. Though not comparable to China's problems, Japan was also experiencing economic difficulties and political instability. In early June, Prime Minister Takeshita resigned in disgrace after being implicated in a financial scandal. Amusingly, a Chinese student in the country remarked that the former prime minister's transgressions were trivial compared to what was common in the PRC.[98]

When the Beijing government's brutal crackdown on the demonstrations occurred, Prime Minister Uno Sōsuke had been in office just over one day. Although the Japanese public reacted with horror at images of tanks pushing through crowds, unarmed demonstrators and passersby being shot, and the brutal repression that followed, Uno refused to condemn Beijing's actions. Nor did he so much as imply that Sino-Japanese relations might be adversely affected by it, even when media accounts were confirmed by hastily evacuated Japanese eyewitnesses. Uno responded to calls from Diet members with different party affiliations to impose sanctions by saying bluntly that he had no intention of doing so.[99] Although he regretted the deaths, taking a stronger position would constitute interference in the internal affairs of another country. He would offer "neighborly" advice to keep China from being isolated by the international community.

As news of the arrest and torture of demonstrators continued, Uno suggested that the Chinese leadership "exercise self-restraint when dealing with their domestic situation."[100] Japan did permit a member of the staff of the Chinese embassy in Tokyo to defect to a third country,[101] but did not agree to extend the visas of students who claimed asylum because while in Japan, they had taken part in demonstrations supporting their countrymen in the PRC.[102]

Uno resigned after little more than fifty days in office, though his attitude toward China was not an important factor. His championing of an unpopular consumption tax, added to revelations that he had failed to properly support a geisha he had been associated with, led to the LDP's defeat in a House of Councillors election that Uno took responsibility for.

Uno's successor Kaifu Toshiki headed an LDP faction too small to implement the reforms Kaifu had promised. He was also tainted by his association with a financial scandal involving the Sagawa Express trucking company's donations to the LDP via organized crime intermediaries. Kaifu resigned after less than two years in office, succeeded by Miyazawa Kiichi. In the interim, Japan's economic position continued to deteriorate in tandem with its unstable political leadership.

AFTERMATH OF THE TIANANMEN DEMONSTRATIONS

The Japanese government's nonjudgmental attitude was appreciated by the new, now more conservative Chinese leadership. Zhao Ziyang was placed under house arrest, replaced by Jiang Zemin, formerly party secretary in Shanghai. Li Peng specifically thanked Tokyo for its understanding.[103] Two days after the events of June 4, a delegation of reporters from major Japanese newspapers began a ten-day visit to the Guangxi Zhuang Autonomous Region, with Beijing Radio reporting that, the rumors they had heard notwithstanding, the group found conditions in that region stable and the investment environment favorable.[104] By two weeks later, 236 Japanese businessmen had registered their return with the embassy in Beijing along with smaller numbers of journalists, volunteer workers, students, and teachers.[105]

While welcomed by the Chinese leadership, Japan's attitude made it an outlier among major international actors, causing considerable anxiety within the country. There was trenchant criticism from international media, more subtle pressure from several governments, and barbed comments from widely respected commentators, including Soviet physicist and human rights activist Andrei Sakharov, who flatly rejected the contention that what had happened at Tiananmen Square should be regarded as an internal affair of the country.[106] China, meanwhile, railed against "gross interference" in the PRCs internal affairs after, for example, a G-7 meeting in Paris that condemned Beijing. Japan signed the Paris declaration though, given its behavior toward the PRC government, apparently half-heartedly.[107]

The Tokyo government's compliant attitude also put it at odds with pro-reform Chinese. Interviewed on Japanese television network NHK, writer Liu Binyan who had been dismissed by *Renmin Ribao* and from the CCP for his support of the 1986–1987 student demonstrations, warned that the Chinese people would remember Japan's support to a repressive regime as a new crime committed by the country's government.[108]

Other Chinese dissident groups were more militant. Japan Airlines received death threats in which a group claiming to be "the Supreme Command for Death Squads" vowed to assassinate one Japanese a week, to include businesspeople, tourists, diplomats, their family members, students, teachers, and any others, excluding journalists, in retaliation against Japan's cooperation with the Chinese government.[109] Another group, identifying itself as the "Xueguang (Bright Blood) Dare to Die Squad," vowed to kill two Japanese each month, this time exempting both journalists and embassy personnel, beginning August 15th, the anniversary of Japan's World War II surrender.[110]

This threat seemed to have credence when, a short while later, a plane crash claimed the lives of two Japanese nationals. The Xueguang group claimed responsibility, though the Civil Air Administration of China (CAAC) denied that the plane, whose crash killed thirty-four persons, had been sabotaged.[111] Other groups including the consulates-general in Shanghai, Shenyang, and Hong Kong, as well as several business establishments, received similar threat letters, some of them advising against Japan's participation in the Asian games that were scheduled for the following year lest "misfortune" befall those who attended. *Kyodo* noted that none of these threats were reported in the Chinese press.[112] After meeting with British Prime Minister Margaret Thatcher, Uno agreed to suspend a $5.8 billion soft loan to the PRC that had been promised the year before, though with no acknowledgment that he was responding to either Thatcher's powers of persuasion or to the threats.[113]

Other, unrelated, issues continued to mar Sino-Japanese relations as well. Discussions on how to rebalance the relationship were complicated by the publication by Japanese historians of a meticulously documented study of the imperial army's use of poison gas in World War II. Its release at this time was almost certainly timed to coincide with the Yasukuni Shrine's annual commemoration of the end of the war. As the professors pointed out, the use of poison gas violated the 1925 Geneva Accords, to which Japan was a signatory.[114] The impetus for the research had come five years before, when one of the authors came across formerly classified documents while conducting research in an American archive.

A second issue arose when boats containing large numbers of persons claiming to be escaping persecution in Vietnam sought asylum in Japan. Investigation showed that an estimated two-thirds of the refugees were Han Chinese from Fujian province,[115] setting in train a lengthy series of negotiations between Tokyo and a Beijing government that seemed reluctant to take them back. Not surprisingly, the poison gas issue was well covered by the Chinese media, while the issue of repatriation of the bogus Vietnamese went unmentioned.

More surprising was the fact that the Chinese press paid little attention to a major development in Japanese defense policy: in August, the staunchly pacifist Japan Socialist Party announced that it now not only accepted the continuation of the U.S.-Japan Mutual Security Treaty "as a means of insuring diplomatic continuity," but also the constitutionality of the Self-Defense Forces (SDF), albeit emphasizing that the SDF were to be under strict civilian control. It continued to maintain, however, that joint U.S.-SDF drills were unconstitutional.[116] The reason for what appeared to be a startling change in ideology was that, having achieved victory in the last House of Councillors election, the JSP now believed that there was a realistic possibility of its taking control of the more powerful lower house, and wanted to attract the support of more independent voters.

Japan continued on the defensive internationally, with those opposed to sanctions arguing, first, that Japan was too deeply involved with the Chinese economy to take strong action without hurting itself. China's cumulative debts to Japan were estimated at $40 billion, and the PRC's continued political as well as economic evolution was heavily dependent on Japanese aid. Second, a stable relationship between the two countries was essential to the security of Asia as a whole. Among other issues, Beijing held the key to a settlement of the troubled situation in Cambodia. They concluded that one should hate the crime but not the persons who committed it.

At a meeting with European countries in October, delegates accused Japan of breaking with the Paris declaration and wondered if it were breaking with the West as well. One delegate commented that

> Japan is once more finding an excuse to justify a selfish, self-centered [i.e., economically motivated] policy. The French risked their diplomatic relations to help smuggle student leaders out of China and hosted the founding of the Foundation for Democracy in China. Japan, which is about to become one of the great powers, has lost yet another opportunity to take the moral upper ground.[117]

Japanese officials' rejoinders that their reluctance to criticize China stemmed from a deep sense of guilt over their country's aggression against China during World War II infuriated some of the Europeans, who wondered why a recent Japanese court decision had upheld the Education Ministry's right to censor textbooks: if such a guilt complex really existed, the Japanese population should rise up in protest against the ruling. European delegates also showed little sympathy for the Japanese position that isolation of China would have a worse effect than trying to convince it that such repressive behavior was counterproductive.

Some Japanese delegates privately—but, importantly, they did not speak out publicly—complained that the Europeans were attempting to force their view of human rights on a culture that looked at the issue differently. Or that it was easy for Europeans to talk about justice because China was so far away from them, but that the view would look different were they, like Japan, close by. There was, they argued, a special relationship between the two that enabled Japan to encourage Beijing to move toward a more open, liberal society, whereas cornering it would have the opposite effect. Another delegate, more critical of his government, stated that Japanese citizens, in contrast to their leaders, had never had a worse view of China.[118]

The 40th anniversary of the founding of the PRC occurred amidst tight security and the announcement of a stringent austerity program to deal with the country's financial difficulties. After three years, the government predicted —accurately—that it would be possible for economic reforms to move forward again. As 1989 closed, the fourth meeting of the Sino-Japanese Friendship Association convened in Tokyo, with Chairperson Sun Pinghua stating delicately that "the recent turmoil in Beijing [has] had a certain influence on the Sino-Japanese friendship movement."[119]

6

Tarnished Gold, 1990-2006

RETURNING TO THE STATUS QUO ANTE

Much of the year following what the Chinese press referred to as "the Tiananmen incident" was spent in trying to return Sino-Japanese relations to their pre-incident status. The Japanese government, caught between foreign governments' pressure for sanctions and Beijing's desire to re-normalize relations, tended to placate China to the extent possible. Loans continued, rationalized with the explanation that they were made for humanitarian purposes: water treatment plants, rural electrification projects, and anti-malaria vaccines. An organization for nongovernmental aid was established "to develop a sound and stable economic relationship between China and Japan" with 120 Japanese banks and trading firms participating and an illustrious board of advisers that included a former prime minister and a former MITI head.[1] In addition to the Japanese government's refusal to extend the visas of Chinese students who claimed that they would face retaliation at home for having participated in pro-democracy demonstrations, the GOJ refused to allow a boat containing avowed pro-democracy advocates from landing, and returned to China an asylum seeker who had hijacked a plane.[2]

While the Beijing leadership must have been pleased with these decisions, it continued to press Tokyo for full resumption of loans while keeping up a barrage of criticism on other issues.

The intent seemed to be to wean Japan away from its dependence on the United States: Japan's future, numerous media commentary stated, was in Asia. At the same time, there was evident unease about the role that Japan might play if it made good on its plans to become a major Asian or international political power.³ The implication appeared to be that, while Japan could be tolerated as a major economic actor, there was cause for concern if economic power were coupled with political clout. When Prime Minister Kaifu made separate trips to Europe, the Middle East, and South Asia, the Chinese press described his hosts as less interested in him than his money: "not Kaifu but *saifu*" (using the Japanese word for wallet) and predicted that loans would result in Tokyo's having more say in the conduct of recipient countries' foreign policies.⁴

After Tokyo, largely responding to American pressure, began talking about contributing troops to the United Nations peacekeeping operations, there were concerns that a Japanese economic, political, and military nexus was being created.

As this was happening, the nationalism that Beijing was encouraging as a way to repair its strained relationship with intellectuals after the Tiananmen demonstrations was proving all too popular.⁵ A group of patriots from Hong Kong and Taiwan set sail to claim the Diaoyu/Senkaku Islands for whichever China they claimed to represent,⁶ but were turned back by Japanese coast guard ships. Beijing's deputy foreign minister issued a protest that students regarded as far too tepid, terming it "appeasement in the guise of protest."⁷ As well, in mid-October, prominent Japanese author and Diet member Ishihara Shintarō announced that the Nanjing Massacre was a lie perpetrated by the Chinese government: it had never happened. Faced with criticism from within Japan as well as from China, Ishihara was adamant, even reiterating his statement a few weeks later.⁸

PRC students declared their intention to demonstrate, as Beijing, anxious to get Japanese loans to help its economy recover from the post-Tiananmen deflation, warned them against doing so. Into this already volatile mix, unconfirmed reports from Taiwan stated that the GOJ was considering officially recognizing a lighthouse that Japanese rightists had built on one of the disputed islands.⁹ This angered the students still more: accusing their own government of capitulating to plans to re-create the Greater East Asian Co-Prosperity Sphere, activists vented their anger in demonstrations proclaiming, "We don't want Japanese money, we want the Diaoyu."¹⁰

Some Chinese intellectuals took the same position, with one Hong Kong paper citing a member of the Chinese Academy of Sciences as criticizing Beijing's "weak" stance "because it badly needs Japanese loans."[11] As it was not in Beijing's interests to allow the situation to escalate, efforts were made to soothe the nationalists. Demonstrations were forbidden; the mainland press did not report what was happening, and outsiders received their information from Hong Kong newspapers with sources inside China.

The long-awaited loan package was finalized in early November 1990,[12] with both sides at pains to restore comity. China also expressed satisfaction with the LDP's decision, reached after strong resistance from opposition parties, to withdraw legislation that would allow Japan to participate in UN peacekeeping operations.[13] And, at the end of November, Premier Li Peng assured a high-level Japanese delegation that China was "full of hope" since the leadership was "strong and the people treasure stability." Despite occasional frictions, bilateral relations calmed.

The two sides began to discuss a visit by the imperial couple to China, which would be a first in the two millennia history of Sino-Japanese contacts. The trip was nearly derailed when, in February 1992, the PRC's National People's Congress passed a law unilaterally annexing the many disputed islands China had claimed, including the Diaoyu/Senkaku group. In the end, the Japanese foreign ministry decided to accept its counterpart's assurance that there had been no change in policy.

Beijing leaders greatly desired the trip, expecting an imperial apology for Japanese conduct during World War II and aware as well of the symbolic implication of his majesty's visit to the capital. A Hong Kong newspaper reported that the government had banned all demonstrations during the emperor's visit;[14] many years later, *Asahi*, citing recently declassified documents, revealed that there had been an agreement on the contentious issue of the comfort women, who had been pressed into prostitution for the benefit of the Japanese military.[15]

In Japan, not only the wording of the apology but also the visit itself was contentious. Right of center critics accused the government of using the emperor to "play the China card," with arch-conservative Ishihara Shintarō shouting that accusation on a popular national television show before the station quickly cut to a commercial. Leftists, many of whom were opposed to the imperial system itself, cited the constitution's denial of any political role for the emperor, and denied the foreign ministry's contention that the trip was not political. The Japanese press reported fierce infighting at the Imperial Household Agency on the exact wording of the statement to be issued.[16]

To considerable relief on both sides, the trip went smoothly. The emperor, speaking at a ceremonial dinner, said only that in the long history of relationships between the two countries, "There was an unfortunate period in which my country inflicted great suffering on the people of China. About this, I feel deep sadness."[17] Though scarcely the apology the Chinese government would have wanted and barely mentioned in the PRC's media, it was apparently enough. Foreign ministry spokesperson Wu Jianmin told *Kyodo* that "it is up to the Japanese side to decide what remarks the emperor will make during his visit to China,"[18] and President Yang Shangkun declared the visit a success.[19]

FAMILIAR TENSIONS RETURN

This era of relatively good feeling began to end in the latter half of 1994 when perennial problems began to assume more salience. One speculation is that, as Western powers loosened post-Tiananmen sanctions against China and restored a full range of contacts, Beijing had less reason to take a low-key attitude toward irritants.[20] The bursting of the Japanese economic bubble in the early 1990s also dimmed its luster in Chinese eyes. In Tokyo, there was resentment that the Chinese government had shown insufficient gratitude toward the support it had rendered.

Complaints spanned a range of issues. Beijing protested that an invitation to Taiwan's vice-premier to attend the Asian Games in Hiroshima was a violation of the one-China policy, cancelling a meeting of the Sino-Japanese Friendship Committee.[21] On the Japanese side, more attention began to be focused on China's rising defense budgets, the PRC's arms sales abroad, and its nuclear testing, with Tokyo warning it would cut aid if they were continued. According to an internal Chinese document procured by a Japanese newspaper in January, the leadership did not take Japanese concerns about nuclear testing and rising military budgets seriously, and was confident that Japan would accept its request for a large loan program.[22]

Whether because of these revelations or not, after the PRC conducted a test in May, Japan made good on its threat. Beijing retorted angrily that these were not gifts but contributions to mutual benefit. Though Japanese aid had long been considered reparations in disguise—a fiction likely agreed upon in order to preserve continuity with Chiang Kai-shek's pronouncement decades before that China would not to ask for reparations (see Chapter 3)—first Premier Li Peng and later President Jiang Zemin now explicitly linked the reparations issue to aid.

Officially, Beijing did not demand compensation, but took no apparent steps to curb the demands of those who were or said they were victims. State-controlled media regularly covered their ongoing remonstrations. This fed into the larger theme of Japan's unwillingness to acknowledge in a sufficiently convincing manner its remorse over its actions during World War II. A crescendo of publicity on Japanese atrocities grew in the months before the anniversary of the end of the war. Archival material was released, museum exhibitions opened, books published, and meetings arranged at which survivors recounted their experiences in horrifying detail. The Chinese media paid close attention to Prime Minister Murayama's "no war resolution" as it was being debated in the Diet. After bitter arguments among different parties and factions, a compromise was reached that substituted "acts of aggression" for "war of aggression" and the resolution passed, albeit in a form that was far less than satisfactory to the Chinese side. *Shijie Zhishi* termed it "like carrying a pipa to cover half one's face," an allusion to an apology made with great reluctance only after repeated requests.[23]

Prime Minister Murayama visited China, making what was the most abject apology China had received heretofore. It was to become the touchstone for all subsequent prime ministers to declare their adherence. Expressing "deep remorse and heartfelt apology for the damage and sufferings caused by [his] country's colonial rule and aggression," Murayama added that Japan must learn from the lessons of history and never repeat the errors of the past. He also promised that no Taiwan ministers would henceforth be allowed to visit Japan. Xinhua termed the statements "positive."[24]

However, the good impression made by Murayama was marred by yet another in the succession of statements by gaffe-prone cabinet members: Education Minister Shimamura Yoshinobu questioned the need for Japan to apologize for its wartime atrocities, saying that "invasion or noninvasion is a question of how you think about it." *Renmin Ribao* responded that these and other officials' remarks that indicated Japan did not sincerely regret its wartime actions: four cabinet ministers in the past decade had made similar remarks, and no less than nine had paid their respects at the Yasukuni Shrine on the anniversary of Japan's defeat.[25]

Murayama, who was Japan's first socialist prime minister in fifty years, resigned after his party, one of three in an unstable coalition, was weakened by criticism for its handling of the Aum Shinrikyo cult's poison gas attack on the Tokyo subway system and poor election results. Though doubtless sorry to see Murayama, whose apology had been the most abject to date, go, Chinese analysts opined that his successor, the LDP's Hashimoto Ryūtarō, was likely to maintain continuity with past policies.[26]

Tokyo, however, had approached the United States for a closer security arrangement prompted by Chinese actions in 1995–1996 that seemed aimed at an invasion of Taiwan (see Chapter 10). Unwilling to publicly acknowledge that its actions played any part in Japanese anxieties, Beijing chose to interpret the agreement as a plot for American dominance of Asia through a revitalized Japanese military. It moved closer to Russia, establishing the Shanghai Cooperative Organization with Moscow and several Central Asian states, and raising the possibility of a Sino-Russian entente that could constrain Japanese interests in access to energy resources and in regaining the Kuril/Northern Territories.

MARITIME ISSUES

Chinese sources also noted that on July 14, six days before the Diet adopted a United Nations Commission on the Law of the Sea (UNCLOS) agreement fixing the nation's exclusive economic zone at 200 miles, the Japanese right-wing youth group Seinenkai had built a lighthouse on the largest of the disputed Diaoyu/Senkaku Islands. On July 29th, China conducted another nuclear test. And Hashimoto elected to pay a visit to the Yasukuni Shrine, becoming the first incumbent prime minister since Nakasone in 1985 to do so. Terming questions on whether he had visited in his public or private capacity and any connection with the test "ridiculous," Hashimoto explained that he had chosen the date because it was his 59th birthday.

A Chinese activist group mobilized to demand that troops be sent to occupy the islands, which, despite a good deal of anti-Japanese invective in the official media and the presence of a few exploration ships in the area near the islands, did not happen. In fact, both governments seemed anxious to cool hot tempers in their respective countries A few weeks after his visit to Yasukuni, at a Nippon Budōkan ceremony to commemorate the end of World War II, Hashimoto expressed "deep remorse" for the victims of Japan's wartime acts.[27]

Attempting to blunt domestic criticism that Beijing was sacrificing its territorial claims in return for financial aid, Ministry of Foreign Affairs spokesperson Shen Guofang denied there was any connection between protecting the PRC's sovereignty over the islands and Japanese loans to China.[28] A few days later, the Japanese foreign ministry announced that it had decided to resume grants since Beijing had promised to suspend testing.[29] Still, a scheduled trip by Vice-Premier Li Lanqing to Tokyo was postponed, accompanied by denials that it was related to strained relations.[30]

Hong Kong sources reported that Jiang Zemin had ordered the country's media not to mention anti-Japanese activities; one Beijing-based activist was sent "on assignment" to Lanzhou, and another, a *Worker's Daily* journalist, was ordered south with instructions to report back to his office at each stop on the Beijing to Kowloon railway. Since the anniversary of the Mukden incident, which provided Japan with a pretext for invading Manchuria in September 18, 1931, the leadership feared a return of the 1989 demonstrations by militants using protests against their government's weak-kneed stance on the islands as their overt cause. University administrators and government officials held meetings with activist groups. The incidence of protests abated,[31] but the atmosphere remained tense into October, amid Hong Kong reports that the activists' real target was their "corrupt, incompetent government."[32]

A curious trend of denunciation and gestures of friendship ensued, with Beijing warning that the Japanese government would have to work harder to improve trade ties at the same time that it eagerly sought Japanese loans and products[33] even as Premier Li Peng repeated the mantra that the two countries were close neighbors separated only by a narrow strip of water.[34] In Japan, approval of loans faced stiff opposition from conservative factions in the LDP, and best-selling author/Diet member Ishihara Shintarō referred to China by the derogatory term "Shina."[35] As the year closed, the two sides announced their intention to upgrade their sporadic security talks to ministerial level,[36] and an agreement on a fourth batch of Japanese loans was signed.[37]

Exchanges of pleasantries by high-ranking officials notwithstanding, a distinct note of disdain for Japan became noticeable. Beijing media reported in detail Japan's ongoing difficulties in pulling its economy out of deflation. Since China had become its largest trading partner in 1996, Japan would need it, and Asia, more than they needed Japan.[38] A poll released in February 1997 indicated that 99.4 percent of the 15,000 respondents vowed that they would always remember the Japanese invasion and 95.0 percent that the Diaoyu Islands belonged to China. "Most" respondents—interestingly, the only item in a long list with no percentages attached—preferred Chinese-made televisions to famous-named Japanese brands.[39] Although Hashimoto did not attend spring festival rites at Yasukuni, Chinese media waxed wroth over the 150 Diet members who did.[40]

In Japan, concerns mounted. There had been a marked increase in illegal immigration, mostly from the PRC, and the recovery of the American economy seemed to have resulted in a decline in Washington's concern with Japan: China might become Washington's top priority and Japan left out.[41] At the same time, there was a spike in the number of Chinese ships into the waters surrounding the disputed islands.[42] A threatened landing by Hong Kong activists prompted a group led by prominent Diet member Nishimura Shingo, to counter that they intended to get the "do-nothing Japanese government back on the right track" of assertively exercising its sovereignty.[43] A few days later, several hundred Hong Kong activists burned the Japanese flag, though event organizers could not explain why their numbers were down from the 14,000 who had done so only a year before.[44]

In China, a memorial hall was opened to commemorate the 60th anniversary of the Marco Polo Bridge incident of 1937,[45] and a multivolume history of World War II was published.[46] The media complained frequently about the revised U.S.-Japan security guidelines. Some conciliatory gestures occurred: for example, the Chinese ambassador to Tokyo suggested that the island dispute be postponed;[47] the Chinese Foreign Ministry office refused to accept a petition from angry Diaoyu protestors in Hong Kong;[48] and the Beijing government ordered a restaurant to remove a sign banning Japanese customers.[49] Nonetheless, *Yomiuri* declared that "in fact each nation's view of the other has never been worse, particularly in the younger generation."[50]

THE ASIAN CURRENCY CRISIS

The Asian currency crisis that emerged in 1997 provided another irritant. Japan, which had been experiencing deflation for several years before the crisis, was criticized for not doing more for Asian countries, while China received credit for not devaluating the nonconvertible yuan.[51] The value of the yen dropped precipitously, raising fears that it could pull the economy of the region down with it. When the Japanese central bank and the U.S. Federal Reserve Bank intervened to bolster the yen, *Wen Wei Po* charged that they had acted only after realizing they had miscalculated the effect that it would have on their own economies.[52] The effect was felt nonetheless, with more than 10,000 Japanese companies declaring bankruptcy in the first half of 1998, the second highest number in the postwar period.[53]

If, as Chinese sources suspected, there was U.S.-Japanese collusion in their response to the financial crisis, it did not extend to other sectors. President Clinton, eager to absent himself from Washington due to a sexual scandal, advanced the date of his scheduled visit from the fall to June. Arousing fears in Tokyo about the U.S. abandoning it in favor of China, Clinton did not visit Japan, giving rise to the phrase "Japan passing." He also publicly praised China for its response to the Asian financial crisis of 1997, remaining silent about Japan's contribution although it was numerically larger.[54]

Possibly as a quid pro quo to his hosts for agreeing to advance the date of his visit, the president, while answering questions on a Shanghai radio show, stated a formula that seemed to soften the American commitment to Taiwan (see Chapter 9). The Chinese foreign ministry then put pressure on Japan to do the same. Prime Minister Obuchi had recently apologized to South Korea for his country's actions in World War II, with its leaders declaring that they had accepted it. This led Chinese officials to expect that a more penitent statement from Obuchi, as well as a statement indicating that Japan accepted the PRC's sovereignty over Taiwan. The Japanese side replied that it would not accede to Beijing's demands, with Jiang Zemin postponing his trip to Tokyo by several months as the two sides conferred privately on the matter.

JIANG ZEMIN VISITS JAPAN

Jiang went to Japan at the end of November, although no understanding had been reached on several contentious matters. He then lectured his audience in a manner that was offensive even to pro-Chinese Japanese. Jiang's choice of venue to do so was especially inappropriate: a ceremonial dinner with the imperial couple that, consonant with the postwar constitution that had stripped the emperor of all but ceremonial power, was supposed to be nonpolitical. Jiang received only a reiteration of Murayama's apology and the statement of Japan's position on Taiwan that was part of the 1972 normalization agreement. Several pre-arranged agreements on such topics as youth exchanges were signed but, tellingly, no joint communiqué was issued. While the Japanese press and public opinion reacted negatively to Jiang's visit, the Chinese media described it as "smooth and successful," with foreign ministry spokesperson Zhu Bangzao stating that "the Chinese side has published similar joint documents with many other countries and many of them were not signed. This will not affect the effect of the document."[55] The disastrous nature of the visit was known to Chinese diplomats and intellectuals, though not publicly spoken of.[56]

There followed a period of each side taking actions that worried the other. Ever-increasing Chinese defense budgets were accompanied by successful tests of new weapons such as the DF-31 ICBM, described by Western sources as giving the PRC a major strike capability that would be difficult to counterattack at any stage of its operation.[57] Larger numbers of Chinese ships appeared in waters around the Diaoyu/Senkaku Islands, prompting fears that the PRC meant to turn the East China Sea into "a Chinese bathtub."[58]

Japan responded in ways that worried China. Firebrand nationalist author Ishihara Shintarō was elected mayor of Tokyo, and at his first post-election press conference criticized both China's human rights record and its treatment of Tibetans.[59] Compounding his previous derogatory reference to China as "Shina,"[60] Ishihara personally went to Taiwan to deliver aid after a devastating earthquake hit the island in September 1999. The PRC also objected vociferously to talk of revising the Japanese constitution and to the Diet passing three defense bills. Ironically, while Chinese media portrayed the closer U.S.-Japanese defense relationship as evidence of a plot to encircle China,[61] the Obuchi administration expressed concern about closer Sino-American ties.[62] Another bill designated the *hinomaru* as the national flag and the Kimigayo as the national anthem.[63] Since both had been used prior to Japan's defeat in 1945, Beijing interpreted the bill as proof of the revival of militarism.

As well, Beijing watched carefully Japanese discussions on joining the U.S. Theater Missile Defense, arguing that "the purpose of making a shield first is to make a sword later"[64] (see Chapter 9). *Xinhua* continued to release counts of how many ministers and Diet members paid their respects at the

Yasukuni Shrine on commemorative and festival days. When Japan, in its ongoing effort to obtain a permanent seat on the UN Security Council, argued that it was one of the largest contributors to the United Nations budget, *Xinhua* asked if the Security Council were "a peddler who sells seats to the highest bidder."[65] Japanese politicians continued to make less than diplomatic statements, such as Nishimura Shingo's pronouncement that Japan should consider having nuclear weapons, with Beijing only slightly mollified by his immediate dismissal from the cabinet.[66]

Trade dropped. Although there were a number of causes, including the Asian currency crisis, Zhu Rongji's attempt to restructure the Chinese economy, and a rising yen, Japanese investment had already begun declining due to a deteriorating investment climate in the PRC. Chinese policy had since the mid-1990s begun removing some of the more attractive tax benefits foreign investors had enjoyed—for example, reducing the refund from the value added tax (VAT). The central government had failed to bail out major provincial investment company GITIC when it defaulted on an $8.75 million payment, thus causing future potential investors to reassess their exposure. And, Japanese business executives complained, worsening local government corruption had increased the costs of doing business.[67]

An anti-Japanese riot broke out at Zhejiang University in Hangzhou when a Japanese student's soccer ball damaged a poster denouncing NATO air strikes against the Federal Republic of Yugoslavia, one of which had hit the Chinese embassy in Belgrade.[68] Speaking off the record, some Japanese officials speculated that the Chinese leadership might be seeking a confrontation to divert from the 10th anniversary of the Tiananmen incident. A Gallup-Yomiuri poll showed that only 33 percent of Japanese and 17 percent of Chinese believed that Sino-Japanese relations were satisfactory, dropping 34 points in China and 32 points in Japan compared to a 1988 poll.[69]

Prime Minister Obuchi paid a fence-mending trip to Beijing that he described cautiously as having obtained "a certain amount of understanding on the defense guidelines."[70] Chinese reaction was more blunt, with a professor at Beijing's College of Foreign Affairs opining that, although the atmosphere of Sino-Japanese relations had improved, none of the bilateral issues had been solved.[71]

Nonetheless, voices of moderation were noticeable on both sides. In a lengthy *Shijie Zhishi* article, author Feng Zhaokui, then deputy director of the Japan Institute at the Chinese Academy of Social Science (CASS), first paid obeisance to the party line by noting that the Japanese government had fired the three arrows of rewriting history, ending the constitution, and strengthening the military all at once. Then, acknowledging the rise of nationalism in both China and Japan, he argued that China and Japan must avoid allowing frictions to form a vicious circle of nationalism inciting nationalism; they should calmly face up to the problems between them and take active steps toward solution.[72] In Tokyo, *Asahi* took a similarly conciliatory view, arguing that the launching of the DF-31 and the threatened launch of a Taepodong-2 long-range missile by its North Korean client state should not arouse calls for a Japanese response. During U.S. President Clinton's visit to Beijing in 1998, the Chinese leadership had agreed that the two sides should mutually dismantle strategic nuclear missiles targeted against each other and, at the meeting of ASEAN foreign ministers in July 1999, had stated its intention to sign the Southeast Asian Nuclear Weapons Free Zone Treaty.[73]

Risking the anger of conservatives, the Obuchi administration made several compromises, agreeing that it would not place the country's flag on the disputed islands[74] and also assenting to concessions in talks on China's accession to the World Trade Organization. The latter annoyed the U.S. negotiators, who felt that Japanese concessions had left more for Washington and others to do.[75]

Mutual irritations continued—appearances of Chinese ships in contested waters, each side seizing on a military upgrade of the other as evidence of hostile intent, and, in a technology-enabled escalation of the diatribes, hacker attacks against government websites of "little Japan" and its companies.[76] In April 2000 Prime Minister Obuchi had a fatal stroke and was replaced by gaffe-prone Mori Yoshihirō, described as having "the heart of a flea and the brain of a shark."[77] The next month, while speaking to a group of Shintō followers, he characterized Japan as a nation of deities (*kami no kuni*) with the emperor at its center, horrifying liberal Japanese and providing the PRC media with additional corroboration for their mantra of reviving Japanese militarism.[78] A few days later, sixteen Diet members plus Tokyo Mayor Ishihara attended the inauguration of Taiwan President Chen Shui-bian in Taipei, with Ishihara telling reporters that if Jiang Zemin attempted to take Taiwan by force, he would be regarded as a Hitler.[79]

On the Chinese side, the government announced its intention to spend $12 million and displace more than a hundred households and ten factories to re-create the site of the infamous World War II Japanese germ warfare unit 731, and to petition for the facility's inclusion on a United Nations list of World Heritage sites.[80] Talks on mutual notification of ships in each other's exclusive economic zone foundered when the two sides could not agree on where the boundaries were. [81]

Doleful references to bilateral relations being at their lowest point since normalization[82] continued until Premier Zhu Rongji, considered more friendly to Japan than Jiang Zemin, visited in October. Public opinion reacted favorably to his less confrontational manner. Unlike Jiang, Zhu did not demand an apology; his public remarks concentrated on the benefits of mutual cooperation. His reputation in China as impatient and short-tempered notwithstanding, Zhu chatted amiably with Japanese citizens, and even played a passage from a Chinese opera on the traditional *erhu*. Chinese media portrayed the visit as a triumph,[83] though Zhu was criticized on social media for not taking a stronger stand on the apology. Japanese sources credited Zhu with a public relations success, with one commentator noting that if bending over backward were an Olympic sport, Zhu and Prime Minister Mori would surely tie for gold. However, he continued, they had not solved any of the problems between the two sides.[84]

Despite occasional allusions to the "narrow strip of water" separating the two nations[85]—a rough barometer of the Chinese government's assessment of bilateral relations—irritations continued to build. While on a visit to Africa, Mori mentioned "the Greater East Asian War," rather than, as the Chinese side saw it, Japan's war of aggression, and referred to China as "Shina."[86] A new textbook that China objected to was approved by the Japanese Education Ministry. Former Taiwan president Lee Teng-hui had applied for a visa,[87] and when a Japan Airlines flight was delayed by bad weather, ninety Chinese passengers had to spend the night on a concrete floor in the Osaka airport, deprived of food or even seats.[88] The impression that Japanese looked down on Chinese was reinforced when brake failures were discovered on Mitsubishi sport utility vehicles being sold in the PRC,[89] and Toyota ran two ads that Chinese netizens deemed condescending.[90]

TRADE DIFFICULTIES

On the Japanese side, a tripling of food imports from the PRC was hurting domestic agricultural producers, as were low-cost products in other areas such as textiles. There was also annoyance at official Chinese statistics that showed bilateral trade as almost equally balanced. Among the creative accounting practices employed were treating Hong Kong separately, even if Chinese-made items were simply transshipped through Hong Kong. Some goods never reached Hong Kong at all, being transshipped on paper only.[91] Illegal immigrants had increased, with a disproportionate number of the newcomers involved in criminal activities.

Although though all of these problems predated the collision between an American reconnaissance plane and an adventurous Chinese fighter pilot on April 1, 2001, Chinese media blamed Tokyo for trying to take advantage of the temporary downturn in Sino-American relations to further its own agenda.[92] This charge was not well received in Japan. An eminent Tokyo University professor issued a scathing critique of the "China School" in the Ministry of Foreign Affairs, saying that it was time that the Japanese government stopped caring about hurting the feelings of China.[93]

Meanwhile in China, Jiang Zemin had introduced the "Three Represents" through which he hoped to secure his legacy in the pantheon of post-1989 leaders. Seemingly innocuous at first glance—decreeing that the Communist Party of China should represent advanced social productive forces, advanced culture, and the interests of the overwhelming majority of Chinese citizens[94]—they were political dynamite, since the more advanced productive forces were clearly capitalist entrepreneurs. Old-line communists were aghast at allowing capitalists to join the party of peasants and workers, with Jiang launching a mass campaign to mobilize support for the plan. At the same time, he had economic worries. At the end of 2001, a *Ta Kung Pao* editorial described the foreign trade situation as "very grim." Predicting that China's exports could fall by 10 percent in the coming year, the paper suggested the solution was to expand electronics exports.[95] It did not mention the obvious: this sector was traditionally dominated by Japanese manufacturers.

THE KOIZUMI ERA

Politically engaged Japanese, noting a succession of short-lived and weak prime ministers, lamented the dearth of strong leadership.[96] They did not have long to wait. When a continuation of the gaffes he had been known for and financial scandals linked to his ministers sent his popularity ratings into single digits, Mori resigned. His successor Koizumi Junichirō immediately asserted himself as the kind of strong figure many Japanese had been hoping for. Announcing bold measures designed to bring the country out of its decade-long malaise ("structural reform with no sacred cows"), Koizumi also assumed a strongly nationalist profile.

As if anticipating what was to come, a Chinese foreign ministry spokesperson stated that it was up to the new prime minister to improve the "fragile" bilateral relationship.[97] A hopeful sign was Koizumi's appointment of Tanaka Makiko as foreign minister. The daughter of Tanaka Kakuei who as prime minister had effected normalization, Makiko was, like her father, markedly favorable to China. She was not, however, popular with the bureaucrats of the foreign ministry, who leaked documents indicating her lack of diplomatic expertise to the press. In addition, Tanaka took policy stands that differed from those of the Koizumi government. After a contentious several months, she was dismissed.

After this, there was little doubt about what direction bilateral relations would take. During his campaign, Koizumi had promised to visit the Yasukuni Shrine once a year if elected, doing so for the first time in August 2001 and eliciting the familiar protests from Beijing, as well as from South Korean President Kim Dae-jung, one of the ROK's more Japan-friendly leaders. Surprisingly, Koizumi was able to pay a visit to Beijing in October, albeit for one day only. After touring the Marco Polo Bridge, the prime minister issued an apology (*owabi*), the first time a Japanese official had used a word with so strong a connotation.[98] Official media expressed approval but noted that since the prime minister had not promised never to visit Yasukuni again, this was but a first step in patching relations but still insufficient.[99] It was to be Koizumi's last visit to Beijing.

When, after the September 11 terrorist attacks, President George W. Bush declared a global war on terror, Koizumi responded positively to the call. Chinese media portrayed the global war on terrorism as a poorly disguised effort to spread America's "tentacles" around the world,[100] and Japan as using the opportunity to further its own interests.[101] Whatever his motives, and in the face of criticism from both Beijing and his domestic political opposition, Koizumi pushed through three anti-terrorism bills that had languished in the Diet for several years. Inter alia, the bills allowed Japan to provide military intelligence and assistance to U.S. military forces, and to dispatch Self-Defense Forces (SDF) troops and vessels out of the immediate area if needed. This, said China, indicated military ambition that threatened East Asian security.[102] In April 2002 Koizumi paid another visit to the Yasukuni Shrine, stating that he felt others would understand that he meant only to commemorate the spirits of the dead.[103]

MUTUAL DISTRUST GROWS

In the following month, a fresh irritant occurred when Chinese police were either permitted to enter or forced their way into the Japanese consulate in Shenyang to arrest a family of North Korean asylum seekers. A major diplomatic incident ensued, with heated words exchanged on both sides. A formal Japanese investigation showed that its ambassador, Anami Koreshige had, shortly before the Korean family tried to take refuge, issued orders to turn away asylum seekers.[104] Further, a videotape showed a Japanese consular official handing one of the police his hat back, since it had fallen off in the scuffle, and an exchange of handshakes between the men. The investigation also revealed that the official had previously dined with one of the Chinese.[105]

Nonetheless, the incident of asylum seekers, including a child, being manhandled by police did not play well with either Japanese public opinion or opponents of the Japanese foreign ministry's so-called China School. Possibly in order to avoid an upsurge in anti-Japanese sentiment, the Chinese press did not comment on the issue. In the end, the Chinese government agreed to allow the asylum seekers to reach their goal of South Korea, via the Philippines.[106]

There was speculation that the decision was made either to avoid unpleasantness ahead of the 30th anniversary of normalization of relations or from concern of damage to its pledge to improve human rights as part of Beijing being chosen as host of the 2008 Olympics.[107] To the annoyance of Japanese conservatives, the GOJ issued relatively light administrative punishments to the consular staff and the ambassador. Reforms were announced, including clarifying the chain of command and enhancing security measures. Cameras would monitor all entrances, and gates were to be kept closed.[108]

The asylum incident had barely been soothed when a remark by Chief Cabinet Secretary Fukuda Yasuō caused further problems in the bilateral relationship. In a meeting with reporters, speaking on background,

Fukuda said that if the Japanese people came to think that the country needed to possess nuclear weapons, he did not know what would happen. Although, as dictated by protocol, he was referred to simply as a top government official, Fukuda admitted he was the source of the remark, adding that it had been a slip of the tongue (*shitsugen*). The Chinese media refused to accept this explanation,[109] while conservative Japanese newspapers argued that the remark had been blown out of proportion.[110] Earlier in the year, Ozawa Ichirō, leader of the opposition Liberal Party, had stated that, in response to Chinese military expansion, Japan could possess thousands of nuclear warheads "overnight" if it wanted, easily surpassing the PRC's military power.[111]

Despite repeated reassurances from Japanese leaders, including both Koizumi[112] and, separately, the Finance Ministry,[113] that China was not an economic threat to Japan, more and more influential sources stated that it was.[114] Contaminated food products, including matsutake mushrooms and spinach, became heated issues, bolstering the arguments of threatened Japanese agricultural interests for protection of their products.

Polls indicated ongoing distrust: 43 percent of Japanese and 67 percent of Chinese did not have a favorable view of each other.[115] Perhaps more worrisome from the Japanese point of view was another poll indicating that, for the first time, a majority of Americans considered China to be economically more important to the United States than Japan.[116] Japanese conservatives, riffing on the title of the 1989 best-seller *The Japan That Can Say No* [to the United States][117] urged that Japan also learn to say no to China.[118]

As the 30th anniversary of the normalization of diplomatic relations between the two approached, a *Yomiuri* editorial declared that relations were at their lowest point since then.[119] In what appeared to be a calculated insult, Beijing announced that it would commemorate the date with an exhibition at the Memorial Hall of the War of Resistance against Japan.[120]

Publicly, and opinion polls notwithstanding, leaders on both sides declared their desire for good relations. As the year ended, difficult negotiations were concluded over how much the Japanese government owed the PRC for permission to raise a North Korean patrol ship, damaged by the Japanese when it intruded into the country's territorial waters but that had sunk in China's exclusive economic zone. China had initially requested 500 million yen, with a settlement of 150 million yen eventually agreed on.[121]

VOICES OF MODERATION IN CHINA

Another positive sign was a lengthy article by *Renmin Ribao* commentator Ma Licheng. Writing in the reformist journal *Zhanlüe yü Guanli* (Strategy and Management), Ma called for new thinking on Sino-Japanese relations. Citing an old Chinese saying that one should return evil with good, he urged China to act like the victorious great power it was. The war had ended nearly sixty years ago: China should not be so harsh on Japan. Tokyo had proved its sincerity by providing large amounts of low-cost loans. Japan's developing military power should not be feared, and its contribution to peace-keeping operations should be welcomed. Arguing that narrow-minded nationalism is not patriotism and should be avoided by both sides, Ma concluded that, since China and Japan are the pivots of Asia, they must work together for its development.[122]

Although Ma's article caused an uproar in the PRC's academic and public opinion circles,[123] it was the forerunner of a spate of other commentaries urging a softer line toward Japan. Despite brief expressions of anger when, in mid-January, Koizumi visited the Yasukuni Shrine a third time while in office, Shi Yinhong, a high-profile professor at Beijing's Renmin Daxue, wrote yet another plea for better relations in the same journal. Shi explained that his ideas were different from Ma's: whereas Ma's analysis was emotional, he, Shi, had begun from the premise that the issue is not whether Japan is good or bad, but rather to suggest ways that the interests of the two countries could be harmonized. China could not, he stated, withstand a hostile Japan as well as a constantly hostile United States, a hostile Taiwan, and a possibly hostile India. Strategic prioritization was necessary: dealing with the United States and Taiwan were primary considerations.

Hence, for the sake of China's own vital interests, a major improvement was imperative. In recent years, what Shi termed Japan's sick economy and high unemployment had fanned the flames of chauvinism, exacerbated by China's condemnations of Japan, the criminal and gangster activities of some immigrants to Japan, and trade and territorial disputes. Right-wingers like Ishihara Shintarō were gaining credence, particularly among the younger generation. Shi proposed that "historical problems" be removed from the diplomatic agenda for "quite a long time," as well as "official and quasi-official propaganda (*piequ guanfang he zunguanfang de xuanchuan*) on the theme."

Chinese leaders had not adequately thanked Japan for its great economic aid, said Shi, and should do so. With regard to the expansion of Japanese military forces, China must be inwardly vigilant while outwardly displaying magnanimity. The mantra of Japan becoming a military power had been exaggerated "to a certain degree." Japan should be treated as a great power, and its aspirations to become a permanent member of the United Nations Security Council should be actively supported.[124] Though Shi had carefully presented his views as the best course for China, he was attacked for the same reasons as Ma. Critics pointed out that Japan had not properly reciprocated the magnanimity that Shi did not seem to believe that China had extended. He ceased giving interviews.[125]

Nonetheless, the cordial meeting that Chinese President Hu Jintao and Koizumi had at ceremonies for the 300th anniversary of Saint Petersburg, Russia, indicated that these calls for better bilateral relations may have had high-level backing. As reported by *Kyodo*, Hu did not mention Yasukuni and said that China would consider both Japan's Shinkansen bullet train system and a German proposal for a high-speed link between Beijing and Shanghai. The two leaders agreed to discuss further high-level meetings, to cooperate to peacefully resolve such problems as North Korean nuclear proliferation and the outbreak of severe acute respiratory syndrome (SARS) in China.[126]

As both sides prepared for the 25th anniversary of the Treaty of Peace and Friendship, conciliatory gestures continued, albeit against a backdrop of resistance in China as manifested in activist efforts to assert sovereignty over the disputed East China Sea islands. Successive articles in *Strategy and Management*'s July and August issues reinforced the need for mutual understanding. The earlier of the two, by Feng Zhaokui of the Japan Institute of the Chinese Academy of Social Sciences, compared one-sided efforts to improve ties with the sound of one hand clapping. Noting that Japan had championed China's entry into the World Trade Organization, had provided generous aid to its economic development, and was the first country to lift sanctions against the PRC after the Tiananmen incident of 1989, Feng opined that Japan's advance toward becoming a political power should be seen as a consequence of the multipolarization of power that followed the end of the Cold War, not as evidence of hostile intent, and that, contrary to Chinese conservatives' opinion, it did not always take orders from the United States.[127]

In the August article, Tsinghua University student Xue Li argued against the popular notion that Japan, unlike Germany, had not shown sufficient remorse over World War II. The two countries' situations were entirely different, rendering comparisons invalid. Trying to extract further apologies was counterproductive: apologies that did not come voluntarily were useless. No nation had contributed more to China's economic development than Japan, yet China had seldom thanked it for doing so. Moreover, China was unlikely to obtain this kind of assistance from other places. Finally, said Li, it was highly improbable that Japan would ever become a military power again.[128]

The Japanese government contributed generously to efforts to stem the SARS epidemic in China and, after Tokyo asked Beijing, through diplomatic channels, Chinese protestors reacting to the Japanese government's leasing some of the disputed Diaoyu/Senkaku Islands from their private Japanese owner, withdrew.[129]

NEW FRICTIONS ARE ADDED TO OLD IRRITANTS

Commemorative activities marking the anniversary of the peace and friendship treaty, which had been signed on August 12 and went into effect on October 23, were cordial but low-key, several incidents having marred the "new thinking" in Sino-Japanese relations. In August, poison gas canisters left behind by the Japanese military after World War II were unearthed by construction workers in Qiqihar, Heilongjiang province. Twenty-nine persons were injured, one of whom later died. Although the Japanese government quickly offered 100 million yen in compensation, anti-Japanese nationalists continued to exploit the incident.[130]

Then, in September, a group of Japanese businessmen on a company outing to free-wheeling Shenzhen, were discovered to have participated in a two-day orgy. The city's brothels were well known and such trysting was not unusual; news of the incident did not even appear until a nonlocal paper, the Beijing-published *Zhongguo Qingnian Bao* (China Youth Daily), printed the story ten days later.[131] Chinese media made much of the incident, stating that, since one of the days was September 18th, the anniversary of the 1931 Mukden/Shenyang incident (see Chapter 2), the indiscretion was a conscious attempt to belittle China.

A few weeks later, yet another inflammatory incident was reported: an "indecent" performance by three Japanese students in Xi'an. Although the students maintained that the signage in their skit, intended to be funny, had been misinterpreted to read "look down on China," the students and a Japanese teacher were expelled from the country in the ensuing outburst of nationalist indignation.[132]

The Beijing government also reacted sharply when Tokyo allowed Tibet's exiled leader, the Dalai Lama, to visit in November 2003, having numerous times accused the Dalai Lama of fostering separatism and "splittism" and warning other countries against allowing him to enter their territories.

In April 2004 a Japanese-owned restaurant in Kunming served a special meal deriving from an ancient court feast, the *nyotai mori*, in which sushi was served on the bodies of nearly naked women. In this case, the women were Chinese, which patriots took as a deliberate insult. The Chinese restaurant manager, a woman, explained to no avail that the women's private parts were covered, that the food was placed on top of leaves rather than on their bodies, and that waitresses had served the food to the guests to avoid any physical contact between them and the women.[133]

New Japanese textbooks were published that glossed over the comfort women issue, underscoring the GOJ's reluctance to accept responsibility for the practice or compensate the victims. Incidents involving Hong Kong residents trying to land on the Diaoyu/Senkaku Islands continued to generate friction. Some Chinese were also angered by discussions within Japan on reducing the PRC's allocation of official development aid. However rational this might seem in light of the rapidly eroding gap in the GDPs of the two countries, the possibility that the aid might be ended aroused considerable resentment.

These issues grew more contentious as Japanese politicians continued to make remarks that angered patriotic Chinese. Among these, the most salient were:

- LDP faction leader Etō Takami calling the Nanjing Massacre "a complete fabrication," with the numbers of those who died greatly exaggerated.[134] Other politicians before Etō had expressed the same thoughts, causing similar adverse reactions.
- Etō's terming Chinese *daisangokujin*, or people from the three countries (that were part of the pre–World War II Japanese empire). [135]
- in response to Chinese elation at the country's first successful manned space launch, Tokyo Governor Ishihara characterized the Chinese as

"ignorant" and their spaceship as outdated. If Japan had wished to have a launch, it could do so within a year.¹³⁶
- LDP Diet member Yamamoto Ichita referred to China as a *yamataoorochi*, a mythical eight-headed, eight-tailed dragon who was reputed to attack a village each year to eat one of its female children.¹³⁷

Such statements bolstered the arguments of critics of the "new thinking."

THE JAPANESE VIEW

Across the sea, Japanese concerns with China were the mirror image of China's concerns with Japan, albeit expressed in a far more restrained manner. Taking note of the PRC's repeated objections to other countries' commenting on its behavior as an infringement of China's sovereign right to do what it wanted within its own territories, Japanese commentators countered that Japan, too, was a sovereign state. As such, it could issue invitations to whomever it deemed appropriate: Chinese objections, therefore, constituted interference in Japan's domestic affairs. Since a large number of Japanese are Buddhists, the appearance of the Dalai Lama, whose unswerving commitment to pacifism and nonviolence had been an important factor in his being awarded the Nobel Peace Prize a decade before, was eagerly anticipated by Japan's peace-loving citizens.

As for the Yasukuni Shrine, while there is disagreement even within Japan regarding the appropriateness of official visits there—since it may violate the constitutional separation between church and state—the shrine clearly honors all Japanese who have fallen in battle anywhere, not just those of World War II. Many Japanese disagree with the judgment that designated some of these as war criminals, pointing out that since no such category had existed until after the war, this was ex post facto justice. The victors of World War II, they felt, were motivated by a desire for revenge rather than justice, condemning military leaders for performing the duties that the social system of the era had instilled in them. The overwhelming majority of the current Japanese population was born after World War II, and sees no reason to feel guilty for deeds they had no part in.¹³⁸ Repeated Chinese statements that their country has shown insufficient remorse strike many Japanese as disingenuous attempts at humiliating their country as well as thinly disguised attempts to extort aid and other concessions from the Tokyo government.

Defenders of the Japanese government pointed out that it has apologized for the poison gas incident in Qiqihar and paid compensation to the victims. Further, the Diaoyu Islands, known to them as the Senkaku Islands, have been under Japanese jurisdiction since 1895, and were *terra nullius* beforehand. Occupied by the United States after the war ended, the Senkakus were returned to Japanese administration decades ago. Beijing had made no claim to the islands until the revelation that the surrounding waters might contain valuable hydrocarbon resources. Worrisomely, whereas PRC authorities had not previously overtly supported the efforts of Chinese—who included persons from Hong Kong and Taiwan—to retake the islands, an effort to do so in April 2004 seemed to have government support.[139]

Moreover, activists from China proper, as opposed to Hong Kong and Taiwan, had spearheaded this latest effort. The "invasion" boats were launched from Xiamen, in Fujian province, and, as one mainland activist stated, "We are going in the same direction as the government. They are not openly supporting us, but it's one eye opened, one eye closed."[140] When Japanese police apprehended the intruders, Chinese mobs surrounded the Japanese embassy in Beijing, burning a Japanese flag. Japanese apprehensions increased when, in November 2004, a Chinese submarine entered waters near Okinawa, prompting the Tokyo government to order the Maritime Self-Defense Force to take security action for only the second time in its history.[141]

As for the PRC's objections to Japan's acquisition of ballistic missile defense systems, these weapons are, by definition, defensive. Hence, many Japanese suspect that China may harbor plans to attack. Toward the end of 2003, a Chinese spy was apprehended in Hyōgo prefecture when he attempted to acquire unspecified cutting-edge technology.[142]

Japanese public opinion is typically embarrassed when the country's politicians make insensitive remarks. But there is also widespread awareness that Chinese nationals have committed a disproportionate number of crimes in the country. Illegal immigrants and visa-overstayers are also disproportionately Chinese. Shooting incidents between Chinese gangs in Tokyo's Shinjuku district are common enough to have become the basis for film and television plots. In the spring of 2004, a family of four was robbed and brutally murdered by Chinese students in Japan.[143]

With regard to the orgy, it is well known that prostitution, though illegal, is common in China. In the highly corrupt culture that evolved as an unintended by-product of Deng Xiaoping's economic reforms, the profits from this publicly proscribed profession form an important part of the revenues of municipalities and of numerous individual officials thereof. That this particular instance occurred on the September 18th anniversary of the Mukden incident of 1931 was almost certainly accidental, since due to repeated PRC admonitions to the citizenry to never forget it, the date has far higher salience in China than in Japan. As for charges that the skit in Sichuan was obscene and insulting, most Japanese accepted the expelled students' explanation that it was an innocent effort at humor that went wrong. In any case, they pointed out, there was no excuse for groups of Chinese to threaten anyone suspected of being Japanese.

An even more troublesome incident that occurred with far less provocation was the mob violence that accompanied a series of soccer matches in several Chinese cities in the late summer of 2004. Chinese spectators booed loudly when the Japanese national anthem was played, and threw garbage both at players and the few Japanese fans who had turned out to watch the games. Internet groups threatened violence. After the final, which the Japanese team won, the players and their fans had to be escorted from the stadium by police and taken to their hotels, from which they dared not venture out.[144]

In September 2004 *Strategy and Management*, the journal in which many of the articles suggesting better relations had been published, was closed, putatively because of an article critical of North Korea.[145] It would later reappear, but in a version with restricted circulation (*neibu*).[146] The call for new thinking on Japan that had been begun by Ma Licheng appeared to have died as well. A month later, a Thai-owned publication declared that "Sino-Japanese ties are back on the rocks."[147]

ANTI-JAPANESE RIOTS IN CHINA

In 2005 anti-Japanese riots broke out in several Chinese cities with considerable damage to Japanese diplomatic and commercial properties. Participants denounced Koizumi's fourth visit to Yasukuni, the Japanese government's approval of a textbook that minimized the country's actions during World War II, and Japan's application for permanent membership in the United Nations Security Council in a reorganization of the Council proposed by then Secretary-General Kofi Annan. All had been heavily publicized in the Chinese press.

At first, leaders seemed to support the students, responding to official protests by saying that it was Japan who owed China an apology, not vice versa. Chinese Vice-Premier Wu Yi abruptly cancelled her meeting with Koizumi when, at a Diet committee meeting, he defended his right to visit the shrine. The Japanese public was offended by this insult to their leader even as the vice-premier became a heroine in China and anti-Japanese protests escalated.

When unrest began to target other grievances, as when an estimated 2,000 retired People's Liberation Army (PLA) men from twenty provinces converged on military headquarters in Beijing to demand pension increases, 30,000 people protested against pollution in northeast China, factory workers in the southeastern special economic zone of Shenzhen demanded unions, and anticorruption signs appeared in Shanghai, the PRC leadership moved to quell the demonstrations.[148] The nationalism that the PRC government had nurtured to repair its damaged legitimacy after the Tiananmen incident of 1989 now appeared to threaten that legitimacy.

After a meeting of foreign ministers, the PRC agreed to repair damage to Japanese diplomatic buildings but not to provide any other compensation or apologize. Two former prime ministers, including Nakasone, urged an end to visits to Yasukuni, and a supra-partisan group of Diet members began to discuss building a new war memorial that would not be freighted by association with war criminals. Collaborative activities continued as when, after the head of the PRC's environmental protection agency described China's pollution problem to a United Nations conference as "the god of death in the air," Japan offered to share its expertise on dealing with the issue.[149]

Some Japanese scholars speculated that the soccer issue was Jiang Zemin's "final offensive," in reference to the dual leadership of Jiang retaining the chairmanship of the Central Military Commission while Hu was president of China and the CCP's general secretary. Jiang, with his perceived animosity toward Japan, having ceded the CMC position to Hu, relations would, they hoped, improve.[150] However, issues were not so much forgotten as downplayed. Hu Jintao warned that Sino-Japanese ties could go cold "in an instant,"[151] the two sides could not agree on a joint declaration over the form of a future East Asian community that proponents hoped would resemble the European Union,[152] and the head of the

DPJ took issue with his own party when he criticized the country's leaders for "chanting that we should be friendly with China while avoiding the real issues."[153] A telecommunications specialist at the Japanese consulate in Shanghai committed suicide, leaving a note explaining that he had been coerced into providing secret information to a PRC operative on his country's policies on the island disputes between them.[154]

RIVALRY FOR ENERGY RESOURCES

With Japan almost completely dependent on imported sources of energy and the PRC, although an important producer of oil, also dependent on imports to sustain current rates of growth, the two countries were unavoidably in competition with each other. Initially, China proposed a pipeline from Angarsk, in Siberia, to Daqing, in northeast China, where the oil would be refined and distributed to the PRC's energy-hungry factories. Japan advocated a much longer route from Angarsk to Nakhodka, on the Japan Sea, from which point tankers could bring the petroleum to Japanese ports. The Tokyo government offered to underwrite the additional costs involved. Russian President Vladimir Putin deftly played one side against another, even arresting and convicting on tax fraud charges the head of the company that had favored the Chinese proposal. In the end, the Japanese side won, but by paying more than it otherwise would have needed to. In an angry outburst, the official news weekly *Beijing Review* described the process thus:

> In 1994, Russian Yukos Oil Corporation put forward the motion of constructing China-Russia crude oil pipelines. In September 2001, China and Russia signed a general agreement on a Sino-Russian pipeline feasibility study. In the following two years, the two sides accomplished the technical aspects. . . . However, just at the moment when the building of the Angarsk-Daqing Route was expected to start, Japan, who [sic] is in dire need of oil, suddenly intervened. . . . Russia's Transneft . . . Company proposed the so-called Angarsk-Nakhodka Route. Japan, aiming to win in the competition with China, began a campaign aimed at Russia on political, economic, media, nongovernmental and other levels to press home [its] . . . proposal. . . . Japan promised to offer "high-sum subscriptions and gifts" worth $14.5 billion. In addition, Japan agreed to invest $8 billion in the oil and natural gas projects of . . . Russia's Far East. . . . At that time, the Angarsk-Daqing pipeline was actually wound up.

> In February 2004, ... Putin claimed ... that the Angarsk-Daqing Route was an issue with strategic significance, which implied that the Russian Government had chosen the oil pipeline route leading to the Pacific Ocean. ... Transneft came up with a new route plan in March 2004, and the outline of the Taishet [a city north of Angarsk]-Nakhodka Route appeared for the first time.[155]

This degree of anger is unusual from the normally bland *Beijing Review*, whose correspondent stopped just short of accusing Japan of having bribed its path to victory. Note also that the author attributed not just money but strategic motives to Putin, strongly hinting that the Russian president wished to constrain Chinese development. Trying to maximize Russia's advantage, Moscow later raised the possibility of running a spur from the pipeline to China. Tokyo immediately responded that, if that were done, it would withdraw its offer to help finance the venture. Notwithstanding Transneft's Vice-President Sergei Grigoriyev's gruff rejoinder that no ousider would decide the destination of a line built within Russian territory, Moscow promised to supply China with oil via truck and rail.[156] Opening a new phase in the ongoing competition, in late September 2005, Moscow and Beijing began negotiations for a gas pipeline between the two countries.[157]

Sino-Japanese economic relations remained good, but the two sides continued to snipe at each other. Summed up in the phrase "hot economy, cold politics," bilateral trade expanded even as Chinese officials decried any Japanese move that could be construed as evidence of remilitarization and Japanese complained regularly about the implications of annual double-digit increases in the PRC's defense budget and each new weapon acquired. It seemed that the stronger China became, the more it sought to avenge itself against past humiliation by Japan, while in Japan nationalism was stimulated by the weakening of the country's economic primacy as the PRC rose in stature both economically and militarily.

Before leaving office, as planned, at the end of September, Koizumi paid one last visit to Yasukuni—on August 15th, the anniversary of the end of World War II. One of the few conciliatory Chinese voices, that of Feng Zhaokui, urged Beijing to "say what needs to be said," but not allow itself to be duped into overreacting, which could push Japanese public opinion into supporting Koizumi. The government should turn its attention to relations under his successors.[158] That is, in fact, what happened.

7

Contradictions Deepen, 2006–2015

EFFORTS TO MEND BILATERAL RELATIONS

When Koizumi retired from politics in September 2006 at the end of his term, Sino-Japanese relations were in one of their periodic downturns,[1] and both sides expressed hopes that his successor would be able to improve relations by assuaging ongoing irritants. Koizumi's defiant attitude notwithstanding, all of these irritants long predated his tenure in office. From Beijing's point of view, the prospect of Abe Shinzō, whom Koiziumi favored as his successor, did not bode well for improvement. Although Abe had said that mending the rift with China would be a priority, he had not specified how he intended to do so, and indeed Japanese public opinion was not unreservedly in favor of accommodation to the PRC. An August 2006 *Yomiuri* poll revealed that 65 percent of the respondents said they did not trust the PRC—the highest figure in the six surveys that the paper had conducted on the topic since 1988. At the same time, 63 percent also named China as a country that was important to the Japanese economy, second only to the United States, at 68 percent, and 56.7 percent felt that China would influence Asia the most in coming years. America was far behind at 14.4 percent.[2] The message was clear: those polled believed that China was becoming increasingly powerful, and an important factor in Japan's prosperity. But it was not well liked.

The results of the Pew Global Attitudes Project, though its questions differed somewhat, were compatible with *Yomiuri*'s findings: 93 percent of Japanese held a negative view of the PRC's growing military might, while 95 percent of Chinese saw it as a good thing. Only 28 percent of Japanese held a favorable view of China, down from 55 percent in a 2002 Pew survey, with 71 percent saying they had little or no confidence in Chinese President Hu Jintao. Only one in five Chinese had a favorable view of Japan, with no comparisons given to previous polls.[3]

Choosing his words carefully, candidate Abe told the sixty attendees of the Tokyo-Beijing Forum that Beijing must make a better effort to understand where Tokyo was coming from. Abe blamed the low opinion that many Japanese had of China and vice versa on "labor pains," which he described as a natural part of developing true mutual understanding. Mutual misunderstanding had, Abe continued, resulted in the public perception that each posed a threat to the other. In order to have a real dialogue, Beijing must first understand that Japan's postwar development was founded on pacifist principles, and that the two countries should not allow single issues to stymie economic ties.

Abe seemed to imply, first, that frequent references in the Chinese media to the resurgence of militarism were counterproductive, and second, that Beijing should overlook Koizumi's visits to the Yasukuni Shrine in the interests of mutual economic prosperity. His remarks did not sit well with his Chinese interlocutors. Among others, Wang Yi, China's ambassador to Tokyo, commented that this attitude "must be altered without further delay" before the Sino-Japanese relationship could get back on the right and productive track. And Jin Xide, deputy director of the Institute of Japanese Studies at the Chinese Academy of Sciences, added that Abe could not write off the shrine visits as mutual misunderstandings.[4]

Abe had been consistently ambiguous about whether he would or would not continue the shrine visits, to the annoyance of the nation's second leading daily, the center-left *Asahi*, which commented that he could not keep "dancing around" the issue forever. He had, the paper noted, visited the shrine in April, but concealed that fact until it was leaked early in August. Abe, it continued, was the grandson of wartime cabinet member Kishi Nobosuke, who had been tried but not convicted of war crimes and later became a prime minister in the postwar government. Although *Asahi* did not say so, Kishi was one of Beijing's most vilified bêtes noirs.

As an additional annoyance to Japanese liberals and an impediment to easing strains with China, Abe had also avoided public statements of his views on war criminals, stating to the Diet that while the Allies had judged that there were fourteen war criminals, the Japanese government had never done so. At another point, he declared that it was up to history to make such judgments.[5]

In a pre-election debate with two other candidates, Abe indicated that he did not support Beijing's contention that Japan's aggressive actions before and during World War II were orchestrated by a small number of military leaders and that the Japanese people were victims, too. Simply puzzling on the face of it, since it seemed counterproductive to insist that more Japanese were guilty than the two sides had heretofore agreed on, Abe's denial had deeper implications that could further complicate Sino-Japanese relations: Beijing's acceptance of the premise that the actions of the militarists were separable from those of the Japanese public had been fundamental to the negotiations on diplomatic normalization that were agreed to in September 1972. This formulation also allowed the PRC to absolve Tokyo of the necessity to pay war reparations.[6]

When asked for his reaction to an apology for Japan's behavior during the war that had been made by a previous prime minister, Murayama Tomiichi, in 1995, Abe's reply was more reassuring. He answered that as long as there was no new cabinet resolution, "[the apology's] spirit would naturally continue." However, he then reiterated a slight variation on his previous contentious statement, that it was "not necessarily appropriate for politicians to make judgments [on history.]"[7]

Despite such portents that did not bode well for amicable Sino-Japanese relations, Abe assumed office in September 2006, becoming Japan's first prime minister born after World War II. He immediately dispatched the president of the House of Councillors, Ohgi Chikage, to Beijing, where she met with senior officials.[8] Ohgi, a well-known film actress before entering politics, was the first female president of the upper house of parliament and a long-time member of peace movements. As such, she was well suited to play the role of bridge over troubled waters.

On the same day, however, *Xinhua* announced that Japan's Jiji press agency had become the first foreign news organization to sign a controversial agreement that restricted foreign news distribution in the PRC. Jiji immediately disputed this, saying it had merely agreed to a slight revision of the contract it had initially signed in 1993. Whether the revision was slight or not, it had the effect of making Jiji an outlier among its counterpart agencies, since all other major international wire services continued to resist. Although there is no evidence that the government of Japan influenced Jiji's decision to sign, the fact that Jiji, and Jiji alone, had agreed to this change was taken as a signal of greater Japanese willingness to have better relations, even at the cost of acquiescing to constraints on the press.[9]

Bilateral subcabinet-level talks began, with an Abe spokesperson announcing confidently that "relations will definitely begin to improve."[10] Chinese Premier Wen Jiabao sent a message to Abe stating that China was willing to make "relentless efforts to develop friendly, neighborly relations of cooperation" and pledging to work "tirelessly" to do so.[11]

Although a number of observers commented on the irony of Beijing's apparent preference for dealing with someone whose views were noticeably to the right of Koizumi, all was not sweetness and light: the PRC's foreign ministry spokesperson challenged Abe to "match his words with deeds," and made clear that his country had not changed its position on the Yasukuni Shrine visits. He also reacted angrily to a comment by Kyūma Fumio, new head of the Japanese Defense Agency, that the PRC's growing military spending posed a threat to Japan.[12]

Abe's first policy message as prime minister did not use words that the Chinese foreign ministry's spokesperson would have wanted to see matched with deeds: Abe spoke of the need to revise the Japanese constitution—code for changing the pacifist language of Article 9, in which Japan foreswore the use of force to settle international disputes—and pledged to create a more assertive Japan,[13] echoing campaign phrases such as the need for a "battling diplomacy," or *tatakau gaikō*. Apart from saying that he planned to work for "future-oriented discussions," Abe did not address relations with China.

One sticking point to Beijing issuing an invitation for Abe to visit was reportedly its insistence on a public statement that neither Abe nor any future prime ministers would visit Yasukuni. The Japanese government reacted testily to what it regarded as interference in the country's domestic affairs, with one official telling reporters that "Japan is not a tributary of China. . . . Such a demand is absolutely unacceptable for a sovereign nation."[14] However, officials confided, it was possible that Abe and Asō Tarō, his foreign minister, might be prepared to make a private commitment that they would not visit during their time in office.[15]

The invitation was, in fact, issued and the meeting duly took place, amid Japanese media speculation that Beijing had succeeded in obtaining the pledge while the country's foreign ministry denied that any such promise had been made. A few months later, the LDP included the desirability of continued visits to the shrine in its party platform to "humbly show our respect for those who became the cornerstone of the country and, vowing never to go to war, reaffirm our determination for eternal peace." It did not, however, specify whether these visits should be made by the prime minister.[16]

Domestic objections to such a conciliatory gesture notwithstanding, Abe was greeted on arrival in Beijing on October 8th with a twenty-one-gun salute and banner headlines about his being the first Japanese leader to visit in five years. The meeting was chiefly important for the fact that it occurred, since little beyond an exchange of pleasantries took place. Those interested in symbolism noted that this was the first time that a new Japanese prime minister had chosen to make his first trip abroad to Beijing rather than Washington.

Hu Jintao declared that the visit marked a turning point in Sino-Japanese relations and, he hoped, a new starting point for the improvement and development of bilateral ties. The two leaders agreed to step up dialogue and announced yet another effort to study their common history as well as to discuss what reforms might be made in the structure of the United Nations.[17] Though unstated in the news coverage of the meetings, the talks must have touched on Japan's long-coveted permanent seat on the UN's Security Council.[18] North Korea's disclosure, as the Hu-Abe meeting was in train, that it planned to detonate a nuclear advice, gave the two leaders an opportunity to jointly condemn the tests.

The tone of relations became more amicable after the meeting, and some steps forward were taken. At the end of November, the Sino-Japanese defense dialogue resumed, after a hiatus of three years, and in February, a Japanese expert was honored for his efforts on behalf of the Chinese environment.[19] In the same month, Foreign Minister Li Zhaoxing, on a visit to Tokyo, avoided sensitive topics, gently alluding to another contentious issue by stating his hope that the two countries could make the East China Sea into "a sea of peace, cooperation, and friendship." Li reportedly offered to help Japan get information on citizens believed to have been abducted by North Korea.[20]

China was also rumored to be considering acquiring Japanese bullet-train technology for its plans to build a high-speed rail system. An agreement for collaborative research on quantum beam studies was reached between the Japan Atomic Energy Agency and the Chinese Academy of Sciences.[21] Abe's New Year's Day address stated that Japan and China were moving toward a strategic relationship based on trust.[22]

On the other hand, North Korea's bellicose actions gave impetus to Japanese who wanted to revise the country's constitution and also rekindled a periodic debate on whether Japan should have nuclear weapons. The unspoken result of the former seems to have been to reinterpret rather than rewrite the constitution.[23] On the latter, Foreign Minister Asō announced that, although Japan definitely had the technical ability to produce nuclear weapons, it had no current intention to do so. The debate, however, continued, and was intensified when in January, an American magazine revealed that China had fired a missile that destroyed an orbiting satellite, its own, thereby achieving an important advance in weapons technology. The air of suspicion deepened when a spokesperson for the PRC's defense ministry said "we" are unaware of the test.[24]

Yomiuri accused Tokyo's space development plans as lacking any real substance and called for immediate action lest we "find Japan has become an underdeveloped country in the realm of space."[25] The following month, the Japanese Coast Guard detected a Chinese ship conducting surveillance activities in an area of Japan's exclusive economic zone that the two sides had previously agreed would require prior notification. Since there had been no notification, a formal protest was issued.[26]

Air Self-Defense Force (SDF) fighter jets were scrambled twelve times over the summer as Chinese fighter bombers made more than forty sorties in the airspace over a disputed offshore gas field known to the Chinese as Chunxiao and by the Japanese as Shirakaba.[27] An American expert on maritime law summarized these and other similar incidents as intended to send strategic messages, to scout venues for operations in the Pacific Ocean, and perhaps to find methods to control access to the littoral waters of East Asia during times of crisis.[28]

Japanese responses to the changing security environment included the establishment of a national security council on the U.S. model, and raising the Japanese Defense Agency, which had been part of the office of the prime minister, to ministry status. *Xinhua* responded with alarm, saying that the slight change in wording belied a fundamental difference. In essence,

> The purpose is to get rid of the constraints set after [Japan] failed in the wartime invasion, shake off the restrictions on the SDF, and

clear the way for justifiably [sic, justifying] interfering in regional and world affairs.[29]

China also expressed "grave concern" about a contingency plan being discussed between Washington and Tokyo in case of a "crisis situation arising in areas around Japan,"[30] a code phrase for Japanese-American coordination to resist a Chinese attack on Taiwan. A few months later, Defense Minister Cao Gangchuan, visiting Tokyo on a goodwill mission, stated that his country was "closely watching Japan-U.S. security arrangements in relation to Taiwan," with his counterpart Kōmura Masahiko replying that Japan was opposed to the use of Chinese military force against Taiwan.[31]

The 70th anniversary of the 1937 Marco Polo Bridge incident brought into focus the two sides' differing interpretations of the history of that era. Commemorations in various parts of the PRC emphasized the heroic struggle of the Chinese people, led by the CCP, against barbaric Japanese cruelty. They also took Japan to task for its perceived lack of sincere contrition. Within Japan, historians concentrated on several miscommunications between the two sides that had allowed what should have been a resolvable misunderstanding to escalate. When Abe failed to appear at the Yasukuni Shrine on the anniversary of the end of the war, conservative groups protested,[32] and a right-wing extremist was arrested after sending to LDP headquarters his severed finger, along with a DVD of the self-mutilation, to express his dissatisfaction.[33]

Japanese investment in China decreased significantly, even as its total overseas investments grew by a wide margin. A Japan expert at the Chinese Academy of Social Sciences (CASS) expressed concern, noting that the PRC was keen on obtaining Japanese technology and funds for sewage treatment, seawater desalinization, and infrastructure projects. He attributed the downturn to exaggerated fears about the political risks of investing in China, the redirection of investment to India and Vietnam, and the fear that Sino-Japanese relations might turn sour again.[34]

Additionally, Japan's official development assistance organization issued a white paper that criticized China for its lack of transparency in extending foreign aid.[35] A foreign ministry official added contentious substance to this somewhat abstract statement, describing the PRC's aid as neocolonialism in the sense that large contributions were made to poor countries in exchange for access to their natural resources.[36] In a break with tradition that was considered meaningful, the new head of the ministry of foreign affairs' China and Mongolia division was not from the ministry's China School.[37]

China agreed to support India's bid for a permanent seat on the UN Security Council, but declined to support Japan's. This appeared to be an attempt to drive a wedge between Japan and India: the two had been drawing closer together in what Beijing perceived as a hedging strategy against the PRC. Abe had advocated bringing India and Australia into an Asian regional cooperation organization as counterweights to the dominance of China; China had opposed their inclusion for the same reason. Japan then recognized India as a nuclear nation, thus contravening its own policy of refusing to recognize states that had not signed the Nuclear Non-Proliferation Treaty.[38]

A columnist for *The Japan Times* ridiculed Abe's policy of reconciliation with China, noting that in a book he had published the year before, *To Be a Beautiful Country*, the prime minister had called for a Japan-India-Australia alliance that, said Abe, was based on shared values. Although Abe clearly had the shared values of freedom and democracy in mind, the columnist riposted, "What shared values—Indian castes, Japanese gangsters, and Australian beer-drinkers?" It was obvious, he concluded, that the target of this incongruous grouping was China.[39] The columnist was not alone in this feeling: Although the joint exercises among Australia, India, Japan, Singapore, and the United States in September 2007 were described as defending sea lane security, Chinese observers suspected that the impressive array of two dozen ships and three aircraft carriers foreshadowed the formation of a new military alliance to contain the PRC. An estimated 60 percent of China's foreign trade and 75 percent of its oil imports pass through the area covered by the training exercise.[40]

Abe's tenure as prime minister lasted only a year—he resigned to take responsibility for the LDP's defeat in a House of Councillors election for reasons that had nothing to do with China. His time in office seemed to confirm the prediction of outspoken former foreign minister Tanaka Makiko that he was "toy fireworks—short-lived and unable to light up the night sky."[41] Though the public tone of Sino-Japanese relations had improved, all of the substantive issues—war guilt, trade, Taiwan, textbooks, and territorial waters—remained. Surprisingly, despite these many contentious issues, China praised Abe's efforts at helping to improve ties.[42] Jia Linbo, senior fellow of the China Institute of International Studies, aptly summarized the Abe administration as although not resolving any of the outstanding problems in the bilateral relationship, at least able to shelve the differences so that the relationship could become more stable.[43]

FUKUDA TAKES THE HELM

Abe was succeeded by Fukuda Yasuō, who held the distinction of being the longest-serving chief cabinet secretary in postwar Japan, thereby bringing his extensive experience to the job. Considered less conservative than either Abe or his chief rival for the prime ministership, Asō Tarō, Fukuda's anointment, followed by his announcement that he would not visit the Yasukuni Shrine, held forth the promise of a better era in Sino-Japanese relations. Still, Chinese sources were circumspect, with Professor Shi Yinhong of Renmin University commenting that, since it would take the Beijing government some time to assess the impact of Fukuda's leadership, he did not expect that any major steps would be taken in the short term. Another Chinese academic opined that, although bilateral problems would no longer be clouded by the history issue, it was unlikely that any major problems between the two powers would be resolved soon.[44]

Some developments gave promise that the placatory policies of the post-Koizumi era would be continued. Japanese observers attended Chinese war games at the end of September,[45] and in the following month, a tenth round of negotiations began in Beijing to discuss the two sides' competing claims to the gas reserves of the East China Sea.[46] In November, a Chinese guided missile destroyer visited Tokyo for the first time since World War II. The two sides pledged cooperation on global warming issues, with Fukuda vowing his intention to turn the Pacific into an "inland sea."[47]

On the other hand, Fukuda also pronounced the maritime SDF's (MDSF's) international support missions to be constitutional, implicitly refuting the Beijing government's contention that they violated it and hence were another step toward the remilitarization of Japan. The Chinese government was also angered when Tokyo issued, several months apart, visas for the exiled Dalai Lama and Rebiya Kadeer, whom they held respectively responsible for riots in Tibet and in Uyghur areas of China.

Fukuda's foreign minister Asō announced a value-oriented diplomacy based on an "arc of freedom and prosperity" among democratic powers. In a major speech in Brussels to the North Atlantic Council, the principal decision-making body of the North Atlantic Treaty Organization (NATO)'s headquarters in Brussels[48] and elsewhere,[49] Asō raised the possibility of cooperation between the SDF and NATO. Although mentioning his awareness that NATO's primary role is collective self-defense, which due to Japan's constitutional "restraint," it could not be part of, Asō suggested that the process begin with what was mutually doable, while aiming for "big and more over time." Neither China nor other observers missed the significance of that statement.[50]

On the Japanese side, government officials were described as "infuriated" by China's deletion of two statements in a joint statement issued on the completion of bilateral economic talks. The first of these had expressed Tokyo's hope that the Chinese government would make efforts to increase the value of the yuan; the second stated that the PRC's participation in the Energy Charter Treaty would be significant, since the PRC remained an observer nation.[51]

The issue of poisoned food that had been imported from China emerged as another irritant. When dumplings contaminated with pesticide sickened a number of Japanese, Tokyo requested an investigation, to which the Chinese authorities agreed. However, after many months of apparent inaction, the Japanese side became frustrated by the lack of response. Japanese media and public opinion turned sharply critical of Fukuda when it was revealed that he had, at Beijing's request, withheld certain information on the investigation. Other poisoned food incidents occurred that involved different pesticides and melamine additives: the cumulative effect was a noticeable drop in Japanese food imports from the PRC.

When, in the spring of 2008, Japan offered to send aid to earthquake-stricken Sichuan, China refused permission because the aid would have arrived aboard an Air SDF (ASDF) cargo plane. Since other countries, including the United States, had sent aid on military carriers, many Japanese were offended. Beijing continued to maintain that the use of the SDF is a violation of Article 9 of the Japanese constitution. Japanese speculated that the true reason for the refusal was Beijing's reluctance to have the Japanese military appear in a favorable light inside China. They felt their hypothesis strengthened when only a year later Beijing agreed, in principle, to joint maneuvers with the MSDF. Tokyo, which had almost certainly suggested that the aid be dispatched on an ASDF plane as a trial balloon to test Beijing's response, then agreed to deliver the aid on civilian cargo planes. Its assistance was reportedly favorably received in the affected areas.

Japanese also reacted negatively to Beijing's decisive suppression of revolts in Tibet and Xinjiang, with even left and center-left newspapers advocating both that the Chinese government hold talks with the Dalai Lama and that it investigate the underlying causes of unrest in ethnic minority areas. Sympathy for minorities also affected the route of the Olympic torch through Japan: Tokyo refused to allow the torch to be protected by the Chinese guards, arguing that its own police were adequate. They noted that the guards' presence had already aroused animosity in several other countries. The abbot of the temple from which the torch was to proceed refused permission for the procession to begin there. Scuffles occurred between Chinese students supporting the PRC and supporters of Tibet, with Beijing registering its displeasure with Japanese authorities for allowing protests to occur.

Irritation even extended to animal exchanges. Ling Ling, the sole panda at Tokyo's large Ueno Zoo, died, some thought symbolically, just before Hu Jintao was due to visit Japan. Hu offered to send two pandas as replacements, thereby inadvertently setting off what the Japanese press termed a panda backlash: vocal popular annoyance with the high rental fees charged for the animals. These had amounted to a million dollars for Ling Ling alone.[52] Protracted negotiations took place on the price.[53]

Concern with China marred Hu Jintao's visit to Japan. To Beijing's annoyance, Japanese television juxtaposed photos of Hu meeting high-level politicians with footage of the unrest in Tibetan areas and interviews with the parents of children killed when the earthquake destroyed shoddily constructed school buildings. The media also expressed annoyance with Fukuda for not pressing Hu on either human rights or the pollution issue. With regard to the latter, Japan's environmental protection agency estimated that more than 40 percent of Kyushu's and over 30 percent of Kantō's pollution came from the PRC.[54] Also, the increasingly frequent sandstorms that accompanied rapid environmental deterioration in China periodically affected air quality in Japan.

Nor were the reciprocal ship visits as problem-free as the Chinese media portrayed them. It was understood that the exchanges would be conducted on the basis of equal treatment. However, the MSDF destroyer *Sazanami* was ordered to dock at Zhanjiang, home of the South China Sea fleet in June, whereas when the *Shenzhen* guided missile destroyer visited Japan the previous November, it was given permission to sail into Tokyo Bay. The level of protocol also disadvantaged the Japanese side. The *Shenzhen* had been met by the head of the MSDF, and Minister of Defense Ishiba Shigeru had attended a reception held for its crew, while the Japanese mariners had to make a separate trip to Beijing, where they were received by lower-level personages. Conservative newspaper *Sankei Shimbun* quoted an unnamed official as saying that China intended to use the exchanges for image enhancement, a sentiment echoed by the center-right *Yomiuri*.[55]

Taiwan remained an irritant as well. A new president, Ma Ying-jeou of the Kuomintang (KMT), took office in May 2008, with twenty-six Diet members angering Beijing by attending his inauguration. Ma had a reputation for favoring China and disliking Japan, in distinct contrast to his pro-Japan predecessor, Chen Shui-bian of the Democratic Progressive Party (DPP). Almost immediately, even leading KMT figures expressed concern that the Japan-Taiwan relationship was deteriorating. The then head of the KMT was dispatched on a week-long trip to Japan to mend fences, so that "Taiwan, Japan, and China can create a win-win-win situation," though without visible improvement in either Taiwan-Japan or Sino-Japanese relations.[56]

Beijing also protested when Chen's predecessor as president of Taiwan, Lee Teng-hui, a graduate of Japan's prestigious Kyōto University whose critics charge is more fluent in Japanese than mandarin,[57] received a visa to visit. Lee delivered a series of lectures on Japanese culture in Okinawa, where he met various high-ranking Okinawan dignitaries. Inter alia, he affirmed his belief that the contested Diaoyu/Senkaku Islands belong to Japan.[58]

Fukuda, who had never enjoyed high popularity ratings, became embroiled in parliamentary wrangles both with opposition parties and within his own LDP. After a particularly contentious debate over a health bill for the elderly, he abruptly announced his resignation.

ASŌ AS PRIME MINISTER

Although Fukuda was no stranger to foot-in-mouth remarks,[59] his successor, former foreign minister Asō Tarō, was still more prone to the problem. While Asō's objectionable comments spanned a wide range that included racial and ethnic sensitivities, several touched directly on issues that were inflammatory to China. In December 2005 he had described China as "a neighbor with one billion people equipped with nuclear bombs that has expanded its military outlays by double digits for 17 years in a row, and it is unclear what this is being used for. It is beginning to be a considerable threat."[60] A month later, Asō called for the emperor to visit the Yasukuni Shrine, later backtracking on the statement but saying that he hoped such a visit would be possible in the future.[61] In March 2006 he referred to Taiwan as a "law-abiding country,"[62] infuriating Beijing by implying that what it considers to be a province of China is a sovereign state.

Asō, though more conservative than Fukuda, made clear that he considered better relations with Beijing to be a priority. The new prime minister lost no time in visiting Beijing, declaring that the two countries' "mission for the next generation must be to reflect on the past in a humble manner and build our futures together." The two sides agreed to set up a hot line,[63] and vowed to work together on such issues as the global financial crisis, environmental degradation, and United Nations reform.[64]

Asō's tenure as prime minister was characterized by other actions that were, in essence, simply continuations of policies pursued by most of his predecessors. Japan and India signed a security cooperation pact whose impetus was widely interpreted as their mutual concern with rising Chinese power. Doubtless hoping to alleviate Beijing's apprehensions, Indian Prime Minister Manmohan Singh attached an unusual disclaimer to the customary statement that the pact was not directed against any third country: "least of all China."[65] A Japan-Australia agreement on security cooperation soon followed that, coupled with the Japan-U.S. security treaty and the agreement with India, could be construed as forming a quadripartite effort to balance growing Chinese military power.[66]

Asō's government also announced its intention to apply to the United Nations Commission on the Limits of the Continental Shelf to make a larger claim. If approved, Tokyo's seabed claims would increase by about 740,000 square kilometers, or nearly double the land area of Japan. This would give it privileged access to, among other resources, methane hydrate that could be used as an alternative to petroleum. Conversely, the claims would disadvantage other energy-hungry economies including that of China.[67]

In apparent response, two Chinese survey ships entered what the Japanese regard as their territorial waters a few weeks later, remaining for nine hours. Tokyo protested to Beijing,[68] though since Beijing also claims jurisdiction over the area, its official reaction was predictable. Lau Nai-keung, who represents Hong Kong on the PRC's Commission on Strategic Development, gave a less official and more blunt response, saying in effect that Japan should get used to it. There was, said Lau, tremendous domestic pressure for Beijing to take action to defend the country's vital national interests; if the government appeared weak on territorial issues, it would have to face nationwide protest. China would not be bullied.[69] Soon afterward, Beijing announced that it would begin building aircraft carriers, and expected to have two 50,000–60,000 ton, that is, mid-sized, vessels completed by 2015. In fact, it had one.[70]

Even as Asō was in Beijing and Toyota announced its intention to invest $586 million into building its seventh auto production plant, in Changchun,[71] fighting broke out between Chinese and Japanese students in Shanghai. The precipitating incident was rather minor—an argument among inebriated students—but quickly escalated into fistfights, bottle-throwing, and racial and ethnic slurs that were indicative of underlying hostility against the Japanese. The blogosphere quickly took up their cause. However, when bloggers began to criticize their own government for taking such a supine attitude toward Japan,[72] Chinese internet censors quickly shut down commentary.

At the same time, however, a Japanese hotel and condominium developer, the Apa Group, published on its company website the article that had taken first prize in an essay contest that the company had sponsored. The award-winning submission had been authored by the ASDF's head, Tamogami Toshio. In what his superiors regarded as a shocking deviation from the organization's standards of professionalism, Tamogami claimed that his country was not an aggressor in World War II, but instead had been trapped into involvement by the United States. Particularly inflammatory to Beijing were statements like, "The current Chinese government obstinately insists that there was a 'Japanese invasion,' but Japan obtained its interests legally under international law through the Sino-Japanese War, the Russo-Japanese War, and so on, and it placed its troops there based on treaties in order to protect those interests."

Tamogami also claimed that life under Japanese occupation had been "very moderate," in sharp distinction to the Beijing government's narrative of the war as well as numerous well-documented instances of barbaric cruelty, some of them recounted by remorseful Japanese who had participated in them. He concluded by urging his fellow countrymen to "take back the glorious history of Japan. A nation that denies its own history is destined to pursue a path to decline."[73] According to press reports, senior air force officers had recommended that ASDF members enter the contest.

Whether or not they did so, submissions from ASDF officers comprised about a third of the essays Apa had received.

Japan's defense minister immediately dismissed the ASDF head, announcing that he himself would voluntarily forfeit a month's pay to take responsibility for the incident. Tamogami, who had reached the legal retirement age of 60, would, the minister continued, leave the defense force. He was expected to voluntarily forego his pension of 60 million yen or approximately $600,000.

Summoned before the Diet for questioning, an unrepentant Tamogami stated that if he could not voice his views openly, Japan was no better than North Korea. He denied that he had urged other ASDF members to enter the contest, saying that there would have been hundreds of entries rather than the reported seventy-eight. Refusing to voluntarily surrender his pension, Tamogami became a darling of the right wing, many of whom shared his views.[74] Perhaps because the Japanese government's actions had been so swift, the Chinese side, while expressing shock and indignation over the incident,[75] did not take stronger retaliatory measures.

This and certain other conciliatory gestures, such as Asō's statement in a CCTV interview that Japan would "humbly review the past and [the two countries would] build the future together" and that the PRC's rapid economic rise would benefit not only Japan but also the whole world, appeared to convince the Beijing leadership that Asō had turned from hawk to moderate.[76] The two sides also reached agreement in principle on the exploitation of the disputed Chunxiao/Shirakaba oil and gas field in the East China Sea. Each party declared that, although it had not surrendered its claims to sovereignty over the disputed area, joint development would proceed.

Western media treated the agreement as an impressive breakthrough—the generally circumspect *Economist*, for example, described it as "profit before patriotism,"[77] while reaction from the parties involved was more nuanced. Japan's *Nikkei Weekly* pointed out that the agreement was "riddled with compromises" and left important details for future negotiations.[78] Despite the PRC's controlled media, many politically aware Chinese citizens expressed strong negative feelings about the pact. A Chinese journalist for an influential Singapore paper summarized his objections as, first, that the agreement had tacitly endorsed Japan's position on the median line; second, that Japan had made no reciprocal gesture for this concession with regard to the disputed Diaoyu/Senkaku Islands; and third, that Japan's "unreasonable" claim to a stake in Chunxiao had been partially met.[79]

Chinese official sources attempted to deflect criticism by arguing that what had been agreed on was not joint development but cooperative development: in the former, the two sides would participate as equal partners, each bound by its own laws and paying taxes to its own government, while under the latter arrangement, Japan would be bound by Chinese law and pay taxes to China.[80] PRC critics were not satisfied with these statements. Chinese official sources had several times used the word "joint" rather than "cooperative."[81] And, while a Japanese official agreed that Japan might pay taxes to China, he added that the details had yet to be finalized. References to the project ceased: patriotism had prevailed over profit.

Although Asō did not visit the Yasukuni Shrine himself, eighty-seven Diet members, including eleven who held government posts, attended the shrine's April 2009 spring festival.[82] Asō did, however, send a *masakaki*, a traditional shrine offering that even Koizumi, who gave a floral bouquet,[83] had not done. The offering was presented under Asō's formal title as prime minister, thereby conferring a degree of official approval. It was, moreover, expensive, costing 50,000 yen, or about $500, though Asō was careful to specify, as had Koizumi, that he had paid the cost himself.[84] Not surprisingly, this did not assuage Beijing. According to a statement read by Beijing's foreign ministry spokesperson, the Chinese government had conveyed its "strong concern and dissatisfaction, and stressed the high sensitivity of historical issues," adding that "any erroneous actions by Japan will have gravely negative consequences for bilateral relations, and we demand that the Japanese side exercise caution in its words and actions and appropriately deal with this."[85]

Despite concern that Beijing would postpone a previously scheduled Asō trip to Beijing, the meeting took place on schedule. The two sides pledged cooperation to combat swine flu, which neither had yet reported cases of. Asō also suggested negotiations on a Sino-Japanese free trade agreement (FTA). The latter proposal was probably more significant for its symbolism than indicative of hopes that it could be quickly concluded. An earlier suggestion by China for such an arrangement had aroused misgivings in Tokyo that an FTA could be a Trojan horse of economic penetration by the PRC. Hu Jintao called on Japan "to properly settle existing problems and disputes between the two countries, especially historical issues" and Asō replied that "a small minority of people in his country feared that

China's growing economic power could translate into military strength," but that he had faith in China's peaceful rise. He remained "very optimistic about the future relations of the two sides."[86]

Domestically, however, Asō's popularity suffered from the effects of the global economic crisis as well as his reluctance to call a lower-house election that the media and many voters thought was long overdue.[87] When, in August 2009, the contest was finally held, a disgruntled electorate that professed itself eager for change gave a rare but decisive victory to a non-LDP party, the Minshutō or Democratic Party of Japan (DPJ).

HATOYAMA

Hatoyama Yukio, standard-bearer of the Minshutō, assumed office in September 2009, having promised to reorganize and rejuvenate the Japanese political and economic structure. While domestic policy was uppermost on this agenda, Hatoyama promised, as had his predecessors, to improve relations with China. To this end, he not only pledged that he would not visit Yasukuni, but that he would urge his ministers to do the same. The new prime minister also announced his intention to end the SDF deployments abroad, to move the controversial Futenma U.S. marine base out of Okinawa, and to conduct a foreign policy that would be more independent from that of the United States. An agreement in principle was reached on military exchanges and joint PRC-Japanese exercises.[88] All of these were compatible with Beijing's previously stated preferences. As Hatoyama was soon to discover, however, implementing the pledges would prove very difficult.

Hatoyama also advocated the formation of an East Asian Community (EAC) that would apparently not include the United States. The Chinese were pleased with the concept of an EAC but had different preferences for its membership. While welcoming a diminution of U.S. influence in Asia, they did not approve of Hatoyama's plan to include India, Australia, and New Zealand, pointing out that none of the three is located in East Asia. Not mentioned but clearly important to Beijing's calculations was the fact that India and Australia have security agreements with Japan that Beijing, among others, believes are directed against the PRC.

Washington, which considers the United States to be a Pacific, though not an East Asian, nation, expressed misgivings about the significance of being excluded from the group. Hatoyama appeared to waffle, saying during a visit to Thailand that there would be "some U.S. involvement in the community" but not specifying what this should be. Nor were Southeast Asian states without reservations about the proposed community. A Singapore newspaper opined that the EAC was being used as a surrogate for Sino-Japanese rivalry, and that Beijing appeared willing to give the Association of Southeast Asian Nations (ASEAN) a role in shaping the community, if only to blunt Japanese influence within it.[89] Singapore's former prime minister Lee Kwan Yew stressed the importance of the United States remaining in Asia to balance China's rise, which Beijing reacted sharply to, again stressing the PRC's commitment to peace and stability in the area.[90] Within Japan, there was bureaucratic resistance to the EAC concept and mockery from critics of the prime minister.

Hatoyama was also criticized domestically for endangering the security treaty with the United States, which, partly due to concerns with rapidly increasing PRC military power, enjoyed recent approval ratings in the 85 percent range. The center-left *Asahi* quoted an unnamed government official as saying that "China is likely maneuvering to prevent Japan from playing a leadership role in East Asia. China might also be trying to drive a wedge between Japan and the United States by taking advantage of this [EAC] issue." The paper's editor in chief faulted Hatoyama for acting before he performed *nemawashi*, which can be loosely translated as sounding out all concerned parties beforehand in order to reach an agreement prior to announcing a policy decision.[91]

Magazines such as *Sapio* and *Shukan Daiyamondo* followed suit, with the former suggesting that the United States would step up its "Japan passing" stance if Hatoyama continued his polices and the latter that the prime minister's foreign policy flip-flops were likely to cause problems for Japan.[92] American Secretary of Defense Robert Gates, visiting Tokyo shortly after Hatoyama took office, pointed out that an agreement on moving the Futenma base had been reached in 2006 after years of negotiation, and that he expected the agreement to be honored. Moreover, he stated, there was simply no alternative location available.[93] Hatoyama then suggested moving the existing U.S. air force base at Kadena, also in Okinawa, causing thousands of residents in that area to demonstrate against the idea.[94] Less than two months after assuming office, Hatoyama found most of his policy initiatives stymied, and relations with China scarcely improved.

When the Japanese government expressed concern about increased Chinese naval activities in waters surrounding Japan, Beijing replied that its actions were no more than it was entitled to. At a meeting of foreign ministers in May, China's then foreign minister Yang Jiechi became so incensed at his counterpart Okada Katsuya's request for a reduction in his country's nuclear arsenal that he seemed ready to walk out, and failed to speak to Okada at dinner that evening.[95] Another hint that Beijing had begun to cool on Hatoyama was *Xinhua*'s description of his meeting with visiting Premier Wen Jiabao as "frank," signaling that it had not gone well.[96] In a meeting before the Yang-Okada exchange, the agency had used the more neutral term "in depth." [97] If the Chinese government had not been pleased with the visit, the Japanese public was. A poll taken after Wen had jogged and performed tai-chi exercises with ordinary Japanese in Yoyogi Park indicated that a majority thought he would make a better prime minister than any likely indigenous candidate.[98] Hatoyama resigned in June 2010, after less than a year in office.

THE DIAOYU/SENKAKU ISSUE REDUX

Hatoyama's successor, the DPJ's Kan Naoto, had campaigned on a slogan adapted from Barack Obama: "Yes, he Kan." Fate was not kind to the implementation of this rhetoric. On September 7, 2010, the captain of a Chinese fishing boat rammed two Japanese Coast Guard (JCG) vessels in waters off the Diaoyu/Senkaku Islands. The JCG arrested the Chinese captain. Instead of deporting him as had been previous practice, the government announced that the captain would be put on trial. This case was indeed different, however, in that expensive government property had been damaged.

Puzzling observers, the Japanese government, which had a videotape of the incident, refused to release it. Later, under pressure, it reluctantly agreed to allow Diet members to view the tape. Eventually, a Japanese coast guardsman uploaded it to the internet, corroborating charges that the captain's actions had been intentional. This, however, was irrelevant to Beijing, which argued that, since the islands were Chinese territory, the Japanese Coast Guard should not have been there. When Tokyo failed to comply with its demand that the captain be immediately released, the Chinese government imposed economic sanctions that included the threat of a cessation of rare earth exports[99] that were crucial to the Japanese automotive manufacturing industry and subjecting Japanese imports to agonizingly lengthy customs inspection procedures. Chinese travel agencies were advised against booking trips to Japan, and four Japanese nationals were arrested and accused of spying.[100]

Japan ultimately capitulated. The Okinawa prosecutor's office stated that it had decided to release the captain "in consideration of Sino-Japanese ties," although reserving the right to prosecute him later—not explaining how this could be done. The captain returned home to a hero's welcome, as all Japanese political parties and major newspapers condemned the Kan administration, using phrases like "adrift in a crisis." A scathing cartoon in center-left *Asahi*, normally sympathetic to China, depicted a poker game in which an astonished Chinese President Hu Jintao is exclaiming, "Why did he throw his trump card down so early?" as Kan tables his "release the captain card."[101]

In a clear signal that it intended to assert its claims to sovereignty in the area, Beijing then announced that its own ships would patrol the waters around the disputed islands, which it has done.[102] Tokyo asked for, and received, a reaffirmation of Washington's commitment to its promises in the security treaty. Beijing, however, had made its point and Kan had backed down, to a cacophony of disapproving voices from across the Japanese political spectrum.

There was much speculation that Beijing had instructed the fishing boat captain to take these actions. However, separate visits from correspondents for two Japanese papers a year later found the captain under house arrest. The local government had purchased his boat, forbidden him to return to fishing, and provided continuous police "protection" to ensure compliance.[103] "From hero to zero," quipped one observer. Whether the captain had acted under orders or on his own volition, given the increase in the numbers of Chinese vessels patrolling the area, there is no doubt that the Beijing government had taken advantage of the collision to strengthen its presence in the area.

Perhaps even more worrisome from Japan's point of view, Russia backed China's stance on the islands, while China continued to back Russia's claim to the Northern Territories.[104] Kan also was faced with opposition from both other parties and within the DPJ on both domestic and foreign policy issues. T-shirts mocked his campaign promise, announcing "No, he Kan't."

Although Chinese government rhetoric was strident, Beijing appeared to be suppressing anti-Japanese demonstrations, even on the sensitive September 18 anniversary of the Mukden/Shenyang incident. The dissident blogger Han Han tweaked the government on this issue, stating that protests against foreigners by people who were not allowed to protest at home were nothing but a group dance, called up by a master when he needed yipping dogs. Authorities erased the item, but not before it was posted to weibo, the Chinese Twitter, where it was seen by millions.[105]

Other, more subdued Chinese voices urged moderation, suggesting such measures as more interaction among nongovernmental organizations. In a lengthy essay for *Jingji Guancha Bao* (Economic Observer), Ma Licheng warned of a "typhoon of nationalism developing violently."[106] His government made full use of this for its own purposes: a Japanese envoy quietly sent to Beijing to negotiate told a Tokyo television station that State Councilor Dai Bingguo told him that, had the fishing boat captain not been released, the Chinese people might have landed on the islands, perhaps even leading to war.[107] Since the statement seemed to rationalize the Kan administration's unpopular decision, it met with considerable skepticism. By the end of 2010, Kan's popularity had fallen to an all-time low of 23.6 percent.[108]

JAPAN'S TRIPLE DISASTER AND NEW PRESSURES FROM CHINA

A few months later, a far greater disaster befell Japan—not a nationalist typhoon in China but an earthquake in Japan accompanied by a tsunami that triggered a nuclear meltdown. In a grotesque twist of fate, the horrendous disaster actually helped prolong the already beleaguered Prime Minister Kan's tenure in office: Partisan politics abated temporarily in response to the magnitude of the recovery effort. American aid in the form of Operation Tomodachi (friend) was rapid and effective, helping to silence the Hatoyama-Ozawa wing of the DPJ that had favored moving closer to China and away from the United States.

While differences of opinion over China policy lost salience, problems of how to finance the massive rebuilding of the devastated Tohoku area and replace nuclear power generation with markedly more expensive alternate energy sources were equally intractable. Kan survived a no confidence vote only by agreeing to step down later after certain legislative measures had passed. With that accomplished, he resigned, being succeeded in September by former Finance Minister Noda Yoshihiko.

Cyberattacks believed to emanate from the PRC increased in intensity, targeting government offices as well as Japan's leading defense contractor, Mitsubishi Heavy Industries. Chinese ships continued to patrol areas around the Diaoyu/Senkaku Islands, with the Tokyo government reluctant to take action. Noda did assent to the naming of nearby islets—the Diaoyu/Senkaku Islands having been named long before. China took umbrage. A *Renmin Ribao* article of January 18, 2012, stating that the action "is a blatant move to damage China's core national interests" (*hexin guojia liyi*) caused particular concern.[109] With "core interests" never explicitly defined but generally construed to mean something Beijing would be willing to fight for, this was ominous news: previously, only Tibet, Taiwan, and Xinjiang had been named as core interests.

A few weeks later, Guangdong province's *Nanfang Zhoubao* (Southern Weekly) stated, with specific reference to the ships' activities "near Okinawa," that although the ultimate mission of China's navy was to build a "harmonious ocean," Japan must understand that it would "go to war to defend the country's core interests."[110] Surprisingly, the next month, Rear Admiral Yin Zhuo, whose past remarks had often been strident, announced that neither the Diaoyu nor Senkaku islands in the South China Sea that China disputes with several other countries were core interests.[111] Subsequent pronouncements by vice-president and heir apparent Xi Jinping and other high-ranking officials tended to be phrased ambiguously, sometimes saying that sovereignty and territorial issues were core interests without specifically naming which territories or coupling "core interests" with another phrase, as when Xi Jinping told visiting Diet members that both sides should be prudent in handling sensitive issues "especially those of great concern and related to core interests."[112] Plainly, Beijing had opted for strategic ambiguity. Chinese maritime patrols continued.

THE ISLANDS CONTROVERSY INTENSIFIES

In April, frustrated with what he regarded as the Noda government's inattention to Beijing's gradual envelopment of the islands, Tokyo Governor Ishihara Shintarō announced in a speech in Washington, DC, that he intended to buy on behalf of Tokyo municipality four of the five islands from their private Japanese owners, the Kurihara family. One island was already owned by the Japanese central government. Since Ishihara had hinted that he would build structures on the islands, which was bound to raise Beijing's response level, the central government responded by saying that it would buy the islands. This was likely to have been Ishihara's intention from the outset: surrounded by reporters while still in the arrival area at Narita airport, the governor said that "if the state takes every possible measure including sovereignty, Tokyo [municipality] will pull out any time."[113] Possibly to ensure that the central government did not procrastinate, he nonetheless pressed on, inviting citizens to contribute to the purchase fund. Within a short time, millions of yen were collected. The Japanese ambassador to China publicly warned that nationalizing the islands would lead to "an extremely grave crisis" with the PRC, thus disputing the wisdom of a government policy and leading to his dismissal a short while later.

After protracted negotiations with both municipal and central governments, the two brothers who owned three of the islands agreed to sell them to the latter, with the sister who owned the fourth declining all offers. Beijing quickly dashed Noda's hope that a central government purchase along with his implied promise that no structures would be erected on the islands would assuage its anger. Some Chinese analysts speculated that the prime minister and the governor had arranged a "good cop–bad cop routine," which Japanese familiar with the level of animosity between the two found ludicrous.[114]

Surprisingly, the Noda government allowed the World Uyghur Congress, an organization advocating Xinjiang's independence from China, to hold its annual meeting in Tokyo in mid-May. Delegates were addressed by, among others, another of China's bêtes noirs, Tamogami Toshio, who had been dismissed as ASDF head after publishing an essay disputing the contention that Japan had been an aggressor nation during World War II.

In China, a new video game called Defend the Diaoyu was introduced. Players were challenged to accumulate "rage" in order to level attacks against zombie-like Japanese soldiers. The game had seventy-one levels, one for each of the islands and islets of the Diaoyu/Sentaku group. Another game on the website of the same company, ZQGame, put players into a virtual 1937 Nanjing, urging them to pay back blood with blood.[115] Although it may be assumed that the game company's motivation was profit, it was hardly conducive to calming troubled waters.

While railing against the Japanese government's "illegal" and outrageous actions, there were also indications that Beijing had no wish to let the altercation escalate. Ta Kung Pao, better known for inflammatory comments than soothing ones, cited CASS Japan expert Lu Yadong's prediction that the recent "spats . . . won't affect their relationship in general" and his suggestion that Beijing increase its contributions to earthquake reconstruction work while working toward a free trade agreement with Tokyo and Seoul.[116] The two sides held quiet talks on the islands, with Chinese sources attributing Japan's hard line on the issue to the country's weakness.[117]

A retired Japanese diplomat privately stated that there were consistent messages from Beijing to Tokyo in August and September that so long as Japan maintained the tacit three no's (no landing, no construction, no research activities), the purchase would not be deemed a fundamental violation of the status quo, and that these messages continued for a while after the purchase.[118] However, this cannot be confirmed, nor can the existence of a tacit three no's understanding. A Japanese Coast Guard official stated to the author that he had never heard of such an agreement.[119]

In this period as well, several trade agreements were concluded and the two countries agreed to exchange information on nuclear safety. Nonetheless, when the islands were formally sold on September 11, 2012, Beijing published its own maritime baselines that included all the disputed islands, and anti-Japanese demonstrations erupted in over a hundred Chinese cities, accompanied by great property damage and minor personal injuries. These bled over into the 81st anniversary of the Shenyang/Mukden incident on September 18th. Some Chinese officials cautioned demonstrators to remember that the enemy was the Japanese government, not Japanese citizens, and some netizens worried that, if Japanese businesses transferred their operations elsewhere and tourists ceased to visit the PRC due to the hostile climate, the real losers would be Chinese workers and, ultimately, social stability.[120] A university professor advised against calls for boycotts since they would fail: consumers the world over vote with their wallets, and Japanese products enjoyed a good reputation among Chinese.[121]

Several foreign international law experts have stated that the Japanese government's purchase of the islands has no relevance to the sovereignty issue: changing the name on the title from individual owners to the state is simply a transfer within the Japanese legal system and has no meaning or force outside that system.[122] This being the case, Noda's action may have done no more than provide the Chinese government with a plausible claim that it had been provoked—an interpretation that would be reinforced by Ishihara's words—and therefore had the right to retaliate by increasing the tempo of its gradual absorption of the islands. However, Ishihara had plainly framed the purchase of the islands as an issue of sovereignty.

Surprisingly, Beijing informed the Japanese government that ceremonies to honor the 40th anniversary of Sino-Japanese normalization would take place as scheduled.[123] So they did, albeit in a lower-key fashion than originally intended, perhaps to avoid rekindling nationalist passions. Nor did Noda and Hu send each other the usual congratulatory anniversary telegrams.[124] Still, the Chinese government made a small gesture of friendship, reversing an earlier decision and allowing Japanese runners to register for the Beijing Marathon.[125]

Chinese aircraft and ships increased their presence in the area around the disputed islands, with several PLA generals outspoken about the need to take action and Vice-Chair of the CCP's Central Military Commission Xu Caihou saying that troops should be "prepared for any possible military combat."[126] A newspaper suggested that Okinawa should not be regarded as belonging to Japan, since it had had a tribute relationship with China for many centuries.[127] The United States responded that its mutual security treaty with Japan "applied to any provocative set of circumstances,"[128] thus seeming to move beyond the language of the treaty, which refers to "armed attacks."[129]

CHINESE DOMESTIC FACTORS

In China, Xi Jinping, designated successor to Hu Jintao as leader of the CCP and of China, disappeared for two weeks in September just prior to the party congress that was to formalize his anointment, and in the midst of what appeared to be a power struggle at the highest levels of government. Xi reappeared, with Chinese netizens expressing disbelief at the explanation that he had injured his back while playing soccer. The party congress had already been postponed until November. When at last it was convened, Xi was duly appointed, with a solid majority of members of his princeling faction in the Standing Committee of the Politburo, though not in the Politburo itself. High-ranking officials were indicted and convicted on corruption charges that many analysts both inside and outside China considered motivated as much by factional affiliations as financial improprieties.

The economy was also a concern. A World Bank report issued earlier in the year had warned that major restructuring was imperative lest the PRC become mired in a middle-income trap.[130] Well before the report was issued, the leadership had expressed concern with the implications of the widening income gap between the country's poorest and wealthiest citizens and the increasing willingness of the disgruntled to protest publicly for what the media delicately referred to as "social stability." Pressures for rapid economic development had paid little attention to the environment, which was deteriorating rapidly.

Xi left no doubt that he intended to be a strong leader, announcing a somewhat vaguely defined China dream. In that this had been the title of a book published by a senior military officer who urged the PRC to surpass the United States as the leading military power in the world, Xi's dream could be interpreted as foreshadowing a higher military profile.[131] However, Xi also equated the dream with peace and prosperity for his country.[132]

ABE RETURNS TO THE PRIME MINISTERSHIP

Meanwhile, in Japan, Noda faced daunting problems of a different sort. Rebuilding from the devastation wrought by the triple disaster had left Japan with debts that were 200 percent of its GDP. A vocal segment of the population demanded that all nuclear power plants be shut down, while other citizens objected to higher electricity bills and business leaders argued that economic recovery depended on the adequate, reliable sources of energy that nuclear power had helped to supply. Noda was forced to devote considerable effort to pushing through an unpopular 5 percent increase in the consumption tax. His popularity suffered and, when the DPJ lost about three-quarters of its seats in the general election in December 2012, Noda resigned to take responsibility. Abe Shinzō, who had led the LDP to an absolute majority in the House of Representatives, became prime minister for a second time.

Chinese authorities, aware that the "battling diplomacy" Abe had promised in his prior campaign for prime minister became noticeably softer after he took office, expressed willingness to improve bilateral relations but only under certain circumstances. A lengthy *Renmin Ribao* article entitled "Let Us See How the Japanese Authorities Clear Up the 'Mess'" set three conditions: no visits to the Yasukuni Shrine, acknowledgment of China's sovereignty over the Diaoyu Islands issue, and no amendment of the Japanese constitution.[133]

It is unlikely that the Chinese side considered the second condition realistic, but no Japanese prime minister, including Abe during his first term in office, had visited Yasukuni, and polls consistently showed that a solid majority of the Japanese public opposed amendment of the constitution. However, Abe's efforts disappointed Beijing on all three criteria. During his earlier term as prime minister, Abe's first foreign trip had been to Beijing; this time it was to Washington, where he declared emphatically, "Japan is back." Within a year, he had strongly affirmed Japan's sovereignty over the disputed islands, begun discussions on amending the constitution, and visited the Yasukuni Shrine. To the expected barrage of criticism from Beijing was added an unusual public criticism by Washington, doubtless prompted by concern that the United States become involved in the issue.

Buoyed by an impressive LDP victory in the House of Councillors election in the summer of 2013, Abe also finalized the formation of a national security council modeled on that of the United States,[134] issued new defense guidelines that called for "proactive pacifism"[135] but stopped short of claiming the right to strike enemy targets overseas,[136] announced his intention to increase defense budgets by 5 percent over the course of five years[137] and to purchase state-of-the art fighter planes and helicopters from the United States. A new secrets protection law was passed.[138]

On the grounds that it was necessary to counter a drift to the left in education, a school district was told to adopt a more conservative textbook than it had originally chosen.[139] Abenomics, an ambitious plan comprising "three arrows" of fiscal stimulus, monetary easing, and economic restructuring, was to return Japan to more robust economic growth. To compensate for demographic contraction, the country should use existing workers more efficiently: less time spent in nonproductive activities like compulsory social events and, in what was immediately dubbed "womenomics," better use of female workers.

China, while railing against revived Japanese militarism, continued with its string of double-digit increases in the defense budget and announced the creation of an Air Defense Identification Zone (ADIZ) that included not only the Diaoyu/Senkaku area but an area disputed with South Korea as well. Foreign analysts sympathetic to Beijing defended the action as motivated not so much by Japan as by the Chinese feeling that every modern country should have an ADIZ;[140] others pointed out that the PRC's ADIZ was quite different from those of other states, amounting to an air control zone rather than an air defense zone.[141]

U.S. maritime law expert Peter Dutton termed China's action "provocative," and that China had "overplayed its hand," noting that no other country had ever proclaimed an ADIZ that overlapped the territory of another country. Whereas civilian aircraft routinely identify themselves to air traffic controllers in the vicinity of their flight paths by filing flight plans with the International Civil Aviation Organization, military planes are a different matter. Since China's ADIZ is in international airspace where Beijing has no jurisdictional authority, they are immune from these requirements. By demanding that planes identify themselves and follow any instructions they are given, China is overstepping the boundary of what is internationally lawful under the customary law that governs ADIZs.[142]

A continuation of the past pattern of chicken-egg stimulus and response was evident—for example, just as Ishihara reacted to increased Chinese incursions around the Diaoyu/Senkakus by suggesting that the Tokyo municipality buy them and Beijing responded by stepping up patrols and, a year later, established an ADIZ that encompassed the islands, Abe may have chosen to pay respects at the Yasukuni Shrine in retaliation for the establishment of the ADIZ. The parties involved typically deny any connection between events, with Abe, for example, vowing that he wished only to pray for the souls of all war dead on the 1st anniversary of his ascension to the prime ministership. In both China and Japan, there were voices urging an end to the stimulus-response-stimulus pattern, but they were obscured by the righteous indignation of nationalists.

The year 2014 began with the Chinese and Japanese ambassadors to London comparing each other's country to Voldemort, with the latter in particular showing an impressive knowledge of the intricate details of the Harry Potter series.[143] As this exchange of barbs was proceeding, the Japanese government announced plans to nationalize 280 islands and islets out of the approximately 400 that serve as markers for determining Japan's territorial waters,[144] and Beijing opened a memorial hall on the site where Korean independence activist An Jung Geung had assassinated former Prime Minister Ito Hirobumi in 1909.¹⁴⁵

A few weeks later, an LDP panel recommended a change in the interpretation of the constitution to allow Japan the right to collective self-defense, despite strong opposition. A poll conducted by the center-left *Mainichi* and Saitama University indicated that 54 percent of respondents were opposed to the change, vis-à-vis 28 percent for it.¹⁴⁶ Still, the need for such a change was reinforced when, shortly thereafter, an American naval intelligence expert stated that Chinese military activities indicated that it was training for a short, sharp war with Japan.¹⁴⁷ Abe did not attend the Yasukuni Shrine's spring festival, but again sent, at his own expense, a *masasaki* offering.¹⁴⁸

In May, in what seemed to be a calculated provocation, Abe was photographed in a plane designated 731—the designation of the unit that had carried out grisly medical experiments in China during World War II.¹⁴⁹ In China, the State Administration of Radio, Television and Film ordered an increase in "patriotic, anti-fascist content."¹⁵⁰ Films in which World War II Japanese soldiers were killed by brave party members became a genre. Some actors make their living "dying" in film after film¹⁵¹ in what South Korean news agency Yonhap termed the CCP's "campaigns to remind its people of the 1937 mass killings and rapes by Japanese troops in . . . Nanjing."¹⁵²

To the amusement of some PRC netizens, several newspapers accused Doraemon, an anime cat, of poisoning the minds of Chinese youth.¹⁵³ If this was an official effort to sway public opinion, it did not work: the big blue cat remained as popular as ever. However, a poll jointly conducted by the official *China Daily* and the Japanese nongovernmental *Genron* in five Chinese cities revealed that 53.4 percent of respondents believed that there would be war, with more than 20 percent believing that it would occur in a few years.¹⁵⁴

The two sides sniped at each other during the Shangri La dialogue in May 2014. Prime Minister Abe, delivering the keynote speech to the gathering, pledged that Japan would play a more active role in making peace in Asia and the world as well as "offer[ing] its utmost support for the efforts of the Association of Southeast Asian Nations countries as they work to ensure the security of the seas and the skies."¹⁵⁵ Given the conflicts between China and several ASEAN states over territorial issues in the South China Sea, Beijing reacted sharply, accusing Abe of creating an imaginary China threat to provide an excuse for remilitarization.

EFFORTS TO MANAGE TENSIONS

Certain events thereafter seemed to indicate that both sides were taking steps to reduce tensions. When Abe presented a special award to a Chinese student who jumped into a river to rescue a drowning Japanese child, Chinese media interpreted the gesture as a sign that he wanted warmer relations.[156] Beijing had reacted less sharply than in previous years to Abe's sending a gift to Yasukuni—saying it "firmly opposed" the action, whereas in 2013 it had issued a "strong protest" and "severe condemnation." For his part, Abe had indicated a desire for a bilateral summit, omitting his previous demands that it be held without preconditions. Quashing rumors that the way was being paved for a state visit, Chinese authorities stated bluntly that "the ball is in Japan's court,"[157] and attention turned to whether the two would talk on the sidelines of the Asia-Pacific Economic Cooperation (APEC) conference in Beijing. A meeting between State Councilor Yang Jiechi and National Security Adviser Yachi Shotarō resulted in what the Chinese foreign ministry described as

> a four-point agreement to improve bilateral ties, agreeing to resume political, diplomatic and security dialogue while acknowledging different positions on the Diaoyu Islands:
> - the two sides have affirmed that they will follow the principles of the four political documents[158] reached between China and Japan and continue to develop the China-Japan strategic relationship of mutual benefit.
> - in the spirit of "facing history squarely and looking forward to the future," the two sides have reached some agreement on overcoming political obstacles in the bilateral relations.
> - *the two sides have acknowledged that different positions exist between them regarding the tensions which have emerged in recent years over the Diaoyu Islands and some waters in the East China Sea, and agreed to prevent the situation from aggravating through dialogue and consultation and establish crisis management mechanisms to avoid contingencies.* [emphasis added]
> - the two sides have agreed to gradually resume political, diplomatic and security dialogue through various multilateral and bilateral channels and to make efforts to build political mutual trust.[159]

Initially, the Chinese press considered the agreement a diplomatic success: the Japanese had at last agreed to acknowledge the existence of a dispute. *Xinhua* cited Deputy Head of the Institute of Japan Study of the Chinese Academy of Social Sciences Yang Bojiang's view that "the hard-earned agreement is a precious step towards a better bilateral relationship. The two countries did it for the sake of a stable, healthy and sustainable relationship and the regional peace and stability." Another CASS Institute deputy head, Gao Hong, opined that "every time when the China-Japan relations went wrong, it was because Japan made wrong moves about historical issues and territorial disputes. That's why this four-point agreement is important." Other unnamed experts added that Abe's concession resulted from mounting domestic and international pressures for compromise.[160]

However, the Japanese side issued a different version of what had been agreed to, its foreign ministry reporting that

> toward the improvement of the Japan-China relations, quiet discussions have been held between the Governments of Japan and China. Both sides have come to share views on the following points:
>
> 1. Both sides confirmed that they would observe the principles and spirit of the four basic documents between Japan and China and that they would continue to develop a mutually beneficial relationship based on common strategic interests
> 2. Both sides shared some recognition that, following the spirit of squarely facing history and advancing toward the future, they would overcome political difficulties that affect their bilateral relations.
> 3. *Both sides recognized that they had different views as to the emergence of tense situations in recent years in the waters of the East China Sea, including those around the Senkaku Islands, and shared the view that, through dialogue and consultation, they would prevent the deterioration of the situation, establish a crisis management mechanism and avert the rise of unforeseen circumstances.* [emphasis added]
> 4. Both sides shared the view that, by utilizing various multilateral and bilateral channels, they would gradually resume dialogue in political, diplomatic and security fields and make an effort to build a political relationship of mutual trust.[161]

In addition to the more informal nature of the encounter connoted by "quiet discussions" and "sharing views," the Japanese side denied the PRC's assertion that Tokyo had recognized the existence of a dispute over the sovereignty of the islands: it had simply taken note of the Chinese view that there was a dispute, without actually acknowledging that there was one.

However, the agreement, or perhaps quiet discussions, did enable a brief meeting between Abe and Xi Jinping at the APEC meeting. It lasted only twenty-five minutes, less than half the time usually accorded to such encounters. The islands were not mentioned, and even the flags of the two countries, normally standard backdrop for such sessions, were absent.[162] In what was to become a defining symbol of the meeting, the photograph of the handshake between Xi and Abe showed both looking as if in pain.

After Japanese Foreign Minister Kishida declared that the agreement was nonbinding,[163] the Chinese side accused the Japanese of duplicity, of having seemed to agree that there was a dispute in order to contrive the meeting.[164] Chinese critics also noted that Abe had not promised to no longer visit the Yasukuni Shrine.[165]

Beijing continued to slowly increase pressure, staging drills that a Chinese commentator described as sandwiching Japan in from north to south, as Tokyo noticed that two Chinese warships were permanently stationed about 200 kilometers north of the disputed islands, sailing in a zigzag pattern or abruptly changing direction as if trying to approach the islands. An official website was launched in Chinese, English, and Japanese, featuring maps and purported copies of ancient documents to support China's claims.[166]

At the same time as these pressures increased, Premier Li Keqiang told a visiting Japanese delegation that bilateral relations could proceed on the basis of the four-point consensus,[167] presumably meaning but not explicitly mentioning the Chinese understanding thereof. Skeptics were unconvinced: the soothing words were meant to anaesthetize the Japanese to a slow but steady imposition of Beijing's will. This tended to reinforce their desire to resist. A record high of 83.1 percent of Japanese declared themselves hostile to China, up 4.2 percent from April 2013; those who felt friendly slipped 5.4 percent to 14.8 percent.[168]

In the opinion of Shi Yinhong, Renmin Daxue's outspoken professor, leaders on all sides—including India, Australia, and the United States as well as Japan and China—were locked into self-reinforcing cycles of aggression with U.S.-anchored "defensive coalitions" that Beijing saw as offensive. Regardless of whether Beijing's strategy is counterproductive, said Shi, it will continue because of popular nationalism, the dynamics of the PLA, and the personal belief of strategic perspectives of the top leaders.[169]

Part Two

8

Economic Rivalry

ECONOMIC RELATIONS BEFORE NORMALIZATION

The Japanese economy was devastated by World War II; that of China heavily scarred by both the war with Japan and the civil war that followed it. A complete reorientation of the trade relations of both took place. The terms of surrender had stripped Japan of 44 percent of its overseas assets, 80 percent of its merchant marine, and large portions of its industrial equipment. More than a quarter of Japanese prewar trade had been with China, the bulk of it in Japan's client state of Manchuria. In the immediate postwar years, the Japanese economy was almost wholly dependent on the United States as the source of aid for reconstruction, needed imports, and markets for its products.[1]

The nation's recovery from wartime devastation was impressive. General MacArthur's 1950 new year's message to Japan reported that coal, utilities, and other basic components of industrial activity were approaching prewar levels, thus establishing the basis of full industrial recovery, and that food production had reached postwar highs.

The Ministry of International Trade and Industry (MITI), established in 1949, was instrumental in the creation of a developmental state, sometimes referred to as "Japan Incorporated" in light of the close ties between government and major corporations. MITI identified and nurtured the industries that seemed best able to provide the engines of overall development. In the 1950s, these were heavy industries like iron and steel, shipbuilding, and electric power; in the 1970s, and 1980s, consumer durables such as automobiles and semiconductors, and in the 1980s, advanced technology electronics and computers. Foreign trade was regulated to protect fledgling domestic industries, and export subsidies provided to them. Strict regulations on foreign direct investment ensured that transnational corporations could not dominate domestic markets at the expense of indigenous companies. A banking system closely tied to the government, and the banks to each other in an intricate system of interlocking relationships known as *keiretsu*, provided capital to industry at preferential interest rates.[2]

Precluded from trade with China after 1949, Japanese businesses reestablished investments in the country's former colony of Taiwan, now reincarnated as the Republic of China. The Korean War was also a tremendous boon to the nation's economy.with Japanese factories providing supplies needed to support the U.S.-led United Nations military effort on the peninsula.

China could not count on a comparable level of generosity on the part of its Soviet ally, whose own economy, never as robust as that of the United States, had suffered badly during World War II. Stalin was, moreover, so suspicious of Mao that he maneuvered the PRC into helping Kim Il-song fight the war in Korea, knowing that it would weaken China and prevent it from taking Taiwan away from Chiang Kai-shek's forces.[3] In addition, Soviet troops denuded north China of most of its Japanese-built industrial facilities. The PRC did, however, possess far more abundant natural resources than Japan and a virtually unlimited supply of manpower to aid in the rebuilding process. With the help of Soviet advisers, large state-owned industries were founded that provided housing and health care for workers as well as education for their children. Small businesses and agriculture were gradually absorbed by the state sector. By 1952 the economy had approached prewar normalcy, albeit a normalcy that was at a level of development far below that of Japan.

Prime Minister Yoshida, though staunchly anti-communist, made the point to U.S. authorities that Japan could live only through trade, and that China was its natural market. American authorities rejoined that Beijing was not interested in buying Japan's consumer goods, but rather the wherewithal to develop its heavy industries, thereby enhancing its war-fighting potential. Some budget-conscious American leaders disagreed with Washington's restrictions on Sino-Japanese commerce, pointing out that unless the U.S. government intended to underwrite the Japanese economy indefinitely, Tokyo should be encouraged to trade with the PRC. More anti-communist decision-makers argued that Japan should seek markets in Southeast Asia instead, which would presumably compensate for the loss of the China market.

Japan did take cautious first steps in this direction, though meeting resistance from potential clients with bitter memories of the Greater East Asian Co-Prosperity Sphere that Tokyo had forced Southeast Asian states into in the 1940s. At one point, Malaysian longshoremen refused to unload a ship carrying goods from Japan.

As seen during the Tokugawa period when Japan was theoretically all but closed off to transactions with China, motivated minds found ways to evade the restrictions. Millions of dollars of trade took place legally through Hong Kong each year. Falsified bills of lading and circuitous shipping routes allowed trade to take place on a less legal basis as well.

While the PRCs media publicly denounced the capitalist war-mongering political-industrial clique that governed Japan, its leadership was fully cognizant that the managerial and technological expertise controlled by this despised clique could be invaluable to the development of the PRC's own economy. In his April 1952 address to the Moscow Economic Conference, China's representative Nan Hanchen mentioned the need for and advantages of Sino-Japanese trade. His words were echoed by Japanese business interests, most enthusiastically by Osaka textile merchants and by the steel industry.

Shortly thereafter, three left-wing Japanese who had attended the conference were invited to Beijing, and on June 1, the first unofficial trade agreement was signed by Han and the three Japanese. Showing the weight that the Chinese government attached to the agreement, Beijing Radio preceded its Japanese-language broadcast with a notice that an important announcement would follow. Although the amount involved, $84 million, was substantial, only 5 percent had actually materialized by the end of the specified period, December 31, due to various restrictions. Items classified in category A of Chinese exports could be exchanged only within category A of Japanese exports, on a barter basis. This meant that the commodities Japan needed most—coal, soybeans, and iron ore—could be imported only in exchange for goods not on the list of items on which sanctions had been imposed during the Korean War. These restrictions remained in place for some time after the war, thereby prohibiting Japan from exporting the steel building materials, railway equipment, and iron ingots that China most needed.[4]

Regional tensions began to ease in the mid-1950s with an armistice in Korea and the death of Stalin in 1953, followed by the Geneva Conference on Vietnam in 1954. The combination of these events allowed both sides a degree of flexibility from their allies' constraints. A Chinese delegate to the Geneva Conference openly acknowledged that trade restrictions had had an adverse effect on the PRC's economic development, and expressed hope that they would be lifted.[5] Since American purchases to prosecute the Korean War sharply decreased after the armistice, the Japanese economy experienced a downturn, providing added impetus to those who wished to trade with China.

Lack of diplomatic relations between the two caused problems for trade despite creative efforts to work around it. According to the memoirs of one of the putatively non-official negotiators, Ikeda Masanosuke of the left-wing Diet Members League for the Promotion of Sino-Japanese Relations, the Chinese side first brought up the concept of separating politics from economics, which under its Japanese name *seikei bunri* became the Tokyo government's guiding principle. Almost immediately thereafter, however, Beijing declared that the idea was unacceptable, surely in order to use Japan's desire for enhanced trade relations as a lever to advance diplomatic recognition. Ikeda also noted that the Chinese suggested the barter trade that was later to become such a hindrance to the development of trade.[6]

Neither side was comfortable with the trade arrangements that were worked out. From Japan's point of view, China's insistence that trade be balanced meant that the Japanese side was often hard-pressed to find suitable imports to balance the exports that China wanted and which Japanese companies hoped to buy. China was irritated because Tokyo refused to allow banks to extend credit to finance the factories it wished to purchase.

Left-wing groups in Japan helped China by pressuring their government to make changes. When restrictions on travel between China and Japan were eased, socialist Diet members and labor union leaders visited Beijing and were warmly welcomed. If the latter sensed any threat to their jobs from competition with Chinese labor, there was no public acknowledgment thereof. Socialist Diet members could bring messages from the conservative government to Beijing, and ostensibly private organizations could set up trade arrangements on mutually agreeable terms. The good offices of Chinese who had studied in Japan in the prewar years, including contacts made since the time of Sun Yat-sen, were useful in this regard. So as well were pro-communist Japanese who had left their country during the period of military domination and taken refuge in the Yan'an base area.

Through such ostensibly private channels, agreements were concluded on such issues as fisheries, allowing for the delineation of zones where each country's ships could seek catches and quotas on how many fish could be taken. Although the compact did not work perfectly, the number of confiscated boats and their cargoes was reduced.

Three subsequent agreements were signed, in October 1953, May 1955, and March 1958. During this period, a series of barter agreement between the two states facilitated a steady increase of trade, reaching a peak in 1956, when the total volume of trade amounted to $151 million, or 3.6 percent of Japan's total foreign trade and 21.9 percent of China's.

The future seemed bright, with the last of the four agreements, that of March 1958, going so far as to allow each side to establish a trade office in the territory of the other, over which the country's national flag could fly. Lest this be interpreted—as Beijing obviously wanted it to be—as representing tacit political recognition of the PRC, the agreement stated that the PRC flag would not receive protection under Article 92 of Japan's penal code. This article prohibits damage, removal, defiling of the national flag or emblem of a foreign state with the intent of insulting the foreign state. When the Chinese flag was torn down (see Chapter 3), Beijing suspended trade for what proved to be four years. However, this hiatus may have had as much to do with setbacks in the Chinese economy as pique at the insult to the PRC's flag: later in 1958, Beijing began a misguided attempt to transform the nation's economic and social structure through communes, close-planting of crops, and backyard steel furnaces. In the disaster that ensured, millions of people starved to death, economic indices plunged downward, and Beijing was unable to afford to purchase the products of Japanese industry.

In 1960 trade with Japan began to seem more feasible again, provided that the Japanese government accepted the PRC's conditions. Premier Zhou Enlai announced to the visiting director of the Japan-China Trade Promotion Association three principles under which trade could be resumed and developed:

1. agreements between the two government covering trade
2. agreements between nongovernmental groups
3. trade by special consideration in case of special difficulties in small and medium industries

Out of the first grew the Liao-Takasaki agreement, negotiated by Liao Chengzhi (see Chapter 3) and Takasaki Tatsunosuke, a businessman and LDP Diet member who had spent his early years in Manchuria. Signed in 1962, the L-T agreement, as it quickly became known, provided for an average two-way trade of approximately $100 million per year, and for the exchange of trade liaison personnel between the two capitals. Japan agreed to accept deferred payment and medium-term credit for Chinese purchases of Japanese industrial plants.

In 1965 Japan's $469 million two-way trade exceeded the 1956 preflag incident postwar peak, surpassing total Sino-Soviet trade as well. The latter had experienced a precipitous decline due to bitter political disputes between the two countries. In 1966 Sino-Japanese trade increased an astounding 132 percent, or 15 percent of the PRC's estimated total foreign trade. With Sino-Soviet trade sharply contracting, Japan became the PRC's largest trading partner and China moved to become Japan's fourth largest partner, after the United States, Australia, and Canada. The outbreak of China's Cultural Revolution the same year had a predictably depressive effect on trade, which dropped to $577 million in 1967, but even so, Japan remained China's largest trading partner.[7]

Agreements between nongovernmental groups were known as friendship trade. Under it, from 1960 on, China traded with "friendly," that is, left-leaning, companies who accepted various PRC positions such as opposition to a "two-Chinas" policy and to the U.S.-Japan Security Treaty. Prices were negotiated at the twice yearly Canton (Guangzhou) trade fair, with the amounts contracted for carefully watched as much as a barometer of Sino-Japanese relations as for their economic implications. Impressive as the increase from $47 million in 1961 to $84 million in 1962 was, with more than eighty Japanese firms participating in the fair, there were deficiencies from Beijing's point of view. The friendly companies tended to be small and economically weak and lacked the substantial capital, extensive commercial experience, and connections with large Japanese corporations that would have facilitated more efficient, low-cost production. Moreover, unlike those major corporations, the friendly firms had little influence on the Japanese government. In time, Beijing relaxed its conditions so as to include so-called dummy corporations: allegedly autonomous spin-offs of major Japanese corporations who received the coveted designation of friendly.[8]

Still, there were problems from Japan's point of view. China continued to insist that the trade be balanced in order to stabilize the PRC's then modest foreign exchange reserves. Since other countries whose products Beijing was interested in, such as Canada and Australia, were not willing to agree to the same terms, this gave Japan an advantage. However, Tokyo was often hard-pressed to find suitable imports to balance the exports that China wanted and that Japanese companies hoped to buy. The Chinese side continued to complain that Japanese banks were forbidden to extend lines of credit so that they could make major purchases.

Trade grew despite these difficulties, albeit subject to downturns due to political circumstances in China. Japan was in the unique position of being able to trade with both the People's Republic of China and the Republic of China on Taiwan. Chinese exports were mainly primary products like soybeans and iron ore, while the majority of Japanese exports to the PRC were fertilizers, steel, machinery, and chemicals. Chafing at existing restrictions nonetheless, big Japanese businesses—a mainstay of support for the ruling Liberal Democratic Party (LDP)—urged the LDP leadership to normalize diplomatic relations. Particularly after Nixon's 1972 trip to Beijing gave added legitimization to Mao's government, Japanese entrepreneurs were convinced that if they did not act quickly, they would lose their privileged position in the China market. A few weeks after a 1972 United Nations report indicated that, with the chaos of the Cultural Revolution abating, the PRC's economic growth was accelerating, three major companies of the giant Mitsubishi conglomerate asked Beijing for permission to send a trade delegation to the Chinese capital.[9] The president of another giant conglomerate, Mitsui, announced that he was going to contact China without using "a webfoot of a duck," that is, outright and formally rather than working through an intermediary with important China connections who would move out of sight and hence figuratively under water.[10]

ECONOMIC CONSEQUENCES OF NORMALIZATION

Bilateral trade grew impressively after the normalization of diplomatic relations removed the restraints the PRC had imposed. Dummy corporations were no longer necessary; corporate groups could travel to China freely to inspect sites for development or joint ventures and did so frequently. Nonetheless, Japanese businesses, like other foreign businesses in the PRC, faced numerous obstacles. China in 1972 had barely begun edging away from a rigidly socialist model. Even those of its decision-makers who saw the benefits to China of foreign trade and investment were extremely wary, lest the country fall under the domination of foreign capitalists. They worried as well about the party line changing, as it had several times in the past, with themselves as targets of a new anti-rightist campaign.

Procedures designed to ensure the safety of those whose careers might be threatened were complicated, and rules were ambiguous. Incredibly, laws and regulations were sometimes even secret: they were revealed to the hapless transgressors only after they had unwittingly committed the offense. Ignorance of the law was not deemed an admissible excuse for breaking the law. Hence, Chinese authorities had considerable discretion, to the discomfort of both would-be Chinese entrepreneurs and those Japanese companies who were interested in doing business in the PRC.

In one sense, mutual diplomatic recognition eased some of the barriers that had hampered the development of Sino-Japanese trade. However, it also aroused concerns in the capitalist West, where the vision of an embrace between big Japanese corporations and a PRC communist government that had been vilifying them for decades was fraught with ominous implications. Both developed and developing countries were already worried about the seemingly invincible "Japan Incorporated" that was outproducing and pricing its products below theirs worldwide: this new partnership had the potential to confer even greater advantages to Japan. Tokyo attempted to soothe these concerns, even dispatching missions to reassure Southeast Asian states that the new relationship with Beijing would not detrimentally affect trade ties with them.

Prime Minister Tanaka appears to have had foreign anxieties in mind when, in his 1973 new year's address he stated:

> The Japanese government will not adopt a policy for expanding Japan's trade share in the Chinese market. What this country seeks in its relations with Peking is to satisfy requirements of China that may arise in carrying out the Chinese economic policy.[11]

There was considerable anxiety in China as well about being taken over by Japan Incorporated. Japanese had other concerns: even though enhanced trade opportunities had been a major factor in the Japanese desire for normalized political relations, some businessmen worried that they might be creating a formidable competitor. As the center-left daily *Asahi*, which had been in the forefront of normalization efforts commented, "The Japanese would be well advised to start thinking of the possibility of eventual relations of economic competition between Japan and China."[12]

Mutual misgivings notwithstanding, Sino-Japanese trade rose sharply, reaching a postwar high in 1972, up 21.9 percent over the previous year for a total of $1.1 billion. Not surprisingly, a disproportionate amount of the increase occurred rather late in the year, in the few months after the September 30, 1972, normalization agreement.[13] In August 1973 the two sides began negotiations on an official trade agreement, a matter of some urgency since the Memorandum Trade Agreement would expire at the end of the year. The importance of having an agreement became still more urgent from Japan's point of view when, in October, the Organization of Petroleum Exporting Countries (OPEC) began an oil embargo. The PRC, though expressing support for OPEC's goals, chose not to become a member of the group, and Chinese officials held forth the promise of an alternate and bountiful source of oil for petroleum-deficient Japan. It was clear to both sides that this would be contingent on receiving equally bountiful Japanese investment to develop the PRC's large oil reserves as well as backing for its other development projects.

Discussions on the details of the agreement were more difficult, involving such issues as the exact terms of Most Favored Nation (MFN) treatment and what currencies to value trade in. As finally agreed on at the end of the year, MFN was accorded on tariffs and surcharges on imports. The Japanese side insisted on some restrictions on exports due to Japan's membership in the Coordinating Committee for Export to the Communist Area (COCOM).[14]

Japanese businesses were reeling due to the oil embargo: its exports were cut 15 to 20 percent, impacting not only the Japanese economy but also those of many Asian countries, including China, since the PRC's agriculture relied on imported petroleum-based fertilizer.[15] At the same time, Japanese government and businesses anxiously watched the latest power struggle playing out in Beijing.[16] Chinese leaders assured Tokyo that contracts would be honored even as reports on arguments between hard-line Maoists and more liberal reformers proliferated.

While Japanese companies were eager to gain access to an alternate source of petroleum, Chinese oil was a mixed blessing. Japanese refineries had been set up to process the "sweet" oil that Japan had been importing from OPEC states in the Middle East and Indonesia, whereas Chinese oil had a much higher sulfur and wax content. This became apparent when a delayed shipment arrived at its Japanese port of destination during colder weather and could not be pumped out because the oil had solidified. Since formally dressed dignitaries, uniformed marching bands, and a large media contingent had assembled for a grand welcoming ceremony, the incident caused considerable embarrassment.[17]

Japan remained interested in Chinese petroleum nonetheless, drawing up plans to build the facilities that were needed to process it and even paying higher prices for the waxy oil than for lighter Indonesian crude, in the interests of Sino-Japanese friendship. Still, a recession in Japan in 1973–1974 reduced the country's overall demand for petroleum.[18]

Year-to-year and even five-year trade agreements, with their need for frequent negotiations and renegotiations, had obvious limitations. One commentator, writing in 1975, worried that if Tokyo missed the chance to conclude such suitable agreements at an early date, it could be outmaneuvered by other major trading powers and might even have to resort to buying Chinese crude, for example, from these countries. Japanese importers had already created a bad impression in the PRC when they failed to import the contracted amount of Chinese oil the previous year due to falling domestic demand. The commentator urged immediate attention, since his sources indicated that Beijing needed quick money to buy more capital goods, such as complete plants, machinery, equipment, and other industrial products in preparation for its next five-year plan. Japan should move quickly lest it miss out on this potentially lucrative opportunity.[19] Japan's imports of other Chinese products did not increase satisfactorily either. PRC spokesmen later blamed the by then purged Gang of Four's policies, earthquakes, and other natural disasters.[20]

It required Deng Xiaoping's re-rehabilitation in 1977 and the ambitious Four Modernizations industrialization program he quickly announced to provide the final impetus for the conclusion of a Long-Term Trade Agreement (LTTA), in 1978. For Japan, the key issue remained securing for Japan a steady supply of Chinese crude; for China, access to Japan's technology, managerial expertise, and whole plants needed to implement its industrialization program.

As concluded, the LTTA had an eight-year period. The years 1978–1985 corresponded to the last three years of the PRC's fifth five-year plan and the entire sixth, and was to have a value of approximately $20 billion. Japan would export technology, plants, construction materials, and machinery worth about $10 billion. In return, it would receive a comparable amount of Chinese crude oil and coking coal, with the amounts to increase for the first five years. Thereafter, quantities were to be decided by consultation between the two sides. Japan agreed to accept deferred payment for its exports. Declaring that the agreement was not only for eight years but "endless," the ebullient Keidanren President Inayama Yoshihiro pressed to have the term extended, which it was, for two more years, with its scope extended to over $80 billion.[21]

Japanese business interests echoed Inayama's enthusiasm, as evidenced by their signing nearly four dozen contracts during the first year. The most spectacular of these centered on the construction of a mammoth, 6-million-ton annual capacity steel complex at Baoshan in the Shanghai area. Japanese media described the prevailing mood as "China fever."

The euphoria did not last long. Difficult as the negotiations to conclude the LTTA had been, its implementation proved still more difficult.[22] There were doubts about whether Japan could absorb all the coal China wanted to export and whether it could efficiently process the PRC's waxy oil. Issues involving interest rates and the details of deferred payments also remained. Additionally, the PRC had not only overestimated the amount of oil it was capable of producing but also, as its economy began to grow rapidly again, domestic needs received preference over exports.[23]

China's complaints about the trade imbalance were accompanied by criticisms of the Japanese themselves as arrogant. As summarized by Chalmers Johnson in 1978,

> It is perhaps not too far-fetched to describe Japanese attitudes toward their continental neighbors as somewhat comparable to the English or German industrialist's attitude toward an Italian or Spanish aristocrat recently gone into commerce. He admires, and is slightly intimidated by, the ancient cultural achievements to which his modern counterpart is heir, but finds it almost impossible in the company board room to suggest seriously that the new boy might become a competitor or threat.[24]

In fact, the new boy wanted to be treated very seriously, perhaps in unconscious re-creation of the Hegelian paradigm of the pupil ("slave" in Hegel's terminology) becoming the master. There was a strong sense of the need to expunge past feelings of humiliation: a new generation schooled in

Mao's belief that China had stood up was unwilling to accept a paradigm in which the Middle Kingdom was only one of the birds flying along in the Japanese government's "V" formation of Asian economic development, with Japan as the leader of the flock.[25]

By 1979 it was Japan's turn to become uneasy at the relationship. The Chinese decision to invade Vietnam, although relatively short in duration, resulted in heavy military expenditures that, when added to the ambitious and not always economically efficient economic development programs begun under Deng Xiaoping's Four Modernizations program, led China to sharply curtail its industrialization plans. Many contracts, a disproportionate number of which were with Japanese companies, were postponed or cancelled outright.

Although several countries' corporations, most notably those of Germany, the United States, and Great Britain, were adversely affected, Japan, which accounted for almost 60 percent of all foreign plant contracts with China from 1978 to 1980, was most heavily impacted. Among the abrogated agreements were commitments to build the Baoshan complex.[26] Several companies had already begun work and demanded compensation for their losses. Eventually, after much bad feeling and numerous mutual consultations, the Japanese government accepted Beijing's explanation that it had moved too quickly and too inefficiently in its modernization plans and agreed to wait out the PRC's retrenchment period. After a few years, Chinese leaders promised, economic growth would resume, with cooperative Japanese companies to be duly rewarded for their understanding. Tokyo agreed to provide $1.33 billion in low-interest development loans for thirty years, with a ten-year grace period. Even so, Sino-Japanese trade fell from $10.38 billion in 1981 to $8.86 billion in 1982.

In 1983 two-way trade recouped its pre-1982 level and was relatively well balanced, though Japan remained wary of the recurrence of the wild swings that had characterized the past.[27] The overwhelming majority of Japanese FDI—82.6 percent according to one estimate—was concentrated in the PRC's coastal areas, much of it in the north. The northern city of Dalian, where the prewar Japanese presence had been substantial, was an especially favored destination.[28] Japanese economists pointed out that investment decisions were not always made for economic reasons.[29]

In addition to direct business relationships with Japanese companies, the government extended loans on concessional terms and official development assistance (ODA) to a variety of Chinese projects ranging from infrastructure and energy development to health-care facilities and environmental projects.

The last-named category became increasingly important to Japanese as the speed of the PRC's industrialization caused a marked increase in pollution, some of which found its way to Japan in the form of heightened concentrations of particulate matter in the air and acid rain.

JAPANESE CONCERNS GROW: RIVALRY REKINDLED

In Japan, there was no unanimity that extending huge credits to the PRC would serve Japan's best interests in the long run. In public pronouncements, government officials tended to emphasize that Japan's assistance in the modernization of China would contribute to the peace and stability of the Asia-Pacific region while paying scant attention to consideration of the risks posed by a PRC that was exhibiting an increased ability to harness its enormous manpower to a modernization program that included agriculture, industry, science and technology, and the military. Aid to China represented 77.5 percent of Japan's total foreign assistance worldwide in 1985, a figure that did not even include massive commercial loans.[30]

Critics of official policy warned of the dangers of Japan inadvertently nourishing a viper, and cautioned against becoming too involved in the China market. Outside of Japan, there were other concerns. Developed countries worried about Japan monopolizing the China trade to their detriment. The Soviet Union, its misgivings about the PRC still present despite a gradual warming trend in relations that began in 1981, was also wary of a Sino-Japanese partnership that might strengthen the PRC. And Southeast Asian states expressed concern that Japan's aid to the PRC would come at the expense of economic assistance to them. Chinese goods were flooding Southeast Asian markets as well as into areas that the Association of Southeast Asian Nations (ASEAN) member states hoped to sell to.[31] In response to their concerns, Japan set an informal ODA allocation ratio of 1:3 between the PRC and the ASEAN states.[32]

Japanese executives had many complaints. Taxes and miscellaneous fees were arbitrarily imposed on foreign companies. The infrastructure was poor, as was the protection of intellectual property rights. Policies changed frequently, often without notification to the affected parties. Because Deng Xiaoping's economic policies had included a degree of flexibility for areas to make their own decisions, these policies could differ widely from one area to another, thus inhibiting long-term planning and the development of a nationwide strategy. Also, Chinese authorities had a maddening habit of trying to renegotiate agreements immediately after the agreements had been signed. Like other foreign companies, Japanese businesses were forced to hire workers and purchase services at higher wages than domestic firms paid, and were charged more for basic items like telephone service. Product quality tended to be unacceptably low, and production deadlines were not always met.

While other countries' companies faced the same obstacles, Japanese firms had the added burden of hostility stemming from memories of World War II. Tales of Japanese war crimes, many of them accurate though others were exaggerated, were publicized by the Beijing government when it suited the government's purposes to do so. Japanese companies also seemed to have a more difficult time in delegating authority to indigenous managers, thus depriving the companies themselves of needed knowledge of the local environment.[33]

With property rights largely unprotected, Japanese companies often found their blueprints and production techniques copied and sold at lower prices than they were able to produce the goods at, even in Chinese factories. This inhibited their desire to transfer more sophisticated technology, which resulted in friction with their Chinese partners. Those Japanese who held a more optimistic view on the transfer of technology and expertise to the PRC argued that their country's firms were moving ahead sufficiently quickly on their own that they could afford to sell or otherwise impart knowledge to China, since they would naturally stay ahead on the technology curve.

TRADE IMBALANCES

After Deng Xiaoping returned to power and instituted an ambitious economic program that necessitated large purchases of plants and technology from Japan, the latter enjoyed large trade surpluses that the Chinese said were insupportable, although privately admitting that there was no alternative short of giving up the ambitious modernization program they had embarked on. One trade official confided to an American visitor that "this is how we keep them [the Japanese, with their reputation for arrogance] in line."[34]

Other frequent complaints were that Japan's investment in China was but a small fraction of its overseas investments, and to the aforementioned reluctance of its companies to transfer advanced technology to the PRC. To which Japanese companies replied that, were the investment environment made more favorable, more investment would be forthcoming, and that better protection for intellectual property rights would ease their reluctance to transfer technology. An inadequate transportation system meant uncertain delivery dates and hence the need to keep large inventories rather than the leaner, more efficient stocks they preferred. Prices for land use, electricity, and labor could triple with neither notice nor explanation, as could duties for component parts vital to the manufacture of items. Contracts were regarded as infinitely negotiable. One frustrated factory manager, who announced that he would stay the course nonetheless, commented that it seemed the Japanese were playing baseball while the Chinese were playing football.[35]

For its part, the Chinese side complained that the Japanese government restricted its markets, making it difficult for Chinese products to enter—a charge the Japanese government was all too familiar with, since it was a major source of ill feeling with the United States and several other important trading partners as well. Aid, the Chinese side charged, was tied to the purchase of Japanese products, and the projects for which it was earmarked seemed to have been chosen for the benefit of Japan Incorporated. Some of the products purchased, including, in 1985, a sizable number of trucks, proved to be of inferior quality, leading to suspicions that Tokyo was trying to hold back China. Instruction manuals that came with the new equipment were often deemed inscrutable. Upon investigation, however, Japanese businesses discovered that a number of problems resulted because the instructions, such as routine maintenance checks and oil changes on vehicles, were simply ignored: those who had little prior experience with maintaining complicated machinery did not understand what was necessary to keep it functioning smoothly.

JAPAN AS NUMBER ONE

By the mid-1980s, Japan's position as a premier economic power seemed unassailable. In sharp contrast to the country Zbigniew Brzezinski had described in 1972 as a fragile blossom, Harvard Professor Ezra Vogel's 1979 work *Japan as Number One* argued that the country had pioneered advanced managerial and production techniques that would propel it to first place in the new global industrial economy.[36] Vogel's book quickly became a best-seller, prompting many other nations besides China to send groups of students hoping to discover how the model might be applied in their countries.

In 1985 the total assets of Dai-Ichi Kangyo edged past the New York–headquartered Citibank to become the world's largest bank. Three of the other banks in the top five, and five of those in the top ten, were Japanese as well.[37] Japan also became the largest creditor nation in the world. Not resting on its laurels, the government announced plans to create an offshore market, an important step in the internationalization of the yen and, in the opinion of commentators both foreign and domestic, emblematic of Japan's premier position in global financial power.[38] Within Japan, land values rose dramatically, most especially in Tokyo, where they doubled within a year.

While some Japanese worried about the PRC catching up to and perhaps even surpassing their country, most statesmen and media commentators believed that the benefits of participating in the vast Chinese market would outweigh any adverse effects from possible future competition between Japan and a more economically developed China.[39] A prosperous China would increase the prosperity of Japan, as well as provide the basis for international, or at least regional, political stability.

In 1984 China's imports exceed its exports by over $1.7 billion, a figure that had risen to $6.41 billion by the first half of 1985. Feelings that Japan was trying to re-create the frequently vilified Great East Asian Co-Prosperity Sphere of its militarist-imperialist 1930s government caused frictions that boiled over into anti-Japanese demonstrations in several parts of China. Banners and shouts accused Japan of an economic invasion, *jingji qinlue* or, for those who spoke Japanese, *keizai shinryaku*. The Beijing government, whose repeated complaints about the issue in the tightly controlled state media had certainly contributed to these reactions, nonetheless made efforts to keep public rage within bounds. One reason seems to have been suspicion that the demonstrations might turn against the government itself; another is that, while objecting to the trade imbalance, the leadership recognized the continued need for Japanese imports.

Japanese sources countered that a structural difference between the two economies was a major factor in the imbalance. China's main export products, such as oil, coal, and farm produce, were not in strong demand in Japan, while China's demand for Japanese steel and machinery was steadily rising. Deng Xiaoping's decentralization of power had also worked toward encouraging local authorities and enterprise managers to expand imports at their discretion. Hence, it was more difficult for the central government to control how much was spent. One solution advocated by several Japanese economists was to shift their country's trade policy from the export of goods to the transfer of technology. Critics objected that this was likely to boomerang against Japan. Instead, they suggested, to prevent economic controversies from seriously undermining bilateral relations, Japan must help the PRC to somehow acquire the ability to produce diversified, attractive export goods.[40]

Whereas Japan posted a record overall trade surplus in 1985,[41] China reported a record trade deficit, initially placed at $7.61 billion[42] and later revised to $13.7 billion, based on calculations more in line with international norms.[43] While Chinese leaders complained about trade deficits, they also urged more trade between the two countries: Deng Xiaoping at one point suggested that rather than constituting 6.2 percent of Japan's foreign trade, trade with the PRC should be 25 percent.[44] Obstacles were numerous, with Japanese business interests repeating previous complaints: Japanese companies that would prefer to keep inventories low had to retain large stocks because of erratic transportation. Duties on crucial imported component parts of items could suddenly triple without explanation, as could land use fees, electricity costs, and labor fees. Yuan could not be easily converted into hard currency, and contracts were not inviolable.

Chinese officials rejoined that Japanese firms were too cautious: it was unrealistic to expect 100 percent guarantees. The Japanese were reluctant to transfer technology, and not prepared to invest in a developing situation. And, they noted, despite their numerous complaints, Japanese companies were staying in China.[45]

Through all of this, Sino-Japanese trade rose, and there was a background mood of optimism: obstacles were acknowledged, but seemed capable of being overcome. Yet, just as if predicted by yin-yang theory, which posits that every success contains within itself the seeds of its own destruction, portents of problems began to manifest themselves. Some noticed the dark clouds accumulating on Japan's horizon, though most observers, particularly in foreign countries, ignored them. In 1986, for example, China took a tentative step toward selling indigenously produced high technology to enhance its foreign exchange reserves. An eleven-day technology export fair in the special economic zone of Shenzhen displayed an estimated 120 items, with special attention given to its Changzheng 3 (Long March) rocket and communications satellites. Chinese officials emphasized that the PRC had become the world's third largest satellite exporter, after the United States and the European Space Agency.

As if to calm those who might have concerns, party leader Hu Yaobang told a visiting group of Japanese industrialists that, although it was an old story in the Orient that after an apprentice is trained and experienced, he would leave his master unemployed, it would not work this way in the new China. Beijing wanted foreign investment and technology in order to raise its people's living standards, "but had no intention of selling or in any way dumping large amounts of its products on the international market. And China means what it says."[46]

While these technological advances were reported by Japanese media, the official response was to reassure those with apprehensions that their fears were without foundation. Whereas prewar Japan had striven for military supremacy, postwar Japan had aimed for, and achieved, economic supremacy, with only the United States, beset by a weak dollar and growing financial deficits, ahead of it. Rather than looking backward at China, these officials seemed to look ahead, concentrating on narrowing the difference between their country and an apparently faltering United States. A schematic diagram of trade networks in the Pacific region that appeared in a 1986 trade study did not even accord a separate sphere to China, which the authors had folded into the category of Asian newly industrializing countries (NICs).[47] See figure 8.1, below.

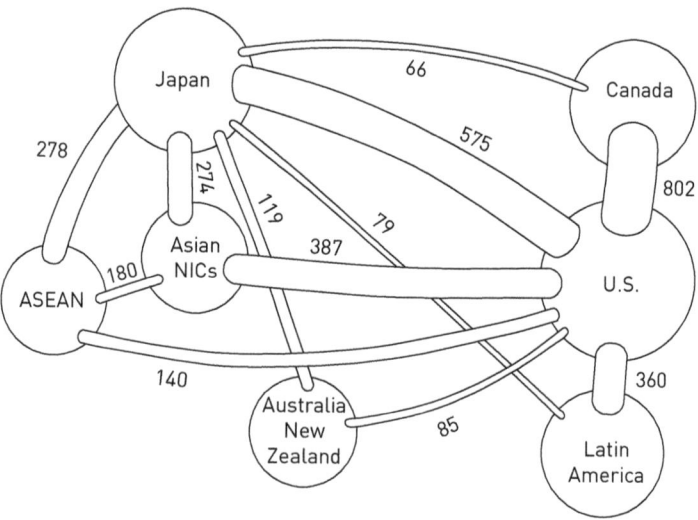

FIGURE 8.1. Trade Network in the Pacific Region: Chinese-Japanese Trade, 2000–2014.
Note: 1982 figures in U.S. $100 million.
Source: Pacific Basin Economic Council (PBEC).

Moreover, the PRC's foreign exchange reserves at that point were reported as a modest $11.91 billion, down 17 percent from the previous year.[48]

EFFECT OF THE TIANANMEN INCIDENT

The next major wrench to economic relations came as a result of the Chinese government's brutal suppression of unarmed demonstrators in and around Tiananmen Square in 1989. Pressed by the United States to join in the sanctions that American public opinion had forced a reluctant President George H.W. Bush to impose, an even more reluctant Tokyo partially acquiesced. Despite Japanese officials' conviction that it would be counterproductive to isolate China, the government agreed to postpone the scheduled third round of yen loans it had promised until there was an improvement in the Beijing leadership's human rights behavior. Tokyo had pragmatic reasons for opposing the sanctions in addition to its feeling that isolation of the PRC would only strengthen the PRC's hard-line extremists: the sanctions caused a sharp drop in Japanese imports to China even as Chinese exports to Japan continued to increase. The result was a rising imbalance of trade in the PRC's favor.

Although the first Japanese business delegation to visit Beijing after the massacres was almost pathetically eager to reinstate business dealings, it reported that the Chinese leaders the group met with made no gesture to encourage removal of the sanctions. Moreover, they were unexpectedly critical of Japan. Prime Minister Li Peng told the delegation that the seven industrialized nations differed among themselves on what they were saying and doing. "Some had a lot to say while doing many things behind the scenes, while others both said little and did little."[49] Subsequent investigations by the Western media revealed that Li's remarks were entirely accurate.

The Beijing government repeatedly expressed its desire for Japanese investment to return to the PRC, arguing that politics must be clearly separated from economics. Ironically, this reversed its pre-normalization position that *seikei bunri* was untenable, since economics and political factors were inextricably intertwined. Japanese companies, anticipating that sanctions would soon be lifted, dispatched exploratory missions to China for discussions on projects to fund. In a relatively short period of time, the loans were indeed reinstated.

New problems bedeviled economic cooperation, however. Beijing, while criticizing the Japanese side for its reluctance to invest, was pursuing a tight money policy in order to damp down the inflation that had been a major precipitant of the 1989 demonstrations. In the words of the head of a major Japanese trading house, this amounted to a driver pressing down on the accelerator and applying the brakes at the same time.[50] Another Japanese commentator advised Beijing to take a careful look at the policies that were responsible for the damaging cycle of inflationary business booms followed by state-mandated busts, and to "stop setting dream deadlines."[51]

There were also frequently voiced concerns about the stability of the post-Tiananmen power structure. With the liberal Party General Secretary Zhao Ziyang removed from office, Japanese business leaders wondered if more orthodox communist leaders would keep the open door to foreign countries open, particularly after the elderly Deng Xiaoping retired.

THE CHINESE ECONOMY RECOVERS

These concerns abated when Deng Xiaoping's highly publicized trip to the special economic zone of Shenzhen in 1992 signaled that the economy could begin to move ahead again: metaphorically, the driver had removed his foot from the brakes. In addition, Deng's chosen heir Jiang Zemin, though remaining in his mentor's shadow, seemed to have established himself as party general secretary. The economy began to grow rapidly again, as if making up for lost time.

AND THE JAPANESE ECONOMY FALTERS

This was not the case in Japan. Problems were becoming more noticeable. The value of the yen escalated rapidly, making Japanese goods more expensive. The home electronics and toy sectors were the first to experience difficulties. Shipbuilders faced bankruptcy, and Sumitomo Steel did the heretofore unthinkable, laying off workers and offering early retirement packages to others. The slide was gradual until 1990, when the property bubble burst, leading to what most people assumed to be a short period of market correction that slipped into what was called the "lost decade." Instead, it stretched into twenty-five years.

Even as Chinese media reported on the Japanese recession with barely concealed schadenfreude, Beijing continued to encourage Japanese investment in the PRC's economy. The product mix began to change. Whereas in the early 1980s, Japan imported mainly raw materials such as oil, coal, and silk, Chinese exports became gradually more labor intensive and higher value–added. Although often of inferior quality, the items were priced far below those produced in Japan. PRC products began to dominate the market in processed foodstuffs, textiles and apparel, footwear, sporting goods, toys, and games.[52] This trend accelerated after China joined the World Trade Organization, which eased the tariff wall that had protected the inefficient Japanese production sector. The balance of trade continued to shift in favor of the PRC.[53]

The long-term effects of this downturn still for the most part unrealized, a Beijing business newspaper in 1992 expressed the hope that the visit of the imperial couple to China would help to persuade reluctant Japanese investors to strengthen their commitment to the PRC's modernization. Thus far, the paper complained, Japan's direct investment in China had been relatively small compared to those made by Taiwan and Hong Kong. The author attributed this to concerns about the stability of China's leadership group and its determination to continue economic reforms. Still, the reporter opined, there was no better time to invest than now, with the economic growth rate having recouped to 10 percent a year.[54] The following year, Beijing's *Business Weekly* reported that, goaded by an appreciating yen, declining overseas investment by Japanese companies in general, and a sober global economic performance with the exception of Asia, Japan had "finally launched a massive investment plan" for the PRC.[55]

Despite continued efforts to attract more Japanese investment to help economic development that indicated the country was still at least partially dependent on the investment, some subtle changes in China's attitude were noticeable. For example, in August 1991, Chairman of the National People's Congress Wan Li told a Chamber of Commerce group that a more prosperous People's Republic would be helpful to Japan,[56] thereby implying that the pupil was now in the position of helping the teacher rather than, as had previously been the case, vice versa. And in October, Vice-Premier Wang Zhen told a visiting Diet member that a prosperous Japan posed no threat to China, nor would a prosperous China threaten Japan.[57]

Since the Japanese economy had rebounded from several setbacks in the past, most notably the oil price shocks of 1973 and 1979, it was expected to be equally resilient in the new millennium. It was not, with the wunderkind economy seeming to settle into what could be a permanent low-growth mode. Briefly summarized, a sharp drop in the GDP's rate of growth from 1991 to 1992 was followed by a period of stagnation, then a modest recovery, and after that, another dip into recession.[58] In one economist's analysis, the very slowness of the decline cushioned the government from making the far-reaching economic restructuring that was necessary to bring the economy back into growth:

> ... [T]he greatest bubble in human history burst in 1989 with no pain, like falling off Everest without breaking a bone. Instead of collapsing, the price of real estate slowly declined at a 7 percent annual rate for two decades, ultimately falling by a total of about 80 percent. There was never a major round of foreclosures or bankruptcies, as the government kept bailing out debtors, ruining its own finances.[59]

In China, the death of Deng Xiaoping in 1997 and the transition to his chosen successor Jiang Zemin caused no major problems for Sino-Japanese economic relations. Within China, there were some difficulties, with major factors being the continued existence of a large number of inefficient state enterprises: their losses were a major factor in the deficits in the central government's budget. So as well were the fiscal effects of Deng's Xiaoping's decentralization of economic decision-making, which had led to a diminution in the proportion of revenue remitted to the state treasury. Under the aegis of activist Premier Zhu Rongji, the number of inefficient state-owned corporations was reduced and a new fiscal system introduced that captured a higher percentage of tax revenues for the central government treasury. After a period of concern about what a World Bank report termed "sinosclerosis"—albeit at annual GDP increases at or near 8 percent—growth rates shot up into double digits beginning in 2000.

Meanwhile, the Japanese economy continued to slide downward. Many industries responded to unprofitability by moving more of their operations to other countries, and disproportionately to China, where labor costs were cheaper and labor unions virtually powerless. The trend continued despite arguments that the advantage of lower labor costs were at least partially offset by such problems as higher worker turnover, indifferent attention to quality, massive intellectual property violations, and unreliable power supplies. This migration of production exacerbated unemployment at home as well as causing a worrisome hollowing out of the country's industrial base.

The PRC became increasingly able to compete with Japanese labor in high-technology fields as well: Chinese software engineers could be hired at a third the cost of their counterparts in Japan.[60] And negotiations on the contract to build the Shanghai to Beijing high-speed rail faltered when the Chinese side proposed to buy only two cars, suggesting to the Japanese that it intended to copy the design and produce its own versions.[61]

THE SEARCH FOR AN EXPLANATION

Economists sought to understand how an economy that had been the envy of the rest of the world managed to falter, and found that the very business strategy that had succeeded so brilliantly was also responsible for its ultimate destruction. MITI's policy of concentrating on promoting the country's giant corporations and encouraging them to compete internationally while shielding the domestic sector from competition by a wall of protectionist measures had resulted in high wages, high prices to consumers, and inability to compete internationally. As major corporations increasingly diverted assets overseas, Japan's industrial regions continued to decline. The nation's overseas investments primarily substituted for domestic production rather than supporting complementary production activities domestically.[62]

At the same time, the intricate structure of state-supported investment encouraged banks to take risks that they might not otherwise have considered. The keiretsu system, in which banks owned portions of each other's shares, and the associated convoy system, in which strong banks were obliged to safeguard weaker ones, meant that bank operations became increasingly asset-expansive. A speculative spiral set in. With property values rising, firms borrowed more because they used their assets as collateral. When the property bubble burst in 1990, banks were left with billions of dollars of nonperforming loans.[63]

The country's largest banks wrote off massive amounts of nonperforming loans, and failed to pay dividends, angering shareholders. They also reduced interest rates to a negligible 0.02 percent. Some progress was made: several of Japan's leading banks merged, and in 2001, as part of the retrenchment effort, MITI was reorganized into METI, the Ministry of Economy, Trade, and Industry.

Protectionism was another response. In 2001 pressure from Japan's farm lobby resulted in tariffs being applied to the import of the fibers used to make tatami mats, as well as on spring onions and shiitake mushrooms. An angry Chinese government imposed counter tariffs on Japanese cars, air conditioners, and cell phones. Since these had much higher value, Japan stood to lose more than it gained from continuation of the tariffs. Tokyo was forced into a humiliating abandonment of the imposts.

OFFICIAL DEVELOPMENT ASSISTANCE TO CHINA IS TERMINATED

ODA was also rethought. Japan had been the largest provider of bilateral aid to China—on average, twice the size of that of Germany, the second most generous contributor, and about ten times that of third-place France. In light of the rapid growth of the Chinese economy while Japan suffered from huge budget deficits, it seemed counterproductive to continue the aid. China had become technologically advanced, even becoming the world's third country to send men into space, whereas Japan had not. Beijing was, moreover, providing aid to other countries at the same time it was receiving aid from Japan. A fair amount of this went to governments that might fairly be described as kleptocracies: ruled by people who used foreign aid to enrich themselves rather than raising the country's living standards, and often with poor records on human rights as well.

Those who opposed continued largesse complained that China did not seem grateful for the ODA, and pointed out that the PRC's behavior failed to conform to the principles of the ODA's charter in such areas as its government's progress toward democracy and its large expenditures for arms, which included the manufacture and proliferation of weapons of mass destruction.[64]

While Beijing might be expected to accept gracefully a discontinuation of aid as symbolic of how far it had come in rivaling its economic tutor, such was not the case. Many Chinese considered ODA as war reparations in disguise, and a poor substitute for what they were owed for the brutal treatment the country had suffered during World War II. Not until March 2005 was an agreement reached to phase out the loans, which would be terminated just prior to the extravagantly produced Beijing Olympics of 2008.

KOIZUMI'S ATTEMPTS AT RESTRUCTURING FALL SHORT

Following a succession of weak prime ministers, the selection of the outspoken Koizumi Junichiro in April 2001 gave hope for a meaningful economic restructuring. Koizumi's five years in office, making him Japan's longest-serving premier since 1972, did indeed include some successes, notably the privatization of the inefficient postal savings system. But opposition from vested interests prevented any overarching reform, and the economy continued its lackluster performance.

The optimistic view that Japanese industry could restructure and upgrade its manufacturing technology by deploying resources into the development of high value–added products to compensate for declining traditional industries being moved offshore was not borne out by events: several countries, including China, were able to innovate their own high value-added products and proved keen competitors. The flaw in the V-formation paradigm had been the assumption that the geese would continue to fly forward but never so quickly as to challenge the position of the leader.

Efforts to set up free trade agreements (FTAs) with the other "geese" also foundered due to opposition by powerful opposition groups, most notably the agricultural sector. Not coincidentally, agriculture was an important voting group that had traditionally supported the LDP and had a number of sympathetic legislators in the Diet. The Beijing government, though mindful that peasant wrath had been instrumental in the demise of several previous dynasties, did not face comparable constraints and quickly took the lead in creating FTAs. Japanese officials fretted, with *Kyodo* quoting an unnamed high official as saying, "China aims to grab the initiative of economic integration in the entire Asian region, including ASEAN."[65]

Keynesian pump-priming fiscal expansion also proved ineffective, apparently due to low business and consumer confidence.[66] In a further humiliation, international rating services in Europe and the United States downgraded Japanese government bonds to the same level as those of Italy, meaning the lowest category among industrially advanced democracies.[67]

At this time also, world petroleum prices rose sharply, with China and Japan becoming bitter rivals for Russian oil, thus enabling President Vladimir Putin to play one off against the other for the benefit of his own country's economy.[68] Competition for oil also exacerbated ongoing contested maritime territorial claims in the East China Sea that involved the rights to oil and gas exploitation, causing intermittent friction between the two sides.[69]

Japan's ever-present sense of rivalry with China was heightened by the painful realization that Japan was no longer the model to emulate. A former vice-minister of MITI lamented that

> whereas in the 1980s, Malaysian Prime Minister Mahathir Mohammed advocated the "Look East Policy" with the aim of adopting the Japanese economic model for his own country's economic development, nowadays, however, no Asian leaders voice such words any more.[70]

METI's white paper on trade and industry as well as the Japanese foreign ministry's blue paper on foreign affairs for fiscal year 2001 noted that the East Asian economy was being pulled by China's development, not Japan's.[71]

CURRENT ECONOMIC RELATIONS

In 2002 China surpassed the United States to become Japan's largest source of imports, simultaneously overtaking Japan as a manufacturing superpower. Some Japanese officials were so alarmed at China's industrial might that they accused the PRC of exporting deflation. Former vice-finance minister for international affairs Kuroda Haruhiko argued that either the yuan should be raised in value or Beijing should take measures to counter domestic deflation. Several rounds of negotiations ensued, but failed to reach a resolution of differences.

In a reversal of past patterns, machinery had accounted for 33.5 percent of total import value from China over the previous year; computer imports had risen by 81.7 percent in 2002 over 2001, and semiconductor imports by 21.5 percent.[72] As Chinese sources pointed out, however, 60 percent of the PRC's exports to Japan were from Japanese companies' factories in the PRC.[73] A poll conducted by *Yomiuri* in August indicated that the chief concern of the majority of respondents was fear of the consequences for Japan of the PRC's rapid economic development.[74] By 2009 the PRC passed the

United States as the largest recipient of Japanese exports, thereby deepening the dependence of Japan on its economy.[75] See figure 8.2 below.

For reasons explained in note 13 (see page 414), Chinese and Japanese statistics differ: for example, according to the latter, China had a $3.7 billion trade surplus with Japan in 2010, rather than a deficit of $55.64 billion; figures for previous years show similar discrepancies.[76] With each side insisting on the superiority of its methods of calculation, resolution of differences becomes more difficult.

As trade with China has become increasingly important to the health of the Japanese economy, trade with Japan has become progressively less important to China. It declined from 42.35 percent in 1981 to 17.22 percent a decade later and is barely 10 percent as of 2015. China, not Japan, became the country to emulate. Interest in the Japanese paradigm was replaced with discussion of a "Beijing consensus" for developing states to emulate. The Beijing consensus, a challenge not so much to a Japanese economic model per se as to democratic capitalism itself and to another somewhat vaguely defined "Washington consensus," was controversial. In its simplest form, the Beijing consensus—which some Chinese economists claimed did not exist— refers to a strong state government whose planners set long-term strategic goals and economic priorities, then systematically pursue them through a commitment to economic and political innovation and experimentation.

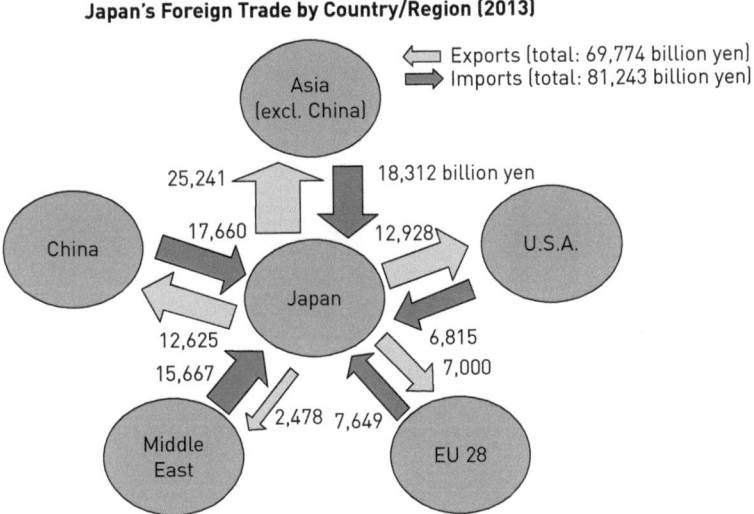

FIGURE 8.2. Japan's Foreign Trade by Country/Region, 2013.
Source: Ministry of Finance.

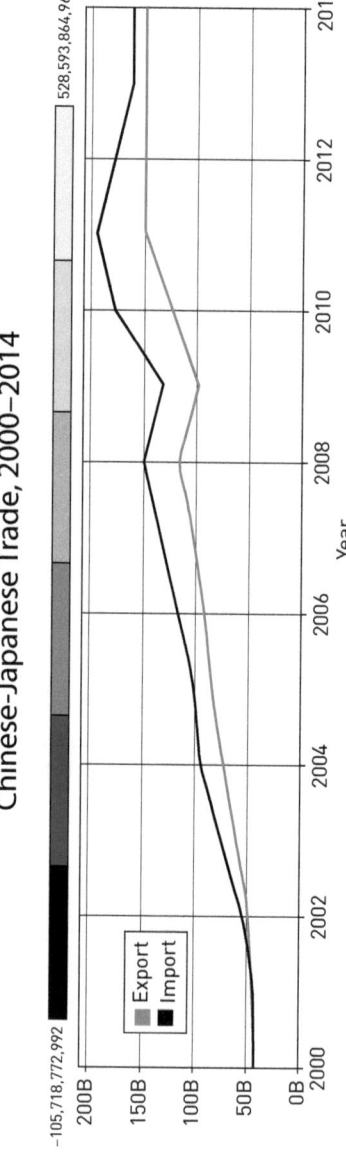

FIGURE 8.3.
Source: Ministry of Finance.

In any case, by the end of 2010, it became clear that the PRC had overtaken Japan as the world's second largest economy, while Japan remained mired in debt. Perhaps because it had been anticipated for so long, the symbolic shift received little attention in Japan. An incident earlier in the year had illustrated Beijing's willingness to use its economic primacy to extract compliance from Japan: in retaliation for the arrest of a Chinese fishing boat captain whose ship had rammed two Japanese Coast Guard vessels, PRC customs began subjecting imports from Japan to an excruciatingly slow inspection procedure. The government also advised the country's travel agencies to discourage tourism to Japan, arrested several of its nationals on spying charges, and announced, although it apparently did not actually do, that it would cease shipments of rare earths to the country, which are essential to the Japanese auto industry.[77] In yet another humiliation, the Japanese government capitulated: the captain was released and welcomed home as a hero.[78] The March 11, 2011, triple disaster of earthquake, tsunami, and nuclear meltdown at Fukushima seemed as if it might be the final blow to Japan's prospects to regain its economic primacy.

Another confrontation between China and Japan began in September 2012, when mass demonstrations broke out following the Japanese government's purchase of three of the five contested Diaoyu/Senkaku Islands from their Japanese owner. The result was considerable damage to Japanese businesses as well as a sharp drop in tourism and the country's auto sales to the PRC. Though painful to the affected businesses, tour operators and auto manufacturers, the losses proved temporary.

The Chinese economy is not without its problems. As its own economists have pointed out, a thoroughgoing restructuring is necessary to keep the country competitive. A study done by University of Chicago economists concluded that the gains achieved by the PRC's post-1978 experimental policies, summarized by Deng Xiaoping as "crossing the river by feeling the stones," may have reached the limit of their effectiveness.[79] And a World Bank study in 2012 warned that without far-reaching structural reform, the PRC faced at best falling into a middle-income trap and at worst a genuine economic crisis. The "demographic dividend" of a large, young population willing to work for low wages has ended, with the PRC's population aging as well and labor costs rising, thereby reducing the nation's attractiveness to foreign investors. Local debt is dangerously high, and banks have a worrisome level of nonperforming loans. Stock market volatility and capital flight out of China have become serious problems.

In November 2013 the Third Plenum of the Eighteenth Party Congress set forth a bold reform program that has been compared to those introduced by Deng Xiaoping in 1978. Plans are to reduce the worrisome level of local debts and nonperforming loans, achieve a more equitable distribution of wealth, and reduce the dangerous level of environmental pollution. At the same time, Xi Jinping began a far-reaching campaign against corruption. Both restructuring and the campaign are apt to depress the rate of economic growth to what has been called "the new normal," something on the order of 7 percent a year. These are causing considerable social pain that arouses resistance from powerful vested interests and could incite an already restive population to more serious forms of opposition that the government delicately refers to as "endangering social stability." Seven percent is believed to be the minimum growth rate necessary to prevent instability. In early 2015 the International Monetary Fund, in a forecast some thought overly generous, predicted that the PRC's growth rate would fall into the 6 percent range.[80]

Japan also undertook ambitious reforms to deal with its quite different problems. The 3/11 disaster left the country with a massively expensive clean-up problem that its stagnant economy was ill-equipped to cope with. Faced with a national debt that was 200 percent of its GDP, Prime Minister Abe Shinzō introduced a "three arrows" strategy that was immediately dubbed "Abenomics": monetary policy, fiscal policy, and structural reforms. The first arrow entailed printing additional money to lower the exchange rate of the yen, making the country's products more competitive internationally and raising the inflation rate from zero to 2 percent. While very modest, this would be Japan's highest inflation rate since 1991. In the second fiscal arrow, the consumption tax was raised from 5 to 8 percent, bringing more money into the treasury. New government spending programs would stimulate demand, thus offsetting the depressive effect of the increased consumption tax. The third arrow, structural reforms, also aimed at making Japanese industries more competitive: it included relaxation of labor market strictures, reduced protection of agriculture, and deregulation of utilities. A "womenomics" program would provide incentives for Japan's female population to enter or rise within the work force to alleviate the depressive effect that a declining population had on productivity.

At first, the program seemed to be working. The yen fell 21 percent against the dollar; the Nikkei 225 stock market index rose 57 percent; and the consumer price index rose to 1.6 percent. Growth was 1.5 percent, 0.9 percent better than had been predicted just before Abe assumed the prime ministership. Abenomics was off to a good start.[81] However, data released in November 2014 unexpectedly showed that the economy had contracted 1.9 percent in the July–September period. The consumption tax increase was believed to be largely responsible. Although it had passed under Abe's predecessor and was therefore technically not part of Abenomics, the tax had not taken effect until several months after he took office. Abe postponed a planned further increase in taxes, amid increasing doubts on the efficacy of his economic program.[82] Still, during the last quarter of 2014, the economy rebounded. GDP increased at an annualized rate of 2.2 percent that, although well below the anticipated 3.6 percent, indicated the worst might be over and the economy launched toward recovery. However, soon after, a slowdown in China's economic growth and plunging oil prices world-wide negatively impacted both Chinese and Japanese economies.

Both China's and Japan's economic reforms had repercussions on bilateral trade, as did frictions over the disputed islands. Even though total foreign direct investment in China increased, that from Japan decreased. Two-way trade declined for two straight years. As reported by the Japan External Trade Organization (JETRO), Japan's total trade with China dropped 6.5 percent in 2013 despite the number of Chinese tourists to Japan and the number of Japanese cars sold in Japan having recovered to what they were before the September 2012 anti-Japanese riots. Exports to China fell 10.2 percent, the second straight year of double-digit decline, while imports from China fell 3.7 percent, the first drop since the world-wide financial crisis year of 2009. Judged by its rather than China's statistics, Japan's trade deficit with the PRC was its highest ever, up 17.8 percent from the previous year.

JETRO noted several factors, principally sluggish Chinese demand due to Beijing's economic structural reforms.[83] Chinese Commerce Ministry spokesperson Shen Danyang, however, noted that "undeniably the severe difficulties in the two countries' political relations also impacted it to a certain level."[84] Japanese companies were also diversifying investments out of China and investing less in the PRC; Japanese direct investment in China fell 25. 2 percent in 2015, its third straight year of decline.[85]

While some observers predicted that the two economies might be decoupling,[86] thereby reducing somewhat the economic consequences of an armed confrontation, diversification seems unlikely to reach that point.

The 23,000 Japanese companies that operate in the PRC employ 10 million Chinese citizens: provincial and local officials want to keep them there, and welcome infusions of Japanese capital and technology. Japanese products enjoy a high reputation among Chinese consumers, many of whom distrust the quality and safety of comparable domestically produced goods. For Japan, the Chinese market remains crucial to efforts to revive the economy.[87] Chinese sources argue that Japan benefits greatly from trade despite the alleged deficit, since many of the profits that balance sheets ascribe to the PRC are produced by Japanese-owned businesses in China.[88]

From being the leader of the V-shaped formation of Asian development, Japan has fallen behind relative to China, with its continued economic prosperity heavily dependent on trade with its larger neighbor. As its population is both declining in numbers and aging, it does not seem likely that even a strongly resurgent Japan can displace the PRC from its place as the world's second largest economy. Yet the Chinese economy is beset with serious problems as well. For the foreseeable future, cooperation, at least on economic matters, seems preferable to the alternatives.

9

Mutual Military Apprehensions

THE DEMILITARIZATION OF JAPAN

Having defeated Japan in World War II, the victors were committed to ensuring that militarism did not arise again. Efforts at demilitarization included the disestablishment of the Shintō religion, since it had been used to reinforce Japan's imperialist agenda; the selection of an American Quaker as governess for the crown prince so as to impart the values of peace and democracy; and the drafting of a so-called peace constitution. Promulgated in 1947, the constitution's preamble states:

> We, the Japanese people, desire peace for all time and are deeply conscious of the high ideals controlling human relationship, and we have determined to preserve our security and existence, trusting in the justice and faith of the peace-loving peoples of the world. We desire to occupy an honored place in an international society striving for the preservation of peace, and the banishment of tyranny and slavery, oppression and intolerance for all time from the earth. We recognize that all people of the world have the right to live in peace, free from fear and want.

This must be read in conjunction with Chapter 2, Article 9, of the same document:

> Aspiring sincerely to an international peace based on justice and order, the Japanese people forever renounce war as a sovereign right of the nation and the threat or use of force as means of settling international disputes.
> In order to accomplish the aim of the preceding paragraph, land, sea, and air forces, as well as other war potential, will never be maintained. The right of belligerency of the state will not be recognized.

The apparently innocuous phrase "in order to accomplish the aim of the preceding paragraph" was a later addition to previous drafts of the constitution, which had prohibited offensive warfare, using forces in self-defense, and maintaining *any* type of military establishment. Inserting this clause, according to its creators, allowed an interpretation of the constitution that permits Japan, consonant with its status as a sovereign nation, to exercise the right of individual self-defense and to maintain Self-Defense Forces (SDF) for that purpose, as long as they were not designed to settle *international* disputes.[1]

There was opposition from both the left and the right of the political spectrum. A retired Japanese ambassador recalled that, shortly after the end of the war, his father received visitors who discussed how Japan could rise again and defeat the Americans. The diplomat's father disagreed, saying that the "Anglo-Saxons" could not be defeated, and that only by allying with them could Japan rise again.[2] This is a sentiment echoed in the diary that an accused war criminal, on trial for his life, wrote while in prison. In it, Kishi Nobusuke opined that, in order to prevent communism from spreading, U.S. troops aided by Japanese volunteers should depose Mao Zedong and his army.[3] Kishi was eventually released from prison and would later become prime minister (February 1957–July 1960) of his country. Another future prime minister, Ashida Hitoshi (March–October 1948), who, unlike Kishi, was widely known as a confirmed liberal, also advocated rearmament and revision of the peace clause.[4]

On the other side of the spectrum were those who would have preferred the earlier draft of the constitution, and strongly disputed the legitimacy of the SDF. Chief among these were supporters of the country's leading opposition party, the Japan Socialist Party and its later incarnation, the Social Democratic Party (SDP) of Japan. The latter gave up its opposition to the SDF only in 1994.

THE KOREAN WAR

Events were to militate in favor of a higher rather than a lower defense posture for Japan. After the government's surrender in 1945, the United States sent in an occupation force headed by the autocratic General Douglas MacArthur. It occupied bases in different parts of Japan. American policymakers held forth a vision of an unarmed Japan living under the supervision of a world government. This image was to prove short lived. The victory of Mao Zedong's communist forces in October 1949 followed by the June 1950 North Korean surprise attack on South Korea dramatically changed the Asian strategic equation. In this new situation, the Japanese bases took on added importance. To the annoyance of Japanese pacifists, American efforts to extirpate the roots of Japanese militarism halted. Conservatives rejoiced, seeing an opportunity to rebuild the country's military with U.S. help.[5]

MacArthur, leading a United Nations–authorized counteroffensive, found his troops confined to a small part of the peninsula around Pusan, facing annihilation by the North Korean army. He responded with a daring amphibious invasion behind North Korean lines at Inchon. This successfully out-flanked the North Korean army, which fled north. In November 1950, after intense negotiations among Stalin, Mao, and North Korean leader Kim Il-song, Chinese forces intervened on behalf of the Pyongyang government.[6] In the face of a long retreat, MacArthur repeatedly requested authorization to strike northeast China and major Chinese cities with nuclear weapons. Fearing that further escalation of the war would bring in the Soviet Union to back its Chinese ally, then president Harry Truman refused.

MacArthur shared a view prominent in the United States at the time: that Truman, who had succeeded to the presidency only after Franklin Delano Roosevelt's death in office, was inadequate for the position. Arguing that the time to strike China was now, while it was weak both militarily and in terms of its economic infrastructure, he warned of a disastrous defeat. After a March 1951 counterattack commanded by General Matthew Ridgway restored equilibrium to the battlefield and disproved MacArthur's claim that the war would be lost unless the United States used nuclear weapons against China, Truman announced his intention to pursue ceasefire talks. MacArthur, whose previous acts had verged on insubordination, then clearly stepped across the line by threatening

China with expansion of the war. In April, Truman relieved MacArthur of command, replacing him with Ridgway, and proceeded with plans for peace talks to end the Korean confrontation.

The sum total of these events, when added to the growing perception that the Soviet Union was becoming a greater threat to world peace than the Axis powers had been, was to confirm the importance of Japan to the defense of American interests in East Asia. John Foster Dulles, appointed to conduct negotiations for a peace treaty with Japan that would conclude the American occupation and return political control to the Japanese government, urged the Japanese to rearm and to conclude a military alliance with the United States. Ironically, it was the Americans who now pressed the Japanese to rearm, while the Japanese government resisted, professing its devotion to the American-inspired constitution.

Within Japan, different views contended. Millions had died during the war and living conditions both during and after it were harsh: many people, even those who did not consider themselves part of any political grouping, felt deceived and betrayed by their former government's aggressive policies. They took a "never again" attitude, and strongly opposed any actions that might result in Japan becoming entangled in military endeavors. Nationalists, some of them on the far right but also including people who were basically pro-American, felt that the proposed treaty would compromise the independence of Japan. Moderate conservatives, who included bureaucratic and business interests, supported the creation of a small self-defense force, but preferred that the United States retain major responsibility for defense. Left-wing organizations such as labor unions argued that any alliance with the United States courted disaster, since it would result in Japan being drawn into a conflict.

In addition to trying to achieve an outcome that would be at least minimally tolerable to these widely divergent domestic concerns, Japanese policymakers wanted to avoid, on the one hand, the dangers of refusal to arm, which might cause a break with the United States, or on the other, a rearmament that resulted in Japan becoming part of larger U.S. geopolitical issues. A security treaty signed in 1951 reflected these concerns. Under it, Japan agreed to provide the United States with bases, and the United States agreed to take responsibility for Japan's security. Tokyo took pains to point out that the agreement, and its 1960 reincarnation, the Treaty of Mutual Cooperation and Security, did not constitute an alliance.

Negotiations over the next thirty-five years would reflect this desire to steer between the Scylla of abandonment by the United States and the Charybdis of entrapment in its wider concerns.[7] In July 1950 the government authorized the establishment of a National Police Reserve, to consist of 75,000 men charged with the defense of the Japanese islands. The police reserve was the genesis of the Self-Defense Forces, which were formally established in 1954. The SDF comprised Ground (GSDF), Maritime (MSDF), and Air (ASDF) arms.

CHINA REARMS ... AND REGRESSES

A few months earlier, the Chinese had entered into an agreement that also impacted military relationships with Japan. The Sino-Soviet Treaty of Friendship, Alliance, and Military Assistance, signed in February 1950, obligated the two contracting parties to

> carry out jointly all necessary measures within their power to prevent a repetition of aggression and breach of the peace by Japan or any other state which might directly or indirectly join with Japan in acts of aggression. Should either [sic] with Japan and thus find itself in a state of war, the other contracting party shall immediately extend military and other assistance with all the means at its disposal. Neither of the contracting parties shall enter into any alliance directed against the other party, or participate in any coalition or in any action of measures directed against the other party.[8]

Beijing's decision to intervene in the Korean conflict necessitated postponement of its plans to take Taiwan and to the solidification of the status of America's bases in Japan. In the years following the ceasefire, China's military, called the People's Liberation Army (PLA), and Japan's SDF developed in parallel. Military relations with each other were essentially non-existent, and both nations had other problems to attend to.

Although China claimed victory in Korea, the war had shown serious deficiencies in its ability to conduct operations. Molded by an ideology that was suspicious of military professionalism, since it reminded communist leaders of the warlordism they had rebelled against, the Red Army, as the PLA was called prior to the founding of the PRC, was characterized by a relatively flat command hierarchy and democratic decision-making. Many commanders were essentially amateurs of varying talent; many of their troops were enthusiastic but illiterate volunteers.

While this configuration worked well against the demoralized forces of Chiang Kai-shek's KMT, it did not perform well against technologically superior U.S./UN forces. In Korea, logistics were poor, supply lines were long, and the local population did not provide the kind of backing that was implicit in the PLA's slogan: "The army is the fish, the people are the water; the fish must support the water and the water must support the fish."

Efforts to incorporate the experience of the PRC's only meaningful ally, the Soviet Union, into the military led to the emergence of class cleavages that bothered party ideologues, who saw in them a slippery slope back to the kind of society they had fought so hard to destroy. Internal arguments about military reform fed into larger conflicts about the transformation of Chinese society as a whole, leading to the disastrous Great Leap Forward of 1958. In addition to causing mass starvation, the Leap, which Soviet leader Nikita Khrushchev had been critical of, added one more factor to a number of preexisting disagreements between the Chinese and the Soviets. This in turn led to a rift in the Sino-Soviet alliance that resulted in Soviet technicians departing en masse. Among other consequences, the break sharply set back China's weapons upgrade program.

By 1962 the PLA had improved again to the extent that it performed well in the Sino-Indian conflict. Then, in 1964, egalitarian ideologues succeeded in abolishing its rank structure. This act presaged the Cultural Revolution, which was characterized by an attack on all professionalism, including military professionalism. Young Red Guards felt free to attack military commanders, both verbally and physically. They succeeded in toppling many from power and intimidating most of the rest. Whether motivated by ideological conviction or a desire for self-preservation, some PLA units took sides in factional struggles among Red Guards. Military training was largely dispensed with, replaced by sessions dedicated to studying Mao Zedong's thought. The chaos abated only after the Soviet attack on Czechoslovakia in 1968. Chinese leaders interpreted the USSR's actions as a warning that the PRC might be next— "killing the chicken to warn the monkey"— and concluded that it was necessary to shift emphasis from domestic strife to preparing to defend against external attack. But the road back to proficiency and expertise was a long one, and the leadership had many other pressing concerns.

The PLA's attack on Vietnam in February 1979 again showed major military deficiencies, with logistical difficulties a particular problem. Deng Xiaoping, reportedly describing the episode as a diplomatic victory but not necessarily a military one, used this to underscore his plans for improvement. However, he placed military modernization last in the priorities of his signature plan, the Four Modernizations, arguing that a strong military could not exist without a strong economy. The strong economy, Deng emphasized, would have to come first. Military training and weapons acquisitions slowly began to improve, but were constrained by tight budgets.

CAUTIOUS SECURITY STEPS IN JAPAN

Japanese defense policy continued along the lines set by the security treaty and the Yoshida doctrine: relying on the United States for defense while concentrating on economic growth. Yoshida Shigeru, who was prime minister from May 1946 to May 1947 and again from October 1948 to December 1954, advocated limited national rearmament and alignment, but not an explicit alliance, with the United States. He did not rule out large-scale rearmament and Japan's reemergence as an independent power at some future date.

In December 1954 an effort at revising Article 9 of the constitution by Yoshida's successor Hatoyama Ichirō was thwarted by a coalition of opposing forces, who also imposed a ban on the overseas dispatch of the SDF and restrictions on arms exports.

Toward the end of the 1950s, the status quo was again challenged by leaders such as Kishi Nobusuke. As prime minister from February 1957 through July 1960, Kishi pushed through a revised security treaty that committed the United States to defending Japan if it were attacked, and to consult with Japan before moving major forces into or out of the country. Either side would be able to abrogate the treaty after 1970 upon one year's notice. These changes, which gave more independence to the Japanese side, were opposed by conservatives as not going far enough, and by the left wing, which opposed any security relationship. The treaty finally passed in a special midnight session of the Diet that the Socialist Party boycotted. Major demonstrations then ensued.

The Chinese press, sympathetic to the left wing, reported the protests in detail, choosing to interpret the changes as a step toward Japan's remilitarization. The atmosphere was such that President Eisenhower cancelled plans for a state visit to celebrate the signing, and Kishi felt obliged to resign. Thereafter, however, opposition trailed off, and the treaty was not, in fact, abrogated in 1970.

Pacifist sentiments remained strong nonetheless. In 1967, under Prime Minister Satō Eisaku, the so-called three principles were established. These prohibited arms exports to communist countries, nations subject to a U.N.-imposed arms embargo, and countries involved in armed conflicts. Satō also introduced the three non-nuclear principles, under which Japan pledged that it would not possess, produce, or introduce nuclear weapons. This plus Japan's accession to the Nuclear Non-Proliferation Treaty were major factors in Satō's being awarded the Nobel Peace Prize in 1974. In 1976 the cabinet of Prime Minister Miki Takeo imposed a total ban on arms exports.[9]

These manifestations of Japan's commitment to peace notwithstanding, throughout the 1960s and early 1970s Chinese sources regularly accused Tokyo and Washington of colluding in a common desire for world domination, and Japan of moving quickly toward remilitarization.[10] Evidence was adduced in the form of rising defense budgets,[11] the hiring of demobilized SDF officers by major Japanese corporations,[12] and the release of films glorifying past battles.[13] In fact, military service was not highly esteemed at the time. Recruits were frequently second sons of rural families. Not expecting to inherit the ancestral land, they hoped to save enough from their military salaries to buy a shop or invest in a small business. When SDF personnel tried to enroll in university classes in the late 1960s, civilian students protested. Those who wore their uniforms on the street risked being spat on: even through the 1980s, SDF members changed out of their military clothing before they stepped outside of Defense Agency facilities.[14]

THE SWORD REEMERGES IN JAPAN

As prosperity increased and Japan regained a more confident international persona, the idea of a more independent defense policy gained adherents. One of Japan's most outstanding writers, Mishima Yukio, argued that the country's culture had been truncated by postwar efforts to suppress and even deny its military tradition. He cited American anthropologist Ruth Benedict's *The Chrysanthemum and the Sword*, based on research she had undertaken on behalf of the American struggle against Japan during World War II. Benedict had hypothesized that both aesthetics, symbolized by the flower that is associated with the Japanese imperial family, and the warrior tradition, *bushidō*, are integral parts of the culture. However, said Mishima, since the end of the war, the sword had been suppressed. Only by reviving it could the true essence of Japanese culture be restored. Shunned by most government officials, Mishima responded by creating his own private army, funding it with a portion of the revenues from his impressive output of plays and novels.

Though he was personally tolerated as a brilliant eccentric by the generally left-of-center literary establishment, Mishima's pleas to restore what he considered a vital part of the Japanese ethos had little resonance in society at large. In a final gesture, Mishima, accompanied by several members of his army, held a GSDF commander captive in his own office until the officer agreed to allow Mishima to address his troops. Mishima succeeded in delivering his address, albeit against a background of jeers and derision from SDF members. Many of them did not actually hear what he had to say. After concluding, Mishima committed ritual suicide, slitting his stomach with a prized traditional sword.

Again, China found evidence for its view that Japanese militarism was on the rise. Although Beijing's reaction was understandable due to Mishima's sometimes flamboyant behavior, this was a misinterpretation of what Mishima stood for. Well versed in the literature and ways of many civilizations, he lived in a Western-style home and incorporated many non-Japanese themes into his literature. According to his biographers, Mishima's aim was to restore the balance of Japanese culture, not to revive militarism. What he wanted was that Japan adopt something like the Swiss system of military service. And, as Chinese policymakers no doubt noticed but did not choose to publicly comment on, SDF members had openly ridiculed his ideas. Moreover, the Japanese government prosecuted members of Mishima's private army who had participated in the incident preceding his death.[15]

As much to reassure Japanese public opinion as official Chinese concerns, the 1970 edition of the annual white paper *Defense of Japan.* used the term "exclusively defense-oriented policy." The government interpreted this phrase to mean that, in the event the nation had to defend itself against a military attack, SDF actions would be limited to Japan's own soil and surrounding areas without making any direct attack on any base of the assailant country.¹⁶ While this explanation sounded innocuous enough, the term "surrounding areas" was ambiguous and would later contribute significantly to the tensions between the two sides, most notably with regard to Taiwan.

Those who believed that an incremental buildup of the SDF was the best way to proceed found it easier to implement when applied to maritime endeavors than for ground forces, since the former did not involve stationing soldiers abroad. Indeed, according to one analyst, the MSDF is a direct descendant of the Imperial Navy in terms of its customs, traditional, and institutional forms. Initially, it absorbed some of the Imperial Navy's personnel as well.¹⁷ Business interests, seeing the need to maintain the nation's economic lifeline and protect Japanese shipping, backed expansion of MSDF tonnage and weapons. In 1970 a more activist individual, Nakasone Yasuhiro, was named head of the Japanese Defense Agency (JDA). Nakasone put forth an ambitious plan to defend his country's sea lanes, out to the Straits of Malacca. While understandable from the point of view of protecting Japan's commercial interests, Nakasone's plan went far beyond the original concept of the SDF as defender of the home territories against external invasion. It was also, according to knowledgeable observers, operationally infeasible.¹⁸

Although Nakasone had made clear that the enemy he had in mind was the Soviet Union, China reacted sharply. An article in the official *Beijing Review* accused Japan of trying to revive its imperial past. Among other charges was that a booklet entitled *Maritime Defense and Japan's Determination* had circulated within the ruling Liberal Democratic Party (LDP) that spoke of the need to build up military strength sufficient to secure a Japanese maritime lifeline. This was the first in a litany of complaints. The visit of the MSDF's new major surface warships to eleven countries was described as not so much a visit as a show of force; the ASDF, China noted, had carried out a large-scale heliborne exercise in Hokkaido; and the 1971 annual fleet review was to be held at the former imperial military port of Sasebo rather than at Yokosuka, as had previously been the case. The author of the *Beijing Review* article inferred some symbolism in this that was hostile to China, but, in fact, both Sasebo and Yokosuka, along with Kure and Maezuru, had been imperial naval ports. The author may have reacted as he did because Sasebo had been the major staging point for the Sino-Japanese War of 1895, but this is likely to have reflected Sasebo's better geographic location for such an endeavor rather than any role as a symbolic epicenter of aggression. Additionally, the article complained that recently released Japanese films had glorified the exploits of persons the Chinese regarded as war criminals.[19]

In the end, Nakasone's plans were defeated, and he was replaced as JDA head by the lower-profile Kubo Takuya. Kubo, whose background had been in police work, reassured the Diet's opposition parties that it would be inconceivable for MSDF vessels to ever operate in the Straits of Malacca or the Indian Ocean. Neither Kubo nor his successors cared to court the controversy spawned by Nakasone's plans. In addition, the JDA's image was diminished when an ASDF fighter collided with a passenger jet during the summer of 1971, and by a scandal involving contracts with Lockheed Aircraft the following year. In September 1972 Prime Minister Tanaka Kakuei visited Beijing in pursuit of the normalization of diplomatic relations. Lectured by his counterpart Zhou Enlai on the evils of reviving Japanese militarism, Tanaka offered to limit the country's defense spending to 1 percent of GNP. This was formalized by the Japanese cabinet in 1976.[20]

However, in 1976, another incident occurred that drew attention to Japan's need for better intelligence and air defense: a defecting Soviet pilot, Lieutenant Viktor Belenko, flew his MiG-25 Foxbat into Hokodate Air Base undetected. This helped ease the passage of the National Defense Program Outline (NDPO) at the end of the next month, with its requirement for full-service surveillance and intelligence capability.[21] The oil shocks of 1973 and 1977 also heightened awareness of Japan's vulnerability to external forces. Tokyo scrupulously abided by its pledge to spend no more than 1 percent of GNP on defense, but since the Japanese economy was growing rapidly in the 1970s and 1980s, this amounted to a finite share of an ever larger pie.

Those who expressed concern at defense spending were typically soothed with the explanation that it resulted from *gaiatsu*. Literally translated as "foreign pressure," it was understood to have the more blunt meaning of "the Americans made us do it."[22] There was considerable truth in this: with the United States suffering from stagflation, relatively high unemployment, and a large trade deficit with Japan, Washington policymakers regularly pressed their Japanese counterparts to agree to bear more of the costs of defense. But at the same time, it gave conservative politicians the excuse they needed to do something they had long favored.

CHINA COMPLAINS

China's official media issued periodic warnings against remilitarization and against the presence of U.S. bases in Japan, but with a ritualistic tone. Privately, Chinese officials seem to have regarded Washington's defense partnership with Tokyo—which at this point Tokyo resolutely refused to call an alliance—as a restraining force on the revival of Japanese militarism. Enjoying better relations with both the United States and Japan during the 1970s and early 1980s, Chinese leaders did not fear that this partnership was directed against the PRC. Moreover, in this period, the Soviet Union was clearly the enemy of all three. In discussions at the time of the normalization of Sino-Japanese relations in September 1972, Zhou Enlai stated that China no longer opposed Japan's security treaty with the United States. China also expressed support for Japan's claims to the Northern Territories seized by the Soviet Union after World War II. And in September 1978, Deng Xiaoping told a Japanese delegation that he was in favor of the SDF buildup.[23] In May 1980, on the first state visit of a PRC leader to Japan, Hua Guofeng told a press conference that

> [a]n independent and sovereign state should have the right to maintain its own defense so as to safeguard its independence and sovereignty. As to what Japan will do, we do not interfere in its internal affairs.[24]

Hua was also quoted as saying that the ASDF should be expanded so that it would be better able to protect shipping routes.[25] Astoundingly, in light of later developments, both a PLA deputy chief of staff and Deng Xiaoping himself stated that Japan should consider raising the percentage of GDP devoted to defense spending to 2 percent.[26]

In actuality, the Japanese government, supported by public opinion, placed effective constraints on the expression of opinions that advocated a more activist approach to defense. In 1978 SDF General Kurisu Hiromi was dismissed for "making controversial remarks about civilian control." More specifically, the general had said that, under certain circumstances, such as the pilot of an ASDF plane being pursued by an enemy fighter plane, it might be necessary for the ASDF pilot to fire first. Commanders might have to take "supra-legal action" in the absence of legal guidelines for exercising the right to self-defense.[27]

In 1981 another SDF general, Takeda Gorō, while making it very clear that he accepted the concept of civilian control of the military—Kurisu's supporters having previously argued that they did not believe Kurisu had ever challenged the concept—stated that a literal interpretation of Japan's self-defense policy would fail to protect the country's territorial interests. He expressed concern that politics seemed to outweigh strategy in policy planning. Takeda's comments were backed by several influential LDP members, but after the opposition parties boycotted the Diet's budget committee hearings, his supporters were persuaded to compromise. A settlement was reached in which Takeda was allowed to retire rather than be dismissed; the prime minister would affirm his support for civilian control of the military, and both he and the head of the JDA would apologize for the general's comments.[28]

The PRC's relatively benign attitude toward Japanese security policy would change due to a number of factors. Beijing was not happy when, in 1981, Prime Minister Suzuki Zenkō pledged to strengthen his country's defense of "several hundred" miles of surrounding waters and the sea lanes to a distance of 1,000 nautical miles.[29] In 1981 as well, Chinese relations with the Soviet Union began to thaw. Beijing also became more wary of the United States after the election of Ronald Reagan as president in late 1980. Reagan undertook to refurbish an American defense establishment that had atrophied in the wake of the Vietnam War.

The elevation of former activist JDA head Nakasone Yasuhiro to prime minister (November 1982–November 1987) was accompanied by policies that indicated Japan was becoming more assertive and nationalistic (see Chapter 5). Nakasone and Reagan enjoyed a warm personal relationship that the media dubbed the Ron and Yasu show, but which seemed to exclude China. With polls showing that 70 percent of the Japanese population opposed revision of Article 9,[30] Nakasone did not return to the ambitious plans he had put forth as head of the JDA. Still, he is credited with raising Japan's defense consciousness, and his policies included a buildup of SDF forces. After 1983 the government eased the ban on weapons exports to allow weapons technology to be shared with the United States.[31]

Japanese defense spending increased by between 5 and 8 percent between 1987 and 1991, even briefly exceeding the 1 percent limit in 1987.[32] Though only just barely breaching the limit, the Chinese media reacted sharply. A red line had been crossed, from which, they predicted, erroneously, there would be no retreat:

> [T]he change can be summarized in one word: the break. Given the first break, it is unavoidable that the second and the third breaks and more breaks will follow, and the state of affairs will get out of control.[33]

TIANANMEN SQUARE INCIDENT AND ITS AFTERMATH

Tokyo did not react sharply to the Beijing government's suppression of unarmed demonstrators at Tiananmen Square and in a hundred other cities in June 1989, soon resuming business as usual. However, the brutality of the suppression sullied the image of Deng Xiaoping's kinder, gentler brand of communism among the general population. The unraveling of the Soviet empire that began the same year was accompanied by the beginning of steady double-digit increases in China's defense budgets at a time when most other countries were reducing theirs.

Initially, this was explained as rewarding the military for its loyalty to the party, albeit after some initial reluctance to intervene, in suppressing the demonstrators. As time and the defense increases continued, the Chinese government sought to assuage foreign concerns by pointing out that the increases were to compensate for a rising inflation rate. However, the rises continued even in years when the economy contracted, and were accompanied by off-budget purchases of ever more sophisticated military equipment, much of it from the former Soviet Union. The PLA's navy and air force began to move away from their previous coastal focus: Chinese ships and planes began to probe into and overfly disputed areas.

Deng Xiaoping's chosen successor Jiang Zemin was the PRC's first leader to have no military experience, and it was rumored that the PLA had hesitations about him. Jiang undertook strenuous efforts to win them over, making frequent trips to military units both near the capital and in remote border areas and difficult terrain. He increased the number of billets for three-star generals, the PLA's highest rank, and raised military pay. Since the military seemed to be advocating a harder line toward disputed international disputes, there was speculation that, in order to gain their support, Jiang tended to acquiesce. Given the closed nature of the PRC's information on such sensitive topics, there is no conclusive proof of this.

Feeling a sense of international isolation after the Tiananmen incident, and always concerned with the possibility of encirclement by enemies, Beijing's policy paradoxically sounded more defensive at the same time as it became more assertive. As the PRC's most powerful neighbor, and a country with which it had a number of disputes, Japan was an important focus of official criticism. A Chinese naval strategist's 1990 article on maritime threats to his country included among his threat scenarios:

- the United States encouraging Japan to take more responsibility for the defense of sea lanes of communication
- Japan's naval expansion exceeding the PRC's ability to counter it
- Japan's claim to the Diaoyutai/Senkaku Islands
- Japan agreeing with Korea to jointly exploit the sea beds in areas the PRC believed to be within its territorial waters[34]

EFFECT OF THE GULF WAR

Elsewhere, Japan was being criticized for not taking a strong enough stand militarily. The Gulf War of 1991 played an important part in moving Japan toward a more active security policy. Japan's initial unwillingness to contribute substantially to the war effort, much less expose its own nationals to risk, was the topic of much criticism from other coalition members, particularly the United States. Japan, they pointed out, was more dependent on Middle Eastern oil than any of the others, and yet disdained meaningful participation in the effort to safeguard the supply thereof. Derogatory comments such as "Other countries sent troops, Japan sent sushi" abounded. A United Nations Peace Cooperation bill sponsored by LDP defense activist Ozawa Ichirō would have permitted the dispatch of SDF and coast guard volunteers overseas to support noncombat activities, but it failed to pass the Diet. In the end, Japan sent minesweepers to the Gulf after the fighting had ceased.

The technological superiority of U.S. forces in the Gulf War did not go unnoticed in Beijing, and was an important factor influencing the PLA to adopt a new strategy of preparation for high-technology regional war.[35] Such techniques would be useful in the event of a confrontation with Japan. These included the creation of "fist" (*quantou*) units whose personnel could be rapidly deployed; several new classes of ships including destroyers, frigates, resupply vessels, and missile patrol craft; and the purchase of state-of-the-art submarines, radars, and fighter planes from the former Soviet Union.

In 1992 Japan received an unpleasant jolt when China's National People's Congress passed a law on the territorial sea. This unilaterally annexed Taiwan and the Diaoyutai/Senkaku Islands, among other areas, as well as reserving for the PLA's navy the right to patrol those waters.[36] While the law had no immediate operational effect and Japan continued to exercise sovereignty over the Diaoyutai/Senkaku group, it did provide a stimulus for those who wished to enhance the role of the SDF.

NORTH KOREAN MISSILE TESTS

The issue of an appropriate Japanese defense policy was given new impetus when, in May 1993, North Korea launched a Nodong-1 missile into the body of water known to Koreans as the East Sea and to Japanese as the Sea of Japan. JDA officials told the Diet that a portion of western Japan was within range of the missile, and that Pyongyang was developing newer versions capable of reaching all of Japan. Moreover, Japan was unable to defend itself against attack. There were also fears that North Korean terrorists could enter Japan and perhaps sabotage its nuclear power plants.[37]

Concerns with abandonment began to eclipse fears of entrapment. Ozawa, reasoning along lines similar to those voiced by Mishima Yukio more than two decades before, argued that Japan should become a "normal" country, *futsu no kuni*: it would not be accepted as a fully functioning member of the international community until it was able to contribute to the defense of that community. A master strategist, Ozawa contrived to destabilize the LDP by forming a splinter party that ended the LDP's thirty-eight year grip on power. A coalition government was formed that included the Social Democratic Party, on the condition that it agree to drop longstanding opposition to the legitimacy of the SDF.[38]

As a result, it became possible for Japan to contribute to peace-keeping activities abroad, which was interpreted as legitimate under Article 9 of the constitution as part of Japan's right to collective self-defense. China protested that this was Tokyo's attempt to "mold" Japanese public opinion for a more aggressive role, and that these changes were causing worry among Asian nations. Chinese ships began to explore waters that were disputed between the two countries with increasing frequency.

Although concerns with both North Korean and Chinese activities had existed for some time, the 1995 edition of the JDA's annual defense white paper was the first to contain explicit mention of this. Media reaction was less than supportive. *Tokyo Shimbun*, for example, commented that "the two countries have some advanced weapons, but their weapons as a whole are quite obsolete. . . . [They] are not making any moves that can be construed as acts of aggression against Japan."[39]

CRISIS IN THE TAIWAN STRAIT

A watershed was reached when, from July 1995 through March 1996, the PLA carried out a series of war games and missile launches in the Taiwan Strait. These menacing activities influenced the negotiations on the revision of the 1976 National Defense Program Outline. In the fall of 1995, the JDA prepared an internal document for the Japan-U.S. Security Consultative Committee, also known as the Two-Plus-Two, meeting, stating that the possibility of a Chinese invasion of Taiwan "cannot be denied," and suggesting an upgraded security relationship between Japan and the United States that included better intelligence gathering and investigation of joint antimissile research.[40] In a security dialogue with Beijing, the Japanese government stated that it had not officially talked about the Chinese threat, but was "objectively analyzing" situations with regard to the People's Republic of China. The Beijing side expressed its hope that Japan would take "a cautious attitude" on theater missile defense (TMD).[41]

With China continuing to test nuclear weapons and the Japanese foreign ministry announcing that it had discovered Beijing planned to begin trial digging at an undersea oil field in disputed waters,[42] Tokyo found Chinese assurances that the PRC's security goals were no threat either to Asia or the rest of the world[43] less than convincing.

In March, as Chinese missile tests took place in the Taiwan Strait, Japanese and American representatives held the fifth in a series of working-level meetings to discuss bilateral cooperation on what was described as a sophisticated antiballistic missile system.[44] On April 17th, Prime Minister Hashimoto and President Clinton signed the Japan-U.S. Joint Declaration on Security Alliance for the 21st Century. The two governments took note of the existence of instability and uncertainty in the Asia-Pacific region, explicitly mentioning "heavy concentrations of military force, including nuclear arsenals," "unresolved territorial disputes," and "potential regional conflicts." The declaration's innocuous-sounding references to the common need to maintain a stable and prosperous environment for the Asia-Pacific region indicated an important shift in the alliance, from a focus on the defense of Japan to one whose goal was the maintenance of peace in Asia. In a related document signed two days before, Japan agreed to provide logistics support in contingencies involving "the areas surrounding (shūhen jitai) Japan."[45]

Discounting the standard disclaimers that the agreement was not directed at any third country,[46] Beijing issued a statement that any act which included directly or indirectly the Taiwan Strait, within the framework of the new guidelines, was an interference in and violation against China's sovereign rights.[47] The accord was "not defensive, but offensive," and whereas the original U.S.-Japan relationship "was simply a bilateral agreement under which the U.S. provided nuclear protection for Japan, the new accord tends to poke its nose into regional affairs."[48]

Indeed, it would have been difficult for the Chinese leadership not to see the documents as an effort at containment of the PRC. As the correspondent for a leading Hong Kong magazine pointed out,

> Who in Asia has the largest nuclear arsenal? Answer China. Where in the region are there unresolved territorial disputes? Answer the South China Sea, where China's claims are disputed by a handful of other countries. As for potential regional conflicts, there is none more destabilizing than China's insistence that Taiwan is one of its provinces. And, of course, the Chinese have been accused by the U.S. on more than one occasion of being guilty of actions that could cause the proliferation of weapons of mass destruction, as well as their means of delivery.[49]

The commitment to defend the shūhen jitai worried many Japanese as well. *Mainichi* worried that the agreement "effectively pushes China out of a previously fairly balanced triangular relationship," while *Asahi* expressed fears of entrapment, arguing that the foreign ministry might not have been aware of what it had landed in by pledging to review defense cooperation guidelines with regard to contingencies in the areas surrounding Japan. The net result of the April 1996 agreements, *Asahi* continued, was to change the security treaty system into one obliging Japan to assist the United States.[50] Other sources replied that it was childish to think that security agreements were not reciprocal: if Japan refused to help the United States, then the United States would have no reason to continue to protect Japan.[51] In this latter analysis, the danger of abandonment was greater than the risk of entrapment.

Beijing, however, must have been disappointed at the reaction of Asian states. Confounding years of predictions that any Japanese moves toward a higher defense posture would be strongly resisted by the numerous states that had experienced its cruelty in World War II, there was no barrage of criticism. Singaporean,[52] South Korean,[53] Indonesian,[54] Filipino,[55] and Hong Kong[56] sources all expressed apprehension over the implication of PRC actions in the Taiwan Strait and seemed cautiously accepting of the new American-Japanese arrangement.

While some Chinese analysts saw the April 1996 agreement as a strengthening of the U.S.-Japanese commitment to the containment of China,[57] another and notably different view was that the arrangement would enable Japan to assume a more independent stance. An article in Shanghai's *Guoji Zhanwang* (World Outlook) posited that, although the U.S.-Japanese security mechanism would exist for a long time, relative Japanese military independence would become ever more obvious, and that the SDF would become a new force for instability.[58] Whether they believed that Japan and the United States were united on an anti-China policy or that Japan would increasingly find an independent path toward militarism, the privately expressed view that the United States would ensure that Japan did not become militarily aggressive simply disappeared. From the Chinese standpoint, the cork was out of the bottle.

The view that Japan would pursue an independent path was bolstered by the statements of certain Japanese commentators. A former director of research at the Ground Self-Defense Force Staff College published an article in which he argued that, because there were situations in which Japan could not expect the United States to come to its aid—he specifically mentioned the Senkaku Islands, claimed by China; and Takeshima, claimed by Korea, which calls it Dokdo— the SDF must be prepared to take independent action. The article's subtitle was "Retreat from the Position of Independent Military Response Will Not Do."[59] A retired SDF general opined that Japan needed to consider seriously the defense of the nation apart from its alliance with the United States. Recent events, he argued, had shown that the "tottering" Japan-U.S. security arrangement had to be redefined; Japan had "reach[ed] the point where the government and people must seriously consider how to protect the security of the nation."[60]

The JDA also announced a decision to deploy its own reconnaissance satellites "to strengthen its ability to collect information on the military situation in neighboring countries" rather than rely solely on the United States. The "unstable Far Eastern situation," including (but apparently not limited to) Korea, was cited as the initial reason;[61] a later statement added that the images Japan received were only those that were in accord with U.S. government policies "and it is not known whether the images have already been revised or if they are originals. Nowadays, images can be made by synthesization."[62]

Even the proponents of a more independent defense posture—and many Japanese strongly opposed it—did not believe that such a defense could easily be mounted. One analyst decried the SDF as "a make-believe force," comparing it to a fire station that does not think of extinguishing fires but exerts efforts only to prevent fires—"a political decoration that cannot fight." Should the SDF decide to retake Takeshima, he opined, it would be unable to do so. And the MSDF existed not to protect Japan, but to protect the U.S. Seventh Fleet.[63]

No appreciable change resulted from this status of adjunct to the American military. A decade later, observers noted that the MSDF had "allowed strategic thought to languish entirely, owing primarily to Japan's close alliance with the United States." Their interviews revealed that, when asked to describe the sources of Japanese seapower thinking, officers invariably called for reinforcing the alliance with the United States.[64]

NEW JAPANESE DEFENSE LEGISLATION

After reaching agreement with the United States on the new defense guidelines, it fell to Prime Minister Hashimoto's government to draft domestic legislation to implement them. Two issues were particularly contentious: the exact nature of what assistance Japan was to render to the United States and the precise geographic area in which it was to be rendered. Although the Social Democratic Party (SDP), with its longstanding opposition to the security relationship with America, was no longer part of the governing coalition, the LDP did not have a majority in either house of parliament and it was necessary to placate other partners.

Not surprisingly in such a situation, circumlocution was used to work around differences of opinion. In the end, it was decided that Japan could not "supply" weapons to American forces, but could "transport" them to American forces so long as the transport remained outside the battle zone. This did not assuage Beijing. Chinese media kept up a steady barrage of criticism on the theme of creeping militarization, sometimes placing the onus on a small clique of ultra-nationalists and sometimes blaming "a certain superpower" (i.e., Washington) for urging Japan on.[65]

Relations, already strained over the Diaoyutai/Senkaku dispute, became incensed when, on August 17th, Chief Cabinet Secretary Kajiyama Seiroku said on Japanese television that the phrase "surrounding geographic areas" did indeed include Taiwan. Although others, including the deputy prime minister, had said similar things, Kajiyama was known as an exceptionally gaffe-prone politician, and the Japanese media gave prominent attention to his remarks. Even those Japanese who were sympathetic to the idea that the Taiwan Strait area should be included in the scope of the law felt that it was impolitic to say so just before Prime Minister Hashimoto's visit to China.

Visiting China for the 25th anniversary of normalization, Hashimoto spoke of the need for a future-oriented relationship. While this might be interpreted as code for ignoring World War II, the prime minister visited the September 18 Museum that commemorated the Japanese invasion of Manchuria (see pp. 68–71), remarking that he had come there to view history correctly to provide a basis for Sino-Japanese relations, signing "peace is what matters" in the museum's guest book.[66]

Although the visit was officially described as a success, Hashimoto was not able to dispel Chinese concerns about the closer Japanese-American defense relationship. Premier Li Peng warned that if Japan were to include Taiwan within the scope of the U.S.-Japan security treaty, the fundamental basis for Sino-Japanese relations would be in jeopardy.[67] Other commentators, presumably hoping that they could influence other countries to object to Japan's actions, took what might be called the slippery slope argument: having asserted its interest in defending the sacred Chinese territories of Taiwan and the Diaoyutai/Senkaku Islands, Japan had abandoned its previously defensive posture of engaging the enemy on the beaches and now aimed to destroy the enemy off its coasts. Might Tokyo also use a trumped-up nuclear threat to abandon its commitment to eschew nuclear weapons? Or might it argue that, in the interests of survival and to ensure the continuation of its Greater East Asian Co-Prosperity Sphere (see Chapter 2), it would send troops to invade and occupy the territory of other countries?[68]

Kajiyama attempted, without visible success, to appease Chinese anger over the Taiwan issue by explaining that he was merely speaking of "broad principles."[69] On his trip, Hashimoto stated in numerous different venues that his country did not support a "two-Chinas" policy or Taiwan independence. At the same time, he did not specifically exclude Taiwan from the scope of defense cooperation with the United States.[70] Hashimoto also took the opportunity to remind his Chinese hosts of the concern with which Tokyo viewed the PRC's rapidly increasing defense budgets as well as the lack of transparency in the budget figures that were released. He and Premier Li Peng agreed to promote high-level bilateral defense ties, including visits by uniformed military officers.[71]

Despite the relatively amicable nature of the Li-Hashimoto discussions on defense, the concerns of neither side were placated. Chinese sources expressed discomfort over a JDA decision to institute a new five-year operational program to cope with "emergencies in neighboring areas," as distinguished from the extant five-year defense programs that covered equipment and spending levels.[72] Included in discussions on streamlining government operations in general were suggestions that the JDA be upgraded to ministry status,[73] though the idea was quickly dropped. The idea of participating in the research and development for America's TMD plan was also discussed, with no clear consensus on whether to do so.

THE NORTH KOREAN MILITARY ISSUE RESURFACES

In 1998 Obuchi Keizō took over as prime minister, amid ongoing but inconclusive discussions on defense. This changed abruptly when, on August 31, North Korea launched a rocket that flew over Japan and landed in the Pacific Ocean. An embarrassed leadership admitted it had not detected the launch, nor would it have been able to protect Japan against the missile if it had been detected. The JDA, after consulting with U.S. intelligence, concluded it was the test of a long-range missile. The incident gave impetus to proponents of TMD. A few days after the launch, the Japanese and American defense ministers agreed to begin joint research into creating such a system, in which satellites, radar, and sea-based missiles would be used to identify, locate, and destroy incoming ballistic missiles. Obuchi sought to forestall criticism from Asian neighbors by announcing that the system was purely defensive, and meant simply to counter threats from rogue states like North Korea. Few, however, doubted, that the system was also being developed in order to counter the PRC's missiles.

A Beijing magazine complained that Tokyo was "behaving like Xiang Zhuang performing the sword dance as a cover for his attempt on Liu Bang's life."[74] Readers familiar with Chinese history would understand this as an allusion to an incident that took place in 206 B.C., when the founder of the Han dynasty narrowly survived an assassination attempt: the author was accusing Tokyo of using North Korea as a surrogate for China in order to persuade the Japanese public to back a stronger defense policy.

China's interpretation of Japan's true motive was essentially confirmed in a series of not-for-attribution interviews conducted by an American congressional commission with high-ranking members of the Japanese defense and foreign ministries in 2003. For example, a JDA official expressed the view that, although North Korea was capable of doing grievous harm to Japan, he believed that the problems between them could be dealt with so that this worst-case scenario would not happen. He described North Korea as a failed state and a short-term problem. China, on the other hand, was a rising power and a long-term threat to Japan's security.[75]

Again speaking off the record shortly after the TMD agreement was reached in 1998, Japanese officials acknowledged that deployment of the system would change the power balance between China and Japan in favor of the latter. They tended to be dismissive of Beijing's argument that TMD would destabilize the region. One official argued that, if TMD forced the PRC to conclude that it could not prevail over the technological primacy of Japan and the United States, the system would help stabilize the region. Another pointed out that China would have no reason to fear TMD unless it were planning to attack Japan:

> If I install an anti-theft alarm system in my house, can anyone say I'm provoking burglars? Unless you are planning to break into my house, why should you criticize me for installing an alarm system?[76]

A particular Chinese concern that Japanese officials did not openly address was that the ship-based upper-tier system part of TMD could be used not only to defend Japan but also Taiwan. Another difficult issue was that, since the research and development of TMD were to be done jointly by the United States and Japan, a longstanding Japanese ban on weapons exports would have to be lifted before any move to mass-produce parts for the system.[77] Recriminations continued on this and other defense-related issues, with Chinese sources seeing this deepening of the U.S.-Japanese defense relationship as a further step toward an Asian version of the North Atlantic Treaty Organization (NATO), one meant to contain the PRC.

In mid-October 1999 nationalist politician Nishimura Shingo, who was then serving as vice-minister of defense, suggested in an interview with the Japanese edition of *Playboy* that the Diet should consider abandoning the country's ban on nuclear weapons. Prime Minister Obuchi immediately demanded, and received, Nishimura's resignation, hoping to blunt the torrent of criticism both domestically and from Asian neighbors, most vocally from China.[78]

DUELING DEFENSE WHITE PAPERS

Japan's 2000 defense white paper, however, reflected increased concern about China's growing military power, in general, and its naval expansion, in particular. It stated that the quantity and quality of the PRC's missile deployments were expanding, noting that China's medium-range missiles were capable of hitting Japan, and that its naval vessels were becoming more active. The paper advocated vigilance against China's military buildup.[79] *Renmin Ribao* responded by accusing Tokyo of ulterior motives: seeking to deflect attention from the expansion of its own military by putting the onus on China. With the easing of tensions between North and South Korea, harping on the ability of the PRC's medium-range missiles to reach Japan was simply Tokyo's new excuse for rationalizing its participation in TMD with the United States.[80]

China published its own defense white paper in October for only the second time in its history—the first one having been published in 1998. Symbolically, it appeared during Zhu Rongji's trip to Japan. Though the tone of Zhu's trip was placatory and the publication was surely intended to address foreign concerns with lack of transparency in the military budget, the white paper was written at a level of generality that did not dispel these concerns. Moreover, it attacked the U.S.-Japanese defense relationship, warning that the peace and stability of the Asia-Pacific region would be imperiled by cooperation between Washington and Tokyo cooperation on TMD.[81]

NEW POWERS FOR THE SDF

In mid-December the Japanese cabinet passed a bill significantly enlarging the roles that the SDF was expected to play. It was to support the American military under the terms of the 1997 guidelines and to cope with various emergencies including attacks by armed guerrillas, weapons of mass destruction, natural disasters, and cyber-terrorism. Approval was granted for equipment to support these missions: large-scale helicopter-carrying destroyers that critics considered to be surrogate aircraft carriers, air-refueling tanker aircraft, additional Aegis-equipped destroyers, and new information technology for patrol aircraft and tanks. While rationalized by the need to transport its nationals in time of emergency, responding to disasters, and participating in UN peacekeeping operations, the acquisitions would simultaneously improve Japan's defense capabilities.

EFFECT OF THE WAR AGAINST TERRORISM

Following a period in which both sides repeated essentially similar and familiar arguments about each other's military buildup, the events of September 11, 2001, served as the catalyst for significant change. A week after the attacks on the World Trade Center and the Pentagon, Japan's newly elected activist prime minister Koizumi Junichirō announced a seven-point plan for assistance to President George W. Bush's war on terrorism. Japan joined Bush's coalition of the willing, and peacekeeping forces were sent to Samawah, albeit under rules of engagement that forbade troops to return fire. Hence, they had to be protected by other coalition forces, giving rise to the taunt "No combat, please; we're Japanese."[82]

Subsequently, counterterrorism legislation gave Japanese forces additional powers. SDF personnel were permitted to use small arms not only to protect themselves, as had been the case in the past, but also individual or facilities in their charge. The SDF could now be used to protect both U.S. and Japanese military installations within Japan. Coast guard forces were permitted to fire directly at hostile ships that had intruded into Japanese waters. Although these additional powers had a two-year time limit, it seemed likely that, in the absence of any blatant misuse of the authority they granted, this expansion of power would be extended; it, in fact, was. In responding so quickly, Koizumi doubtless wanted to avoid the criticisms of free-riding on defense that were made about Japan in 1991, and also wanted to enhance Japan's chances of obtaining a permanent seat on the UN Security Council by raising the country's profile in international peacekeeping activities. But he was also deeply suspicious of the Chinese leadership, and they of him. In the PRC's official interpretation, the United States was using the September 11 attacks as an excuse to extend its global hegemonic agenda, and Koizumi was using the U.S. plea for help as a pretext for his remilitarization agenda.

Given the control that party and government are able to exercise over information on sensitive topics like Japan, it is likely that the Chinese population at large has internalized this view. There are exceptions. A *Renmin Ribao* editor writing in the liberal (for the PRC) journal *Strategy and Management* argued that Chinese should respect Japan's right to recover militarily, calling fear of Japan "irrational and uncivilized." The reasoning behind the editor's conclusion was, however, unlikely to have pleased Japanese patriots: he believed that, because Japan was fading while the PRC was forging ahead, there was no reason for concern.[83]

Domestic opposition was also a factor. In July 2002, after a specially extended session of the Diet, the government had to shelve efforts to pass legislation intended to strengthen Japan's defense against major attack in the face of ongoing concerns about entrapment versus abandonment. Opponents charged that the definition of external attack was too vaguely worded. Under it, Japanese forces could be inadvertently drawn into a conflict through conflation of proposed new measures with legislation passed in 1999 that allowed Japanese logistical support for U.S. forces outside Japanese territory.[84]

Although Japan was not drawn into conflict, in late 2002, the GOJ agreed to dispatch an Aegis-equipped destroyer to the Indian Ocean to provide additional surveillance and logistical support to the United States. It took this action despite domestic opposition based on the longstanding principle that, while Japan has the right of collective self-defense through the UN Charter, the constitution bars the country from using it.[85] A few weeks later, the LDP and its two coalition partners, New Kōmeitō and the New Conservative Party, reached agreement to raise the JDA to ministerial status, though without a definite timetable for doing so.[86]

The year 2003 saw the launch of Japanese reconnaissance satellites with better resolution than those the SDF heretofore possessed. A small step away from reliance on imagery from the United States, the new equipment had resolution capabilities that were nonetheless inferior to those of commercially available items. According to experts, the newly deployed satellites would still leave Japan dependent on the United States for credible missile launch indications.[87] Debate began on three so-called contingency bills to enhance the country's ability to deal with emergencies. A notable feature thereof was to give the prime minister the power to order the mobilization of the SDF after obtaining verified evidence that an armed attack was mounting.

In May, *Yomiuri* editorialized that the exclusively defense-oriented policy first articulated in 1970, and under which SDF planes had been denied air-to-air refueling capability and precision bombing apparatus, was outmoded. It cited former prime minister Hatoyama Ichirō's 1956 statement that "inaction that would bring the nation to ruin can never be considered something that is dictated by the constitution," adding that current Deputy Chief Cabinet Secretary Abe Shinzō had stated that the rapid progress of weapons technology and changing military strategy warranted a review of the conventional idea of an exclusively defense-oriented policy. Hence, a rethinking of strictures against allowing the SDF to strike enemy bases was worthy of study. JDA Director-General Ishiba Shigeru had already argued for considering the advisability of allowing the SDF to have the capability to strike an enemy military base.[88]

There were strong disagreements on what to do about the discrepancy between what was legal under the constitution and what might protect the nation's security in time of emergency. Ballistic missiles launched from North Korea could reach Japan within ten minutes. But under current law, the prime minister had to get approval from the security council and cabinet before issuing a mobilization system that would allow the military to activate the country's missile defense system—a procedure that was estimated to take half an hour at the least. Those who worried more about defense than internal controls argued that the law should be changed.[89] Opponents replied that preparing for a threat was apt to actually encourage one, and wondered if the Diet would truly be able to contain the SDF under the new legislation.[90]

In the end, the bills passed easily. China's official media predictably condemned the legislation as preparation for war. Ishiba, *Renmin Ribao* pointed out, had indicated that, were the United States to launch a preemptive strike in the Pacific, "It is by no means impossible that Japan would invoke the emergencies legislation" to help. This was tantamount to the collapse of the "traditional" policy of an exclusively defense force. The paper advised that, out of consideration for its own security and that of East Asia, Tokyo should construct a new security concept based on pacifist values, and explore with East Asian nations the establishment of a collective security arrangement.[91] Shortly thereafter, the two sides announced that they planned, for the first time, to exchange warship visits.[92]

THE THIRD NATIONAL DEFENSE PROGRAM OUTLINE

The year 2004 saw further steps that reinforced Chinese fears. In discussions during the Diet debate on emergency bills, government officials indicated that they had decided to view any attack on U.S. forces defending Japan as an act of aggression against the nation, which would constitutionally allow Japan to counterattack. The government would even consider an attack on U.S. forces outside Japanese territory as an attack on Japan if it feared that the act of aggression could escalate into Japanese territory.[93] In February, the Diet passed a revised U.S.-Japan bilateral Acquisition and Cross-Servicing Agreement (ACSA) that allowed the U.S. military and SDF to better share goods and services.

The report of an advisory panel to the prime minister, the Araki Commission, advocated an integrated security strategy that called for the use of state-of-the art information technology, overhauling the chain of command, and improved training programs.[94] These suggestions generated considerable debate, but were, with some modifications, incorporated into Japan's revised 2005 National Defense Program Outline. Released in December 2004, the NDPO 2005 broke precedent by naming China and North Korea as security concerns. Though criticized by domestic defense analysts as a patchwork of bureaucratic compromises that lacked a guiding philosophy, the document nonetheless represented a transitional step toward a security posture that better addressed the country's perception of threat.[95]

The focus of Japan's defense policy began to shift from countering an increasingly unlikely land-based invasion to preparing for a variety of threats from the sea, or by ballistic missiles, terrorists, guerrillas, special operations forces, and weapons of mass destruction. The JDA's Joint Staff Council was also reorganized to better integrate the operations of the three self-defense forces so that they could respond more rapidly to unspecified contingencies.⁹⁶ The repeated presence of Chinese ships in waters claimed by Japan, including, in November 2004, a nuclear submarine, tended to reduce domestic opposition to moving ahead with these plans. Moreover, as the Japanese press frequently noted, it would take only about ten minutes for Nodong missiles launched in North Korea to reach Japan.⁹⁷

Further angering China, in February 2005, Tokyo and Washington issued a statement that a peaceful Taiwan Strait was a common strategic directive. Seeing a thinly veiled warning that the two might cooperate militarily to forestall any Chinese attempt to seize Taiwan by force, Beijing railed against this "unprecedented" interference in its domestic affairs.⁹⁸ Japan's 2006 defense white paper repeated the ritualistic tone of its immediate predecessors, noting that North Korea's nuclear program had caused grave concern, that the Chinese navy and air force were becoming more active, and that it would be desirable for the PRC to be more transparent on the aims of its rapidly increasing military buildup and spending.⁹⁹

A bilateral agreement on joint naval exercises and port calls was reached in 2007. Although touted as opening a new phase in defense exercises, it was not an entirely happy experience. The Japanese later complained that the Chinese side evaded reciprocal treatment of visiting Japanese in subtle ways.¹⁰⁰ (See Chapter 7.)

The mid-September 2009 transition from an LDP-led government to one headed by the Democratic Socialist Party (DSP) brought an immediate change in the tone of defense policy. Beijing was pleased by new Prime Minister Hatoyama's explicit wish for a more independent foreign policy, meaning moving away from close reliance on the United States, and toward Asia. Hatoyama also vowed to close the U.S. marine base at Futenma within a hundred days, and end Japan's eight-year-long participation in the refueling operation in the Indian Ocean. He accomplished the latter, which critics had opposed because it seemed to violate the prohibition against collective self-defense, though to pacify Washington. Hatoyama offered $5 billion in civilian aid for Afghanistan reconstruction.¹⁰¹ However, he was unable to consummate the closing of Futenma, which was governed by a 2006 agreement between the United States and Japan. Apologizing for this failure, and caught in a campaign finance scandal, Hatoyama resigned in June 2010.

Despite Hatoyama's efforts, Chinese defense policy appeared no more conciliatory. Less than two weeks after the new prime minister took office, Chinese media gave much publicity to the new weapons that were featured in an impressive parade, as well as the higher educational level of the country's officer corps.[102] Though unacknowledged by the Hatoyama government, concern grew with the PRC's strategy for its naval forces breaking out of the first island chain, past Japan, into the Pacific.[103] Influential Fudan University Professor Shen Dingli advocated setting up overseas military bases.[104] And a team of Chinese naval surveyors completed a series of permanent structures such as lighthouses and memorial tablets to delineate a maritime baseline through which to bolster its sovereignty claims in the East China Sea.[105]

Chinese assertiveness in the East China and South China seas became increasingly noticeable in 2010. PRC officials, including military officials whom the government claimed were speaking in their private capacity and not necessarily on behalf of the government, became outspoken both in bilateral meetings and international fora.[106] In May 2010 then Foreign Minister Yang Jiechi became enraged when his counterpart Okada Katsuya suggested that China "at least make efforts not to increase the number of its nuclear weapons" and "show its commitment" to nuclear disarmament. In the end, Yang decided not to storm out of the meeting but did file a diplomatic protest against Okada, saying he had been rude.[107] In a meeting of the Association of Southeast Asian Nations (ASEAN) security forum in July, Yang responded to then American Secretary of State Hillary Clinton's call for settling territorial claims through negotiations on legitimate claims to land features by abruptly leaving for an hour. On returning, he delivered what was described as a rambling half-hour speech accusing the United States of plotting against China.[108]

The collision of a Chinese fishing boat with two Japanese coast guard vessels set off a confrontation between the two countries that Hatoyama's successor Kan Naoto was widely believed to have badly mishandled. Asserting the right to patrol waters China regarded as its own, the PRC's ships and planes became an increased presence in areas around the disputed islands in what PLA General Zhang Zhaozhong termed a "cabbage strategy": gradually surround a claimed area with multiple layers of vessels including nonmilitary hulls, essentially daring rivals to break through, thereby denying them access.

Since the incremental movements were small and often not sustained—fleets of fishing vessels backed up by China Maritime Surveillance ships, the equivalent of a coast guard, and provincial maritime militias—would appear, sometimes in force, and then recede, it was difficult for Japan to craft a response.[109] Some U.S.-Japan military exercises aimed at retaking unspecified islands took place. There was a greater SDF presence in the southwestern part of Japan nearest the disputed areas, and an initiative to train an amphibious force along the lines of the U.S. marine corps.[110] The number of submarines was to be increased to twenty-two from the existing sixteen, and more E-2C early warning aircraft sent to patrol the area.[111] These had no noticeable deterrent effect.

After the triple disaster of earthquake, tsunami, and nuclear meltdown of September 11, 2011, little thought could be given to anything but disaster relief, with the inevitable recriminations against the hapless incumbent prime minister. In September, Kan resigned, and was succeeded by Noda Yoshihiko.

As predicted by a leading Chinese newspaper, Noda would be preoccupied by the recovery effort from the 3/11 disaster.[112] His first press conference indeed dwelled on his plans to do so, devoting only a sentence to saying that Japan would have to adjust to the security environment. He gave no details. The reciprocal visits by PLA and SDF forces funded by Japan's Sasakawa Peace Foundation resumed, having been suspended since the fishing boat–coast guard ship collision a year before.[113] Still, the Chinese media excoriated Noda for a speech to the SDF in which the prime minister mentioned that failing to prepare for war would lead to crisis,[114] and ridiculed an SDF exercise as "clumsy."[115]

Other signs indicated, however, that the Chinese leadership was more concerned than it publicly acknowledged. A Hong Kong newspaper cited respected Beida academic Liang Yunxiang as terming the government-organized commemorations of the 80th anniversary of the Japanese invasion indicative of Beijing's increasing emphasis on nationalism as a means to enhance the cohesion of the Chinese people.[116] And PRC media took note of Noda's reaching out to India and Southeast Asian states who were feeling similar pressures from China, as well as of Australia agreeing to accept a contingent of American marines.

While visiting Australia in 2011, U.S. President Barack Obama announced that the United States would move away from its focus on the Mideast and pivot to Asia. The term "pivot," which had appeared in a *Foreign Policy* article just before his visit by then Secretary of State Hillary Clinton,[117] was later modified to "rebalance." Underlying the pivot/rebalance was a preexisting AirSea Battle operational concept, later renamed the more unwieldy but less controversial Joint Concept for Access and

Maneuver in the Global Commons or JAM-GC.[118] Under whatever name, the clear aim was to counter China. Collectively, these developments reinforced always present Chinese fears of being encircled by hostile powers. State media railed against those who propounded the theory of a "China threat" to serve their own underhanded purposes.

Goaded into purchasing three of the five disputed Diaoyu/Senkaku Islands by nationalistic Tokyo Governor Ishihara Shintarō, Noda incurred China's wrath. (See Chapter 7.) At the same time, Noda's efforts to raise the sales tax angered many Japanese voters. Although the tax increase passed, the DPJ suffered a disastrous defeat in the 2012 general election: Noda resigned to take responsibility.

BEIJING RESPONDS

Beijing, citing the nationalization of the three islands as its rationale, increased the tempo of its cabbage strategy, sending more fishing boats, China Maritime Surveillance ships, and planes into the area. The PRC's first aircraft carrier, the *Liaoning*, built by completing the hull of the Ukrainian *Varyag* and adding Chinese weapons and sensors, was commissioned in 2012. Its subsequent voyages prompted one observer to comment that the ship seemed to be marking its territory. The navy also deployed Jin-class ballistic missile nuclear submarines equipped with more accurate and longer-range missiles that provided the PRC with its first credible sea-based nuclear deterrent.

In March 2013, in an effort to eliminate overlap in command and functions, four of the country's five maritime enforcement agencies were merged into the China Coast Guard under the aegis of the State Oceanic Administration. In November of the same year, Beijing announced that it intended to establish the country's first National Security Commission (NSC) to coordinate security policy formation and provide strong central leadership. Though believed to have been inspired by that of the United States, the PRC's version seems to have as strong a role in domestic security as in foreign affairs.[119] In a further indication that Xi Jinping, who had been named head of the CCP just a month before Abe was elected prime minister, intended to be a strong leader, Xi became the NSC chair as well. In the same month, the PRC declared the formation of an Air Defense Identification Zone (ADIZ), with critics, noting the differences between it and other ADIZs, charged was less an air defense zone than an air control zone.[120]

ABE'S DEFENSE PROGRAM

Beginning his second time as prime minister, the LDP's Abe Shinzō vowed to transform his country, from a reactive stance to playing a more active part in the international community. Unspoken but unmistakable was Abe's desire to counter Chinese aggression. Despite the palliative name of "proactive pacifism," most of the initiatives he took in this effort met opposition not only from Beijing but also from elements within the Japanese public.

Defense budgets began to rise, albeit glacially and only after more than a decade of actual decline. That for fiscal year 2013 was up 0.8 percent, 2.2 percent in 2014, and 2 percent in 2015.[121] These were exceedingly modest by comparison with the double-digit increases the PLA has enjoyed since 1989, and in Japan's case, came after eleven straight years of declining allocations for defense.

Japan's largest warship since World War II, the *Izumo*, was launched in 2013. Although technically a helicopter destroyer, the ship bore a strong resemblance to a conventional aircraft carrier, which Beijing immediately accused it of being. However, since the *Izumo* has neither a ski-jump nor a catapult, it can accommodate only short-takeoff and vertical landing (STOVL) planes. Conversion would be both expensive and time-consuming.[122]

Chinese analysts, describing the ship as a "hybrid carrier warship," called attention to the date of the launch, August 6, the 68th anniversary of the American nuclear attack on Hiroshima.[123] Foreign pundits with marginal expertise on the subject made much of the fact that a ship named *Izumo* had taken part in World War II.[124] In fact, the original *Izumo*, like other vessels of the Japanese Imperial Navy such as the *Yamato* and the *Mutsu*, are named after ancient administrative divisions of Japan. Laid down in 1898, *Izumo* saw service in the Russo-Japanese War of 1905 and in World War I. After sinking a Chinese ship in the 1937 battle of Shanghai, the superannuated *Izumo* spent the remainder of the war as a training ship until sunk in port by the U.S. navy. As one frustrated observer commented, "Perhaps we should've named [the ship] the 'Hello Kitty.'"

A month after China established its National Security Commission, Japan announced the formation of a national security council modeled after that of the United States.[125] At the same time, three documents were issued that, according to American analyst of the Japanese military Toshi Yoshihara, systematically align Japanese policy, strategy, and capabilities. The "National Security Strategy," the first such document of its kind, articulated Japan's intention to participate in regional and global security, while the National Defense Program Guidelines dealt with longer-term defense policy and force structure. The Medium Term Defense Program sets forth acquisition goals for the next five years.[126]

In April 2014 Japan's self-imposed, three-decade-long ban on selling arms abroad was lifted, albeit with significant restrictions: exports were prohibited to countries violating international treaties or rules signed by Japan or United Nations Security Council rules, and countries involved in conflicts. There were to be no third party transfers without prior consent from Japan.[127]

Predictably, and despite the PRC's much larger arms export activities—the PRC is now the world's third largest exporter, behind the United States and Russia— Beijing interpreted the change as a dangerous alteration of the status quo in the Asia-Pacific region although "fortunately ... China has become capable of managing strategic risks in East Asia and could mount a counterattack against any military provocations."[128] Retired major general and well-known hawk Luo Yuan was more blunt, declaiming that a war with Japan was becoming increasingly likely, that the United States would not intervene, and that China would prevail.[129]

To the surprise of foreign observers who expected that Japan would at first export only component parts, entire systems quickly became available,[130] with both Australia and India expressing interest in buying Japanese submarines. Thirteen Japanese companies including giant Mitsubishi Heavy Industries exhibited at Paris's 2014 Eurostatory, one of the world's largest defense and security industry trade shows.

Chinese companies were present as well, prompting a regional security analyst, speaking on condition of anonymity, to compare the two: China, he said had "a couple of big toys" such as the *Liaoning*, refitted after purchase from Ukraine, but "doesn't know how to use them." By contrast, "Japan is building up capabilities the other way round, steadily building knowledge, capability, operational know-how, and integrating steadily more advanced platforms and missions with the U.S."[131]

THE DEBATE ON AMENDING THE CONSTITUTION

Since meeting the stringent procedures for amending the constitution was nearly impossible,[132] Abe instead opted for cabinet ruling that reinterpreted its meaning so as to allow Japan the right of collective self-defense. Proponents argued that, under the old interpretation of the constitution, the SDF could not perform many actions conducive to the defense of Japan, such as protecting U.S. naval vessels under attack in seas near Japan. Nor could they shoot down missiles passing through Japanese air space but targeting an ally, rescue foreign contingents under attack in United Nations peacekeeping operations, or provide rear support to foreign contingents.[133] However, a former chief cabinet secretary in Abe's own party declared the decision "preposterous," and others worried that the new interpretation, rather than making Japan safer, would drag it into war.[134]

The prime minister's popularity ratings have suffered, particularly after pushing through controversial security bills in September 2015 that allowed the SDF to serve in combat overseas, albeit under carefully circumscribed criteria: when Japan is attacked, or when a close ally is attacked; when the result threatens Japan's survival; when the attack poses a clear danger to people; when there is no other appropriate means available to repel the attack and ensure Japan's survival and protect its people; and where the use of force is restricted to a necessary minimum.[135]

A state secrets law aimed at tightening the government's control over sensitive classified information, favored by Washington, was equally controversial due to concerns that it would lead to restrictions on freedom of the press and allow the government to conceal its misdeeds.[136] Impressive though these developments may collectively seem, and as much as Beijing expresses concern, they cannot be much help against a cabbage strategy.

Each side regularly continues to criticize the other's defense budget. China points out that Japan's is one of the highest in the world after the United States and that, apart from the United States itself, Japan is the only country in the world to possess F-15 fighter planes and Aegis class destroyers as well as impressive numbers of other modern combat platforms. China's defense budget is, they note, per capita, one of the smallest in the world.

Japanese commentators respond that the constitution forbids the use of these weapons except under clearly demarcated defensive conditions. Unlike the PRC's defense budget, Japan's has remained essentially stationary, even actually declining for more than a decade.[137] And a much larger proportion of it goes for personnel expenses than in China. Also included in the defense budgets are payments for the upkeep of American bases in Japan. Moreover, because China has the largest population in the world, a per capita divisor is not a valid way to look at the budget. And the PRC's defense expenditures continue to rise despite the fact that the PRC faces no threat of armed invasion.

Additionally, China's defense budget conceals more than it reveals. Among the items not included are the cost of weapons procured from abroad; state subsidies to the defense industry; certain research and development programs; and the funding of paramilitaries. The PRC's actual defense expenditures are apt to be two to three times the stated amounts.[138]

THE NUCLEAR DEBATE REKINDLED

The issue of whether Japan should possess nuclear weapons has begun to change. Memories of raging atomic firestorms and bodies hideously distorted by radiation remain etched into the collective consciousness, but so is the thought that both China and, putatively, North Korea, could use them against Japan in the near future. A Kyōto University professor has suggested that serious debate on the issue be initiated should any one of three scenarios take place: the American defense commitment to Japan weakens; China's navy begins regular patrols around the country; or the North Korean nuclear threat worsens.[139]

A popular conservative magazine solicited essays from more than forty writers on the topic, discovering that even dovish contributors believed that it was acceptable for Japan to use the option of going nuclear as a lever against other, potentially hostile, states. One compared the ban on nuclear weapons to a one-sided fight: "For a nation to entirely foreswear nuclear weapons is like taking part in a boxing match and promising not to throw hooks." Others, however, believed that the country was safer without nuclear weapons, since "no one would shoot an unarmed man."[140]

North Korea's October 2006 nuclear test did not lead to any immediate change in Japan's pledge not to acquire a nuclear capability of its own. Nonetheless, Foreign Minister Asō Tarō declared that the issue of whether or not to do so should be publicly discussed.[141] This in itself represented a marked change from less than a decade before, when Nishimura Shingō was forced to resign his defense position in the Liberal Party after mentioning the same issue. The taboo on discussion had, in effect, been tacitly lifted. To be sure, there had been intermediate steps. Discussions on the advantages and disadvantages of possessing nuclear weapons had been taking place privately and intermittently for half a century.

Though little noticed at the time they were promulgated, the three non-nuclear principles had never been linked with Article 9, since the constitution was regarded as too difficult to amend. As early as 1957, Prime Minister Kishi had noted that Article 9 did not prohibit Japan from possessing small defensive nuclear weapons. The issue, however, remained incendiary. In June 2002 Chief Cabinet Secretary Fukuda Yasuo stated in off-the-record remarks to journalists that "circumstances and public opinion" could require Japan to possess nuclear weapons. Although this provoked a public outcry and a sit-in protest at Hiroshima, Fukuda merely amended his remarks and did not resign.[142] Whether in favor of the idea or opposed to it, most observers agreed that, to the extent that North Korea continues its nuclear tests, the probability of Japan acquiring nuclear weapons is likely to increase.

A Hong Kong affiliate of China's official news agency predicted that Japan would have the ability to make nuclear bombs within three years. The country was, the agency stated, using its inadequate energy resources as a cover for developing nuclear technology, and intended to step outside the umbrella of nuclear protection that the United States had given it.[143] The news agency might have been reacting to the fact that discussions over whether or not to acquire nuclear weapons are no longer proscribed, though so far there have been no serious calls to actually acquire them.

Given the impressive level of Japanese technology, few doubted that the country lacks the expertise to produce such weapons. But Japan's next moves were expected to be not the acquisition of nuclear weapons, but the enactment of permanent laws on overseas dispatches for the SDF,[144] as in fact was the case.

Beijing also reacted negatively to discussions between Tokyo and Washington on contingency plans for an attack on Japan. Although the two sides mentioned only North Korea, Chinese analysts interpreted the contingency plans as a strengthening of the U.S.-Japanese alliance that was targeted against China. Tokyo had, in their opinion, moved from listing Taiwan as a common strategic objective with Washington in the mid-1990s, to active discussions on a joint war plan for the Taiwan Strait.[145]

CONCLUSIONS

The gradual movement of Japan toward becoming a "normal" country with a standard military force seems irreversible, though the measured pace of this movement could be either slowed down by changes in government and economic reverses or speeded up in response to external events. Similarly, the PRC's military buildup is apt to continue so long as political stability and the impressive economic gains of the past two decades are maintained. International pushback has been minimal, and most observers agree that the Beijing government has the ability to control the domestic social disruptions engendered by rapid economic development.

Exchanges between the China and Japan on military issues have become highly predictable. Tokyo notes the increase in military spending and asks for clarification on China's intentions and spending. Beijing responds that the PRC's defense budget is small compared to that of Japan, whose arsenal is second only to that of the United States in terms of size and sophistication. China, it avers, is developing peacefully while Japan is becoming increasingly militaristic.[146]

Tokyo replies that to possess a regular military is not to become militaristic; its defense spending has remained stable; its forces are for defense only; and it is unthinkable that the country could ever return to the militarism that preceded World War II. Moreover, what the SDF has developed are essentially niche capabilities, enabling it to fight along with the United States, but not apart from it. China's claimed intention of developing peacefully is belied by its analysts' attention to Mahanian concepts of military assertiveness, the sorts of weapons it has been acquiring, and China's activities in and around disputed areas.[147] There are suspicions that the PRC's actual goal is to reestablish control over all the territories held by the Qing dynasty.[148]

Of course, for those Chinese who believe that a combined U.S-Japanese alliance to establish America's global hegemony is precisely what Washington has in mind, this is hardly consoling. Chinese commentators also evince skepticism about Japan's stated desire to be a normal country, since they choose to define a normal country as one that maintains harmonious ties with its neighbors, has a correct attitude toward historical problems, and takes actions conducive to mutually beneficial economic cooperation while seeking joint security with its neighbors.[149] They find Japan lacking on all criteria.

The Taiwan Strait and disputed territorial waters, including the Diaoyutai/Senkaku Islands, remain potential flashpoints. Still, rising military capabilities do not necessarily result in actual combat or war. Much will depend on how the two governments manage the tensions between them on other issues. Joint military exercises and officer exchange programs, while they may prove marginally helpful to establishing trust, cannot solve the larger issues between the two countries.

10

Taiwan between Two Powers

MULTICULTURAL INFLUENCES AND THE QING/ MANCHU ANNEXATION

Situated between continental China and the islands of Japan, Taiwan is believed to have been first settled by Polynesian aboriginal peoples. Genetic analysis indicates that they may have been the ancestors of the large Austronesian dispersion that includes native Hawaiians as well as the Maori of New Zealand.[1] There is also archaeological evidence of prehistoric settlements from the south of present-day China.[2] Historically, the island was regarded as wild and outside the cultural ambit of the Middle Kingdom. Early Chinese geographical sources considered Taiwan to be part of the Ryukyu Islands, which now belong to Japan.

With the age of European exploration and maritime conquest, Taiwan soon felt Western influence as well. In 1582 a Dutch sailor spied the island from the crow's nest of his Portuguese ship, exclaiming "Ilha Formosa," or beautiful island, in recognition of its scenic landscape. In 1624 ships of the Dutch East India Company, forced out of the Penghu Islands (Pescadores) by the Chinese, arrived and established a colonial capital in southern Taiwan's Tainan. Two years later, the Spanish came and set up bases in the northern part of the island, at Keelung (Jilong) and Tamsui (Danshui). The present-day city of San Dian owes its name to local attempts to pronounce the name of the fort, San

Diego, that the Spanish built in the area. Defeated by the Dutch in 1642, the Spanish departed.

A Dutch clergyman who was among the first of his countrymen to live on Taiwan for any length of time did a survey of the island in 1628. He described a variety of aboriginal villages with palisades in the foothills, subsisting largely through hunting and primitive agriculture. Along the coast, he found in all a few hundred Chinese from Fujian province, directly opposite the island. Scattered among the aboriginal villages, the Fujianese fished and traded pottery, salt, and ironware for deer skin and meat.[3]

The East India Company set about developing the island's agriculture, establishing plantations and an infrastructure. This facilitated the immigration of many more Fujianese to Taiwan. After 1636 the Dutch began to rent out rice and sugar plantation to Chinese contract workers, most of whom initially returned home after they had earned enough to establish themselves there.[4] Dutch missionaries established churches and schools that taught their language and developed a written script for the aboriginal tongues while converting local people to Christianity.

Meanwhile, in China, the Ming dynasty was weakened by internal disorder and lawlessness, finally succumbing to ethnically Manchu invaders from the north. The Manchus proclaimed Beijing the capital of their Qing dynasty in 1644, though resistance continued in the south, to which many Ming loyalists had fled, until 1661. The most celebrated of these was the half-Japanese scion of a leading pirate family, Zheng Chenggong, known in the West as Koxinga. Zheng expelled the Dutch from Taiwan in early 1662 and, though given credit for Sinicizing Taiwan, actually died in May or June of the same year.

Under his son and grandson, the island gained its first Confucian temple. Chinese customs and laws were instituted. The Zheng regime conducted intermittent forays on the Chinese coast that, although sometimes described as loyalist attempts to dislodge the Qing, looked remarkably like profit-seeking pirate raids in the family tradition. The Zheng family also imposed burdensome taxes on the local population, and became riven with internal quarrels. In 1683 the Qing were able to defeat the Zheng forces.

Far from heralding a strong presence on the island, the conquest began a debate within the Qing court about what to do with Taiwan. One faction advocated abandonment, arguing that it was an isolated island far across the seas from China, and a hideout for pirates, escaped convicts, deserters, and ruffians. Having no value, Taiwan should be left to its own devices. Han immigrants currently living in Taiwan should be shipped back to their homes in China. The Penghu (Pescadores) Islands were, by contrast, an important military strongpoint that must be retained.

The other side argued that China could not be defended from the Penghu Islands alone: Taiwan was a natural shield for the southeastern provinces. Moreover, the dynasty could use its rich soil and natural resources. The policy of shipping immigrants back to China was impractical: to avoid capture, they would flee to the mountains that form the spine of the island. Impossible to track down there, the immigrants would join with the aborigines and escaped convicts who already inhabited these mountainous areas, and might eventually attack coastal China as Koxinga's family had done. Hence, any attempt to repatriate would create greater problems in the future. The Dutch might also be tempted to return, jeopardizing the status of the Penghu Islands. The retention view won out, with the Kangxi emperor issuing a proclamation in 1684 that Taiwan had officially become a territory of the Qing dynasty.

The Qing ruled the island, at least nominally, for the following two centuries. However, the officials dispatched there tended to be of low quality, and they were poorly paid as well. The result was corruption and bribery on a scale even beyond that seen in China. Rebellion was endemic, with records indicating about a hundred major and minor uprisings during the 212 years of Qing administration. This plus the diseases that thrived in the island's semi-tropical climate and its reputation for being home to poisonous snakes combined to keep Beijing's interest in the area low. Immigration from China was forbidden until 1760, although the law apparently succeeded only to the extent of slowing the flow. In theory, passage to Taiwan was restricted to government officials and approved merchants; their families, if any, were not permitted to join them. Quite a few intermarried with the aboriginals.

Schools existed to teach the Confucian classics to children of officials and other families of status. In 1883 records indicate that more than 2,000 Taiwan residents were preparing to sit for the Chinese civil service examination. Still, the veneer of Sinic civilization was thin. The literati totaled less than half of 1 percent of the population, or far less than in continental China.[5]

By the nineteenth century, the West returned to Asia, aggressively seeking markets and, in some cases, territorial acquisitions. A British fleet appeared off Keelung harbor in 1841, but did not attempt to take the port.

In 1854 an American fleet under Commodore Perry, who had just signed a treaty with Japan, anchored at Keelung and used a search for missing sailors as an excuse to land. In follow-on to Perry's observation that the island was well suited to serve the U.S. navy as a trade station, the American government asked Beijing if Taiwan were part of China. The Qing government, ignorant of the implications in international law, and probably wishing to evade responsibility for the frequent incidents in which shipwrecked sailors were killed by Taiwan's headhunter aboriginals, replied that it was a barbaric region whose residents were beyond its control.

Through its consul in Amoy, Washington arranged a treaty with a Taiwan aboriginal chief to help its shipwrecked sailors.[6] Although a convenience for marooned seafarers, the treaty also implied nonrecognition of the dynasty's title to the island. The United States did not take advantage of the Qing statement to assume control of Taiwan. But the Japanese, who were acquainting themselves with international law, took note.

Renewed Western interest in the area stimulated modernization efforts in both China and Japan. In contrast to the failure of China's attempt, Japan's succeeded impressively. With its longstanding warrior tradition now enhanced by modern ships and arms, Japan, like the West, began to seek markets and territories. In 1871, after the Qing initially disclaimed responsibility for the actions of aboriginals against Ryukyuan sailors, the Japanese government invaded Taiwan, extracting a sizeable indemnity before it withdrew. France also became active in the area, sending a fleet to Keelung in 1884 during the Sino-French war, and attacking both Keelung and Tamsui the following year.

In recognition of Taiwan's role as a shield for China's southeastern provinces, the Qing dispatched a reformist official, Liu Ming-chuan, to the island. Liu's recommendation that the island be made a separate province rather than, as previously administered, a part of Fujian, was accepted. This was accomplished in October 1885, with Liu named Taiwan's first governor. Unfortunately, Liu's ambitious plans for infrastructure, administrative, and educational reforms were thwarted by the same kind of bureaucratic indifference that had characterized previous Qing attitudes toward the island. In 1891 Liu resigned in frustration, and was replaced by an official in the more traditional, that is, less effective, mold. In 2004 China Central Television ran a version of good governor Liu's life as part of a campaign to stress Taiwan's ties with China.[7]

Three years later, the Sino-Japanese War began. Interestingly, the Japanese government sought out the same American consular official, by then retired from service with Washington, who had negotiated the U.S. treaty with the Taiwan aboriginals. Hired as a foreign affairs adviser, he helped to formulate Tokyo's invasion plan.[8] Quickly defeated, the Qing ceded Taiwan to Japan in the Treaty of Shimonoseki in April 1895, its status as a province of Qing China having lasted less than a decade.

In Taiwan, there was anger and, after anticipated help from France failed to materialize, despair. In May, a Taiwan Democratic Republic was proclaimed. The declaration designated a president and a national flag, even issuing postage stamps. However, the new republic endured for only three weeks. Japanese troops found heavier resistance than expected, but by November 1895, Tokyo was informed that Taiwan was pacified. Although this was basically true, small-scale and sporadic resistance continued throughout the early years of Japanese colonization.

TAIWAN UNDER JAPANESE RULE

As the era's only non-Western colonial power, it was important to Japan to produce a model colony worthy of the Empire of the Rising Sun. Not only would Japan prove itself equal or superior to the West as an administrator, but the experience would also provide valuable lessons for future territories that the ambitious empire might want to colonize.[9] This activist attitude was in sharp contrast to the passive possession of the Qing.

Japanese rule is usually divided into three periods. The first, from annexation until the end of World War I, involved suppressing resistance and setting up an administrative system. The new government announced that those who wished to leave the island would be given two years to do so. A number, variously estimated at 4,500 to 6,500, actually did so. This included many of the malcontents, thus taking the edge off resistance. After the expiration of the two-year grace period in May 1897, the government strictly controlled traffic between China and Taiwan. In a further effort to restrict contact between the two sides of the strait, the Qing court's request for a consulate in Taipei, now called Taihoku according to the Japanese pronunciation of the characters, was refused.

The colonizers arrived equipped with mandarin-speaking translators, but quickly discovered that most people did not understand the language. Substitutes were eventually located who could communicate in the Taiwanese (basically Fujianese), Hakka, and aboriginal tongues of the inhabitants. Police controls were established, a thorough land survey carried out, and standardized measurements and currencies introduced. Census data were collected, an ethnological survey of the island's peoples conducted, and monopolies created for the manufacture and marketing of the island's major products.

The winding, dusty streets of the capital city were straightened, rationalized, paved, and given Japanese names. Buildings were constructed for the colonial administration, many of them designed by leading Japanese architects and bearing strong resemblances to recently built edifices in Tokyo. A transportation system was created: railroads and better roads soon linked the island's major cities.

The educational system was also totally revamped. In Japan, the reforms of the Meiji Restoration had included the establishment of a modernized educational system aimed at providing everyone with basic literacy, numeracy, and loyalty to the imperial government. Specialized education in science, engineering, medicine, and the social sciences was available to an elite few, chosen through an objective examination.[10]

A similar, though not quite equal, system was applied to Taiwan: Children would be trained to read, write, compute, and be unquestioningly obedient to the wishes of the mother country. Japanese educators deemed Taiwan's existing Confucian schools both too low in quality and too few to serve in this capacity. They introduced plans for an islandwide system of modern primary schools that would replace the Chinese learning they deemed backward with the modern scientific principles that had been introduced in Meiji-era Japan. The Chinese academies were allowed to continue, but both children and their parents tended to prefer the modern educational schools, with their sports programs and instruction in a wider range of topics. The most promising students, selected as in Japan by objective examination,[11] would be educated into an elite of physicians and civil servants. These would form a stabilizing class to serve as intermediaries between the Japanese rulers and their colonial subjects.

Most Taiwanese children attended so-called common schools that included instruction in reading both Chinese and Japanese. Japanese children attended elementary schools where all instruction was in Japanese. Though the quality of the latter substantially exceeded that of the former, all schools emphasized instruction in the Japanese language, arithmetic, and ethics. The last category focused on Confucian principles that fit the goals of empire, such as loyalty and obedience to one's superiors. Confucian principles that educational bureaucrats thought might lend themselves to identification with China were omitted.

Another aspect of Confucianism that was excluded was its negative attitude toward manual labor: Taiwanese were taught that there was honor in even the lowliest of tasks. Also unlike Confucianism were the efforts to educate both boys and girls. Care was taken to see that Taiwanese were not educated beyond their station in life, which was several steps below that of the Japanese colonizers. Although education for Taiwanese focused on the primary levels, there were two exceptions. In addition to the aforementioned elite, normal schools were founded in order to train Taiwanese as Japanese-language teachers.[12]

A debate grew up between those who wanted to assimilate (*dōka*) the Taiwanese and those who for felt it sufficient to make them good citizens of the empire (*kōminka*).[13] Taiwan's first civil administrator Goto Shimpei came down firmly on the side of kōminka, famously stating that "it is impossible to change the eyes of a flatfish [whose eyes are on top of its head] into those of a sea bream [whose eyes are on either side of the head]."[14] In this period, Gotō's kōminka prevailed.

During the second period, from 1918 to 1937, Japan consolidated its hold on Taiwan. World War I had created an economic boom for Japan, with Taiwan participating in the prosperity. The expanded infrastructure and economic base created more opportunities for Taiwanese to participate in modern industry. Pressures for dōka gained ground. Upper-class Taiwanese families, in particular, became annoyed at the inferior education given to their children, which put them at an immediate disadvantage in competition for jobs in the new economy. Some of these were open to both Taiwanese and Japanese, though the latter received higher pay for what seemed to be the same work. Taiwanese families who could afford to sent their children to Japan to study.

Demands grew for the establishment of a Taiwanese middle school. Those who favored its establishment argued that it would be preferable to keep promising young men—the overwhelming majority of students sent abroad were male—in Taiwan than expose them to the intellectual atmosphere of Japan, which they considered dangerous. Such young men were apt to return with ideas that could prove subversive to the colonial regime.[15] Indeed, one of the most influential figures in the Taiwan independence movement, Peng Ming-min, reports exactly such an experience in his sojourn at a Kyōto middle school. In a class on Western philosophy, he came across the writings of Ernest Renan, whose views that nations were based not on race, language, nor culture, but on a felt sense of community and shared destiny convinced Peng that there should be a separate Formosan (Taiwanese) state.[16] The argument for keeping young men at home proved persuasive, with Taiwanese middle schools duly founded. In 1928 the island's first university, Taihoku (Taipei) Imperial University, came into being.

Resistance to Japanese rule was replaced by demands for greater equality within the Japanese polity. While in theory dōka had integrated the school system, it was obvious to all that opportunities for Taiwanese students were not the same as those for Japanese. Education officials, who were Japanese, favored those of their own "race," as it was then termed, in deciding admissions, and many continued to worry about the consequences of overeducating the natives.

With stated policy contradicting actual experience, pressures for change began to increase. Problems arose because, although colonization had separated the residents of Taiwan from China and its culture, however tenuously they had been part of it, they found themselves unable to be accepted as true Japanese. In the 1930s, for example, only six of Taiwan's 1,074 public schools had native principals.[17] Feeling neither Chinese nor Japanese, some of the more articulate of the colonized began to refer to Taiwan as "Asia's orphan." A more positive view, espoused by Chiang Wei-sui, someone who would later be dubbed the Sun Yat-sen of Taiwan, was that the Taiwanese could serve as intermediaries between Japan and China.[18]

What appeared to be a different view can be seen in the founding of the Taiwanese Assimilation Society in December 1914. Its stated aim was to "organize Japanese and Taiwanese for friendly relations and to promote a perfect assimilation in compliance with the imperial wish for equal treatment of all nationals." However, despite its name, the society's real objective seemed to be equal treatment rather than assimilation.[19] Though the colonial government dissolved it a few months later on grounds that the organization was harmful to public safety, the founders had made their point. Other groups with similar aims arose. Ironically, Taiwanese studying in Japan were freer to express such views, and did so. By 1921 there were calls to establish a Taiwan parliament. Advocates did not aim at liberation from Japanese rule, which would have been regarded as subversive, but at reforming the colonial government in order to gain autonomy within it.

In this period also, the Tokyo government devised what it termed a southern strategy, meaning expansion into Southeast Asia. In view of its location, Taiwan was considered a springboard. The founding of Taihoku Imperial University reflects this motive as well as the government's desire to satisfy Taiwanese demands for better education. The new university was to be a center for research focusing on the subtropical regions of south China and the South Pacific, since this information would support future Japanese expansion in those areas.[20]

The third period was, in essence, an outgrowth of Japan's success at implementing its aggressive southern strategy. Dating from Japan's expanded aggression against China in 1937 until its defeat in World War II in 1945, the period was characterized by greater pressure for assimilation. Chinese-language publications, which had been tolerated, though not encouraged, in the past, were now forbidden. Speaking Taiwanese, even in the workplace, could result in punishment or even loss of one's job. Taiwanese were obliged to take Japanese names, wear kimonos, and participate in Shintō rituals.

At first, the government did not impose military service obligations on the Taiwanese. However, as the war progressed and Japanese losses mounted, Taiwanese were enlisted as volunteers. Beginning in September 1944, they began to be conscripted as well. Records indicate that 80,533 non-Japanese residents of Taiwan served in the military and 120,775 served in noncombat roles. The death rate was high: one in seven.[21]

Considerable efforts were made in order to mobilize patriotic feelings. A classic "national policy film" (*kokusaku-eiga*), *The Bell of Sayon*, is illustrative. Based on a real-life incident, the heroine, portrayed as the product of Japan's enlightened treatment of primitive tribes, helps with the ceremony to celebrate the conscription of her village's young men. Despite a drenching rainstorm, Sayon insists on accompanying the men to their mobilization point. En route, she falls into a raging river and drowns—an emblem of colonial sacrifice and loyalty for others to emulate.[22] Aboriginals proved to be especially impressive fighters. One of the last Japanese soldiers known to have survived the war but refused to surrender was a Taiwanese aboriginal. Nakamura Teruo, aka Sunion, was discovered in a remote area of Indonesia in late 1974.[23]

Along with the dubious privilege of serving in the Japanese military came Tokyo's acceptance of Taiwanese demands for true equality. Three Taiwanese were named members of the House of Peers, and plans were announced for Taiwanese representation in the lower house of the Diet as well. Japanese and Taiwanese youth were henceforth permitted to attend the same schools. In 1945 the governor-general announced that Taiwanese and Japanese officials on the island would receive the same salary.[24] These changes were justified with the argument that, although Taiwanese were not Japanese, they, like the Japanese, were subjects of the emperor. That, of course, had been true since 1895.

Success for the Taiwanese came too late; the war ended before these long sought-after changes could be implemented. Told to turn on their radios on August 15, 1945, for an important announcement, Taiwanese heard the emperor announce Japan's defeat. Due to wartime censorship, most had not realized that the war was going badly, and the news came as a shock. So was the subsequent revelation that Taiwan was to be turned over to China, then under the jurisdiction of Chiang Kai-shek's Kuomintang (KMT) government. Japan's wartime propaganda had portrayed Chiang, as well as China, as the enemy. Now he was to be the ruler.

Moreover, there was a huge discrepancy between living standards on Taiwan vis-à-vis China. Though relatively few Taiwanese were yet aware of it, they soon would be. While the geography of the island's position between Japan and China was a constant, the psychological position of Taiwan's inhabitants between the two was to undergo another and major change.

THE KUOMINTANG ASSUMES CONTROL

Although the Japanese government relinquished control over Taiwan in the peace treaty that ended the war, it did not specify to whom sovereignty was to devolve. Chiang Kai-shek's claim to exercise jurisdiction for the Republic of China elicited mixed reactions on the island, as well as from some Japanese. Many Taiwanese were reluctant to "re"join a China they had never really felt part of, or that they felt had long ago rejected and abandoned them. Some Japanese Army officers were sympathetic to them. Within hours of the emperor's speech, a small group headed by one Gu Chen-fu met with two Japanese officers to proclaim an independent nation. A roster of officials, including president, vice-president, and some lower-level positions, was presented.

The movement did not last long, in part because Governor-General Andō Rikichi, acting on orders from Tokyo, opposed it. The central government's reasoning was that the movement might endanger the safety of the nearly 500,000 ethnic Japanese on the island, and that any GOJ involvement might offend the United States.[25] This abortive attempt at independence confirmed the KMT government's suspicions about the lack of loyalty of the Taiwanese, which was to cause the Taiwanese much grief later and create a significant degree of nostalgia for the days of Japanese rule.

Both Chinese and Japanese governments gave attention to the problems of de-mobilization and repatriation. Tens of thousands of Taiwanese soldiers and civilian workers in the Japanese military who were serving in China and Southeast Asia would have to be returned to the island. Additionally, the half-million Japanese residents of Taiwan were expected to return to Japan. About 200,000 of them expressed reluctance to leave, since it meant abandoning homes, property, and a relatively secure existence. Postwar Japan offered few attractions as an alternative. Extensive Allied bombing had all but leveled most major cities, and there were severe food shortages. Unlike the home islands, Taiwan had been spared from most bombing, and food stocks were more than adequate. Although Chiang Kai-shek's government took pains to avoid retaliation against the Japanese, Chiang, already suspicious of the allegiance of the Taiwanese, had no desire to allow such large numbers of them to remain on the island. In the end, about 460,000 were repatriated, with an estimated 28,000 who were deemed to possess special technical expertise allowed to stay.[26]

The new Chinese government of the ROC took control of the colonial administrative structure, staffing it with KMT members sent from the mainland. Among these were several hundred *banshan* or half-mountain people: Taiwanese who had lived in China during the war and joined the KMT. Troops were also sent, though there was no violent resistance. The pleasure that a number of Taiwanese took at being liberated from Japanese rule was, however, short-lived.

Those who went to greet the liberators were appalled. Eyewitness accounts describe men pushing or shambling their way off the ships, looking more like coolies than soldiers, some with shoes and some without. With shaggy hair that reminded onlookers of the taro—which, when harvested from the ground, is covered with coarse black root hairs—the men appeared hesitant to face the neatly attired and well-groomed Japanese, who lined up and saluted smartly.[27] Unfortunately, the imagery turned out to faithfully mirror the reality of the early KMT presence. It also represented an emerging rift. "Taro" became a common term of disrespect for the Chinese on Taiwan; Chinese reciprocated by calling the locals "yams," which are not only a staple of the Taiwanese diet but also happen to resemble the shape of the island itself.

The KMT/ROC gained control of Taiwan's economy by requisitioning major public and private industries that had been established under Japanese rule. While a certain amount of disruption was probably inevitable, given the difficulties of transferring title from one group to another, the process was in this case disastrous. In contrast to the draconian but relatively honest Japanese bureaucracy, the KMT administrators were exceedingly corrupt. Additionally, they tended to regard all Taiwanese as collaborators with the enemy, and to treat them accordingly. Many believed that their sojourn on Taiwan would be temporary, and hence looked at it as an opportunity to extract as much wealth as possible in order to create a comfortable existence for themselves and their families when they returned to China.

The infrastructure that the Japanese had created was destroyed as, for example, railroad ties and even the rails themselves were ripped up and shipped to the mainland to be sold as scrap. Once-high standards of sanitation sank to abysmal levels. Exorbitant prices were set for inoculations, which had been free under the Japanese, and diseases unheard of for decades began to return. Numerous burdensome taxes were imposed even as civil services deteriorated.

Whereas the Qing dynasty's policy toward Taiwan had been passive, Chiang Kai-shek was determined to turn the Taiwanese into good Chinese. Talk of independence was strictly forbidden, with the leaders of the brief August 1945 attempt to establish a Taiwan republic receiving stiff prison sentences. Chiang provided no option comparable to the two-year grace period Japan had offered Taiwanese in 1895, during which residents could choose to stay or leave. Hence, there was no legal escape mechanism.

A KMT Youth Corps provided indoctrination in the party's principles and to the Republic of China. Chiang also required the islanders to learn mandarin, imposing penalties on those who dared speak either their native languages or Japanese. Radio, film, and later television programming with native language content was severely limited, with parts for native speakers tending to be confined to such roles as maids and menial laborers.

In February 1949 the tensions generated by this situation burst into prominence. A policeman's abusive behavior toward a poor woman he found selling cigarettes without a license attracted an angry mob who supported her. The officer responded by calling in reinforcements, who shot indiscriminately into the crowd, thus fanning the flames of discontent. Public order quickly disintegrated, being restored only after Chiang Kai-shek promised a full investigation. The public's trust in his pledge proved ill-founded. Troops sent from China began firing at bystanders before they even disembarked from the transport ships.

A full-scale massacre ensued that aimed at destroying an entire generation of Taiwanese intellectuals—nearly all of whom had been educated under the Japanese. Tens of thousands—the precise number is still a matter of controversy—died.[28] The ensuing repression was so severe that what came to be called the February 28th Incident could not be spoken of openly for decades. This era forms the background for the acclaimed *City of Sadness* (Beiqing Chengshi), which won the Venice Film Festival's Golden Lion Award in 1989.

What could not be spoken of openly nonetheless remained in the public consciousness and was discussed quietly among trusted groups of friends. The slogan "The dogs [Japanese] have gone, but the pigs [mainland Chinese] have come" became common among them, and were sometimes vented in ways that even vigilant censors had a difficult time with. For example, in a society where rural festivals are common and pork a staple of the cuisine, one could not be sure whether the ritual killing of a pig was simply that or whether it had an intentional double entendre. An American scholar in Taiwan during the late 1950s for a research project found many of his most valuable contacts by walking the city streets at night and saying, in Japanese, "Taiwan under the pigs is hell" or "Taiwan is a police state, but Japan is a democracy." While mainlanders did not understand, Taiwanese did, and would invite him into their homes to confide their experiences and offer to introduce him to other like-minded individuals.[29]

The initial events of the February 28th Incident occurred within view of the headquarters of the American diplomatic mission in Taipei and were transmitted to Washington by the mission's horrified officials. Since American support was crucial to the KMT's ability to prosecute its civil war with the Chinese communists on the mainland, the United States was able to force the Chiang government to make reforms that somewhat bettered the lot of the Taiwanese.

After the KMT was defeated on the mainland, its leaders fled to Taiwan. There, they were forced to confront the reality that, since the island might be their home for the foreseeable future, it was unwise to treat it as a place to be looted. In the short run, this did not help locals: huge numbers of refugees arrived from China, bidding up housing prices and causing food shortages.

Some Taiwanese were able to leave, many of them for Japan. A number of them did so simply to get away. For example, Lin Hsien-tang (1881–1956), who had been one of the more important Taiwanese during the colonial era, withdrew entirely from public life when he emigrated to Japan. Other exiles became part of activist groups that plotted to overthrow the KMT government and create a Taiwan for the Taiwanese. The Chiang regime sent spies to infiltrate the Taiwanese community in Japan, whose members soon became vigilant against them. Over time, Japan became less important than the United States as a destination for such subversive groups, as more young people opted for study in the United States.

Paradoxically, while working to root out all vestiges of Japanese influence on the Taiwanese, the Chiang government enjoyed good relations with the Tokyo government. Chiang had tried to ensure that Japanese troops could depart from the mainland in a dignified manner. Given the hatred that existed against the Japanese there, this was no easy task and his efforts were appreciated by the Japanese leadership. A pro-Taiwan, or perhaps more accurately, pro-KMT, faction within Japan's preeminent Liberal Democratic Party (LDP) served Taiwan's interests well. Chiang Kai-shek had, its supporters maintained, returned Japan's wartime malice with virtue, citing four particulars:

- Chiang had opposed the abolition of the Imperial Household Agency after the war.
- he had been "strict but generous" toward Japanese soldiers and civilians in China after Japan's surrender, greatly assisting their repatriation.
- he had strongly opposed suggestions that Japan be divided into zones of occupation.
- he had refused the opportunity to exact reparations from Japan.[30]

Both prior ties to Taiwan developed during the colonial era and hostility to the mainland's government because it was communist and allied with the Soviet Union contributed to the level of Japanese support for the ROC. Cooperation was fostered in other ways as well. Although it would have been considered treasonous to say so in the 1930s and 1940s, many

KMT members admired the Japanese system of military and police, especially their ability to suppress communism. On the mainland, as many as 20,000 Japanese troops, wearing KMT uniforms but under the command of their former officers, fought *with* KMT General Yan Xishan against communists until 1948.[31] In 2006 a left-wing Japanese filmmaker gained prominence for a documentary critical of this. While the Tokyo government maintained that the men left their units and volunteered to join the KMT, the surviving soldiers replied that being told to volunteer by a Japanese officer was the same as being given an order, and that they continued to be bound by Japanese army regulations.[32]

After Chiang had consolidated power in Taiwan, a Japanese presence of sorts returned. Retired Japanese military officers began arriving in Taipei in the 1949–1950 period. Known as the White Group, putatively because the Chinese surname of their leader, Tomita Naosuke, was Pai (Bai in pinyin transliteration), meaning white, the officers helped create the Yuan Shan Training Institute north of Taipei.

General Peng Mengji, known as the Butcher of Kaohsiung for his role in the February 28th massacre, was named the institute's director, with Chiang Kai-shek's elder son and heir Chiang Ching-kuo also influential therein. Ching-kuo seemed closer to those who had studied in Japan, such as Peng, than those who had studied in the United States. However, the activities of the Japanese were limited to supplying military advice; the new government preferred to shield most Taiwanese from contact with former colonial rulers.[33]

Under the influence of U.S. policy, Japan accorded diplomatic recognition to Taipei rather than Beijing. Japanese corporations had lucrative investments in Taiwan, where rapid economic growth was creating increasing demand for Japanese products. As time went on, these corporations found ways to trade with the People's Republic of China through so-called dummy corporations, but it was not easy to maintain this balancing act: Taiwan continued to be an irritant in relations between China and Japan, and China an irritant in relations between Taiwan and Japan. Beijing attempted to use trade as a lever to attenuate Tokyo's ties with Taipei, demanding, for example, the participation of the Japanese government in the signing of trade agreements and official guarantees of their implementation, and diplomatic privileges for its trade representatives. Sometimes the government of the Republic of China on Taiwan was able to deflect them, helped by the United States, and sometimes not.[34]

Beijing also protested strongly when Prime Minister Kishi Nobusuke, who favored close coordination with the United States (see Chapter 3), paid his first state visit to Taipei as prime minister in 1957. In 1957 as well, a Japan-ROC Cooperation Committee (Nikka Kyōryoku Iinkai or JRCC), was formed within the Diet, serving, among other functions, as a mechanism for soothing China-Taiwan-Japan relations over such irritants as the status of PRC-ROC defectors and the resolution of Import-Export Bank credits. Representatives of leading Japanese business interests were also members of the JRCC, as well as some prominent nonpolitical figures.[35]

THE DE-RECOGNITION OF THE ROC AND SINO-JAPANESE RELATIONS

Although Mao Zedong had said in the 1930s that he did not consider Taiwan to be part of China, Henry Kissinger found in 1970 that the party leadership was now adamant that it was, insisting the resolution of Taiwan's status be part of any agreement that normalized diplomatic relations between the two countries. From time to time, Chinese media accused Japan of wanting to regain control of Taiwan.[36]

While it is unlikely that Tokyo ever contemplated a restoration of its colonial relationship, Beijing had some grounds for apprehension. In his talks with Zhou Enlai about normalization, Henry Kissinger reported that Zhou seemed at least as concerned with Japan taking over the role of defender of Taiwan as he was with Taiwan independence. According to Kissinger, he repeatedly came back to the theme that, as the United States withdrew from Taiwan, Japan would try to replace it militarily and otherwise. Arch-conservative Sasakawa Ryōichi, Zhou charged, had several times held secret talks with "Chiang gang chieftains" who had close ties to the Taiwan independence movement.[37] At a later date, Zhou added that after the "Nixon shock," three Taiwan officials visited Japan for "a very significant talk" with Prime Minister Satō and former prime minister Kishi, who had transmitted a "closely guarded message" to Chiang Kai-shek that the only hope for the Republic of China's future was to give up all claims to the mainland.[38]

During the following year, *Renmin Ribao* cited the assertion in a Japanese journal *Gunji Kenkyu* (Military Research) that Taiwan had a stranglehold on the maritime trade route that maintained Japan's life, and that its loss would directly endanger the safety of Japan and Korea. In 1978 defense agency head Kanemaru Shin, the *eminence grise* of Japanese politics at the time, told then American Defense Secretary Harold Brown that Taiwan was vital to the defense of Japan and Korea.[39] Under pressure from Prime Minister Fukuda, who was trying to get the Diet's approval of the controversial Sino-Japanese Peace and Friendship Treaty, Kanemaru retracted his remarks, but then told a press conference that "what has always been in my mind unwittingly slipped from my mouth."[40]

Incidents like this continued to occur. Indeed, given the geopolitical significance of the waterways surrounding Japan and Taiwan, and the fact that Taiwan's northernmost island is a few minutes' boat trip from Japan's Yonaguni Island, it is clear that Japan has a strong geopolitical interest in keeping Taiwan out of the control of a potentially hostile power, just as it is in China's geopolitical interest to gain control.

In the end, Kissinger was able to finesse the issue by acknowledging the Chinese position without actually saying that the United States agreed with it. Japan, which effected recognition in 1972, did so with a similar formula. However, Japan's decision to recognize the People's Republic of China and de-recognize the Republic of China did not end these trilateral irritants. In a case involving air travel, Tokyo acceded to Beijing's request to terminate flights to Taiwan, but the route was lucrative, and after a short hiatus, flights were resumed. Since such agreements are reciprocal, this meant allowing Taiwan's flag carrier, misleadingly named China Airlines (CI), to land in Japan. Although the PRC's state carrier, CAAC (Civil Air Administration of China), had ticket counters in Los Angeles and San Francisco that were in close proximity to those of CI, Beijing announced it could not share a Japanese airport with the Taiwan carrier. Tokyo then allowed China Airlines to use Haneda, formerly the international airport until Narita, far away from Tokyo and much less convenient to use, opened. Knowledgeable air travelers who preferred a brief monorail commute to Haneda over a longer and far more expensive bus or car trek to Narita, boosted CI's bookings.[41] However, for those making connections to other international air destinations, which left from Narita, flying into Haneda was less preferable.[42]

Unofficial, but substantive, ROC-Japanese diplomatic relations were carried out through Japan's Interchange Association (Jiaoliu Xiehui in Chinese; Kōryū Kyōkai in Japanese) in Taipei and Taiwan's Association of East Asian Relations (Yadong Guanxi Xiehui or Yatō Kankei Kyōkai) in Tokyo. Taiwan staffed its embassy-equivalent with regular foreign service officials; Japan, in order to maintain the fiction that relations were informal, seconded officers from the foreign ministry to the Interchange Association. The JRCC was disbanded in 1973 after the PRC voiced strong objections to it, but a new group, the Nikka Kankei Giin Kondankai, generally referred to by its abbreviated name Nikkakon, was founded in the same year. Another organization, the Seirankai (Young Storm Association), consisting of thirty-one young, vociferously anti-communist LDP members, railed out against the recognition of the PRC, describing the termination of relations with the ROC as shameless acts by diplomatic Quislings. Seirankai, however, proved short-lived.

While Taipei chafed under various restrictions posed by the unofficial nature of the new arrangement, Beijing was irritated that Tokyo-Taipei ties continued at all and made numerous attempts to further attenuate them. Pressure from pro-Taiwan elements within the ruling LDP such as Nikkakon, from anti-communist right wing groups in the public, and to the Taiwanese community in Japan succeeded in delaying or blocking many of these. As a case in point, the Taiwan faction of the LDP was able to complicate Prime Minister Miki Takeo's desire to sign a peace treaty with Beijing by demanding the deletion of the word "peace" from the treaty. They further pointed out that an anti-Japanese clause in the Sino-Soviet treaty of 1950 was still in force, therefore, in their opinion, precluding the signing of a treaty with the PRC. In the end, a modified treaty was signed. In another instance, pressures from this faction succeeded in persuading the Japanese foreign ministry to refuse China's request that Tokyo refrain from issuing visas to residents of Taiwan.[43] Japan remained the largest foreign investor in Taiwan from 1952 to the 1990s,[44] and two-way trade between them remains robust.

RESTORATION OF JAPANESE INFLUENCE IN TAIWAN

Taiwan's Chiang dynasty ended with the death of Chiang Ching-kuo in January 1988. The younger Chiang, who had already taken important steps toward democratization, was succeeded by the vice-president he had personally chosen. Lee Teng-hui, a Hakka whose first language was Taiwanese, had been educated under Japanese rule and received his undergraduate degree from Japan's prestigious Kyōto University as well as a doctorate from Cornell University in the United States. As anticipated, Lee quickened the pace and scope of his predecessor's democratic reforms.

Given the far larger number of native-born vis-à-vis mainlanders in the population, democratization inevitably involved Taiwanization. Beijing, eager to absorb Taiwan but realizing that non-mainland-born Taiwan leaders would be loath to agree to such an arrangement, opposed many of Lee's reforms, suspecting that they aimed at establishing Taiwan's de jure independence. Stating that it wished to solve what it referred to as "the Taiwan problem" peacefully, Beijing warned that it would invade if Taiwan declared itself independent. Though Lee never publicly stated that this was his intent,[45] independence could easily be construed as the motive for many of his actions. Whether his goal was actual independence, continued separation from the mainland, or a better bargaining position on the terms for unification with the mainland, Japan was an important part of Lee's strategy.

In 1991 Taipei succeeded in changing the name of its de facto embassy in Tokyo from the potentially misleading Association of East Asian Relations to the Taipei Economic and Cultural Representative Office (TECRO). Japanese culture, already very popular in Taiwan despite Chiang Kai-shek's efforts to replace it with Chinese forms, got a boost when, in 1993, Lee's administration lifted the ban on Japanese-language programs. Alice King, also known as Jing Mei-ling, a popular Japanese television figure born in Taiwan but educated in Japan and an outspoken proponent of her native land's right to independence, did much to popularize the culture of each country in the other.

Japanese products gained wide favor, particularly among the younger generation. Parents dressed toddlers in the latest fashions from such emporia of kiddie couture as Miki House, and themselves in the haute couture of Kenzō and Rei Kawakubo. 'Tweens and teenagers purchased a full array of Japan's Hello Kitty merchandise, ranging from backpacks and lunchboxes to customized Kitty credit cards and, later, cell phones.

When cable television arrived in Taiwan—it had been resisted by KMT interests, since the three major network channels were all owned by party or party-affiliated interests—Japanese offerings increased markedly. Most of Taiwan's popular variety shows are copied from Japanese models. A Taiwanese word, *harizu*, means "Japan mania," and the April 1997 cover of the widely read *Hsin Hsin-wen* (The Journalist) showed two pretty teenagers dressed in the latest fads from Japan under a headline that roughly translates "Watch out: your children are turning into Japanese."[46]

Cultural exchanges occurred in both directions. Films from Taiwan played to enthusiastic audiences in Japan, and several of the island's pop stars were sensations in Japan as well. Theresa Teng Li-jun, also known as Theresa Teng, whose songs in Japanese were regularly at the top of the hit parade, was a particular favorite. Teng's songs were also popular in the PRC, where a popular saying was that "the day belongs to Deng Xiaoping, but the night belongs to Teng Li-jun."[47]

TAIWAN POLITICS POISED BETWEEN CHINA AND JAPAN

While *Hsin Hsin-wen* did not intend its warning about the younger generation turning into Japanese to be taken seriously, not all of Taiwan's citizens were happy with Lee's reforms. Many of those who had emigrated from the mainland to Taiwan during the 1945–1949 period were resistant to what amounted to de-sinicization. In 1991 Lee's administration announced that the Republic of China no longer claimed the right to rule the mainland. The two entities were separate and co-equal parts of China.

As time went on, Lee went further. His policy of *bentuhua*, usually translated as "localization," included such moves as reducing the Chinese content of history and geography courses—students had up until that point been made to memorize long lists of ancient emperors and the names of rivers and rail lines in a country they had never been to—substituting the history and geography of Taiwan instead. While mandarin remained the medium of instruction in schools, instruction was also made available in Hoklo (Taiwanese), Hakka, and aboriginal languages.

Lee described his goal as the creation of a "new Taiwanese," who would be a blend of the many cultures that had impacted Taiwan over the years. Unstated but clearly understood by all, including the Beijing leadership, was that this was to be a separate identity that was only partially Chinese in nature. As time and intermarriage softened the divide between mainland-born and Taiwan-born families, the nationalistic feelings of native Taiwanese evolved from a desire to rid themselves of the KMT carpetbaggers to a desire to be free of the mainland's pressure for unification.

Lee's policies were opposed by a well-organized and powerful group within the KMT, most of them with recent mainland origins. Referred to as the nonmainstream KMT, they at one point threatened to run a rival slate of candidates against Lee, including the former head of the ROC armed forces at its head. Lee, a shrewd politician, was typically able to outmaneuver them.

Adroitly using his Japanese, as well as his American, connections, Lee advanced his reform agenda in a variety of ways. An avid golfer, he was able to address political issues while on the course with Japanese officials, many of whom shared his passion for the game. In addition to this "vacation diplomacy," Lee also sought to avail himself of Japan's excellent medical facilities for treatment.

In an interview with Japanese history professor and well-known writer Shiba Ryōtarō in the spring of 1994, Lee incurred Beijing's ire on a number of issues. One of the most irksome, his statement that he had been a Japanese citizen for twenty-two years, is factually true. Beijing, however, chose to interpret it as evidence that Lee had always thought of himself as a Japanese rather than a Chinese, and that he continued to do so. When he praised what Japan had done for its former colony—which is also factually true—the Chinese press accused Lee of ignoring the hardships of the Taiwanese people under Japanese rule.

Further upsetting was Lee's comparison of himself, a devout Christian, to Moses leading Taiwan into the promised land. Beijing interpreted the statement as a clear attempt to assert the island's independence from the Egypt of the pharaohs of the Chinese leadership. Also intensely annoying to Beijing, and in the same year, 1994, Lee told Tokyo University Professor Nakajima Mineo that it was no longer necessary for the Japanese prime minister to apologize for World War II: what was more important was that Japan should acquire a clear view of the future as the leader of Asia. This contradicted both the Chinese leadership's clearly stated insistence that past Japanese apologies had been insufficient and its tacit conviction that China is the natural leader of Asia. *Xinhua* accused Lee of unburdening his mind to Japanese friends who were "keen on splitting up China" and of "prostrating himself in praise of Japanese rule."[48]

Members of Taiwan's leading opposition party, the Democratic Progressive Party (DPP), went even further than Lee in cultivating relations with Japan. In April 1995 a leading DPP politician who would later become the nation's first female vice-president hosted a commemoration of the 100th anniversary of the Treaty of Shimonoseki at the very same Japanese inn at which the document had been signed. Attendees, who included political figures from each country as well as Japanese raised in Taiwan and Taiwanese educated in Japan, noted that China had ceded Taiwan "in perpetuity" to Japan, and emphasized the shared history of the two island nations.[49]

While Beijing expressed great annoyance at this event, Taiwan was to cause even greater tensions in Sino-Japanese relations during 1995. Lee Teng-hui was able to utilize his American connections to obtain a visa from a reluctant State Department so that he could visit Cornell University to receive its distinguished alumnus of the year award. Secretary of State Warren Christopher had imprudently given his Chinese counterpart personal assurances that the visa would never be granted. Congressional anger at the denial of a visa to Lee led it to countermand Christopher, thus drawing maximum publicity to what would normally have been a minor event.

Beijing, in turn, decided that it would have to retaliate for the disrespect it had been shown. The People's Liberation Army began a year of war games and missile launches that resembled scenarios for an invasion of Taiwan. The proximate aim of these actions appeared to be the disruption of Taiwan's first direct presidential election. (Lee had previously been elected under an indirect system.) The PRC's media heaped opprobrium on Lee, hinting at dire consequences that would follow his reelection.

While this venom was understandable given Beijing's anger over Lee's visit, observers were somewhat puzzled. His leading opponent Peng Ming-min was an outspoken proponent of Taiwan independence of long standing, whereas Lee had never publicly advocated it. Preelection tracking showed that Beijing's anger made Lee more popular. Initially predicted to get between 33 and 38 percent of the vote against three opponents, Lee actually received 52 percent, with Peng drawing less than half that total. Not surprisingly, Lee claimed a mandate for the very policies that had so upset Beijing. To save face, Beijing claimed, correctly but misleadingly, that *openly* pro-independence forces had been defeated.

China's belligerent behavior caused alarm in Tokyo, due to its concern for maritime security, the country's important investments in Taiwan, and the feeling that it, like Taiwan, was a democratic island nation dependent on international trade for its survival in the shadow of a rising China.[50] It was subsequently revealed, but never officially confirmed, that the Japanese Defense Agency (JDA) had plans to provide noncombat support to American forces if an armed conflict broke out in the strait.[51] At some point in the crisis, Tokyo approached Washington to explore an upgrading of the security relationship between the two. Barely a month after the arrival of two U.S. aircraft carrier battle groups in the waters off Taiwan and the cessation of Beijing's war games, the Japan–United States Joint Declaration on Security Alliance for the 21st Century was issued. In it, the two countries agreed to cooperate "in dealing with situations in the areas surrounding Japan which would have an important influence in the peace and security of Japan."[52] Beijing demanded, but did not get, Tokyo's assurances that the areas around Japan, *shūhen jitai*, did not include Taiwan. In China, there was no public acknowledgment of how the PRC's behavior might have contributed to this change on Japan's part.

The Tokyo government's decision to play a more active part in the defense of Taiwan was not universally popular in Japan. Hosokawa Morihiro, a former prime minister regarded as pro-China, argued for a narrow definition of the U.S.-Japan Security Treaty as being solely for Japan's defense, and that its commitment should be restricted to situations within the country's national boundaries. He specifically rejected the American view that the alliance constituted the cornerstone of regional security.[53] Others argued that any notion that the United States intended to protect Japan without any reciprocal gestures from Japan was not only untenable but also childishly naive.[54]

Two years later, Taiwan again figured in the tensions between China and Japan. China, having persuaded U.S. President Bill Clinton to iterate the "three no's"—no support for two Chinas, no support for one China, one Taiwan, and no support for Taiwan's entry into international organizations for which sovereignty is a prerequisite—sought the same assurances from Japan. This was to occur during President Jiang Zemin's visit to Tokyo. The Japanese foreign ministry stated pointedly beforehand that Japan would not do so, and would not go beyond the language of the 1972 normalization communiqué in which Tokyo said it "understands and respects" the Chinese position on Taiwan.[55] Either ignoring or disbelieving these statements, Jiang delivered a twenty-five-minute diatribe demanding a number of concessions, including that Tokyo accede to Beijing's position on Taiwan. Prime Minister Obuchi reiterated the language of the 1972 communiqué and said that Tokyo did not support Taiwan independence, but declined to state explicitly that Tokyo opposed Taipei's membership in the United Nations and similar international organizations. Observers speculated that the two countries might be headed for a clash of wills over Taiwan.[56]

The following year, with relations between both Beijing and Washington and Beijing and Tokyo strained, Lee told a correspondent for Germany's *Deutsche Welle* that, since the ROC had been a sovereign state since it was founded in 1912 and amendments to its constitution in 1991 had designated cross-strait relations as "state to state or at the very least special state-to-state relationships," there was no need to declare independence.[57] Since Lee's statement implied a sovereign status for the island rather than, as Beijing contended, classifying Taiwan as a province of the mainland, it prompted further anger from the Chinese leadership.

Also in 1999, the right-wing politician Ishihara Shintarō was elected mayor of Tokyo. Outspoken and articulate—in a previous career as a writer, he had been ideologically aligned with Mishima Yukio (see Chapter 9)—Ishihara proved very helpful to Lee. He invited Lee to visit Tokyo, and himself visited Taiwan, seemingly relishing Beijing's angry reactions.

By this time also, retired Japanese diplomats and Self-Defense Force (SDF) officers had begun to visit Taiwan regularly. The latter provided advice to the Taiwan military and tours of Japanese military facilities. Certain think tanks in Japan, Taiwan, and the United States that were associated with right-of-center views began holding regular Track Two–type meetings along the general theme of how to protect Taiwan from invasion by the mainland. With careful planning, it was hoped, an informal security arrangement could be achieved by combining the U.S.-Japan Security Treaty with the United States' Taiwan Relations Act (TRA). The TRA, passed by the U.S. Congress after President Jimmy Carter's surprise normalization of relations with the PRC, states that the establishment of diplomatic relations with the PRC rests on the expectation that the future of Taiwan will be determined by peaceful means and pledges that the United States will supply Taiwan with such defensive arms as are necessary to maintain a balance of military power in the Taiwan Strait.[58]

A related idea, that the U.S.-Japan treaty should become the cornerstone of a U.S.-centered Pacific alliance based on shared democratic values, and to which Taiwan might someday be admitted, was also discussed.[59] The TT (Tokyo-Taipei) and Trilateral (U.S.-Japan-Taiwan) dialogues exemplified this kind of discourse.[60] At the time, talk of trilateral military arrangements was private and low-key. In late 2006, however, Taiwan's president spoke openly of it in a meeting with the head of Japan's unofficial embassy in Taipei.[61]

The year 1999 was also the run-up to the presidential election of March 2000. Lee, who declared that he would not run again, indicated that he wanted his vice-president Lien Chan to succeed him, and the KMT duly ratified his choice. Lien had superb credentials. In addition to his experience as vice-president, the nominee was a *banshan*—born in China to Taiwanese parents—and had married a mainland woman. Hence, he could presumably bridge the gap between the two groups. Dignified and impeccably tailored, Lien had earned a doctorate in political science from the prestigious University of Chicago.

In contrast to Lee, who had been comfortable with life under the Japanese—even expressing his pride that his brother had died fighting for the Japanese during World War II, Lien came from a strongly pro-China family. His given name was suggested by his patriotic grandfather because the combination of Lien and Chan means "successive battles." The patriarch's hope was that the boy would revive the Chinese nation and "reorganize the light and hope of our homeland" after the struggle with Japan. Lien, however, lacked charisma and proved a lackluster campaigner. And, in choosing Lien, Lee passed over a former protégé, mainlander-born James Soong Chu-yü. The more popular Soong also controlled substantial organizational resources, and decided to run as an independent. He founded the People First Party (PFP) to provide an institutional base for his candidacy, taking significant amounts of these resources as well as party members with him.

This split the KMT. With polls showing Soong running far ahead of Lien but approximately equal to the opposition DPP's pro-independence candidate Chen Shui-bian, the PRC issued a white paper on Taiwan. Apparently a last-minute attempt to help Soong, it hinted that an unspecified deadline had been set for unification which, if not met, "will only force the Chinese government to adopt all drastic measures possible, including the use of force, to safeguard China's sovereignty and territorial integrity."[62]

This threat may have been the reason that Chen, a native-born Taiwanese whose mandarin is noticeably accented, was able to win, though by barely three points. A popular, if unverified, theory on Taiwan is that Lee had chosen Lien in a deliberate attempt to ensure that the KMT did not win the election, and put the DPP candidate, whose anti-unification views were far more compatible with his own, into office.

Whether Lee did or did not purposely skew the election in Chen's favor, the KMT blamed him for its loss. He was replaced as party leader by

Lien Chan. The antimainstream of the KMT now became the mainstream, and exhibited a markedly less antagonistic attitude toward the PRC.

This view sharply distinguished the KMT from the new DPP administration, which was unreceptive to Beijing's insistence that it accept Beijing's interpretation of the one-China policy—that there is but one China and its capital is in Beijing—before talks could be held. The DPP viewed this as tantamount to Taipei giving up its negotiating position as a precondition for negotiations. Nor would the party agree with an alleged 1992 consensus that had been agreed upon by the KMT administration: that both sides agreed there was but one China, with each side free to define how it wished to view that one China.[63]

Chen explained to two visiting Japanese parliamentarians that he was willing to resume dialogue with the PRC as long as it took place with both sides on an equal footing.[64] In that this might imply Taiwan was a state co-equal with the PRC rather than, as Beijing contended, a province, this would have been difficult for the Chinese authorities to accept.

In an effort to soothe relations with the PRC, Chen's inaugural speech promised that, assuming Beijing did not intend to use military force against Taiwan, he pledged not to declare independence, change the nation's title, seek to include the "state-to-state" designation in the constitution, promote a referendum to change the status quo on independence or unification, or abolish either the National Unification Council or the Guidelines for National Unification.[65] Chen's words were artfully crafted, since the Beijing authorities had repeatedly stated that they reserved the right to use force to bring about unification.

Taiwan's new vice-president, Harvard-educated Annette Lu Hsiu-lien, was the same woman who had hosted a ceremony to commemorate the hundredth anniversary of China ceding jurisdiction of Taiwan to Japan. A longstanding opponent of unification, she was less inhibited than Chen about speaking her mind on the topic. Beijing apparently decided to ignore the Chen administration in hopes that it would be voted out of office in 2004. In the interim, it concentrated on the opposition, hosting several delegations thereof to the mainland.

In the 2004 election, Lien Chan and James Soong ran on a combined KMT-PFP ticket as president and vice-president, respectively. Although their combined totals in the 2000 election would easily have put them in office, polls in the run-up to the 2004 election showed Lien and Soong in a virtual tie with Chen. An apparent assassination attempt on Chen and his vice-president the day before the election may have created a sympathy vote sufficient to allow them to win, albeit by a scant 0.2 percent margin. Rather than conceding, Lien and Soong became contentious, charging that the incident had been contrived. Although the Central Election Commission certified the results, a series of noisy demonstrations, scuffles, and court cases ensued, undermining the legitimacy of the government in a manner favorable to Beijing.

During the following March, China's National People's Congress passed an Anti-Secession Law reasserting in a more strident form Beijing's right to employ nonpeaceful means to effect unification.[66] A month later, Lien went to China, visiting his grandmother's grave and being cheered by schoolchildren chanting "Grandfather Lien, you have returned, you have finally returned!" Lien, as head of the KMT, and Hu Jintao, in his capacity as head of the Chinese Communist Party, signed a five-point communiqué whose most salient feature was their opposition to Taiwan independence.[67] Perhaps because the communiqué embodied Beijing's positions, ceding nothing to Taipei, on the eve of his departure, Lien was given some presents to take back: the promise that Taiwan fruit could enter China duty-free, and that two pandas would be made available to one of the island's zoos.

Taiwan citizens were divided on how beneficial these might be. While fruit farmers were pleased, there would be little benefit to the economy of the island as a whole. Taiwan's hi-tech sector had long ago eclipsed agriculture in export value: agricultural products comprise less than 2 percent of Taiwan's exports, and fruit is a still smaller portion of that. Since most fruit farming is done in southern Taiwan, a DPP stronghold, the "gift" seemed intended to lure support away from the DPP and toward the KMT. Moreover, both the pandas and the duty-free fruit would presumably take place as domestic transfers, thereby constituting tacit acceptance that Taiwan was part of China. According to a poll taken by the pro-independence Taiwan Thinktank, 40.9 percent of respondents felt that Lien's trip aimed at creating goodwill, with 45.2 percent believing that it aimed at dividing the country.[68] Critics ridiculed the set-piece nature of Lien's trip, among other things turning a recording of the schoolchildren's chant into a ringer for their cell phones.

Shortly after Lien's return, James Soong made a separate visit to China, also paying his respects at ancestral tombs, being serenaded by schoolchildren, and denouncing Taiwan independence. The leader of the smaller, but most pro-unification, New Party, Yok Mu-ming, was similarly entertained in Beijing in July.[69]

The Chen administration worried that China would be able to subvert its policies by negotiating with opposition parties, as did officials in both the United States and Japan. The Japanese and U.S. governments announced their intention to upgrade a strategic dialogue that had been held at vice-ministerial level in previous years: the stated purpose of the change was "to develop common approaches to deal with the tension over the Taiwan Strait and other potential crises in Asia."[70]

Some Taiwan citizens feared that the Chen administration was unnecessarily provocative and relied more heavily than it should on tenuous gestures of support from the United States and Japan. They favored more conciliatory behavior toward Beijing and, for economic reasons, direct transportation links between Taiwan and the PRC. The KMT and PFP promised both. The more-right-wing elements thereof seem to have replaced the anti-communism of previous years with a kind of great-Han feeling that does not exclude unification with the PRC, although carefully adding that China will have to become democratic before this can be contemplated.

Nonetheless, a series of incidents indicate that despite the generally warm feelings toward Japan in Taiwan, they are not universally held. When outspoken Japanese Foreign Minister Asō Tarō said in February 2006, "Thanks to the significant improvement in educational standards and literacy [during colonization], Taiwan is now a country with a very high education level and keeps up with the current era," an uproar ensued. While even the angriest could not deny the truth of Asō's statement, they felt that it gave only a partial picture of the imperial era. The generally pro-Japan and pro-independence *Taipei Times* editorialized against "Trading One Nationalism for Another," pointing out that the Japanese did not embark on their colonial adventure because of some idealistic *mission civilisatrice*, and that there had been a dark side of imperialism as well.[71]

The PRC's official response was much angrier. Japan's so-called education had "strained every nerve to suppress the spread of Chinese traditional culture, enslaving and assimilating Taiwan people through ideological and spiritual movements."[72] PRC bloggers not only threatened bodily harm to the Japanese foreign minister, but also had harsh words for their own foreign ministry for what they regarded as a weak response—"What's the use of expressing indignation . . . this is not just about feeling outraged—taking action is the most important thing."⁷³ Asō, complaining that his remarks had been misconstrued, won back many friends in Taiwan, and angered Beijing still more, during the following month when he referred to Taiwan as a "country."⁷⁴

In the interim, and illustrating the KMT's ambivalence on relations with Japan, the magistrate of Taipei County, a KMT member, ordered the demolition of a memorial to Taiwan aborigines who had died fighting for Japan during World War II. Funded by donations from Japan and inaugurated only weeks before by Lee Teng-hui, the scenic spot on which it was built had been a favorite of Japanese tourists for many years. The land on which it was built, however, belonged to the county. The magistrate deemed Japanese flags and stones inscribed with "the souls of the fallen are hoping that the spirit of Yamato can be restored," insulting, while the DPP's director of ethnic affairs accused the magistrate of trying to revive authoritarian rule and being insensitive to the nostalgia that many people feel for the colonial era.⁷⁵

Relations between Japan and Taiwan remained warm, with the various manifestations of this continuing to draw angry Chinese ripostes. In May 2005 the United States and Japan reaffirmed their commitment to treat the security of Taiwan as a common strategic objective, reiterating it a year later.⁷⁶ In August, the Diet dropped the visa requirement for Taiwan tourists,⁷⁷ and Lee Teng-hui made his third trip to Japan since retiring from the presidency. And, despite the furor that erupted from the PRC, accompanied by American expressions of concern, when Chen Shui-bian announced that the National Unification Council would cease to function, Tokyo expressed no misgivings. According to Taiwan's former de facto ambassador to Tokyo, "Japanese officials understand Taiwan's stance."⁷⁸

Quietly, the equivalent of a military attaché was dispatched to Japan's de facto embassy in Taipei. Speaking cautiously when interviewed, the attaché said he participated in meetings with Taiwanese government and military officials and sent dispatches to Tokyo.⁷⁹ Tokyo also dispensed advice on cross-strait relations: the head of Taiwan's Mainland Affairs Council reported on his return from a June 2006 visit to Tokyo that he was warned to be cautious of the united front tactics that Beijing was using.⁸⁰ Many KMT leaders, however, saw Japan's motive in support of Taiwan as its desire to use the island as a pawn in the triangular relationship with the United States and the PRC.⁸¹

A few months after Lien's visit, the KMT elected a new chair, Taipei Mayor Ma Ying-jeou. Hong Kong–born to a pro-unification mainland family,[82] the Harvard-educated Ma and his principal rival, Wang Jyn-ping, Taiwan-born Speaker of the Legislative Yuan, ran on similar platforms of promising to better relations with the mainland, Wang representing the *bentuhua* (localization) wing of the KMT. Therefore, Ma's victory, with more than 70 percent of the ballots cast, seemed to portend a more significant move in the direction of sinification as well as better relations with the mainland. He was widely regarded as less favorably disposed, and even hostile, toward Japan. Ma's overwhelming victory also made Ma the clear favorite for the KMT's candidate for the presidency in 2008.

Ma stated that unification is the KMT's stated aim, and that he did not think Taiwan should be included in the scope of the U.S.-Japan Security Treaty.[83] Since no responsible member of either the Japanese or the American governments had advocated including Taiwan therein, this was a moot point. Ma later modified his statement on unification by adding that China would have to become a democracy first, and also called for Beijing to reverse the verdict on Tiananmen as a prerequisite to negotiations.[84]

Commensurate with his newly acquired status as KMT leader, Ma visited Japan in July 2006. A major motive was to dispel his image as anti-Japanese, which he attributed to slander by the opposition DPP. Yet Ma criticized the Japanese prime minister's visit to the Yasukuni Shrine and said that he hoped Japan would take a "broader view of history"—statements that seemed designed to please Beijing rather than Tokyo.[85] Confronted with probing questions in meetings with Diet members, Ma gave evasive answers. Noisy right-wing demonstrators outside a press conference denounced him for acting as an agent of China and interfering in Japan's internal affairs.[86]

With Taiwan about to be hit by a typhoon, Ma cut short his trip, pronouncing it a success despite reports to the contrary.[87] His party did attempt to make amends after the trip, creating a Japanese-language version of its official website and translating major local news stories to send to Diet members and Japanese media via daily emails, saying it would help Japanese gain a better understanding of Taiwan "from an unbiased source."[88]

The PRC leadership viewed a Ma administration as preferable to a continuation of DPP rule, but took note of apparently contradictory statements—for example, Ma saying on the one hand that Taiwan should not engage in talks before China removes its missiles targeting Taiwan and on the other that unification is the end goal of his party, and also pledging to maintain the status quo of the Republic of China while stating that independence is an option.[89]

Ma won the presidency in 2008 handily nonetheless, campaigning on promises to improve the economy and improve relations with China. His inauguration speech did not mention Japan, to Tokyo's dismay.[90] It had reportedly been removed from an earlier draft.[91] The new president proceeded to make good on his promise to improve cross-strait relations, stating that he accepted the alleged 1992 consensus of one China, two different views thereof, and signing numerous agreements with Beijing that critics regarded as aimed at integrating the island's economy so tightly with that of the PRC's that an autonomous, much less an independent, existence would be precluded.

Despite these actions, the economy, which had been the major issue in the 2008 election rather than cross-strait or Sino-Japanese relations, did not improve. While the downturn of the world economy was a significant factor, Ma's critics argued that he had surrendered important indicators of Taiwan's sovereignty in exchange for meager benefits from the PRC.

When, during the following year, Japan's de facto ambassador to Taipei, Saitō Masaki, stated in a private meeting that his government regarded Taiwan's status as undetermined, Ma became infuriated, saying that it had been finalized in the 1952 treaty between the ROC and Japan.[92] Although Saitō was correct—Beijing had made abrogation of the 1952 treaty a condition of the 1972 normalization agreement between China and Japan, and Tokyo did so—he apologized. Ma, however, excluded Saitō from subsequent press conferences and other activities, leading him to resign a few months later.[93]

A 2010 visit from Abe Shinzō, an important force in Japanese politics who was at that time between prime ministerships, was badly handled. Among other gaffes, Ma addressed Abe as "deputy prime minister," and Taiwan's ministry of foreign affairs refused his request to schedule a meeting with the head of the opposition DPP. When the DPP invited Abe to dinner, the ministry provided neither a car nor a staff member to accompany him, which would have been normal procedure: Abe took a cab.[94]

In addition, Taiwan's premier decreed that government documents referring to Japanese "rule" be changed to Japanese "occupation," as well as ordering other changes that implied Taiwan was part of China.[95] In

2014 these modifications were extended to textbooks, prompting protests by students and academics. The mayor of one large city replied that his municipality would not adopt the books.

The following year, it was Taiwan's turn to be disrespected. Taiwan was the largest contributor to relief efforts after the March 11th earthquake-tsunami-nuclear meltdown, yet received no public thanks from the government. According to *Kyodo*, the Japanese government ran thank-you notices in the major newspapers of all countries whose government and citizens had made contributions, except Taiwan.[96]

The Ma administration did conclude certain agreements with Japan, most of them trade-related. A consulate-equivalent was opened in Hokkaido, Taiwan's sixth in Japan and the first new one in many years. Direct flights were initiated that connected Taipei's Songshan airport, hitherto reserved for domestic flights and conveniently located within Taipei city, with Haneda in Tokyo. And a park commemorating Hattori Yayoi, a Japanese engineer who built an irrigation waterway and reservoir in Taiwan in the pre–World War II period, was dedicated.[97]

Most importantly, a fishing agreement was concluded in April 2013, delineating the areas in which each country's fleet was allowed to operate. Negotiations on the matter had dragged on for years, with the Japanese government's decision to accede at this time raising questions on its motives. It is probable that Tokyo wished to retaliate against provocative Chinese actions in the area, though in order to preserve the appearance of adherence to a one-China policy, the text appeared in Japan as a private agreement between the two countries' fishing associations,[98] whereas it was carried on Taiwan's ministry of foreign affairs website.[99]

Mounting opposition to Ma's cross-strait initiatives burst into full-scale demonstrations in March 2014 after he attempted to remove Wang Jin-pyng, the speaker of the Legislative Yuan, from office and tried an irregular maneuver to ensure the passage of a Cross-Strait Services Trade Agreement (CSSTA), which the speaker, his erstwhile rival for KMT chair and leader of the KMT's localization wing, had delayed. Protestors occupied the Legislative Yuan for a month, as hundreds of thousands of their supporters jammed the streets of central Taipei.

Although what became known as the Sunflower Movement received relatively modest coverage in Western media, it was major news in Japan. The protest was peaceful, with the occupiers even cleaning up the legislative chambers before they left. Nonetheless, its scale and depth of emotion made it clear to Ma, and to Beijing, that future progress toward unification would be very difficult. The elections of 2014 were a devastating loss for the KMT,[100] with its prospects for the general election of 2016, and continuation of its China policy, seemingly grim as well.

Ma's dilemma was well illustrated in his reaction to the PRC's extravagant parade to commemorate the 70th anniversary of the end of World War II. To the extent that either KMT or CCP forces fought the Japanese, the former had borne the brunt of hostilities, which even the pro-unification Ma would have found it politically unwise to deny. Meanwhile, former KMT presidential candidate Lien Chan announced his intention to attend the Beijing festivities even as Lee Teng-hui declared his pride, as a Japanese citizen at that time, in supporting Japan. Caught in a difficult position, Ma criticized Lien's visit as "inappropriate" and Lee's actions as "debasing himself."[101]

The DPP's overwhelming victory in the January 2016 election, taking not only the presidency but achieving, for the first time, an absolute majority in the Legislative Yuan, cast doubt on the viability of the future of the KMT as well as its pro-China policies. It also opened the way for closer cooperation between Taiwan and Japan.

CONCLUSIONS

The better relations with the mainland that the Ma administration promised in 2008 were achieved at the cost of linking Taiwan more closely to the PRC on the PRC's terms and alienating localization forces in Taiwan as well as harming relations with Japan.

Beijing's options are limited: to push the government further risks returning the pro-independence, pro-Japanese DPP to power or, at best, the pro-localization wing of the KMT, which from Beijing's point of view would be nearly as bad. A large majority of the population now identifies as Taiwanese only, as opposed to both Taiwanese and Chinese, with those who believe themselves to be Chinese in the low single-digits. Economic integration has not been accompanied by a desire for political integration, and Japanese support, however tacitly expressed as, for example, in a commitment to help the United States defend the "nearby waters" constitutes an obstacle to unification.

The split in the Taiwan electorate should not be construed as starkly pro-China versus pro-Japan. Polls show overwhelming bipartisan support for the status quo of neither de jure independence—since that would invite attack from the PRC—and opposition to unification with the PRC. The underlying concern is what to do to keep China from invading, while at the same time maintaining Taiwan's economic growth.

For this, trade and good relations with both the PRC and Japan are important, suggesting that a policy of equidistance would optimize the country's best interests.[102] However, establishing better relations with one has come at the cost of poorer relations with the other. In sum, Chang Wei-sui's dream of Taiwanese as intermediary between China and Japan seems now to be the reverse: it may be pushing them further apart. While Japan has no desire to absorb Taiwan, it has a clear geopolitical interest in not allowing Taiwan to be absorbed by China. As stated by leading journalist and former deputy head of Taiwan's National Security Council Antonio Chiang, "Taiwan can neither stay neutral nor play the role of balancer. This is international reality, and Taiwan must make a choice."[103]

Part Three

11

Conclusions

Although the issues of war guilt, territorial jurisdiction, and the terms of trade are important, they are insufficient as explanations of the level of animosity between China and Japan, and are unlikely to be solved by apology or capitulation. The roots of Sino-Japanese tension are deep, going back to the earliest days of contact between the entities that became known as China and Japan. While feeling indebted to China for having borrowed important parts of its culture from China, Japan also sought to be recognized as an equal, and was rejected, as seen in the pique of the Sui emperor at the assumption of equality implicit in a 607 A.D. letter addressed to the emperor of the Land of the Setting Sun from the emperor of the Land of the Rising Sun. There was but one Middle Kingdom, and one Son of Heaven. Japanese were regarded as lesser beings and expected to comport themselves as such, presenting tribute to the emperor and performing the ketou of obedience.

The same attitude of haughty disdain is evident in Ming dynasty Emperor Hong Wu's 1380 missive to the Ashikaga shogun, referring to him as a stupid Eastern barbarian who, living so far across the sea, was haughty and disloyal. Should this behavior continue, he warned, disaster might follow. Challenging the cosmology of the centrality of the Middle Kingdom, the Ashikaga replied that heaven and earth were not monopolized by one ruler; the world did not belong to a single person. The prince who wrote the reply continued that, if a threatened invasion were to materialize, the emperor's forces might receive an unpleasant surprise: the Japanese would not kneel to pay respect to China's best generals. The two backed different sides in the dynastic wars of the Korean peninsula, with China's ally emerging triumphant.

Instances of amicable relations can be found in the historical record as well. The Middle Kingdom did make some accommodations to Japanese feelings. At some Chinese ports of entry, though not all, Japanese emissaries were admitted with gifts only, rather than gifts and documents, because they found the requirement to bring tribute to the emperor and make gestures of loyalty to him to be distasteful. For a variety of reasons, the number of tribute missions declined beginning in the ninth century, even as a distinctive Japanese culture took shape that combined the extensive borrowings from Chinese civilization with indigenous elements.

When an envoy of the thirteenth-century Yuan/Mongol empire demanded tribute, he was refused, leading to an attempted invasion of Japan. Shintō priests interpreted the defeat of the expedition to a divine wind, kamikaze, conjured up by indigenous Japanese gods to protect the country. By the fourteenth century, Japanese scholars were proclaiming the superiority of Japan over China because its allegedly single line of emperors had descended in an unbroken line from the gods, whereas China had experienced numerous changes of dynasty and lacked sacred ancestry. Others went so far as to argue that these gods were the original substance of Buddha.

In the late sixteenth century, a war that began with an ill-fated Japanese invasion of Korea was rekindled when a Ming dynasty envoy arrived in Japan for the investiture ceremony of Toyotomi Hideyoshi as king of Japan and vassal of the Ming emperor. Hideyoshi, deeming the process patronizing, reopened hostilities. A combination of Chinese and Korean forces defeated Japan once again. Hideyoshi passed away soon thereafter.

His successor Tokugawa Ieyasu attempted to establish a tribute system that paralleled China's, with mixed success: Korea was resistant; Okinawa more amenable. Though the Tokugawa and Ming governments found common cause in certain endeavors such as antipiracy operations, relations between the two were poor. In 1621 the Tokugawa rejected official government-to-government relations, relegating China to the lowest rung of foreign relations and referring to its representatives as barbarians, just as Chinese had hitherto regarded Japanese envoys. In the nineteenth century, the nativist *kokugaku* movement aimed to return to the roots of a putatively purer, more authentically Japanese culture unsullied by not only Confucian influences but also those of China in general.

The arrival of the West, with its Westphalian conception of theoretically equal sovereign states, was initially rejected by China, at this point under the aegis of the Qing, Manchu, dynasty. Resisting even the notion of establishing a foreign office, much less the concept of equality, proved costly. Superior technology enabled the Western powers to defeat the Qing in several confrontations, forcing its leadership to acquiesce to their demands. The Japanese were somewhat acquainted with this technology through the presence of the Dutch: aware of the setbacks their larger neighbor had suffered, they more quickly realized the need to respond to Western pressures rather than try to ignore them. It has been argued that because they had borrowed so heavily from China in the past, Japanese were better psychologically prepared to do so from the West. Having long acknowledged the existence of what would now be called a peer competitor, it was easier to accept the existence of others.

The arrival of U.S. Commander Matthew Perry's ships in Edo Bay in 1853 led to a rapid and impressive Japanese effort to emulate the strengths of the Western states. Fifteen years later, helped by advocates of kokugaku, who argued that Japan must return to the ancient tradition of imperial rule, the Tokugawa shōgunate was overthrown and power restored to the emperor, at least nominally. During the reign of the Meiji emperor, Japan's modernization was rapid and impressive. An effort to form a partnership against the West under the rubric "same culture, same race" (*dōbun, dōshu*) failed, as Chinese reformers were unable to gain traction within their own society and Japanese reformers came to see them as hopeless.

A scant four decades after the appearance of Perry's appearance, Japan went to war with China, defeating its much larger neighbor with relative ease. For many Chinese leaders and intellectuals, the contempt they felt for Japan became tinged with envy. When, a decade later, Japan defeated Russia as well, Western powers, too, became alarmed. Japan had learned the lessons of Western imperialism too well.

From the Japanese point of view, however, their country was not accepted as an equal member of the Westphalian configuration of sovereign states regardless of its accomplishments. Japan had been forced into signing unequal treaties and even, in the case of the settlement with Russia, retroceding part of it. Many Japanese products, though competitive, were barred from Western markets; some passed laws forbidding its nationals to immigrate there. At this point, the concern became the achievement of equality with the West and, for some, primacy over it. The lesson learned was that Japan would have to fight to get it.

Again, there were efforts at Sino-Japanese cooperation: reformers who escaped from China after the failure of the 1898 reform found at least temporary refuge in Japan; at a later date, Sun Yat-sen did as well. Sun formed genuine friendships there, albeit occasionally tinged with opportunism as when in 1907 he hinted that, in return for Japanese help in overthrowing the Qing, he would not object if Japan claimed Manchuria—the homeland of the Qing Manchus—in return for its help. Other, more conservative, Japanese felt that the Qing, as a fellow monarchy, should be supported.

The Qing dynasty fell nonetheless, resulting in a China ruled by warlord governments and, later, at least nominally unified by the Kuomintang under Chiang Kai-shek. In Japan, a highly nationalistic military clique gained influence, partly through assassinating more liberal statesmen who objected. Shintō was reformulated in support of their extremist nationalist agenda, in line with kokugaku theorists' more strident views of Japanese exceptionalism.

Absorbing Taiwan in 1898 and Korea in 1905, Japan moved into Manchuria in 1931, followed by invasions of coastal China, India, and Southeast Asia. Its troops behaved with arrogance and cruelty, thus antagonizing even those who initially welcomed their homelands' liberation from Western colonial rule. Imperial overstretch led to abject defeat, and a reset of Sino-Japanese relations.

Soon after Japan's defeat, Japanese troops were fighting with Chiang Kai-shek's forces against the Chinese Communist Party (CCP)'s troops. Even after relocating his government to Taiwan, Chiang hired Japanese officers as advisers. The old enemies established rapport, if not actual friendship, in their common opposition to communism. Clearly, this did not endear Japan to the winner of the confrontation, the Chinese Communist Party. With the CCP now in charge in China and, in its earlier years, dominated by the Soviet Union, dislike of Japan was reinforced by ideology. Only when the Beijing leadership broke from Moscow and sought allies against it was a degree of cordiality established, albeit against the backdrop of a continuing stream of Chinese criticism of Japan's alleged intentions to revive militarism, re-create the Greater East Asian Co-Prosperity Sphere, and serve as the Asian avatar of American imperialism.

Evidence of all of these could be found in several Japanese films that seemed to glorify war, the rapid revival of the country's economic strength, and the gradual bending of the antiwar provisions of its constitution, generally as a response to American pressure. But these indictments ignored strong pacifist pressures within Japan, the existence of antiwar films, and resistance to any actions that would entangle it in U.S. commitments elsewhere, whether in Asia or beyond.

In Japan, there were different fears. According to a 1954 *New York Times* analysis, "Japan always had one eye on China."[1] Prime Minister Yoshida, who would have liked to establish diplomatic relations with Beijing but was prevented by Washington from doing so, proposed the equivalent of an Asian Marshall Plan, reasoning that, were the less developed countries of the area to find themselves unable to raise living standards, they would fall into the Chinese orbit. Speaking before the National Press Club in Washington, Yoshida declared that, as an Eastern nation, Japan understood the area and wanted to help. Still, even allocating $400 million a year to Southeast Asia would, he estimated, be about a tenth of what was required to keep pace with China.[2]

Already Japan saw the PRC beginning to displace it in major Southeast Asian markets. Foreign ministry analysts became concerned that, rather than being a promising market for Japanese products, China would be its greatest competitor in the rest of Asia.[3] However, an American academic took a somewhat more optimistic tone, noting that, while feeling culturally indebted to China, Japanese also seemed to have a strong feeling of superiority toward the Chinese. "Japanese seem quite confident of their ability to understand the Chinese and to handle them."[4]

In 1956 Japan was admitted to the United Nations with broad domestic support: membership was regarded as emblematic of its return to the community of nations and commitment to world peace. As its economy prospered, Japan soon became the second largest contributor to the United Nations, after the United States.

The International Olympic Committee's 1959 decision to award the 1964 Olympic Games to Tokyo was yet another affirmation of Japan's status. These were the first games to be held in Asia—Tokyo had actually been chosen as the venue in 1940, but the committee later rescinded its decision in favor of Helsinki because of Japanese aggression in China. In a poignant symbol of the nation's rise from the ashes of defeat, the young man chosen to bear the torch into the stadium had been born in Hiroshima on the day the atomic bomb was dropped there. Showcasing Japanese technological acumen, the Shinkansen bullet train was inaugurated a few days before the games began. So as well did another marker: the 1964 games were the first to feature computer recording and calculation of statistics.

In 1964 also, Japan became the first non-Western member of the Organization for Economic Cooperation and Development.[5] At his first press conference after being chosen prime minister in November, Satō Eisaku declared that Japan's international voice had been too small, citing his predecessor as saying that the country was one of the three pillars of the world, along with the United States and the Soviet Union.[6]

However, despite these achievements, Japanese confidence seems to have eroded. Both trade and security considerations were involved. As for the first, Chinese Premier Zhou Enlai's successful visit to Africa, in which he declared China would "roll it up like a mat," proved disquieting. Japan's envoys to Africa and France, still a major influence in its former colonies there, met to discuss a response to the PRC's increased propaganda activities and checkbook diplomacy. While Japan's exports to the continent had been rising at about 20 percent annually, its imports were negligible, thus placing it at a disadvantage in the competition. Trade agreements would have to be concluded. In addition, Japanese foreign aid had heretofore been concentrated in Asia.

With regard to security, the PRC's successful detonation of a nuclear device, making it the first Asian member of the nuclear club, also had a profound effect. Although the notion of Japan building nuclear weapons was unthinkable at the time, China's success provided Tokyo with the incentive to move quickly to produce a satellite "to ameliorate any dismay over the PRC's nuclear explosion." Plans also took shape to produce a nuclear-powered ship, the *Mutsu*.[7]

Japanese decision-makers tended to downplay strident Chinese rhetoric as that of a gawky adolescent who would someday mature and join the family of nations.[8] Trade would provide the soft pillow, as one senior official put it, that would aid the transition. Conversely, in the assessment of U.S. Ambassador Edwin Reischauer, the Chinese viewed Japan, to which they paid "scant and largely contemptuous attention . . . in their eyes is a late and distorted offshoot of China's ancient civilization."[9]

The open break between Beijing and Moscow led to more cordial relations between Japan and the PRC, with Tokyo being courted by both sides. China was the more successful of the two suitors, taking the position that the Kurils belonged to Japan while the Soviet leadership remained adamantly opposed to returning all but the lesser islands. Sino-Japanese trade began to rise, raising concerns in both Washington and, for reasons other than the obvious satisfaction of the country's business community, in Tokyo as well. The United States, becoming further drawn into the conflict with Vietnam, feared China might choose to intervene, as it had in the war in Korea and did not want closer Sino-Japanese ties that might aid Beijing to pursue the conflict. Conversely, Japan feared being drawn into the conflict, due to the presence of U.S. bases on its territory.

Many Japanese expressed unhappiness with the manner in which their government conducted negotiations with China. After *Xinhua* cited the head of a quasi-unofficial trade mission to Beijing as attacking his government for "pursuing an anti-China policy in subservience to American imperialism," an editorial in *Tokyo Shimbun* said the communiqué "reminded us not of a negotiation between equals, but of a master-servant relationship."[10]

Ambassador Reischauer urged Japan to take a leadership role in Asia, hoping it would help to stabilize the area against further communist expansion.[11] While, in the abstract, most Japanese welcomed a larger role for their country, they did not want to take the risk of becoming enmeshed in conflict that might be a consequence of a higher international profile. Tokyo's view of a larger role involved an aid program for Southeast Asia. However, Beijing denounced the program, construing it as a plan to re-create the Japanese dominance of the area that ended with its defeat in World War II. In addition to its aid project, Japan also began to develop a peace corps–like program whereby young people and retirees with needed specialties could volunteer for service in developing nations.[12]

Although generally supportive of Prime Minister Satō's plans to reclaim Japanese prestige through trade and diplomacy, some within Japan began to argue that these initiatives would be insufficient: the country would never regain the international stature it felt entitled to as long as it remained a military nonentity.[13]

At the time, such views had little support and could be harmful to those who articulated them publicly. Competition with China was expressed primarily in economic rather than military terms. In a prescient analysis, the U.S. National Intelligence Estimate (NIE) released in 1968 stated that Japan saw China as a long-range competitor of influence, but that Japan would avoid provoking China while working mainly through economic means to limit its influence. Japan would try to foster a less militant and more realistic view of the outside world while taking care not to impair its own relationship with the United States.[14] Attaching an addendum to the NIE, the director of the State Department's Intelligence and Research Division remarked that the estimate had given inadequate weight to the emerging regional and global importance of Japan, that the country was increasingly aware that it would have to take more and more active steps to contain and compete with China and, in doing so, would be drawn into the more dynamic view to which its leadership already aspired. However, if China, already in possession of nuclear weapons, should take on a more menacing aspect, pressures to compete would build within Japan.[15]

Framers of the 1970 NIE, by contrast, saw in the PRC's post–Cultural Revolution return to active diplomacy a China whose aspirations were blocked by a vastly superior Soviet Union and United States "and the growth in economic strength and self-confidence of . . . traditional rival Japan." Japan, the NIE continued,

> poses special problems in Peking because it too is an Asian power, is outstripping China in economic growth, and is strongly resistant to Maoist subversion or Chinese threats. And the Chinese, who remember Japanese imperialism in China during World War II, wonder what threat the Japanese may become to their security over the long term and fear Tokyo will one day take on the role of protector of Taiwan. The Chinese answer so far has been to continue with a rather rigid and vituperative propaganda attack on Japan's leaders, their policies, and their alleged ambitions in Asia. While this may impress the North Koreans and some people in Southeast Asia, it does little good for China's cause in Japan itself.[16]

A survey taken of Tokyo students in 1971 indicated that a majority felt superior to Indonesians, Mexicans, Chinese, and French and slightly superior to Americans. Despite their country having surpassed Germany as the number two economy in the non-communist world, respondents indicated that they felt Germans were slightly superior to Japanese.[17]

The issue of rivalry arose again only a few months later when it became known that Washington and Beijing had begun discussions on reestablishing relations. Following President Nixon's announcement, without prior consultation with Tokyo, that he would be visiting China six months hence, a Japanese analyst opined that the manner in which the announcement was made—that Nixon would not be visiting Tokyo, and the fact that the U.S. president was going to Beijing rather than the Chinese leader visiting Washington—indicated that "the historical past in which China was the central kingdom where the world paid proper homage appears to be in the process of being revived."[18]

These feelings were intensified when the People's Republic of China was awarded the permanent membership seat on the United Nations Security Council formerly held by the Republic of China on Taiwan. Japan's aspirations for a seat, despite its large contributions to the UN's budget and impeccable record as a peaceful member of the international community, were ignored.

Comments by Japanese academics and in the country's newspapers at the time indicated a feeling of being slighted, and an air of "What about us?" A representative comment was that it was not that Japan should aspire to a place among the superpowers, but that the contrast in treatment between China and Japan could not but be noticed. In his press conference announcing the trip, Nixon had mentioned Japan only once, and that in the context of the textile agreement being negotiated.[19] In discussions between National Security Adviser Henry Kissinger and President Richard Nixon, Kissinger discounted the president's concern that Japanese would be attracted to China after mutual recognition, thinking it more likely that the two would begin to compete.[20]

In the period of amicable relations that followed the 1972 Sino-Japanese normalization agreement, friction was present but latent. A particular concern was the Chinese side's penchant for imposing conditions for negotiations. Although one of these was the recognition of equality on both sides, Japanese conservatives pointed out that accepting these conditions in the first place was hardly a recognition of equality and, in fact, constituted what they regarded as "humiliating diplomacy."

While the Chinese accused the Japanese of attempting to re-create the country's pre–World War II dominance of Asia, Japanese saw China as trying to re-create the tribute system of the imperial era. Speaking of negotiations for the Peace and Friendship Treaty, a columnist for the *Japan Times* characterized his country as "known to be particularly weak-kneed with regard to China, which is now emerging once again as the Middle Kingdom with emissaries from the surrounding countries paying their respects in visits to Beijing."[21]

The feeling of rivalry extended even to sports, as when Japanese media reported that China had dethroned Japan in the tally of gold medals for the first time in the 31-year history of the Asian Games: the PRC's teams had taken home 61 first-place finishes to Japan's 57.²² In general, Japanese seemed to fit Ambassador Reischauer's characterization of them as inveterate naval-gazers, while the Chinese attitude—publicly, at least, since the media were at this time still under strong party/state control—exuded serene self-confidence.

Still, occasional hints of a sense of rivalry with Japan were evident despite the state-controlled press. A Guangdong wall poster of 1977 observed that the Chinese economy was being strongly outperformed by that of Japan, and suffered from "broken down social order and rising crime." Signed "Gong Ren," a homonym for "worker," the anonymous writer asked whether the Chinese people were truly inferior to Japanese or whether the socialist system was to blame.[23]

Japanese concerns were muted during these heady days of impressive annual increments in the GDP, and some even spoke of a "bigemonic" system, an era of "Amerippon."[24] The anti-Japanese demonstrations that broke out in China during the summer of 1985 included complaints against Japanese economic imperialism and the arrogance of its nationals. Although the students' feelings of hostility toward Japan appeared to be sincere, party and government were to some degree complicit.[25]

Mixed signals came from the Beijing leadership. At the same time that Japanese investment was being encouraged, youth groups feted, and even defense exchanges discussed, the government-announced preparations to commemorate the 40th anniversary of the Japanese defeat in World War II by staging exhibits that included photographs and detailed descriptions of war atrocities.[26] Media commentary dwelled on the relevance of such cruelties for the present situation, hinting that as long as the Japanese refused to sincerely repent the past, there was potential for repeating the mistakes in the future.[27]

It is also possible that the demonstrations were encouraged by at least one faction of the Chinese government, perhaps hoping for leverage with Tokyo in dealing with the large trade deficit China was running with Japan. The demonstrations were quickly suppressed when the students' demands began to oppose the larger issue of how their own officials were profiting, which the protestors saw as selling out China for their personal advantage (see Chapter 5). In any case, the genie of anti-Japanese protests was out of the bottle.

Students' concerns notwithstanding, Chinese government leaders took pains to assuage Japanese worries that they were creating a force that would eventually destroy it. Less than a year after the demonstrations, then president Hu Yaobang told a group of Japanese industrialists that China would not behave as in the old tale of the Orient, in which after an apprentice was trained and experienced, he would leave his master unemployed. China wanted investment and technology solely to better the living standards of its people. "And China means what it says."[28]

Whether or not Hu was sincere, he was out of power a few months later, accused, among a number of crimes, of being excessively favorable to Japan. And Japanese fears that their country was lagging behind the PRC intensified. They blamed a compartmentalized market that disadvantaged Japan in the race to build Pacific rim communications systems.[29] Already in 1988, President Zhao Ziyang had announced an export-led economic plan that would hasten rivalry with Japan.[30]

The bursting of the Japanese economic bubble at the beginning of the 1990s was a bad period for China as well, with the brutal suppression of demonstrations in Tiananmen Square and elsewhere in China denting its international image and necessitating an austerity program to damp down the inflationary pressures that were an important cause of the demonstrations. But whereas China recovered quite rapidly, Japan did not. An additional cause of concern for Tokyo was the February 1992 unilateral decision of the Chinese legislature to declare sovereignty over the Diaoyu/Senkaku Islands disputed between the two as well as over Taiwan, always a sensitive issue in Japan, and a number of islands the PRC contests ownership of with Taiwan and several Southeast Asian states. Yet another cause for concern was the long sequence of annual double-digit increments to the Chinese defense budget that began in 1989, even as those of most other powers were being cut due to the end of the Cold War.

Although the Chinese leadership remained eager for Japanese aid and expertise, even expressing gratitude for Japanese understanding in the wake of sanctions imposed by many countries after the Tiananmen incident, a shift in attitude, subtle at first, was noticeable. One trigger was Japan's decision to take part in UN peacekeeping operations. Ignoring the pressure Japan had been under to do so, a lengthy article in *Guoji Wenti Yanjiu* in April 1992 strongly opposed the decision, accusing Tokyo of using participation in such operations as a springboard to become a political power. The implication seemed to be that, although Beijing accepted the economic strength of Japan, it was strongly opposed to Japan taking on an enhanced political and military role—even though the PRC was moving ahead rapidly on all three fronts. In this analysis, Japan was seeking to regain great power status by taking advantage of the disintegration of the Cold War balance of power combined with the strength of its economy.[31]

As its economy failed to regain momentum, Japanese concerns with China increased. A series of weak prime ministers characterized by brief terms in office and meager accomplishments contributed to the loss of morale. A 1994 *Yomiuri* editorial opined that, whereas Japan's diplomacy toward China after 1972 had been motivated by feelings of guilt over its conduct in World War II, younger Japanese politicians had no alternative but to look on it as a competitor or even a potential superpower, given the PRC's evolution into a strong and wealthy nation.[32]

By 2001 Japanese sources began to notice that the quality of Chinese products had improved, thereby enhancing their ability to compete with more expensive Japanese items. The country's leading business newspaper observed that, whereas the PRC's manufactures had been low-cost but low-quality, they had become low-cost high-quality.[33] This view was reinforced when, a few weeks later, the Sony Electric Group announced that, contrary to its past practice of first manufacturing new products at home and only later transferring production overseas, it had decided to produce its new home-use multicolor printer at a Guangzhou joint venture plant from start to finish.[34]

The advent of a strong prime minister, Koizumi Junichirō, the same year heightened Sino-Japanese tension. Although able to do little to restructure the country's economy, he defied Beijing through such acts as visiting the Yasukuni Shrine each year throughout his entire five-year time in office, the last instance on August 15th, which, since it was the anniversary of Japan's surrender, seemed chosen to cause maximum irritation to the Chinese. Koiziumi also continued efforts to gain permanent membership for Japan on the UN Security Council.

In 2001 as well, with the founding of the Bo'ao Forum for Asia, China implicitly claimed the role of leader of Asian development, displacing Japan from its self-appointed position as leader of the V-shaped formation of geese flying toward a modern, industrialized future. In what might have been regarded a tacit acceptance of this, Prime Minister Koizumi attended. METI's 2002 white paper on manufacturing reported that about half of Japanese companies predicted that within five years, the technology level of not only China but also other nations in the region would be on a par with Japan; 17 percent believed the PRC had already reached this level.[35]

In 2004 the conservative *Sankei Shimbun* opined that Japan was increasingly coming to regard China as a geopolitical rival.[36] Although the primary arena of competition was economic, as seen in the sports and space competition examples above, the feeling of losing out in rivalry with China was spread across many other areas as well. In 1987 *The Japan Times* lamented the fact that the country was lagging behind in the number of places chosen as world historical areas.[37] A few years later, *Yomiuri Shimbun* announced proudly, if defensively, that the discovery of a 12,000-year-old Jōmon pottery had "overcome[e] the strong feeling most Japanese have had that everything old about Japan's culture came from mainland China."[38] The unearthing of the ancient Fujiwara-kyō was likewise described as indicating that it was "larger than any city in China or Korea at the same time."[39] It was also noticed that fewer foreign students were opting to study Japanese, preferring instead to learn Chinese.[40] And that Chinese students studied much harder than their Japanese counterparts.[41]

As Chinese awareness of the change in relative power relations rose, so did anti-Japanese feelings, which surfaced in various incidents. When a young Chinese actress appeared in a skirt made of material depicting Japan's wartime flag—albeit the creation of a foreign designer—she was pilloried in the social media and accused of being a traitor. The same was said of a Chinese actor when it was learned that he was being considered for a role involving the Yasukuni Shrine. A few intellectuals such as Ma Licheng and Shi Yinhong argued against such reactions, calling for new thinking on Sino-Japanese relations. Since Japan was in decline, they pointed out, there was no longer reason to fear it.

In Ma and Shi's view, vindictive feelings were unbecoming to a great power. China should understand that it was natural for Japanese to be upset about the reversal in power relations; while rising to the top, the PRC should cultivate peaceful foreign relations and domestic stability, and keep a low profile, *taoguang yanghui*, while it gained strength. Their voices were quickly drowned out by angry nationalists saying that Japan was responsible for the rise of anti-Japanese sentiments and there was no need for the PRC to be gentler toward or more embracing of it.[42]

As Ma predicted, he and other proponents of the "new thinking on Japan" were attacked and their ideas receded from the public discourse. In Japan, apprehension grew, with the Japan Defense Agency's 2002 white paper indicating that it saw China as a military threat. The two countries vied for leadership in Southeast Asia, with the PRC easily besting Japan in the competition to set up free trade agreements (FTAs) due to the ability of Japan's powerful agricultural lobby to block them. A frustrated METI official commented that the purpose of FTAs was to form alliances: should Japan continue to fail to create them, the area would be dominated by China. He also observed that Sino-Japanese competition gave the countries that each side negotiated with leverage to maneuver against each other.[43]

Although Chinese state councilor and former foreign minister Tang Jiaxuan told visiting Social Democratic Party leader Doi Takako that China accepted Japan's becoming a political power,[44] no official actions corroborated this. A typical Chinese comment was that

> Japan has always been watching China's rapid development within its own political standard. In fact, Japan does not sincerely embrace China as a rising regional power. By now, Japan still regards itself as the most important country in Asia. In diplomatic language, Japan repeats again and again that it welcomes China's reform and development and is willing to participate in China's modernization. Yet these words represent only Japan's sense of superiority. That is why Japan stresses that it is the most important part of the West (the second world economic power) and Japan is the only Asian country to join the G8 club.[45]

The two competed for energy supplies, allowing Moscow to play one off against the other for Russia's benefit, something both sides realized.[46] An internationally respected columnist for the generally China-friendly *Asahi Shimbun* remarked that "China acts and Japan reacts. Now we are losing the oil race."[47] A series of ugly incidents, sometimes seemingly government-encouraged, involving such triggers as sports events, textbooks, student skits, and the conduct of Japanese businessmen that Chinese found offensive, began to occur with regularity. In October 2005 the PRC launched *Shenzhou 6*, its second manned space mission, into orbit.[48]

With a candor rare among diplomats, then Deputy Foreign Minister Yachi Shōtarō stated that neither China nor Japan was willing to acknowledge that they were struggling for leadership and locked in a rivalry that would last a long time.[49] While the rivalry spread across many fields and regions, a particular focus was Southeast Asia. Singapore's *Straits Times* reported that, though it had largely escaped international attention, the region had become yet another theater of contention for China and Japan, already enmeshed in several other bilateral disputes. One of these theaters is the Greater Mekong Sub-region (GMS), an organization supported by the Asian Development Bank and several other regional donors as well as Japan. It comprises two provincial-level Chinese divisions, each of which sends a representative, and five contiguous Southeast Asian states. At a 2005 meeting of the GMS, most of the fifty-odd foreign journalists covering the summit were Japanese nationals, even though no Japanese officials were present. Very much present and active was China's then premier Wen Jiabao as well as the leaders of other participating countries. Nonetheless, Japanese development loans totaling over 27 billion yen were funding a 1,500-kilometer east–west highway from Da Nang in Vietnam to Mawlamyine (Moulmein) in Myanmar. At the same time, an undisclosed sum from China was underwriting a 2,500-kilometer north–south highway from Kunming, capital of Yunnan, to Bangkok.[50]

When Burma upgraded its national telephone systems from analog to digital, it changed from Japanese to Chinese technology; Japan was also lagging behind China in getting contract approvals from the Myanmar government. Although Japan remained the largest trading partner and investor in neighboring Thailand, Chinese investors were moving into more sectors of the economy. Whereas twenty years ago, the foreign language many Thais were trying to learn was Japanese, it was now Chinese.[51]

The South Pacific also became an area of concern. Shortly after Beijing presided over a Pacific Islands forum in Fiji, Tokyo hosted a two-day summit of presidents and prime ministers in Tokyo. The stated aim of this, the fourth Pacific Island forum Japan had sponsored, was to enhance sustainable development and security in the region. However, according to the Voice of America, competition with China was evident behind the scenes.[52]

Central Asia, rich in mineral resources, was avidly courted by both sides. Beijing made much of the area being China's "back door" and the route of the ancient Silk Road. Japan emphasized its generous loans, expertise in mining and other technology,[53] and also practiced "sumo diplomacy." The quintessentially Japanese sport is particularly popular in Mongolia, several of whose nationals have reached the highest rank of *yokozuna*. As an unnamed Japanese official commented to a Hong Kong newspaper, "Of course, China's role and ambitions feed into that thinking. We can't ignore that."[54]

Africa also received increased attention. It was noted that Chinese trade with the continent totaled $40 billion in 2005, up 36 percent year on year, whereas African-Japanese trade was only $18 billion, with a concomitant gain in Chinese influence.[55] To counter this, and despite the strenuous budget-cutting measures then being taken by the financially stressed Tokyo government, the foreign ministry received additional funding of 450 million yen to build seven new embassies, three of them in Africa and another in Micronesia, to raise Japan's diplomatic profile in those areas.[56]

According to the Organisation for Economic Co-operation and Development (OECD), in 2006, China surpassed Japan to become the world's second largest funder of research and development, investing $136 billion to the latter's $130 billion. There had also been a marked increase in the number of patents granted to China.[57]

The official attitude in China was to be dismissive of the manifestations of anti-Japanese sentiment, the advances China was making into traditional Japanese markets, and the sustained increases in its defense budgets. The "China threat" had been manufactured by right-wing Japanese extremists to provide an excuse for the re-militarization of their country. A few months after unruly soccer fans vented their anger over Japan's victory in a match with China, Sun Ling, a scholar at the Institute of Japan Studies at the Chinese Academy of Social Sciences, argued that Japan's sense of crisis was purely imaginary. In truth, the security environment in East Asia was relatively relaxed. Japan enjoyed a "consolidated status" as the world's second-largest economy. Although its military had only 250,000 members, they were technologically advanced, well equipped, and well trained. As an important ally of the world's sole superpower, the Japanese homeland and "so-called neighboring areas" were covered by the umbrella of the United States-Japan security alliance. Therefore, no threat to Japan's security existed. In what was almost certainly meant to be reassuring but could also be read as an assertion of the Middle Kingdom mentality, Sun closed by saying that "the reality is that China has never regarded any country as a rival."[58]

In a thoughtful essay, Professor Shi Yinhong of Renmin University distinguished between the immediate causes of Sino-Japanese tension, meaning demonstrations and riots occasioned by particular events such as conciliatory gestures to Taiwan, Prime Minister Koizumi's visits to the Yasukuni Shrine, and what he termed remote causes. He attributed the latter to a dual change in the structure of power relations (*quanshi guanxi jiegou*) between the two, with strong emotional dynamics interacting with the power dynamic induced by the change in relative strength between them. Particularly since the beginning of 2004, "due to the urgent desire to make Japan an 'equal' and 'normal' political power, there has been strong resistance to China's rise. The Japanese government generally refrained from taking the initial step of offering major concessions in political and strategic disputes. Hence, many major political and strategic disputes erupted, almost none of which could be resolved in the foreseeable future. In fact, every one of them seems to be deteriorating progressively."[59]

Again, some voices in China dissented from the view that Japan was at fault. In a lengthy commentary entitled "Are We Demonizing Japan?" from a *Xinhua* forum that was broadcast by Hong Kong's Phoenix TV, author Ai Xin argued that, whereas the Western media, and especially the U.S. media, were demonizing China, Chinese were demonizing Japan. Citing a lengthy list of extreme statements, he asked what had happened to the sensitive Japanese films and books that had seemed so attractive to Chinese only a few years ago. Why was it that Chinese in Hong Kong and in Taiwan had an open-minded attitude toward Japanese, while only those in the mainland condemned them mercilessly? Ai Xin answered the question: "We have become a bully toward a country whose national strength has grown smaller. We do it to build our often fragile national confidence. Must we act like a rags-to-riches ruffian?" The author closed by asking his compatriots to reflect on this, asking if China were drifting toward moral corruption.[60] Any speculation that Ai Xin's views might indicate a softening of official attitudes was short-lived. Shortly thereafter, *Freezing Point*, a weekly magazine associated with the China Youth Daily, was suspended and its editorial staff replaced when it published an article noting that, although Japan was criticized for distorting history, Chinese textbooks did so as well.[61]

The end of Koizumi's term in office in 2006 was followed by another round of weak Japanese prime ministers, with incumbents averaging only a year in office apiece. Each promised to establish better relations but, after brief periods that appeared to herald a better relationship—for example, efforts to try to develop a common view of history—were unable to do so, and a preliminary agreement to share the resources of a disputed oil field that could not be finalized, all failed.

As China's need for Japanese expertise abated, Beijing's attitude hardened and nationalist voices in Japan grew stronger. In China, confidence rose while morale in Japan declined in tandem with indicators in measurable areas of decline. In 2007 the Bank of China announced that the country's foreign exchange reserves had surpassed those of Japan to become the largest in the world.[62]

Official declarations that China and Japan should not be rivals since they shared responsibility for the integration of Asia were not accompanied by accomplishments that indicated a desire for cooperation to this end. Chinese media tended to dwell on Japan's resentment that it was losing its competitive edge to China. A military journal said bluntly that China would not accept Japan as the leader of Asia, and that if Japan wanted to play an important part in the region, it would need Chinese help,[63] thus clearly indicating that Japan would play a subordinate role.

Taking note of the disparity between the size of Japan and that of China, and the fact that the nation's population was shrinking at the same time as it was aging, some Japanese were inclined to accept a lesser role for their country. Japan could become a lifestyle great power, *seikatsu taikoku*, rather than an economic great power, *keizai taikoku*. Soft power was a more attractive alternative to hard power, making use of the international popularity of its manga, anime, cuisine, architecture, and haute couture.[64]

In early 2006 the foreign ministry allocated an additional 1.16 billion yen for a fund specifically aimed at improving its image in China. The fund would underwrite the cost of distributing selected animated series and Japanese popular songs, known as J-pop, to provincial broadcasters.[65] Nearly 2 billion yen was allocated for the promotion of soft power generally; English-language newspapers began to carry regular columns like "Cool Japan," and covered new anime and manga productions in more detail. Citing the more than 200 Confucius Institutes that Beijing had established over the preceding four years and the fact that junior and senior high schools in the United States were switching foreign-language classes from Japanese to Chinese, Tokyo announced plans for a tenfold increase in the number of Japanese-language instruction facilities abroad, from 10 to 100.[66]

How effective these efforts would be was problematic. Referring to the promotion of Japanese soft power globally, Singaporean sources pointed out that Japan faced competition not only from China but from South Korean soft power as well.[67] The pageantry of the opening and closing ceremonies of the 2008 Beijing Olympics, orchestrated by one of China's leading filmmakers who had only recently been the target of censors, was watched by tens of millions around the world, as was the meticulously executed 2015 parade to commemorate the 70th anniversary of the country's victory over Japan in World War II. A Japanese company employee expressed concern that the railway being constructed along the border with North Korea would drastically change the flow of goods in the northeast, adding that Japanese companies "could not ignore" the implications thereof.[68] Nor did the implications of Xi Jinping's "one belt one road" overland and maritime reimagined Silk Roads.

For many Japanese, even successful soft power was insufficient. They were determined to resist, intensifying complaints from China that Japan was trying to hold it back. This attitude was epitomized by an end-of-2015 article by the international correspondent for the generally pro-China *Asahi*: "China Outpacing Japan Arouses the Patriot in Me." Summarizing a list of Chinese triumphs over his country in trade deals, air, space, and defense, the journalist concluded that, although Japanese have been comfortable with chasing after the United States and European nations since the dawn of the Meiji era, "our hearts, by comparison, cannot remain calm when China is pulling ahead of us in anything."[69] Interestingly, and despite Beijing's opposition to allowing Japan a permanent seat on the United Nations Security Council, Japanese do not seem to have complained that China was trying to hold back Japan.

Small but collectively meaningful slights accumulated, as when former Singaporean prime minister Lee Kwan Yew, speaking at a meeting to commemorate the 40th anniversary of the Association of Southeast Asian Nations (ASEAN), spoke of the rise of China but failed to even mention Japan.[70] The same year, and even more humiliating, the Swiss-based International Institute's 2007 World Competitiveness Index ranked China above Japan for the first time, raising the PRC to 15th among the top fifty-five, while dropping Japan eight places to 24th.[71]

Japan's fears of marginalization were magnified as the United States also seemed to be turning away from it and toward China. Addressing this question directly and offering China integration into global institutions as a responsible stakeholder,[72] Harvard professor and former U.S. Assistant Secretary of Defense Joseph Nye provided two reasons that America should not abandon Japan in favor of China: their common democratic values and the challenge both countries face from China's rise, to assure that it did not become a threat. Nye advocated a policy that combined liberal and realist approaches: reinforcing the U.S.-Japan alliance while offering China integration into global institutions as a responsible stakeholder.[73]

Part of Nye's formula, however, meant considering Chinese membership in the G8,[74] meaning that Japan would lose its position as the group's only

Asian member. Hence, Tokyo was not pleased with then French President Nicolas Sarkozy's plan to expand the group. It remained a sore point that despite generous contributions to the United Nations, Japan had been unable to obtain permanent membership on the UN Security Council. Yet four of the five permanent seats on the body—all but China's—are held by G8 members.

Then chief cabinet secretary Machimura Nobutaka pointed out that the group started as a gathering of mature advanced democracies—which, although he refrained from explicitly saying so, Russia was not. Nor, were the PRC to be included, would it be.[75] In yet another blow to Japanese pride, President Obama himself announced Jon Huntsman's appointment as his administration's envoy to Beijing, but left notification of John Roos's assignment to Tokyo to an impersonal statement.[76]

Noting that the United States itself seemed to be in a state of decline whereas China was rising, some Japanese analysts advocated moving away from the United States to a position of equidistance as a better option. This view became more prominent when in 2009 the Democratic Party of Japan (DPJ) replaced the more America-friendly LDP as the ruling party. Newly elected Prime Minister Hatoyama Yukio stated his desire for the country to act as a bridge between the Orient and Occident, clearly having the United States and China in mind.[77] To that end, he advocated an East Asian Community (EAC) that excluded the United States, and also declared his intention to end bases on Okinawa. In an interview with London's *Financial Times*, Foreign Minister Okada Katsuya stated bluntly that under the LDP, his country's foreign policy had become excessively dependent on Washington.[78]

While Beijing responded warmly to the DPJ's overtures, concrete gestures that would indicate an easing of tension did not follow. The Chinese leadership may have sensed that Hatoyama's initiative was less than it seemed. A cable from the U.S. Embassy in Tokyo to Washington that was released by Wikileaks assessed the real intent of the EAC as an effort to "lock" China in by encouraging Beijing to abide by international norms and "encircle" it by strengthening ties with Asian neighbors. The DPJ itself, the cable continued, was divided on the initiative to China, with some favoring Hatoyama's initiatives as a way to curb China's growing regional influence and others favoring a more hard-line stance that included opposition to the PRC's human rights record, and support for Taiwan's entry into international organization. The Japanese public's position on sovereignty-related issues, as well as ongoing concerns about China's food and safety record, would further constrain Hatoyama's efforts.[79] In any event, the results were meager.

In hindsight, 2010 may have been an inflection point. This was the year in which it was announced that the Chinese economy would soon pass Japan's to become second largest in the world. Friendly overtures to Beijing did not seem to be reciprocated and, in fact, China's actions during the year indicated a hardening of Beijing's attitude. These included Foreign Minister Yang Jiechi's anger at a meeting with Okada in May when the latter brought up the issue of the PRC's expanding nuclear arsenal; Yang's strident rebuff at an ASEAN meeting during the summer with regard to a suggestion that territorial disputes should be settled through negotiation; and the September collision between a Chinese fishing boat and two Japanese coast guard ships. The net effect was to stiffen positions on both sides as well as undercutting support for the DPJ's more accommodating stance.

In Japan, the widespread perception that the government had badly mishandled the ship collision incident led to a nationalist effort to force it to buy the islands. This, in turn, stoked Chinese nationalism into riots in 2012, even though the Beijing leadership must have been aware that the purchase was simply a domestic transfer of ownership that had no effect on the sovereignty issue. Japanese voters turned the DPJ out of office in favor of a far more conservative government. Beijing increased patrolling around the disputed islands, and declared an Air Defense Identification Zone (ADIZ) around the area, with Tokyo responding that its military aircraft would not comply with the ADIZ regulations. It also sought a closer defense relationship with the United States, commenced exercises to train marines in retaking islands, and prepared to station troops on nearby islands.

Although a stimulus-response-stimulus pattern in postwar Sino-Japanese relations has been ongoing, the intervals between confrontations have become shorter, positions more intransigent, and the probability of reaching compromises progressively reduced. Tension seemed to have become the default mode for bilateral relations. Both Beijing and Tokyo are aware of the horrendous cost that war would bring to themselves as well as the other side, yet neither wants to surrender its position. Although a partial emollient, the trade relationship has fallen short of the integrating function initially hoped for, generated frictions of its own, and, as characterized by one analyst, "helping little to alleviate tensions in other troubled areas of the bilateral relationship."[80]

The two sides can cooperate and compromise, as evidenced by the successful conclusion of the 1978 Peace and Friendship Treaty and, albeit briefly, by the 2008 agreement on oil field sharing. More optimistic observers believe that they can also develop a common view of history, though others are dubious. When asked about this, Singapore's prime minister is said to have laughed aloud and pronounced agreement "impossible. On one side, nothing has been forgotten and, on the other, nothing is remembered."[81] This is not quite true: the Chinese side has forgotten much about its own history, as several of its nationals agree.[82] Cases in point include the PRC's 2015 celebration of a mythical version of World War II, and its continued silence on such unflattering topics as the Great Leap Forward–induced famine of 1958 and the slaughter of unarmed civilians at Tiananmen in 1989. A correspondent with many years residence in the PRC titled her book *The People's Republic of Amnesia*.[83]

In Japan, nationalists have been able to rework history in ways that are inimical to the development of a common view. Though the major issue of Japanese aggression cannot be doubted, research, much of it done by non-Japanese, has cast doubt on the Chinese account of the Marco Polo Bridge incident,[84] on which nation bore responsibility for actually starting the war,[85] on the comfort women,[86] and on the number of casualties of the Nanjing Massacre,[87] though not on the occurrence of the massacre itself. Factual accuracy notwithstanding, they have had no noticeable effect in modifying the Chinese narrative of the war.

On the issue of the disputed islands, it is possible that, with a certain amount of forbearance, each side can abide by what a retired Japanese diplomat characterized as a tacit agreement not to land on the islands, conduct research on them, or build on them.[88] On the other hand, in a discussion on protecting the islands from Chinese encroachment, a Japanese Coast Guard authority told the author that he had never heard of such an agreement.[89] Assuming the agreement does exist, expecting adherence to it is problematic, since China's salami tactics appear to be reducing Tokyo's control. If conflict should break out, Beijing will be in a better position that it otherwise would have been; if it does not, it will have incrementally gained much of what it sought without a fight.

Negotiating any agreement will be compounded by the perception that one power is rising and another declining. Assuming that the rising power will continue to rise and the other continue to decline—which is not a given—time is on the side of the rising power. Yet mutual acceptance of equality will be crucial to the success of negotiations to resolve problems. This will be difficult in view of the longstanding feelings of superiority/inferiority on both sides. Perhaps recalling the traditional Chinese wisdom that a mountain does not accommodate two tigers, Singapore's then senior minister Lee Kwan Yew warned the 1997 Shangri-La gathering that "this region has never at the same time experienced both a strong China and a strong Japan."[90]

While, with the exception of the period from the late nineteenth to mid-twentieth century, it was Japan that felt inferior, suspicions of inadequacy are not absent in China, even today. In a thoughtful interview with a Japanese paper, the highly regarded dean of Beijing University's School of International Relations described a "very interesting combination of superiority and inferiority. On the one hand, some people say we are stronger than before, China is a rising power, and China may dominate the world in the future. On the other hand, when unpleasant things happen, they say China is being humiliated and still a victim of world politics." He was not optimistic that insecurities could be resolved: "This kind of complexity and ambivalence will last almost forever." [91]

As adherents to the constructivist paradigm of international relations argue, national images are not immutable: states can change their perceptions of each other and, consequently, their behavior. Speaking abstractly, the problems that exist between China and Japan are capable of resolution; it is possible that the world's second and third largest economies can, as their ceremonial rhetoric has repeatedly proclaimed, work together for the peace and prosperity of all.

Currently, the determination to do so does not appear to exist. Given the unlikelihood that problems can be resolved, it may be more realistic to hope that they can be managed. The two can cooperate on issues such as energy, health, and environmental issues, as well as increase people-to-people contacts. The question is whether this will be enough. Or whether they will be able to find ways to encourage cooperation in other spheres.

Both sides are aware that the losses of a conflict are likely to outweigh the benefits, even to the victor, and that the tyranny of geography makes it impossible to escape each other. Insofar as emotions allow a rational guide to policy, an uncomfortable peace is preferable to armed conflict. Much depends on the two nations' ability to control tensions, alleviate periodic crises, and maintain basic stability. If the will can be developed, there may be a way. In the words of an ancient Chinese proverb, *qiēcuōzhuómó*: stones that cannot escape each other rub each other smooth.

12

Epilogue

MANAGING A FRAGILE RELATIONSHIP

Three years after the hardback version of this book went to press, an uneasy calm had settled over Sino-Japanese relations. There were no pyrotechnics, but neither was there discernible progress in resolving the issues between them. The Japanese government continued to press for a summit, even as the Chinese government held fast to its conditions that Japan do more to atone for its conduct in World War II and admit that the status of the Diaoyu/Senkaku islands was contested.

This did not prevent periodic high-level meetings from occurring on the sidelines of multinational gatherings, although press reports of the content of the conversations were not enlightening. There was no mention of substantive issues and many bland anodynes such as the two looking forward to the commemoration of the normalization of relations in 1972 or the anniversary of the Japan-China Treaty of Peace and Friendship of 1978, and agreeing, albeit abstractly, on such matters as the need to deal with North Korean nuclear proliferation, to cooperate on clean energy, and to "promote productive discussions and manage pending issues in an appropriate manner." Or they spoke past each other in code: the Japanese side typically mentioning the need to control national emotion and sentiment, thus hinting at the Chinese government's role in instigating anti-Japanese feelings, and the Chinese side reiterating the need to remember history and learn from it, its standard request for deeper apologies about Japan's conduct in World War II.

The media of each country tended to describe the meetings differently: the Chinese press took pains to say that the Japanese side had requested the meeting, while the Japanese media generally either did not mention how it had taken place or, in the case of the 2016 Asia-Pacific Economic Cooperation (APEC) meeting in Lima, that Prime Minister Abe Shinzō and President Xi Jinping had "stepped a couple of paces toward each other" after a group meeting of the 21 leaders in "a natural movement." Official photographs showed the two looking stiff, but nothing like the pained faces of the much-remarked-on picture from the 2014 APEC meeting.

Just below the top level, diplomatic interchanges could be more testy. At a meeting of the foreign ministers of ASEAN, Kono Tarō voiced his opposition to unilateral attempts to change the status quo based on military power and endorsed the U.S. freedom of navigation exercises in areas where sovereignty was contested. His counterpart, Wang Yi, responded by calling Konō's remarks "completely like a mission the United States has assigned to you," and contrasting Konō unfavorably with his father, a previous foreign minister, who had been "an honest politician." Konō replied by suggesting that China "learn how to behave like a big power."

TWO STRONG LEADERS SOLIDIFY THEIR INTERNAL POSITIONS

Xi Jinping and Abe consolidated their leadership positions domestically in nearly simultaneous political events. A brief early 2017 flurry of high-level dissent against Xi's centralizing too much power in his person ended rather quickly. In mid-October 2017, the 19th Congress of the Central Committee of the Chinese Communist Party (CCP) not only confirmed a second five-year term for Xi, but amended the party's constitution to give him a status hitherto reserved for Mao Zedong alone. His "Xi Jinping Thought on Socialism with Chinese Characteristics for a New Era" was elevated to parity with Chairman Mao's oeuvre and far above the accords given to the three intervening party secretaries, even including Deng Xiaoping, the architect of China's reforms. Deng is memorialized only for his "theory," and the names of his two successors are not mentioned at all.

Because age limits preclude any member of the new Standing Committee of the Politburo, from which party heads are typically chosen, from succeeding Xi, there is talk that he intends to stay on for an unprecedented third term.

A week later, a snap election in Japan gave Abe a supermajority in the Diet, with voter turnout unexpectedly high despite driving rains that heralded a typhoon. As anticipated, Abe announced that he now had a mandate to change the constitution, and that doing so would be a centerpiece of his 2018 legislative agenda. Chinese media noted resistance from both the Japanese public at large and from opposition parties. With opposition parties in disarray, the latter were not expected to be a major obstacle. Disagreements within Abe's Liberal Democratic Party (LDP) over the exact wording of the changes are, however, liable to be substantial. Abe, already one of Japan's longest-serving prime ministers, is likewise thought to be interested in serving for a third term. The two cases are not quite comparable, of course, since the Japanese prime minister and his party must stand for election, while Xi and the CCP do not. And three-term prime ministers, though uncommon in recent Japanese history, are not unprecedented.

POLICY IMPLICATIONS

With each leader seemingly firmly in control in his respective country, one might argue either that this freed them to negotiate a breakthrough or that it enabled them to take a hard line toward the other side. The signals were mixed. Chinese media continued to snipe at Japan, noting with no trace of regret the failure of its mission to clear space junk, and reporting in detail about the difficulties encountered by sundry Japanese companies, charging that the country's traditional shame culture was being replaced by a "falsification culture."

There was no diminution of the familiar theme of Japanese unwillingness to acknowledge, and make amends for, its behavior in World War II. Sirens sounded in many Chinese cities on September 18th, to mark the anniversary of the 1931 Mukden Incident. In December 2017, a series of major events marked the 80th anniversary of the Nanjing Massacre. In the weeks before what has been a national holiday since 2014, a documentary recounting the atrocities in graphic detail, modern dramas, and traditional Chinese operas with appropriate themes were staged; and testimonial meetings were held in which relatives of survivors shared family stories of the horror. Flags flew at half-staff as monks from China, Japan, and South Korea chanted prayers for the victims. Xi Jinping attended the formal ceremony but, strangely, did not give a speech.

THE ECONOMIC COMPETITION

The Japanese economy continued its longest continuous streak of growth since 2006 with the inflation rate rising slightly, giving hope that Abenomics was finally lifting the economy out of more than a quarter century of stagnation. In the first trading day of 2018, the Nikkei closed above 27,000 for the first time in 26 years. Still, GDP grew at less than 2 percent, and there were other problems: electronics giant Toshiba registered record losses, eventually agreeing to sell its semiconductor subsidiary to a consortium comprising its U.S. business partner Western Digital and two Japanese government-backed funds. An earlier feeler from a Chinese company had raised national security concerns. Issues of quality control at airbag manufacturer Takata and Nissan Motors as well as Kobe Steel's admission that it had falsified product data threatened to tarnish the country's reputation for meticulous production standards. Additionally, a population that was aging and declining in numbers did not bode well for the future.

The Chinese economy, though slowing to what Xi Jinping referred to as "the new normal," nonetheless grew at official figures in the mid-6-percent range. Chinese economists pointed out, however, that growth figures were being artificially inflated and were unsustainable; postponing the inevitable crash could only make it more severe. In 2017, international credit rating agencies Moody's and Standard & Poor separately downgraded China, with the former saying it expected the financial strength of the economy to continue to erode and the latter lowering its outlook from positive to negative. China's finance ministry accused the ratings agencies of using "inappropriate methodology" and underestimating the resilience of the PRC's economy. Nonetheless, in the midst of Xi Jinping's triumphant moment at the 19th Party Congress, Zhou Xiaochuan, the highly respected governor of China's central bank, warned of a "Minsky moment": a sudden collapse of asset prices after a long period of growth that is sparked by debt or currency pressures. In China, local government debt is worrisomely large and getting worse, household debt is rising quickly, and corporate debt levels are high. China, is facing the end of its demographic dividend of young people willing to work for low wages. Like Japan, it has an aging population, but one that has a much lower per capita income level than that of Japan.

Bilateral trade was strong, with demand from China for such high-value products as industrial robots, construction machinery, and smartphone components being an important factor offsetting declining sales of vehicles and electronics following a rise in the PRC's consumption tax. Uniqlo, one of Japan's most iconic clothing brands, now has more stores in China than in Japan. Trade had its frictions, as when China Central Television charged, erroneously, that food from the radiation-contaminated Tohoku area was being sold in local supermarkets. The lucrative tourist trade also caused problems: Japanese found the deportment of many Chinese visitors upsetting, and, more seriously, several ancient temples were found to have been deliberately defaced by two Chinese tourists.

On a macro level, Japanese leaders debated the wisdom of joining the China-led Asian Infrastructure Development Bank (AIIB) and whether to participate in its ambitious One Belt One Road (OBOR) economic development plan. The warmth of American President Donald Trump's reception of Xi Jinping at Mar-a-Lago revived old fears of "Japan passing" among some Japanese, who worried that the United States and China might form a G-2 condominium to the exclusion of Japan. Chinese analysts were generally cynical of Japanese motives, some believing that the Tokyo government wanted to try to control the AIIB from inside and that participation in OBOR was a desperation move representing the country's last hope to extricate itself from the mire of continued economic decline. Foreign commentators opined that, unsure of its options after the United States had withdrawn from the Trans-Pacific Partnership, Japan felt a greater need for cooperation with China.

Doubts about the wisdom of this course persist. Japanese analysts are not convinced by Beijing's assurances that the AIIB does not seek to compete with the Asian Development Bank, in which Japan has been the major player. And the Japanese government has made plain that its participation in OBOR would not support upgrades to the Pakistani port of Gwadar, where China has a military base, and that its commitment to helping Kenya to develop the port of Mombasa was in order to avoid having PRC ships enter the port.

DEFENSE

Each side continued to express apprehension over the other's military preparations. In 2017, China's official defense budget, believed to substantially understate the actual figure, dropped from double-digit growth to about 7 percent, although that was still in excess of the rise in the country's GDP. China continued fortifying the artificial islands it had built from reefs in the South China Sea, and constructing military bases at Gwadar in Pakistan and Obock in Djibouti, both of which are of considerable strategic importance. The Chinese military continues to make advances in technology that include testing hypersonic glide vehicles and cruise missiles. Japanese sources also reported cyberhacking attacks believed to have emanated from China.

Japanese defense specialists, while acknowledging these impressive advances, seemed more concerned with the PRC's cabbage strategy of slowly encircling and in essence osmosing the territories disputed between them. Japanese fishermen have complained that they dare not fish in the areas, and that overfishing by Chinese boats was depleting their catches elsewhere. According to the country's defense ministry, Chinese government ships had entered the waters contiguous to the Senkaku/Diaoyu Islands more than a thousand times since late 2012. At one point, they were accompanied by a drone.

Responding to expressions of Japanese concern, CCTV accused the Abe administration of playing up the increased passage of Chinese air force planes through the Miyako Strait and circling Taiwan air space in order to divert attention from the country's poor economy and domestic scandals while encouraging support for change in the constitution and higher defense budgets. The "new normalized training" would include an increase in the frequency of training, a change in the area of training to beyond the first island chain, and more intense training and methods. Neighboring countries "should be prepared" for such changes. In December 2017, Chinese air force planes flew through the Strait of Tsushima for the first time, conducting drills in the Sea of Japan. Xinhua explained these as intended to improve the air force's maneuvering capabilities. Observing that there had been interference from another country's aircraft, the press agency pointed out that, since Tsushima is considered an international waterway, its flights conformed to the strictures of the United National

Convention on the Law of the Sea. In a first for the Russian military, it exercised with Chinese forces in the Sea of Okhotsk, off Japan's northernmost island of Hokkaido.

Japan's defense budget also increased, albeit by far more modest increments: 1.5 percent for 2017. The Ministry of Defense is reportedly mulling refitting its largest helicopter destroyers to carry short takeoff and landing (STOVL) planes, in effect transforming the ships into aircraft carriers. Japanese left-of-center forces object, saying that doing so will mean the end of Japan's defense-only military, with PRC media enthusiastically endorsing their opinions. The Japanese coast guard has received enhanced funding to deal with China's much larger coast guard vessels, and Ishigaki City, which administers the Diaoyu/Senkaku Islands, proposes to change the names of areas to include "Senkaku" to emphasize its ownership. The Chinese foreign ministry responded that this would not change China's irrefutable claim to ownership, and warned that it could only hurt the improvement of bilateral relations.

The Japanese government has also negotiated a lease to expand a small base it established at Djibouti in 2011; the current facility does not provide docking for ships, though it does provide access to a joint civilian/military-use airport as well as access to the American, French, and Italian expeditionary bases. Tokyo also made efforts to solidify ties with the other major players in the region—India, Australia, and the United States—to create an informal quadrilateral against the PRC's advances. The Chinese press has described such efforts as an attempt to preserve the group's hegemony, reframed as "the rules-based international order, on the pretext of supporting a peaceful and stable Indo-Pacific."

TAIWAN

As predicted in Chapter 10, the victory of Taiwan's Democratic Progressive Party (DPP) began a warming trend in bilateral relations with Japan that irritated China. A few weeks after the election, the Japanese government changed the name of its quasi-official organization for handling relations with Taiwan from the Taipei Economic and Cultural Office to the Japan-Taiwan Exchange Organization, with a parallel adjustment from the Taiwan side. The Chinese foreign ministry lodged an immediate protest, warning Japan against "sending any wrong message to the Taiwan authorities or the international community and causing new interference in Sino-Japanese ties." Japan and Taiwan are also cooperating in search-and-rescue training.

Beijing also objected strenuously to the annual report of Japan's National Institute for Defense Studies (NIDS). Among other criticisms mentioned at a Chinese Foreign Ministry press briefing, the report had treated Taiwan as a political entity similar to that of China and had furthermore referred to Taiwan under its formal name, the Republic of China. According to a source in the Japanese Foreign Ministry, the Chinese government had received an advance text of the report and stated its objections, but was told that the wording of the NIDS report was not the government's official opinion. It was published without change. The Chinese government also reacted badly to a simulated defense exercise in which American and Japanese forces fought against an invasion of Taiwan, calling it "gross interference in China's domestic affairs that fomented intentional strife in cross-strait relations, especially defense relations" and warning that such "tricks" would harm others—clearly meaning Taiwan—as well as Japan.

THE FUTURE OUTLOOK

There have been several hopeful signs. Xi Jinping's not making a speech at the commemorative for the Nanjing Massacre can be construed as positive, as has the fact that Abe neither visited the Yasukuni Shrine in December 2017 nor sent his traditional masasaki offering. In the same month, Chinese and Japanese negotiators reached a tentative agreement designed to avoid clashes in the Diaoyu/Senkaku area, though the details have not been finalized and Japanese officials have voiced concerns that China might interpret the agreement as giving the PRC a legitimate right to approach the islands.

However, the sum total of recent developments does not bode well for a breakthrough. Abe's eagerness for a summit meeting has surely provided Xi with leverage in continuing to insist that such a meeting can take place only if Beijing's conditions are met. Since they have not been, Xi has tacitly precluded a summit by declaring his willingness to enhance better ties through party-to-party diplomacy. Typically this has meant invitations to opposition party leaders and to LDP members known to be favorable to China---in other words, not empowered to negotiate on behalf of the government. It is also likely that Beijing would demand an additional communique as a quid pro quo, presumably including an affirmation that the Tokyo government recognizes China's claim to Taiwan. Capitulation on this point would bring the PRC's territorial waters uncomfortably near to Japan as well as angering the United States, meaning that it is highly unlikely. In sum, the best that can reasonably be hoped for is a continuation of the present uneasy calm.

Acknowledgments

This book grew out of my efforts to understand the delicate and often fraught relations between what are now the world's second and third largest economies. Ironically, the topic was first suggested to me by my husband as a dissertation topic way back when—perhaps he is even now thinking, correctly, that it took me long enough. But how different the position of the two countries seems now than they were three decades ago.

I have many people to thank for their help in the course of the decade-plus that I have been working on the issue. First and foremost, to the librarians of the University of Miami who processed what must have seemed an endless stream of interlibrary loan requests for microfilms and hard copies of newspapers and documents in unfamiliar languages. Student workers cheerfully trundled back and forth heavy boxes of periodicals that had been consigned to off-campus storage facilities. A Cooper Fellowship, grant from the Center for Humanities, and a sabbatical leave freed me from teaching for several semesters and enabled trips to Beijing, Shanghai, and Tokyo for interviews. Those who graciously shared their thoughts with me are cited where possible, though most individuals interviewed requested anonymity.

I also profited from conversations with others doing research on related topics. Listservs of China and Japan watchers introduced me electronically to those I call e-quaintances. Steve Tsang generously shared his research on Chiang Kai-shek; Gerrit van der Wees suggested Dutch sources for the chapter on Taiwan, even supplying translations for relevant passages; Ogihara Mitsunori guided me through the nuances of some particularly opaque, to me, Japanese sources. I have additionally learned much from the work of Jim Holmes, Toshi Yoshihara, Yu Maochun, Sally Paine, Bruce Elleman, my late husband Edward L. Dreyer, Ed Friedman, Don Keyser, Arthur Waldron, and the many others whose books and articles I have cited. As well as from the comments of several anonymous readers. Stephen Halsey supplied much-needed optimism and an ironic sense of humor when it was most needed. Alan Luxenberg of the Foreign Policy Research Institute also provided encouragement, as did, in a somewhat different form, my former student Chris Torres, whose periodic calls began with "Hi Doc, that manuscript done yet?"

The editors at Oxford University Press have been wonderful to work with; I mention, in particular, Dave McBride, Kathleeen Weaver, and Stacey Victor. As always, the responsibility for errors and omissions is mine alone.

Jane Teufel Dreyer
Coral Gables, Florida
December 2015

Notes

CHAPTER 1

1. For a fuller explanation of how the system functioned in theory and practice, see June Teufel Dreyer, "The '*Tianxia* Trope': Will China Change the World?," *Journal of Contemporary China* Vol 24, no. 6(Fall 2015), http://dx.doi.org/10.1080/10670564.2015.1030951.

2. Mark Mancall, "The Ch'ing Tribute System: An Interpretive Essay," in John King Fairbank, ed., *The Chinese World Order: Traditional China's Foreign Relations* (Cambridge, MA: Harvard University Press, 1968), pp. 64, 76.

3. Ronald Toby, *State and Society in Early Modern Japan: Asia in the Development of the Tokugawa Bakufu* (Princeton, NJ: Princeton University Press, 1984), p. 181.

4. John F. Cady, *Southeast Asia: Its Historical Development* (New York: Houghton-Mifflin, 1964), p. 594.

5. Ryusaku Tsunoda, William Theodore de Barry, and Donald Keene, *Sources of Japanese Tradition* (New York: Columbia University Press, 1965), pp. 15–35.

6. Kate Wildman Nakai, *Shogunal Politics: Arai Hakuseki and the Premises of Tokugawa Rule* (Cambridge, MA: Council on East Asian Studies, Harvard University, 1988), p. 249.

7. Nakai, 1988, pp. 237–238.

8. *Xinhua*, August 3, 2011.

9. In 1931 the seal was designated a national treasure of Japan, and is on permanent exhibition at the Fukuoka City Museum.

10. Edwin O. Reischauer, *Ennin's Travels in T'ang China* (New York: Ronald Press, 1955), pp. 41–42.

11. *Asahi*, March 2, 2015, http://ajw.asahi.com/article/behind_news/social_affairs/AJ201503020035.

12. George Sansom, *A History of Japan to 1334* (Stanford, CA: Stanford University Press, 1958), p. 21.

13. Robert Borgen, *Sugawara no Michizane and the Early Heian Court* (Cambridge, MA: Council on East Asian Studies, Harvard University, 1986), p. 227.

14. As recorded in the Sui Shu 隨書 81. 15b-16a, the original of this passage is "其國書曰日處天子致書日沒天子無恙云云帝覽之不悅謂鴻臚卿曰蠻夷書有無禮者勿復以聞."

15. Tsunoda et al., p. 37.

16. In 2004 Chinese sources aroused a furor among patriotic Koreans when they referred to Koguryŏ as a kingdom in China. Koguryŏ's domains had indeed straddled the Yalu River, which today forms the boundary between China and North Korea.

17. Bruce L. Batten, "Foreign Threat and Domestic Reform: The Emergence of the Ritsuryō State," *Monumenta Nipponica* 41, no. 2 (Summer 1986): 209–210.

18. Batten, p. 215.

19. This argument is cogently made by Batten, pp. 199–217.

20. Sansom, p. 69.

21. Borgen, p. 71.

22. Borgen, pp. 6–7.

23. Borgen, p. 35.

24. Reischauer, *Ennin's Travels*, p. 71.

25. Edwin O. Reischauer, trans., *Ennin's Diary: the Record of a Pilgrimage in Search of the Law* (New York: Ronald Press, 1955), passim.

26. Receiving embassies from abroad was not, however, a cost-free enterprise for the Japanese government, since the envoys were lavishly entertained.

27. Borgen, pp. 247–248.

28. Sansom, p. 271.

29. Yi-t'ung Wang, *Official Relations Between China and Japan, 1368–1549* (Cambridge, MA: Harvard-Yenching Institute Studies, IX, Harvard University Press, 1953), pp. 16–17.

30. Translated in Wang, p. 17.

31. Translated in Kwan-wai So, *Japanese Piracy in Ming China During the 16th Century* (East Lansing: Michigan State University Press, 1975), pp. 164–165; Wang, pp. 18–19; see also George Sansom, *A History of Japan 1334–1615* (Stanford, CA: Stanford University Press, 1961), pp. 168–169.

32. Wang, p. 19.

33. Wang, p. 38.

34. On the Ming sea voyages, see Edward L. Dreyer, *Zheng He: China and the Oceans in the Early Ming Dynasty, 1405–1438* (London: Longman, 2006); Geoff Wade, "The Zheng He Voyages: A Reassessment," Asia Research Institute, National University of Singapore, Working Paper No. 31, October 2004, http://www.ari.nus.edu.sg/docs/wps/wps04_031.pdf.

35. Wang, p. 2.

36. So, passim, has an excellent summary of these activities. Pages 15–36 are particularly germane to this discussion.

37. Sansom, 1961, p. 170.

38. Xie Jie, Minister of Revenue in Nanjing, quoted in So, p. 214.

39. Wang, p. 50.
40. Toby, p. 24.
41. Stephen Turnbull, *Samurai Invasion: Japan's Korea War, 1592–1598* (London: Cassell, 2002), is the only book-length work on this war.
42. Kenneth W. Swope, "Crouching Tigers, Secret Weapons: Military Technology Employed During the Sino-Japanese-Korean War, 1592–1598," *Journal of Military History* 69 (January 2005): 11.
43. See Toby, pp. 76–80, for a more detailed account of these events.
44. *Hayashi Razan Bunshu*, cited by Toby, p. 197.
45. Toby, p. 199.
46. Toby, p. 200.
47. Sansom, 1961, p. 403.
48. Toby, pp. 12–13.
49. See, for example, the analysis of Professor Nakamura Hidetaka in Toby, p. 87.
50. Nakai, 1988, p. 310.
51. Nakai, 1988, pp. 343–344.
52. See Lynne Struve, *The Southern Ming, 1644–1662* (New Haven, CT: Yale University Press, 1984), for details.
53. This period is summarized in Toby, pp. 118–140. The allusion is to Li Bo (701–762 A.D.), one of China's greatest poets. According to legend, Li drowned while leaning out of a boat in an attempt to embrace the reflection of the moon in the water.
54. Mark McNally, *Proving the Way: Conflict and Practice in the History of Japanese Nativism* (Cambridge, MA: Harvard University Asia Center, 2005), p. 89.
55. Peter Nosco, *Remembering Paradise: Nativism and Nostalgia in Eighteenth Century Japan* (Cambridge, MA: Council on East Asian Studies, Harvard University, 1990), p. 46.
56. This point is made in Nosco, pp. 79–80.
57. The classic Foucaultian analysis of *kokugaku* is Harry Harootunian's *Things Seen and Unseen: Discourse and Ideology in Tokugawa Nativism* (Chicago: University of Chicago Press, 1988).
58. McNally, p. 216.
59. Masahiro Wakabayashi, "Taiwanese Nationalism and the Unforgettable Others," in Edward Friedman, ed., *China's Rise, Taiwan's Dilemmas, and International Peace* (London: Routledge, 2006), pp. 4–5.
60. Kate Wildman Nakai, "The Naturalization of Confucianism in Tokugawa Japan: The Problem of Sinocentrism," *Harvard Journal of Asiatic Studies* 40, no. 1 (June 1980): 173.

CHAPTER 2

1. This memorandum is translated in full in Franz Schurmann, *Imperial China: The Decline of the Last Dynasty and the Origins of Modern China* (New York: Random House, 1967), pp. 105–113.
2. Under which a foreigner accused of a crime would be tried according to the laws of his or her own country rather than those of China. In 1822 Francis Terranova, an American seaman, had tossed an earthenware jug overboard, knocking a woman in a small boat below into the water. Unable to swim, she drowned. The Chinese court

ordered Terranova strangled to death. Foreign outrage over the barbarous nature of the punishment led to pressure for extraterritoriality.

3. Under which privileges granted to other nations would automatically be extended to the nation that was receiving most favored nation status.

4. The Taiping, Nien, and Muslim rebellions, affecting large swaths of different areas of the country.

5. Ssu-yu Teng and John Fairbank, *China's Response to the West: A Documentary Survey, 1839–1923* (Cambridge, MA: Harvard University Press, 1954), pp. 77–79.

6. Mary Claubaugh Wright, *The Last Stand of Chinese Conservatism: The T'ung Chih Restoration of 1862–1874* (Stanford, CA: Stanford University Press, 1957), p. 178.

7. Teng and Fairbank, p. 116.

8. Albert Feuerwerker, *China's Early Industrialization* (Cambridge, MA: Harvard University Press, 1958), passim, deals with this issue in detail.

9. Franz Michael, "Introduction: Regionalism in Nineteenth Century China," in Stanley Spector, *Li Hung-chang and the Huai Army: A Study in Nineteenth Century Regionalism* (Seattle: University of Washington Press, 1964), pp. xl–xliii.

10. Kwang-Ching Liu, "Li Hung-chang in Chihli: The Emergence of a Policy, 1870–1875," in Samuel C. Chu and Kwang-Ching Liu, *Li Hung-chang and China's Early Modernization* (Armonk, NY: M.E. Sharpe, 1994), p. 11.

11. See. e.g., Arthur Walworth, *Black Ships Off Japan* (Hamden, CT: Archon Books, 1966); George Feifer, *Breaking Open Japan: Commodore Perry, Lord Abe, and American Imperialism* (New York: Smithsonian Books, 2006); and Perry's own account of his voyage, Matthew Calbraith Perry, *Narrative of the Expedition of an American Squadron to the China Seas and Japan, 1852–1854* (New York: D. Appleton and Company, 1856). Also available in several other editions, abridged and unabridged, that give examples of the care with which Perry planned and carried out his strategy for impressing the Japanese government.

12. Ôkuni Takamasa, *Shinshin kōhōron* (1866/1867), cited by Harry Harootunian, "The Functions of China in Tokugawa Thought," in Akira Iriye, ed., *The Chinese and the Japanese* (Princeton, NJ: Princeton University Press, 1980), pp. 26–27.

13. Marius B. Jansen, *China and Japan: From War to Peace, 1894–1972* (Chicago: Rand-McNally, 1975), p. 5.

14. Jansen, 1975, p. 130.

15. Kwang-Ching Liu in Chu and Liu, p. 6.

16. However tenuous that unbroken line had at times been.

17. Motoori Norinaga, cited in Harootunian, p. 24.

18. Takasugi Shinsaku, cited in Harootunian, p. 35.

19. Edwin Pak-wah Leung, "Li Hung-chang and the Liu-ch'iu (Ryukyu) Controversy, 1871–1881," in Chu and Liu, p. 165.

20. Michael Auslin, *The Unequal Treaties and the Culture of Japanese Diplomacy* (Cambridge, MA: Harvard University Press, 2005); Louis G. Perez, *Japan Comes of Age: Mutsu Munemitsu and the Revision of the Unequal Treaties* (Madison, NJ: Fairleigh Dickenson Press, 1999), passim.

21. A decade before, Kim Ok-kyun had led an abortive coup that resulted in the death of several members of the royal family. Kim then fled to Japan, which refused the Korean king's requests for extradition. The king then employed a more devious strategy: hiring an individual to gain Kim's trust and invite him to Shanghai, where the assassination could more easily be carried out. There are unsubstantiated, though

plausible, rumors that Chinese military leader Yuan Shikai, who was Li Hongzhang's representative in Seoul, was also involved. In any case, from the point of view of the Korean king and the Chinese government, Kim was a traitor, and dismemberment was standard punishment for that crime.

22. Edward A. Falk, *Togo and the Rise of Japanese Sea Power* (New York: Longmans, Green and Co, 1936), pp. 165–170; Georges Blond, *Admiral Togo* (New York: Macmillan, 1950), pp. 100–105.

23. See, for example, "China's Declaration of War," *The Japan Weekly Mail* (Yokohama), August 11, 1894, p. 178; "Declaration of War by the Emperor of China," *The North-China Herald* (Shanghai), August 3, 1894, p. 191; "The Wo-jen," *The Peking and Tientsin Times*, September 1, 1894, p. 102, cited in S.C.M. Paine, *The Sino-Japanese War of 1894–1895: Perceptions, Power, and Primacy* (Cambridge, UK: Cambridge University Press, 2003), pp. 135–136.

24. Paine, p. 137.

25. These and other blunders are detailed in John Lang Rawlinson, *China's Struggle for Naval Development, 1839–1895* (Cambridge, MA: Harvard University Press, 1967), passim. On the matter of regional navies' unwillingness to fight in another region, Rawlinson quotes a Maritime Customs official as saying "the war with Japan affected the province of Zhili to a light degree only and, as far as one could see, the people of Tianjin regard it as a matter of no moment to them" (p. 202).

26. Yi Shunding, *Tao Riben Xiwen*, November 1894, cited in Samuel C. Chu, "China's Attitudes Toward Japan at the Time of the Sino-Japanese War," in Iriye, pp. 74–75.

27. Jansen, 1975, p. 131.

28. Ding's options were not attractive. His punishment on returning to Beijing would almost certainly have been death, probably by decapitation.

29. Paine, pp. 228–232; Jansen, 1975, pp. 9–10.

30. Jansen, 1975, p. 23.

31. George A. Lensen, *Balance of Intrigue: International Rivalry in Korea and Manchuria, 1884–1899* (Tallahassee: University Presses of Florida, 1982), Vol. 1, p. 239.

32. Paine, p. 229.

33. "Peking Pride," *The Peking and Tientsin Times*, February 9, 1985, in Paine, p. 254.

34. The negotiations are covered in detail in Lensen, Vol. 1, pp. 231–255.

35. A Kuping (Treasury) tael equaled about 37.3 grams of silver.

36. See, for example, http://wwi.lib.byu.edu/index.php/The_Willy-Nicky_Telegrams.

37. On Kang Youwei, see Yu-wei K'ang, *Ta T'ung Shu: The One-World Philosophy of K'ang Yu-wei* (London: Allyn and Unwin, 1958); Jung-pang Lo, ed., *Kang Yuwei: A Biography and a Symposium* (Tucson: University of Arizona Press, 1967); Kung-chuan Hsiao, *A Modern China and a New World: K'ang Yu-wei, Reformer and Utopian, 1858–1927* (Seattle: University of Washington Press, 1975).

38. See Joseph Levenson, *Liang Ch'i-ch'ao and the Mind of Modern China* (Cambridge, MA: Harvard University Press, 1953).

39. Urs Matthias Zahmann, *China and Japan in the Late Meiji Period: Chinese Policy and the Japanese Discourse on National Identity, 1893–1904* (London: Routledge, 2009), pp. 89, 132.

40. For an excellent example of this, see Arthur N. Waldron, "The Warlord: Twentieth Century Chinese Understandings of Violence, Militarism, and Imperialism," *American Historical Review* 96, no. 4 (October 1991): 1073–1100. Waldron traces the

origin of *junfa* in Chinese from the Japanese *gunbatsu*, a Japanese neologism for "military clique," since the Japanese saw parallels between the Prussian Junkers and their own samurai class. In Chinese, however, the same characters meant, and continue to mean, "warlord," an entirely different concept.

41. The paragraphs on Hattori are summarized from Paula Harrell, "Guiding Hand: Hattori Unokichi in Beijing," in Joshua A. Fogel, ed., *Crossing the Yellow Sea: Sino-Japanese Cultural Contacts 1600–1950* (Norwalk, CT: Eastbridge Press, 2007), pp. 183–192.

42. Harrell, 2007, p. 186.

43. Harrell, 2007, p. 189.

44. Aida Y. Wong, "The East, Nationalism, and Taishō Democracy: Naitō Konan's History of Chinese Painting," in Fogel, pp. 281–304; quote appears on pp. 298–299; Yue-him Tam, "An Intellectual's Response to Western Intrusion: Naitō Konan's View of Republican China," in Iriye, pp. 161–183.

45. Paula Harrell, *Sowing the Seeds of Change: Chinese Students, Japanese Teachers, 1895–1905* (Stanford, CA: Stanford University Press, 1992), p. 211.

46. Marius Jansen, *The Japanese and Sun Yat-sen* (Cambridge, MA: Harvard University Press, 1954), pp. 9–11.

47. Marius Jansen, "Konoe Atsumaro" in Iriye, pp. 116–117.

48. Harrell, 1992, p. 214.

49. Jansen, 1954, p. 122.

50. *Asahi*, July 7, 2010.

51. Jansen, 1954, p. 130.

52. Jansen, 1954, p. 56.

53. For the details of the Russian military enhancement program, see Paine, p. 328.

54. Shumpei Okamoto, *The Japanese Oligarchy and the Russo-Japanese War* (New York: Columbia University Press, 1970), p. 74.

55. The completion of the trans-Siberian railway had enabled the Russians to bring in fresh troops to Manchuria. Japanese troops, whose ranks had been depleted by the fierce fighting, would have had a difficult time matching their numbers. Unbeknownst to all but a few key decision-makers, the Japanese position in Manchuria was deteriorating.

56. James L. Huffmann, *Creating a Public: People and the Press in Meiji Japan* (Honolulu: University of Hawaii Press, 1997), pp. 310–358; Joel E. Hamby, "Striking the Balance: Strategy and Force in the Russo-Japanese War," *Armed Forces and Society* 30, no. 325 (Spring 2004): 345–346; Okamoto, pp. 196–223.

57. The individual was Mori Kaku, an official of the giant Mitsui conglomerate and official of the China Industrial Company, which had been founded with substantial investment by Mitsui. Jansen, 1954, pp. 165–166.

58. Jansen, 1954, pp. 190–191.

59. "Japan Curbs War Talk: Agitators Using California Incident to Embarrass the Government," *New York Times*, April 22, 1913, p. 2.

60. Jansen, 1954, p. 189.

61. Text of the agreement is available at http://connection.ebscohost.com/c/articles/21213160/lansing-ishii-agreement-1917.

62. For details, see John Albert White, *The Siberian Intervention* (Princeton, NJ: Princeton University Press, 1950), passim. White describes Japanese policy as devious—agreeing with its allies on backing Kolchak while supporting rival

Siberian factions including that of Semonov, with the ultimate aim of producing anarchy that Tokyo could use to Japan's benefit. At the same time, the other states, and the United States in particular, wanted to prevent Japan from gaining power in the area.

63. "Japan Grants China Autonomy on Tariff," *New York Times*, April 25, 1930, p. 14.

64. James B. Crowley, *Japan's Quest for Autonomy: National Security and Foreign Policy 1930-1938* (Princeton, NJ: Princeton University Press, 1966), p. 186.

65. Hugh Byas, *Government by Assassination* (New York: A.A. Knopf, 1943); see especially pp. 22-31.

66. *The Times* (London), January 11, 1932, cited in Crowley, p. 156.

67. Crowley, p. 168.

68. A district in Tianjin.

69. Steve Tsang, "Chiang Kai-shek's 'Secret Deal' and Xian and the Start of the Sino-Japanese War," Palgrave Communications, January 20, 2015. doi:101057/palcomms.2014.3.

70. Ben-Ami Shillony, *The Young Officers and the February 26, 1936 Incident* (Princeton, NJ: Princeton University Press, 1973), passim.

71. Crowley, p. 343, citing United States Department of State, *Foreign Relations of the United States, (FRUS), 1937*, p. 385.

72. See, for example, David Askew, "The Nanjing Incident: Recent Research and Trends," *Electronic Journal of Contemporary Japanese Studies* (April 2002), passim.

73. Crowley, p. 375.

74. These and other battles in the Second Sino-Japanese War are discussed in detail in Edward L. Dreyer, *China at War: 1901-1949* (London: Longman, 1995), pp. 206-306.

75. Gerald E. Bunker, *The Peace Conspiracy: Wang Ching-wei and the China War, 1937-1941* (Cambridge, MA: Harvard University Press, 1972), p. 102.

76. David P. Barrett, "Introduction: Occupied China and the Limits of Accommodation," in David P. Barrett and Larry N. Shyu, eds., *Chinese Collaboration with Japan: The Limits of Accommodation* (Stanford, CA: Stanford University Press, 2001), p. 6.

77. See, for example, Jian-Yue Chen, "American Studies of Wang Jingwei: Defining Nationalism," *World History Review* 2, no. 1 (2004): 10.

78. John F. Melby, *The Mandate of Heaven: Record of a Civil War; China 1945-49* (Toronto, Canada: University of Toronto Press, 1968), p. 124.

79. Timothy Brook, "The Creation of the Reformed Government in Central China, 1938," in David P. Barrett and Larry N. Shyu, eds., *Chinese Collaboration With Japan, 1932-1945: The Limits of Accommodation* (Stanford, CA: Stanford University Prsss, 2001), p. 100.

80. Stephen Mackinnon, "Conclusion: Wartime China," in Stephen R. Mackinnon, Diana Lary, and Ezra F. Vogel, eds., *China at War: Regions of China, 1937-1945* (Stanford, CA: Stanford University Press, 2007), p. 335.

81. See, for example, Sheldon H. Harris, *Factories of Death: Japanese Biological Warfare 1931-1945 and the American Cover-Up* (New York: Routledge, 2002), pp. 289, 263, 283; Toshiyuki Tanaka, *Hidden Horrors: Japanese War Crimes in World War II* (Boulder, CO: Westview Press, 1996), passim.

82. Melby, p. 15.

83. Melby, p. 145.

84. Mackinnon, p. 349.
85. David P. Barrett, *Dixie Mission: The United States Army Observer Group in Yenan, 1944* (Berkeley: University of California Press, 1970), p. 13.
86. Bunker, p. 278, makes this point with regard to Japanese negotiations with Wang Jingwei and Chiang Kai-shek.
87. James Auer, ed., *From Marco Polo Bridge to Pearl Harbor: Who Was Responsible?* (Tokyo: Yomiuri Shimbun Press, 2006), p. 66.

CHAPTER 3

1. In December 1951. Hints of Yoshida's reluctance and eventual agreement may be found in United States Department of State, Washington D.C., *Foreign Relations of the United States*, hereafter *FRUS, East Asia and the Pacific*, Japan, Vol. 6, 1951, pp. 1393, 1400, 1431, 1448.
2. Kurt Radke, *China's Relations with Japan, 1945-83: The Role of Liao Chengzhi* (Manchester, UK: Manchester University Press, 1990), p. 10.
3. The details remain murky to this day. See Jay Taylor, *Generalissimo: Chiang Kai-shek and the Struggle for Modern China* (Cambridge, MA: Belknap Press, 2009), pp. 34–37.
4. Shigeru Yoshida, *Yoshida Shigeru: Last Meiji Man* (Lanham, MD: Rowman & Littlefield, 2007), p. 46; Richard Finn, *Winners in Peace: MacArthur and Yoshida, and Postwar Japan* (Berkeley: University of California Press, 1992), p. 52.
5. Yoshida, p. 290.
6. C. Martin Wilbur, "Japan and the Rise of Communist China," in Hugh Borton et al., *Japan Between East and West* (New York: Council on Foreign Relations, 1957), p. 206.
7. Wilbur, pp. 207–208.
8. Wilbur, pp. 219–220.
9. Decades later, doubts were raised as to whether Mao had actually used this phrase, it being stated that the sound system was poor and that only those nearest the chairman heard what he actually said. In any case, the statement expresses sentiments that Mao made in other venues, and has been widely attributed to him.
10. http://www.fmprc.gov.cn/mfa_eng/ziliao_665539/3602_665543/3604_665547/t18011.shtml; "The Texts of the Agreements Concluded Between the Soviet Union and Communist China," *New York Times*, February 15, 1950, p. 11.
11. Jirō Bessho, "Hokkaido 'Kaihō Kenkyu'" (Hokkaido Research Bulletin), *Kaizō*, January 10, 1952, pp. 154–165, in C. W. Braddick, *Japan and the Sino-Soviet Alliance, 1950-1964* (Basingstoke, UK: Palgrave Macmillan, 2001), p. 218.
12. Lindsay Parrott, "Tokyo Parties Hit Separate Treaty," *New York Times*, April 27, 1950, pp. 1, 13
13. Yoshida, p. 230.
14. In the third of the three incidents, known as the Matsukawa case after the train station near where the derailment occurred, twenty persons were found guilty, five of whom were sentenced to death. The sentences were reversed in 1961 after the defense showed that some confessions had been coerced, and that the investigation had been poorly conducted. It has been called the worst miscarriage of justice in postwar Japan. *Japan Times*, December 2, 2009.
15. *Dagong Bao*, August 21, 1951, cited in Shao Chuan Leng, *Japan and Communist China* (Kyoto: Doshisha University Press, 1958), p. 4.

16. Richard Finn, *Winners in Peace: MacArthur and Yoshida and Postwar Japan* (Berkeley: University of California Press, 1992), p. 300.

17. A spate of such articles appeared with numbing regularity in *Renmin Ribao*, *Dagong Bao*, and other papers as well as on numerous Radio Beijing broadcasts in September and early October 1951.

18. Enlai Zhou, *Riben wenti wenjian huibian* (Compilation of Documents on the Japan Question) (Beijing: Shijie Zhishi [World Knowledge], 1955), pp. 62–66.

19. Braddick, pp. 15–16.

20. Mariko Asano Tamamori, "Victims of Colonization: Japanese Agrarian Settlers and Their Repatriation to Japan," *Asia-Pacific Journal* 6, no. 1 (February 2009): 24–52, especially 41–43.

21. Kai-shek Chiang, *Statements and Speeches by Generalissimo Chiang Kai-shek, August–September 1945* (Shanghai: International Press, 1945), Vol. I, p. 3.

22. "Repatriation of Wartime Japanese Emigrants Marked in China," *Xinhua*, June 26, 2006; "China Repatriation Remembered," *Japan Times*, June 26, 2006.

23. *Japan Times*, June 26, 2006.

24. *Asahi*, August 4, 2011, http://ajw.asahi.com/article/asia/china/AJ201108045480.

25. "Peiping Seeking Talks on Japanese It Holds," *New York Times*, December 25, 1952, p. 6.

26. *Asahi*, January 8, 1953; *Asahi*, Janurary 24, 1953, cited in Seiichiro Takagi, "An Analysis of Chinese Behavior Toward Japan, 1950–1965: An Examination of Three Models of International Behavior," unpublished dissertation, Stanford University, Stanford, CA, 1977, p. 90.

27. William J. Jorden, "First Repatriates Return to Japan," *New York Times*, March 23, 1953, p. 5.

28. William J. Jorden, "Reds Greet Exiles at Homes in Japan," *New York Times*, March 28, 1953, p. 2.

29. A book detailing these facts, Kurihara Toshio's *Siberia Yokuryū Mikan No Gigeki* (Japanese Detainees in Siberia: Unfinished Tragedy) (Tokyo: Iwanami Shinsho) went into its fourth printing in 2009.

30. "335 Repatriates Return to Japan," *New York Times*, July 4, 1955, p. 3.

31. Toshio Arai, "Kyōjutsusho wa kōshite kakareta" (Testimonies Were Written as Such), *Sekai* (World, Tokyo), no. 648 (May 1998): 69–78, in Takashi Yoshida, *The Making of the "Rape of Nanking": History and Memory in Japan, China, and the United States* (New York: Oxford University Press/Weatherhead Institute of Columbia University, 2006), pp. 67–68.

32. Lindsay Parrott, "Japan to Ask US for 17 Warships," *New York Times*, March 13, 1954, p. 2.

33. Lindsay Parrott, "Japan Restricts Fisheries Guard," *New York Times*, April 8, 1954, p. 11.

34. *Kyodo*, (Tokyo), December 27, 1954.

35. *Kyodo*, April 15, 1955.

36. Renamed Almaty after the disintegration of the Soviet Union.

37. Text in *New York Times*, October 12, 1954, p. 8.

38. "Japan Refuses the Bait," *New York Times*, October 15, 1954, p. 22; *FRUS, East Asia and the Pacific*, Vol. 14, 1952–1954, p. 377.

39. Kuo-kang Shao, "Zhou Enlai's Diplomacy and the Neutralization of Indo-China," *China Quarterly*, no. 107 (September 1986): 483–504, citation from pp. 501–502.

40. See, for example, *Xinhua*, February 14, 1954.

41. William J. Jorden, "Sabotage by Reds Feared in Japan," *New York Times*, February 27, 1954, p. 3.

42. *Kyodo*, December 12, 1954.

43. *Kyodo*, March 14, 1955.

44. "Two Top Japanese Chide Red Lands," *New York Times*, February 6, 1955, p. 6.

45. "Texts of Address and Statement by Chou (Zhou) at the Bandung Conference," *New York Times*, April 25, 1955, p. 7.

46. *Kyodo*, March 21, 1955.

47. Robert Trumbull, "Hatoyama Plans Peace Diplomacy," *New York Times*, April 26, 1955, p. 8.

48. The opening scene of *Godzilla* shows a fishing trawler whose sailors are playing musical instruments until seared by the monster's breath. In the background is a life preserver with the number five, as in the *Lucky Dragon*'s name.

49. See, for example, http://www.antiatom.org/GSKY/en/discription_gensuikyo.htm.

50. Robert Trumbull, "Japan Becomes a Field for Communist Pressure," *New York Times*, May 5, 1957, p. 213.

51. Trumbull, p. 213.

52. *Kyodo*, July 16, 1955.

53. *Xinhua*, August 16, 1955.

54. "Hatoyama's Foes Unite," *New York Times*, July 12, 1955, p. 8.

55. *Xinhua*, August 17, 1955.

56. Robert Trumbull, "Tokyo-Peiping Tie Appears Far Off," *New York Times*, August 18, 1955, p. 1.

57. For example, a fifteen-person scientific delegation headed by Japanese-educated vice-premier Guo Moro, in his role as president of the Chinese Academy of Science, was described as having spent three weeks in Japan to promote scientific relations between the two countries. *Xinhua*, December 24, 1955.

58. *FRUS*, Vol. 6, 1951, pp. 94–95.

59. *FRUS*, Vol. 6, 1951, p. 73.

60. *FRUS*, Vol. 6, 1951, pp. 55–56.

61. *FRUS*, Vol. 6, 1951, p. 47.

62. *FRUS*, Vol. 6, 1951, p. 48.

63. *FRUS*, Vol. 6, 1951, p. 5.

64. *Kyodo*, April 27, 1957.

65. *Xinhua*, July 26, 1957.

66. *Kyodo*, August 1, 1957.

67. "Peiping's Attacks Puzzle Japanese: Propaganda Barrage Seen as Effort to Hinder Tokyo's Trade with South Asia," *New York Times*, August 4, 1957, p. 18.

68. *Kyodo*, August 7, 1957.

69. *Kyodo*, August 17, 1957.

70. "Japanese Link 12 to 'Red' Spy Ring," *New York Times*, December 3, 1957, p. 14.

71. *Kyodo*, March 5, 1958.

72. *Central News Agency* (CNA), Taipei, April 5, 1958.

73. "Japanese Pact Scored: Group Asks Reconsideration of Peiping Trade Accord," *New York Times*, April 3, 1958, p.5.

74. Robert Trumbull, "Red China Warns Tokyo Reporters," *New York Times*, March 1, 1958, p. 6.
75. *Kyodo*, March 22, 1958.
76. *Kyodo*, April 4, 1958.
77. *Xinhua*, April 13, 1958.
78. "Tokyo Reaction Is Mild," *New York Times*, April 14, 1958, p. 6.
79. *Xinhua*, May 7, 1958.
80. *Xinhua*, May 10, 1958.
81. *Reuters*, (Hong Kong), June 28, 1958.
82. *Xinhua*, June 11, 1958.
83. *Kyodo*, June 20, 1958.
84. *Kyodo*, July 9, 1958.
85. *Reuters*, July 27, 1958.
86. *Xinhua*, August 1, 1958.
87. Braddick, p. 129.
88. A partial transcript of the Mao–Khrushchev conversations is available at http://digitalarchive.wilsoncenter.org/document/112083.
89. Yoshida, p. 175.
90. Chillingly documented, based on provincial and local archival data, by Jisheng Yang, translated by Stacy Mosher and Guo Jian, edited by Edward Friedman, Stacy Mosher, and Guo Jian. *Tombstone: The Great Chinese Famine, 1958–1962* (New York: Farrar, Straus and Giroux, 2012).
91. "Japan Again Tops World Shipyards," *New York Times*, January 26, 1958, p. 12.
92. *Asahi*, March 28, 1959.
93. Details appear in Braddick, p. 180.
94. *Kyodo*, March 21, 1959.
95. *Kyodo*, March 30, 1959.
96. *Kyodo*, April 15, 1959.
97. Tillman Durdin, "China Tied to Soviet by Need for Vast Aid," *New York Times*, September 27, 1959, p. E4.
98. Richard Johnston, "Japanese Left-Wing Group Split by Debate on Future Strategy," *New York Times*, July 6, 1960, p. 17.
99. *Xinhua*, July 26, 1960.
100. *Kyodo*, July 19, 1960.
101. *Xinhua*, September 12, 1960.
102. *Kyodo*, December 25, 1960.
103. E. W. Kenworthy, "Tokyo Aides Greet Humphrey," *New York Times*, December 29, 1965, p. 3.
104. *Japan Times*, April 11, 1964.
105. *Asahi*, July 18, 1964.
106. *Kyodo*, June 24, 1964.
107. *Kyodo*, September 26, 1964.
108. "A Tariff Dilemma Confronts Tokyo," *New York Times*, January 13, 1964, p. 40.
109. *Japan Times*, April 8, 1964.
110. Seymour Topping, "France Disappointed at Relations with Red China," *New York Times*, September 27, 1964, p. 7.
111. *Japan Times*, February 1964.
112. *Japan Times*, March 1, 1964.

113. *Xinhua*, March 2, 1964.
114. *Tokyo Shimbun*, March 5, 1964.
115. *Japan Times*, March 21, 1954.
116. *Japan Times*, April 11, 1964.
117. *Japan Times*, April 11, 1964.
118. "Japanese in Space Technology: Satellite in Orbit Due in Three Years," *New York Times*, January 18, 1965, p. 41.
119. The brothers, born to the Satō family, were adopted into their respective wives' families, one of which was also named Satō, and the other named Kishi. This is a common practice in Japan when the wife has no brother to carry on the family line. The eldest of the three Satō brothers, who remained in his birth parents' household, had been a vice-admiral in World War II.
120. *Kyodo*, November 9, 1964.
121. *Renmin Ribao*, November 24, 1964, reprinted in *Xinhua*, November 24, 1964.
122. See, for example, Robert Trumbull, "Sato Hopeful of U.S. Sympathy on Japan's Chinese Dealings," *New York Times*, January 1, 1965, p. 2; "Sato, in U.S., Calls Washington 'Rigid' in Stand on China," *New York Times*, January 11, 1965, p. 3.
123. *Asahi*, January 21, 1965; *Yomiuri*, January 21, 1965.
124. Robert Trumbull, "Closer China Ties Big Issue in Japan," *New York Times*, December 6, 1964, p. 23.
125. *Xinhua*, December 7, 1964; *Kyodo*, December 7, 1964.
126. Seymour Topping, "Peking Attacks Tokyo 'Hostility,'" *New York Times*, December 9, 1964, p. 2.
127. *Japan Times*, January 22, 1965.
128. *Xinhua*, April 30, 1965. The reason for the lag between the Satō administration's decision and Beijing's cancellation was the efforts made in the interim by Nichibō executives to have Eximbank credit for the sale made available.
129. *Asahi*, May 1, 1965, editorialized that it did not understand the GOJ's attitude.
130. *Yomiuri*, December 22, 2008; *BBC*, December 23, 2008.
131. Robert Trumbull, "Size of Military Debated in Japan," *New York Times*, June 27, 1965, p. 2.
132. *Xinhua*, January 21, 1965.
133. *Japan Times*, June 8, 1965. Chiang Kai-shek had waived any claim to negotiations at the end of World War II, but the CCP government had announced it would not be bound by Chiang's action.
134. *Japan Times*, June 9, 1965.
135. *Japan Times*, May 1, 1965.
136. *Japan Times*, May 9, 1965.
137. *Nihon Keizai Shimbun*, May 7, 1965.
138. "Japanese Are Disturbed," *New York Times*, October 2, 1965.
139. Seymour Topping, "Mao's 'Infallibility,'" *New York Times*, February 10, 1965, p. 11.
140. *Japan Times*, January 7 and 19, 1966.
141. *Japan Times*, April 28, 1966.
142. See, for example, Robert Trumbull, "Japanese Reds Said to Rebuff Peking," *New York Times*, June 1, 1966, p. 6.
143. Summarized in *Japan Times*, February 3, 1967.

144. *Japan Times*, January 9, 1966; Robert Trumbull, "China Said to Use Troops in Curbing Red Guards' Foes," *New York Times*, September 13, 1966, p. 1; Kurt Radke, *China's Relations With Japan, 1945-83: The Role of Liao Chengzhi* (Manchester, UK: Manchester University Press, 1990), pp. 170-183.
145. Emerson Chapin, "Closer Ties to China Urged for Japan," *New York Times*, June 5, 1966, p. 2.
146. *Asahi*, June 23, 1966.
147. *Japan Times*, January 17, 1967.
148. *Sankei*, February 3, 1968.
149. See, for example, *Xinhua*, September 19, 1967, announcing the expulsion of correspondents from *Mainichi*, *Sankei*, and *Tokyo Shimbun* for "smearing the Great Proletarian Cultural Revolution," "directing their personal spearhead against ... Chairman Mao," and "exceedingly arousing the indignation of the Chinese people."
150. *Japan Times*, April 30, 1967; John M. Lee, "Japan's Press Attacked for Its Peking Reporting," *New York Times*, May 1, 1972, p. 4. For Samejima's release, see *Japan Times Weekly*, December 27, 1969.
151. *Kyodo*, March 8, 1968.
152. *Japan Times*, February 15, 1966.
153. *Japan Times*, February 18, 1966.
154. For some examples, see *Xinhua*, March 5, 1968; March 11, 1968; and March 16, 1968—involving the expansion of Haneda, the building of Narita, and the enlargement of a U.S. military airfield.
155. *Xinhua*, December 31, 1967.
156. See, for example, Shanghai Radio, October 28, 1967. For more on the Haguruma troupe, consult Xiaomei Chen, *Acting the Right Part* (Honolulu: University of Hawaii Press, 2002), pp. 156-157.
157. *Xinhua*, March 6, 1969; *Kyodo*, March 6, 1968.
158. *Kyodo*, March 14, 1968.
159. Fred Greene, INR/READ to Thomas Hughes, January 8, 1968, appended to NIE January 11, 1968, *FRUS*, Vol. 29, (2006), p. 256.
160. *FRUS*, Vol. 29 (2006), p. 258.
161. *FRUS*, Vol. 29 (2006), pp. 270-271.
162. *FRUS*, Vol. 29 (2006), p. 280; telegram dated June 5, 1968.
163. *FRUS*, Vol. 29 (2006), p. 281; telegram dated June 5, 1968.
164. *Xinhua*, March 10, 1968.
165. *Xinhua*, March 25, 1968.
166. Memorandum from National Security Council staff member Alfred Jenkins to President's Special Assistant Walter Rostow, June 18, 1968; *FRUS*, Vol. 29, p. 288.

CHAPTER 4

1. *Kyodo*, January 27, 1969.
2. Takashi Oka, "Italy's Plan to Recognize Peking Dismays Japan," *New York Times*, January 26, 1969, p. 16.
3. *Japan Times Weekly*, February 22, 1969.
4. *Renmin Ribao*, January 27, 1969,
5. *Renmin Ribao*, February 28, 1969.
6. See, for example, *Kyodo*, March 7, 1969; *Asahi*, March 8, 1969.

7. *Kyodo*, March 22, 1969.
8. *Xinhua*, March 22, 1969.
9. *Xinhua*, April 12, 1969.
10. *Kyodo*, February 16, 1969.
11. *Kyodo*, April 2, 1969.
12. *Xinhua*, April 4, 1969; *Kyodo*, April 4, 1969.
13. *Tokyo Shimbun*, April 6, 1969.
14. The term refers to a tablet with a crucifix on it that the Tokugawa shōgunate forced people to stamp their foot on to prove that they were not Christians. In the case of the seventeenth-century crucifix tablet stampers, the issue was personal survival; in the modern case, it was maintaining the Sino-Japanese relationship. Sometimes the political career of the contemporary *fumie* diplomats was, in fact, sacrificed by failing to be re-elected or resigning under pressure.
15. Takashi Oka, "Tokyo-Peking Tie Defended by Sato," *New York Times*, April 12, 1969, p. 2.
16. *Xinhua*, February 22, 1969.
17. Takashi Oka, "Soviet Is Pursuing 'Smiles' Policy toward Japan," *New York Times*, July 14, 1969, p. 6.
18. Oka, p. 6.
19. *Xinhua*, December 1, 1969.
20. *Xinhua*, June 22, 1969.
21. *Xinhua*, May 22, 1969.
22. Rumors to this effect circulated in Japan for many years, most of them apparently emanating from leftist sources. Even after confirmed by the declassification of U.S. documents, the Japanese foreign ministry continued to sidestep the issue with statements such as "we know of no such documents." In August 2009, with the opposition Minshutō, which had promised a full investigation of the matter, on the verge of an overwhelming electoral victory, the foreign ministry began to relent. *Asahi*, August 25, 2009.
23. *Renmin Ribao*, November 28, 1969.
24. These are themes repeated constantly in the late fall and winter of 1969. For a representative sample, see *Renmin Ribao*, November 28, 1969; *Xinhua*, November 26, 1969; *Xinhua*, December 5, 1969.
25. Takashi Oka, "Sato, Home, Says Okinawa Will Remain Free of A-Arms After '72," *New York Times*, November 27, 1969, p. 6.
26. *Xinhua*, May 27, 1969.
27. *Xinhua*, December 23, 1969.
28. *Kyodo*, May 31, 1969.
29. *Asahi*, April 9, 1969.
30. Peter Grose, "Study Finds China's Growth Rate Stunted by 3 Years of Turmoil," *New York Times*, May 19, 1969, p. 10.
31. *Japan Times*, January 3, 1970.
32. *Japan Times*, February 7, 1970.
33. Takashi Oka, "Sato Foresees Major Role for Japan in 1970s," *New York Times*, February 14, 1970, p. 3.
34. "Japan Welcomes U.S.-Chinese Talks," *New York Times*, January 10, 1970, p. 3.
35. Philip Shabecoff, "China Raises Orders for Japanese Steel; Impact on U.S. Is Seen," *New York Times*, February 17, 1970, p. 59.

36. Robert Walker, "Heavy Chinese Buying Keeps World Steel Demand High," *New York Times*, May 17, 1970, p. 14.
37. *Japan Times*, April 25, 1970, pp. 1, 2.
38. *Japan Times Weekly*, May 2, 1970.
39. *Japan Times Weekly*, February 21, 1970.
40. Tillman Durdin, "Peking Accuses Japanese of Developing War Rockets," *New York Times*, February 19, 1970, p. 4.
41. Tillman Durdin, "Communist China Orbits Satellite: Gains Seen," *New York Times*, April 26, 1970, p. 1.
42. *New York Times*, May 25, 1970, p. 65.
43. *New York Times*, May 25, 1970, p. 65.
44. "Patience Is Stressed by Sato in Replying to Peking's Attack," *New York Times*, April 21, 1970, p. 3.
45. *Japan Times Weekly*, October 31, 1970; *Japan Times*, November 14, 1970.
46. Takashi Oka, "New China Policy Is Urged in Japan," *New York Times*, March 22, 1970, p. 4.
47. "Japan's 'Private Ambassador' Leaves Peking After 12 Years," *New York Times*, August 19, 1970, p. 3.
48. *Japan Times Weekly*, October 24, 1970.
49. *Japan Times Weekly*, October 31, 1970.
50. *Japan Times Weekly*, November 28, 1970.
51. Herman Kahn, *The Emerging Japanese Superstate: Challenge and Response* (Englewood Cliffs, NJ: Prentice Hall, 1970), p. 130.
52. *Kyodo*, January 1, 1970.
53. *Kyodo*, February 19, 1971; Takashi Oka, "Japan's Reaction Is Pride and Disquiet," *New York Times*, February 20, 1971, p. 14.
54. Max Frankel, "Subtle Shifts by the President," *New York Times*, February 26, 1971, p. 14.
55. *Japan Times*, January 2, 1971.
56. National Intelligence Estimate, November 12, 1970, in *FRUS*, Vol. 17: *China* Washington, DC, 1997), p. 243.
57. *Japan Times*, January 2, 1971.
58. Seiji Hasegawa, "The World Will Revolve Around Beijing," in Morinosuke Kajima, ed., *Japan in International Affairs* (Tokyo: The Japan Times, 1971), pp. 138, 140.
59. Edwin O. Reischauer, "Premier Chou's Fear: A Resurgent Japan," *New York Times*, August 15, 1971, p. E3.
60. *Japan Times Weekly*, June 26, 1971.
61. *Reuters*, April 1, 1971.
62. Tad Szulc, "New Gesture to China," *New York Times*, June 11, 1971, p. 9.
63. *Kyodo*, July 21, 1971.
64. *Japan Times Weekly*, July 3, 1971.
65. Takashi Oka, "China Invites Opposition Party in Japan," *New York Times*, June 10, 1971.
66. *Asahi*, September 21, 1971.
67. *Japan Times*, January 23, 1971.
68. Takashi Oka, "Ex-Minister Pursues Criticism of Sato," *New York Times*, October 19, 1971, p. 26.
69. *Japan Times Weekly*, March 27, 1971, citing Kasushige Hirasawa.

70. *Japan Times Weekly*, April 3, 1971.
71. *Japan Times Weekly*, May 1, 1971.
72. *Japan Times*, July 18, 1971. For Satō's response to Nixon's new China policy, see professors Tanaka Akihiko and Murata Koji's interview with Satō's personal secretary Kusuda Minoru, November 16, 1995, at http://nsarchive.gwu.edu/japan/kusudaohinterview.htm.
73. *Asahi*, July 17, 1971.
74. *Japan Times*, July 18, 1971.
75. Editorial, "Tokyo Before Peking," *New York Times*, August 9, 1971, p. 28.
76. Richard Halloran, "China Discussed by Tokyo's Envoy," *New York Times*, August 12, 1971.
77. Editorial, "Squeeze on Japan," *New York Times*, August 20, 1971, p. 32.
78. *Japan Times Weekly*, July 31, 1971.
79. Takashi Oka, "Japan Faces Major Shift in Policy Toward China," *New York Times*, July 23, 1971, pp. 1, 5.
80. *Japan Times Weekly*, July 24, 1971.
81. *AP*, August 24, 1971.
82. *Kyodo*, August 21, 1972; UPI, August 21, 1972.
83. *Japan Times Weekly*, May 29, 1971.
84. *Japan Times Weekly*, January 2, 1971.
85. *Japan Times*, July 31, 1971.
86. See, for example, Editorial, "Chou En-lai Speaks," *New York Times*, August 10, 1971, p. 30; James Reston, "China's Nightmare," *New York Times*, August 11, 1971, p. 29.
87. *Sankei*, August 13, 1971.
88. Richard Halloran, "China Discussed by Tokyo's Envoy," *New York Times*, August 12, 1971, p. 4.
89. *Kyodo*, August 24, 1971.
90. *Kyodo*, August 25, 1971.
91. *Nihon Keizai Shimbun*, September 3, 1971.
92. *Japan Times*, September 28, 1971.
93. *Japan Times*, October 8, 1971.
94. *Japan Times*, October 14, 1971.
95. *Renmin Ribao*, October 27, 1971; the same phrases appear in several *Xinhua* reports.
96. Richard Halloran, "Tokyo: Sato Role on China Assailed," *New York Times*, October 27, 1971, p. 1.
97. *Japan Times*, October 28, 1971; Richard Halloran, "Sato Foils Foes in Upper House," *New York Times*, October 29, 1971, p. 11.
98. *Mainichi*, November 22, 1971.
99. *Japan Times*, November 27, 1971.
100. John Lee, "Display of U.S.-China Goodwill Causing Apprehension in Japan," *New York Times*, February 24, 1972, p. 1.
101. *Asahi*, February 28, 1972.
102. *Beijing Review*, March 6, 1972, pp. 2–4.
103. "Satō Clashes with Newsmen in Final Parlay," *New York Times*, June 18, 1972, p. 2.
104. *Japan Times*, April 30, 1972.
105. *Sankei*, July 11, 1972.

106. *Asahi*, July 7, 1972. *Asahi* named neither its source nor the name of the intermediary.
107. *Japan Times*, July 15, 1972.
108. *Japan Times*, July 19, 1972.
109. *Japan Times*, July 20, 1972.
110. *Japan Times*, August 12, 1972.
111. *Japan Times*, August 8, 1972.
112. *Japan Times*, August 10, 1972.
113. *Japan Times*, August 12, 1972.
114. *Japan Times*, August 22, 1972.
115. *Japan Times*, August 23, 1972.
116. *Japan Times*, August 29 1972.
117. *Kyodo*, September 2, 1972.
118. *Kyodo*, September 8, 1972.
119. *Kyodo*, September 16, 1972.
120. Text is available at http://www.mofa.go.jp/region/asia-paci/china/joint72.html.
121. *Japan Times*, October 2, 1972.
122. *Japan Times*, October 20, 1972.
123. Richard Halloran, "Tanaka Cautious on Chinese Ties," *New York Times*, October 1, 1972, p. 13; *Japan Times*, October 14, 1972.
124. *Asahi*, September 30, 1972.
125. *Japan Times*, October 1, 1972.
126. *Japan Times*, October 13, 1972.
127. *Japan Times*, special normalization supplement, October 27, 1972, pp. B1, B2.
128. Chalmers Johnson, "The Patterns of Japanese Relations with China, 1952–1982," *Pacific Affairs* 34, no. 3 (Autumn 1986): 403.
129. Johnson, p. 409, says that the Japanese public heard only one side of the China story. While this is basically true, some reporters did manage to print more forthright stories, for which several were expelled and at least one, Samejima Keiji, was imprisoned for a lengthy period of time.

CHAPTER 5

1. See *The Golden Age of the U.S.-China-Japan Triangle, 1972–1989*, edited by Ezra F. Vogel, Yuan Ming, and Tanaka Akihiko (Cambridge, MA: Harvard University Asia Center, 2002). While the authors have Sino-American-Japanese relations as their focus, the term is an accurate description of the Sino-Japanese dyad as well.
2. In election periods, the pear-shaped doll—designed so that if tipped over it immediately rights itself—has one eye not yet painted in; that is done if/when victory is announced.
3. *Japan Times*, September 23, 1972; September 24, 1972.
4. *Japan Times*, August 27, 1974.
5. *Sankei*, October 5, 1974.
6. A detailed discussion thereof can be found in Chalmers Johnson, "Tanaka Kakuei, Structural Corruption, and the Advent of Machine Politics in Japan," *Journal of Japanese Studies* 12, no. 1 (Winter 1986): 1–28.
7. *Japan Times*, January 21, 1975.

8. *Asahi*, February 4, 1975.
9. *Japan Times*, February 8, 1975.
10. *Sankei*, February 7, 1975.
11. *Tokyo Shimbun*, February 16, 1975.
12. *Mainichi*, April 11, 1975.
13. *Sankei*, May 5, 1975.
14. Kazuo Ogura, "How the 'Inscrutables' Negotiate with the 'Inscrutables': Chinese Negotiating Tactics Vis-à-vis the Japanese," *China Quarterly*, no. 79 (September 1979): 552.
15. Composite of Japanese press reports, January–February 1977.
16. *Xinhua*, February 16, 1978; *Kyodo*, February 16, 1978.
17. *Japan Times*, March 16, 1978.
18. *Reuters*, February 24, 1978.
19. *Beijing Radio*, February 25, 1978.
20. *Xinhua*, March 14, 1978.
21. *Japan Times*, June 24, 1978.
22. *Kyodo*, July 21, 1978.
23. *Japan Times*, August 10, 1978.
24. *Kyodo*, July 16, 1978.
25. *New York Times*, July 23, 1978.
26. *Kyodo*, July 19, 2011
27. *Kyodo*, July 11, 1978.
28. *Japan Times*, July 25, 1978.
29. *Wen Wei Po* (Hong Kong), July 25, 1978.
30. *Kyodo*, August 14, 1978.
31. Text in *Kyodo*, August 12, 1978.
32. See, for example, *Renmin Ribao*'s editorial of August 14, 1978.
33. *Ta Kung Pao*, August 14, 1978.
34. *Xinhua*, October 23, 1978.
35. "There Is No Tacit Consent Regarding the Diaoyu," *Hsin Wan Pao*, August 16, 1978.
36. *Asahi*, August 16, 1978.
37. Paragraph 7 of the 1972 joint declaration stated that "neither of the two countries should seek hegemony in the Asia-Pacific region, and each country is opposed to efforts by any other country or group of countries to establish such hegemony," while Article 2 of the 1978 treaty said, "The contracting parties declare that neither of them should seek hegemony in the Asia-Pacific region and that each is opposed to efforts by any other country or group of countries to establish such hegemony."
38. *Kyodo*, March 6, 1979.
39. See Chapter 8 for a more detailed treatment of these events.
40. *Xinhua*, March 29, 1979.
41. *Japan Times*, April 22, 1979.
42. *Japan Times*, April 22, 1979; *Japan Times*, April 29, 1979.
43. *Japan Times*, May 23, 1979.
44. *Kyodo*, May 25, 1979.
45. *Japan Times*, December 19, 1979.
46. *Kyodo*, May 31, 1979.
47. *Japan Times*, August 2, 1979.
48. *Japan Times*, September 7, 1979.
49. *Kyodo*/*Reuters*, September 27, 1979.

50. *Xinhua*, November 29, 1979.
51. Author's interviews, Research Institute for Peace and Security (RIPS), November 1979.
52. *Japan Times*, May 1, 1980.
53. *Tokyo Shimbun*, May 4, 1980.
54. *Asahi*, May 26, 1980.
55. *Kyodo*, May 27, 1980. *Xinhua* did not report this statement.
56. *Nihon Keizai Shimbun*, December 9, 1981.
57. *Xinhua*, December 29, 1981.
58. Phoenix Net, May 14, 2013, http://news.ifeng.com/shendu/xmzk/detail_2013_05/14/25273256_0.shtml.
59. Chalmers Johnson, "The Patterns of Japanese Relations with China, 1952–1982," *Pacific Affairs* 59, no. 3 (Autumn 1986): 419, details the charges and countercharges and their probable motivations.
60. Seiichi Momura, *The Devil's Gluttony*, Tokyo. The original was serialized in the JCP's flagship newspaper *Akahata* (Red Flag) in 1981 and then published in two volumes by Kobunsha in 1981 and 1982, but withdrawn because of concerns about a particular photograph. Kodokawa Shoten then issued a one-volume version in 1982, without the photograph.
61. *Kyodo*, September 28, 1982.
62. *Japan Times*, October 10, 1982.
63. UPI, November 8, 1982.
64. Composite of reports from the Japanese newspapers *Xinhua* and *Renmin Ribao*, November 22–December 2, 1986.
65. Reuters/*Kyodo*, May 18, 1984.
66. *Zhongguo Xinwenshe* (Beijing), August 13, 1985.
67. *Cheng Ming* (Hong Kong), no. 16, Special Issue, November 16, 1985.
68. *Kyodo*, December 13, 1985.
69. *Japan Times*, October 13, 1985.
70. *Xinhua*, September 27, 1986.
71. This is a complicated issue; apparently some of the women were, as the GOJ argued, prostitutes. Others, however, were innocent victims who became, in essence, sex slaves to the troops. In a page 1 article in its September 12, 2014, issue, the left-of-center *Asahi Shimbun*, which had all along backed the comfort women, admitted that its source had falsified data and issued a formal apology, available at http://ajw.asahi.com/article/views/vox/AJ201409130014.
72. See Julia Wong, "The 1986 Student Demonstrations in China: A Democratic Movement?," *Asian Survey* 28, no. 9 (September 1986): 970–985 for details of the demonstrations.
73. See, for example, the *Hong Kong Standard*, February 8, 1987.
74. *Japan Times*, February 1, 1987.
75. See, for example, *Beijing Review*, April 27, 1987.
76. *Xinhua*, April 11, 1986; *Japan Times*, April 3, 1986.
77. See *Japan Times*, August 13 and 16, 1987; *Xinhua*, September 6, 1986; *Renmin Ribao*, September 10, 1986.
78. *Renmin Ribao*, June 11, 1987.
79. *Xinhua*, June 22, 1987.

80. Although Shaanxi is better known for its cave dwellings than Shanxi, where they also exist, *Wei Wei Po* and, apparently, Watanabe both referred to Shanxi.
81. *Xinhua*, February 26, 1988.
82. *Wen Wei Po*, February 26, 1988.
83. *Xinhua*, February 26, 1988.
84. *Japan Times*, April 23, 1988.
85. *Xinhua*, March 12, 1988; *Japan Times*, March 13, 1988.
86. *Liaowang* (Beijing), September 1, 1986.
87. *Xinhua*, April 9, 1986.
88. *Xinhua*, October 30, 1986
89. *Xinhua*, June 10, 1988.
90. *Xinhua*, February 14, 1989.
91. *New York Times*, January 5, 1989.
92. Author's interviews, Tokyo, April 1989.
93. *The Military Balance, 1989–1990* (London: International Institute for Strategic Studies, 1990).
94. *Beijing Radio*, January 29, 1989.
95. *Xinhua*, March 21, 1989; *Japan Times*, March 25, 1989.
96. *Beijing Review*, April 10–16, 1989.
97. *Xinhua*, April 14, 1989.
98. *Japan Times*, June 6, 1989.
99. *Japan Times*, June 24, 1989.
100. *Japan Times*, June 27, 1989.
101. *Japan Times*, June 17, 1989.
102. *Japan Times*, July 8, 1989.
103. *Renmin Ribao*, July 4, 1989; *Japan Times*, July 4, 1989.
104. *Beijing Radio*, June 17, 1989.
105. *Japan Times*, June 25, 1989.
106. *Japan Times*, August 18, 1989.
107. *Kyodo*, July 19, 1989.
108. *Nihon Hōsō Kyōkai* (NHK; Tokyo), June 23, 1989.
109. *Kyodo*, July 18, 1989.
110. *South China Morning Post* (Hong Kong), July 19, 1989.
111. Agence France-Presse (AFP), September 3, 1989.
112. *Kyodo*, August 8, 1989.
113. AFP, July 14, 1989.
114. Kentaro Awaya and Yoshiaki Yoshimi, *Doku Gasu Sen Kankei Shiryō* (Documents on Poison Gas Warfare) (Tokyo: Fuji Shuppan, 1989). Reviewed in *Japan Times*, August 12, 1989.
115. *Mainichi*, August 30, 1989.
116. *Asahi*, August 22, 1989.
117. *Japan Times*, October 11, 1989.
118. *Japan Times*, October 11, 1989.
119. *Radio Beijing*, November 21, 1989.

CHAPTER 6

1. *Xinhua*, March 29, 1990.
2. *Xinhua*, April 30, 1990.
3. Though, after discussing the dangers, *Shijie Zhishi* added a slightly hopeful note with the statement that as long as both China and Japan abided by the Pancha Shila, friendly relations could be restored and developed. Weilong Luo, "Japan Holding Overall Detente Does Not Equal Post-Cold War Detente Cycle," *Shijie Zhishi*, January 1, 1990, pp. 7–8.
4. *Zhongguo Qingnian Bao* (China Youth Daily, Beijing), May 7, 1990, p. 2, citing a Japanese television program.
5. On Chinese nationalism, see, for example, Peter Hays Gries, *China's New Nationalism: Pride, Politics, and Diplomacy* (Berkeley: University of California Press, 2004); Suisheng Zhao, *A Nation-State by Construction: Dynamics of Modern Chinese Nationalism* (Stanford, CA: Stanford University Press, 2004).
6. The so-called blue camp in Taiwan, members of the Kuomintang and People First parties, claim the islands on behalf of the Republic of China. The greens, represented by the Democratic Progressive Party and Taiwan Solidarity Union, state that the islands belong to Japan.
7. *South China Morning Post*, October 31, 1990, p. 15.
8. *Renmin Ribao*, October 14, 1990, p. 6.
9. A rightist youth group originally constructed the lighthouse in 1978, after a flotilla of Chinese fishing boats, many of them armed, appeared off the islands. It was upgraded a decade later, but had never received official recognition from Tokyo, which was at pains to avoid confrontation on the sovereignty issue. AP, October 30, 1990.
10. *Cheng Ming* (Contending, Hong Kong), November 1, 1990, pp. 8–9.
11. *Hong Kong Standard*, October 31, 1990, p. 10.
12. *Xinhua*, November 2, 1990. The Japanese government had been quietly telling Beijing for several months of its intentions, rendering the actual announcement somewhat anticlimactic.
13. *Xinhua*, November 8, 1990. However, a few weeks later, *Xinhua* reported that Kaifu planned to submit another bill in the next Diet session. *Xinhua*, December 10, 1990.
14. *Ming Pao*, October 21, 1992.
15. *Asahi*, December 10, 2014, http://ajw.asahi.com/article/behind_news/politics/AJ201312100053.
16. *Chicago Tribune*, October 22, 1992, http://articles.chicagotribune.com/1992-10-22/news/9204050552_1_imperial-visit-empress-michiko-emperor-akihito.
17. Text of the emperor's address in *Kyodo*, October 23, 1992; I am unable to find mention of it in *Xinhua*.
18. *Kyodo*, October 23, 1992.
19. *Xinhua*, October 25, 1992.
20. I am indebted to an anonymous reader for this suggestion.
21. *Nihon Keizai Shimbun*, August 17, 1994.
22. *Sankei*, January 4, 1995.
23. *Shijie Zhishi*, July 1, 1995, p. 2. The allusion comes from Tang dynasty satirical poet and government official Bai Juyi whose work frequently drew on his experiences

in government. I am indebted to Professor Qiang Zhang for directing me to the locus classicus.

24. *Xinhua*, August 14, 1995.
25. *Renmin Ribao*, November 8, 1995.
26. According to an analysis in *Xiandai Guoji Guanxi* (Contemporary International Relations, Beijing) February 20, 1996, Hashimoto would probably continue Murayama's policy of "self-independence," hoping to exercise more leadership in Asia.
27. *Kyodo*, August 15, 1996.
28. *Zhongguo Xinwen She*, September 3, 1996.
29. *Asahi*, September 6, 1996.
30. Agence France-Presse (AFP), September 11, 1996.
31. *Hong Kong Standard*, September 16, 1996; *Hong Kong Standard*, September 17, 1992.
32. *Cheng Ming*, October 1, 1996.
33. AFP, November 10, 1996.
34. *Xinhua*, December 4, 1996.
35. *Sankei*, November 5, 1996.
36. *Sankei*, December 1, 1996.
37. *Xinhua*, December 24, 1996.
38. *Guoji Wenti Yanjiu*, January 13, 1996.
39. *Zhongguo Qingnian Bao*, March 18, 1997.
40. *China Daily*, April 24, 1997.
41. *Ekonomisuto*, March 4, 1997.
42. *Kyodo*, April 24, 1997.
43. *Sankei*, May 8, 1997.
44. AFP, May 11, 1997.
45. *Xinhua*, July 7, 1997.
46. *Xinhua*, July 13, 1997.
47. *Kyodo*, July 4, 1997.
48. *Hong Kong Standard*, September 5, 1997.
49. *South China Morning Post* (Hong Kong), January 4, 1998.
50. *Yomiuri*, September 25, 1997.
51. Glenn D. Hook, Julie Gibson, Christopher Hughes, and Hugo Dobson, *Japan and the East Asian Financial Crisis: Patterns, Motivations, and Instrumentalization of Japanese Regional Economic Diplomacy* (Warwick, UK: University of Warwick, 2002) argue persuasively that Japan was doing all that it could, given its own financial constraints. For an analysis of the Chinese response, see Wayne M. Morrison, *China's Response to the Asian Financial Crisis: Implications for U.S. Economic Interests* (Washington, DC: Congressional Research Service, U.S. Library of Congress), Rept. 98-220, 2002, available at http://congressionalresearch.com/98-220/document.php?study=CHI.
52. *Wen Wei Po*, June 18, 1998.
53. *Yomiuri*, November 1, 1998.
54. See, for example, Saori N. Katada, *Banking on Stability: Japan and the Cross-Pacific Dynamic* (Ann Arbor: University of Michigan Press, 2001), p. 255.
55. *Xinhua*, December 9, 1998.
56. The disastrous nature of the visit, with oblique criticism of Jiang Zemin, is discussed in Zhaokui Feng and Lin Chang, *Zhong-ri Guanxi Baogao* (Report on Sino-Japanese Relations) (Beijing: China Foundation for International and Strategic Studies, 2007).

57. See, for example, *Federation of Atomic Scientists Newsletter*, August 14, 1999, http://fas.org/nuke/guide/china/icbm/df-31.htm.
58. *Sankei*, July 2, 1999.
59. *Yomiuri*, April 24, 1999.
60. *Yomiuri*, April 13, 1999.
61. *Jianchuan Zhishi* (Ship Construction Knowledge, Beijing), July 5, 1999.
62. *Mainichi*, April 30, 1999.
63. *Yomiuri*, August 18, 1999.
64. *Shijie Zhishi*, April 1, 1999, p. 19.
65. *China Daily*, September 25, 1999.
66. *Liaowang*, November 1, 1999.
67. See, for example, *Xinhua*, February 4, 1999; *Nikkei Telecom Database*, April 18, 1999; *Kyodo*, June 12, 1999
68. *Asahi*, May 12, 1999; AFP, May 13, 1999. Both cite conflicting stories on whether the damage to the poster was deliberate. *Asahi* added that the student demonstration had originated to protest the NATO bombing of the Chinese embassy in Belgrade, but that the students turned their anger against Japan.
69. *Kyodo*, September 30, 1999.
70. *Kyodo*, May 10, 1999.
71. Professor Zheng Qirong, cited in *Hong Kong Standard*, July 10, 1999.
72. *Shijie Zhishi*, June 6, 1999, pp. 8–10.
73. *Asahi*, August 4, 1999.
74. *Ming Pao*, August 4, 1999.
75. *Kyodo*, July 14, 1999, citing U.S. Trade Representative Charlene Barshevsky and her deputy Richard Fisher.
76. AFP, February 14, 2000; *Asahi*, February 18, 2000. The hackers said their motivation was to protest an Osaka conference of nationalists who did not believe that the Nanjing Massacre had occurred.
77. BBC, November 20, 2000, among other references.
78. See, for example, *Xinhua*, May 16, 2000, and *Xinhua*, May 20, 2000. The latter noted that although Mori had issued a retraction, he had not actually apologized.
79. *Xinhua*, May 21, 2000. Foreign Minister Kono Yohei apologized to Beijing and reprimanded Ishihara for his "inappropriate remark." Beijing was not soothed, and Ishihara stood by his remark. *Yomiuri*, May 24, 2000.
80. *Xinhua*, August 15, 2000.
81. *Kyodo*, September 28, 2000.
82. *Nihon Keizai Shimbun*, August 27, 2000.
83. See, for example, *Ta Kung Pao*, October 17, 2000.
84. *Nikkei Telecom*, October 21, 2000.
85. *Xinhua*, January 16, 2001.
86. *Zhongguo Xinwen She*, January 10, 2001.
87. *Xinhua*, April 20, 2001. The visit was controversial within Japan as well, with *Asahi* arguing, in essence, that the harm done to Sino-Japanese relations would outweigh the right of Lee, now a private citizen, to seek medical attention in the country. *Asahi*, April 19, 2001.
88. *China Daily*, February 21, 2001.
89. *Xinhua*, February 18, 2001.

90. In one, a traditional Chinese stone carved lion appeared to be saluting the Prada GX; since stone lions are carved along the Marco Polo Bridge, some saw a hidden allusion to the event that marked the beginning of the Sino-Japanese War. In the other, a Land Cruiser was shown pulling a Chinese-made truck along a bumpy road. Toyota, denying any derogatory intent, apologized. http://auto.sina.com.cn/news/2003-12-03/51714.shtml.
91. *Xinhua*, February 19, 2001.
92. *Renmin Ribao*, April 22, 2001.
93. AFP, April 18, 2001, interview with Tokyo University Professor Wakabayashi Masahiro.
94. *Selected Works of Jiang Zemin* (Beijing: Foreign Languages Press, 2013), Vol. 3, pp. 1–2.
95. *Ta Kung Pao*, December 18, 2001.
96. Author's interviews, June 2000.
97. AFP, April 24, 2001.
98. See James Przystup, *Japan-China Relations: From Precipice to Promise* (Washington, DC: Institute for National Strategic Studies, U.S. National Defense University, December 2001). Chinese media account is available at http://news.sohu.com/87/64/news146856487.shtml.
99. *Xinhua*, October 8, 2001.
100. *Xinhua*, September 20, 2002.
101. *Renmin Wang*, November 2, 2001, citing then-director of the Japanese Foreign Relations Office of the Chinese Academy of Social Sciences Jin Xide.
102. *China Daily*, November 2, 2001.
103. Government of Japan, Ministry of Foreign Affairs, April 21, 2002, http://www.mofa.go.jp/announce/pm/koizumi/observe0204.html.
104. *Kyodo*, April 15, 2002.
105. *Kyodo*, May 17. 2002.
106. *Nihon Keizai Shimbun*, May 23, 2002.
107. *Bungei Shunjū* (Literary Arts Spring and Autumn, Tokyo), July 1, 2002.
108. *Yomiuri*, July 3, 2002.
109. *Renmin Ribao*, June 7, 2002.
110. *Yomiuri*, June 7, 2002.
111. *Jiefang Junbao* (Liberation Army Daily, Beijing), April 14, 2002.
112. *Kyodo*, April 12, 2002.
113. *Nihon Keizai Shimbun*, June 25, 2002.
114. See, for example, *Nikkei Management*, August 1, 2002.
115. *Kyodo*, September 22, 2002.
116. *Yomiuri*, December 6, 2002.
117. Akio Morita and Ishihara Shintarō, *The Japan That Can Say No* (Tokyo: Konbunsha Publishing, 1989).
118. *Bungei Shunjū*, July 1, 2002.
119. *Yomiuri*, September 23, 2002.
120. *Xinhua*, September 28, 2002.
121. *Kyodo*, December 27, 2002.
122. *Zhanlüe yü Guanli* (Strategy and Management), December 1, 2002.
123. *Guangzhou Ribao*, June 12, 2003.
124. *Zhanlüe yü Guanli*, March 1, 2003, pp. 71–75.

125. *Nanfang Zhoumo* (Southern Weekend), June 12, 2003.
126. *Kyodo*, May 31, 2003.
127. *Zhanlüe yü Guanli*, July 1, 2003.
128. *Zhanlüe yü Guanli*, August 1, 2003. For a detailed account of this period, see Peter Hays Gries, "China's 'New Thinking' on Japan," *China Quarterly*, no. 184 (December 2005): 831–850.
129. *Jiji*, June 14, 2002, quoting Vice-Minister of Foreign Affairs Takuchi Yukio.
130. *Kyodo*, September 4, 2003.
131. *Zhongguo Qingnian Bao*, September 28, 2003.
132. *Asahi*, November 3, 2003; AFP, October 31, 2003.
133. *Straits Times* (Singapore), April 7, 2004.
134. *Asahi*, July 13, 2003.
135. *Kyodo*, July 14, 2003.
136. *Yomiuri*, November 3, 2003.
137. Fong Tak-ho, "Old Rivalry Fired Up as Economic Dragon Stirs," *South China Morning Post*, April 3, 2003.
138. According to polls, this is the majority view. However, some Japanese are horrified and apologetic when they learn what their country did during the war, and profess profound guilt. See, for example, "One Japanese on a Quest of Atonement: A Tour of Horror Sites in China Is a History Lesson for Visitors," *New York Times*, September 5, 2004, p. I4.
139. See June Teufel Dreyer, "Sino-Japanese Territorial and Maritime Disputes," in Bruce Elleman, Stephen Kotkin, and Clive Schofield, eds., *China and Its Borders: Twenty Neighbors in Asia* (Armonk, NY: M.E. Sharpe, 2012), p. 91.
140. Charmaine Chan, "Territorial Rites," *South China Morning Post*, April 23, 2004; Michael Richardson, "The Treasure Islands of Southeast Asia," *South China Morning Post*, May 28, 2004.
141. *Kyodo*, November 10, 2005. The first instance occurred in March 1999, in response to two North Korean vessels approaching the Noto peninsula in northern Japan. Such orders are issued to the MSDF when it is deemed impossible or extremely difficult for the Japanese Coast Guard to secure maritime safety.
142. *Sankei*, November 11, 2003.
143. *Asahi*, March 24, 2004.
144. *Asahi*, August 5, 2004.
145. *South China Morning Post*, September 22, 2004. The journal had been affiliated with the State Development Planning Commission, which was merged with the State Economic and Trade Commission into the National Development and Reform Commission, leaving it without a sponsoring organization. Unable to find a new one, it became illegal, and was closed down by the CCP's Publicity Department.
146. I am indebted to Professor Tony Saich for this information.
147. *Asia Times*, October 18, 2004. The paper is published in both Bangkok and Hong Kong.
148. Susan Shirk, *China: Fragile Superpower* (Oxford: Oxford University Press, 2007), p. 175.
149. *Xinhua*, May 12, 2005; *Yomiuri*, May 12, 2005.
150. *Shokun!* (You!, Tokyo), October 1, 2004; author's interviews, Tokyo, November 2004.
151. *Xinhua*, May 23, 2005.
152. *Asahi*, November 25, 2005.

153. *Yomiuri*, December 15, 2005.
154. *Yomiuri*, December 30, 2005.
155. See Feng Yujun, "Russia's Oil Pipeline Saga," *Beijing Review*, July 29, 2004, pp. 10–13; the passage quoted here appears on p. 13.
156. Isabel Gorst and David Pilling, "Tokyo Threatens to Withdraw From $11 Billion Oil Pipeline," *Financial Times*, April 30, p. 8; "Russia Reconstructs Oil Tank Farm for Far East, China," *Itar-Tass* (Moscow), October 6, 2005.
157. "China, Russia in Talks Over New Gas Pipeline," *Kyodo*, September 21, 2005.
158. *Ming Pao*, August 15, 2006.

CHAPTER 7

1. Other notable downturns had occurred during the prime ministerships of Kishi Nobusuke (1957–1960), his brother Satō Eisaku (1964–1972), and Nakasone Yasuhiro (1982–1987).
2. *Yomiuri*, August 11, 2006.
3. *International Herald Tribune*, September 22, 2006.
4. *Asahi*, August 4, 2006.
5. *Asahi*, September 17, 2006.
6. A summary of the debate appears in *Asahi*, September 13, 2006. The reparations issue is a good deal more complicated than the newspaper's terse references to it might indicate. Chiang Kai-shek, head of the government of the Republic of China that Tokyo broke relations with in order to establish relations with the PRC in 1972, had long ago agreed not to ask for reparations. Since the PRC leadership claimed to be the successor government to the Republic of China, it was legally, though not necessarily morally, bound to observe this arrangement. Beijing's acceptance of the separation between militarists and the general Japanese public allowed it a face-saving reason not to demand reparations. Conversely, its insistence on reparations would have provided the influential Japanese opponents of normalization with a powerful argument against concluding the normalization agreement.
7. Reuters, September 18, 2006.
8. Agence France-Presse (AFP), September 21, 2006.
9. *Straits Times*, September 21, 2006. The government had established a subsidiary of *Xinhua*, the China Economic Information Service (CEIS), and then issued regulations that not only allowed CEIS to impose fees on foreign media but also gave it the power to regulate and censor them. They were forbidden to solicit mainland subscribers directly and were required to distribute news content only through agents approved by *Xinhua*, which received a 30 to 40 percent commission for doing so.
10. *Kyodo*, September 25, 2006.
11. AFP, September 27, 2006.
12. *Xinhua*, September 28, 2006.
13. *Financial Times*, September 29, 2006.
14. A reference to the tribute system of the traditional Chinese empire, in which a prerequisite for relations with the Middle Kingdom was acceptance of the position of vassal state as symbolized by performing the *ketou* (kowtow) of three kneelings and nine prostrations. Some states, such as Korea, appear to have been comfortable with the relationship; others, like the Thais, participated in the ritual but without

internalizing its underlying premises. Japan, the most outwardly resentful of China's vassal states, sometimes went to great lengths to resist the tribute system, even at one point attempting to set up a parallel system with itself as the center. See, for example, Ronald Toby, *State and Society in Early Modern Japan* (Princeton, NJ: Princeton University Press, 1984), pp. 118–140 and passim.

15. *Financial Times*, October 1, 2006.
16. Reuters, January 16, 2007.
17. See, for example, *Renmin Ribao, Japan Times, New York Times*, and *Washington Post*, all on October 9, 2006.
18. In addition to the obvious success of the Japanese economy, there is an element of rivalry with the PRC. When China was admitted to the UN in October 1971, Tokyo lobbied hard and unsuccessfully for a seat, arguing that Japan was far more important internationally than the about-to-be admitted China.
19. *Yomiuri*, February 19, 2007.
20. AFP, February 16, 2007.
21. *Nikkei Telecom 21 Database*, July 20, 2007.
22. *Asahi*, January 1, 2007.
23. The pacifist segment of the population is adamantly opposed to rewriting the constitution, considering any change to Article 9 to be another step on the slippery slide to reversion to the militarism of the 1920s and 1930s. Successive governments have aborted efforts at revision in favor of reinterpretation in the direction of allowing them more freedom to deploy troops in international scenarios. The euphemism for instituting a standard military force is "making Japan into a 'normal country,'" or *futsū no kuni*.
24. AFP, January 19, 2007.
25. *Yomiuri*, January 21, 2007.
26. AFP, February 5, 2007.
27. *Asahi*, January 2, 2008.
28. Peter Dutton, *Scouting, Signaling, and Gatekeeping: Chinese Naval Operations in Japanese Waters and the International Law Implications* (Newport, RI: U.S. Naval War College, February 2009), China Maritime Studies, no. 2, p. 6.
29. *Xinhua*, January 10, 2007.
30. *China Daily* (Beijing), January 5, 2007.
31. *Yomiuri*, August 31, 2007.
32. *Yomiuri*, August 16, 2007.
33. *Kyodo*, August 23, 2007.
34. *China Daily*, August 21, 2007.
35. http://www.mofa.go.jp/POLICY/oda/white/2006; Chapter 3, Section 2.
36. *Yomiuri*, November 20, 2006.
37. Hiroyasu Akutsu, "Tokyo and Taipei Try to Tango," *Far Eastern Economic Review* (January/February 2007): 32. The "China School" of MOFA refers to career bureaucrats who favor accommodation with the PRC. Their detractors criticize the China School's attitude as "kowtow foreign policy."
38. *Yomiuri*, January 10, 2007. The GOJ justified its decision by indicating that India was a democracy with a stable political system, that it had announced its intention to allow IAEA inspections, and that its switching energy demand to nuclear power, with Japanese help, would contribute to the prevention of further global warming.
39. *Japan Times*, January 18, 1967.

40. *Straits Times*, September 2007.

41. Tanaka, the daughter of former Prime Minister Tanaka Kakuei and, like her father, a strong proponent of close Sino-Japanese ties, made the prediction just before Abe's ascension to the post. *Straits Times*, September 17, 2006.

42. *Xinhua*, September 13, 2007.

43. Cited in *Straits Times*, September 13, 2007.

44. Cited in *Straits Times*, September 24, 2007.

45. *Xinhua*, September 26, 2007.

46. *Yomiuri*, October 11, 2007.

47. Fukuda speech to the 14th International Conference on the Future of Asia, Tokyo, May 22, 2008, http://www.mofa.go.jp/region/asia-paci/speech0805-2.html.

48. Asō's speech of May 4, 2006, is available at http://www.mofa.go.jp/announce/fm/aso/speech0605.html.

49. Asō's speech to the Japan Institute of International Affairs, November 30, 2006, http://www.mofa.go.jp/announce/fm/aso/speech0611.html.

50. Asō's speech to the Japan Institute of International Affairs, November 30, 2006, is available at http://www.mofa.go.jp/announce/fm/aso/speech0605.html.

51. *Asahi*, December 10, 2007.

52. *Financial Times*, May 12, 2008.

53. *Jiji*, November 6, 2009.

54. *Yomiuri*, April 25, 2008.

55. *Sankei*, June 25, 2008; *Yomiuri*, June 25, 2008.

56. *Taipei Times*, December 7, 2008.

57. Lee's first language is Hoklo, known in its Taiwan variant as Taiwanese. Growing up when Taiwan was a Japanese colony, he learned excellent Japanese and has many times been criticized by Beijing for, in essence, being a Japanese.

58. *Sankei*, September 25, 2008. This runs counter to the policy of the KMT government as well as that of the PRC. According to *Tzu-yu Ji-pao* (Liberty Times, Taiwan), Taiwan Foreign Minister Francisco Ou called Lee's remarks "his personal opinions."

59. For example, in June 2003, after a widely publicized gang rape case involving students at prestigious Waseda University, Fukuda indicated that the young women's choice of clothing indicated that they were to blame.

60. BBC, December 22, 2005.

61. *China Daily*, January 29, 2006.

62. *Mainichi*, March 9, 2006.

63. AFP, October 24, 2008.

64. *Asahi*, October 24, 2008.

65. *Straits Times*, October 23, 2008.

66. *Yomiuri*, December 18, 2008.

67. *Yomiuri*, November 1, 2008.

68. *Yomiuri*, December 8, 2008.

69. *South China Morning Post*, December 26, 2008.

70. *Asahi*, December 31, 2008.

71. *Yomiuri*, October 27, 2008.

72. ChinaSMACK, October 14, 2008, carried many of these, in which the "dwarfs" were castigated in obscene language. They included such predictions as this: in twenty years Japan, "already a has-been, will go down the toilet and be the third rate power

it always was in most of history." http://www.chinasmack.com/2008. The offending posts were removed.

73. APA Group (Tokyo), http://www.apa.co.jp/book_report/index.html#sakuhin.
74. *Yomiuri*, November 12, 2008.
75. *Xinhua*, November 1, 2008.
76. *Shijie Zhishi*, December 1, 2008.
77. *Economist*, June 21, 2008.
78. *Nikkei Weekly*, June 23, 2008.
79. Ching Cheong, "Tokyo Seen as Having the Upper Hand," *Straits Times*, June 21, 2008.
80. *South China Morning Post*, June 28, 2008.
81. See, inter alia, *China Daily*, June 20 2008; transcript of Ministry of Foreign Affairs statement, June 18, 2008, at http://news.xinhuanet.com/english/2008-06/18/content_8394206.htm.
82. *Kyodo*, April 23, 2009.
83. Presumably considered less provocative because it did not have the same Shintō significance as the masasaki.
84. *Yomiuri*, April 21, 2009.
85. *Xinhua*, April 23, 2009.
86. *Straits Times*, May 1, 2009.
87. According to Articles 45 and 46 of the Japanese Constitution, elections for the House of Councillors are fixed, occurring every three years, with members serving six-year terms. Terms for the House of Representatives are four years but, unlike the House of Councillors, the lower house can be dissolved before the end of its term and new elections held. The DPJ had obtained a majority in the House of Councillors in the August 2007 election, prompting Prime Minister Abe to resign to take responsibility.
88. *Yomiuri*, November 27, 2009.
89. *Straits Times*, November 11, 2009.
90. *Straits Times*, November 5, 2009.
91. *Asahi*, November 10, 2009.
92. *Sapio*, December 16, 2009, pp. 91–93; *Shukan Daiyamondo* (Tokyo), November 28, 2009, pp. 132–134.
93. *Kyodo*, October 21, 2009.
94. Reuters, November 8, 2009.
95. *Kyodo*, May 18, 2010; *Financial Times*, May 18, 2010.
96. *Xinhua*, May 31, 2010.
97. *Xinhua*, April 12, 2010.
98. *Business Times* (Singapore), June 5, 2010.
99. Exactly what happened is controversial. On September 23, 2010, the *New York Times* reported that the Chinese government had said it would halt rare earth exports to Japan—which would have been a clear violation of World Trade Organization rules; on the same day, Reuters reported that the Chinese Ministry of Commerce denied doing so; the *Times* stuck to its story. It is possible that the announcement was made to send a message to the Japanese government, which did indeed react sharply, immediately seeking out other sources of supply.
100. *Xinhua*, September 23, 2010.
101. *Global Times*, September 25, 2010; *Asahi*, September 26, 2010.

102. *Xinhua*, September 17, 2010.
103. *Mainichi*, September 6, 2011; *Asahi*, September 8, 2011.
104. *Yomiuri*, September 29, 2010.
105. *International Herald Tribune*, September 29, 2010.
106. *Jingji Guancha Bao* (Economic Observer, Beijing), November 20, 2010.
107. TBS (Tokyo Broadcasting System) Television, December 6, 2010.
108. *Global Times* (Beijing), December 27, 2010.
109. *Kyodo*, January 22, 2012.
110. *Nanfang Zhoumo*, February 9, 2012.
111. Yin Zhou, interviewed by *Nihon Keizai Shimbun*, March 11, 2012.
112. Cited in *China Daily*, May 4, 2012.
113. *Mainichi*, April 12, 2012.
114. Author's interviews: Miami, November 2012, and Ottawa, October 2013.
115. *Wall Street Journal*, July 4, 2012. Reportedly, the game was removed, not by China's censors but by Apple. Users were still able to play the Nanjing Massacre game. *Wall Street Journal*, July 11, 2012.
116. *Ta Kung Pao*, May 5, 2012.
117. *Global Times*, May 16, 2012.
118. Kazuhiko Togo post to National Bureau of Asian Research's Japan Forum, July 5, 2014.
119. Author's interview, November 2014.
120. A selection of comments from Weibo (the Chinese equivalent of Twitter), as reported by *Global Times*, September 20, 2012.
121. John Gong, associate professor at Beijing University of International Business and Economics, cited in *South China Morning Post*, September 19, 2012.
122. Donald Clarke, professor, George Washington University School of Law, personal communication with the author, December 6, 2014.
123. *Kyodo*, September 21, 2012.
124. *Yomiuri*, October 1, 2012.
125. *Kyodo*, November 25, 2012.
126. *Washington Free Beacon*, September 18, 2012, http://freebeacon.com/chinese-general-prepare-for-combat/.
127. *Financial Times*, July 23, 2012.
128. *Bloomberg*, September 12, 2012.
129. http://www.mofa.go.jp/region/n-america/us/q&a/ref/1.html, Article 5.
130. http://www-wds.worldbank.org/external/default/WDSContentServer/WDSP/IB/2013/03/27/000350881_20130327163105/Rendered/PDF/762990PUB0chinao0Box374372B00PUBLIC0.pdf.
131. Mingfu Liu, *Zhongguo meng: Hou meiguo shidai de daguo siwei zhanlue dingwei* (China Dream: The Great Power Thinking and Strategic Positioning of China in the Post-American Age) (Beijing: Zhongguo youyi chuban gongsi, 2010).
132. *Washington Post*, June 8. 2013.
133. *Renmin Ribao*, December 17, 2012.
134. http://www.nippon.com/en/simpleview/?post_id=16037, December 25, 2013.
135. *Yomiuri*, December 18, 2013.
136. *Christian Science Monitor*, December 18, 2013.
137. *Japan Times*, December 15, 2013.

138. *Open Democracy* (London), December 20, 2013, http://www.opendemocracy.net/opensecurity/saul-takahashi/japans-designated-secrets-bill-sound-of-jackboots.

139. Authorities in Taketomi, a small rural township, believe that they were chosen as an example. *New York Times*, December 29, 2013.

140. Bonnie Glaser, analyst at the Center for Strategic and International Studies, Washington, DC, quoted in *Los Angeles Times*, November 23, 2013; *AsiaTimes*, November 25, 2013.

141. Michael Auslin, *Politico*, November 26, 2013.

142. *Christian Science Monitor*, December 5, 2013,

143. See, for example, *The Guardian*, January 9, 2014; AP, January 19, 2014; the two also debated on BBC.

144. *The Japan News*, January 9, 2014.

145. *Xinhua*, January 19, 2014.

146. *Mainichi*, February 12, 2014.

147. *U.S. Naval Institute News*, February 18, 2014. Captain Fanell's speech can be viewed in full at http://www.youtube.com/watch?v=wWhwm4SJxTw. He was relieved of command and shortly thereafter announced his retirement.

148. *Bloomberg*, April 22, 2014.

149. Sina.com, May 13, 2013, http://english.sina.com/world/2013/0513/589996.html.

150. Sina.com, August 15, 2014, http://english.sina.com/entertainment/p/2014/0815/728223.html.

151. *New York Times*, September 11, 2014; *Kyodo*, December 12, 2014.

152. *Yonhap* (Seoul), December 10, 2014.

153. *South China Morning Post*, September 26, 2014, http://www.scmp.com/news/china-insider/article/1601029/beware-chubby-blue-guy-chinese-dailies-warn-public-against-japans; *New York Times*, September 29, 2014, http://sinosphere.blogs.nytimes.com/2014/09/29/a-warning-in-china-beware-the-blue-fatty-cat/.

154. AFP, September 10, 2014.

155. Shinzō Abe, keynote address at the Shangri La Dialogue, May 30, 2014, http://www.iiss.org/en/events/shangri%20la%20dialogue/archive/2014-c20c/opening-remarks-and-keynote-address-b0b2/keynote-address-shinzo-abe-a787.

156. Xinhuanet, November 14, 2013, http://news.163.com/13/1114/07/9DKHKSII0001121M.html?from=tag.

157. AFP, October 15, 2014, citing Chinese Ambassador to Tokyo Chang Yonghua; Reuters, August 28, 2014, http://www.reuters.com/article/2014/08/28-us-japan-abe-china-idUSKBN0GS02O20140828.

158. The four documents refer to the China-Japan Joint Statement of 1972; the China-Japan Treaty of Peace and Friendship of 1978; the China-Japan Joint Declaration of 1998; and a joint statement on advancing strategic and mutually beneficial relations in a comprehensive way signed in 2008.

159. http://news.xinhuanet.com/english/china/2014-11/07/c_133773116.htm.

160. http://news.xinhuanet.com/english/china/2014-11/07/c_133773116.htm.

161. Japanese Ministry of Foreign Affairs, November 7, 2014, http://www.mofa.go.jp/a_o/c_m1/cn/page4e_000150.html.

162. *New York Times*, November 11, 2014, http://www.nytimes.com/2014/11/11/world-asia/leaders-of-china-and-japan-hold-long-awaited-meeting.html?_r+t.

163. *Jiji*, November 14, 2014.

164. *Ming Pao*, November 14, 2014.
165. *Xinhua*, November 7, 2014.
166. http://www.diaoyudao.org.cn/index.htm. The site went online December 30, 2014.
167. *China Daily*, December 5, 2014.
168. *Bloomberg*, December 22, 2014.
169. Interviewed by the *Sydney Morning Herald*, July 3, 2014.

CHAPTER 8

1. Shigeru Yoshida, "Japan and the Crisis in Asia," *Foreign Affairs* 20, no. 2 (January 1951): 177.
2. Chalmers Johnson, *MITI and the Japanese Miracle: The Growth of Industrial Policy 1925–1975* (Stanford, CA: Stanford University Press, 1982).
3. On the basis of recently declassified cables among Stalin, Mao, and Kim, Zhihua Shen and Danhui Li conclude that Kim's offensive in Korea was a perfect means for Stalin to achieve both his goals of unifying Korea and keeping China's military at the service of Soviet strategy. Shen and Li, *After Leaning to One Side: China and Its Allies in the Cold War* (Washington, DC: Woodrow Wilson Center and Stanford University Press, 2011), p. 28.
4. Seiichiro Takagi, "An Analysis of Chinese Behavior Toward Japan, 1850–1965: An Examination of Three Models of International Behavior," Ph.D. dissertation, Stanford University, Stanford, CA, 1977, p. 78. Microfilm 78-2247 available through University of Michigan, Ann Arbor.
5. *New York Times*, May 16, 1954.
6. Kurt Radke, *China's Relations With Japan, 1945–83: The Role of Liao Chengzhi* (Manchester, UK: Manchester University Press, 1990), pp. 101–105.
7. Chae-Jin Lee, "The Politics of Sino-Japanese Trade Relations, 1963–68," *Pacific Affairs* 42, no. 2 (Summer 1969): 131.
8. Lee, p. 130.
9. *Kyodo*, July 12, 1972.
10. *Asahi*, June 12, 1972.
11. *New York Times*, January 1, 1973.
12. *Asahi*, September 30, 1972.
13. *Kyodo*, February 7, 1973. A caveat on statistics is necessary, since the two countries report their statistics in different ways: both report larger volumes of imports from the other than the other reports as exports. In trade statistics, exports are classified by country of destination and registered on a free on board (FOB) basis, whereas imports are registered on the basis of country of origin, and cost, insurance, and freight (CIF). Hence, the transport share of the value of the goods is included in the import, but not the export, statistics. A second discrepancy results from the Chinese practice of over-invoicing as a way to avoid foreign exchange control. A third issue results from the way shipments to and from both sides through Hong Kong are recorded. For a more complete explanation, see Hans Gunter Hilpert, "China and Japan: Conflict or Cooperation? What Does [sic] Trade Data Say?," in Hanns Günther Hilpert and René Haak, *Japan and China: Cooperation, Competition, and Conflict* (Houndsmill, UK: Palgrave, 2002), pp. 35–38.

14. *Asahi*, December 15, 1973; *Japan Times*, January 6, 1974. *Asahi*, which opposed the COCOM restrictions, noted that Australia, despite its membership in COCOM, had refused to comply with the restrictions in concluding a similar treaty with the PRC.
15. *New York Times*, January 4, 1974,
16. *Japan Times*, February 25, 1984.
17. Author's conversation with an observer at the ceremony, October 1979.
18. *Kyodo*, January 26, 1975.
19. Masanori Tabata in *Japan Times*, October 13, 1975.
20. *Asahi*, January 18, 1977.
21. *Asahi*, October 12, 1978.
22. Robert E. Bedeski, *The Fragile Entente: The 1978 Japan-China Peace Treaty in a Global Context* (Boulder, CO: Westview Press, 1983), pp. 86–88, provides details on the LTTA negotiations and its problems.
23. Yoshihide Soeya, *Japan's Economic Diplomacy with China, 1945–1978* (Oxford: 1998, Clarendon Press), p. 154.
24. Chalmers Johnson, "How China and Japan See Each Other," *Foreign Affairs* 50 no. 4 (July 1972): 713.
25. The flying geese pattern posited that East Asian economies would be developed from Japan to the newly industrializing economies (Taiwan, South Korea, Singapore, and Hong Kong) and then to China and the ASEAN states. Counties specialize in exporting products in which they have a comparative advantage, utilizing the capital gained to upgrade their industrial structures, helped as well by foreign direct investment (FDI) from more advanced economies, in this case, Japan. C. H. Kwan, *Economic Interdependence in the Asia-Pacific Region* (London: Routledge, 1994), passim.
26. For a good summary of the issues surrounding Baoshan, see Ryosei Kokubun, "The Politics of Foreign Economic Policy-Making in China: The Case of Plant Cancellations with Japan," *China Quarterly*, no. 109 (March 1986): 19–44.
27. Allen S. Whiting, *China Eyes Japan* (Berkeley: University of California Press, 1989), p. 97.
28. For example, Japan's participation in the massive Dalian Economic and Technological Development Area. The Dalian Industrial Park was the country's first joint project to develop a plot of land. *Xinhua*, October 19, 1992.
29. Katsuji Nakagame, "Japanese Direct Investment in China," in Hilpert and Haak, p. 57.
30. *Japan Times*, February 4, 1987.
31. *Japan Times*, December 2, 1979, pp. 1, 3.
32. Junichi Inada, "Japan's ODA and Sino-Japanese Relations," in Hilpert and Haak, p. 123.
33. C. H. Kwan, "The Rise of China as an Economic Power: Implications for Asia and Japan," in Hilpert and Haak, p. 24.
34. Author's conversation with Allen Whiting, September 1988.
35. *Japan Times*, October 14, 1986.
36. Ezra F. Vogel, *Japan as Number One* (Cambridge, MA: Harvard University Press, 1979), passim.
37. AP, August 1, 1986.
38. See, for example, the collection of articles in *Japan Times*, December 1, 1986.
39. Goto Noboru, cited in *Xinhua*, March 4, 1985; in *FBIS-CHI*, March 5, 1985, p. D2.

40. *Japan Times*, November 7, 1985.
41. *Japan Times*, January 17, 1986.
42. *Japan Times*, January 23, 1986.
43. *Japan Times*, January 25, 1986.
44. *Xinhua*, September 27, 1986.
45. *Japan Times*, October 14, 1986.
46. *Xinhua*, July 18, 1986; in *FBIS-CHI*, July 22, 1986, p. D1.
47. *Japan Times*, January 10, 1986.
48. *Kyodo*, April 27, 1986.
49. *Yomiuri*, November 12, 1989.
50. *Yomiuri*, October 1, 1990.
51. *Yomiuri*, May 6, 1990.
52. Hanns Günther Hilpert, "Japanese Direct Investment in China: Its Effect on China's Economic Development," in Hilpert and Haak, p. 46.
53. *Yomiuri*, March 13, 2001.
54. Xinhua, November 1, 1991.
55. *China Business Weekly* (Beijing), July 11–17, 1993.
56. *Xinhua*, August 18, 1991.
57. *Xinhua*, October 16, 1991.
58. See David Bailey, Dan Coffey, and Philip Tomlinson, "Introduction: The Attributes of the Crisis," in Bailey, Coffey, and Tomlinson eds., *Crisis or Recovery in Japan: State and Industrial Economy* (Cheltenham, UK, and Northampton, MA: Edward Elgar, 2007), pp. 1–8, for a fuller treatment.
59. Andy Xie, formerly chief Asia-Pacific analyst for Morgan Stanley, cited in Ruchir Sharma, *Breakout Nations: In Pursuit of the Next Economic Miracles* (New York: W.W. Norton, 2012), pp. 252–253.
60. *Yomiuri*, March 7, 2003.
61. *Yomiuri*, August 1, 2003.
62. Ulrike Schaede discusses this issue in detail in "Globalization and the Japanese Subcontractor System," in Bailey, Coffey, and Tomlinson, pp. 82–105.
63. Terutomo Ozawa, "Institutionally Driven Growth and Stagnation—and Stuggle for Reform," in Bailey, Coffey, and Tomlinson, pp. 106–132.
64. According to its charter, preconditions for the grant of ODA are:

> (1) Environment and development will be pursued in tandem. (2) Use of ODA for military purposes or for aggravation of conflicts will be avoided. (3) Full attention will be given to trends in military expenditures, development/production of weapons of mass destruction and missiles, export/import of arms in the recipient country and other matters in the recipient country. (4) Full attention will be given to the efforts for democratization and the introduction of market economy, and protection of basic human rights in the recipient country. http://www.id.emb-japan.go.jp/oda/en/whatisoda_05.htm.

65. *Kyodo*, October 9, 2003.
66. Keith Cowling and Philip Tomlinson, "Transnational Monopoly Capitalism, the J-Mode Firm, and Industrial 'Hollowing Out' in Japan," in Bailey, Coffey, and Tomlinson, p. 73.
67. *Yomiuri*, December 18, 2001,

68. June Teufel Dreyer, "Sino-Japanese Rivalry and Its Implications for Developing Nations," *Asian Survey* 56, no. 4 (July/August 2006): 544–545.
69. June Teufel Dreyer, "Sino-Japanese Territorial and Maritime Disputes," in Bruce Elleman, Stephen Kotkin, and Clive Schofield, eds., *China and Its Borders: Twenty Neighbors in Asia* (Armonk, NY: M.E. Sharpe, 2012), pp. 80–95.
70. Shinji Fukukawa, cited in *Yomiuri*, October 10, 2002.
71. *Yomiuri*, May 22, 2001.
72. *Asahi*, January 29, 2003.
73. This is corroborated in a 2003 study by Paul Ryan, "Is China Exporting Deflation Globally, Hollowing Out Japan?," Marubeni Corporation Economic Research Institute (Tokyo), 2003.
74. *Yomiuri*, September 23, 2002.
75. http://www.stat.go.jp/english/data/handbook/c0117.htm.
76. http://www.jetro.go.jp/en/news/releases/20110512035-news.
77. Rare earths are essential to the production of powerful magnets used in hybrid and electric-vehicle traction motors. The Japanese auto industry has been at the forefront of their development. "Vehicle Electrification," SAE International, November 17, 2001, http://ev.sae.org/article/10435.
78. *Asahi*, September 25, 2010.
79. Wendy Dobson and Anil Kashyap, "The Contradiction in China's Gradualist Banking Reform," http://faculty.chicagobooth.edu/anil.kashyap/research/papers/Contradiction-in-Chinas-gradualist-banking-reforms.pdf unpublished paper, October 2006.
80. AP, January 20, 2015.
81. Joshua K. Hausman and Johannes F. Wieland, "Abenomics: Preliminary Analysis and Outlook," Brookings Papers on Economic Activity, Washington, DC: Brookings Institution, Spring 2014, pp. 1–63, passim, but see especially p. 4.
82. *International Business Times*, December 8, 2014.
83. JETRO Survey, "Analysis of Japan-China Trade in 2013 and Outlook for 2014," February 28, 2014, http://www.jetro.go.jp/en/news/20140228009-news.
84. *The China Post*, January 30, 2015, http://www.chinapost.com.tw/business/asia-china/2015/01/30/427731/Political-tensions.htm.
85. Jiji, January 22, 2016.
86. Gordon G. Chang, "The Chinese and Japanese Economies Are Delinking: Prelude to Conflict?," *Forbes*, February 16, 2014, http://www.forbes.com/sites/gordonchang/2014/02/16/the-chinese-and-japanese-economies-are-delinking-prelude-to-conflict/.
87. Reuters, February 11, 2014, http://blogs.reuters.com/ian-bremmer/2014/02/11/is-the-china-japan-relationship-at-its-worst/.
88. *Guoji Shangbao* (Shanghai), January 17, 2011.

CHAPTER 9

1. See, for example, Christopher W. Hughes, *Japan's Security Agenda: Military, Economic, and Environmental Dimensions* (Boulder, CO: Lynne Rienner, 2004), pp. 135–136.
2. Hisahiko Okazaki, "China Has More Cards Up Its Sleeve," *Yomiuri*, August 26, 2002, http://www.okazaki-inst.jp/08262002yomiuri-E.html. This article is derived

from a speech by Okazaki four days earlier; in the speech, the speaker was his father; in the article, the speaker is not identified.

3. Yoshibumi Wakamiya, *Sengo Hoshu No Ajia Kan* (The Postwar Conservative View of Asia: How the Political Right Has Delayed Japan's Coming to Terms with Its History of Aggression in Asia) (Tokyo: LTCB Library Foundation, 1999), pp. 55–56.

4. Wakamiya, pp. 59–60.

5. See, for example, Wakamiya, pp. 110–111.

6. See Zhihua Shen and Danhui Li, *After Leaning to One Side: China and Its Allies in the Cold War* (Washington, DC: Woodrow Wilson Center Press and Stanford University Press, 2011), passim, for details of these negotiations.

7. This terminology is borrowed from Christopher W. Hughes, *Japan's Emergence as a "Normal" Military Power* (London: International Institute for Strategic Studies [IISS], 2004), pp. 22–23. Adelphi Paper 368-369.

8. The Sino-Soviet Treaty of Friendship, Alliance, and Mutual Assistance, Ministry of Foreign Affairs of the People's Republic of China, http://www.fmprc.gov.cn/eng/ziliao/3602/3604/t1801.1.htm.

9. *Yomiuri*, July 23, 2004.

10. *Renmin Ribao*, September 18, 1971, p. 3.

11. "Facts on File: Japanese Militarism Back in the Saddle," *Peking Review*, January 29, 1971, pp. 20–22. After 1978, the publication was renamed *Beijing Review*.

12. "Indisputable Evidence of Revival of Japanese Militarism: Zaibatsu Stage Comeback," *Beijing Review*, January 22, 1971, pp. 11–13.

13. Ti-wen Tao, "Striking Revelation of Japanese Militarism's Ambitions for Aggression: On the Reactionary Japanese Film, 'Battle of the Japan Sea,'" *Beijing Review*, February 5, 1971, pp. 13–17.

14. Sebastian Moffet, "Back to the Barracks: Okinawa Keeps Fighting, but Japan Quietly Rearms," *Far Eastern Economic Review*, September 19, 1996, pp. 16–17.

15. See, for example, John Nathan, *Mishima: A Biography* (Boston: Little Brown, 1974), passim, and Henry Scott-Stokes, *The Life and Death of Yukio Mishima* (New York: Farrar, Straus and Giroux, 1974), passim. Reference to the Swiss military system may be found in Scott-Stokes, p. 281.

16. *Yomiuri*, May 26, 2003.

17. Euan Graham, *Japan's Sea Lane Security, 1940–2004: A Matter of Life and Death?* (London: Routledge, 2006), p. 102.

18. Graham, p. 109.

19. "Japanese Reactionaries Step Up Naval Expansion," *Beijing Review*, October 29, 1971, pp. 18–19.

20. Japan Defense Agency, "Japan: A Web Guide. Defense Spending," http://www.mod.go.jp/e/about/answers/budget_h25/index.html.

21. See Graham, p. 114, for a fuller discussion of the NDPO.

22. The phrase is Michael Chinworth's, in *Inside Japan's Defense* (New York: Brassey's U.S., 1992), p. 9.

23. *Kyodo*, September 6, 1978. See also *Japan Times*, September 7, 1978.

24. *Xinhua*, May 26, 1980; see also Victor Cha, *Alignment Despite Antagonism: The U.S.-Korea-Japan Security Triangle* (Stanford, CA: Stanford University Press, 1990), p. 105.

25. Reinhard Drifte, *China's Security Relations with China Since 1989: From Balancing to Bandwagoning?* (London: Routledge Curzon, 2003), p. 46.

26. Tatsumi Okaba, "Nitchu kankei no kako to shōrai" (The Past and Future of Japanese-Chinese Relations), *Gaikō Forum*, February 2001, p. 15; *Yomiuri*, November 10, 1982, quoted in Drifte, pp. 46–47.

27. Tsuneo Watanabe, "The Bankruptcy of Civil-Military Relations in Japan," *NIRA Review*, Summer 1996, p. 4, http://www.nira.go.jp/publ/review/96summer/watanabe.html.

28. Watanabe, p. 4.
29. Graham, p. 323.
30. Graham, p. 143.
31. *Yomiuri*, July 23, 2004.
32. Hughes, *Japan's Security Agenda*, p. 149.
33. *Xinhua*, February 12, 1987.
34. Shengzhu Lu, "Lianqian Nianqian de Zhongguo Haiyang Huanjing" (Two Thousand Years of China's Maritime Environment), *Junshi Zhanwang* (Military Outlook, Beijing), Spring 1990, pp. 33–34.

35. A reader of this manuscript, resident at a Chinese military academy, recalls cadets watching a documentary on U.S. military superiority, and that officer-teachers frequently mentioned in their lectures that the PLA was being left far behind.

36. In addition to the areas named, the law claimed Chinese jurisdiction over islands in the South China Sea. In conjunction with Beijing's 9-dashed line, which has no basis in international law, the cumulative effect was to lay the basis for bitter later disputes over both the East China and South China seas.

37. *Yomiuri*, June 12, 1993.
38. *Yomiuri*, September 4, 1994.
39. *Tokyo Shimbun*, July 3, 2005.
40. *Sankei*, October 16, 1995.
41. Japanese Ministry of Foreign Affairs release, January 19, 1996, http://www.mofa.go.jp.
42. *Tokyo Shimbun*, February 12, 1996, p. 1; in *FBIS-EAS*, February 14, 1996, p. 5.
43. *China Daily*, March 4, 1996.
44. *Kyodo*, March 26, 1996.
45. The text appears at http://www.mofa.go.jp/region/n-america/us/security/html; see Reinhard Drifte, *China's Security Relations With China Since 1989: From Balancing to Bandwagoning?* (London: Routledge Curzon, 2003), pp. 93–94, for a discussion of the background of the declaration.

46. *Kyodo*, April 1, 1996.
47. *Kyodo*, April 1, 1996.
48. *China Daily* (Beijing), May 23, 1996, p. 4, citing "experts at a recent conference sponsored by the Chinese Association for International Understanding," held on an unspecified date.

49. Frank Ching, "U.S.-Japan Ties Reinvigorated," *Far Eastern Economic Review*, May 2, 1996, p. 40.

50. A summary of press comments from several Japanese newspapers was published by *Kyodo*, April 18, 1996.

51. *Yomiuri*, April 18, 1996, p. 3.
52. *Business Times* (Singapore), April 23, 1996
53. *NHK News Program*, April 17, 1996; in *FBIS-EAS*, April 18, 1996, p. 19.
54. *Kompas* (Jakarta), April 25, 1996, p. 4.

55. *Financial Times*, April 25, 1996.
56. *South China Morning Post*, March 9, 1996.
57. Hiroyuki Akita interview with Yunling Zhang, director of the Institute of Asian and Pacific Studies under the Chinese Academy of Social Sciences, *Nihon Keizai Shimbun*, April 29, 1996, p. 8; in *FBIS-EAS*, April 30, 1996, pp. 1–2; see also Guocheng Zhang, "Japan's Constitution Is Facing a Test," *Renmin Ribao*, April 23, 1996, p. 6.
58. Lineng Chen, "The Japanese Self-Defense Forces Are Marching Toward the 21st Century," *Guoji Zhanwang* (World Outlook, Shanghai), February 8, 1996, pp. 18–20. Although this article was published prior to the announcement of the treaty, Chen was clearly familiar with the parameters of what was being negotiated.
59. Kotarō Kamei, "Asian Military Frontline," *Gunji Kenkyu* (Military Research, Tokyo), April 1996, pp. 126–138; *FBIS-EAS*, May 17, 1996, pp. 3–12.
60. Toshiyuki Shikata, *Far East Emergency: How Japan Will Be Drawn into War* (Tokyo: Crest, April 1996), unpaginated preface; in *FBIS-EAS*, June 6, 1996, pp. 5–6.
61. *Nihon Keizai Shimbun*, May 5, 1996, p. 1; in *FBIS-EAS*, May 7, 1996, pp. 5–6.
62. Shunji Taoka, "A Plan to Have a Domestic Reconnaissance Satellite Has Emerged: Japan Seeks Intelligence Independence," *Aera* (Tokyo), June 3, 1996, pp. 62–63; in *FBIS-EAS*, June 4, 1996, pp. 7–9; quote appears on p. 9.
63. Tsutomo Matsumura, "Politicians Should Question Self-Defense Forces' Operational Abilities Before Debating on the 'Right of Collective Self-Defense,'" *Sapio*, June 12, 1996, pp. 105–107; in *FBIS-EAS*, June 17, 1996, pp. 26–29; quote appears on p. 26.
64. Toshi Yoshihara and James R. Holmes, "Japanese Maritime Thought: If Not Mahan, Who?," *Naval War College Review* 59, no. 3 (Summer 2006): 32.
65. See, for example, *Beijing Radio*, August 22, 1996.
66. *Xinhua*, September 6, 1997.
67. *Kyodo*, August 28, 1997.
68. Yaqiang Li, "What Is Japan Doing Southward?," *Jianchuan Zhishi* (Naval and Merchant Ships, Beijing), September 8, 1997, p. 4.
69. *Yomiuri*, August 20, 1997.
70. Todd Crowell, "Soothing China: During a High-Profile Visit, Japan's Leader Plugs a Message of Peace," *Asia Week*, September 19, 1997.
71. *Kyodo*, September 4, 1997.
72. *Yomiuri*, August 19, 1997.
73. *Yomiuri*, August 19, 1997.
74. Xiangqing Meng, "A Strategic Measure with Ulterior Motives: Background and Attempt of Japan's Participation in the Theater Missile Defense System," *Shijie Zhishi*, April 1, 1999, pp. 18–19.
75. Interviews conducted by the United States-China Economic and Security Review Commission, Tokyo, March 2003. The author, as a commissioner, took part.
76. *Straits Times*, November 7, 1999, citing an unnamed official.
77. *Asahi*, November 24, 2003.
78. *Hong Kong Standard*, October 21, 1999; *Yomiuri*, October 21, 1999.
79. Japan Defense Agency, *Defense of Japan, 2000*, p. 68.
80. *Renmin Ribao*, August 4, 2000.
81. "China Defense White Paper, 2000," *Xinhua*, October 16, 2000, p. 3, http://www.xinhuanet.com.

82. James Simpson, "Ten Years Ago, Japan Went to Iraq ... And Learned Nothing," *War Is Boring*, April 10, 2014, https://medium.com/war-is-boring/ten-years-ago-japan-went-to-iraq-and-learned-nothing-b7f3c702dd1f.
83. *Straits Times*, November 30, 2002.
84. *Yomiuri*, July 14, 2002.
85. *Yomiuri*, November 19, 2002.
86. *South China Morning Post*, December 15, 2002.
87. *Straits Times*, March 27, 2003; *Straits Times*, April 3, 2003.
88. *Yomiuri*, May 26, 2003.
89. *Straits Times*, December 29, 2003.
90. *Asahi*, June 7, 2003.
91. *Renmin Ribao*, May 20, 2003, p. 3.
92. Agence France-Presse (AFP), August 18, 2003.
93. *Yomiuri*, January 26, 2004.
94. *Financial Times*, October 5, 2004, p. 10; *South China Morning Post*, October 26, 2004.
95. Text of the NDPO 2005 is available at http://www.jda.go.jp/e/index http://www.mod.go.jp/e/d_act/d_policy/pdf/national_guidelines.pdf.htm; for commentary, see *Yomiuri*, December 11, 2004; David Fouse, "Japan's FY 2005 National Defense Program Outline: New Concepts, Old Compromises," *Asia-Pacific Security Studies* 4, no. 3 (March 2005): 1–4.
96. *Yomiuri*, May 8, 2004.
97. *Yomiuri*, April 8, 2004.
98. *New York Times*, February 20, 2005, p. 3.
99. Japanese Defense Agency, *White Paper 2006*, http://www.mod.go.jp/e/publ/w_paper/2006.html.
100. *Japan Times*, November 20, 2009.
101. *AP/Navy Times*, January 25, 2010, http://www.navytimes.com/article/20100115/NEWS01/1150320/Japanese-refueling-mission-Indian-Ocean-ends.
102. *Xinhua*, October 1, 2009.
103. Tadahiko Furusawa, "The Chinese and the Sea," January 2001, *Defence Research Centre* (Tokyo), unpaginated.
104. Dingli Shen, "Don't Shun the Idea of Setting Up Overseas Military Bases," January 28, 2010, http://www.china.org.cn/opinion/2010-01/28/content_19324522_2.htm.
105. *South China Morning Post*, February 10, 2010.
106. Author's conversations at U.S. Pacific Command, Honolulu, February 14, 2011.
107. *Kyodo*, May 18, 2010; *Financial Times*, May 18, 2010.
108. *Washington Post*, July 30, 2010.
109. For a discussion of the cabbage strategy as it concerns Japan, see Harry Kazianis, "China's Expanding Cabbage Strategy," *The Diplomat*, October 29, 2013, http://thediplomat.com/2013/10/chinas-expanding-cabbage-strategy/.
110. *Asahi*, September 1, 1010.
111. *Kyodo*, November 25, 2010.
112. *Zhongguo Qingnian Bao*, August 31, 2011.
113. *Asahi*, October 2, 2011.
114. *Guoji Xianqu Daobao*, October 21, 2011.
115. *Jiefang Junbao* (Liberation Army Daily, Beijing), November 16, 2011.
116. *Ming Pao*, September 19, 2011.

117. Hillary Clinton, "America's Pacific Century," *Foreign Policy*, November 2011, pp. 56–83.

118. *U.S. Naval Institute News*, January 20, 2015, http://news.usni.org/2015/01/20/document-air-sea-battle-name-change-memo.

119. The Ministry of Foreign Affairs does not have a strong presence on the NSC, which mirrors the relatively low degree of influence it is believed to exercise over foreign policymaking.

120. Maritime law expert Professor Peter Dutton cited in *Christian Science Monitor*, December 5, 2013.

121. Japanese Ministry of Defense, January 15, 2015, http://www.mod.go.jp/e/d_budget/pdf/270206.pdf.

122. See, for example, Corey Wallace, "Does the Izumo Represent Japan Crossing the 'Offensive' Rubicon?," *Japan Security Watch*, August 13, 2013, http://jsw.newpacificinstitute.org/?p=11000.

123. *Xinhua*, August 7, 2013.

124. For example, Gideon Rachman, "A Gaffe-Prone Japan Is a Danger to Peace in Asia," *Financial Times*, August 12, 2013.

125. Joji Haranō, "Japan Launches Its Own National Security Council," December 25, 2013, http://www.nippon.com/en/genre/politics/l00050/.

126. Toshi Yoshihara, "Japanese Hard Power: Rising to the Challenge," American Enterprise Institute, August 2014.

127. *The Japan News*, April 2, 2014.

128. *Global Times*, April 3, 2014.

129. MGN Luo Yuan, cited in *South China Morning Post*, April 3, 2014.

130. *Wall Street Journal*, July 28, 2014.

131. *Wall Street Journal*, July 28, 2014.

132. Article 96 of the constitution stipulates that revisions must be initiated by the Diet through a concurring vote of two-thirds or more of all the members of each house, allowing the legislature to propose a national referendum on the issue.

133. Shinichi Kitaoka, "The Turnabout of Japan's Security Policy: Toward 'Proactive Pacifism,'" www.nippon.com, April 2, 2014.

134. Nonaka Hiromu, quoted in *Asahi*, August 14, 2014.

135. *BBC News*, September 18, 2015, http://www.bbc.com/news/world-asia-34287362.

136. Reuters, December 6, 2013, http://www.reuters.com/article/2013/12/06/us-japan-secrets-idUSBRE9B50JT20131206.

137. *Kyodo*, December 24, 2006.

138. Calculating the true Chinese defense budget has become, in the words of one economist, a virtual cottage industry, with estimates ranging from 30 percent to ten times official figures. Most fall in the two times to four times of stated amounts. See, for example, the International Institute for Strategic Studies, *The Military Balance 2006* (London: Routledge, 2006), pp. 249–253, for a cogent treatment of this issue.

139. *South China Morning Post*, July 12, 2003, quoting Professor Terumasa Nakamichi.

140. "Japan Begins to Express Doubts about Nuclear Plan," AP, August 8, 2003, citing the Tokyo-based magazine *Shokun*.

141. *International Herald Tribune*, October 24, 2006.

142. *Asia Times*, June 13, 2002.

143. *Zhongguo Tongxun She* (Hong Kong), December 26, 2006.

144. *Yomiuri*, June 10, 2006.
145. *China Daily*, January 5, 2007.
146. See, for example, China's 2015 "Defense White Paper," *Xinhua*, May 26, 2015, http://english.chinamil.com.cn/news-channels/2015-05/26/content_6507716.htm.
147. Yoshihara and Holmes, pp. 41–42.
148. Yoshihiko Sakurai, "Proposal to Prime Minister Koizumi: The Enemy Is Within Japan," *Sankei*, January 12, 2006, quoted in Yoshihara and Holmes, 2006, p. 43; see also James Holmes and Toshi Yoshihara, *Red Star Over the Pacific: China's Challenge to U.S. Maritime Strategy* (Annapolis, MD: U.S. Naval Institute Press, 2010), passim.
149. Yuanying Pei, "Military Power Ambition," *Beijing Review*, July 29, 2004, p. 15. Pei formerly served as Chinese ambassador to India and Poland.

CHAPTER 10

1. Jared M. Diamond, "Taiwan's Gift to the World," *Nature*, Vol. 403, February 17, 2000, pp. 709–710.
2. "Earliest Inhabitants," in *Taiwan 2005 Yearbook* (Taipei: Government Information Office, 2005), p. 44.
3. Leonard Blussé, *Trubuut aan China, View Eeuwen Nederlands-Chinese Betrekkingen* (*Tribute to China: Four Centuries of Chinese-Dutch Relations*) (Amsterdam: Otto Cramwinckel Uitgever, 1989), p. 47. I am indebted to Dr. Gerrit van der Wees for bringing this to my attention, and for his translation.
4. Blussé, p. 54.
5. E. Patricia Tsurumi, *Japanese Colonial Education in Taiwan, 1895-1945* (Cambridge, MA: Harvard University Press, 1977), p. 8.
6. Kiyoshi Ito, *Taiwan Lishi* (History of Taiwan), translated by Walter Chen (Taipei: Qianwei Chubanshe, 2004), pp. 81–82.
7. I am indebted to an anonymous reviewer for this information.
8. Ito, pp. 88–89.
9. Unfortunately, the experience did not serve Japan well in its colonization of Korea, whose citizens have bitter memories of their years under imperial rule.
10. With exceptions made for the children of peers.
11. Like most generalizations, this is true but should be understood to have qualifiers. Mishima Yukio, arguably Japan's most famous writer, was able to attend the Gakushu-in, or Peers School, by virtue of his passing an examination, which the children of aristocrats were not required to take. They, unlike he, paid no tuition, were excused from examinations, and addressed by teachers using a more polite form of Japanese than used for the commoners. Still, when Mishima graduated first in his class, the emperor personally presented him with an award. See, for example, John Nathan, *Mishima: A Biography* (Boston: Little, Brown, 1977), pp. 14–15.
12. Tsurumi, pp. 22–25.
13. Leo T. S. Ching, *Becoming "Japanese": Colonial Taiwan and the Politics of Identity Formation* (Berkeley: University of California Press, 2001), passim. These terms, which form the framework for Ching's book, are defined on pp. 12–13.
14. Ito, p. 34.
15. Tsurumi, p. 66.

16. Ming-min Peng, *A Taste of Freedom* (New York: Holt Rinehart and Winston, 1972), p. 26.

17. Steven E. Phillips, *Between Assimilation and Independence: The Taiwanese Encounter with Nationalist China, 1945–1950* (Stanford, CA: Stanford University Press, 2003), p. 24.

18. Ching, p. 79.

19. Ito, p. 167.

20. Tsurumi, p. 123.

21. Ito, p. 217.

22. Emilie Yueh-yu Yeh and Darrell William David, *Taiwan Film Directors: A Treasure Island* (New York: Columbia University Press, 2005), p. 16.

23. http://www.wanpela.com/holdouts/registry.html.

24. Phillips, p. 39.

25. Ito, p. 221; Phillips, p. 95.

26. Ito, pp. 222–223.

27. Peng, p. 51.

28. George H. Kerr, *Formosa Betrayed* (London: Eyre and Spottiswoode, 1965), passim.

29. Douglas Mendel, *The Politics of Formosan Nationalism* (Berkeley: University of California Press, 1970), p. 7.

30. Okinori Kaya, "Taiwan kirisute no bokyō o omashimeru," in *Senzen sengo hachijunen* (Tokyo: Keizai Ourai Sha, 1976), pp. 337–354, in Phil Deans, "Taiwan in Japan's Foreign Relations: Informal Politics and Virtual Diplomacy," *Journal of Strategic Studies* (London) 24, no. 4 (December 2001): 167.

31. Donald G. Gillin, *Warlord: Yen Hsi-shan in Shansi Province, 1911–1949* (Princeton, NJ: Princeton University Press, 1967), p. 285.

32. Colin Joyce, "Ex-Soldier Fights to Make Japan Remember Its Past," *Daily Telegraph* (London), June 7, 2006, http://www.telegraph.co.uk. Joyce mentions more than 2,000 soldiers; a zero may have been omitted, since U.S. military records put the figure at close to 20,000. James Mitchell, personal communication to the author, January 17, 2007.

33. Ito, p. 167; Tsurumi, pp. 301–302; Phillips, pp. 113–114.

34. Gene T. Hsiao, *The Foreign Trade of China: Policy, Law, and Practice* (Berkeley: University of California Press, 1977), pp. 45–47.

35. Phil Deans, "Taiwan in Japan's Foreign Relations: Informal Politics and Virtual Diplomacy," *Journal of Strategic Studies* (London) 24, no. 4 (December 2001): 156.

36. See, for example, *Xinhua*, July 11, 1969.

37. *Foreign Relations of the United States* (FRUS), Vol. 17 China 1969-1972 Washington, DC United States Department of State, pp. 514–558; see also Jay Taylor, *The Generalissimo: Chiang Kai-shek and the Struggle for Modern China* (Cambridge, MA: Belknap Press, 2009), pp. 514–515, 566, 602.

38. FRUS, Vol. 17, *China, 1969-1972*, p. 602.

39. *Japan Times*, August 1, 1978.

40. *Japan Times*, August 2, 1978.

41. Despite the disadvantages of obtaining connecting international flights, since the traveler would have to go from Haneda to Narita, the traffic between Taipei and Tokyo was substantial. Hence, the flights from Haneda to what was then called Chiang Kai-shek International Airport and, after 2007, Taoyuan International Airport, made good business as well as political sense.

42. In 2011 Haneda was re-opened to international routes.

43. Cited in Joint Publications Research Service, *China Report (JPRS-CAR)*, August 1, 1983, pp. 2–3.

44. Ito, p. 339.

45. Richard C. Bush, *Untying the Knot: Making Peace in the Taiwan Strait* (Washington, DC: Brookings Institution Press, 2005), passim.

46. Koichi Iwabuchi, *Recentering Globalization: Popular Culture and Japanese Transnationalism* (Durham, NC: Duke University Press, 2002), pp. 125–126.

47. Theresa Teng Li-jun was also popular in China.

48. *Xinhua*, August 23, 1995.

49. Hsiu-lien Annette Lu, with Ashley Esarey, *My Fight for a New Taiwan: One Woman's Journey from Prison to Power* (Seattle: University of Washington Press, 2014), p. 228.

50. Benjamin Self, "The Rise of China and the Role of the U.S.-Japan Alliance in Taiwan's Security," paper presented at a conference entitled "The Rise of China Revisited," National Chengchi University (Taipei), December 11, 2003.

51. Jason Blatt, "Scheme to Back Troops," *South China Morning Post*, July 28, 1997, quoting *Tokyo Shimbun*.

52. Signed on April 17, 1996. Text appears at http://www.mofa.go.jp/region/n-america/us/security/security.html.

53. Cited in Yoshifumi Nakai, "Policy Coordination on Taiwan," in Masashi Nishihara, *The Japan-U.S. Alliance: New Challenges for the 21st Century* (Tokyo: Japan Center for International Exchange, 2000), p. 80.

54. Hisahiko Okazaki, personal communication to the author, July 17, 2001.

55. "Japan Flatly Rebuffs Pressure over Taiwan, War Apology," *Hong Kong Standard*, October 29, 1998.

56. Peter Landers and Susan V. Lawrence, "Sorry, No Apology," *Far Eastern Economic Review*, December 10, 1998, p. 21.

57. http://www.dw.com/de/ein-china-zwei-staaten/a-17180562.

58. 96th Congress, Public Law 96-8, H.R. 2479, April 10, 1979, Taiwan Relations Act.

59. See, for example, Pi-chao Chen, "The Redefined U.S.-Japan Alliance and Peace over the Taiwan Strait: A Taiwanese Perspective," paper presented at the International Forum on Peace and Security in the Taiwan Strait, Taipei, July 26–28, 1999, p. 16.

60. *CNA* (Taipei), February 20, 2006.

61. *Taipei Times*, November 30, 2006, p. 1.

62. *Xinhua*, February 21, 2000.

63. The term "1992 consensus" refers to an agreement that may or may not have been reached that year between the PRC and Taiwan, aka the ROC, that both belong to one China, and each can have different interpretations of what constitutes the one China. The negotiators for Taiwan were chosen by the then ruling party, the KMT. When the DPP came to power in 2000, it stated that no consensus was ever reached on the issue. There is no documentation of this agreement, which even the PRC agrees was "verbal," as in *Renmin Ribao*, October 13, 2004. In February 2006 Su Chi, who headed Taiwan's Government Information Office at the time of the 1992 meeting, admitted he had made up the term as a replacement for "each side with its own interpretation" of China, because he thought it could benefit cross-Strait development. *Taipei Times*, February 22, 2006. Raymond Burghardt, who headed the Taipei office of the American Institute in Taiwan at the time of the meeting, said, "... some language [in the faxes

that went back and forth between the two sides] ... overlapped and some differed [so that it was] confusing and misleading. To me, I'm not sure why you could call that a consensus." CNA and *Taipei Times*, February 28, 2006, http://www.taipeitimes.com/News/taiwan/archives/2006/02/28/2003295010.

64. CNA, May 5, 2000. The Japanese parliamentarians were Hattori Minao and Watanuki Tamisuke, both of the LDP.

65. Chen Shui-bian, "Taiwan Stands Up: Toward the Dawn of a New Era," Office of the President, Republic of China, May 21, 2000, http://th.gio.gov.tw/pi2000/dow_2.htm.

66. According to Article 8 of the Anti-Secession Law, "In the event that 'Taiwan independence' secessionist forces should act under any name or by any means to cause the fact of Taiwan's secession from China, or that major incidents entailing Taiwan's secession from China should occur, or that possibilities for a peaceful reunification should be completely exhausted, the state shall employ non-peaceful means and other necessary measures to protect China's sovereignty and territorial integrity." *Xinhua*, March 14, 2005.

67. For full text, see *Xinhua*, April 29, 2005. Following the meeting, a joint communiqué was issued agreeing on five points: the resumption of cross-Strait negotiations based on the "1992 consensus"; establishment of a "military mutual trust mechanism"; establishment of a cross-Strait common market; promotion of consultations on Taiwan's participation in international activities; and establishment of periodic party-to-party contact and other exchanges. On May 5, 2005, People First Party Chair James Soong arrived in China for similar talks.

68. *Taipei Times*, May 8, 2005, p. 2.
69. *South China Morning Post*, July 13, 2005.
70. *Yomiuri*, May 5, 2005.
71. Associated Press and *Taipei Times*, February 6, 2006.
72. *Xinhua*, February 6, 2006.
73. *South China Morning Post*, February 7, 2006.
74. "The Chinese Foreign Ministry Makes Solemn Representations With Japan Over Asō's Remarks on Taiwan," March 11, 2006, http://www.fmprc.gov.cn.
75. *South China Morning Post*, February 21, 2006; *South China Morning Post*, February 23, 2006.
76. *Yomiuri*, May 5, 2005, p. 2; *Taipei Times*, May 3, 2006.
77. AP, August 3, 2005.
78. CNA, May 26, 2006.
79. *Washington Post*, March 24, 2006.
80. *Taipei Times*, June 9, 2006, p. 3.
81. *Taipei Times*, July 17, 2006, p. 8.
82. Ma's father requested that "fight against independence and for the unification of China" be inscribed on his burial urn.
83. *Taipei Times*, January 25, 2006, p. 8.
84. *South China Morning Post*, August 7, 2005.
85. *Taipei Times*, January 13, 2006.
86. *South China Morning Post*, July 12, 2006.
87. *Taiwan News*, July 13, 2006.
88. *Taipei Times*, July 20, 2006.
89. *Feng Huang Wei Shih Chung Wen Tai* (Phoenix TV, Hong Kong), February 17, 2006.

90. Author's interview with Japanese government official, June 12, 2008. The source actually used the word "infuriated."
91. Author's interview with a former employee of Taiwan's Ministry of Foreign Affairs, May 22, 2008.
92. *Taipei Times*, May 3, 2009.
93. *Kyodo*, December 1, 2009; *China Times*, December 2, 2009; *Taipei Times*, December 2 and 3, 2009.
94. *Taipei Times*, November 8, 2010.
95. *Taiwan Communiqué*, January/February 2014, pp. 14–16, http://www.taiwandc.org/twcom/145-index.htm; *Taipei Times*, January 30, 2014, http://www.taipeitimes.com/News/editorials/archives/2014/01/30/2003582456/2.
96. *Kyodo*, April 20, 2011.
97. *China Post*, June 5, 2012, http://www.chinapost.com.tw/print/343332.htm.
98. As explained by Deputy Press Secretary Saiki Naoko, May 5, 2013, http://www.mofa.go.jp/press/kaiken/kaiken24e_000001.html.
99. Ministry of Foreign Affairs, Republic of China, April 15, 2013, http://www.mofa.gov.tw/en/News_Content.aspx?n=539A9A50A5F8AF9E&sms=37B41539382B84BA&s=E80C25D078D837BB.
100. See, for example, Ricky Yeh, "Why the KMT Failed in Taiwan's Local Elections," *The Diplomat*, December 9, 2014, http://thediplomat.com/2014/12/why-the-kmt-failed-in-taiwans-local-elections-2/.
101. *Want China Times* (Taipei), August 15, 2015, http://www.wantchinatimes.com/news-subclass-cnt.aspx?id=20150821000107&cid=1101.
102. In 2006 Ma Ying-jeou declared, to considerable skepticism, that this would be his policy as president. *Taiwan News*, July 28, 2006.
103. *P'ing-kuo Jih-pao* (Apple Daily, Taipei), July 12, 2006.

CHAPTER 11

1. *New York Times*, November 9, 1954.
2. Text of Yoshida address, *New York Times*, November 9, 1954, p. A4.
3. *New York Times*, October 28, 1957.
4. C. Martin Wilbur, "Japan and the Rise of Communist China," in Hugh Borton et al., *Japan Between East and West* (Berkeley: University of California Press, 1975), p. 225.
5. *Japan Times*, April 30, 1964, p. 16.
6. *Kyodo*, November 9, 1964.
7. *Kyodo*, January 17, 1965; *New York Times*, January 18, 1965, section IV, p. 1.
8. *New York Times*, June 27, 1965.
9. *New York Times*, August 15, 1971, p. E3.
10. *New York Times*, April 12, 1969, p. A2.
11. *New York Times*, October 6, 1965, p. A1.
12. *New York Times*, September 6, 1965, p. A2.
13. *New York Times*, June 27, 1965, p. A2.
14. National Intelligence Estimate (NIE) 41-68, January 11, 1968, in *Foreign Relations of the United States (FRUS)*, Vol. 29: *1964–1968* (1968), p. 256.

15. Memorandum from Fred Greene INR/REA to Hughes, January 8, 1998, in NIE 41–68, January 11, 1968, in *FRUS*, Vol. 29, United States Department of State, Washington, D.C., p. 256.
16. NIE 13-7-70, November 12, 1970, Document 95, *FRUS*, Vol. 17: *1969–1976*, unpaginated.
17. *Japan Times*, July 17, 1971.
18. *Japan Times Weekly*, July 17, 1971.
19. *Japan Times*, October 14, 1971.
20. Nixon-Kissinger conversation of February 14, 1974, in *FRUS*, Vol. 17, *October 1971–February 1972*, p. 665.
21. *Japan Times*, June 22, 1975, p. 4.
22. *Japan Times*, December 4, 1982.
23. *New York Times*, February 2, 1977.
24. Akira Kato, "Collapse of Big-Power Self-Confidence in Japan's Diplomacy," *CEAC (Council on the East Asian Community) Commentary*, December 18, 2014, http://www.ceac.jp/e/commentary/141218.pdf.
25. For a fuller treatment of this, see Jessica Chen Weiss, *Powerful Patriots: Nationalist Protest in China's Foreign Relations* (New York: Oxford University Press, 2014), pp. 82–103.
26. See, for example, the discussion of preparations to open a museum on the site of the infamous germ warfare Unit 731 carried by *Xinhua*, March 6, 1985.
27. *Beijing Review*, March 11, 1985, p. 13.
28. *Xinhua*, July 18, 1986.
29. *Nihon Keizai Shimbun*, July 5, 1987.
30. *Japan Times*, January 26, 1988.
31. *Guoji Wenti Yanjiu*, April 13, 1992, pp. 18–24.
32. *Yomiuri*, January 1, 1994.
33. *Nihon Keizai Shimbun*, September 10, 2001.
34. *Nihon Keizai Shimbun*, October 14, 2001.
35. *Asahi*, June 12, 2002.
36. *Sankei Shimbun*, August 5, 2004.
37. *Japan Times*, July 8, 1987.
38. *Yomiuri*, May 12, 1997.
39. *Yomiuri*, May 16, 1997.
40. *Yomiuri*, August 10, 2004.
41. *Yomiuri*, March 15, 2002.
42. *Straits Times*, November 30, 2002; article by Ma appears in *Zhanlüe yu Guanli*, December 1, 2002, pp. 41–47.
43. *Nihon Keizai Shimbun*, September 14, 2002.
44. *Jiji*, April 30, 2003.
45. *Zhongguo Wang*, June 20, 2003.
46. See June Teufel Dreyer, "Sino-Japanese Rivalry and Its Implications for Developing States," *Asian Survey* 46, no. 4 (July/August 2006): 538–557 for further details.
47. *New York Times*, January 3, 2004.
48. *Xinhua*, October 13, 2005.
49. Japan Ministry of Foreign Affairs, press release, December 13, 2005, http://www.mofa.go.jp/announce/press/2005/12/1213.html.
50. *Straits Times*, August 17, 2005.

51. *Straits Times*, August 17, 2005.
52. *Voice of America*, May 25, 2006.
53. *Associated Press*, August 10, 2006; *Yomiuri*, August 11, 2006.
54. *South China Morning Post*, August 26, 2006.
55. *Asia Times*, August 15, 2006.
56. *Kyodo*, December 24, 2006.
57. *Kyodo*, December 4, 2006.
58. *China Daily*, November 4, 2005.
59. *Ming Pao*, April 21, 2005.
60. *Feng Huang (Phoenix) Wang*, January 18, 2006, http://www.phoenixtv.com.
61. *The Telegraph* (London), February 27, 2006.
62. *South China Morning Post*, January 18, 2007.
63. *Heping yü Fazhan* (Peace and Development), May 1, 2006.
64. This theme, and Chinese efforts to compete with it, are explored in Jing Sun, *Japan and China as Charm Rivals: Soft Power in Regional Diplomacy* (Ann Arbor: University of Michigan Press, 2012), passim.
65. *Asahi*, January 1, 2006.
66. *Kyodo*, April 17 2008.
67. *Straits Times*, March 17, 2007.
68. *Asahi*, January 27, 2007.
69. *Asahi*, December 29, 2015.
70. *Straits Times*, August 8, 2007.
71. *Yomiuri*, May 11, 2007.
72. *Taipei Times*, May 17, 2008.
73. *Taipei Times*, May 17, 2008.
74. Now again the G7, with Russia's exclusion due to its actions in the Crimea and Ukraine.
75. *Asahi*, July 2, 2008.
76. *Straits Times*, July 25, 2009.
77. *Asahi*, September 26, 2009.
78. *Financial Times*, September 17, 2009.
79. "Prime Minister Hatoyama's Focus on China," October 7, 2009, https://wikileaks.org/plusd/cables/09TOKYO2344_a.html.
80. Denny Roy, "Stirring Samurai, Disapproving Dragon: Japan's Growing Security Activity and Sino-Japanese Relations," *Asian Affairs* 31, no. 2 (Summer 2002): 5.
81. Prime Minister Lee Hsien Loong cited in *Straits Times*, February 8, 2015.
82. In addition to the sentiments that forced the closing of *Bingqian*, Wang Jisi, dean of Beijing University's School of International Studies, stated that "our history books have not provided very balanced and comprehensive interpretations. That's why I think we should restudy history." Cited in *Asahi*, June 12, 2010.
83. Louisa Lim, *The People's Republic of Amnesia: Tiananmen Revisited* (New York: Oxford University Press, 2014).
84. See, for example, James Auer, ed., *From Marco Polo Bridge to Pearl Harbor: Who Was Responsible?* (Tokyo: Yomiuri Shimbun, 2006), p. 66.
85. See Professor Steve Tsang's study, as noted in Chapter 2, of the revelation in Chiang Kai-shek's diaries and presidential papers he had, in fact, decided on war, not because he reached an agreement with the CCP to resist but because he had received a signal from Josef Stalin that the USSR would support him in a war

with Japan. Steve Tsang, "Chiang Kai-shek's 'Secret Deal' and Xian and the Start of the Sino-Japanese War," *Palgrave Communications*, January 20, 2015, doi:101057/palcomms.2014.3.

86. According to a report from the United States Office of War Information dated August 19, 1944, and declassified in 1973, interrogation of a number of these women indicated that they were, in fact, prostitutes. In 2014 *Asahi* retracted all the stories on the comfort women it had printed in previous decades that quote a Japanese man who claimed he had kidnapped about 200 women and forced them to work in wartime brothels: the source, Yoshida Seiji, was a fraud, as had been shown by *Sankei Shimbun* more than twenty years before. See, for example, *Japan Times*, August 5, 2014.

87. For example, the publications of Japan's Society for the Dissemination of Historical Fact, http://www.sdh-facts.com.

88. Togo Kazuhiko, personal communication, July 5, 2014.

89. Interview with author, November 14, 2014.

90. Speech by then Senior Minister Lee Kwan Yew to the International Institute for Strategic Studies Conference, Hotel Shangri-La, Singapore, September 12, 1997. I am indebted to Mr. William Whaley of IISS for providing me with a copy of the speech in its entirety.

91. Wang Jisi, cited in *Asahi*, June 12, 2010.

CHAPTER 12

1. *South China Morning Post*, November 21, 2016.
2. *Japan Times*, August 8, 2017. The elder Kono, while serving as chief cabinet secretary in 1993, had issued as abject an apology on the comfort woman issue as China has received.
3. See June Teufel Dreyer, "Connecting the Dots: Will Xi Stay the Course?" *Foreign Policy Research Institute* e-note, April 26, 2016, https://www.fpri.org/article/2016/04/connecting-dots-will-xi-stay-course/ for the details of the brief public display of discontent.
4. *Global Times*, February 6, 2017.
5. *Xinhua*, October 11, 2017.
6. *Reuters*, May 23, 2017.
7. *Reuters*, October 19, 2017.
8. *Nikkei*, December 28, 2017.
9. *Yomiuri*, December 31, 2017.
10. *Nikkei*, September 21, 2017.
11. *Sankei Shimbun*, November 21, 2017.
12. *CCTV-4*, November 22, 2017.
13. *Xinhua*, December 18, 2017.
14. *TASS*, September 25, 2017; *South China Morning Post*, October 5, 2017.
15. "Foreign Ministry Spokesperson Geng Shuang's Regular Press Conference, December 4, 2017. http://www.fmprc.gov.cn/mfa_eng/xwfw_665399/s2510_665401/2511_665403/t1516395.shtml
16. Michael Edward Walsh, "The Expansion of the Japan Self-Defense Force Base in Djibouti," *CSIS Islands Society*, November 23, 2017.
17. *Global Times*, January 4, 2018.
18. "Foreign Ministry Spokesperson Geng Shuang's Regular Press Conference, January 3, 2017," http://www.fmprc.gov.cn/mfa_eng/xwfw_665399/s2510_665401/t1428102.shtml
19. Author's interview, February 15, 2017.
20. *Kyodo*, December 6, 2017.

Bibliography

Akutsu, Hiroyasu. "Tokyo and Taipei Try to Tango." *Far Eastern Economic Review*, January/February 2007.
Askew, David. "The Nanjing Incident: Recent Research and Trends." *Electronic Journal of Contemporary Japanese Studies* (April 2002). http://mt7kx-4ww9u.search.serialssolutions.com/?sid=sersol%3ARefinerQuery&rft.aulast=Askew&url_ver=Z39.88-2004&l=MT7KX4WW9U&SS_ReferentFormat=JournalFormat&rft.genre=article&rft_val_fmt=info%3Aofi%2Ffmt%3Akev%3Amtx%3Ajournal&rft.atitle=The+Nanjing+Incident%3A+Recent+Research+and+Trends&rft.title=Electronic+Journal+of+Contemporary+Japanese+Studies&citationsubmit=Look+Up&rfr_id=info%3Asid%2Fsersol%3ARefinerQuery&SS_LibHash=MT7KX4WW9U&rft.aufirst=David.
Auer, James, ed. *From Marco Polo Bridge to Pearl Harbor: Who Was Responsible?* (Tokyo: Yomiuri Shimbun Press, 2006).
Auslin, Michael. *The Unequal Treaties and the Culture of Japanese Diplomacy* (Cambridge, MA: Harvard University Press, 2005).
Awaya, Kentaro, and Yoshiaki Yoshimi. *Doku Gasu Sen Kankei Shiryō* (Documents on Poison Gas Warfare) (Tokyo: Fuji Shuppan, 1989).
Bailey, David, Dan Coffey, and Philip Tomlinson. "Introduction: The Attributes of the Crisis." In Bailey, Coffey, and Tomlinson, eds., *Crisis or Recovery in Japan: State and Industrial Economy* (Cheltenham, UK, and Northampton, MA: Edward Elgar, 2007), pp. 1–8.
Barrett, David P. *Dixie Mission: The United States Army Observer Group in Yenan, 1944* (Berkeley: University of California Press, 1970).
Barrett, David P., and Larry N. Shyu, eds. *Chinese Collaboration with Japan: The Limits of Accommodation* (Stanford, CA: Stanford University Press, 2001).
Batten, Bruce L. "Foreign Threat and Domestic Reform: The Emergence of the Ritsuryō State." *Monumenta Nipponica* 41, no. 2 (Summer 1986): 209–210.
Bedeski, Robert E. *The Fragile Entente: The 1978 Japan-China Peace Treaty in a Global Context* (Boulder, CO: Westview Press, 1983).
Beijing Review, Vol 15, no. 9 March 6, 1972.
Blond, Georges. *Admiral Togo* (New York: Macmillan, 1950).

Blussé, Leonard. *Tribuut aan China, View Eeuwen Nederlands-Chinese Betrekkingen* (Tribute to China: Four Centuries of Chinese-Dutch Relations) (Amsterdam: Otto Cramwinckel Uitgever, 1989).
Borgen, Robert. *Sugawara no Michizane and the Early Heian Court* (Cambridge, MA: Council on East Asian Studies, Harvard University, 1986).
Braddick, C. W. *Japan and the Sino-Soviet Alliance, 1950–1964* (Houndsmill, Basingstoke, UK: Palgrave/Macmillan, 2001).
Brzezinski, Zbigniew. *The Fragile Blossom: Crisis and Change in Japan* (New York: Harper and Row, 1972).
Bungeshunjū (Literary Arts Spring/Autumn, Tokyo), June 1, 1972.
Bunker, Gerald E. *The Peace Conspiracy: Wang Ching-wei and the China War, 1937–1941* (Cambridge, MA: Harvard University Press, 1972).
Bush, Richard C. *Untying the Knot: Making Peace in the Taiwan Strait* (Washington, DC: Brookings Institution Press, 2005).
Byas, Hugh. *Government by Assassination* (New York: Alfred A. Knopf, 1943).
Cady, John F. *Southeast Asia: Its Historical Development* (New York: Houghton-Mifflin, 1965).
Cha, Victor. *Alignment Despite Antagonism: The U.S.-Korea-Japan Security Triangle* (Stanford, CA: Stanford University Press, 1990).
Chang, Gordon G. "The Chinese and Japanese Economies Are Delinking: Prelude to Conflict?" *Forbes*, February 16, 2014. http://www.forbes.com/sites/gordonchang/2014/02/16/the-chinese-and-japanese-economies-are-delinking-prelude-to-conflict/.
Chen, Lineng. "The Japanese Self-Defense Forces Are Marching Toward the 21st Century." *Guoji Zhanwang* (World Outlook, Shanghai), February 8, 1996, pp. 18–20.
Chen, Pi-chao. "The Redefined U.S.-Japan Alliance and Peace over the Taiwan Strait: A Taiwanese Perspective." Paper presented at the International Forum on Peace and Security in the Taiwan Strait, Taipei, July 26, 1999.
Chen, Xiaomei. *Acting the Right Part* (Honolulu: University of Hawaii Press, 2002).
Cheng Ming (Contending, Hong Kong). http://www.chengmingmag.com/.
Chiang, Kai-shek. *Statements and Speeches by Generalissimo Chiang Kai-shek, August–September 1945* (Shanghai: International Press, 1945).
China Business Weekly (Beijing). http://www.chinadaily.com.cn/english/bw/.
Ching, Leo T. S. *Becoming "Japanese": Colonial Taiwan and the Politics of Identity Formation* (Berkeley: University of California Press, 2001).
Chinworth, Michael. *Inside Japan's Defense* (New York: Brassey's U.S., 1992).
Chu, Samuel C., and Kwang-Ching Liu. *Li Hung-chang and China's Early Modernization* (Armonk, NY: M.E. Sharpe, 1994).
Clinton, Hillary. "America's Pacific Century." *Foreign Policy*, November 2011, pp. 56–83.
Cowling, Keith, and Philip Tomlinson. "Transnational Monopoly Capitalism, the J-Mode Firm, and Industrial 'Hollowing Out' in Japan." In David Bailey, Dan Coffey, and Philip Tomlinson, eds., *Crisis or Recovery in Japan: State and Industrial Economy* (Cheltenham, UK, and Northampton, MA: Edward Elgar, 2007), pp. 61–81.
Crowell, Todd. "Soothing China: During a High-Profile Visit, Japan's Leader Plugs a Message of Peace." *Asia Week*, September 19, 1997. http://www-cgi.cnn.com/ASIANOW/asiaweek/97/0919/nat1.html.
Crowley, James B. *Japan's Quest for Autonomy: National Security and Foreign Policy 1930–1938* (Princeton, NJ: Princeton University Press, 1966).
Deans, Phil. "Taiwan in Japan's Foreign Relations: Informal Politics and Virtual Diplomacy." *Journal of Strategic Studies* (London) 24, no. 4 (December 2001), pp. 151–176.

Dent, Christopher. *China, Japan, and Regional Leadership in East Asia* (Cheltenham, UK: Edward Elgar, 2008).
Diamond, Jared M. "Taiwan's Gift to the World." *Nature*, vol. 403, February 17, 2000, pp. 709–710.
Dreyer, Edward L. *China at War: 1901–1949* (London: Longman, 1995).
Dreyer, Edward L. *Zheng He: China and the Oceans in the Early Ming Dynasty, 1405–1438* (London: Longman, 2006).
Dreyer, June Teufel. "Sino-Japanese Rivalry and Its Implications for Developing Nations." *Asian Survey* 56, no. 4 (July/August 2006): 544–545.
Dreyer, June Teufel. "Sino-Japanese Territorial and Maritime Disputes." In Bruce Elleman, Stephen Kotkin, and Clive Schofield, eds., *China and Its Borders: Twenty Neighbors in Asia* (Armonk, NY: M.E. Sharpe, 2012), pp. 81–97.
Dreyer, June Teufel. "The '*Tianxia* Trope': Will China Change the World?" *Journal of Contemporary China* (Fall 2015), http://dx.doi.org/10.1080/10670564.2015.1030951.
Dobson, Wendy, and Anil Kashyap. "The Contradiction in China's Gradualist Banking Reform." Unpublished paper, October 2006, http://faculty.chicagobooth.edu/anil.kashyap/research/papers/Contradiction-in-Chinas-gradualist-banking-reforms.pdf.
Drifte, Reinhard. *China's Security Relations With China Since 1989: From Balancing to Bandwagoning?* (London: Routledge Curzon, 2003).
Drifte, Reinhard. "From 'Sea of Confrontation to Sea of Cooperation'?—Japan Facing China in the East China Sea." *Japan Aktuell*, no. 3, 2008, pp. 27–51.
Drifte, Reinhard. "The Japan-China Confrontation over the Senkaku-Diaoyu Islands—Between 'Shelving' and 'Dispute Resolution.'" *Asia-Pacific Journal* 12, issue 30, no. 3 (2014): 1–28.
Dutton, Peter. *Scouting, Signaling, and Gatekeeping: Chinese Naval Operations in Japanese Waters and the International Law Implications* (Newport, RI: Naval War College: February 2009). China Maritime Studies no. 2.
Ekonomisuto (Tokyo). www.shukan ekonomisuto.co.jp. Falk, Edward A. *Togo and the Rise of Japanese Sea Power* (New York: Longmans, Green and Co, 1936).
Far Eastern Economic Review (Hong Kong), 1946-2009. http://www.feer.com.
Federation of Atomic Scientists Newsletter, August 14, 1999. http://fas.org/nuke/guide/china/icbm/df-31.htm.
Feifer, George. *Breaking Open Japan: Commodore Perry, Lord Abe, and American Imperialism* (New York: Smithsonian Books, 2006).
Feng Zhaokui, and Lin Chang. *Zhong-ri Guanxi* Baogao (Report on Sino-Japanese Relations) (Beijing: China Foundation for International and Strategic Studies, 2007).
Feuerwerker, Albert. *China's Early Industrialization* (Cambridge, MA: Harvard University Press, 1958).
Finn, Richard. *Winners in Peace: MacArthur and Yoshida, and Postwar Japan* (Berkeley: University of California Press, 1992).
Fogel, Joshua A., ed. *Crossing the Yellow Sea: Sino-Japanese Cultural Contacts 1600–1950* (Norwalk, CT: Eastbridge Press, 2007).
Fouse, David. "Japan's FY 2005 National Defense Program Outline: New Concepts, Old Compromises." *Asia-Pacific Security Studies* 4, no. 3 (March 2005): 1–4.
Gillin, Donald G. *Warlord: Yen Hsi-shan in Shansi Province, 1911–1949* (Princeton, NJ: Princeton University Press, 1967).
Graham, Euan. *Japan's Sea Lane Security, 1940–2004: A Matter of Life and Death?* (London: Routledge, 2006).

Gries, Peter Hays. *China's New Nationalism: Pride, Politics, and Diplomacy* (Berkeley: University of California Press, 2004).
Gries, Peter Hays. "China's 'New Thinking' on Japan." *China Quarterly*, no. 184 (December 2005): 831–850.
Guoji Wenti Yanjiu (Research on International Issues, Beijing).
Guoji Zhanwang (International Outlook, Shanghai), February 8, 1996, pp. 18–20.
Hamby, Joel E. "Striking the Balance: Strategy and Force in the Russo-Japanese War." *Armed Forces and Society* 30, no. 325 (Spring 2004): 345–346.
Haranō, Joji. "Japan Launches Its Own National Security Council." December 25, 2013, http://www.nippon.com/en/genre/politics/l00050/.
Harootunian, Harry. *Things Seen and Unseen: Discourse and Ideology in Tokugawa Nativism* (Chicago: University of Chicago Press, 1988).
Harrell, Paula. *Sowing the Seeds of Change: Chinese Students, Japanese Teachers, 1895–1905* (Stanford, CA: Stanford University Press, 1992).
Harrell, Paula. "Guiding Hand: Hattori Unokichi in Beijing." In Joshua A. Fogel, ed., *Crossing the Yellow Sea: Sino-Japanese Cultural Contacts 1600–1950* (Norwalk, CT: Eastbridge Press, 2007), pp. 183–192.
Harris, Sheldon H. *Factories of Death: Japanese Biological Warfare, 1931–1945 and the American Cover-Up* (New York: Routledge, 2002).
Hasegawa, Seiji. "The World Will Revolve Around Beijing." In Morinosuke Kajima, ed., *Japan in International Affairs* (Tokyo: The Japan Times, 1971), pp. 34–51.
Hausman, Joshua K., and Johannes F. Wieland. "Abenomics: Preliminary Analysis and Outlook." Brookings Papers on Economic Activity, Washington, DC: Brookings Institution, Spring 2014.
Heping yü Fazhan (Peace and Development, Beijing), May 1, 2001.
Hilpert, Hanns Günther. "Japanese Direct Investment in China: Its Effect on China's Economic Development." In Hanns Günther Hilpert and René Haak, eds., *Japan and China: Cooperation, Competition, and Conflict* (Houndsmill, UK: Palgrave, 2002), pp. 1–11.
Hilpert, Hanns Günther, and René Haak. *Japan and China: Cooperation, Competition, and Conflict* (Houndsmill, UK: Palgrave, 2002).
Holmes, James, and Toshi Yoshihara. *Red Star Over the Pacific: China's Challenge to U.S. Maritime Strategy* (Annapolis, MD: U.S. Naval Institute Press, 2010).
Hook, Glenn D., Julie Gibson, Christopher Hughes, and Hugo Dobson. *Japan and the East Asian Financial Crisis: Patterns, Motivations, and Instrumentalization of Japanese Regional Economic Diplomacy* (Warwick, UK: University of Warwick, 2002).
Hoppens, Robert. *The China Problem in Postwar Japan: Japanese National Identity and Sino-Japanese Relations* (London: Bloomsbury Press, 205).
Hsiao, Gene T. *The Foreign Trade of China: Policy, Law, and Practice* (Berkeley: University of California Press, 1977).
Hsiao, Kung-chuan. *A Modern China and a New World: K'ang Yu-wei, Reformer and Utopian, 1858–1927* (Seattle: University of Washington Press, 1975).
Hughes, Christopher W. *Japan's Emergence as a "Normal" Military Power* (London: International Institute for Strategic Studies [IISS], 2004), Adelphi Paper nos. 368–369.
Hughes, Christopher W. *Japan's Security Agenda: Military, Economic, and Environmental Dimensions* (Boulder, CO: Lynne Rienner, 2004).

Huffmann, James L. *Creating a Public: People and the Press in Meiji Japan* (Honolulu: University of Hawaii Press, 1997).
Inada, Junichi. "Japan's ODA and Sino-Japanese Relations." In Hanns Günther Hilpert and René Haak, eds., *Japan and China: Cooperation, Competition, and Conflict* (Houndsmill, UK: Palgrave, 2002), pp. 121–139.
International Institute of Strategic Studies (London), Strategic Survey, published annually. http://www.iiss.org/en/publications/strategicsurvey/issues/strategic-survey.
Iriye, Akira, ed. *The Chinese and the Japanese* (Princeton, NJ: Princeton University Press, 1980).
Ito, Kiyoshi. *Taiwan Lishi* (History of Taiwan), translated by Walter Chen (Taipei: Qianwei Chubanshe, 2004).
Iwabuchi, Koichi. *Recentering Globalization: Popular Culture and Japanese Transnationalism* (Durham, NC: Duke University Press, 2002).
Jansen, Marius B. *The Japanese and Sun Yat-sen* (Cambridge, MA: Harvard University Press, 1954).
Jansen, Marius B., ed. *Changing Japanese Attitudes Toward Modernization* (Princeton, NJ: Princeton University Press, 1965).
Jansen, Marius B. *China and Japan: From War to Peace, 1894–1972* (Chicago: Rand-McNally, 1975).
Jansen, Marius B. *China in the Tokugawa World* (Cambridge, MA: Harvard University Press, 1992).
Jianchuan Zhishi (Ship Construction Knowledge, Beijing), www.pjdl.me/jczszzs.html.
Jiang, Zemin. *Selected Works of Jiang Zemin* (Beijing: Foreign Languages Press, 2013), vol. 3.
Johnson, Chalmers. "How China and Japan See Each Other." *Foreign Affairs* 50, no. 4 (July 1972), pp. 711–721.
Johnson, Chalmers. *MITI and the Japanese Miracle: The Growth of Industrial Policy 1925–1975* (Stanford, CA: Stanford University Press, 1982).
Johnson, Chalmers. "The Patterns of Japanese Relations with China, 1952–1982." *Pacific Affairs* 34 no. 3 (Autumn 1986), pp. 402–428.
Johnson, Chalmers. "Tanaka Kakuei, Structural Corruption, and the Advent of Machine Politics in Japan." *Journal of Japanese Studies* 12, no. 1 (Winter 1986), pp. 1–28.
Kahn, Herman. *Japan: The Emerging Superstate: Challenge and Response* (Englewood Cliffs, NJ: Prentice-Hall, 1970).
K'ang Yu-wei. *Ta T'ung Shu: The One-World Philosophy of K'ang Yu-wei* (London: Allyn and Unwin, 1958).
Katada, Saori N. *Banking on Stability: Japan and the Cross-Pacific Dynamic* (Ann Arbor: University of Michigan Press, 2001).
Kato, Akira. "Collapse of Big-Power Self-Confidence in Japan's Diplomacy." *CEAC (Council on the East Asian Community) Commentary*, December 18, 2014, http://www.ceac.jp/e/commentary/141218.pdf.
Kazianis, Harry. "China's Expanding Cabbage Strategy." *The Diplomat*, October 29, 2013, http://thediplomat.com/2013/10/chinas-expanding-cabbage-strategy/.
Kerr, George H. *Formosa Betrayed* (London: Eyre and Spottiswoode, 1965).
Kokubun, Ryosei. "The Politics of Foreign Economic Policy-Making in China: The Case of Plant Cancellations with Japan." *China Quarterly*, no. 109 (March 1986), pp. 19–44.

Kwan, C. H. *Economic Interdependence in the Asia-Pacific Region* (London: Routledge, 1994).

Kwan, C. H. "The Rise of China as an Economic Power: Implications for Asia and Japan." In Hanns Günther Hilpert and René Haak, eds., *Japan and China: Cooperation, Competition, and Conflict* (Houndsmill, UK: Palgrave, 2002), pp. 12–31.

Landers, Peter, and Susan V. Lawrence. "Sorry, No Apology." *Far Eastern Economic Review*, December 10, 1998, p. 21.

Lee, Chae-Jin. "The Politics of Sino-Japanese Trade Relations, 1963–68." *Pacific Affairs* 42, no. 2 (Summer 1969), pp. 129–144.

Leng, Shao Chuan. *Japan and Communist China* (Kyoto: Doshisha University Press, 1958).

Lensen, George A. *Balance of Intrigue: International Rivalry in Korea and Manchuria, 1884–1899* (Tallahassee: University Press of Florida, 1982).

Leung, Edwin Pak-wah. "Li Hung-chang and the Liu-ch'iu (Ryukyu) Controversy, 1871–1881." In Samuel C. Chu and Kwang-Ching Liu, eds., *Li Hung-chang and China's Early Modernization* (Armonk, NY: M.E. Sharpe, 1994), pp. 162–175.

Levenson, Joseph. *Liang Ch'i-ch'ao and the Mind of Modern China* (Cambridge, MA: Harvard University Press, 1953).

Li, Yaqiang. "What Is Japan Doing Southward?" *Jianchuan Zhishi* (Naval and Merchant Ships, Beijing), no. 6, June 6, 1997, pp. 7–8.

Liaowang (Outlook, Beijing). Weekly newsmagazine affiliated with the official Xinhua News Agency, published since 1981.

Lim, Louisa. *The People's Republic of Amnesia: Tiananmen Revisited* (New York: Oxford University Press, 2014).

Liu, Kwang-Ching. "Li Hung-chang in Chihli: The Emergence of a Policy, 1870–1875." In Samuel C. Chu and Kwang-Ching Liu, eds. *Li Hung-chang and China's Early Modernization* (Armonk, NY: M.E. Sharpe, 1994, pp. 49–76.

Liu Mingfu. *Zhongguo meng: Hou meiguo shidai de daguo siwei zhanlue dingwei* (China Dream: The Great Power Thinking and Strategic Positioning of China in the Post-American Age) (Beijing: Zhongguo youyi chuban gongsi, 2010).

Lo, Jung-pang, ed. *Kang Yuwei: A Biography and a Symposium* (Tucson: University of Arizona Press, 1967).

Lu, Hsiu-lien Annette, with Ashley Esarey. *My Fight for a New Taiwan: One Woman's Journey from Prison to Power* (Seattle: University of Washington Press, 2014).

Lu, Shengzhu. "Lianqian Nianqian de Zhongguo Haiyang Huanjing" (Two Thousand Years of China's Maritime Environment). *Junshi Zhanwang* (Military Outlook, Beijing), Spring 1990.

Luo Weilong. "Japan Holding Overall Detente Does Not Equal Post-Cold War Detente Cycle." *Shijie Zhishi*, January 1, 1990.

Manicom, James. "Japan's Ocean Policy: Still the Reactive State?" *Pacific Affairs* 83, no. 2 (June 2010): 307–326.

Manicom, James. *Bridging Troubled Waters: China, Japan, and Maritime Order in the East China Sea* (Washington, DC: Georgetown University Press, 2014).

Mancall, Mark. "The Ch'ing Tribute System: An Interpretive Essay." In John King Fairbank, ed., *The Chinese World Order: Traditional China's Foreign Relations* (Cambridge, MA: Harvard University Press, 1968), pp. 63–89.

Matsumura, Tsutomo. "Politicians Should Question Self-Defense Forces' Operational Abilities Before Debating on the 'Right of Collective Self-Defense.'" *Sapio*, June 12, 1996, pp. 105–107.

McNally, Mark. *Proving the Way: Conflict and Practice in the History of Japanese Nativism* (Cambridge, MA: Harvard University Asia Center, 2005).
Mendel, Douglas. *The Politics of Formosan Nationalism* (Berkeley: University of California Press, 1970).
Meng, Xiangqing. "A Strategic Measure with Ulterior Motives: Background and Attempt of Japan's Participation in the Theater Missile Defense System." *Shijie Zhishi*, April 1, 1999, no. 7, pp. 18–19.
Michael, Franz. "Introduction: Regionalism in Nineteenth Century China." In Stanley Spector, ed., *Li Hung-chang and the Huai Army: A Study in Nineteenth Century Regionalism* (Seattle: University of Washington Press, 1964), pp. xl–xliii.
Millett, Allan R. *The Korean War* (Washington, DC: Potomac Books, 2006).
Momura, Seiichi. *The Devil's Gluttony*. Vols. 1 and 2 (Tokyo: Kobunsha, 1981, 1982).
Morita, Akio, and Ishihara Shintarō. *The Japan That Can Say No* (Tokyo: Konbunsha Publishing, 1989).
Morrison, Wayne M. *China's Response to the Asian Financial Crisis: Implications for U.S. Economic Interests* (Washington, DC: Congressional Research Service, U.S. Library of Congress, 2002). Rept. 98–220.
Nakagame, Katsuji. "Japanese Direct Investment in China." In Hanns Günther Hilpert and René Haak, eds., *Japan and China: Cooperation, Competition, and Conflict* (Houndsmill, UK: Palgrave, 2002), pp. 52–71.
Nakai, Kate Wildman. "The Naturalization of Confucianism in Tokugawa Japan: The Problem of Sinocentrism." *Harvard Journal of Asiatic Studies* 40, no. 1 (June 1980): 157–199.
Nakai, Kate Wildman. *Shogunal Politics: Arai Hakuseki and the Premises of Tokugawa Rule* (Cambridge, MA: Council on East Asian Studies, Harvard University, 1988).
Nakai, Yoshifumi. "Policy Coordination on Taiwan." In Masashi Nishihara, ed., *The Japan-U.S. Alliance: New Challenges for the 21st Century* (Tokyo: Japan Center for International Exchange, 2000), pp. 71–94.
Nanfang Zhoumo (Southern Weekend, Guangzhou; 1981–present), http://www.infzm.com/.
Nathan, John. *Mishima: A Biography* (Boston: Little Brown, 1974).
Nishihara, Masashi. *The Japan-U.S. Alliance: New Challenges for the 21st Century* (Tokyo: Japan Center for International Exchange, 2000).
Nosco, Peter. *Remembering Paradise: Nativism and Nostalgia in Eighteenth Century Japan* (Cambridge, MA: Council on East Asian Studies, Harvard University, 1990).
Ogura, Kazuo. "How the 'Inscrutables' Negotiate with the 'Inscrutables': Chinese Negotiating Tactics Vis-à-Vis the Japanese." *China Quarterly*, no. 79 (September 1979), pp. 529–552.
Okamoto, Shumpei. *The Japanese Oligarchy and the Russo-Japanese War* (New York: Columbia University Press, 1970).
Ozawa, Terutomo. "Institutionally Driven Growth and Stagnation—and Struggle for Reform." In David Bailey, Dan Coffey, and Philip R. Tomlinson, eds., *Crisis or Recovery in Japan: State and Industry Economy* (Cheltenham, UK: Edward Elgar, 2007), pp. 106–132.
Paine, S. C. M. *The Sino-Japanese War of 1894–1895: Perceptions, Power, and Primacy* (Cambridge, UK: Cambridge University Press, 2003).
Peng, Ming-min. *A Taste of Freedom* (New York: Holt Rinehart and Winston, 1972).
Perez, Louis G. *Japan Comes of Age: Mutsu Munemitsu and the Revision of the Unequal Treaties* (Madison, NJ: Fairleigh Dickenson Press, 1999).

Perry, Matthew Calbraith. *Narrative of the Expedition of an American Squadron to the China Seas and Japan, 1852–1854* (New York: D. Appleton and Company, 1856).

Phillips, Steven E. *Between Assimilation and Independence: The Taiwanese Encounter with Nationalist China, 1945–1950* (Stanford, CA: Stanford University Press, 2003).

Przystup, James. *Japan-China Relations: From Precipice to Promise* (Washington, DC: Institute for National Strategic Studies, U.S. National Defense University, December 2001).

Radke, Kurt. *China's Relations with Japan, 1945–83: The Role of Liao Chengzhi* (Manchester, UK: Manchester University Press, 1990).

Rawlinson, John Lang. *China's Struggle for Naval Development, 1839–1895* (Cambridge, MA: Harvard University Press, 1967).

Reischauer, Edwin O. *Ennin's Travels in T'ang China* (New York: Ronald Press, 1955).

Reischauer, Edwin O., trans. *Ennin's Diary: The Record of a Pilgrimage in Search of the Law* (New York: Ronald Press, 1955).

Rose, Caroline. *Sino-Japanese Relations: Facing the Past, Looking to the Future?* (London: Routledge Curzon, 2005).

Roy, Denny. "Stirring Samurai, Disapproving Dragon: Japan's Growing Security Activity and Sino-Japanese Relations." *Asian Affairs* 31, no. 2 (Summer 2004), pp. 86–101.

Ryan, Paul. "Is China Exporting Deflation Globally, Hollowing Out Japan?" Marubeni Corporation Economic Research Institute, www.marubeni.co.jp/research/eindx/0303.

Sansom, George. *A History of Japan to 1334* (Stanford, CA: Stanford University Press, 1958).

Sansom, George. *A History of Japan, 1334–1615* (Stanford, CA: Stanford University Press, 1961).

Sapio (Tokyo).

Schaede, Ulrike. "Globalization and the Japanese Subcontractor System." In David Bailey, Dan Coffey, and Philip R. Tomlinson, eds., *Crisis or Recovery in Japan: State and Industry Economy* (Cheltenham, UK: Edward Elgar, 2007), pp. 82–105.

Schurmann, Franz. *Imperial China: The Decline of the Last Dynasty and the Origins of Modern China* (New York: Random House, 1967).

Scott-Stokes, Henry. *The Life and Death of Yukio Mishima* (New York: Farrar, Straus and Giroux, 1974).

Self, Benjamin. "The Rise of China and the Role of the U.S.-Japan Alliance in Taiwan's Security." Paper presented at conference entitled "The Rise of China Revisited," National Chengchi University, Taipei, December 11, 2003.

Sharma, Ruchir. *Breakout Nations: In Pursuit of the Next Economic Miracles* (New York: W.W. Norton, 2012), pp. 252–253.

Shen, Zhihua, and Danhui Li. *After Leaning to One Side: China and Its Allies in the Cold War* (Washington, DC: Woodrow Wilson Center and Stanford University Press, 2011).

Shijie Zhishi (World Knowledge, Beijing). July 1, 1995. www.xinhuanet.com/world/sjzs.

Shillony, Ben-Ami. *The Young Officers and the February 26, 1936 Incident* (Princeton, NJ: Princeton University Press, 1973).

Shirk, Susan. *China: Fragile Superpower* (Oxford: Oxford University Press, 2007).

Shokun! (You!, Tokyo) October 1, 2004, pp. 52–59.

Shukan Daiyamondo (Diamond Weekly, Tokyo), November 28, 2009, pp. 132–134.

Simpson, James. "Ten Years Ago, Japan Went to Iraq . . . And Learned Nothing." *War Is Boring*, April 10, 2014, https://medium.com/war-is-boring/ten-years-ago-japan-went-to-iraq-and-learned-nothing-b7f3c702dd1f.
Smith, Sheila A. *Intimate Rivals: Japanese Domestic Politics and a Rising China* (New York: Columbia University Press, 2015).
So, Kwan-wai. *Japanese Piracy in Ming China During the 16th Century* (East Lansing: Michigan State University Press, 1975).
Soeya, Yoshihide. *Japan's Economic Diplomacy with China, 1945–1978* (Oxford: Clarendon Press, 1998).
Spector, Stanley. *Li Hung-chang and the Huai Army: A Study in Nineteenth-Century Regionalism* (Seattle: University of Washington Press, 1964).
Stueck, William. *The Korean War: An International History* (Princeton, NJ: Princeton University Press, 1995).
Struve, Lynne. *The Southern Ming, 1644–1662* (New Haven, CT: Yale University Press, 1984).
Sun, Jing. *Japan and China as Charm Rivals: Soft Power in Regional Diplomacy* (Ann Arbor: University of Michigan Press, 2012).
Swope, Kenneth W. "Crouching Tigers, Secret Weapons: Military Technology Employed During the Sino-Japanese-Korean War, 1592–1598." *Journal of Military History* 69 no. 1 (January 2005): 11–41.
Takagi, Seiichiro. "An Analysis of Chinese Behavior Toward Japan, 1850–1965: An Examination of Three Models of International Behavior." Unpublished Ph.D. diss., Stanford University, Stanford, CA, 1977. Microfilm 78-2247 available through University of Michigan, Ann Arbor.
Tam, Yue-him. "An Intellectual's Response to Western Intrusion: Naitō Konan's View of Republican China." In Akira Iriye, ed., *The Chinese and the Japanese* (Princeton, NJ: Princeton University Press, 1980), pp. 161–183.
Tamamori, Mariko Asano. "Victims of Colonization: Japanese Agrarian Settlers and Their Repatriation to Japan." *Asia-Pacific Journal* 6, no. 1 (February 2009).
Tanaka, Toshiyuki. *Hidden Horrors: Japanese War Crimes in World War II* (Boulder, CO: Westview Press, 1996).
Taoka, Shunji. "A Plan to Have a Domestic Reconnaissance Satellite Has Emerged: Japan Seeks Intelligence Independence." *Aera* (Tokyo), June 3, 1996, pp. 62–63; in U.S. Department of Commerce, *Foreign Broadcast Information Service*, East Asia (*FBIS-EAS*), June 4, 1996, pp. 7–9.
Taylor, Jay. *Generalissimo: Chiang Kai-shek and the Struggle for Modern China* (Cambridge, MA: Belknap Press, 2009).
Teng, Ssu-yu, and John Fairbank. *China's Response to the West: A Documentary Survey, 1839–1923* (Cambridge, MA: Harvard University Press, 1954).
Toby, Ronald. *State and Society in Early Modern Japan: Asia in the Development of the Tokugawa Bakufu* (Princeton, NJ: Princeton University Press, 1984).
Tsang, Steve. "Chiang Kai-shek's 'Secret Deal' and Xian and the Start of the Sino-Japanese War." *Palgrave Communications*, January 20, 2015. doi:101057/palcomms.2014.3.
Tsunoda, Ryusaku, William Theodore de Bary, and Donald Keene. *Sources of Japanese Tradition* (New York: Columbia University Press, 1965).
Tsurumi, E. Patricia. *Japanese Colonial Education in Taiwan, 1895–1945* (Cambridge, MA: Harvard University Press, 1977).

Turnbull, Stephen. *Samurai Invasion: Japan's Korea War, 1592–1598* (London: Cassell and Company, 2002).
United States Congress. *Congressional Record*, 96th Congress, Public Law 96-8, H.R. 2479, Taiwan Relations Act.
Vogel, Ezra F. *Japan as Number One* (Cambridge, MA: Harvard University Press, 1979).
Vogel, Ezra F., Yuan Ming, and Tanaka Akihiko, eds. *The Golden Age of the U.S.-China-Japan Triangle, 1972–1989* (Cambridge, MA: Harvard University Asia Center, 2002).
Wade, Geoff. "The Zheng He Voyages: A Reassessment." Asia Research Institute, National University of Singapore, Working Paper No. 31, October 2004, http://www.ari.nus.edu.sg/docs/wps/wps04_031.pdf.
Wakabayashi, Masahiro. "Taiwanese Nationalism and the Unforgettable Others." In Edward Friedman, ed., *China's Rise, Taiwan's Dilemmas, and International Peace* (London: Routledge, 2006), pp. 3–31.
Wakamiya, Yoshibumi. *Sengo Hoshu No Ajia Kan* (The Postwar Conservative View of Asia: How the Political Right Has Delayed Japan's Coming to Terms with Its History of Aggression in Asia) (Tokyo: LTCB Library Foundation, 1999).
Waldron, Arthur N. "The Warlord: Twentieth Century Chinese Understandings of Violence, Militarism, and Imperialism." *American Historical Review* 96, no. 4 (October 1991): 1073–1100.
Wallace, Corey. "Does the Izumo Represent Japan Crossing the 'Offensive' Rubicon?" *Japan Security Watch*, August 13, 2013, http://jsw.newpacificinstitute.org/?p=11000.
Walworth, Arthur. *Black Ships Off Japan* (Hamden, CT: Archon Books, 1966).
Wang, Yi-t'ung. *Official Relations between China and Japan, 1368–1549* (Cambridge, MA: Harvard University Press, 1953). Harvard-Yenching Institute Studies, no. 9.
Watanabe, Tsuneo. "The Bankruptcy of Civil-Military Relations in Japan." *NIRA (National Institute for Research Advancement) Review* (Summer 1996): 4, http://www.nira.go.jp/publ/review/96summer/watanabe.html.
Weiss, Jessica Chen. *Powerful Patriots: Nationalist Protest in China's Foreign Relations* (New York: Oxford University Press, 2014).
White, John Albert. *The Siberian Intervention* (Princeton, NJ: Princeton University Press, 1950).
Whiting, Allen S. *China Eyes Japan* (Berkeley: University of California Press, 1989).
Wilbur, C. Martin. "Japan and the Rise of Communist China." In Hugh Borton et al., *Japan Between East and West* (New York: Council on Foreign Relations, 1957), pp. 213–240.
Wong, Aida Y. "The East, Nationalism, and Taishō Democracy: Naitō Konan's History of Chinese Painting." In Joshua A. Fogel, ed., *Crossing the Yellow Sea: Sino-Japanese Cultural Contacts 1600–1950* (Norwalk, CT: Eastbridge Press, 2007), pp. 281–304.
Wong, Julia. "The 1986 Student Demonstrations in China: A Democratic Movement?" *Asian Survey* 28, no. 9 (September 1986), pp. 970–985.
Wright, Mary Claubaugh. *The Last Stand of Chinese Conservatism: The T'ung Chih Restoration of 1862–1874* (Stanford, CA: Stanford University Press, 1957).
Xiandai Guoji Guanxi (Contemporary International Relations, Beijing), February 20, 1996.
Yang, Jisheng, Edward Friedman, Jian Guo, and Stacy Mosher. *Tombstone: The Great Chinese Famine, 1958–1962* (New York: Farrar, Straus and Giroux, 2012).
Yeh, Emilie Yueh-yu, and Darrell William David. *Taiwan Film Directors: A Treasure Island* (New York: Columbia University Press, 2005).
Yeh, Ricky. "Why the KMT Failed in Taiwan's Local Elections." *The Diplomat*, December 9, 2014, http://thediplomat.com/2014/12/why-the-kmt-failed-in-taiwans-local-elections-2/.

Yoshida, Shigeru. "Japan and the Crisis in Asia." *Foreign Affairs* 20, no. 2 (January 1951), pp. 171–181.

Yoshida, Shigeru. *Yoshida Shigeru: Last Meiji Man* (Lanham, MD: Rowan & Littlefield, 2007).

Yoshida, Takashi. *The Making of the "Rape of Nanking": History and Memory in Japan, China, and the United States* (New York: Oxford University Press/Weatherhead Institute of Columbia University, 2006).

Yoshihara, Toshi. "Japanese Hard Power: Rising to the Challenge." American Enterprise Institute, August 2014, https://www.aei.org/publication/japanese-hard-power-rising-to-the-challenge/.

Yoshihara, Toshi, and James R. Holmes. "Japanese Maritime Thought: If Not Mahan, Who?" *Naval War College Review* 59, no. 3 (Summer 2006), pp. 23–51.

Zahmann, Urs Matthias. *China and Japan in the Late Meiji Period: Chinese Policy and the Japanese Discourse on National Identity, 1893–1904* (London: Routledge, 2009).

Zhanlüe yü Guanli (Strategy and Management, Beijing), December 1, 2002, pp. 41–47.

Zhao, Suisheng. *A Nation-State by Construction: Dynamics of Modern Chinese Nationalism* (Stanford, CA: Stanford University Press, 2004).

Zhou, Enlai. *Riben wenti wenjian huibian* (Compilation of Documents on the Japan Question) (Beijing: Shijie Zhishi [World Knowledge], 1955).

NEWSPAPERS, PRESS AGENCIES, NON-OFFICIAL WEBSITES

Agence France-Presse (AFP)
APA Group (Tokyo)
Asahi Shimbun (Tokyo)
Associated Press (AP)
Beijing Radio
Brigham Young University, World War I Archive
British Broadcasting System (BBC, London)
Business Times (Singapore)
Central News Agency (CNA, Taipei)
Cheng Ming (Hong Kong)
Chicago Tribune
China Daily (Beijing)
China Post (Taipei)
ChinaSMACK
Christian Science Monitor (Boston)
Council on the East Asian Community (CEAC, Tokyo)
Dagong Bao (Shanghai)
East Asian Studies News, University of California at Los Angeles
ET Today (Taipei)
Far Eastern Economic Review (Hong Kong)
Federation of Atomic Scientists Newsletter (Washington, DC)
Financial Times (London)
Global Times (Beijing)
Guardian, The (London)
Guoji Xianqu Daobao (International Herald Leader, Beijing)

Guoji Shangpao (International Business, Beijing)
Guoji Wenti Yanjiu (Research on International Questions, Shanghai)
Hong Kong Standard
Hsin Wan Pao (New Evening Post, Hong Kong)
International Business Times (New York)
International Herald Tribune (Paris)
Itar-Tass (Moscow)
Japan News, The (English-language version of *Yomiuri Shimbun*, Tokyo)
Japan Times, The (Tokyo)
Japan Times Weekly (Tokyo)
Japanese Holdouts Registry, *Jiefang Junbao* (Liberation Army Daily, Beijing)
Jiji (Tokyo)
Jingji Guancha Bao (Economic Observer, Beijing)
Kyodo (Tokyo)
Los Angeles Times
Mainichi Shimbun (Tokyo)
Ming Pao (Hong Kong)
New York Times
Nihon Hōsō Kyōkai (NHK, Japan Broadcasting Association, Tokyo)
Nihon Keizai Shimbun (*Japan Economic News*, Tokyo)
Nikkei Telecom (Tokyo)
Nippon.com (Tokyo)
Phoenix Net (Hong Kong), Phoenix Television (Feng Huang, Hong Kong), *P'ing-kuo Jih-pao* (Apple Daily, Taipei)
Politico (Arlington County, VA), Open Democracy (London), *Renmin Ribao* (People's Daily, Beijing)
Renmin Wang (People's Daily Internet, Beijing)
Reuters (London)
Sankei Shimbun (Tokyo)
Shanghai Radio
Sina (Beijing), http://sina.com.cn
Society of Automotive Engineers (SAE) International (New York)
Society for the Dissemination of Historical Fact (Tokyo) *South China Morning Post* (Hong Kong)
Straits Times (Singapore)
Sydney Morning Herald (Sydney, Australia)
Ta Kung Pao (Hong Kong)
Taipei Times (Taipei)
Taiwan Communiqué (Washington, DC)
Taiwan News (Taipei)
Tokyo Broadcasting System Television (TBS)
Tokyo Shimbun
United Press International (UPI)
United States Naval Institute News (Annapolis, MD)
Want China Times (Taipei)
Washington Free Beacon (Washington, DC)
Washington Post
Wen Wei Po (Hong Kong)

Wikileaks *Xinhua* (New China News Agency, Beijing)
Yomiuri Shimbun (Tokyo)
Yonhap (Seoul)
Zhongguo Qingnian Bao (China Youth Daily, Beijing)
Zhonghua Xinwenshe (Beijing)

GOVERNMENT WEBSITES AND ARCHIVES

China, People's Republic of, Foreign Ministry
China, Government of the People's Republic of
 Diaoyu: The Inherent Territory of China
China, Republic of Taiwan, Ministry of Foreign Affairs
Gensuikyo (The Japan Council against Atomic and Hydrogen Bombs) Archive, Japan External Trade Organization (JETRO). Japan Statistics, Japanese Defense Agency, (up to January 9, 2007)
Japanese Defense Ministry (since January 9, 2007)
Japanese Foreign Ministry
Taiwan, Republic of China on
Taiwan Yearbook, 2005
United States Department of Commerce, Foreign Broadcast Information Service, China (FBIS-CHI)
United States Department of Commerce, Foreign Broadcast Information Service, East Asia (FBIS-EAS)
United States Department of Commerce, Joint Publications Research Service, China Report (JPRS-CAR)
United States Department of State
United States Department of State:
 Foreign Relations of the United States (FRUS)
 Vol. 6: *Japan*, 1951
 Vol. 29, Part 2: *Japan*, 1968
 Vol. 17: *China*, 1969–1972
United States National Security Archive at George Washington University
United States Office of War Information
 "Psychological Warfare Team Report on Korean Comfort Girls," Rept. no. 49, October 1, 1944
Voice of America
World Bank

Index

Abe Shintarō 175, 179
Abe Shinzō 215, 216, 217, 218, 219, 220, 221, 222, 223, 240, 241, 242, 243, 244, 245, 246, 279, 307, 312, 313, 315, 350
Abenomics 241, 278, 279
Acquisition and Cross-Servicing Agreement, U.S.-Japan 308
Adenauer, Konrad 101
ADIZ See Air Defense Identification Zone
Ai Xin 373
Aiichi Kiichi 104
Air Defense Identification Zone (ADIZ) 242, 312–313, 377
AirSea battle concept 311
Akahata 99. 110, 123
Akutagawa, Ryunosuke 124
Amaterasu, sun goddess 7, 15, 29, 30
An Jung Geung 243
Andō Rikichi 329
Angarsk pipeline 213, 214
Anti-Secession Law 346
Apa Group 228
APEC. *See* Asia-Pacific Economic Cooperation conference
Arai Hakuseki 25, 26, 27
Araki Commission 308
Asanuma Inejirō 101, 108. 109, 110, 114, 141

ASEAN. *See* Association of Southeast Asian Nations
Ashida Hitoshi 282
Ashikaga, Ashikaga bakufu 16, 18, 19, 22, 357
Asia-Pacific Economic Cooperation (APEC) conference 244, 246
Asō Tarō 218, 220, 223, 224, 226, 227, 228, 229, 230, 231, 316, 347, 348
Association of Southeast Asian Nations (ASEAN) 169, 199, 232, 243, 261, 273, 310, 375, 377
Asukata Ichirō 167
Aum Shinrikyo 193

bakufu 14, 15
Ball, George 143
Bandung Conference 97, 98
banshan 330, 344
Baoshan steel complex 259, 260
Beijing consensus 275
Belenko, Viktor 291
Bell of Sayon, The 328
Benedict, Ruth 288
bentuhua 339, 349
Bo'ao Forum 368
Borah, William 70
Boxer Rebellion 51–52, 53, 57, 60
Brezhnev, Leonid 158

456   Index

Brzezinski, Zbigniew 158, 263
Buddhism, Buddhists 9, 15, 18, 30, 31, 41, 164, 209, 358
Bush, George W. 202, 305
bushido 289

Carter, Jimmy 343
Canton (Guangs=zhou) trade fair 254
Cao Gangchuan 221
Chen Shui-bian 199, 226, 344, 345, 348
Chen Yi 110, 118
Chen Yonggui 165
Chiang, Antonio 353
Chiang Ching-kuo 334
Chiang Kai-shek 66, 67, 68, 69, 71, 73, 76, 78, 103, 151, 152, 331, 332, 333, 335, 360
Chiang Wei-sui 327, 353
"China fever" 153, 157, 165, 259
"China School" 201, 203, 222
"China threat" 243, 270, 312, 372
Chōshū 40
Chōson 10
Christians, Christianity 20, 41, 51, 52, 53, 66, 167
Christopher, Warren 341
Chrysanthemum and the Sword, The 288
Chunxiao 220, 229
"yellow peril" 50
City of Sadness (Beiqing Chengshi) 332
Cixi (empress dowager) 36, 51, 52
Clinton, Bill 196, 199, 297, 342
Clinton, Hillary 310
COCOM. *See* Coordinating Committee for Export to Communist Countries
cohong 34
Confucius, Confucian 4, 5, 6, 9, 11, 12, 17, 25, 30, 31, 36, 37, 38, 45, 51, 54, 56, 64, 160, 321, 322, 325, 326, 359, 374
Confucius Institutes .
Coordinating Committee for Export to Communist Countries (COCOM) 129, 257
Cross-Strait Services Trade Agreement (CSSTA) 351
Cultural Revolution 119, 128, 254, 364

Daimyo 20, 22., 31, 40–41
daisangokujin 208

Dalai Lama 208, 209, 223, 225
datsu-a ron 44, 117
de Gaulle 111
Democratic Progressive Party (DPJ, Minshutō) 231, 233, 234, 376, 377
Democratic Progressive Party (DPP) 226, 340, 344, 350, 352
Democratic Socialist Party (DSP) 108, 112, 113, 213, 309, 312
Deng Xiaoping 159, 160, 163, 166, 168, 170, 172, 176, 177, 178, 180, 181, 211, 258, 260, 261, 262, 264, 265, 268, 270, 277, 278, 287, 292, 294
DF-31 ICBM 197, 199
Diaoyu/Senkaku islands 160, 163, 166, 167, 189, 190, 193, 195, 197, 207, 208, 210, 226, 230, 233, 236, 237, 241, 242, 244, 277, 295, 296, 301, 312, 319, 367
Ding Ruchang 47, 48
dōbun; dōshu / tongwen;tongzhong (same culture same race) 43, 52, 162, 165, 339, 359
dogeza gaikō *See* ketou (kowtow) diplomacy
Doi Takako 370
dōka (assimilation) 326, 327
Dokdo (Takeshima) 299
DPJ *See* Democratic Party of Japan
DPP *See* Democratic Progressive Party
DSP *See* Democratic Socialist Party
Dulles, John Foster 83, 101, 284
Dutch, Dutch learning 23, 24, 34, 321, 359
Dutton, Peter 242
dwarfs, dwarf pirates, *wokou*, 9, 19, 46, 48, 49, 50

EAC *See* East Asian Community
East Asian Community (EAC) 231, 232, 376
Eisenhower, Dwight 110, 288
Emerging Japanese Superstate, The: Challenge and Response 138
Ennin 13

February 28 Incident 331, 332
Feng Yuxiang 67
Feng Zhaokui 198, 206, 214

fengshui 38
fingerprinting issue 103, 112
Five Classics of Shintō 15
Foucault 31
Four Modernizations 260
Fragile Blossom, The 158
Fujio Masayuki 179
Fujiwara 9
Fujiyama Aiichirō 101, 103, 137, 141
Fukuda Takeo 162, 165, 166, 167
Fukuda Yasuō 203–204, 223, 224, 226, 227, 317
Fukuryū Maru Number 5 98, 113
Fukuzawa Yukichi 44, 45, 117
fumie diplomacy 129, 155
Furui Yoshimi 128, 135, 137
futsu no kuni 296

gaiatsu 191
Gang of Four 258
Gates, Robert 232
Geneva Conference 252
genrō 40, 60
Gensuikyō 98–99, 113
germ warfare 200
Go-Daigo 16
Godzilla films 98
Gotō Shimpei 326
Great Leap Forward 112, 286, 378
Greater East Asia Co-Prosperity Sphere 77, 189, 264, 302, 360
Greater Mekong Sub-Region (GMS) 371
Greene. Fred 124
Grotius, Hugo 39
Gu Mu 168
Guangxu emperor 51, 52, 55
Guo Moruo 85, 122

Haguruma 124
hakkō ichiu 66, 68, 77
Hakusan Maru 105
Han dynasty 7, 8
Hashimoto Ryūtarō 193, 194, 297, 300, 302
Hatoyama Ichirō 97, 98, 100, 287, 297, 307
Hatoyama Yukio 231, 232, 233, 235, 309, 310, 376, 377

Hattori Unokichi 53, 54
Hattori Yayoi 351
He Xiangning 84, 85
Hebei-Chahar Political Council 71
Hideoyoshi Toyotomi 20, 21
Himiko 8
hinomaru 179, 197
Hiranuma Shū, 56
Hirasawa Kazushige 153
Hirohito, Emperor 79, 139, 143, 146
Hiroshima 79, 99, 110, 113. 191, 313, 317, 361
Hirota Koki 74
Hori Shigeru 159–160
Hosokawa Morihiro 342
Hotaru 181
Ho-Umezu accord 71
Hong Wu emperor 357
Hu Jintao 206, 212, 216, 219, 225, 230, 234, 239, 246
Hu Yaobang 170, 173, 177, 179, 265, 367
Hua Guofeng 162, 292
Huang Hua 164
Hughes, Thomas 125
Hundred Days' Reforms 51, 52, 55
Hundred Regiments Campaign 78
Huntsman, Jon 376

Ikeda Hayato 110, 111, 114
Ikeda Masanosuke 252
Inayama Yoshihiro 259
Ishiba Shigeru 226
Ishibashi Tanzen 147
Ishihara Shintarō 139, 189, 199, 208, 236, 237, 312, 343
Ishii, Kikujirō.
Ishii, Mitsutada 120
Itō Hirobumi 41, 44, 48, 52, 53
Itō Yūkū 48
ittō koku 66
Iwakura mission 41
Izanagi 7, 26
Izanami 7, 26
Izumo 313

Japan As Number One 263
Japan Communist Party (JCP) 83, 93, 97, 99, 103, 105, 109, 110, 113, 114, 118, 120, 121, 123, 137, 146, 150, 151

458 Index

Japan Defense Agency 220. 288, 290, 293, 296, 297, 302, 303, 306, 307. 308, 341, 369
Japan External Trade Organization (JETRO) 162, 279
"Japan Incorporated" 249, 256, 263
Japan Socialist Party (JSP) 84, 99, 108, 109, 110, 113, 117, 118, 119, 122, 134, 137, 141, 150, 161, 169, 186
Japanese Exclusion Act 65
JCP. See Japan Communist Party
JETRO. See Japan External Trade Organization
Jia Linbo 222
Jiang Zemin 184, 192, 194, 196, 199, 200, 201, 212, 268, 270, 294, 342
Jimmu Tennō 7, 66, 77
Jin Xide 216
Jin-Doichara accord 71
Jing Mei-ling. See King, Alice
Johnson, Chalmers 259
Johnson, Lyndon 125
Johnson, U. Alexis 124
Joint Declaration on Security Alliance for the 21st Century (U.S.-Japan) 297–298; 342
JSP. See Japan Socialist Party
Jurchen 27

Kahn, Herman 139
Kaifu Toshiki 184, 189
Kaifusō 12
Kajiyama Seiroku 301, 302
Kamakura 15, 16
kamikaze 15, 358
Kamiya Fuji 154
Kamiyo (Age of the Gods) 25, 26
Kamo no Mabuchi 21, 31
Kan Naoto 233, 234, 235, 236, 310, 311
Kanenaga, Prince 17
Kang Youwei 51, 55, 56
Kangxi emperor 321
Kawakami Jōtarō 118
ketou (kowtow) (dogeza gaikō) foreign policy 155
Khrushchev, Nikita 95, 106, 109, 286
Kiesinger, Kurt 131
Kim Dae-jung 202

Kim Ok-kyun 45
Kimigayo 179, 197
Kimura Toshio 142
King, Alice (Jing Mei-ling) 338
Kirov Ballet 130
Kishi Nobusuke 102, 104. 105, 110, 115, 216, 282, 287, 288, 335
Kishida Fumio 246
Kissinger, Henry 142, 143, 146, 154, 335, 365
Kitabatake Chikafusa 15
Kiyokimi 13
Koguryō 10
Koito Chūgo 121
Koizumi Junichirō 202, 203, 204, 205, 206, 211, 212, 214, 215, 216, 218, 223, 230, 273, 305, 306, 368, 372,373
Kojiki 11, 26
Kokinshū.
Kokugaku (national learning) 29, 30, 32, 66, 358
Kokuryūkai (Black Dragon, Amur River Society) 58
Kōmeitō; New Kōmeitō 112, 141, 151, 306
Kōminka.
Kōmura Masahiko 221
Konoe Fumimaro 77
Korean War 88, 90
Kowshing 46
Koxinga See Zheng Chenggong
Kubo Takuya 291
Kuno Chūji.
Kuomintang (KMT) 63, 67, 68, 71, 72, 73. 75, 76, 77, 78, 80, 84, 86, 92, 331
KMT Youth Corps 331
Kurihara family 237
Kurils See Northern Territories
Kurisu Horomi 292
Kuroda Haruhiko 274
Kwantung Army 70

Lansing, Robert 63
Lansing-Isshi agreement 63
Lau Nai-keung 227, 228
"lean to one side" policy 86
LDP See Liberal Democratic Party
League of Nations 70
Lee Kwan Yew 232, 375, 379

Index 459

Lee Teng-hui 200, 226, 337, 339, 340, 341, 343, 344, 348, 352
Lei Renmin 103
Li Hongzhang 38, 42, 43, 44, 45, 46, 48
Li Keqiang 246
Li Lanqing 194
Li Peng 183, 192, 267, 301
Li Zhaoxing 219
Liang Qichao 51, 55, 56, 57
Liang Yunxiang 311
Liao Chengzhi 84, 85, 114, 118, 122, 144, 165
Liao Zhongkai 84
Liaoning 314
Liao-Takasaki (L-T) Agreement 124, 254
Liberal Democratic Party (LDP) 84, 107, 108, 115, 116, 119, 121, 122, 126, 128, 134, 135, 137, 138, 141, 142, 146, 147, 149, 150, 155, 156, 157, 158, 159, 160, 163, 165, 170, 184, 194, 208, 209, 219, 221, 226, 231, 240, 241, 243, 254, 255, 273, 290, 293, 295, 296, 300, 306, 309, 313, 333, 337, 376
Liberal Party 205
Li-Itō Convention 44, 46
Lien Chan 344, 345, 346, 352
likin 37
Lin Biao 119, 132, 144, 157, 160
Liu Bang 303
Lin Hsien-tang 333
Liu Ming-chuan 323
Liu-Song dynasties 8
Lockheed scandal 15
Long March 71
Long Term Trade Agreement (LTTA) 258, 259
L-T Agreement See Liao-Takasaki Agreement
Lu, Annette Hsiu-lien 345
Lu Xun 85
Lu Yadong 238
Luo Fenglu 48

Ma Licheng 205, 211, 369
Ma Ying-jeou 226, 349, 350, 351, 352
MacArthur, Douglas 84, 88, 249, 283, 284

Macartney mission 34
Macmillan, Harold 101
Machimura Nobutaka 376
Mahathir Mohammed 274
Mainland Affairs Council 348
Man'yōshū 12, 13
Manchukuo 69, 70, 73, 74, 76, 91, 249
Manchus, Qing dynasty 22, 29, 32, 35, 37, 38, 43, 50, 55, 56, 57, 60, 63, 66, 69, 321, 323, 324, 331, 343, 359, 360
Mao Zedong, Maoists 4, 34, 37, 79, 80, 82, 83, 84, 85, 86, 87, 102, 106, 109, 120, 123, 128, 129, 133, 143, 144, 155, 157, 160, 162, 174, 177, 250, 255, 257, 260, 282, 283, 286, 335, 364
Maori 320
Marco Polo 33
Marco Polo Bridge incident 72, 195, 202, 221. 378
Marx, Karl 64, 106
Matsumura Kenzō 121, 122, 137, 146
Matsuoka, Yōsuke 70
May 4th Movement 64
Mayer, Armin 148
Mei Lanfang 85
Meiji period, Meiji emperor 10, 40–41, 44, 47, 52, 57, 60, 325, 359, 375
Memorandum Trade Agreement 257
Mencius 4, 17
METI. *See* Ministry of Economy, Trade, and Industry
Miki Takeo 141, 159, 160, 166, 288
Minamoto 14
Ming dynasty 15, 16, 17, 18, 19, 22, 23, 42, 321, 357, 358
Ministry of Economy, Trade, and Industry (METI) 272, 274, 368
Ministry of International Trade and Industry (MITI) 91, 110, 169, 188. 249, 271, 272, 274
Minshutō. *See* Democratic Party of Japan
Mishima, Yukio 288, 289, 343
MITI. *See* Ministry of International Trade and Industry
Mito 31
Miyamoto Kenji 120, 123
Miyazaki Seimin 84

Miyazaki Tōten 56, 84
Miyazawa Kiichi 184
Mongols, Yuan dynasty 16, 17, 28, 29, 33, 358
Mori Yoshihiro 199, 200, 202
Mukden (Shenyang) incident 67, 235
Murayama Tomiichi 192, 193
Mutsu 114, 313, 362
Mutsu Munemitsu 45
Mutual Security Treaty(U.S.-Japan) 186, 254, 301

Nagasaki 22, 23, 24, 29, 79, 104, 105, 167
Nagasue Eiichi 112
Nagata Tetsuzan 72
Naitō Konan 54
Nakajima Mineo 153, 340
Nakamura Teruo (Sunion) 328
Nakasone Yashiro 169, 173, 174, 176, 177, 178, 180, 193, 212, 290, 291, 293
Nan Hanchen 251
Nanjing (Nanking) massacre 74–75, 78, 180, 189, 208, 243, 378
Narita Tomomi 137
National Defense Program Outline (NDPO) 291, 308
National Police Reserve 285
National Unification Council 345, 348
nativism, nativists 12, 13, 30
NATO. *See* North Atlantic Treaty Organization
NDPO. *See* National Defense Program Outline
Nehru, Jawaharlal 98
New Conservative Party 306
New Fourth Army 78
"new thinking" in Sino-Japanese relations 207, 211
Nihon Shoki 11, 26, 66
Ninigi 7
Nishimura Kumao 90
Nishimura Shingo 195, 198, 304, 317
Nishio Suihiro 108
Nixon, Richard 131, 132, 138, 139, 140, 141, 142, 143, 145, 146, 147, 148, 151, 154, 335, 364, 365
Nobel Peace Prize 209, 288

Noda Yoshihiko 236, 237, 239, 240, 311, 312
North Atlantic Treaty Organization (NATO) 224, 304
Northern Expedition 67
Northern Territories (Kurils) 109, 118, 131, 158, 159, 160, 162, 163, 173, 193, 234, 292, 362
Nosaka Sanzō 83, 88, 104
Nuclear Non-Proliferation Treaty 288
Nye, Joseph 375

Obama, Barak 311
Obuchi Keizō 196, 198, 199, 302, 342
ODA. *See* Official Development Assistance
Oda Nobunaga 20
OECD. *See* Organization for Economic Cooperation and Development
Official Development Assistance (ODA) 260, 261, 272, 360, 362
Ogata Taketoru 96
Ohgi Chikage 217
Ohira Masayoshi 165, 167, 169
Okada Kastsuya 233, 310, 376, 377
Okazaki Kaheita 140
Okinawa (Ryūkyūs), 22, 32, 43, 79, 99, 127, 130, 131, 132, 135, 147, 148, 158, 210, 226, 231, 232, 234, 236, 239, 320, 323
Ōkubo Toshimichi 43
Ōkuma Shigenobu 62
Okune Seisuke 181
Ōnin War 20
Ono no Takamura 13
Operation Tomodachi 235
Opium War 35
Organization for Economic Cooperation and Development (OECD) 114, 362, 372
Overseas Chinese Affairs Commission 85
Ozawa Ichirō 204, 235, 295, 296

Paekche 7, 10, 11
Paine, S.C.M. 46
Pancha Shila 113

Parhae 14
Peace and Friendship Treaty 159, 378
Peace Preservation Corps 73
Pearl Harbor 78–79
Peking Gazette 49
Peng Mengji 334
Peng Ming-min 327, 341
People First Party (PFP) 344, 345
People's Liberation Army (PLA) 212, 246, 285, 286, 287, 289, 294, 310, 311, 313, 341
Pepin, Jean-Luc 145
Perry, Matthew 10, 38–39, 323, 359
PFP. *See* People First Party
pirates, piracy 18, 19
PLA. *See* People's Liberation Army
Portsmouth, Treaty of 59
Prairie Fire, 124
Putin, Vladimir 213, 214

Qian Qichen 281
Qin dynasty, Qin Shi Huangdi 20, 27
Qing dynasty. *See* Manchus

Reagan, Ronald 293
Rebiya Kadeer 223
Records of the Legitimate Succession on Divine Sovereignty 15
Reischauer, Edwin 117, 363, 366
Renan, Ernst 327
reparations 74, 90, 118, 151, 191, 192, 217, 272, 333
Reston, James 145
Ricci, Matteo 33
Ridgway, Matthew 284
Roos, John 376
Roosevelt, Franklin 84, 283
Roosevelt, Theodore 59
Rusk, Dean 125
Russo-Chinese War 57–59
Ryūkyū islands, Ryūkyū kingdom. *See* Okinawa

Sadao Miyahiro 31
Sagawa Express scandal 184
Saint Francis Xavier 33
Saionji Kinkazu 137

Saionji Kinmochi 137
Saitō Masaki 350
Sakhalin 59, 131
Sakharov, Andrei 185
sakoku period 24
salami tactics 378
Samejima Keiji 123
Sarkozy, Nicolas 376
San Francisco Peace Conference 88, 90
sankin kōtai 22, 29, 41
Sasakawa Peace Foundation 311
Sasakawa Ryōichi 335
Sasaki Kōzoō 118, 150
Sata Tadataka 105
Satō Eisaku 114, 115, 116, 118, 121, 122, 124, 125, 127, 128, 129, 130, 131, 132, 134, 135, 136, 137, 138, 139, 141, 142, 144, 146, 147, 148, 149, 150, 151, 288, 335, 362
Satsuma 21, 40, 41
Sazanami 225
Schall, Johann 33
SDF. *See* Self Defense Forces
SDP. *See* Social Democratic Party of Japan
seikei bunri 91, 252, 267
Seirankai 337
Seinenkai 193
Sekigahara, Battle of 21
Self Defense Forces (SDF) 165, 186, 202–203, 209, 210, 220, 223, 224, 225, 226, 228, 229, 231, 237, 282, 285, 288, 289, 290, 291, 292, 293, 295, 296, 299, 300, 305, 306, 307, 308, 311, 315, 317, 318, 343
Sengoku (Warring States) era 20
Shanghai Cooperation Organization 193
Shen Danyang 279
Shen Guofang 194
Shenzhen 225
Shenzhou 6 370
Shi Yinhong 205, 206, 246, 369, 372
Shidehara Kijūrō, Shidehara diplomacy 65, 69
Shigemitsu Mamoru 97, 100
Shimamura Yoshinobu 192
Shimonoski, Treaty of 48, 49, 324, 340

Shin Kanemaru 336
Shina 27, 42, 200
Shinkansen 206, 361
Shintō 9, 15, 30, 31, 41, 159, 281, 328, 358, 360
Shirakaba 220, 229
shōen 12
shogun 14, 15, 22, 23, 24, 25, 27, 28, 40
Shōtoku, Prince 9, 11
Shu Jing (Book of History) 26
shuhen jitai 298, 342
Shun 5, 26, 28
Siberian Intervention 64
Silk Road(s) 375
Silla 10
Singh, Manmohan 227
Sino-Japanese War, 1894–1895 45–50
Sino-Soviet Treaty of Friendship, Alliance, and Mutual Assistance 86, 285, 337
"sinosclerosis" 270
Social Democratic Party of Japan (SDP) 282. 296, 300, 370
soft power 374
Soga 9
Sōhyō (General Council of Trade Unions of Japan) 84, 99
Sōka Gakkai 112
Song Zheyuan 71, 73
Soong, James Chu-yü 344, 345, 346
sonnō jōi.
Soong Qingling 84
Stalin, Josef 4, 67, 72, 82, 86, 95, 250, 252, 283
Stimson, Henry 69
Suetsugu Nobumasa 74
Sui dynasty 8, 9
Sun Pinghua 187
Sun Yat-sen 52, 56, 60, 61, 62, 63, 66, 84, 138, 252, 327, 360
Sun Zi 17, 37
Sunflower Movement 352
Sunada Shigemasu 100, 101
Sun-Joffe Manifesto 64
Sunion. *See* Nakamura Teruo
Sunoda Sunao 163
Suzuki Zenkō 293

Taihō ritsuryō 11
Taika reforms 9–10
Taira 14
Taishō emperor 60
Taiwan Democratic Republic 324
Taiwan Relations Act 343
Taiwan Thinktank 346
Taiwanese Assimilation Society 327
Takasaki Tatsunoke 110
Takeda Gorō 293
Takeiri Yoshikatsu 141
Takeshima. *See* Dokdo
Takeshita Noboru 183
Tale of Genji 13
Tamogami Toshio 228
Tanaka Chigaku 66
Tanaka Giichi 67
Tanaka Kakuei 149, 150, 151, 152, 153, 154, 156, 158, 159, 160, 161, 202, 256, 291
Tanaka Makiko 202, 222
Tang dynasty 10, 11, 12. 13, 24
Tanggu Truce 70, 73
taoguang yanghui 369
Teng, Theresa Li-jun 339
Terauchi Masatake 63
Theater Missile Defense (TMD) 197. 297, 302, 303, 304
Three Non-Nuclear Proliferation Principles 288
Three Principles of the People 64
Tiananmen Square incident 184, 185, 188, 189, 191, 198, 206, 212, 267, 294, 367
Tianjin, Treaty of 44
tianxia 66
TMD. *See* Theater Missile Defense
To Be a Beautiful Country 222
Tōgō, Heihachirō 59
Tōjō Hideki 131, 136
Tokugawa 21, 23, 24, 27, 29, 31, 32, 39. 40, 41, 42, 251, 358, 359
Tokyo War Crimes Trials 78
Tomita Naosuke 334
Tonghak rebellion 46
Tongji Restoration, 36–38, 51
Tongmenghui 56, 66
tongwen;tongzhong/dōbun;dōshu (same culture same race) 43
Toraijin 8

Toyotomi Hideyoshi 20, 21, 358
Triple Intervention 49, 50, 61
Trotsky, Leon 67
Truman, Harry 283
Tsushima, Battle of 59
turtle boats 21
Twenty-One Demands 62

Uchida Ryōhei 62
UN. *See* United Nations
UNCLOS. *See* United Nations Convention on the Law of the Sea
United Front Work Department 85, 182–183
United Nations (UN) 88, 96, 103, 115, 147, 148, 150, 166, 190, 198, 222, 286, 305, 306, 367, 368, 376
United Nations Convention on the Law of the Sea (UNCLOS) 159, 193
Uno Sōsuke 183, 184
Ushiba Nobuhiko 142. 143, 145
Utsunomiya, Tarō 138
Utsunomiya, Tokuma 138

Verbiest, Ferdinand 33
Versailles Conference 65
Vogel, Ezra 263
von Dirksen, Herbert 75, 80

Wa 7, 8
Wan Li 269
Wang Guochuan 146
Wang Jingwei 66, 68, 75, 76, 77, 78
Wang Jyn-ping 349, 351
Wang Yi 216
Wang Zhen 269
Washington consensus 275
Washington naval treaties 65, 71
Watanabe Michio 181
Wei dynasty 8
Wen Jiabao 218
Whampoa Military Academy 64, 66
White Group 334
White-Haired Girl 124
Wikileaks 376
Willy-Nicky letters 50

World Trade Organization (WTO) 199, 206, 269
World War I 60, 61, 65, 326
World War II 4, 80, 82, 87, 89, 90, 94, 101, 107, 109, 119, 131, 140, 152, 158, 162, 167, 171, 174, 179, 180, 181, 185, 186, 187, 190, 192, 194, 195, 196, 199, 207, 208, 209, 211, 214, 217, 222, 237, 243, 249, 250, 262, 273, 281, 289, 292, 299, 301, 313, 318, 328, 340, 344, 348, 351, 352, 363, 364, 365, 366, 368, 374, 378
Wu Qi, 17
Wu Xueqian 169, 179
Wu Xuewen 113, 114
Wu Yi 212

Xi Jinping 236, 239–240, 246, 278, 312, 375
Xi'an incident 71, 78
Xiang Jiang 303
Xue Li 206–207

Yachi Shōtarō 370
Yamamoto Ichita 209
Yamato (Great Peace) 9, 348
Yamato 313
Yan'an base area 71, 83, 253
Yanagiya Kensuke 180
Yang Bojiang 245
Yang Jiechi 233, 244, 310, 377
Yang Shangkun 191
Yao 5, 26, 28, 47
Yasukuni Shrine 1, 166, 167.172, 174, 175, 178, 179, 181, 186, 192, 193, 195, 198, 202, 203, 205, 206, 209, 211, 212, 211, 212, 214, 216, 218, 221, 223, 227, 230, 231, 241, 242, 243, 244, 246, 249, 368, 369, 372
"yellow peril" 50
Yi dynasty 43, 44
Yin Zho 236
Yok Mu-ming 347
Yoshida Shigeru 82, 84, 90, 111, 114, 250, 287, 361
Yoshihara, Toshi 314
Yoshikawa Mitsutade 120
Yuan dynasty. *See* Mongols
Yuan Shikai, 46, 51, 60, 61, 62, 63, 64

Zengakuren 110
Zhang Xueliang 68, 71
Zhang Zhaozhong 310
Zhang Zuolin 67, 69
Zhao Anbo 112, 113, 118
Zhao Ziyang 183, 184, 268, 367
Zheng Chenggong (Koxinga) 321, 322
Zhou dynasty 4, 27
Zhou Enlai 89, 96, 97, 100, 102, 105, 110, 123, 127, 133, 136, 137, 143, 142, 144, 145, 147, 149, 150, 151, 152, 153, 155, 160, 162, 253, 291, 292, 335
Zhu Bangzao 197
Zhu De 105
Zhu Rongji 198, 200, 270, 304

www.ingramcontent.com/pod-product-compliance
Ingram Content Group UK Ltd.
Pitfield, Milton Keynes, MK11 3LW, UK
UKHW041307180426
11947UKWH00009B/746

9 780190 692209